Precarious Solidarities
Artists for Democracy 1974–77

Edited by Wing Chan and David Morris

With contributions by Rasheed Araeen, Guy Brett, Virgil Calaguian, Wing Chan, Cường Minh Bá Phạm and George Clark, Charles Esche, Hannah Healey, Susan Hiller, Eileen Legaspi-Ramirez, María José Lemaitre Mujica and Caroll Yasky, David Medalla and Brandon Taylor, David Morris, Annabel Nicolson, Nii Kwate Owoo, Vijay Prashad and Cecilia Vicuña

Exhibition Histories

Exhibition Histories

Afterall's *Exhibition Histories* book series, published since 2010, addresses what happens when art becomes public. Research led, it is committed to presenting a plurality of voices and critical perspectives, while bringing archival and other primary materials to bear on current and future practice. The series to date has focussed on curatorial experimentation; exhibitionary activity led by artists; and contested articulations of the 'global' and the 'located'. Complementing the books are online publications at afterall.org, discussion events and a research-based masters course in Exhibition Studies at Central Saint Martins, University of the Arts London. As researchers, publishers and teachers at Afterall, we will continue to explore situations that productively challenge and refine our understandings of 'art', 'exhibition' and 'history', mindful of what those terms might mean for the present. This would not be possible without the collaboration of our project partners: Asia Art Archive, based in Hong Kong; the Center for Curatorial Studies at Bard College, New York; documenta Institut, Kassel; and the Faculty of Fine, Applied and Performing Arts, University of Gothenburg.

Precarious Solidarities
Artists for Democracy 1974–77

Exhibition Histories

Contents

8 Introduction: Precarious Solidarities
Wing Chan, Charles Esche and David Morris

16 Precarious Solidarities: Artists for Democracy in Historical Perspective
David Morris

50 Art in a Solidarity Continuum: Winnowing Loose Transnational Threads
Eileen Legaspi-Ramirez

66 Before Art and Politics: Regarding the Precarious Documents of Artists for Democracy
Wing Chan

86 A Museum for the People: On the Museo de la Solidaridad Salvador Allende
María José Lemaitre Mujica and Caroll Yasky

98 Following *Chile Vencerá*
Hannah Healey

116 Everything is suspended in thin air
Cường Minh Bá Phạm and George Clark

130 'We are going to win': On Artists for Democracy and the 1970s Conjuncture
Vijay Prashad

137 Artists for Democracy 1974–77

163 Organized Dreaming
Cecilia Vicuña, 2013

185 Agriculture, Field, Decoration
Guy Brett, 1976

198 Commentary: You Hide Me
Nii Kwate Owoo, c.1970

213 Paul Burwell and David Toop at Artists' For Democracy
Annabel Nicolson, 1975

266 Performance art – it breathes and grows
Virgil Calaguian, 1977

278 Sacred Circles: 2,000 Years of North American Indian Art
Susan Hiller, 1977

292 David Medalla in Conversation with Brandon Taylor, 1977

303 Preliminary Notes for a Black Manifesto (extract)
Rasheed Araeen, 1975–76

Voices from AFD

Rasheed Araeen, Conrad Atkinson, Anne Bean, Guy Brett, Virgil Calaguian, Hugh Cave, Stephen Cripps, John Dugger, Rose English, Charles Hustwick, Tina Keane, Roberta Kravitz, Lynn MacRitchie, Kathleen McCreery, David Medalla, Jonathan Miles, Ife Nii Owoo, Nii Kwate Owoo, Nick Payne, Stephen Pusey, Saleem Arif Quadri, Steve Sprung, Sylvia Stevens, Jun Terra, Anna Thew, Giles Thomas, Cecilia Vicuña

321 Acknowledgements

322 Authors' Biographies

327 Image and Text Credits

330 Index

Introduction: Precarious Solidarities

Wing Chan, Charles Esche and David Morris

Precarious Solidarities is the fourteenth book published under the *Exhibition Histories* rubric, a constantly evolving series that positions art as a public activity. The evolution of the book series has been marked by a number of methodological shifts that are worth accounting for in the context of a plurivocal project such as Artists for Democracy (AFD). The series has thus far addressed art's public aspect by focussing on moments when artworks are exposed, open to shared experience and perhaps curatorially captured within the context of group showings. It began with a focus on singular exhibitions often addressed in pairs, so that an analysis of difference, both proposed and unwitting, could be the basis to consider what made these presentations exceptional. An early criterion for us as editors was to consider exhibitions that we felt had created something not previously possible. This was a rather loose concept, to be sure, but it was useful in rejecting exhibitions that simply delivered predetermined goals for their national, regional, commercial or artist initiators. It was also a criterion that distracted us from the inevitable reprimand of constructing a canon of the best, most successful or most important. We were and remain in pursuit of exhibitions that have made a difference, in the ways that we hope each book describes. Fairly rapidly, the field of exhibitions and biennials expanded for us to include festivals and then the political and institutional contexts in which public art activity has always taken place. We became drawn to something we hesitated to call 'institutional histories', because it sounded too sociological, but which could more adequately account for the varieties of long-term organisation through which art emerges. While looking at wider contexts, we also want to stay close to artists and the impacts that artworks can have on our perceptions and opinions. After all, this is still what makes art and exhibitions worthwhile as public endeavours.

This brings us quite naturally to Artists for Democracy. Co-founder Cecilia Vicuña writes in this publication that revolutionary politics in South America is 'collective dreaming-acting that transforms society', and that transformation is something for which many artists strive. That hyphenated phrase 'dreaming-acting' also points to the need for organisation, and AFD was, through its many informal transformations, ultimately a structure that held a dream around which to build solidarity with others. The fact that AFD was largely embodied by artists is equally important to its value in thinking about artistic work in the public sphere, as is the way that an organisation born in the wake of the Chilean repressions became such an international call to action, from Vietnamese liberation to colonial discriminations in Britain. Vijay Prashad says very clearly here that the fascist/neoliberal coup d'état in Chile was different from other reassertions of coloniality in that it came at a moment where the forces of emancipation thought they were winning. Such a perspective is beyond our imagination in the twenty-first century, but it bears reflecting on for a moment. Chile was a turning point and, even though there were a few more victories, the power of reaction never lost its grip again. No wonder, then, that artists were highly motivated to defend the rights that had been won after 1945. In Chile, they saw what the future had in store. Today, the world confronts a new radicalism of the right that departs from neoliberalism and wishes to erase whatever remains of plurality and communality in society. We can learn much from what worked, and didn't, in the solidarities that developed to oppose the last rightist turn of the screw.

We live in precarious times. This can operate at different scales – from immigration status, to ecosystems in crisis, to daily means of subsistence – which makes the need for new solidarities ever more urgent. Resistance to the increasing precarity of life engendered by globalised capitalist modernity has galvanised social movements across many different contexts in recent years; in our own workplace, University of the Arts London, we have been on strike more times than we can count in recent years, with an end to precarious working conditions a headline demand. Recent years have seen the largest wave of public sector strikes in the UK for decades. This has drawn superficial comparisons to the 1970s, but may be understood as just the latest phase in a declining nation-state's various postimperial convulsions – seen also in the grotesque spectacle of its monarchy, its xenophobic authoritarian imaginaries and its abrupt exit from the European Union, which the UK voted to join around the same time that AFD began.

AFD's position in history is complex: its core events took place in London, but its orientation connected personal and artistic trajectories spanning Africa, Asia, Europe and the Americas, and it aimed to give 'material and cultural support to liberation movements worldwide' as a 'broad artistic front'. To include AFD in the *Exhibition Histories* book series is to test the possibility of decentring our studies of art and its publics while being physically sited in the UK. As David Morris suggests in his essay contextualising

AFD, 'A project such as AFD exceeds narratives of "Britishness" or "British art history"; it happened in spite of, rather than because of, the imperial nation state.' Morris's writing guides us to explore the twin senses of artistic and political possibility at the very moment of 1974 to 1977 in London, when, as now, imperial power was in crisis and the environment for migrants hostile.

AFD's inaugural and best-known event is the 'Arts Festival for Democracy in Chile' at the Royal College of Art, London, in October 1974: a multifaceted two-week gathering of performance, exhibition and discussion. Following a split in the founding group, a second phase of AFD began in a squat at 143 Whitfield Street in early 1975, establishing itself as an experimental artist-to-artist space. More festivals, solo and group exhibitions, performances, gatherings and organising followed. During this period, AFD renamed itself the Fitzrovia Cultural Centre; its members numbered at least 50 artists and cultural workers across visual art, literature, dance, experimental theatre, film, video, improvised music and other common grounds. After the group was evicted from Whitfield Street in 1977, it was unable to find a new home; some last traces of AFD could be found in events such as 'Mayfair Illuminations' at 41 Berkeley Square in August 1978, or in the call-out that same year for a 'Grand Artists Banquet'. Invoking a tradition of famous artists' banquets alongside Ho Chi Minh's early culinary training with the great chef Auguste Escoffier, the invitation was for a thousand artists to cook their favourite recipes together – a reaction to the over-seriousness and puritanism of British political circles.

We have developed this research as much as possible through dialogue, primarily with the protagonists and those with personal connections to AFD's histories, as well as with wider circles of comrades and collaborators. The result is multivocal and *partial* – in the double sense of being fragmentary and shaped by affinity. AFD has no central archive, official or otherwise, and its documents are scattered across many personal collections, where they are not lost or long forgotten. AFD events were often programmed and publicised unbeknownst to their announced participants, with primary documents no guarantee of whether an event actually happened. Moreover, storytelling, myth-making and information-interventions are all constants in AFD's artistic repertoire. As such, the research led us into a complex dance with facticity. This became a creative challenge – as well as a point of inspiration – for organising the present publication. ('If we don't know for sure if the 1000-artist banquet ever happened, why not organise our own?') Wing Chan's contribution here addresses the questions raised by the precarious documents of AFD; from Michel-Rolph Trouillot's injunction to ask how history works, rather than what it is, Chan demonstrates how artistic practices can offer alternative forms of history-making and collective political education. Such fragmented archives offer a lens through which to view our precarious present.

From the start we felt compelled to seek perspectives from those places AFD's solidarities are expressed towards. The conversational contribution of María José Lemaitre Mujica and Caroll Yasky from the Museo de la Solidaridad Salvador Allende (MSSA) invites us to approach 'from the "outside" in', offering entry points from their base in downtown Santiago. They trace the Chile-UK connection by reconstructing the institutional history of this museum; its ideal since 1971 of becoming a museum for the people; and the extended intellectual, diplomatic, institutional and artistic networks it has accumulated. They also address how museum workers have translated the institution's founding commitments to address current sociopolitical urgencies. Eileen Legaspi-Ramirez's essay begins with the context of the Philippines, and the bastardisation and instrumentalisation of 'solidarity' in the present-day times of Ferdinand Marcos Jr. Taking AFD as a point of departure to trace through-lines, frictions and tangents – and with close attention to works by Rasheed Araeen, David Medalla and Cecilia Vicuña – Legaspi-Ramirez highlights modes of self-hybridisation, self-acknowledgement and self-education as survival strategies for diasporic artists. The fraught ephemerality of AFD's histories is read as part of a long continuum of creative solidarity work, across disparate times and locations, exceeding its moments of public coalescence.

Continuing these transnational movements, Hannah Healey follows the two-year journey of a single work, John Dugger's *Chile Vencerá,* across multiple contexts of presentation. Dugger's monumental banner has become one of the most recognisable visual icons of AFD, in large part due to its circulation via a photograph that shows it at the head of the major solidarity rally in Trafalgar Square in London in 1974, the occasion for its making. Healey explores how the work's meanings accumulated and shifted across such diverse contexts as a Labour Party rally in

London, a counterculture church in San Francisco and a Chilean-refugee-led community centre in Berkeley, California. By considering the banner across these different moments – the rally, the protest, the concert – the text is a compelling invitation to an expanded understanding of what we could mean by 'exhibition'. Returning us to London in this more speculative mode, artists Cường Minh Bá Phạm and George Clark consider the archive of AFD's festival 'People of the World Learn from Indochina, Homage to Ho Chi Minh and the Victory of the Indochinese Peoples', held in London in 1975 to mark the end of the Second Indochina War, alongside that of the An Việt Foundation (AVF), established in 1981–82 as an infrastructure to support Vietnamese post-war settlement in London. Their text taps into the circulations of experimental music and revolutionary song, exploring questions of belonging, memory, exile, tradition, war and love through a sonic sensibility. Finding moments of resonances and discord across the entangled archives of AFD and AVF, they foreground the shared complexity of interpersonal histories and the necessity of community and gathering. Their questions echo some of our own in thinking about what we are to make of AFD's collective histories now: 'What is the sound of a group? What are the sounds left behind, and what sounds can be brought with us?'

The extended 'Archives and Voices' section of this book is a starting point to answer such questions. It collates primary materials including leaflets, invitations, posters, letters and photographic documentation of AFD activities spanning its years of activity from a range of personal and public archives. The documents are loosely chronological and punctuated by key texts from Rasheed Araeen, Guy Brett, Virgil Calaguian, Susan Hiller, David Medalla (in conversation with Brandon Taylor), Annabel Nicolson, Nii Kwate Owoo and Cecilia Vicuña. In dialogue with these archival documents is an edited selection of voices from over 25 members of AFD. These first-person narratives complement or contradict the primary materials, adding texture and complexity, or simply filling gaps in the stories and capturing aspects that the archive is otherwise unable to reach.

This book builds on our past research, and indicates future directions. It may be seen as a companion to another long-standing *Exhibition Histories* project, on the histories and archives of ruangrupa, which we are developing for future publication. In that project the 'dreaming-acting' described by Vicuña is seen in a very different context, taking it forwards in time to *reformasi*-era Jakarta and beyond. The cultural situation in Indonesia bears traces of the actions of AFD, if only as a memory of an international, decolonising resistance active in Southeast Asia. Cultural workers faced a very different set of circumstances in the post-Suharto moment, but what both organisations share is a call for solidarity and collectivity as key aspects of artistic practice. If ruangrupa claim to 'make friends not art', they mean it in terms of building real, meaningful relations with others, where solidarity is not an abstract term of endearment but a shared struggle. They choose to act on their dream of solidarity by changing the terms under which art and friendship are built, in ways that are comparable to how AFD turned the slaughter of Salvador Allende into a common cause and a means to activate a transnational community of values.

We give our heartfelt thanks to all the contributors to this publication and to our steadfast partners in *Exhibition Histories*: John Tain and Sneha Ragavan at Asia Art Archive; Lauren Cornell and Tom Eccles at the Center for Curatorial Studies, Bard College; and Mick Wilson at the Faculty of Fine, Applied and Performing Arts, University of Gothenburg. We are also delighted to welcome a new partner to our midst, the documenta Institut, and to welcome Felix Vogel and Mi You to our editorial group. We look forward to where this collective research takes us.

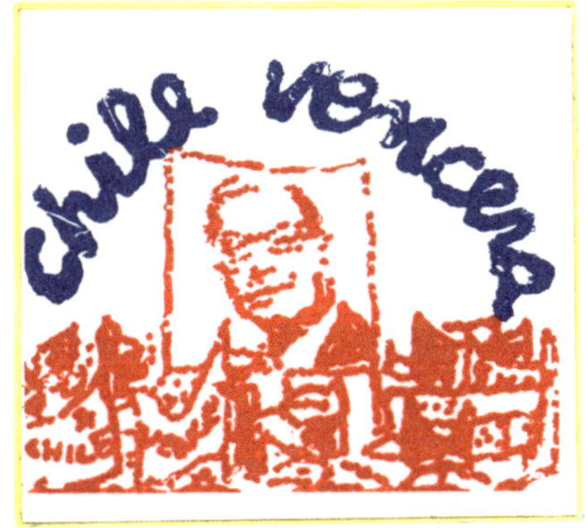

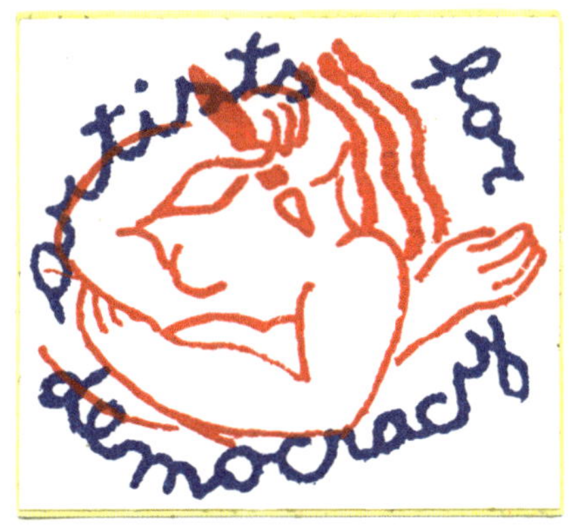

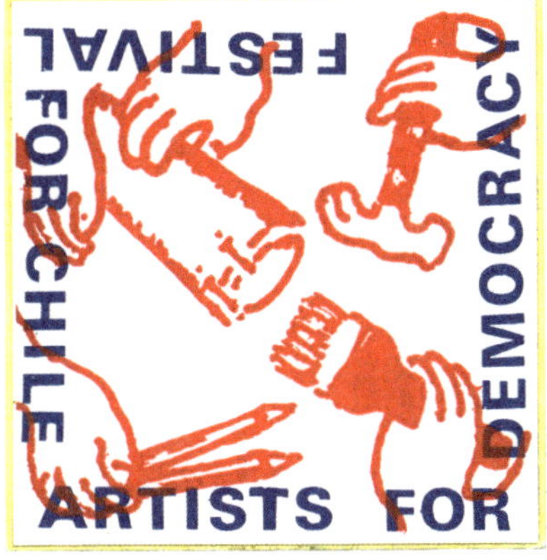

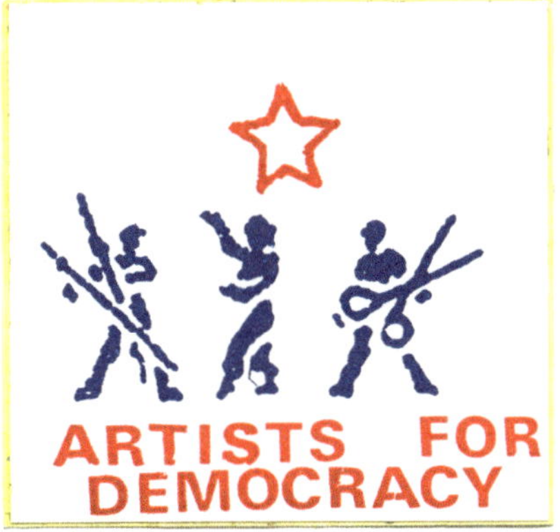

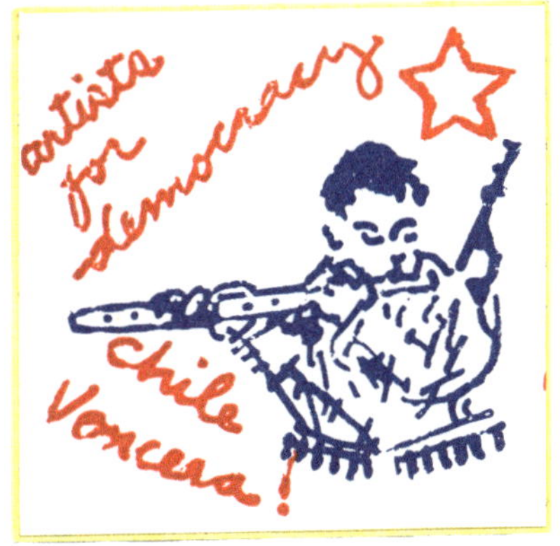

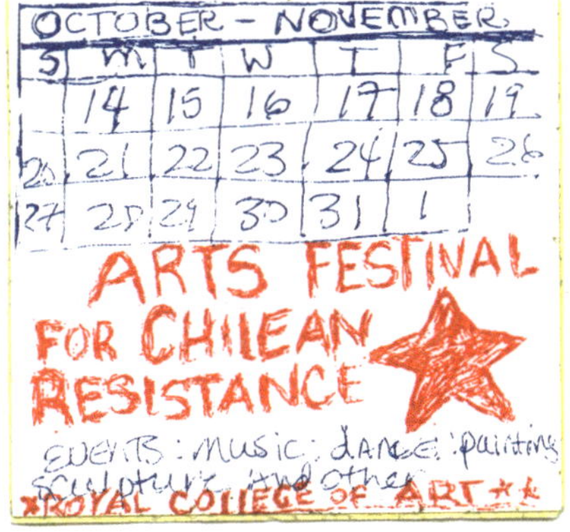

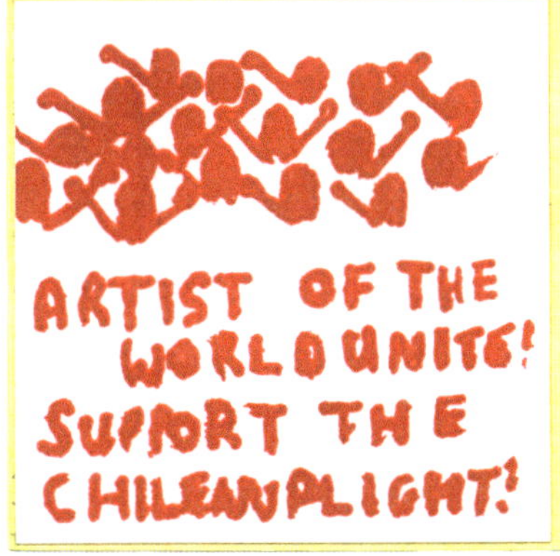

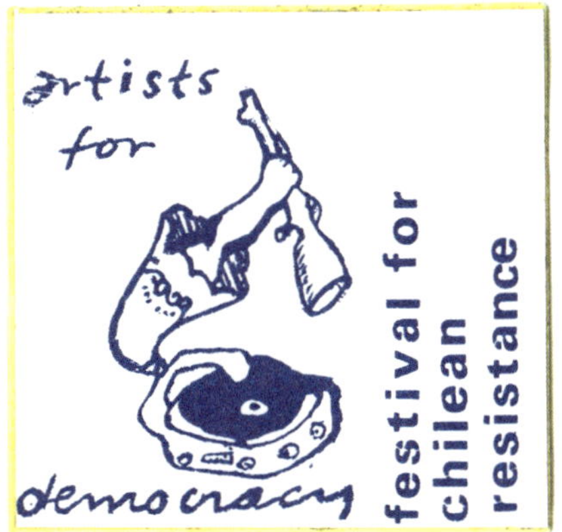

Artists for Democracy, stickers created by artists including John Dugger, David Medalla and Cecilia Vicuña, for 'Arts Festival for Democracy in Chile', Royal College of Art, London, 1974

Precarious Solidarities: Artists for Democracy in Historical Perspective

David Morris

> Struggle is hazardous and proceeds in spirals and zig-zags…
>
> 'THE AIMS OF ARTISTS FOR DEMOCRACY', 1974[1]

1 'THE AIMS OF ARTISTS FOR DEMOCRACY, and some suggestions for our organisation, with proposals for immediate and long-range tasks', dated 26 November 1974, Guy Brett collection, Tate Archive (TGA 20208).

In his 'Preliminary Notes for a Black Manifesto', Rasheed Araeen writes:

> What is important now is not WHAT WE WERE IN THE PAST, but WHAT WE ARE TODAY. ... [F]inding ourselves surrounded and dominated by the forces which either demand our return to ethnic traditions or make us accept the hegemony of Western developments, WE HAVE NO CHOICE BUT TO OPPOSE THEM BOTH; AND OUT OF THIS CONFRONTATION WILL EMERGE NEW FORMS THAT TRULY REFLECT OUR PARTICULARITY IN THE WORLD TODAY.[2]

Araeen's 'TODAY' can be read historically, in the context of the times and places in which he was working on the text, in Karachi and London during 1975 to 1976. It can also be read indexically, the 'TODAY' invoking the present, wherever and whenever that may currently be. I was not alive in the 1970s and the London I live in is a very different city. But in what follows I try to explore the long 'today' across the points suggested by Araeen's words – to talk historically about the present, about particularity in its world(s), and to do so by way of this 1970s 'today'.

Contemporary might be another word for this sense of 'today'. Our particularity in the world today is the expression of the spirals and zigzags of history, and the globalised present is a reflection of a world map shaped by colonialism. *Contemporary* is a description of the disjunctive coexistence of multiple temporalities, characteristic of globalisation.[3] But if contemporaneity – the condition or quality of being contemporary – is an articulation of the temporal logic of global capitalist modernity, it is not reducible to it; hence the Zapatismo call for *un mundo donde quepan muchos mundos*: a world where many worlds fit.[4] In his 'Preliminary Notes', Araeen asks: 'How are Third World people trying to enter into the modern era or/and create their own contemporary history? If their voice is muted or not heard at all, what are the underlying causes? And what are the alternatives open to them?' He goes on to note a handful of examples of organised attempts by the Third World to find a direction other than that imposed by the West. The three examples he gives are FESTAC '77 (The Second World Black and African Festival of Arts and Culture), which took place in Lagos, Nigeria in 1977; Centro de Arte y Comunicación (Center for Art and Communication, CAyC), formed in Buenos Aires, Argentina in 1968; and Artists for Democracy (AFD).

2 Rasheed Araeen, 'Preliminary Notes for a Black Manifesto', *Black Phoenix*, no.1, Winter 1978, p.11; and in this volume, p.306.

3 See Peter Osborne, 'Existential Urgency: Contemporaneity, Biennials and Social Form', *Nordic Journal of Aesthetics*, vol.24, no.49–50, 2016, pp.175–88.

4 I am grateful to Migrants in Culture for introducing me to *un mundo donde quepan muchos mundos*. See www.migrantsinculture.com.

Artists for Democracy is the expression of a very particular time and place. In London in 1974, a small group of artists and cultural workers from Chile, the Philippines, the United States and Britain agreed to form an organisation to offer material and cultural support to liberation movements worldwide. Their immediate context was a declining imperial power in a state of deep crisis. In the words of one contemporary analysis: 'There is no doubt that the old British state is going down.'[5] Legislation such as the 1968 Commonwealth Immigrants Act and the 1971 Immigration Act, introduced by respective Labour and Conservative administrations, introduced a racialised two-tier citizenship system – 'unashamedly racist', in the words of then-premier of India Indira Gandhi – that provided the blueprint for Britain's current 'hostile environment' for migrants.[6] For many of those arriving in London from elsewhere, this did not appear to be a place with especially favourable conditions for the creation of revolutionary new cultures. AFD co-founder Cecilia Vicuña, for instance, quickly realised that 'the real thing' was happening back in Latin America.[7]

Artists, writers and intellectuals from all over the world have long gathered in imperial centres for reasons often antithetical to the project of empire.[8] Just as the economic status of a city such as London is based on the labour of peoples from elsewhere, so too is its cultural capital. A project such as AFD exceeds narratives of 'Britishness' or 'British art history'; it happened in spite of, rather than because of, the imperial nation state. As co-founder David Medalla wrote at one point: 'We are the expatriates of a future world.'[9] (Several AFD members had problems with obtaining visas to live and work in Britain; one of them narrowly avoided deportation.[10]) Nadine El-Enany argues that contemporary Britain *in toto* may be understood as 'the spoils of empire', rightfully belonging to those whom Britain has historically dispossessed.[11] The British state itself can therefore be considered an object of restitution alongside its many stolen artefacts; to echo the words of Nii Kwate Owoo in his 1970 film *You Hide Me*, it should 'immediately and unconditionally be returned to us!'[12] There is nonetheless a critical tension between the persistence of London's position within international art circuits – hence its gravitational pull for artists – and its distance from where 'the real thing' was actually happening. These tensions would both expand and circumscribe AFD's field of activity.

5 Tom Nairn, *The Break-Up of Britain: Crisis and Neo-Nationalism*, London: New Left Books, 1977, p.13.

6 See Ian Sanjay Patel, *We're Here Because You Were There: Immigration and the End of Empire*, London: Verso, 2021.

7 Cecilia Vicuña, conversation with Courtney J. Martin, 'Precarious Solidarities: Artists for Democracy 1974–77', online symposium, 2 February 2023.

8 See, for instance, Benedict Anderson, *Under Three Flags: Anarchism and the Anti-Colonial Imagination,* London: Verso, 2006; *Chimurenga Chronic*, 'imagi-nation nwar – genealogies of the black radical imagination in the francophone world' issue (April 2021).

9 See the drawing for David Medalla's performance *Tatlin at the Funeral of Malevitch*, (1976), in this volume, p.269. This is not to suggest that these artists should not be included in national canons, but to emphasise the expansive horizons their work demands.

10 See Dom Sylvester Houedard, letter to Jun Terra, 16 February 1975; C. Vicuña, conversation with C.J. Martin, *op. cit.*

11 See Nadine El-Enany, *Bordering Britain: Law, Race and Empire*, Manchester: Manchester University Press, 2020.

12 See Nii Kwate Owoo, 'Commentary: You Hide Me', in this volume, p.201.

The group itself was a precarious formation. The founders broke apart within six months; further splits would occur during its subsequent tenure at 143 Whitfield Street; and overall, it managed to sustain itself for a little over three years. A level of volatility is not uncommon in the context of collective political and artistic endeavours; group initiatives that last into the medium-long term are a comparative rarity. Histories of AFD have thus far been largely told in relation to individual artists' biographies, a fact that might tell us more about the dominant ways of constructing art's histories than about the history of AFD itself. In practice, the role of the 'artist' was a highly fluid one within their activities. What is important to attend to now is not just whatever was being produced under the name of 'art' but everything happening around it or made possible by it. Paradoxically, the 'artist' may appear as a rather incidental character in the present story – a collective fiction, perhaps, and one that helps map a different set of possibilities.

The story of AFD may also serve as a reminder of alternative, pre-identitarian political sensibilities. This can be seen, for instance, in the group's ready expression of common cause with peoples across vast cultural, geographic and geopolitical differences (and regardless of participation-or-not from members of those communities); or in the way their Whitfield Street squat was a 'queer' space without ever considering itself as such.[13] Undoubtedly there are tensions within such approaches, but they suggest a politics grounded in relationships within and across difference, and an understanding that individualised identities may function as barrier rather than basis for solidarity.

AFD's story is in no respect a singular one; as one participant observed of their milieu:

> [A] feature of this period was the formation of groups. Their history has never been written. Typically, the establishment never acknowledged their importance while, belatedly and dilutedly, appropriating many of their ideas. ... There were the artists' self-help groups: SPACE (which secured St Katherine's Dock for artistic experiment and discussion), Art Meeting Place, Arts Labs, Acme, Pavilions in the Parks (with its curious 'random' selection procedure), and later on Bonnington Square, and the Brixton Artists Collective. There were pressure groups such as Facop, discussion and theoretical groups such

13 Charles Hustwick, conversation with the author, 22 June 2023; see also his account of AFD as queer space in this volume, p.297.

as the Women's Art History Collective, the Anti-University, the Free International University, Tone Place Seminars, and the many groups whose agitation was combined with new ideas of artistic practice, such as Exploding Galaxy, Artists Placement Group, Scratch Orchestra, Destruction in Art Symposium, Monkey Theatre, O Productions, Ting Theatre of Mistakes, Event Structure Research Group, London Calling, London Film-makers Co-op, Beau Geste Press, Coracle Press, and later on, Artists for Democracy, Poster Collective, Banner Arts and Pan-Afrikan Connection.[14]

14 Guy Brett, 'Internationalism among artists in the 1960s and 1970s', in R. Araeen (ed.), *The Other Story: Afro-Asian Artists in Post-War Britain* (exh. cat.), London: Hayward Gallery / South Bank Centre, 1989, pp.112–13.

15 See Richard Cork, *Everything Seemed Possible: Art in the 1970s*, New Haven: Yale University Press, 2003.

16 *Ibid.*, back cover.

17 Killian Fox, 'Naeem Mohaiemen: "I wanted to take the documentary form and jar it', *The Observer*, 22 September 2018. Emphasis added.

The present publication is a call for another kind of history: one that recognises art and culture as a wholly non-individuated activity, grounded in the mess of group work and its exponential interrelations.

*

From the perspective of one London-based critic, the 1970s was a decade in art where 'everything seemed possible'.[15] This was a moment where 'nothing seemed off-limits' – where 'young artists emerged with a host of heretical alternatives in mind, including film, video, performance, raw documentation, photography and texts'.[16] Naeem Mohaiemen, another keen observer of the 1970s, has remarked that the decade was also 'a moment when anything seemed possible *politically*, particularly if you're from the left. And it's a moment of promise because of decolonisation. But then it pivots and everything starts going dark, by my estimation ... it's the period when things didn't work out.'[17] AFD is the outgrowth of these two moods of possibility – political and artistic. Its story is of the contradictions and mixed fortunes of both.

Fascination with the artistic-solidaristic complexes of the 70s is a more contemporary mood. The present publication is no exception to this, and it is in good company. 'The International Art Exhibition for Palestine' (1978) in Beirut; the pan-Arabism of the first two Arab biennials (in Baghdad in 1974 and Rabat in 1976); post-'68 artists of the Salon de la Jeune Peinture in Paris; the Museo de la Solidaridad Salvador Allende (MSSA, established 1971–73) in Chile; the Japan, Asian, African and Latin American Artists' Association (JAALA, established 1977); the Art Against Apartheid collection (established early 1980s); the Museo de Arte Latinoamericano Contemporáneo de Managua / en Solidaridad con

Nicaragua (established 1983) – all these initiatives and more have been brought together in recent years in the exhibition project 'Past Disquiet'.[18] FESTAC '77 and earlier major pan-African festivals in Dakar (1966) and Algiers (1969) have been the focus of Chimurenga's panoramic forays; and more broadly, the cultural politics of the decolonisation era and legacies of the 1955 Bandung Conference have been explored through exhibition projects including 'After Year Zero: Geographies of Collaboration' (2013) and 'Southern Constellations: The Poetics of the Non-Aligned' (begun 2019).[19] Other recent exhibitions have taken 'solidarity' as a keyword to gather a range of kindred curatorial/artistic projects, including several of the above.[20]

What happens when the transnational networks of anti-imperialism from the not-too-distant past are brought into the contemporary contexts of the 'global' contemporary? Noting the tendency, 'Southern Constellations' hazarded that 'in this time of increasing global inequalities, crises, and the widening chasm between the rich and the poor, artists are seeking new ways and means of expression with which to overcome such divisions and perhaps re-establish different, more just global relations'.[21] Yet the critical concern is what relationship the 'solidarity' expressed in this earlier moment, with its overlapping horizons of decolonisation, liberation and revolutionary struggle, can hold with respect to contemporary manifestations, i.e., the distance between then and now. Are such manifestations predicated on 'the absence of a context of political practice that might give such exhibitions an effective extra-artistic political force' (as Peter Osborne has argued in another context)?[22] Or, to turn to Artists for Democracy more concretely: Is this story of a politicised and particularly worldly group of artists remarkable most of all for its anticipation of art's 'global' turns that were just around the corner? Or could there be other reasons to return to it now; other lessons we might learn; other ways we might extend it in the present?

*

At a conference in 1978 on 'The State of British Art', Richard Cork would acknowledge the prevailing attitude in British art at the time: 'We are guilty of appalling British imperialist provincialism with regard to the Third World.'[23] Araeen's 'Preliminary Notes for a Black Manifesto', published in the journals *Black Phoenix* and

18 See Kristine Khouri and Rasha Salti (ed.), *Past Disquiet: Artists, International Solidarity and Museums in Exile*, Warsaw: Museum of Modern Art in Warsaw, 2018.

19 See *FESTAC '77 – decomposed, an-arranged and reproduced by Chimurenga*, Cape Town and London: Chimurenga and Afterall Books, 2019; Bojana Piškûr (ed.), *Southern Constellations: The Poetics of the Non-Aligned* (exh. cat.), Ljubljana: Moderna galerija, 2019; Annett Busch and Anselm Franke (ed.), *After Year Zero: Geographies of Collaboration* (exh. cat.), Warsaw: Museum of Modern Art in Warsaw, 2013.

20 For instance, 'Actions of Art and Solidarity' (2021), curated by Office for Contemporary Art Norway (OCA) and organised in collaboration with Kunstnernes Hus, Oslo; 'Solidarity Spores' (2020), Asia Culture Centre, Gwangju.

21 B. Piškûr, *Southern Constellations*, *op. cit.*, p.5.

22 P. Osborne, 'Living with Contradictions: The Resignation of Chris Gilbert', *Afterall*, issue 16, Autumn/Winter 2007, p.113.

Studio International that same year, offered a trenchant critique of predominant understandings of 'internationalism', as something anchored in Europe and North America to the exclusion of the majority of the world. In Araeen's analysis, 'international art' may as well be described as 'imperialist art', a Western model imposed on the Third World. We may thus think of the prevailing aesthetic model in European and American art contexts at that moment as *international-imperial* aesthetics. This may be contrasted with what Sanjukta Sunderason terms 'partisan aesthetics', to describe artistic practices that were politicised through their adjacency to left-wing activism in Calcutta through the 1940s and 50s.[24] The *partisan* here describes a political position-making for artists that could support and promote the intersecting political positions of modernity, nationalism and socialism, through different examples of participation in and disassociation from India's Communist Party. This conjuncture is precisely the shift from a colonial to a postcolonial condition, and the formation of the modern Indian state post-independence; for Sunderason, *partisan aesthetics* refers those modes of artistic and intellectual practice that articulate the relationships between socialism and modernity in the context of decolonisation.

AFD's anti-imperialism was advanced within a still-imperial metropole, and the concept of the *partisan* offers a point of contrast for understanding how AFD took shape as part of a critical dialogue with *internationalist-imperialist* aesthetics. As a collective, they were *not* partisan, and deliberately so. They were a self-described 'broad front' group of cultural workers operating under the banner of 'democracy', and as such they held various political affiliations. (In fact, partisanship towards the Revolutionary Left Movement (MIR) at the close of the Chile Festival was one of the major factors that led to an initial split in the group.) 'Democracy' held a range of meanings – from specific opposition to the military coup in Chile and commitment to anti-imperialist solidarity with the Third World, to a more general sense of affinity with democratic politics of different types. This extended, in particular, to socialism in its various 'really existing' varieties in the mid-1970s, as well as being the expression of a general principle of collective political organisation.

The 'broad front' strategy extended to AFD's aesthetics, characterised by an experimental spirit realised through a great diversity of artistic approaches. It was unusual in its combination

23 R. Cork, quoted in John A. Walker, *Left Shift: Radical Art in 1970s Britain*, London: I.B. Tauris, 2002, p.212.

24 See Sanjukta Sunderason, *Partisan Aesthetics: Modern Art and India's Long Decolonization*, Redwood City, CA: Stanford University Press, 2020. I am grateful to May Adadol Ingawanij for her recommendation of Sunderason's work.

of various and often incompatible tendencies and approaches – many of which can be seen in diagrams drawn up by Su Braden and Frank Popper respectively. Certain features mark AFD out as an outlier within the contemporary art scene at the time. These are not easily separated, and they intertwine and combine across AFD's many activities in different ways: (1) its aesthetic agenda, tending towards performative, literary and poetic forms; (2) its embrace of 'amateur'/DIY/non-art forms[25] (3) its queer experiment-in-living at Whitfield Street; (4) its demographic make-up; (5) its internationalism in artistic and political terms. All of this combined in a mercurial admixture of agitprop and avant-garde.

AFD's specific political outlook could only have taken the shape that it did in the years it existed, the mid-to-late 1970s.

25 The group included numerous non-artists and hosted a range of 'non-art' activities, such as writing, cooking, homeopathy, poetry, education, political meetings and organising.

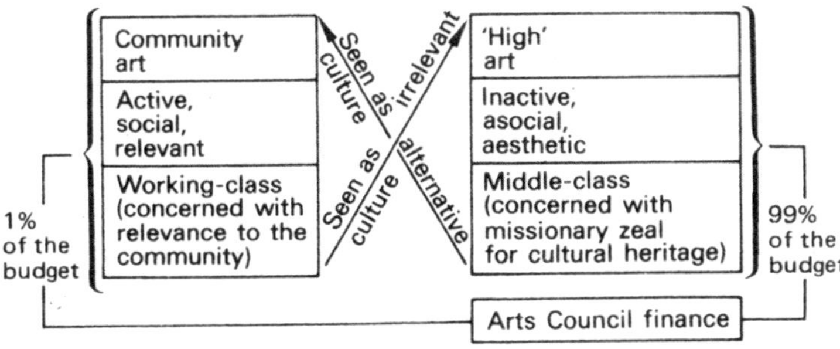

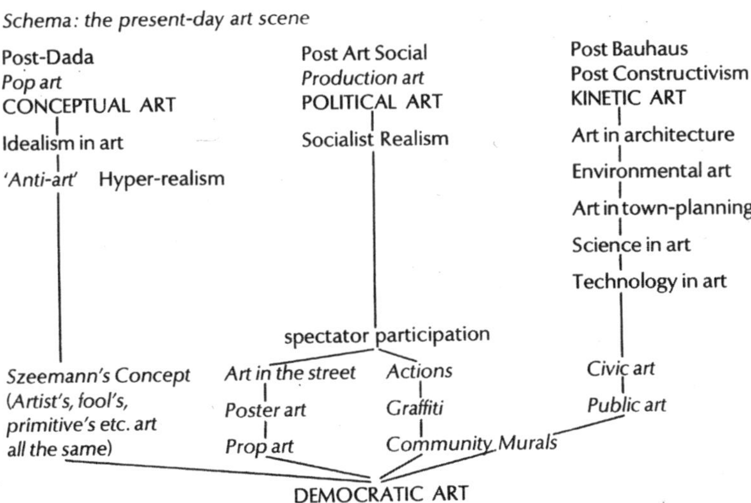

top: from Su Braden, *Artists and People* (1978); bottom: from Frank Popper, *Art – Action and Participation* (1975)

At this point, the era of national liberation and formal decolonisation from European powers was reaching its end. During the first phase of this process, post-1945, a large part of the formally colonised world won independence. Yet many parts of the world remained under the domination of colonial rule through this time, and many national liberation movements turned to armed struggle as the only means to secure their freedom, with the Chinese and Cuban revolutions (in 1949 and 1959 respectively) providing powerful examples to follow. The years 1973–75 saw a number of successes in this regard. The African Party for the Independence of Guinea and Cape Verde (PAIGC) declared independence in Guinea-Bissau in September 1973, and the following year the Carnation Revolution in Portugal saw the collapse of Estado Novo and the acceleration of the decolonisation process in Angola, Mozambique, Cape Verde and São Tomé and Príncipe. The period saw revolutions in Ethiopia (1974), Laos (1975), Afghanistan (1978), Grenada (1979) and Nicaragua (1979), while the cause of national liberation movements was being advanced at the United Nations, notably in the 1974 New International Economic Order, which highlighted 'the interdependence of all members of the world community' and put forward a set of proposals to end the economic colonialism that newly decolonised nations still faced.[26] But above all, the independence of Vietnam, hard won against the forces of United States imperialism, defined the moment. For the Third World and its supporters, much indeed seemed possible.

But the geopolitical outlook was by no means clear. Hopes for the coming British revolution were raised, while reactionary forces beckoned Pinochet-style military takeover in Britain.[27] AFD was a response to the overthrow of Allende's democratic route to socialism, with support from the US, and the imposition of national debt and structural adjustment programmes was already beginning to shape the neocolonial dynamics between the First and Third Worlds (or what would come to be known as the Global North and South). The preceding decade, military coups in Brazil (1964) and Indonesia (1965) had seen the destruction of progressive governments, also with the support of the US and UK, with terrible consequences. And in Southeast Asia, the years following 1975 took increasingly violent turns, defined by the genocide in Cambodia (1975–79), the Vietnamese-Cambodian war in 1978 and the Vietnamese-Chinese border war in 1979. With anti-imperialism no longer a common cause after 1975, the interference of Cold War

26 See United Nations General Assembly, 'Declaration on the Establishment of a New International Economic Order', 1 May 1974.

27 Tariq Ali, *The Coming British Revolution*, London: Jonathan Cape, 1972; Patrick Cosgrave, 'Could the Army Take Over?', *The Spectator*, 22 December 1973. See also Andy Beckett, *Pinochet in Picadilly: Britain and Chile's Hidden History*, London: Faber & Faber, 2002, in particular chapter 13, on the formation of far-right 'civil defence group' Civil Assistance, involving various establishment and ex-military figures.

geopolitics in Southeast Asia combined with old prejudices and ambitions for regional dominance, with devastating effects. A festival in homage to the victory of the Indochinese peoples, such as that organised by AFD in 1975, could only have happened at that moment. As the 1970s drew to a close, the triumphant mood was no longer possible to maintain. And this is also the point at which AFD dissolved.

In a conversation published in a 1979 issue of *Black Phoenix*, Araeen and Medalla discuss the 'failure' of AFD's project. In Araeen's analysis, it lay in its inability to deal with cultural imperialism, particularly at the level of artistic practice; for Medalla, it was instead to be found in the disconnect between cultural workers, who had little knowledge of politics but saw it as an opportunity to exhibit, and political radicals, who had little or no interest in art or poetry. These critiques offer some coordinates for thinking about what we might consider 'successes' in relation to AFD, namely, how it dealt with cultural imperialism at the level of its practice (or failed to do so), and how it reconciled (or not) the conflicting priorities of its collective.

With this in mind, we may ask: What was the relationship between the twin senses of artistic-political possibility at this very particular moment of 1974 to 1977? What was its relationship to those to whom it dedicated its activity – 'the people', 'the masses', 'the international working class'?[28] What publics did it in fact gather? What practices and languages were established towards its aim of giving 'material and cultural support to liberation movements worldwide' and towards democratic and progressive cultures?

28 See 'THE AIMS OF ARTISTS FOR DEMOCRACY', *op. cit.*

*

The 'Arts Festival for Democracy in Chile' (Royal College of Art, 14–30 October 1974) is a place to start answering these questions. As the first and largest event organised under the banner of AFD, the Chile Festival may be the clearest instance of a collective artistic manifestation developing from, and contributing to, progressive political movements. The central role of culture in Salvador Allende's 'peaceful route to socialism' provided a model for artists and cultural workers, and the shock of the 1973 coup saw a great wave of organising solidarity across the world. In Britain, the national Chile Solidarity Campaign, with its basis in a strong trade union movement, quickly took the lead in efforts to campaign for democracy to be restored for the Chilean people, and in support, too, of the several thousand Chileans exiled in the UK. One of those exiles was Cecilia Vicuña, who writes:

> AFD's revolutionary attempt was to dream on the scale of the Americas by reversing the colonial order of the art world, where the metropolis dictates the aesthetic language the colonies must follow. It offered an alternative model of creativity generated from South America and the Third World … where revolutionary politics and experimental art merge with ease.[29]

29 C. Vicuña, 'Organized Dreaming', trans. Christopher Winks, in *Artists for Democracy: El Archivo de Cecilia Vicuña*, Santiago: Museo de la Memoria y los Derechos Humanos/ Museo Nacional de Bellas Artes, 2013, unpaginated; and in this volume, pp.163–67.

Vicuña's retrospective account emphasises the Festival's debt to the examples of 'new forms of collective participation' provided by 1960s–70s Chile, including Allende's agrarian reforms and Project Cybersyn, the pioneering experiment in cybernetic governance. In this account, the Chile Festival is seen as extending the alternative models of creativity that developed during the Chilean revolutionary process. And this represented a reversal of the prevailing internationalist-imperialist dynamic, where cultural-political developments of the supposedly 'peripheral' world could provide models for cultural workers worldwide, and especially in the imperial metropole. In an interview towards the end of the AFD collective's life, Medalla would emphasise the group's purpose as a space to learn from what was happening in the Third World (giving Guinea-Bissau and Vietnam as examples): 'New types of culture are being created, you see, and because one is away from these places doesn't mean one should be blind to what is happening there.'[30]

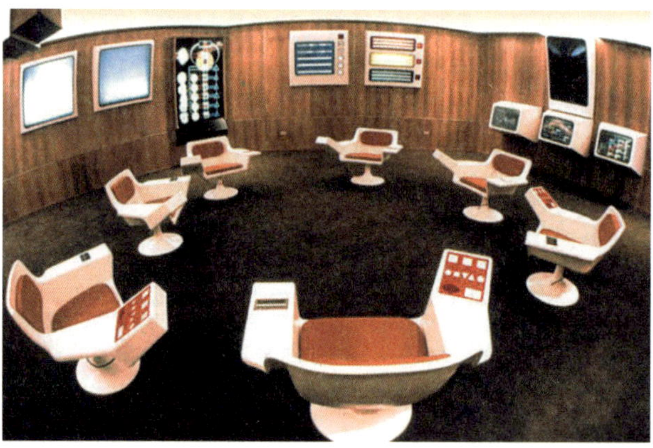

The operations room of Project Cybersyn, developed in Chile in 1971–72 during the government of Salvador Allende

Besides Allende's Chile, AFD drew from different cultural-artistic models. European-American avant-garde traditions, still-dominant within art schools and the art system at large, operated as genuine inspiration and critical foil; and these were complemented by understandings of avant-garde developments within a wider geographical scope, such as the internationalism championed as part of Signals gallery in London, and its accompanying publication *Signals Newsbulletin*, particularly with respect to Latin America. In the Philippines in the late 1960s, the Ermita district of Manila was a formative context for several core AFD members; 'happenings' took place in unexpected venues, from streets, parks and by the sea wall, to cafes, bars, restaurants, churchyards and cemeteries. These events mingled with marches against the Vietnam War and the activities of the communist youth organisation Kabataang Makabayan.[31] We may also speculate about AFD's continuity with what Patrick Flores describes as a wider 'installative' tendency in art in Southeast Asia, a 'relationality activated by multiple forces' and motivated by the desire 'to convene an art world, or a relational or transpersonal world of art, by creating conditions for people to assemble along the various axes of dissent, development, nationalism and solidarity'.[32]

Cultural models from elsewhere opened up significant space for invention and projection. China was of special interest to the post-'68 generation internationally, as a powerful locus of inspiration, fantasy and orientalist misunderstanding through which political and artistic questions could be advanced. Jun Terra recalls the Maoist influence on his cultural-political milieu in Manila, and Guy Brett and John Dugger each participated in Society for Anglo Chinese Understanding (SACU) tours of the People's Republic during the 1970s; these experiences furnished a range of new ideas on art, which were elaborated in writing and exhibition-making. This included Brett's championing of non-professional 'spare-time artists' and the touring exhibition 'Peasant Painting from Huhsien [户县] County';[33] Terra's Maoist readings of the art of his contemporaries;[34] Caroline Tisdall's *Guardian* article based on Dugger's experiences in China and the social and economic position of artists there;[35] and 'People Weave a House!', Dugger's 1972 exhibition collaboration with Medalla and others at the Institute of Contemporary Arts (ICA), London, in which visitors were invited to collectively weave architecture

30 David Medalla, interview by Steven Thorn, 1977, Guy Brett collection, Tate Archive (TGA 20208).

31 Jun Terra, correspondence with the author, 19 July 2022 and 28 April 2023.

32 Patrick D. Flores, 'A Changing World', in David Teh and David Morris (ed.), *Artist-to-Artist: Independent Art Festivals in Chiang Mai 1992–98*, London: Afterall Books, 2018, pp.269 and 278.

33 In Brett's account: 'The paintings convey a great sense of adventure in the large-scale collective undertakings of irrigation systems, terracing climbing the mountains, the density of healthy crops. And at the same time delight in the small scale – the workers' tea cups, a book, a newspaper, shoes left behind to enter the soggy field – material details of real life.' G. Brett, 'China's Spare-time Artists', *Studio International*, vol.189, no.973, January/February 1975, p.14. See also *Peasant paintings from Hu county, Shensi province, China* (exh. cat.), London: Arts Council of Great Britain, 1976.

34 J. Terra, '"From the Masses to the Masses": The Art of David Medalla', unpublished manuscript, 1972.

35 Caroline Tisdall, 'Chinese Agitscape', *The Guardian*, 15 December 1972.

THE MASSES HAVE BOUNDLESS CREATIVE POWER.
MAO TSETUNG

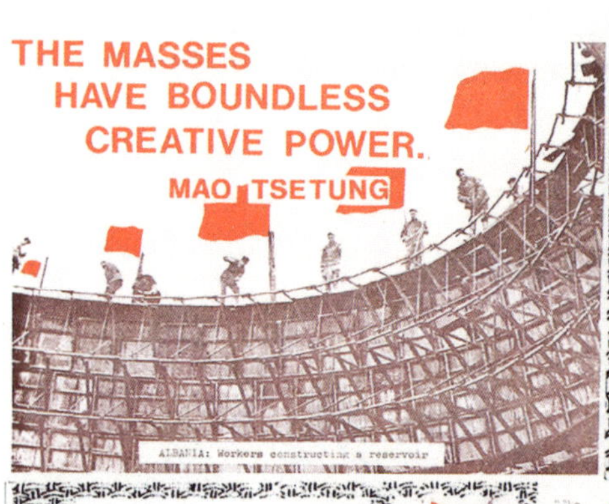

ALBANIA: Workers constructing a reservoir

PEOPLE WEAVE A HOUSE!

VIETNAM: Women's militia fighting the U.S. aggressors

VIETNAM: Woven bridge

MARX

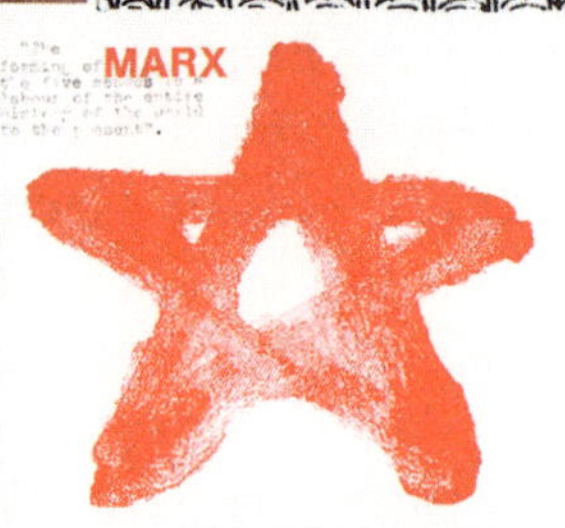

a participation–production project by

JOHN DUGGER

cultural workers team led by

DAVID MEDALLA

of

ARTISTS LIBERATION FRONT

ENGELS "It is not that the solution of the housing question simultaneously solves the social question, but that only by abolition of the capitalist mode of production, is the solution of the housing question made possible". from THE HOUSING QUESTION by F. ENGELS (1872-3)

NORTH AMERICA: Woven scaffolding (American Indian)

"Mythology", said MARX, "is the unconscious artistic assimilation of natural and social phenomena". MARX also said, "society cannot demand from the artist an imagination independent of that society's mythology. Today there are two contending world mythologies: the decadent mythology of moribund capitalism, which produces bourgeois cosmopolitan culture, and the progressive mythology of the rising world proletariat, which is creating an international socialist culture. The question "FOR WHOM?" is fundamental in discovering the mythical content of artistic works.

INDOCHINA: Mat-weaving

SOUTH AMERICA: Woven houses, Lake Maracaibo, Venezuela

LENIN said, "there are democratic and socialist elements in every national culture". To serve the people, it is the task of all progressive artists to discover these democratic and socialist elements, encourage their growth, concentrate them, transform them through struggle, and bring them to a higher stage of artistic development. These elements reflect the revolutionary experiences of the masses through different historical epochs; they are the seeds from which will grow the bright flowers of proletarian socialist culture, when the masses win liberation and end the exploitation of man by man. Revolutionary theory and the inevitable victory of world communism guide our artistic practice.

HOLLAND: Polderboys weaving a dyke

CHINA: Women bridge-builders

COME AND WEAVE A HOUSE OF TRANSPARENT PLASTIC TUBING AT THE INSTITUTE OF CONTEMPORARY ARTS

ICA

NASH HOUSE THE MALL LONDON SW1
01-930 6393

Daily noon to 7pm except Monday

Open to the public

24 NOVEMBER-24 DECEMBER 1972

part of an integrated programme The Body as a Medium of Expression

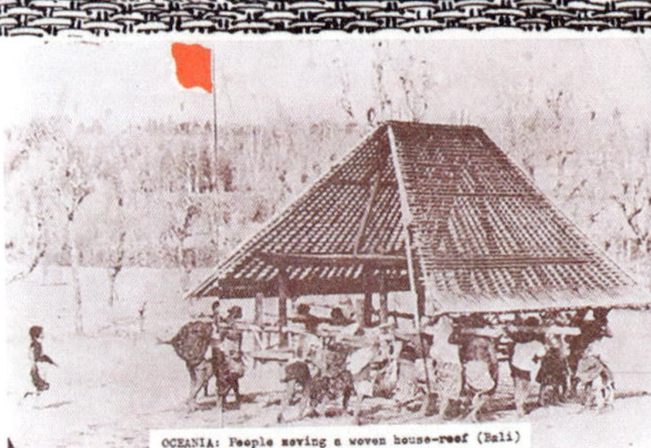

OCEANIA: People moving a woven house-roof (Bali)

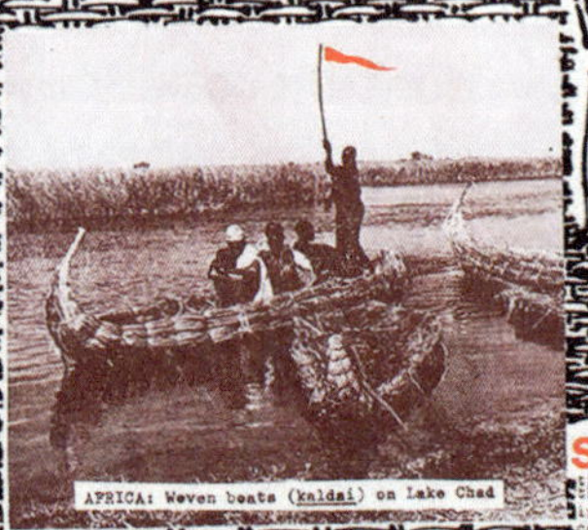

AFRICA: Woven boats (kaldai) on Lake Chad

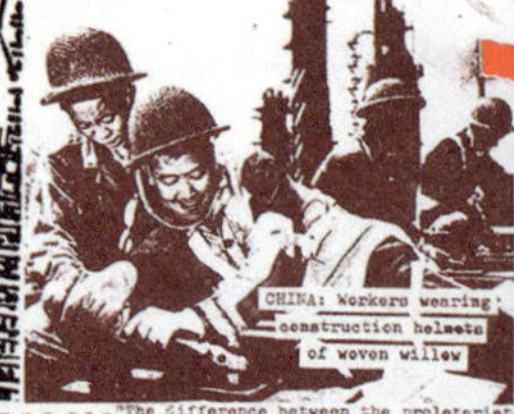

CHINA: Workers wearing construction helmets of woven willow

STALIN "The difference between the proletariat and the other classes which at any time in the course of history revolutionized the relations of production consists in the fact that the class interests of the proletariat merge with the interests of the overwhelming majority of society, because proletarian revolution implies the abolition not of one or another form of exploitation, but of all exploitation". ECONOMIC PROBLEMS OF SOCIALISM IN THE USSR

right: Li Feng-Lan discussing and developing the second version of her painting *Springhoeing*, Huhsien [户县] County, c.1972–73

facing page: Exhibition poster for 'People Weave a House!', Institute of Contemporary Arts, London, 1972

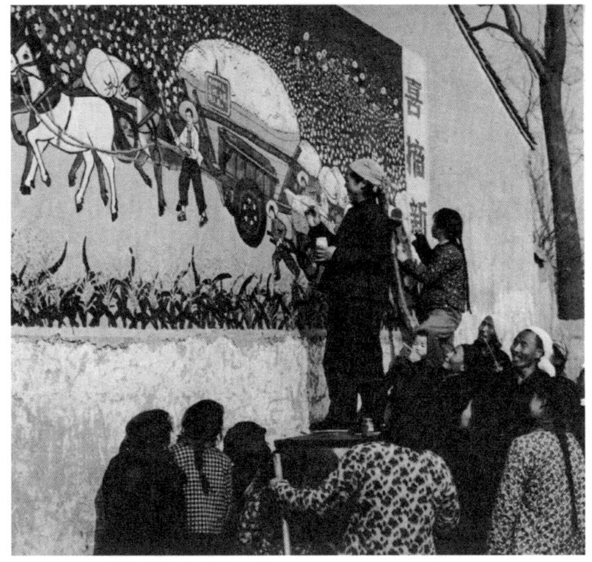

using a large loom and transparent plastic tubes. Altogether China appeared to offer an example the British art world should learn from – 'the basis for a completely new culture', as one critic put it[36] – constructing an irresistible image of the artist-in-society, however distant its realities may be. Cultural work in general is prioritised over individual careers; artists are unalienated in their work and receive government salary and expenses; popular involvement is encouraged through 'a general demystification of the different branches of culture – philosophy, science, art';[37] and the emphasis is 'on community, or the sensual contact of bodies, or food, or the earth'.[38]

Dugger and Medalla's collaboration first developed through shared interests in Buddhism and interconnected South Asian intellectual traditions, and their mutual involvement in the Exploding Galaxy (1967–68), the multidisciplinary collective and 'dance-drama' group based at 99 Balls Pond Road.[39] Their aim was to 'break down the invisible barrier between "creator" and "spectator" … and art be a living process in which one, two or several people formulate suggestions that others take up and develop in different directions'.[40] Dugger and Medalla would travel together to visit the Kerala Kathakali dance company, a major influence on the collective, spending time in India and Sri Lanka as part of an eighteen-month journey via ship with additional stops in Dakar, Senegal, Durban, South Africa, Mombassa, Kenya, Pakistan and, finally, Manila.[41] The experience was formative

36 Adrian Rifkin, 'The Chinese Exhibition at the Warehouse Gallery', *Artscribe*, no.5, February 1977, p.17. The critical reception to the 'amateur painters' was generally favourable; after London, the exhibition went to Nottingham, Birmingham and Edinburgh, and received interest from venues in Essex, Bradford, Sheffield, Glasgow, Brighton and Portsmouth. See Emily Williams, 'Exporting the Communist Image: The 1976 Chinese Peasant Painting Exhibition in Britain', *New Global Studies*, vol.8, no.3, 2014, pp.279–305.

37 G. Brett, 'China's Spare-time Artists', *op. cit.*, p.12.

38 C. Tisdall, 'Chinese Agitscape', *op. cit.*

39 See Jill Drower, *99 Balls Pond Road: The Story of the Exploding Galaxy*, London: Scrudge Books, 2014. The scholarship of Heinrich Zimmer, especially *Myths and Symbols in Indian Art and Civilization* (ed. Joseph Campbell, Bollingen Foundation: New York, 1946), was a shared point of reference.

40 D. Medalla, 'The Exploding Galaxy', 1968, Guy Brett collection, Tate Archive (TGA 20208).

– it was said they 'left England as Buddhists and came back as Maoists'.[42] Dugger and Medalla would draw heavily on Mao's writings in their articulation of their art practices back in London, individually and through the Artists Liberation Front (ALF, a precursor to AFD formed in 1971). Maoist precepts offered a new rationale for their ongoing experiments in participatory art-making: 'the masses have boundless creative power' indicated mass participation as the basis of a revolutionary people's culture; participation art offered 'a democratic form of proletarian cultural internationalism'.[43] Or, as the banner that hung at the entrance of their People's Participation Pavilion at documenta 5 (1972) boldly proclaimed: 'Socialist Art through Socialist Revolution!'

ALF's (over)identification with certain orthodoxies of 'socialist art' is particularly curious because in general the work they were producing is barely recognisable in terms of the aesthetic agendas of 'really-existing-socialism'. The British art context of the time included a wide spectrum of leftist practices, including the League of Socialist Artists and their Communard Gallery at 18 Camberwell Church Street, London, a group whose rhetorical style bore strong similarities to ALF, but whose arguments and practice favoured orthodox socialist realist aesthetics. By contrast, ALF's aesthetics continued to develop according to their interest in experimental and participatory artistic forms. It is possible that some still saw a vanguard role for the ALF group within the 'broad front' movement that AFD sought to build – this might explain certain conflicts that would later emerge in the group. In any case, in Brett's estimation the major difference was that 'AFD was open to more people and therefore more ideas',[44] and its 'broad front' aesthetics allowed the coexistence of 'orthodox' and 'experimental' styles (of which more below). At the entrance to the Chile Festival hung a large-scale painting by AFD co-founder Stephen Pusey, whose practice would develop into civic activism and the community mural movement – visitors were thus greeted by Allende, Pablo Neruda and the Chilean masses, in grand socialist-realist style.[45]

The Chile Festival's numerous symposia reflect the scale of the group's transnational ambitions: 'Cultural Imperialism and Latin American art and culture'; 'Art and Culture in Asia'; 'Art and Culture in Africa and the Black culture of the Caribbean'; and 'Third World culture'. AFD's geopolitical map, as seen through its exhibitions, would further include: Vietnam and

41 Their trip was financed by film producer, director and underground patron Sylvina Boissonnas, who also supported other members of the Galaxy with travel to India and various other projects. I am grateful to Eva Bentcheva for sharing her research on John Dugger's experience of this time.

42 J. Drower, *99 Balls Pond Road*, *op. cit.*, p.339.

43 D. Medalla, 'On the Elements of Democratic and Socialist Culture', 3 March 1972; John Dugger, 'On Participation', 22 February 1972. Guy Brett collection, Tate Archive (TGA 20208).

44 See *Artists for Democracy: El Archivo de Cecilia Vicuña*, *op. cit.*

45 Stephen Pusey, correspondence with the author, 27 April 2023.

Stephen Pusey,
People Build a Garden,
Earlham Street,
London, 1977

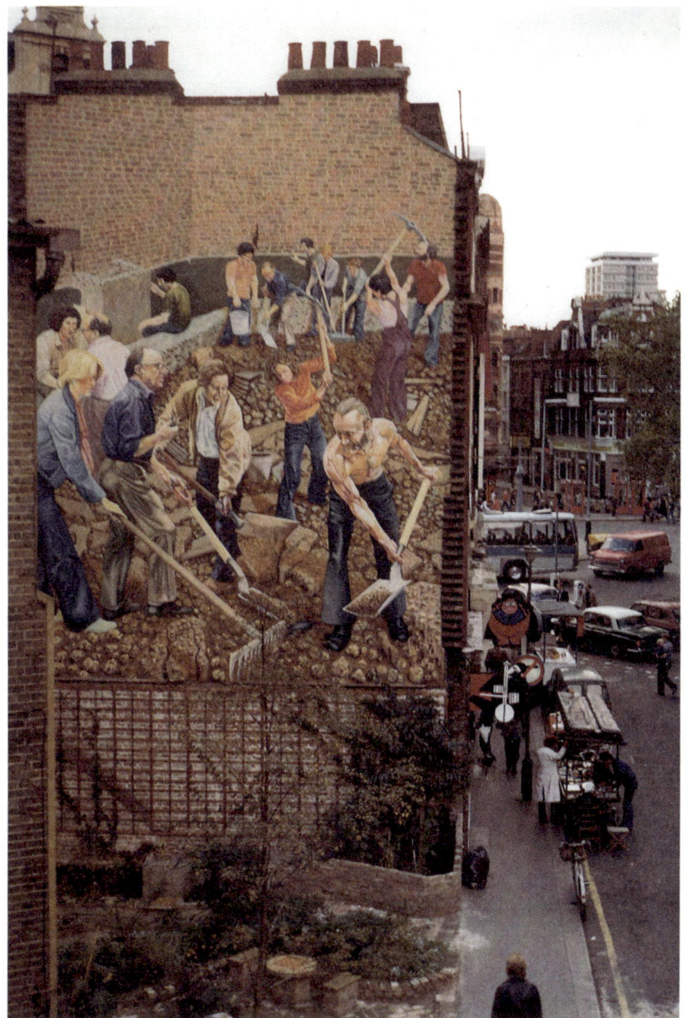

Indochina, as reflected in 'People of the World Learn from Indochina' (1975); the independence struggles in Angola, Mozambique, Guinea-Bissau and Zimbabwe, as seen in 'Victory to People's War' (1975); China, which was the focus of 'China Show' (1976); and the Indigenous struggle in North America, in 'American Indian Movement 1976 Exhibition' (1976–77). Additional events, meetings and performances addressing a wider range of imperial and post-imperial contexts took place as part of these exhibitions or ran parallel to them. Whitfield Street hosted political meetings on East Timor and Albania; and a group of students supporting the revolutionary movement in Iran used the space to meet regularly.[46]

The group also turned its attention to its immediate colonial context: the United Kingdom of Great Britain and Northern Ireland. A 1974 planning document drafted by Medalla includes plans for a travelling exhibition that would 'examine the history of working class culture in England, from the beginning of capitalism to the present day'.[47] The exhibition, never realised, was to address the legacy of British colonialism within the nation itself: 'Historically, English imperialism systematically destroyed or denigrated the national cultures of its colonies; how did the English imperialists launch cultural aggression against the culture of the working classes at home in England?' It also set out to explore the potentials of 'minority cultures' within the imperial nation – 'Among the non-English people who work in England, what effective roles do their different national cultures play in resisting the cultural penetration of the English bourgeoisie?' – and planned to involve cultural-political groups working in Britain such as Cinema Action, Red Ladder Theatre Company, May First Movement, Third World Troubadours, Art Combine and 7:84 Theatre Company.

The programme for the Chile Festival's opening night, on 14 October 1974, reveals a number of significant connections to Black history in Britain. The night began with an invocation on conga drums by Trinidadian artist Roy Caboo, who had been amongst those on trial in 1971 as part of the infamous Mangrove Nine case, a landmark in the struggle against racist policing in Britain.[48] Poems were read by Accabre Huntley, who had published her poetry that same year for the first time, at age seven; Accabre was the daughter of Eric Huntley and Jessica Huntley, founders of Bogle-L'Ouverture Publications, one of the first independent Black-owned publishers and booksellers in the UK, and she joined the festival at the invitation of writer Andrew Salkey, co-founder of the Caribbean Artists Movement (1966–72), who would give a poetry reading the following evening.[49] Barbadian poet and communist Peter Blackman also featured in the opening programme, reading from his 1952 poem *My Song is for All Men*.[50] The festival went on to include a symposium, 'Art and Culture in Africa and the Black Culture of the Caribbean', chaired by Saint Vincent–born Lester Lewis, who would found the Hackney Black People's Association, and with contributions from groups including the UHURU Arts Group, who developed theatre, dance, poetry, exhibitions and participatory 'Grounding' events with the Black community in Chapeltown, Leeds.[51]

46 AFD's archive includes a letter expressing solidarity on behalf of the Philippines liberation committee, chaired by Medalla.

47 'THE AIMS OF ARTISTS FOR DEMOCRACY', *op. cit.*

48 Roy Caboo was also was part of a drumming workshop alongside Agor-Mmba at the Festival; he would have an exhibition the following year at the Keskidee Centre, London. See 'Caboo: The Making of a Caribbean Artist', *Race Today*, vol.7, no.2, February 1975, pp.36–39.

49 Accabre Rutlin, communication with the author, 6 July 2023.

50 Peter Blackman, *My Song is for All Men*, London: Lawrence & Wishart, 1952. Blackman does not appear in Lynn MacRitchie's footage of the opening, although not all parts were captured on film. L. MacRitchie, correspondence with the author, 27 July 2023.

Various 'local' issues register in AFD's archive, including campaigns on housing, healthcare services and abortion; and were the focus of performances such as Araeen's 1977 *Paki Bastard*, which refracted Britain's (post)imperial conjuncture through the racism of British society. AFD overlapped with numerous other left political groupuscules in London at the time, including the ALF; the British Black Panthers, via Araeen and H.O. Nazareth; and trade unionism and British second-wave feminism – Lynn MacRitchie, for instance, was a union representative at the hospital where she worked as a cleaner and a regular at feminist meetings throughout her time with AFD. The conflict in Ireland was a live issue, as a mainstay on the national news and the focus of large-scale campaigns such as Troops Out, and as a reference in the events programme at AFD's festival for Vietnam, which involved a durational performance by Limited Dance Company (including Rose English, Sally Potter and Jacky Lansley). Ireland was amongst the concerns that led to another split in the group, with some feeling it was necessary to focus on the struggle 'on their doorstep' rather than the more 'distant' concerns of Third World liberation – a dynamic reproduced across the British left in the mid-1970s.[52]

The intent behind AFD's unrealised exhibition on the history of the working class in England may be understood with reference to a number of common theoretical sources. One is the work of Amílcar Cabral. AFD participants were familiar with his work following a talk at Westminster Central Hall in 1971, and it would inform Araeen's 'Black Manifesto' as well as the strategy of the American Indian Movement (AIM) at the United Nations (Jimmie Durham having met Cabral in Geneva in the early 70s), to which I will return in the following section.[53] Cabral's emphasis on culture as integral to anti-colonial liberation movements offered a powerful example for cultural workers worldwide – whatever their proximity to armed struggle (a fundamental part of his theory with reference to the revolutionary process in Guinea-Bissau).[54] Cabral's strategy of a 'return to the source' – the development of popular, 'indigenous' cultural forms as a tool to resist colonial domination – resonates with another reference point common to AFD members, the Maoist principle 'from the masses to the masses' (also known as 'the mass line'). This recommended a cyclical process: listening to the 'scattered and unsystematic' ideas of the people, concentrating them into

51 *Chapeltown News*, no.18, July 1974, available at https://harehills111.files.wordpress.com/2016/12/july-1974.pdf; and Imruh Bakari, conversation with the author, 15 June 2023.

52 L. MacRitchie, conversation with the author, 7 October 2020. See also Ian Birchall, '"Vicarious Pleasure"? The British far left and the third world, 1956–79', in Evan Smith and Matthew Worley (ed.), *Against the Grain: The British Far Left from 1956*, Manchester: Manchester University Press, 2014, pp.190–208.

53 Amílcar Cabral's lecture was published as *Our People are our Mountains: Amílcar Cabral on the Guinean Revolution*, London: Committee for Freedom in Mozambique, Angola and Guiné, 1972.

54 See A. Cabral, 'National liberation and culture', in *Unity and Struggle: Speeches and Writings*, New York: Monthly Review Press, 1979, pp.138–54.

systematic ideas, taking them back to explain to the people and using them as a guide for action – and then repeat: 'And so on, over and over again in an endless spiral, with the ideas becoming more correct, more vital and richer each time. Such is the Marxist theory of knowledge.'[55]

In the early 1970s, Dugger and Medalla would position their experiments in participation art as direct expressions of this principle. The 1974 planning document reiterates AFD's commitment to the mass line, but raises the need to determine more precisely how 'progressive' art should be defined, including: '(1) a meaningful and qualitative definition of the *new* in art (beyond formal terms); (2) ability to distinguish *progressive* vs *retrograde* examples of experimental art'. Noting that 'the "new" and the "experimental" do not necessarily confer upon an artistic production the quality of being truly progressive', the text surveys historical examples of progressive tendencies (Dadaists, Cubists, Russian Constructivists, Fernand Léger, John Heartfield, Vladimir Tatlin, Bertolt Brecht, Vladimir Mayakovsky) as well as retrograde (some expressionists, symbolists, Futurists, Ezra Pound, F.T. Marinetti), with reference to a fundamental question: 'FOR WHOM?'[56] The statement rejects 'poster-and-slogan' style art, referencing Lenin's and Mao's remarks ('both of whom vigorously opposed it') and acknowledging that there are also many significant artists who nonetheless fall short in their commitments to scientific socialism. It argues instead for an attitude of *critical assimilation*: to 'broaden and extend their *formal* artistic discoveries, and infuse them with *proletarian content*'; to 'distinguish what Lenin called "*the democratic and socialist elements in every national culture*", concentrate them and bring them to a higher stage in our artistic production'; and to 'follow in a living way Chairman Mao's teaching: "Make the past serve the present" (culturally speaking, the *past* here means all valuable artistic heritage of *every* culture in the world, and the *present* refers to the progressive forces of our time).'[57]

What was AFD's relationship to 'the masses' in practice? In the estimation of one Exploding Galaxy member, the 1960s counterculture was heavily skewed towards British elites and white almost without exception.[58] The core members of AFD came from a wider mix of social backgrounds and a significant number were from other parts of the world. Amongst the British were aristocratic, bourgeois and working-class individuals.[59] Members not from the

55 See *Quotations from Chairman Mao Tsetung*, Beijing: Foreign Languages Press, 1976, p.129.

56 'THE AIMS OF ARTISTS FOR DEMOCRACY', *op. cit.*

57 *Ibid.*

58 J. Drower, *99 Balls Pond Road*, *op. cit.*, pp.44–45, describing the scene around London's UFO club.

59 The planning document includes a call to AFD members from working-class backgrounds to lead study meetings and seminars with a view to 'informing all members on the working class struggle in England'.

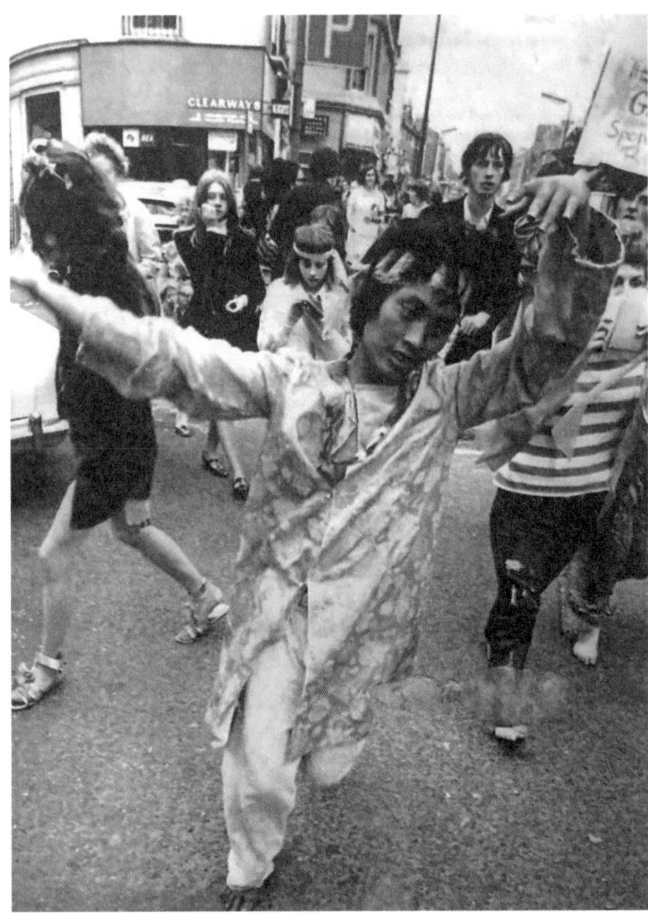

David Medalla (front) with the Exploding Galaxy, *The Kinetic Ballet of the Kings Road*, 22 July 1967

UK came from a comparable range of class backgrounds, but their 'foreignness' presented additional barriers for Britain's overwhelmingly white, parochial art establishment.

These dynamics could produce curious alliances between radical and conservative tendencies in the art institutional landscape. Signals gallery, for instance, clashed with the narrow nationalist agenda of the Arts Council of Great Britain in the mid-1960s, which would have had no interest in providing support for such a conspicuously internationalist project. Medalla and Signals co-founder Paul Keeler would therefore turn to other sources of support, sustaining the gallery through more old-fashioned, private means – Signals relied on an 'enlightened' elite patronage (e.g. Keeler's father, an optical instruments manufacturer, and others brought in by Brett and poet Hugo Williams, both alumni of the boarding school Eton).[60] While the

60 See Paul Overy, 'Other Stories', in *Art History*, vol.20, no.3, 1997, p.494. Keeler, who adopted the name Ahmed Paul Keeler following his conversion to Islam in the mid-1970s, would organise the 'Festival of Islam' at the Institute of Contemporary Arts, London in 1971; and the large-scale 'World of Islam Festival', at various London venues, in 1976.

agenda of the Arts Council did change by the 1970s, when AFD received some project- and artist-specific grants, the group was still not able to achieve the necessary support to make their project sustainable long-term.[61]

In such circumstances, what material support was AFD able to offer to liberation movements? The Chile Festival did not receive any state funding, but the initiative was supported by prominent figures in the establishment; the Royal College of Art was secured as a venue (Lord Esher, the Rector and Vice Provost, was Brett's father) and the list of sponsors included British Members of Parliament, a Fellow of the Royal Society and Nobel Prize–winning scientist, diplomats, ambassadors and international cultural figures. Material support for Chile was to be raised in an auction of works donated by artists, with proceeds split fifty-fifty, half to the artist and half to the Chilean cause. The auction raised £300, from 30 artworks sold, which was given to Álvaro Bunster, English representative of the Chile Anti-Fascist Front in Rome, with the recommendation that the full amount be given to MIR as an organisation within the front.[62] A further £100 was raised by a later ICA auction. For a group of unwaged cultural workers operating without a budget, £400 was not an insignificant amount; but to put it in perspective, a Trade Union Congress campaign for Chile that same year raised £3928.90 in total, with AFD's total closer to the lower-middle range of donations by individual trade union branches.[63]

Beyond AFD's moderate financial contribution to liberation struggles, how else was its material and cultural support enacted? Much can be said for the simple gesture of a festival in solidarity (of which more below). Another powerful example is provided by Dugger's *Chile Vencerá* banner, as seen in probably the most widely circulated photograph of AFD, of the Chile Solidarity Campaign rally in London's Trafalgar Square in 1974. The scale is extraordinary: this monumental banner proclaiming 'Chile will prevail' at the head of a 10,000 strong gathering for the Chilean people. But the image also speaks to the interdependence of artistic practice and social movement, for the scale of the rally is what makes the scale of the work possible.

Yet material-cultural support can also ripple out in more subtle ways. The Chile Festival took place at the crest of a wave of energy generated by the optimism of Allende's victory in Chile and the subsequent shock and outrage generated by the coup. By way of

61 AFD were awarded £250 in 1976 for 'The Hand in Life and Art'; and £500 in 1977 for 'Vernacular Art in Camden'; a request of £5000 per annum to rent a new premises following the group's eviction from Whitfield Street, made directly by Medalla to Peter Bird, Assistant Art Director at the Arts Council, was refused. See Arts Council of Great Britain, 'Value for money: Thirty-second annual report and accounts 1976/77', 1977; and Peter Bird, letter to Lord Esher, 27 May 1977, Guy Brett collection, Tate Archive (TGA 20208).

62 Adjusted for inflation, the total is equivalent to around £5000 in today's money. The proceeds of the sale were a contentious issue for some time, with Lord Esher and Roland Penrose earlier insisting that the donation be made to Amnesty International; the circumstances around the subsequent decision to divert the funds to MIR was the basis of a bitter split in the founding AFD group.

63 From 31 trade unions, £3928.90 was raised in total for the Fund for Chilean Relief between December 1973 and May 1974. The Society of Lithographic Artists, Designers, Engravers and Process Workers gave £75; the National Union of Public Employees and the Transport and General Workers' Union each gave £1000. See Ann Jones, *No Truck with the Chilean Junta!: Trade Union Internationalism, Australia and Britain, 1973–1980*, Canberra: ANU Press, 2014, p.50.

contrast, we may consider AFD's homage to Ho Chi Minh and the Indochinese Peoples, which took place the following year at a much-reduced scale compared to the Chile Festival. By 1975, Vietnam was no longer the subject of widespread campaigning in Britain – though it had been just a few years earlier, as seen in major rallies organised by the Vietnam Solidarity Campaign (VSC) in 1967 and '68. In its celebration of Vietnam's victory, the AFD group were more in tune with the mood of the US left – where 50,000 joined an end-of-war rally in New York in May 1975 – and, more generally, the anti-imperialist mood across the world, in stark contrast to the generally muted response in Britain. Having left the UK for Colombia, Vicuña would produce her own homage to the Vietnamese people through a series of paintings and banners. One such work, *Chile saluda a Vietnam!* (*Chile Salutes Vietnam!*, 1975), depicts a Mapuche woman and a female Vietnamese guerilla, passing on a rifle and revolutionary book. It is a banner cut into strips – echoing *Chile Vencerá* – and was shown in Vicuña's 1977 solo exhibition at the Fundación Gilberto Alzate Avendaño, Bogotà: 'Homenaje a Vietnam' ('Homage to Vietnam').

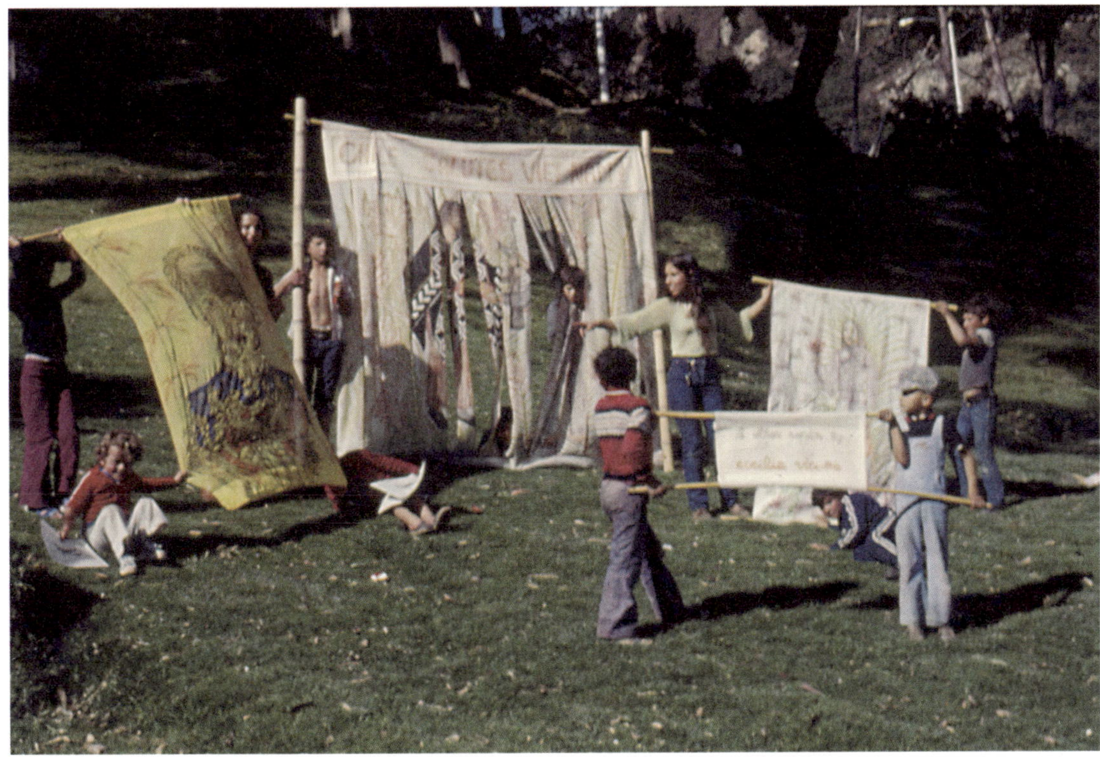

Cecilia Vicuña and her works from the exhibition 'Homenaje a Vietnam' ('Homage to Vietnam') during a workshop with children, Bogotá, Colombia, 1977

*

The 'American Indian Movement 1976 Exhibition' took another approach to material-cultural support, by producing a show directly with the liberation movement in question. Organised by AFD and the UK committee of the American Indian Movement, it was staged in part to protest 'Sacred Circles: Two Thousand Years of North American Indian Art' at the Hayward Gallery in London, and the United States Bicentennial, marking the signing of the Declaration of Independence – also marking 200 years of Indigenous resistance to US land theft and settler colonialism, as AIM highlighted. Originally planned to last for around six weeks between September and October 1976, the show was extended into January 1977, making it the longest-running exhibition at the Whitfield Street space. It received significant press attention, including in *The Times*, *Evening Standard* and *Studio International*, as a counterpoint to 'Sacred Circles', and it has become an example often raised in retrospective accounts of AFD. Indeed, people travelled long distances to see it.[64] Yet documentation on the exhibition – and on AIM UK itself – remains scarce. Said to be 'small but eloquent' by one reviewer, it consisted of photographs, protest leaflets, drawings and posters, with a large-scale reproduction of a graphic showing an Indigenous American imprisoned within the stripes of the US flag.[65] In the image, the figure's hand rests upon on a pipe tomahawk emerging through bars – an ambiguous symbol of diplomacy in the encounter between Europeans and Indigenous peoples.[66]

These were critical years in the project of Indigenous internationalism. As Nick Estes recounts in *Our History Is the Future* (2019), the summer of 1977 saw a delegation of 120 led by Indigenous elders from Six Nations, Oceti Sakowin Nation, Hopi, Panama, Guatemala, the Amazon, Mexico and Chile march through Geneva for a historic gathering at the United Nations to establish formal recognition for Indigenous peoples. This occasion was built on a long tradition of radical organising, with roots in the Red Power movement in the early 1960s as well as many earlier articulations of an Indigenous internationalist agenda.[67] The American Indian Movement, founded in 1968, was a successor to these. AIM's occupation of Wounded Knee in 1973, which followed actions such as the Trail of Broken Treaties (1972) and the occupation of Alcatraz

64 'David Medalla in conversation with Brandon Taylor', *Artscribe*, no.6, 1977, p.23; and in this volume, pp.292–95.

65 The image was originally a poster produced by Swedish artist Christer Themptander in 1970, titled *We Will Never Forget Wounded Knee*, and featured in publications including the long-running *Akwesasne Notes* as well as *The Black Panther*. See Louise Siddons, 'Red Power in the 'Black Panther': Radical Imagination and Intersectional Resistance at Wounded Knee', *American Art*, Summer 2021, p.17.

66 *Ibid.*

67 Nick Estes, *Our History Is the Future: Standing Rock Versus the Dakota Access Pipeline, and the Long Tradition of Indigenous Resistance*, London: Verso Books, 2019, p.265.

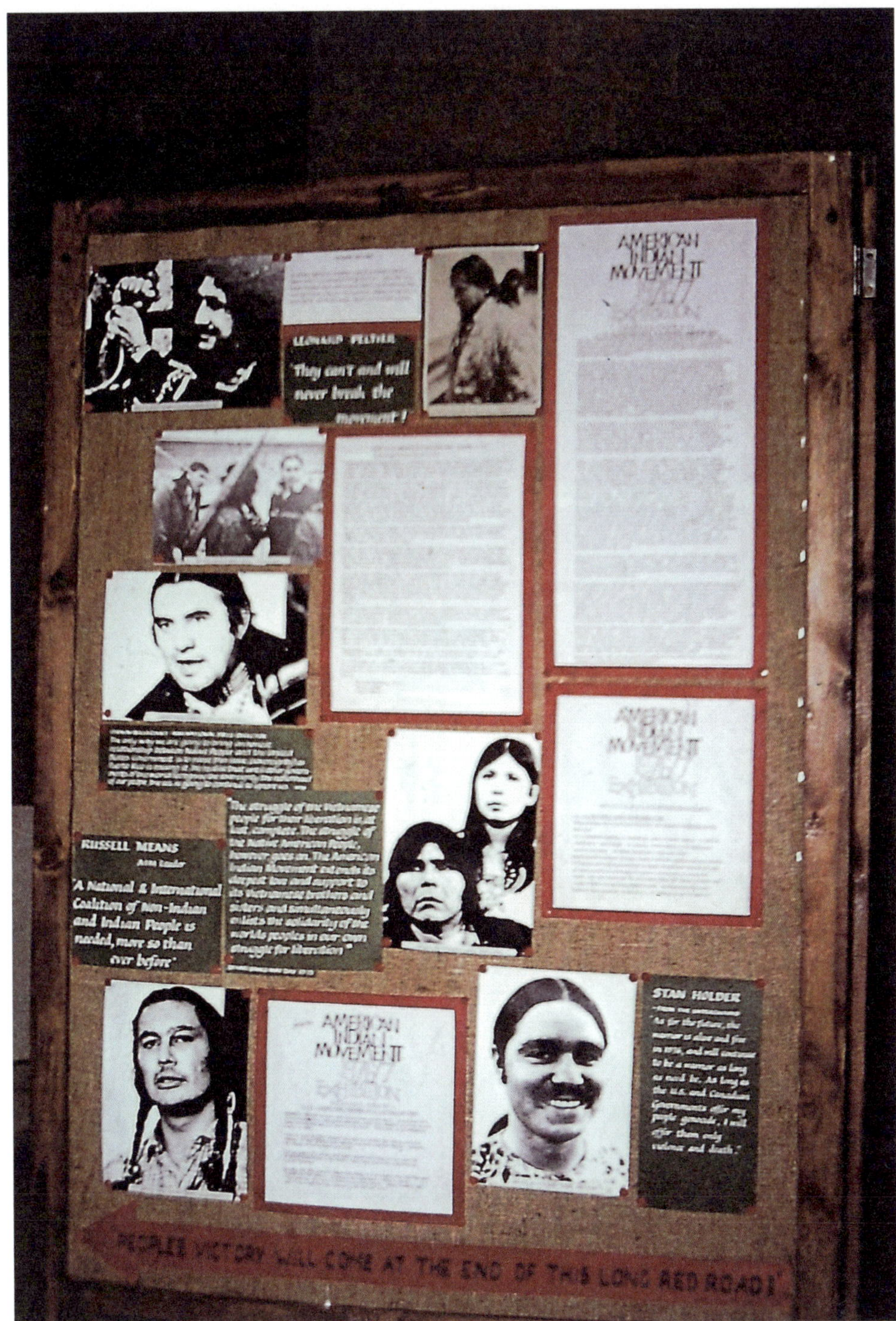

American Indian Movement displays at the Crucible Theatre, Sheffield, 1977.
The displays were included in AFD's 'American Indian Movement 1976 Exhibition', 143 Whitfield Street, 1976–77

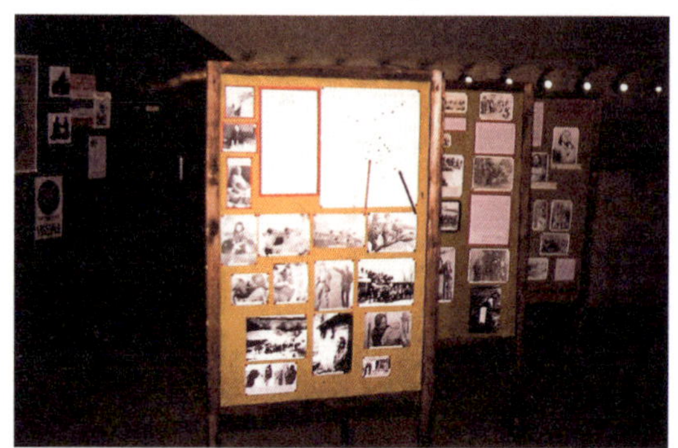

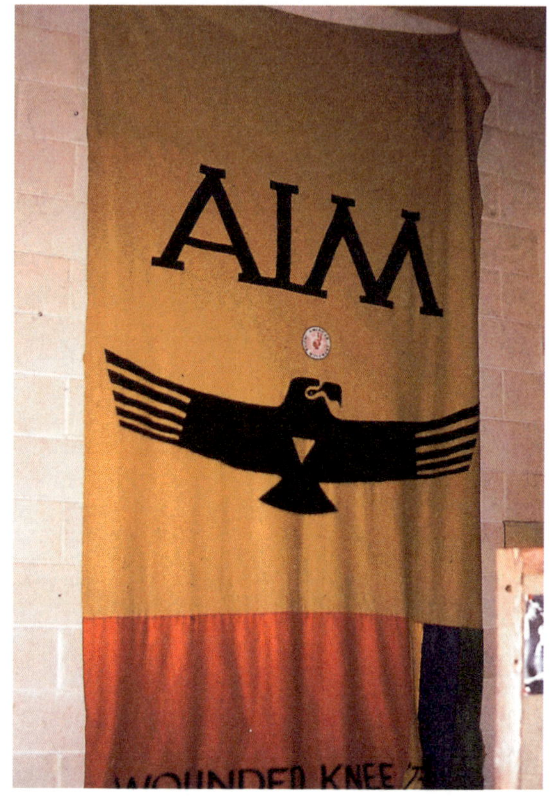

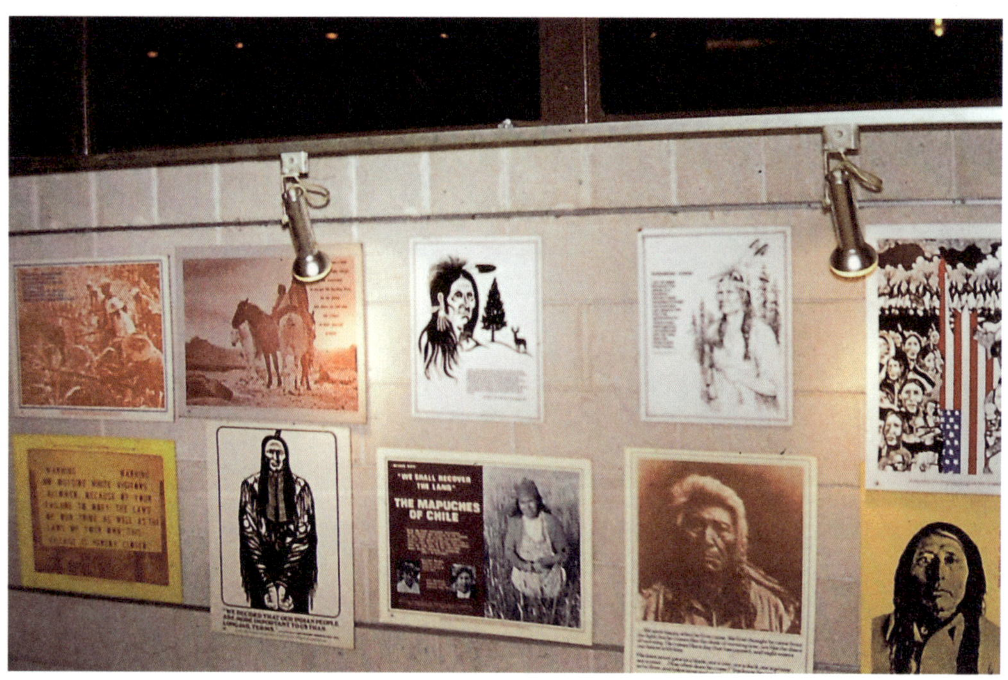

American Indian Movement displays at the Crucible Theatre, Sheffield, 1977.
The displays were included in AFD's 'American Indian Movement 1976 Exhibition', 143 Whitfield Street, 1976–77

(1969), saw the organisation's leaders arrested and subjected to legal processes that took momentum from the movement. It was in the context of this, and wider attacks from US counter-intelligence on domestic radical movements, that AIM established the International Indian Treaty Council (IITC) in 1974, as a platform to advance the cause of Indigenous peoples worldwide.[68] The transnational connections, and the regional AIM offices consequently established, found significant support in the socialist bloc in particular.[69]

In this context of Indigenous internationalism, the UK committee of AIM formed to join together the AIM Support Committee, based in Birmingham, and the AIM Support Group, in Derbyshire. Headquartered in the Northfield area of Birmingham and headed by Terry Lewis, the group found common cause with the colonised nations of the British Isles: they strengthened links with the independence parties Plaid Cymru (Wales) and Sinn Fein (Ireland), meeting up on tours with AIM activists from the US such as Madonna Thunder Hawk.[70] During one such tour, AIM representatives came to 143 Whitfield Street (in the company of Jane Fonda, according to one AFD member living there at the time).[71] An announcement calling for donations to support the 'American Indian Movement 1976 Exhibition' gives details of its scope: to 'show the true situation in the United States today, of the struggle by the American Indian Movement / Native American Nations for sovereignty and self-determination', as well as 'the spirit of the American Indian People, still alive today despite everything, still following the true Indian Way and still producing beautiful poetry and artwork'. The exhibition gathered photographic documentation, posters, poetry, artworks and graphics on AIM, and was intended to tour across Britain.

What are we to make of this singular exhibition today? The contemporary art market has turned towards Indigenous art and thought in recent years, as reflected in many shows, publications and art initiatives. As Candice Hopkins observes, such 'discovery' of Indigenous ideas often indexes a moment when Western cultures and ideologies are in crisis – in times of environmental collapse, Indigenous knowledge is turned to, again and again, for possible solutions.[72]

The AIM exhibition does not coincide with a broader interest in Indigenous art in the mid-1970s; it emerges from an understanding

68 See Roxanne Dunbar-Ortiz, 'How Indigenous Peoples Wound Up at the United Nations', in Dan Berger (ed.), *The Hidden 1970s: Histories of Radicalism*, New Brunswick, NJ: Rutgers University Press, 2010, pp.115–34.

69 See György Ferenc Tóth, *From Wounded Knee to Checkpoint Charlie: The Alliance for Sovereignty between American Indians and Central Europeans in the Late Cold War*, Albany, NY: SUNY Press, 2016.

70 See Kate Rennard, 'Becoming Indigenous: The Transnational Networks of the American Indian Movement, Irish Republicans, and Welsh Nationalists', *Native American and Indigenous Studies*, vol.8, no.2, Fall 2021, pp.92–124.

71 Details remain sketchy on how the exhibition plan came together. There was a Brixton office of AIM that may have played a role; AIM representatives' visits were connected to the Geneva initiative, and Jimmie Durham, who was a key figure through the International Indian Treaty Council, visited London in 1976 (although the exhibition's connection to *Akwesasne Notes* suggests that he was not involved). The AIM exhibition would subsequently travel to Sheffield. I am grateful to Maria Thereza Alves and Richard Hill for their comments on these points.

72 Candice Hopkins, quoted in Lucy R. Lippard, 'Floating Between Past and Future: The Indigenisation of Environmental Politics', *Afterall*, issue 43, Spring/Summer 2017, p.34.

of the politics of culture, of the forms of imperialism that may be conducted in the name of art, and of exhibition-making as part of a critical battleground. The AIM initiative also demonstrates how exhibitions may speak to one another. In this case, it functioned to expand the context for the larger 'Sacred Circles' show, and offered a critical intervention into its interpretation and understanding. This may be seen in the fact that the press reaction to 'Sacred Circles' broadly followed the critique advanced by the AIM show, and as such the exhibition operated as critical counterpoint – a 'more urgent and committed revelation of the state of the American Indians today'.[73] For instance, writing in *The Times*, Richard Cork used the AIM show in his opening paragraphs to introduce the problematics of 'Sacred Circles', including the framing of Indigenous life and history as something of the past, and complicating, to some extent, the settler narrative; Paul Overy, in the *Evening Standard*, concluded that 'Sacred Circles' reflected 'our desire to enclose Indian culture inside the white man's notion of art'; and in *Studio International*, Susan Hiller offered a comprehensive analysis of the exhibition as a document of the sustained destruction of Indigenous cultures. In particular, Hiller implicated the exhibition strategies of 'Sacred Circles' in this process – how its display, framing and contextualisation advanced a European-American colonial viewpoint while also insisting on this as a natural and neutral position, 'using "art" to cover up some historical truths ... voiding symbols of their complexity by eliminating their context; [and] valuing art objects more than societies'.[74]

What comes across in these texts is a remarkable consensus forming around 'Sacred Circles', with AIM's 'small but eloquent' exhibition providing the critical context to understanding. It steered its visitors in this direction and produced an intervention into mainstream discourse on Indigenous art – a rare opportunity, given British culture's characteristic occlusion of its imperial legacies. It is curious, perhaps, that in these reviews the AIM show features in a largely instrumental way – to register a point of reference for the reviewer's critique – and so it is treated only cursorily as an exhibition in its own right. Its presentation of a political imaginary of its own – 'the spirit of the American Indian People' – at this crucial moment of Indigenous internationalism for the movement is a history still to be told.

73 Richard Cork, 'The Indigenous Americans', *The Times*, 12 October 1976.

74 Susan Hiller, 'Sacred Circles: 2,000 Years of North American Indian Art', *Studio International*, vol.193, no.985, January/February 1977, p.58; and in this volume, pp.278–80.

*

AFD's 'broad front' was artistic as much as it was political, aimed at including 'the entire spectrum of artistic expression and production in the world, traditional and new, with the distinct emphasis on the new, i.e., the experimental.'[75] So far I have focussed on some concrete examples of how AFD offered material-cultural support to liberation struggles, but this agenda is inseparable from a parallel commitment towards evolving experimental and collective cultural forms through which to enact said support. The dynamic relationship between these twin aims might be understood in terms of what one AFD participant later described as the 'seeds of a new popular culture': 'Artistic ideas are in the air, and ripe for use. Nor is it a question of putting art first, as a kind of prime mover. ... [T]he really significant fact is the relationship between the people, the event, and the means of expression.'[76] If this essay's previous sections have addressed AFD's relationship to 'the people', and to its historical moment, I now turn to its means of expression.

As a group of cultural workers, AFD occupied various roles through an artist-led sensibility – the curatorial/organisational function was informally shared, where 'solo' presentations were directed by the artists themselves, and group shows collectively assembled into ad-hoc installation environments, often without any clear sense of authorship. Sometimes its presentation strategies were borrowed from elsewhere, for instance the Chile Festival's planned inclusion of 'wall newspapers' familiar from various socialist contexts: one contextualising the situation in Chile; one for visitors to leave criticisms and comments in response to the exhibition; one containing messages of solidarity for the Chilean people (including translations 'in all the languages of the world' of excerpts from Allende's final statement and a Neruda poem – translations being solicited by post). There was often a pedagogical agenda: several participants were in formal education at the time, as students or teachers, and AFD offered space for many more informal kinds of learning, research and 'mutual apprenticeship'.[77]

AFD's later exhibitions continued to develop an understanding of exhibition-making as a didactic and pedagogical tool. Exhibitions could include a surfeit of information, giving context to the

75 'THE AIMS OF ARTISTS FOR DEMOCRACY', *op. cit.*

76 G. Brett, *Through Our Own Eyes: Popular Art and Modern History*, London: Heretic Books, 1986, p.153.

77 C. Vicuña, 'Organized Dreaming', *op. cit.*

'message' the show aimed to deliver (supplemented by lectures, screenings and workshops with children, as mentioned above), but these didactics could come in idiosyncratic ways – a far distance from the sober museological and/or assertive agitprop modes of presentation that might be expected. At the festival for Vietnam, historical background was blockily hand-drafted, mirroring the show's DIY-ramshackle environments; in a photograph taken at Whitfield Street, Medalla can be seen narrating from a handwritten sequence of key dates in Chinese revolutionary history, on a scroll so long that it extends through a trap-door and into the space below; notice boards and reading spaces were set up at various times, to which visitors could add their own contributions, and theses were often elaborated through semi-improvised performances and dance-dramas. One exhibition plan captures the general approach: 'Our exhibition, if we do decide to bring it about, will have mainly a didactic character. At the same time, we can evolve many different experimental ways of presentation.'[78]

A 1975 investigation into the agricultural bases of social organisation, presented at AFD's Whitfield Street space, is another example. Its thesis unfolded via two interrelated exhibitions, by Lynn MacRitchie and Guy Brett respectively. MacRitchie's 'The World in a Grain of Sand' occupied the main part of the space as a complex participatory environment constructed out of various found materials, including clippings from the *Financial Times*, dishes of water and germinating seeds. Flanked by images of grain production in China, India and Russia, alongside images of bread and bread-making, visitors were invited to explore the material bases of industrialised food and image consumption. The work is remarkably contemporary, but its intent to convey a specific message, and the analytical clarity of that message, sets it apart from more recent comparable examples: 'people will be encouraged to sift through the symbolic grain where they will find quotations, poems and statements illustrating the fact that it is the labour of the people which produces the grain which is the basis of the food we eat'.[79] Brett's small complementary presentation, 'Fruits of the Earth in Decorative Art', developed the speculation that decorative art came into existence with the invention of agriculture by making visual connections between pattern, repetition and agricultural labour: 'The little metal ribbons of electric circuitry echo the branches in a Persian carpet which echo the conduits of irrigation: a lively energy flows through each.'[80]

78 'THE AIMS OF ARTISTS FOR DEMOCRACY', *op. cit.*

79 L. MacRitchie, 'The World in a Grain of Sand', undated handwritten notes shared with the author.

80 G. Brett, 'Agriculture, Field, Decoration', in *Carnival of Perception: Selected Writings on Art*, London: Institute of International Visual Arts, 2004, p.157; and in this volume, pp.185–89.

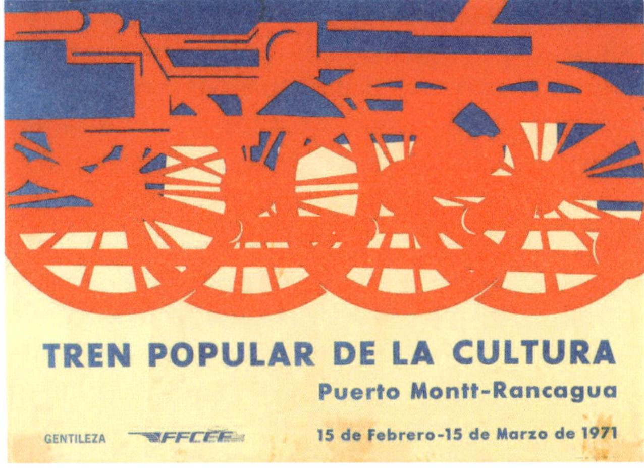

Talleres gráficos FF. CC del Estado de Chile, poster for 'El tren popular de la cultura' ('The Popular Culture Train'), 1971, offset lithograph, 69 × 53.5 cm

Considered from the context of today's global food crisis, MacRitchie's and Brett's critical investigations of the nexus of art, agriculture and social life could not be more timely.[81]

AFD's experimental presentations of cultural-historical analysis and research – what we may term *experimental didactics* – anticipate more recent exhibition projects such as the aforementioned 'Past Disquiet', and research-led approaches in exhibition-making such as 'the project exhibition', the 'thesis exhibition' and the 'self-reflexive exhibition format' or 'essay exhibition'.[82] We might also project a lineage back to the radical approaches that evolved at different moments of social-political upheaval. Museology of the early Soviet era evolved various experiments in this regard: dialectical-materialist analysis of historical narratives or the daily news; exhibitions of contemporary industrial processes, or advancing religious and philosophical ideas (such as the cosmism of Nikolai Fedorov); and 'itinerant exhibitions' designed to travel on mobile 'agit-trains'.[83] The latter, as well as 'popular museums' of the Second Spanish Republic, provided inspiration for the mobile exhibitions of Allende-era Chile, such as 'El tren popular de la cultura' ('The Popular Culture Train'), which brought 'high culture' to people living in remote localities.[84] These precedents suggest an alternative lineage of exhibition-making, with emphasis on exhibition as a tool of collective research, popular education, political engagement and critique of prevailing ideologies.

Also significant is the primary form AFD chose to advance its agenda: the festival. Festivals have a lineage in left-wing cultural

81 See Food and Agriculture Organisation of the United Nations, 'The State of Food Security and Nutrition in the World 2023', available at https://www.fao.org/documents/card/en/c/cc3017en. Economic and agricultural ecosystems provided the basis for one the most inspiring large-scale exhibition models in recent years, ruangrupa's organisation of documenta 15 (2022) based on the principle of *lumbung*, and agrarian reform, land justice and food security are core to the activities of Philippines cultural workers' organisation SAKA (Sama-samang Artista Para sa Kilusang Agraryo), to give just a couple of notable recent initiatives in this regard.

82 See, for instance, Marion von Osten, 'Another Criterion… or, What Is the Attitude of a Work in the Relations of Production of Its Time?', *Afterall*, issue 25, Spring/Summer 2010; Manuel Borja-Villel, in *Really Useful Knowledge*, (ed. Mafalda Rodríguez et al.), Madrid: Museo Nacional Centro de Arte Reina Sofía, 2014, p.6; Anselm Franke, 'On Fichte's Unlimiting and the Limits of Self-reflexive Institutions', in *Love and Ethnology: The Colonial Dialectic of Sensitivity (after Hubert Fichte)*, Berlin: Sternberg / HKW, 2019, p.13; Simon Sheikh, 'A Conceptual History of Exhibition-Making', presentation at the first Former West congress, 2009.

83 See Arseny Zhilyaev (ed.), *Avant-Garde Museology*, New York: e-flux Books, 2015.

84 See Maria Berríos, '"Struggle as Culture": The Museum of Solidarity, 1971–73', *Afterall*, issue 44, Autumn/Winter 2017, pp.133–43.

politics, a certain repertoire of coming-together that includes various artistic activities alongside gathering, discussion and debate.[85] Certain festival features deserve particular attention here: (1) multiple arts rather than art in the singular; (2) performativity; (3) artist-to-artist / absence of curatorial authority ('if you wanted to take part, you came along'[86]); (4) connection to the everyday; (5) modes of conviviality, celebration, hospitality and joy; (6) processionality, related to process, procession and a coexistence of temporalities and worlds.[87] The group's installational environments anticipate Raymundo Albano's equation of Philippine fiesta displays and contemporary installation art some years later.[88] AFD's Chile Festival, for instance, included two large-scale environments, the 'campamento Nueva Havana' and 'campamento La Luega of Santiago de Chile', which hosted much activity and were modelled on autonomous centres 'set up by people all over Chile where they democratically evolved new ways of doing things socially, politically and culturally'.[89]

Unlike the Exploding Galaxy's psychedelic commune at 99 Balls Pond Road, AFD's experiment-in-living was open to the public. The makeshift residence and 'cultural centre' at Whitfield Street hosted a succession of guests alongside its public programmes – visiting artists, friends, lovers, local children, stray cats – and its later years became increasingly improvised through ever-changing displays and happenings, evolving into a kind of continuous performance, 'a rolling sequence that did not really separate out into distinct exhibitions'.[90] One of these was a brief improvisation titled *Sweeping Gestures*, by two performers of different generations: Charles Hustwick, a young artist finding his way in London; and Trevor Thomas, a prominent figure in the Campaign for Homosexual Equality (CHE), a distinguished curator and the father of AFD artist Giles Thomas.[91] Although AFD was not affiliated with organisations such as CHE or the Gay Liberation Front (GLF), it resonates with kindred initiatives in queer exhibition-making and institution-building in a number of ways; for many of its number, Whitfield Street performed vital functions as community and stage for artistic-and-otherwise manifestations of queer life.[92]

85 We might also think of its particular related forms, such as the slogan, the speech and the banner.

86 L. MacRitchie, conversation with the author, 7 October 2020.

87 I am grateful to David Teh and Grace Samboh for conversations on the festival-exhibition continuum. See D. Morris and D. Teh (ed.), *Artist-to-Artist*, *op. cit.* On 'procession', see Tonika Sealy Thompson and Stefano Harney, 'Ground Provisions', *Afterall*, issue 45, Spring/Summer 2018, pp.121–25.

88 Raymundo Albano, 'Installations: A Case for Hangings', *Philippine Art Supplement* 2, no.1, January–February 1981, p.3.

89 J. Terra, correspondence with the author, 8 April 2021. The *campamentos* played host to much activity during the Festival, such as the Paddington Printshop and Terra's Red Star Shadow Puppet Theatre workshops, based on the Indonesian shadow puppet theatre *wayang kulit*. The particular energy and symbolism of makeshift dwellings in urban contexts was something Brett had elsewhere noted with reference to Resurrection City, U.S.A., a large-scale temporary encampment built in 1968 on the National Mall in Washington DC by the Poor People's Campaign. See G. Brett, 'Avant-Garde Art and the Third World', in Brandon Taylor (ed.), *Art & Criticism: Proceedings of a Conference Held in London on 23rd and 24th April 1976*, Winchester: Winchester School of Art Press, 1979, p.71.

90 C. Hustwick, correspondence with the author, 29 June 2023.

91 Trevor Thomas was curator-director of the Leicester Museum and Art Gallery (1940–46) until his persecution and dismissal as a result of anti-homosexuality laws; he also had the distinction of being Britain's youngest museum curator when he joined Liverpool Museum in 1931 aged 23. On *Sweeping Gestures*, see Hustwick's account in this publication, p.297.

92 See, for instance, Bas Hendrikx (ed.), *Queer Exhibition Histories*, Amsterdam: Valiz, 2023.

AFD's commitment to *the experimental* took many forms. In artistic terms, it formed an uneasy alliance with various 'traditional', 'folk' or 'popular' forms. This can be understood as a pragmatic extension of AFD's 'broad front' politics, to be as inclusive as possible with respect to artists and audiences, but it can be also understood in terms of aesthetic strategy. Some context for this may be given by the critical confrontation between Naseem Khan's 1976 report *The Arts Britain Ignores: The Arts of Ethnic Minorities in Britain* and Araeen's vehement critique of it. Khan's report highlighted a systematic lack of state support in Britain for artists and communities categorized as 'minority ethnic', meaning, largely but not exclusively, those with heritage in nations colonised by Britain.[93] Araeen's critique charged that the report simply reinforced a set of crude colonial assumptions about art, where 'advanced', 'avant-garde' art is the preserve of white European-Americans, as opposed to the 'traditional' culture and/or arts (plural) of the colonised world.

As a Black avant-gardist, Araeen clearly rejected this.[94] Yet in many respects, his critique of Khan upholds the modernist line of 'advanced' versus 'traditional' art; a line that becomes much blurrier in AFD's incorporation of a range of creative practices, including artisanal 'handicrafts' (as featured in the Chile exhibition), 'traditional' woodblock prints (in 'China Show') and various performances of music, theatre, poetry and dance drawing from popular and classical traditions. Popular song was often rendered as performance-poetry, as in the lyrics to revolutionary songs read at the opening of the festival for Vietnam, or the words of Buffy Sainte-Marie read to inaugurate the AIM exhibition at Whitfield Street. And what emerges overall is a contradictory but nonetheless complex understanding of 'avant-garde' and 'traditional' arts as co-extensive – or at least, not mutually exclusive.

Retrospective accounts also emphasise 'non-artistic' elements such as Araeen's Sunday cooking sessions, the various contributions of beloved AFD elder Andrew 'Pop' Kim or the homeopathic experiments of Peter Fisher.[95] Many such stories surround AFD, of creative practices not so obviously compatible with the commonsense understanding of what an artist is and does. For Araeen, the group's 'amateurism' – its failure to attract many 'professional' artists – was a problem.[96] But this was also part of its aesthetic, as one of their contemporaries observed: 'AFD productions tend towards an informal style that oscillates from the embarrassingly

93 See Naseem Khan, *The Arts Britain Ignores: The Arts of Ethnic Minorities in Britain*, London: Commission for Racial Equality, 1976.

94 Araeen's point is that the distinction is not racially coded, as Khan's report seemed to suggest. In a comparable critique of racialised aesthetic criteria, Araeen has argued for Jonathan Miles's work with the Poster-Film Collective (shown at AFD's Chile Festival and 'Victory for People's War' at Whitfield Street) as a forerunner to the British Black Arts Movement of the 1980s: 'Being a white artist, [Miles] also demolished the general notion that only blacks were involved in antiracist struggles or should produce such work.' R. Araeen, 'A Very Special *British* Issue? Modernity, Art History and the Crisis of Art Today', *Third Text*, vol.22, issue 2, March, 2008, p.136.

95 Kim was a retired policeman from Hong Kong and a regular presence at Whitfield Street; at the Chile Festival he would 'perform rhythmic movements with illuminated Chinese clubs', a technique he taught to others along with Tai Chi. Fisher, a doctor in training, was very close to Kim and would test his homeopathic inventions on other members of the group; he later become the personal homeopathic physician to Queen Elizabeth II. L. MacRitchie, correspondence with the author, 27 July 2023.

96 R. Araeen, correspondence with the author and Wing Chan, 15 April 2023.

amateur to stunning moments which usually benefit from an oriental sense of pace and timing.'[97] And if AFD's enthusiasms contain notes of exoticism, this is by no means limited to those cultures 'other' to Britain; for instance, in the context of his 1977 installation *Eskimo Carver* at AFD, Medalla enthuses about the Derbyshire tradition of 'well dressing', where public sources of water such as wells are decoratively adorned.[98] Other times, AFD's position might appear more contradictory – in the ironically titled 'Vernacular Art in Camden' (1977); in the rejection of so-called 'poster-and-slogan art' by significant factions within the group; in certain tendencies towards the 'creative genius' myth, which had a special closeness to Medalla.

Geeta Kapur, speaking in Havana for its 1989 biennial, talks about artists' and intellectuals' task 'to bring existential urgency to questions of contemporaneity', observing that '[s]ufficiently historicised, either tradition or contemporaneity can notate a "radical" purpose in the cultural politics of the Third World'.[99] This connects AFD's broad front with Araeen's comments that open the present essay. For Araeen, AFD's 'failure' was its inability to deal with cultural imperialism at the level of artistic form – its failure, ultimately, to express 'what we are today'. If *the contemporary* is to be understood as the coexistence of different times in a disjunctive conjuncture, in which different social and historical times meet in the present's non-unity, festive gatherings such as those organised by AFD may express the messy possibilities of shared presence in non-unity. And if we expand Araeen's analysis from the focus on expression via individual artworks in the modernist sense, to what we might see as the total assemblage of the group, its potential to express 'what we are today' increases: to articulate, again, relationships between the people, the event and the means of expression, with an expansiveness of the 'we' in 'what we are today'. AFD's articulation of such relationships was singular in its combination of different, often incompatible approaches to connect concrete and imagined political groupings and world-historical events in the context of anti-imperial struggle. The outcome was necessarily contradictory and unresolved.

So I leave the question open as to whether, ultimately, AFD 'succeeded' in its task. In Vicuña's view: 'The failure of the original AFD is its greatest beauty, as failure seeds the birthing of new forms.'[100] Vijay Prashad notes that it is unwise to think about the past in terms of success or failure.[101] To do so is to make the

97 Marc Camille Chaimowicz, 'Performance', *Studio International,* vol.193, no.985, January/ February 1977, p.14.

98 D. Medalla, interview by Steven Thorn, *op. cit.*

99 Geeta Kapur, 'Contemporary Cultural Practice: Some Polemical Categories', in R. Weiss et al., *Making Art Global (Part 1)*, London: Afterall Books, p.203.

mistaken assumption of a linear progression of history, which can lead to feelings of nostalgia and melancholic impasse, when in reality the course of events is anything but straight. AFD's activities were most powerful within the energy of social movement – a fact that speaks to the inseparability of 'art' and 'politics', but also the necessity of directing artistic energies towards the kind of revolutionary 'extra-artistic political force' that the present moment demands. How to do this, today, is still far from straightforward. Struggle proceeds in spirals and zigzags.[102]

100 C. Vicuña, 'Organized Dreaming', *op. cit.*

101 See Vijay Prashad, *Struggle Makes us Human: Learning from Movements for Socialism* (ed. Frank Barat), Chicago: Haymarket Books, 2022.

102 'THE AIMS OF ARTISTS FOR DEMOCRACY', *op. cit.* This is a paraphrasing of Friedrich Engels, also often cited by Prashad in recent years. See, for instance, 'History Often Proceeds by Jumps and Zig-Zags', *Tricontinental: Institute for Social Research Newsletter*, no.33, 15 August 2019.

Art in a Solidarity Continuum: Winnowing Loose Transnational Threads

Eileen Legaspi-Ramirez

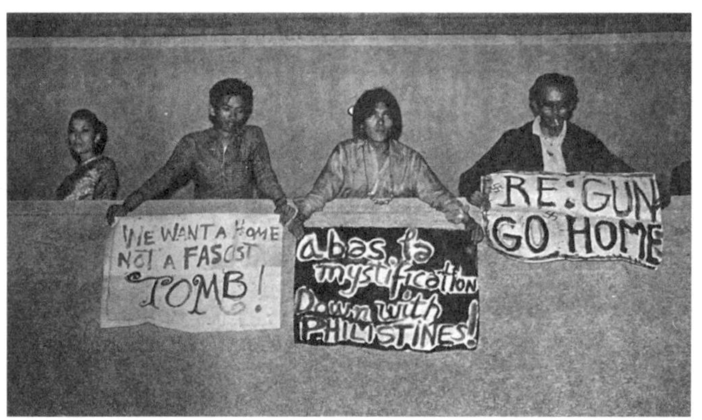

Mars Galang, David Medalla and Jun Lansang protesting at the opening of the Cultural Center of the Philippines, Manila, 1969. From *Philippines Free Press*, 20 September 1969

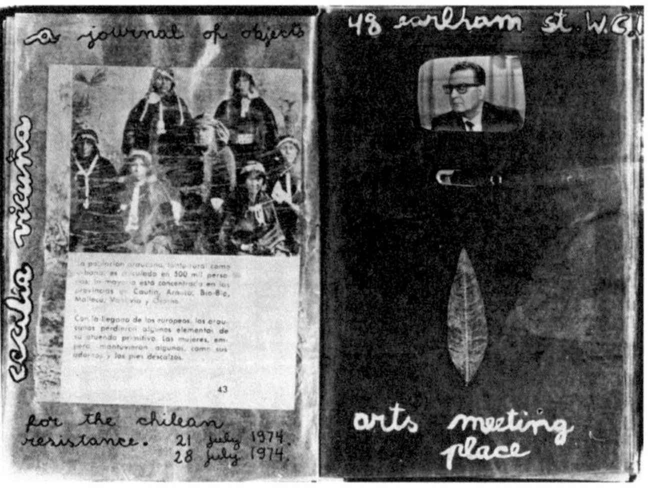

Invitation to Cecilia Vicuña's installation *A Journal of Objects for the Chilean Resistance* at Art Meeting Place, London, 1974

I write this with a distinct sense of resignation, of knowing that generational memories of what and whom propelled Artists for Democracy (AFD) have become more muted in the years since COVID-19 wreaked havoc on this planet.[1] I am inevitably looking at AFD and manifestations of solidarity from a rather dire, albeit distanced, Philippine perch, where incumbent President Ferdinand Marcos Jr and his public information machinery raise attenuated calls for 'solidarity' in its most bastardised form. Instrumentalised support has returned the Marcos family to the highest levels of power, looking past 'divisive' trespasses purportedly to rechannel energies toward stubborn urgencies actually wrought by fumbling pandemic fascism and elite largesse. In writing this text, I have taken comfort in AFD co-founder Cecilia Vicuña's poignant foregrounding of 'disrupted social bonds' and the iterative unraveling and reweaving manifest in her writing and installations to date.[2] Vicuña's perspective remains pertinent four decades down the line, as we push against unequivocal surrender to neoliberal greed amidst wavering radicality.

In 1974, Chile was spoken of as laboratory from which fascism could be exported as well as testament to intersectional resistance.[3] At the time, this axis was taken as a chance to test tactics and alliances. The present text comes at a parallel juncture, marked by a resurgence in local crises and struggles, alongside much global anxiety regarding dismal transcultural and climate futures. At such momentous intersections, when so much is awry, looking back at episodes of promise pushes raggedy emergency rafts against sheer melancholia. At least part of the wager is that revisiting past bursts of aggregated creative sociopolitical energy, thrust at crises not entirely alien to ours today, surfaces how diverse configurations such as those seen in AFD enable the fleeting but potent congealing of sentiments and empathy-driven work that still resonates across space and time.

Trawling through the traces of AFD in Vicuña's archive hits me as mildly analogous to picking through survivor troughs and untidied barracks evidencing struggles in medias res. The understandably perspectival traces surface multifaceted disparity in capacities to exercise power and variably victorious attempts at weathering erasures of ways of knowing and doing. I take cues to look at untidy seams, unintentional diversions to otherwise untried or underexplored paths born of *newen* (often translated from Mapuche as 'the force of people from the land')

1 Recent departures of the AFD core membership include David Medalla (1938–2020), Guy Brett (1942–2021) and John Dugger (1948–2023).

2 See Miguel A. Lopez (ed.), *And if I devoted my life to one of its feathers?: Aesthetic Responses to Extraction, Accumulation, and Dispossession*, Berlin: Sternberg, 2023.

3 Ariel Dorfman, speaking at the opening of 'Arts Festival for Democracy in Chile', Royal College of Art, London, 1974. See also Lynn MacRitchie's video documentation of the festival, available at http://lynnmacritchie.com/AFDChile.html.

– tangents generated through excesses of force asserted by language, art and bodies laid on the line without promise of definitive comeuppance.[4]

4 For an extended discussion of *newen*, see Magnus Course, 'The Birth of the Word: Language, Force, and Mapuche Ritual Authority', *HAU: Journal of Ethnographic Theory*, vol.2, no.1, Spring 2012, pp.1–26.

Doing and Knowing

Solidarity relations are undeniably fluid and contingent – conflicts are prone to appear within temporal peer structures, despite repeated assertions of operative multiplicity and robust simultaneity. The often-intuitive interfacing of creative energy instigates voids and pauses, which can morph or veer in unlikely directions and produce nascent and arguably incomprehensible positionalities. Expectedly, both urgency and artistry keep things on the fly.

It is worth remembering that the relational precarity in solidarity formations such as AFD is a product of considerable movement and migration. Hence the agitational character of migrant artists expressing solidarity elsewhere whilst experiencing othering where they are at. What I hadn't quite anticipated in

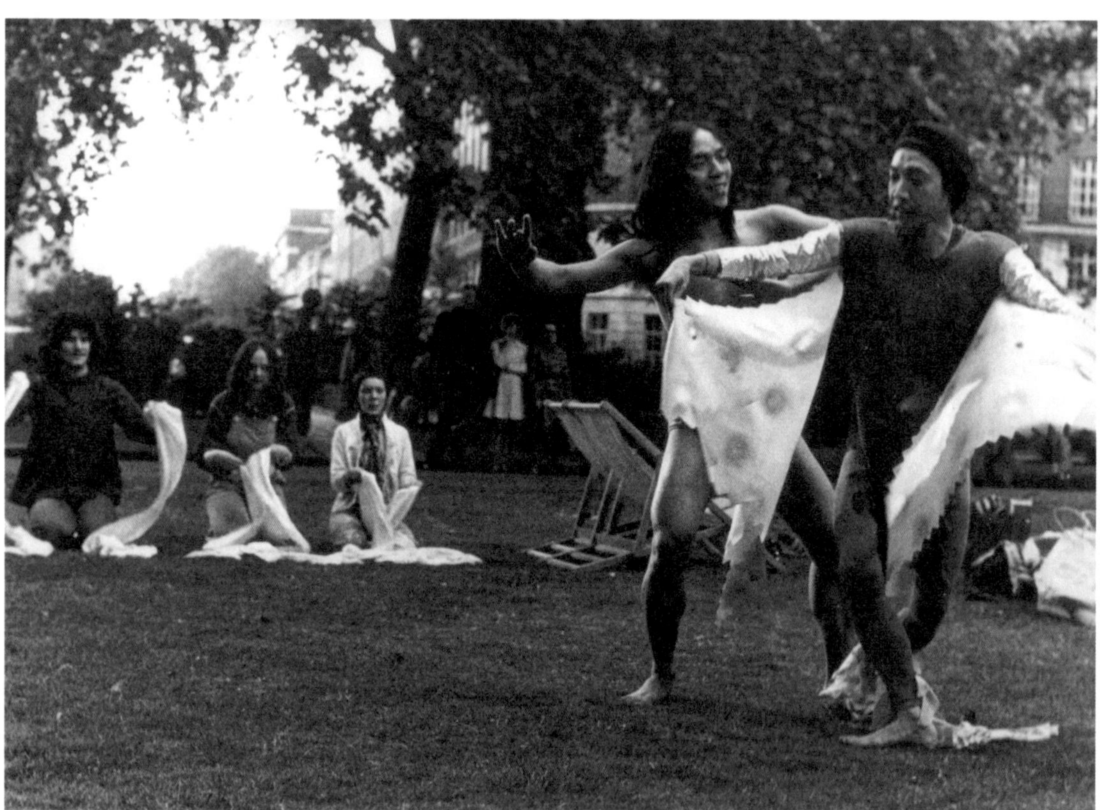

Virgil Calaguian (left foreground) and Jun Terra performing Mao Tse-tung's poem 'Swimming', Puck Festival, Russell Square, London, May 1975

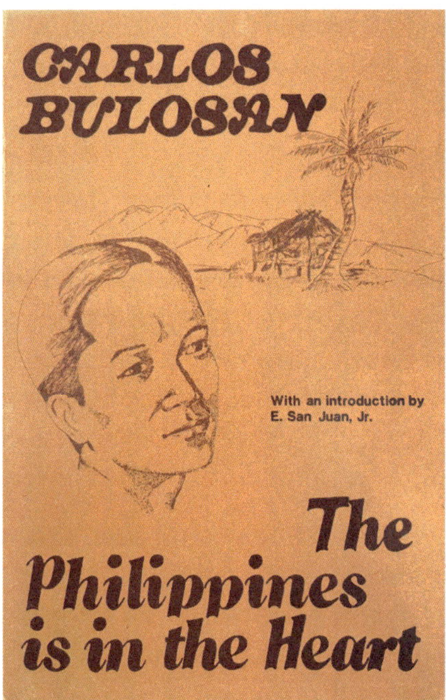

Cover of Carlos Bulosan's *The Philippines is in the Heart* (New Day Publishers, 1978)

revisiting the histories of the participants in AFD was a mild distantiation from nation-laden originary discourse, which I sensed via David Medalla's protracted AFD activities, alongside fellow Filipinos Jun Terra and Virgil Calaguian. My sense is that their shifting roles as interlocutors of homeland narratives were dialectically shaping how and why they applied themselves to solidarity causes elsewhere – possibly as a viable response to the fraught situation of local culturati visibly becoming instrumentalised by a fascist state back in the Philippines.

The distantiation of the politically exiled Medalla may have been tactical as much as strategic. 1974 was also the year Ferdinand Marcos Sr institutionalised the en masse trafficking (more benignly called 'warm body export') of Filipinos through the Labor Export Policy (Presidential Decree 442). This state-sanctioned mobility of individual labour continues as a key Philippine development track and plays very well into volatile political dynamics within the extant diasporic and migrant communities that still exercise a stake on what happens to and in the republic. Self-identification is embodied flex, responding to morphing demographics as well as political realignments.

On a hunch, I turned to the experiences of two other diasporic Filipino figures, the novelist Carlos Bulosan (1911–56) and the artist Carlos Villa (1936–2013), both of whom I'm fairly certain Medalla had contact with prior to his settling in Europe. Bulosan described his experience of living in the class- and race-divided United States thus:

> I realized how foolish it was to believe then that I could define roots in terms of places and persons. I knew, then, that I would be as rootless in the Philippines as I was in America, because roots are not physical things, but the quality of faith deeply [ingrained] and clearly understood and integrated in one's life. The roots I was looking for were not physical but intellectual and spiritual things. In fact, I was looking for a common faith to believe in and of which I could be a growing part.[5]

The deep empathy Bulosan felt for and amongst once-colonised but eventually resisting subjects also surfaced in Carlos Villa, whose need to flex – 'to self-hybridize', as art historian Margo Machida puts it – underpinned his will to survive.[6] Villa described himself as 'growing up Filipino and acting black' in the belly of the beast – the USA – which resonates with Medalla's and Rasheed Araeen's assertion to Blackness in Britain in the 1970s.[7] In the case of Araeen, this effectively positioned him within a politically inclusive social category, encompassing his Pakistani heritage within shared experiences of racism and oppression; and to a certain extent it perhaps eased his own reckoning with reductive misidentifications of his work as stylistically Islamic.[8] I see these indicative self-performances as means to enable relational mobility, avowedly cultivating the capacity to empathise with those similarly oppressed within the logics of structural disenfranchisement.

Writing in the mid-1970s, Araeen spoke of the need for a 'constant ideological position vis-à-vis the Third World, rather than taking actions only at "critical moments"'.[9] And we revisit this through Medalla's assertion that 'a struggle is not a model; it's a movement', taken from the repartee, a few years later, between Araeen and Medalla on AFD and identity politics.[10] Therein implicitly lies the idea of an iterative limbo preceding posited radical change. Vicuña, for her part, in 1974 declared: 'We are forming AFD to educate artists on how to create work in the service of the people.'[11]

This push to self-learning was a collective anchor with continued significance for the AFD group. Lynn MacRitchie

5 Carlos Bulosan, quoted in E. San Juan Jr, *Between Empire and Insurgency: The Philippines in the New Millennium, Essays in History, Comparative Literature, and Cultural Politics*, Quezon City: University of the Philippines Press, 2015, pp.115–16. The quotation is from Bulosan's short story 'My Education' (1995).

6 Margo Machida, 'Transcultural Sampling: The Reimagined Worlds of Carlos Villa', in *Carlos Villa: Worlds in Collision*, Oakland: University of California Press, 2021, p.55.

7 Carlos Villa, quoted in Lucy R. Lippard, 'Making the World Smaller: Carlos Villa's Polyculturalism', in *ibid.*, p.13.

8 See Kylie Gilchrist, 'Rasheed Araeen's Bismullah', *MAVCOR Journal*, vol.6, no.2, 2022.

9 Rasheed Araeen, 'Conversation with David Medalla', *Black Phoenix*, no.3, Spring 1979, p.18.

10 See *ibid.*

11 Cecilia Vicuña, in *Artists for Democracy: El Archivo de Cecilia Vicuña*, Santiago: Museo de la Memoria y los Derechos Humanos / Museo Nacional de Bellas Artes, 2013, unpaginated.

has affirmed the vibrant curiosity felt as she was herself documenting the Chile Festival in 1974 – they were all 'so eager to learn'.[12] The festival and AFD itself obviously tended to those bemoaning the limits of art school, and the European bubble that was fully implicated in its empiric impulses. Having barely handled camera equipment, MacRitchie set out to translate images into tight, zoomed-in shots, as if leaning in to listen and closely engage. She has shared how they were avidly joining multiple reading groups and propelling 'constant discussion' – 'we wanted to base our politics on something solid'. This picture parallels the present-day DIY self-publishing and narrativising that is feverishly happening through zines and the many platforms proliferating through a spectrum of self-organised autonomous/collectivist movements across networked global points. In the 1970s, the shared desire to think and act beyond London – 'small, grey and miserable', in MacRichie's words, yet enlivened by the international mix of peoples rippling through it – mitigated the 'wasteland' feel that artist-activists were pushing back against.

With this in mind, I have come to approach AFD as part of a *solidarity continuum*. We could pencil in precedents such as Vicuña's early work as part of the Santiago-based Tribu No collective, founded in 1967, and her book *Sabor a Mí* (*Taste of Me*, 1973), and her later involvement in the Heresies Collective (founded 1976 in New York City); Medalla's early 1970s collaboration with John Dugger in Artists Liberation Front (ALF), and, much later, his initiation in 2000 of the London Biennale, involving Terra and others; Araeen's ties with the Black Panther movement and involvement in establishing of the journals *Black Phoenix* in the late 1970s and *Third Text* a decade later – these are amongst many threads of life and passionate advocacy that far exceed the few years of AFD's mid-70s coalescence.

The continuum also emphasises solidarity as a drawn-out process – requiring persistent labour to exceed the instances when coalescing actually happens. In the aforementioned statements by Araeen and Villa, I recognize their respective self-acknowledgment of the internalised oppression that has to be unlearnt daily.[13] This labouring within, of remaking self, is key to building knowledge-driven alliances, and reveals a keen analysis of structural impediments as well as internal contradictions. In the case of Vicuña, her creative work has proceeded from being mindful of the intangible;

12 L. MacRitchie, conversation with Adeena Mey, 2 February 2023.

13 See Rasheed Araeen's statements as recounted in Christopher Turner, '"There is an element of optimism inmy work"'. *Apollo*, 27 January 2018, available at https://www.apollo-magazine.com/there-is-an-element-of-optimism-in-my-work/.

14 Courtney J. Martin, 'Rasheed Araeen, Live Art, and Radical Politics in Britain', *Getty Research Journal*, no.2, 2010, p.114.

her art is inclined to the lyricism of the poetic and the contingencies of the relational just before they are transformed into invitations to the everydayness of surfacing commonality. I sense this particularly in Vicuña's underlining of non-activity and creative leisure during her Tribu No years, but also in the more elaborate instantiations, or materialisations, of relating viscerally, as manifest in AFD's Chile Festival and beyond.

I now turn to developing these threads via schematic intertextual readings of Araeen's *Paki Bastard: Portrait of the Artist as a Black Person* (1977), Medalla's *Eskimo Carver* (1977) and Vicuña's *Precarios* (1966–2017).

The Artist as Cipher of Agitation and Pain

In a 2007 communication with the art historian Courtney J. Martin, Araeen described *Paki Bastard*, first performed at AFD's Whitfield Street squat in 1977:

> I began with a sound of my playing flute. But then I changed this track with Handle's [*sic*] Messiah, followed by a song from an Indian film, a song by Asian folk singer, a voice of NF [National Front] saying 'Paki go home', and finally the speech of a trade union leader complaining about the lack of support for the strike at Grunwick.

Martin's essay recounting the conversation continues to offer the context:

> The sound gathered the cacophony of noise on London's streets as they were altered by the addition of immigrants. For example, open-air markets with stalls selling Asian music in Brixton, Southall, or Brick Lane comingled with ringing church bells. At night, these sounds turned sinister, as members of the National Front shouted down immigrants before pursuing them. As Araeen noted, the chant that he heard most often was 'Paki'.[14]

I invoke this evocative description of Araeen's *Paki Bastard* as it plays up the layering of ambient aural buzz around what was already a sensorially provocative action. As I was trying to make sense of AFD, I was struck by the unevenness of accessible tellings, with readier references to Chile (and sometimes also Vietnam) but not as much about solidarity work with regard to, for instance, Native Americans. The gnawing feeling that there were indeed more stories to look into became bodily and mentally triggering.

Rasheed Araeen performing *Paki Bastard* at 143 Whitfield Street, London, 31 July 1977

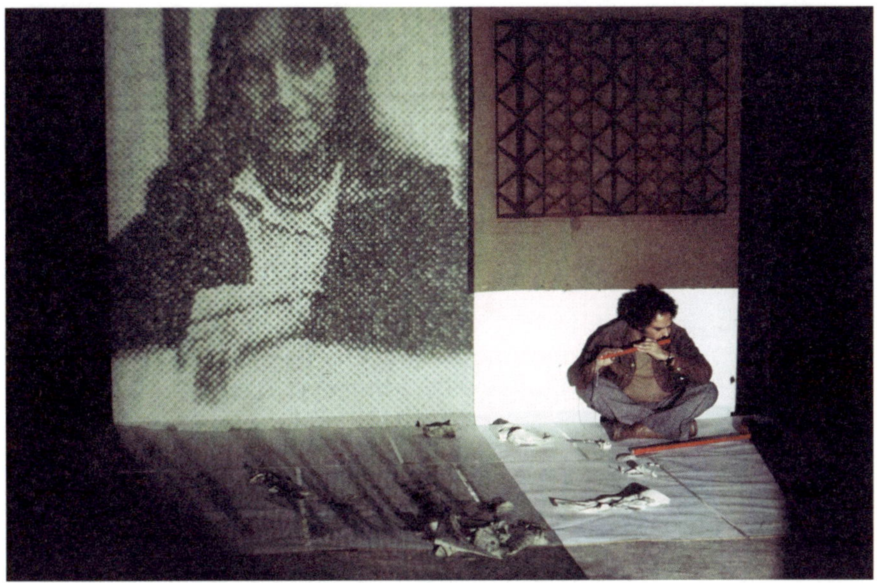

This made me ask: What accounts for these memory skews in attention and focus, apart from happenstance in archiving?

AFD's Anne Bean has this to share about Araeen's performance (via a chain of association from another work she had made for Medalla, titled *The Cure of Wounds*):

> the cure of wounds made me think of the title of Araeen's *Paki Bastard* which had a huge impact on me whilst the memories are vague with slide projections over Rasheed as he spoke with some images of Brick Lane and racist paper headlines but the title *Paki Bastard* still shouts boomingly into my ear as it stingingly forced an awkward complicity with this deeply derogatory insult as one said it out loud and it made one question the implications of the words emerging from one's own mouth into the world, and although I did not aspire to make work in this directly activist mould I pondered a work I would do called *White Kaffir* which girls in my convent school in Zambia had called me for being a Jew and soon after Paul Burwell and I did a version of The Last Poets song 'White Man's Got a God Complex'...[15]

15 Anne Bean, untitled reflection on AFD, from correspondence with David Morris, 22 September 2022.

Bean's reflection here captures something of the complexly overlapping positionalities that precariously gathered around AFD. Writing on the position of artists in diaspora, Epifanio San Juan Jr evokes an ideal of 'tribal cosmopolitanism' that he finds in the work of James Clifford. Diaspora 'serves as the site of contingency *par excellence*. [Clifford] conceives of a "polythetic field of diasporic forms expressed in multiple discourses of travels, homes, memories, transnational connections."'[16] Clifford proceeds to describe the possibilities of 'adaptive constellations of responses to dwelling-in-displacement"'.[17] Such 'tribal cosmopolitanism' may be read alongside a passage from Jean Fisher's analysis of 'The Other Story: Afro-Asian Artists in Post-War Britain' (1989–90), which reads in part: '[T]his generation of artists introduce[d] a "postcolonial" cosmopolitanism of multiple spatio-temporal attachments.'[18] That Araeen himself would take on the fraught mission of positing such a counternarrative, through his curation of the project, suggests another reason for the volatility of mutually felt, albeit asymmetric, alienation.

Solidarities are not just wrought through grand gestures (like exhibitions or festivals) but also more mundane, subtle, small actions; making room for ambiguity *vis-à-vis* specificity/legibility, and the anticipation of response (both from immediate and distanced contexts of circulation) as well as reckoning with disparate material conditions. Such could be seen in Medalla's participatory work *Eskimo Carver*, realised at AFD's Whitfield Street space. With its performative and installation aspects referencing Indigenous oral poetry and news accounts of a pipeline impinging on Inuit territory in Alaska, I see this as a less directly political enacting of Medalla's predilection for collaboration. The late AFD co-founder Guy Brett noted:

> Medalla's participatory installations were from the beginning a means of breaking with certain ingrained taboos and restrictions governing the artistic scene. Through them he put forward the startling idea of invading the monocultural, monological, monolithic institutions of the art world by the sheer pressure of a latent creativity.[19]

This potentially unwieldy polyvalence comes through the transformation of text and material form done at Medalla's bidding to use whatever was on hand. The work evoked embodied memories from those who took up its charge to fashion 'knives' to symbolically and literally slice through spoken, written and sung narratives as well as ideational and material limits.

Brett pointed to 'the variety of minds or psyches that devised them (the makeshift knives) within the arena of expectation

16 E. San Juan Jr, *Between Empire and Insurgency*, *op. cit.*, p.149.

17 *Ibid.*

18 Jean Fisher, 'The Other Story and the Past Imperfect', *Tate Papers*, no.12, Autumn 2009, available at https://www.tate.org.uk/research/tate-papers/12/the-other-story-and-the-past-imperfect. 'The Other Story' opened at the Hayward Gallery in London before touring to Wolverhampton and Manchester.

19 Guy Brett, 'Elasticity of Exhibition', *Tate Papers*, no.12, Autumn 2009, available at https://www.tate.org.uk/research/tate-papers/12/elasticity-of-exhibition.

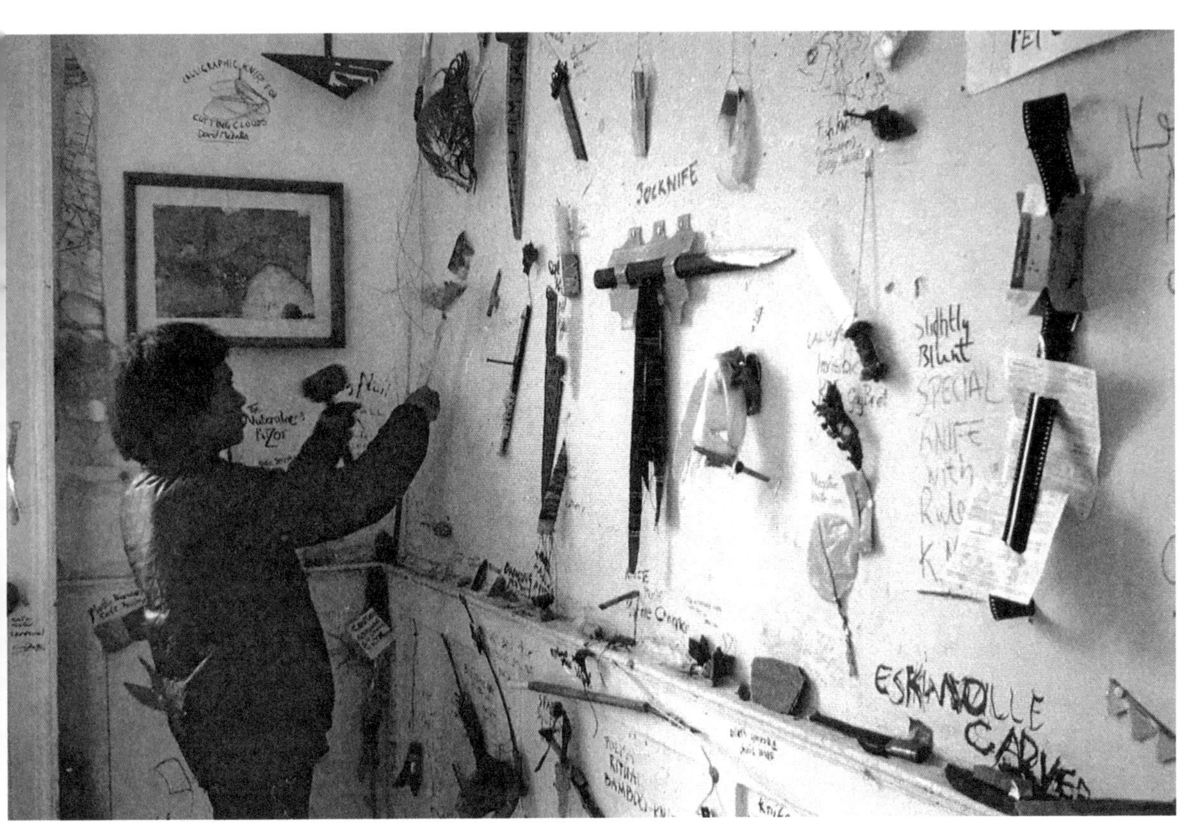

David Medalla installing *Eskimo Carver,* 143 Whitfield Street, London, 1977

and challenge that the artist created'.[20] As both primary critic and de facto biographer, Brett established the work's immediate situational triggers; yet ironically, *Eskimo Carver*'s appended history has since become tainted with the charge of employing a slur that had yet to be flagged at that early juncture of AFD. In this, it surfaces a wound that in Bean's recollection of both *Paki Bastard* and *Eskimo Carver* raises her own self-indicting reflections on whiteness and power. These appear in her stream of consciousness alongside a reference to Joseph Beuys – 'When you cut your finger, bandage the knife' – another subtle gesture suggesting a more oblique approach to social wounds.[21]

20 *Ibid.*

21 A. Bean, untitled reflection on AFD, *op. cit.*

One might even find some uncanny resonances between the objects that eventually made up Medalla's *Eskimo Carver* and Vicuña's *Precarios*. Given the falling out between artists following the Chile Festival, we could say that the sensorial resonances outlived human alliances. Yet clearly there are earnest affinities. We see as much in Vicuña's own description of her *Precarios* as 'installations and *basuritas*, objects composed of debris, structures that disappear, along with quipus and other weaving metaphors. [...] Created in and for the moment, they reflect

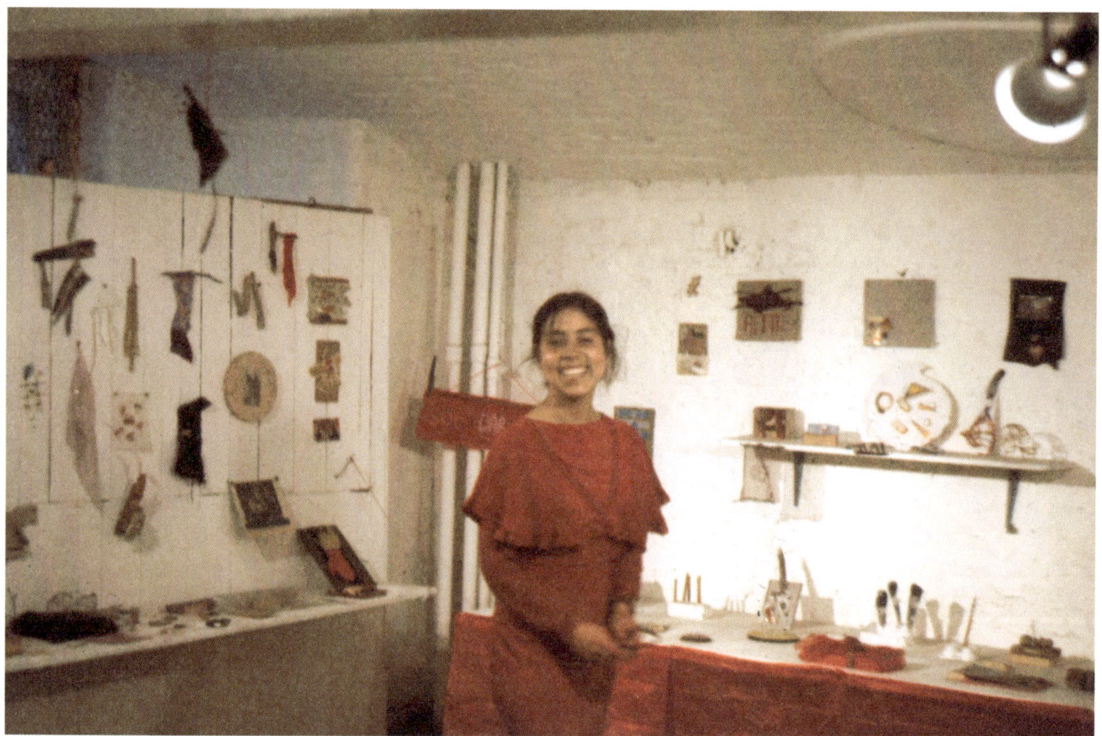

Cecilia Vicuña with her installation *A Journal of Objects for the Chilean Resistance* at Art Meeting Place, London, 1974

ancient spiritual technologies – a knowledge of the power of individual and communal intention to heal us and the earth.'[22] In considering these works together, my point is that the undoing of AFD's early relational threads did not thwart the shared ends and equivocating sympathies toward mindful regard for post- and non-human beings nor the privileging of participatory democracy. These continue to be invoked in reckonings with AFD's work, as well as with Vicuña's vibrant current practice,[23] and this recognition of sustained association surfaces, in my mind, potencies of intersectionality relevant to broader liberation aesthetics foregrounded in AFD and even more widely.[24]

The intractability and volatility of relations seen in Vicuña's *Precarios* also indicate dispersal as a tactic to thwart complete capture. Exposed to the vicissitudes of climactic change and attendant disaster, as well as to the extractive designs of capital, the *Precarios* exist between object and site, between bodies and minds moving in common, between elements of endangered ecologies. Candice Amich, writing on how Vicuña's performativity has demonstrated this potency, vividly phrases it as 'the unlocatable as a strategy of resistance'.[25] And so this is a generative volatility that is lived out, I would say, with exceedingly fragile affinities opening up to the subtly radial as well as more readily recognisable resonances.

This also invites other routes into study. My own research on AFD has led me to trail off into looking at crossed paths, at possibly germinal but understudied encounters: between Villa showing in California and Canada in 1996–97 alongside the young Filipino social realist Norberto Roldan, now gone home to Capiz province, doing a biennale counterposed against the Centre that is Manila; or Villa showing at the Havana Biennial in 1991, after the French-Filipino Lani Maestro had done so in 1986, at about the same time that Chilean critic Nelly Richard and other Latin American thinkers started figuring prominently in her thinking; in '86 we also interestingly find Vicuña simultaneously showing within the same exhibition platform, posed as counterfoil to Euro-American monolithic narratives of art. All these stories suggest unfolding webs of more stories, sans tidily sewn-up ends.

Such tempting speculations may offer a powerful counterforce with respect to formerly marginalised histories – indeed, they may be the only recourse in the absence of more 'official' documentation. Yet they also invite historiographic dilemmas, as Eleanor

22 See Vicuña's statement at http://www.ceciliavicuna.com/introduction.

23 See Francisco Villaroel and Lucy Quezada, 'A Conversation with Cecilia Vicuña: Artists for Democracy's "Future Archive"' (trans. Phillip Penix-Tadsen), *Artishock*, 23 June 2014, available at https://artishockrevista.com/2014/06/23/conversation-with-cecilia-vicuna/.

24 See, for example, Louise Siddons, 'Red Power in the "Black Panther": Radical Imagination and Intersectional Resistance at Wounded Knee', *American Art*, vol.35, no.2, Summer 2021, pp.2–31.

25 Candice Amich, 'From Precarity to Planetarity: Cecilia Vicuña's Kon Kon', *The Global South*, vol.7, no.2, Fall 2013, p.136.

Roberts highlights in her analysis of Araeen's and Medalla's parallel trajectories:

> The political transformation of the quotidian in both artists' practices prompts consideration of ways in which more typical, centralised sources of evidence (such as the institutional archive and authoritative first-hand accounts) might be unseated in favour of the seemingly extraneous or dubious indices of the misremembered, the excessive, the unbalanced, the automythological, and the spatially or temporally dispersed. Within these parameters, alternative historiographical methods emerge which in turn create new possibilities for understanding practices which are uncertain, difficult, or otherwise elusive to historical documentation, and enable interrogation of the aesthetic and political effects of performances that may or may not have even happened.[26]

Roberts raises Medalla's and Araeen's critical engagement with visibility politics: how they appeared to be counting on solidarity as both survival and performative undoing – posing this more as a way through than a way into institutional memory-making and singular tellings, and eventually bringing together strands of Black arts movements, ethnic/migrant minority/race-ethnicity underpinned discourse, as well as transnational liberation impulses – all of which may be seen to culminate in parallel with the mid-1970s moment of AFD. Needless to say, this weaving of expansive, even if interlaced, resonance brings a push-and-pull dynamic upon such stagings of shared resistance.

If AFD's coalescence was brief and contentious, its actions can still be taken as coordinates for potential tangents and smartened realignments. Here we might turn again to San Juan, who invokes the 'labor of acquiring self knowledge', in an echo of AFD's charge to self-education cited above.[27] Citing Antonio Gramsci, he asserts how solidarity remains essentially cumulative:

> [E]very revolution has been preceded by a long process of intense critical activity, of new cultural insight and the spread of ideas through groups of men initially resistant to them, wrapped up in the process of solving their own immediate economic and political problems, and lacking any bonds of solidarity with others in the same position.[28]

26 Eleanor Roberts, 'Black Sheep: Rasheed Araeen, David Medalla, and Reconfigurations of Visibility in the 1970s', *Contemporary Theatre Review*, vol.31, no.1–2, p.54.

27 *Ibid.*

28 Antonio Gramsci, quoted in E. San Juan Jr, *Between Empire and Insurgency*, *op. cit.*, p.10.

We could conceive of Vicuña's *Precarios* as indicative of the highly contingent and sometimes flailing but often fascinating possibilities of solidarity work. As Juliet Lynd suggests, such precarious reckoning, 'as failed memory trace', may be cast against the disappointments of the Chilean revolution, and, by extension, all our present complicities.[29] With this, we might hope to continue embarking on a shared quest for intersecting empathetic alliances not necessarily conjoined in specificities of geography or reductively legible junctures of history, but by the capacity to converge in spaces made permeable by the vivacity summoned by bodies, minds and work brushing up against each other, possibly bristling at the friction at the onset, yet ultimately finding workable chemistry amidst the ensuing melee.

29 Juliet Lynd, 'Precarious Resistance: Weaving Opposition in the Poetry of Cecilia Vicuña, *PMLA*, vol.120, no.5, October 2005, pp.1588–607.

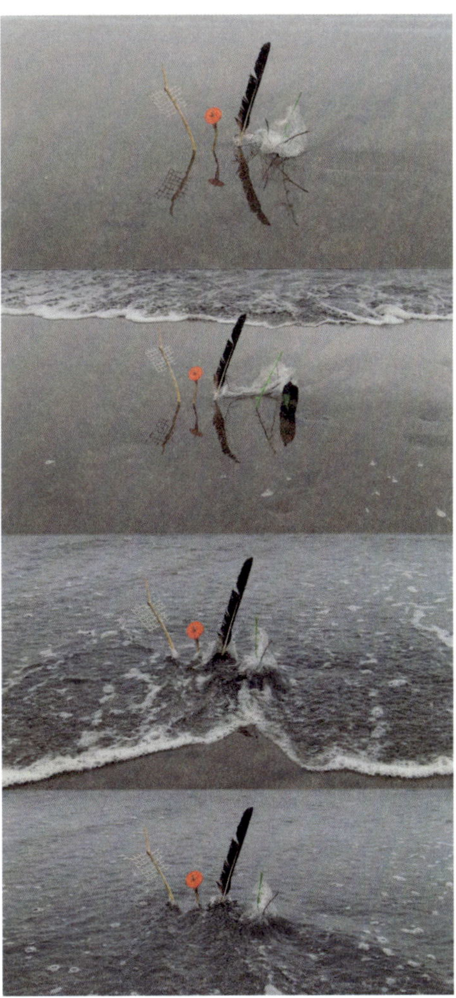

Cecilia Vicuña, *Dissolution*, precarious site-specific performance installation, Concón, Chile, 2009

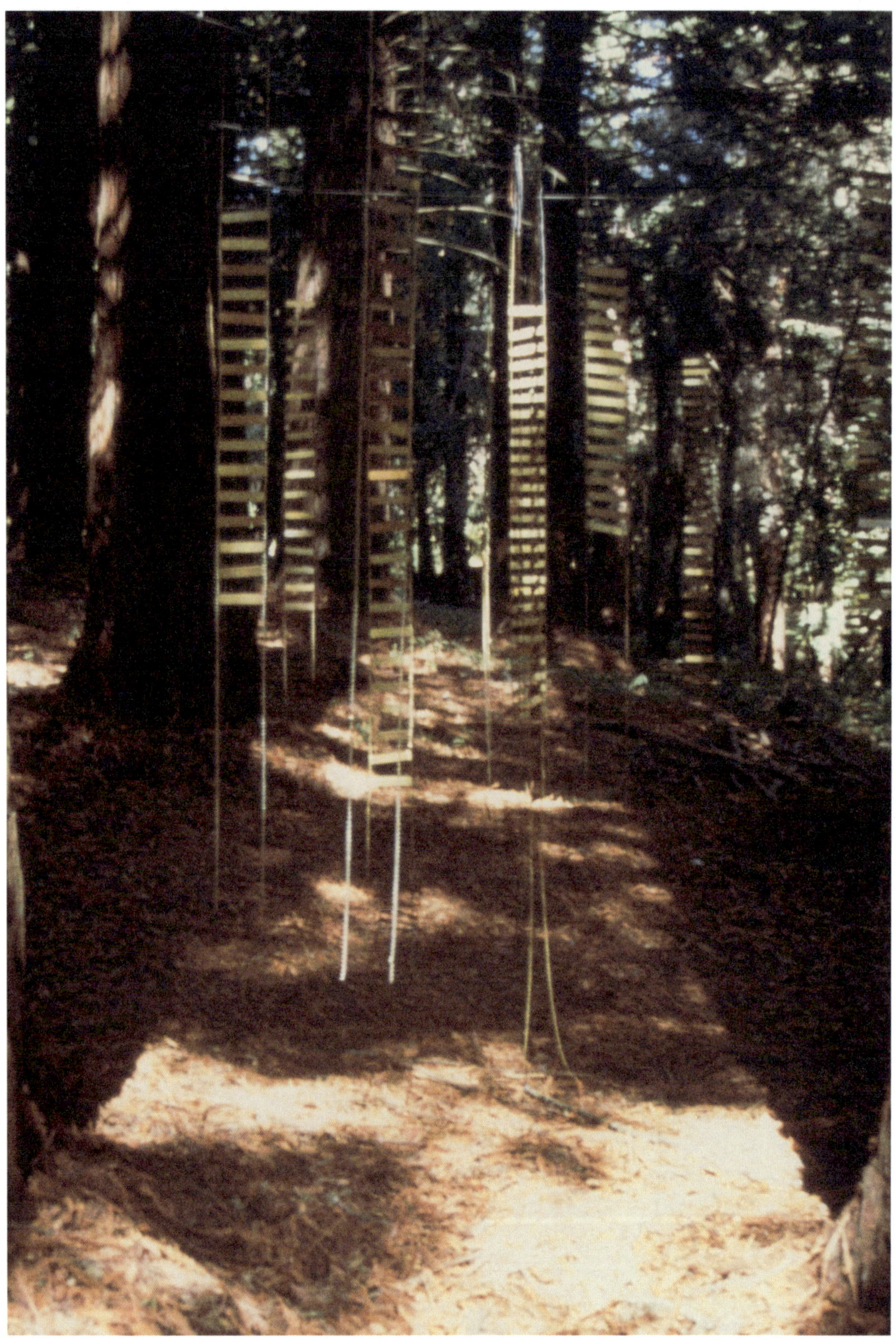

Carlos Villa, *Campo Santo*, 1999–2004, engraved brass plaques and chains, dimensions variable. Installed at Soquel, California

Thus, indeed, the struggle is through and with form, as Vicuña has put it: 'The search for a structure in society is analogous to the search I undertake for form in my works. The social form is easier to find, it's obviously socialism, self-sufficient communities, but is harder to do it. The form I search for is harder to find, but easier to do.'[30] This could easily be taken as an acknowledgement of the non-sensicality of monolithic knowledge forms as well as the viability of collectivity that operates across broader spheres of struggle – therefore making room even for deep division regarding tactics, immediacy, militancy, risks of co-optation and instrumentalisation. We could then further conceive this as *newen*, the excess of force (both of language and art) surpassing ideology, and mobilising multiplicities of means and ends.

30 C. Vicuña, *Saborami*, Cullompton, Devon: Beau Geste Press, 1973, p.65.

In many ways, AFD's eventual fraying at the seams occasions the activation of this can-do, must-do impulse, albeit in dispersed sites and unplanned resurfacings. Over time, when the politics of recognition and identity become less critically potent *vis-à-vis* the traversing of difference for solidarities to survive, the make-do and symbolic AFD *camposantos* might imaginably shape-shift into structures made of sturdier, crisis-tested relational armatures, sealed off with adhesives that formidably bear the tug and pull of specificities – the crevasse of particularities (crossing from the certain toward the contingent) that makes the deploying of the *trans-* prefix performatively open-ended and boundary-crossing.

Before Art and Politics: Regarding the Precarious Documents of Artists for Democracy

Wing Chan

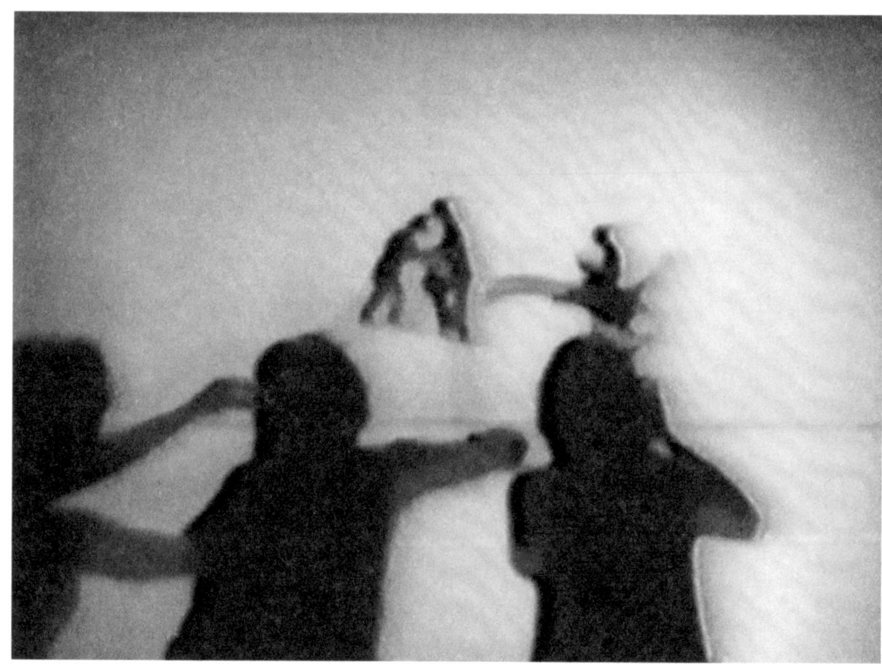

Red Star Shadow Puppet Theatre performing Lu Xun's 'An Incident'. From the video *Statements from the Arts Festival for Democracy in Chile*, shot and edited by Lynn MacRitchie (recorded at the 'Arts Festival for Democracy in Chile', Royal College of Art, London, 1974)

In October 2022 I travelled to the south bank of the River Thames to attend a ritual guided by Artists for Democracy (AFD) co-founder Cecilia Vicuña. I was trying to find answers to the question of what constitutes a political mobilisation in the field of art. The experience shook my understanding of this question. Being there was electrifying. In my diary, looking at a photograph I took that day on my phone, I wrote that I had witnessed a *becoming anonymous* artist.

> Last Friday. Participating in the guided ritual marching to the River Thames from the Turbine Hall and back I became a tree. There were almost two hundred of us there, a crowd bigger than I expected. Everyone didn't know everyone. But as we saw [Vicuña] make movements with a tree branch in hand, we followed and made sounds with the branches in our hands. It's magical to see how tiny physically Cecilia Vicuña is, and gentle her voice, and then two hundred people were motivated simply by her gesturing and speech. As she spoke in the last three minutes of the 1.5-hour ritual, she became even tinier. She asked people in the Turbine Hall to investigate the Brazil election and the future of the rain forest. She didn't talk about her sculpture in the hall. Rarely do I see artists shrink themselves to make room. Her hands also shrank. The moment she raised the tree branch and made a small dance I noticed her age. The dance was still smooth and light, but the baby fat in her hands was gone. My impression of her before the tree ritual was still the 1970s her. As a document, the photo that I took is terrible. I keep only capturing her back. Her face isn't shown. She's anonymous there. I kept standing behind her, literally following her. I found myself unable to witness on the side and take a good profile shot that can tell a story of her and the site we were in. It really made me think afterwards how the bad photo I took is at performing my understanding of her in the moment, including her playing down her persona in public.

The ritual took place in London, but our attention was directed towards Brazil and Amazonia. I thought of AFD's exhibitions and performances in London in the 1970s, often directed towards places where communities were resisting imperialism, colonialism and fascism, in North America, Angola, Chile, China, Ireland, Mozambique, Vietnam, Zimbabwe and elsewhere. Was there any resemblance? Holding my symbolic tree branch, I sensed that the space I occupied was changing in size: as the artist shrank and became anonymous in the mass gathering, space was exposed, to be filled up by other empathetic selves. As viewers-turned-participants, we took up the space. We were moved, detached from our own biographies and guided to internalise the fate of a tree and, by extension, the artist's political calling – however distant from our origins and the location of the ritual. I realised that the mobilisation of the people in situ in art spaces concerned imitation, muscle memory and, above all, a sense of scale not only optically perceived but also physically and spatially experienced.[1] I interpreted the artist's action as fostering social communication; in moving beyond pure individual and aesthetic achievement, it was akin, perhaps, to the ideological position that many 'cultural workers' choose to take. I was left with the impression of the artist's presence fading and shrinking, and thereby increasing the participants' strength and volume for mobilisation.

Five months later, I encountered another document of the ritual; an official photograph in Tate's accompanying monograph.[2] The image shows the artist's magnificent, singular presence with a mass of blurry bodies behind her. I recognised my own face, captured by the museum's camera. Comparing my own narrative to this 'official', or institutional, record, I was perplexed. Through the Tate photograph, I became aware of myself performing in the production of a particular ideal, the 'political artist'. Yet what was most uncomfortable to me was the realisation of how loudly this institutional representation spoke – how it now got in the way of my own bodily experience and interpretation. To me, it seemed that the purpose of the institution's camera – to bring the artist into sharper focus – produced a number of distortions: it collapsed distances and manipulated the relative size of the figures within the frame; it centred an individualistic narrative of the artist and belied the collective experience I and others had experienced; and it obscured the exchange between the artist and audience-participants that co-produced the mobilisation in their simultaneous experience of space and time. In effect, rather than documenting the ritual, the institutional technology produced a document of the artist's ego.

These experiences forced me to rethink my approach to the history of AFD. Using 'art meets politics' as an index of their actions suddenly felt insufficient. I needed a different set of questions. I would need to suspend the powerful categories with

1 Here I take inspiration from two major volumes studying scale in regard to material properties, artistic production and the reception of art: Joan Kee and Emanuele Lugli (ed.), *To Scale*, Chichest, West Sussex: Wiley-Blackwell, 2015; Jennifer L. Roberts (ed.), *Scale*, Chicago: Terra Foundation for American Art, 2016.

2 Catherine Wood (ed.), *Cecilia Vicuña: Brain Forest Quipu*, London: Tate Publishing, 2023.

which I set out to study AFD – 'art' and 'politics' – to see what more I could see.[3] The story that emerged concerns, for me, the artist's role in helping us rethink how meaning is produced in history. This includes an awareness of the publics involved and their perspectives; a critical understanding of power and framing; and a consideration of the boundaries between exposure and anonymity.

3 Here I am adopting Saskia Sassen's method of destabilising settled categories. See S. Sassen, 'Before Method: Analytic Tactics to Decipher the Global – An Argument and Its Responses, Part II', *The Pluralist*, vol.8, no.3, Fall 2013, pp.101–12.

4 Michel-Rolph Trouillot, 'The Power in the Story', in *Silencing the Past: Power and the Production of History*, Boston: Beacon Press, 1995, pp.1–30.

Withdrawing from the document

Historian Michel-Rolph Trouillot talks about the researcher's responsibility to track power, to ask 'how history works' instead of 'what is history'. As researchers, we are encouraged to identify the meeting points between history as social process and history as knowledge, to see where some processes are accepted as knowledge and others are not. Such meeting points, Trouillot posits, are indicative of power exercised, because the system of acceptability cannot work without power.[4] Extending Trouillot's idea into thinking about AFD, for the process of political mobilisation to be accepted as knowledge in art, either the artist must take control of knowledge production or the art world must sit with the uneasiness of the uncentred, *becoming anonymous* artist.

Looking at documentation of the performance of Jun Terra's Red Star Shadow Puppet Theatre on 25 October 1974, during AFD's 'Arts Festival for Democracy in Chile' at the Royal College of Art (RCA), London, we find another instance of the artist figure withdrawing from view. Terra's choice of media drew from popular traditions to tell stories through a backlit screen, with moveable silhouetted forms. His theatre also incorporated mime, with performers sometimes joining him behind the screen to illustrate parts of the story through their gestures. As the performers moved towards the light source and away from the screen, their projected shadows increased in size and also blurred and faded out, almost disappearing.

At the festival, Terra talked about the precise social context and function of shadow puppets:

> The cultural arm of the National Liberation Front in the Philippines are also fighters. They are not only performers and actors. They put forward the line of the party and the line of the liberation front in every work that they do. It's always the line of fighting against American imperialism and establishing a national democratic government, and this is expressed in many forms, through puppet shows, paintings, songs and

dances. [...] In Southeast Asia, shadow puppets were used to perform the function of making people concentrate on a certain ethos. It used to be performed after harvest time when people have time to rest and reflect on their own lives. It played the role of unifying the whole collectively. This was a time when the agricultural communities of Southeast Asia were self-sufficient and stable. But, with the encroachment of colonialism and imperialism in the area, the old society started to deteriorate, and now it's completely destroyed. So the shadow puppets started to lose relevance and to lose audiences. But now, because of the National Liberation Movement in the area, they have slowly revived. Puppets are now being used by the National Liberation Movement to convey the message of the revolution. So shadow puppets as an art form is performing a great function in the task of the whole people to build a new kind of society. [...] According to Lenin, there are democratic and socialist elements in various cultures, and certainly, shadow puppets is one of the democratic and socialist forms, one that you can appropriate by putting in content that could be understood in the West. If I knew more of the Western popular forms of art, I would have used them.[5]

Terra's performance at the RCA was based on Lu Xun's 1920 short story 'An Incident', chosen to parallel the context of class consciousness and the hope for social reforms in the 1970s.[6] 'An Incident' employs a first-person narrator to propagate a moral lesson. He recalls an incident from 1917, at the beginning of the intellectual revolution of the May Fourth Movement in China, to contrast the virtue of a rickshaw man with the indifference of the narrator himself, the rickshaw's wealthy rider. Seeing the rickshaw man walk an injured old woman towards the gate of a police station, the narrator diminishes. He confesses: 'Suddenly I had a strange feeling. His dusty, retreating figure seemed larger at that instant. Indeed, the further he walked the larger he loomed, until I had to look up to him. At the same time he seemed gradually to be exerting a pressure on me, which threatened to overpower the small self under my fur-lined gown.'[7]

As Terra noted, shadow puppetry historically functioned to mobilise people in recognition of their larger-than-life roles and duties in society. But Terra's puppet theatre, being only 'one of the democratic and socialist forms' of art, carried a particular indeterminacy, or blurriness, perhaps as a consequence of

5 From the video *Statements from the Arts Festival for Democracy in Chile*, shot and edited by Lynn MacRitchie (at the Royal College of Art, London, 1974), archive of Lynn MacRitchie.

6 By 1974, Lu Xun's stories had been translated into English and published by Foreign Languages Press in Beijing. Jun Terra recalls encountering an English translation in Manila in the 1960s. Conversation with the author, 27 April 2023.

7 Extracted from Lu Xun, 'An Incident', in *Selected Works of Lu Xun: Volume One*, Beijing: Foreign Languages Press, 1956, p.50.

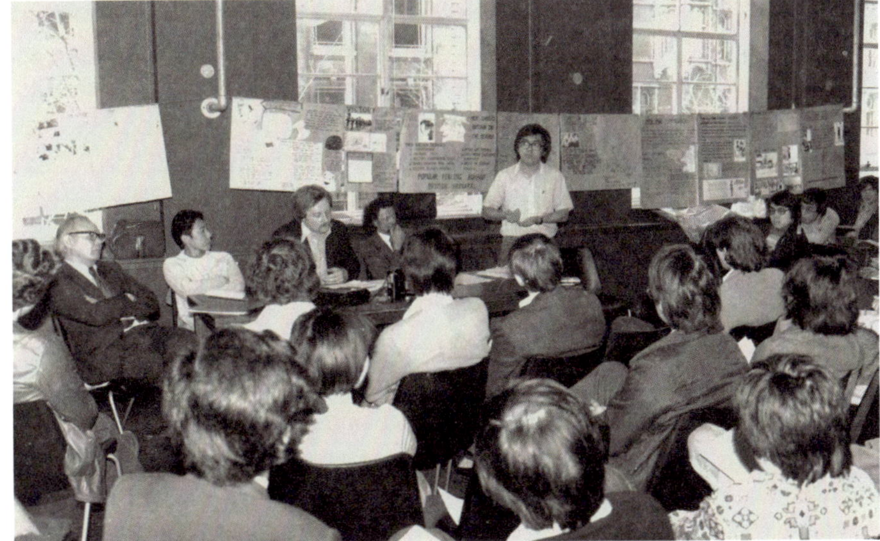

Meeting of the Association for Radical East Asian Studies, including Jun Terra (second from left), early 1970s

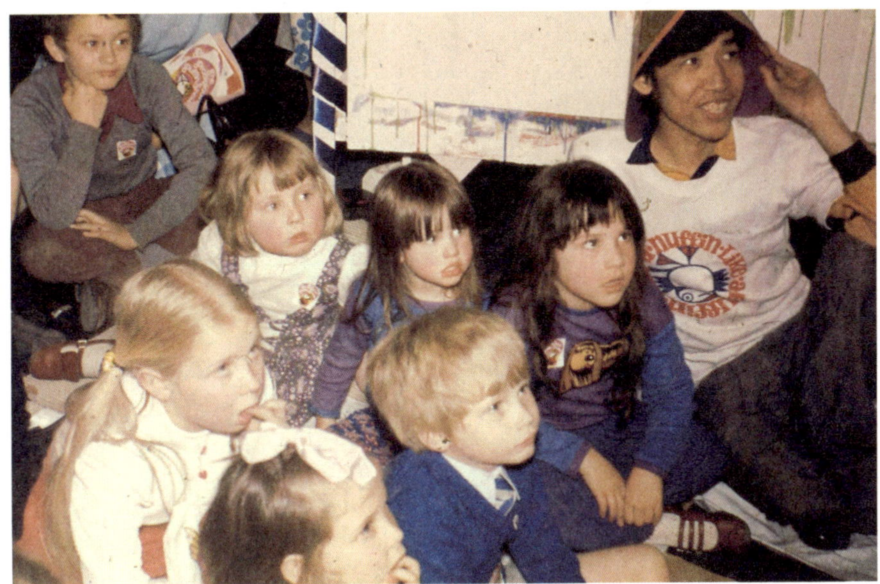

Jun Terra (far right) narrating a collaborative shadow puppet performance for Puffin Books, London, early 1970s

emphasising the political urgency of aesthetic decisions in an art practice. Terra's stories of AFD and beyond extend this sense of an indeterminate and expansive artistic-political practice: they recall his time in Manila, in his leadership role on the cultural bureau of Kabataang Makabayan in the late 1960s; in London, in his participation in the Association for Radical East Asian Studies (AREAS) at the School of Oriental and African Studies (SOAS, University of London), and his puppet theatre children's workshops for Puffin Books in the early 1970s; in Leith, Scotland, in his involvement in a 1973 event with workers and artisans that resulted in a children's playground and a conference on the problematics of housing demolitions, which the community, the council, artists and construction workers joined for;[8] in London again, in his impromptu performances with David Medalla at multiple iterations of the London Biennale in the 2000s; and in his ongoing practice of poetry and essay writing on, and not limited to, art, culture, books, history and the environment.

Meaning and feeling

At the time AFD was established, wider discussions were emerging on the museum as 'information centre'.[9] Curator Pontus Hulten was theorising the museum as a 'site of communication' in relation to the new function and operation of contemporary art spaces in the West after May 1968.[10] Indeed, across various exhibition contexts the influence of cybernetics was pervasive. AFD did not see itself as a formal institution, but its activities reflect an understanding and engagement with these issues, including the problematics of representation/documentation and the politics of how information is projected and perceived.

The politics of information would also have been palpable from the wider political context. The manipulation and suppression of information has long been a feature of the British press and its adherence to governmental-imperial agendas – the war in Oman being a case in point in the 1970s.[11] Launched in 1971, the counter-information campaign 'Operation Truth' emphasised the lived experience of the Chilean revolution in order to defend Salvador Allende's Unidad Popular (Popular Unity) government against attacks by national and international press; it unexpectedly resulted in the founding of the Museo de la Solidaridad Salvador Allende in Santiago.[12] Given that truths and fictions were obscured in the 1970s political context, how aware were AFD artists of the construction of history?

At AFD's base at 143 Whitfield Street, Lynn MacRitchie's environment 'The World in a Grain of Sand' (2–19 March 1975) aimed to develop its participants' capacity to interrogate information and discern alternative historical truths, particularly with regard to heated debates around the Green Revolution. Entering the space, visitors passed through a screen made of plastic strips showing popular media images of package tours and tourist attractions; beyond the screen, they encountered hanging baskets filled with

8 Arianna Mercado in conversation with J. Terra, 'Symposium: Precarious Solidarities: Artists for Democracy (1974–77)', Afterall, London, 2 February 2023.

9 Pierre Gaudibert, Pontus Hulten, Michael Kustow, Jean Leymarie, François Mathey, Georges Henri Rivière, Harald Szeemann and Eduard de Wilde, 'Exchange of views of a group of experts', *Museum*, vol.24, no.1, 1972, pp.5–14.

10 P. Hulten, cited in Yuk Hui and Adeena Mey, 'The Exhibition as Medium: Some Observations on the Cybernetisation of the Institution and the Exhibition', *Afterall*, issue 53, 2023, p.80.

11 See Gulf Committee, 'British Troops in Oman', *New Left Review*, July/August 1975, pp.109–12.

12 See Maria Berrios, 'Struggle as Culture: The Museum of Solidarity', in *Art and its Worlds: Exhibitions, Institutions and Art Becoming Public*, London: Afterall Books, 2021, pp.350–52.

Lynn MacRitchie, 'The World in a Grain of Sand', 143 Whitfield Street, London, 1975

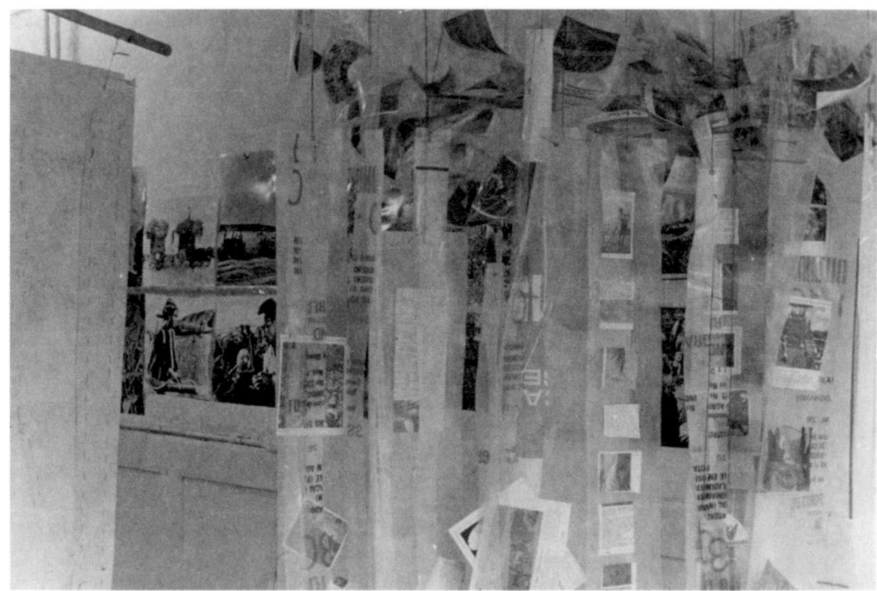

a mix of grains and confetti made from copies of the *Financial Times*, which they were invited to sift through with riddles to retrieve buried pieces of paper printed with poems and commentaries on food production. MacRitchie's set-up exposed the complicated relation between politics, labour and the agricultural production of grain – an analysis seemingly absent in the popular media. The installation demanded the public to partake in it, including through a designated study area and information centre of collected news clippings and criticism contributed by visitors and fellow artists. Art critic Margaret Richards affirmed the investigative nature of the project in a letter to MacRitchie:

> Reality is always half objective fact and half conditioned or spontaneous emotion. Interpretations are part observation and part feeling. This exhibition exposes realities that are hidden by conventional responses. Most of us lay 'art-consumers' are unconsciously conditioned, and it takes a socially sensitive, as well as an aesthetically sensitive artist to show us how to look at what we see, and sense what lies behind it.[13]

13 Margaret Richards, handwritten private letter to L. MacRitchie, titled 'Meaning and Feeling', March 1975, archive of Lynn MacRitchie.

In an article subsequently published in the left-leaning newspaper *Tribune*, Richards addressed the artist's role in making material realities explicit in order to address labour and class:

> The common theme is the gap between product and process, consumer and producer, commercial glamour and natural

> beauty. The imagery makes us re-see our wrapped loaf as the end-product of real wheat grown in a field by real workers, processed by other real workers and sold to us as a convenience food. And package tours to exotic places are another aspect of the same selling technique, feeding our dreams but keeping us out of contact with the Real Venice, Bali or South Africa.[14]

'The World in a Grain of Sand' shares strategies with initiatives by groups such as Equipo de Contrainformación (Counter-Information Team), based in Rosario, Argentina, which assigned effective communication and political urgency as key values in their audio-visual documentary work. In 1973, Equipo de Contrainformación made *Ezeiza* as a multi-layered narrative constructed from photographs and drawings of the massacre that took place at the Ezeiza airport in June of that same year, on the occasion of a mass gathering to mark Juan Domingo Perón's return from exile. To tell the truth of the event and reinforce the ideological position of the politicised artists, the work gathered images found in magazines or taken by the group's members, along with a sequence of colour cartoons by group member Juan Pablo Renzi that illustrated a worker-witness's oral account.[15] If Equipo de Contrainformación used the process of collective work and juxtapositions to denounce political violence in Argentina, MacRitchie used the process of participation, sifting actions and the organisation of information to denounce the epistemological violence in the memory-making of media. Meanwhile, in London, artists Margaret Harrison, Kay Hunt and Mary Kelly organised the project *Women and Work: A Document on the Division of Labour in Industry 1973–1975* to study gender and labour issues in a factory in the Bermondsey district. Displayed as data, charts, documents and photographs, it was presented at South London Gallery in 1975. In these various exhibition contexts, the influence of cybernetics and the notion of feedback were felt though unnamed: through a guided reading of images, accounts and data collected from real life, the artists demonstrated, with visual aids, how information can be manipulated to construct meanings or analysed to reveal power, thereby activating the viewers to reconsider the world they live in and how they perform their civil duties in their respective socio-political realities.

Applying communication theories to visual culture against cultural imperialism, Belgian sociologist Armand Mattelart,

14 M. Richards, 'Squatter-artists with a social purpose', *Tribune*, 14 March 1975 (see p.183).

15 See Graciela Carnevale Archive, hosted by Archivos en Uso. For introducing me to the work of Equipo de Contrainformación, I am grateful to John Beeson for the presentation 'Cultural Politics at the End of Third World Nationalisms', 49th Annual Conference of the Association for Art History, London, 13 April 2023.

who worked with Allende's Popular Unity party on media reform prior to the military coup in September 1973, had co-authored *Para leer al Pato Donald* (*How To Read Donald Duck*) with critic and writer Ariel Dorfman in Santiago in 1971.[16] The latter, along with other Chilean exiles, spoke at the symposium 'Cultural Imperialism and Latin American Art and Culture', during AFD's Chile Festival at the RCA in October 1974. Soon after, in 1975, the English edition of Mattelart and Dorfman's book was released in London by International General, a publishing house and distribution initiative overseen by curator Seth Siegelaub, who had founded the interrelated research institute and library for Marxist studies on communication and culture, the International Mass Media Research Center, in Bagnolet, outside of Paris, in 1973.[17] This is yet another example of the proximity of information and communication in the arts and how they were crucial to extending the notion of artistic and exhibition-making projects in the 1970s across geographies.

With this in mind, we can zoom in on the notice board at MacRitchie's exhibition – a collectively assembled and abundant locus of information. Among the items posted was a call for the public to demonstrate at the UK Prime Minister's offices at 10 Downing Street against British and Iranian troops in Oman on 9 March 1975, a week after the exhibition's opening date. Accompanying this call was the notice for a one-day programme of talks and films co-organised by the Polytechnic of Central London Students' Union, the Arab Society, the Gulf Committee, Palestine Action and the Palestine, Gulf, Yemen Solidarity Committee. The organising groups would meet at the AFD space continuously. The programme listing included a lecture by Fred Halliday, co-founder of the Gulf Committee, who had published his seminal work *Arabia without Sultans* in 1974.[18] He would co-edit the July/August 1975 issue of *New Left Review*, which reported on the suppression of information by the British press regarding events in Oman.[19] The first issue of Gulf Committee's *The Gulf Bulletin* in June 1971 was already naming Oman 'Britain's Vietnam'.[20] Around this time, his brother the historian Jon Halliday contended, in a 1972 publication produced by AREAS in London to investigate the Korean Revolution of 1945 to 1953, that the British press was supinely complying with the flood of misinformation put out by the Park Chung Hee regime.[21] In short, the access to information and the capacity to interrogate it became shared skill sets in art and politics. Political-action

16 Ariel Dorfman and Armand Mattelart, *Para leer al Pato Donald*, Valparaíso, Chile: Ediciones Universitarias de Valparaíso, 1971.

17 Leontine Coelewij and Sara Martinetti, *Seth Siegelaub: Beyond Conceptual Art*, Amsterdam and Köln: Stedelijk Museum Amsterdam and Verlag der Buchhandlung Walther Koenig, 2016, p.282.

18 Fred Halliday, *Arabia without Sultans*, Harmondsworth: Penguin, 1974.

19 See Gulf Committee, 'British Troops in Oman', *op. cit.*

20 *The Gulf Bulletin* was the periodical of the Gulf Committee, co-founded by Fred Halliday, Helen Lackner, Fawwaz Traboulsi and others mostly from SOAS. See *The Gulf Bulletin*, no.1, June 1971, p.1, British Library.

planning and discursive activities directed towards distant places and inwardly to reflect an anti-imperialist spirit converged in London in the 1970s, with many such activities taking place at the AFD space at 143 Whitfield Street. Through them, information became the protagonist, and each artist's input was not singular but instead formed as a part of a collective feedback process.

21 Jon Halliday, *Three Articles on the Korean Revolution (1945–1953)*, London: Association for Radical East Asian Studies, 1972, p.ii.

Collective political education

The range of 'information' AFD took in – its collective library – was vast. The festival 'Living Words, Living Images: Festival of Progressive Poetry and Art' (8 June – 10 July 1975), for example, featured 'poems by Mao Tse-Tung, Ho Chi Minh, Lu Xun, Kuo Mo-Jo, Bertolt Brecht, Vladimir Mayakovsky, Nizam Hikmet, Arthur Rimbaud, Josina Machel, Kim U Cha, Amado Hernandez, Pablo Neruda, Miguel Hernandez, Nicolas Guillen, Rafael Alberti, Nakano Shigeharu, Nguyen Quang Than, Clarita Roja, Cesar Vallejo, Jorge Rebelo, Dsh, Nazareth, as well as Albanian, Palestinian, Chilean, Filipino, Irish, African, Iranian, Korean, Somali, Indian, Vietnamese poems'. Artists were visiting London bookshops to find publications such as *China Pictorial* and *Peking Review*, which concerned developments in China during the Cultural Revolution; political newspapers such as *Red Weekly*, published by the International Marxist Group; *South Vietnam in Struggle*, produced by the National Liberation Front, *Phụ nữ Việt nam*, the newspaper of Vietnam Women's Union, and *Vietnam International*; and *Freedom News*, which concerned Black struggles. The outlets for these included Guanghwa Bookshop in Soho's Chinatown, Collets on Charing Cross Road, Banner Books & Crafts on Camden High Street and Unity Bookshop on Railton Road.

Many AFD events began with poetry recitals, highlighting the potential role of the poet as a writer of political history. On the programme for the July 1975 festival 'People of the World Learn from Indochina, Homage to Ho Chi Minh and the Victory of the Indochinese Peoples', one poet's name caught my attention in particular: Jose Maria Sison. It came as a surprise that they were already reading Joma, as he is known in the Philippines, in London. Seeing his name on the AFD document brings AFD out of the 1970s context and forms a connection with present struggles and political education in the Philippines. Best known as the founder of the Communist Party of the Philippines (CPP), Joma composed poetry and political writings. By 1969, he had written the first versions of *Philippine Society and Revolution* and released it serially in the student paper of the University of the Philippines, *The Philippine Collegian*; these writings were then published as a book in Tagalog by the press Pulang Tala Press in the Philippines in 1971, and in English translation in Hong Kong by Ta Kung Po that same year. In *Philippine Society and Revolution*, Joma integrated Marxist-Leninist-Maoist ideologies into his history writing of the Philippines on behalf of Kabataang Makabayan and the CPP. It disclosed the historical causes of the country's land problems and defined the semi-colonial and feudal ruling systems as the common enemies of the people.[22] The volume progresses from the presentation of the essential history of the Filipino people; to an investigation of the three basic problems that the people are facing (imperialism, domestic feudalism and bureaucratic capitalism); and concludes with waging the people's war for a democratic revolution as a solution. Though Joma was later exiled, the influence of his writings in the Philippines has lasted. His writings are still read and referenced by cultural workers organising in the Philippines for agrarian reform and food security.

22 Amado Guerrero, *Philippine Society and Revolution*, Hong Kong: Ta Kung Po, 1971.

> You
> Stand midway
> Between the crumbling of empires
> And the rising of the workers world.

These are the closing lines of the poem 'You', by Jun Terra. Terra shared space with Joma in the progressive review magazine *Eastern Horizon*, published by Ta Kung Po in Hong Kong from 1960 to 1981, as well as a leadership role in Kabataang Makabayan in Manila in the 1960s. Reading between the lines, I wonder if AFD projected an understanding of itself through the milieu of poet-leaders in political history and the Marxist theorisation of an internationalist approach to literature and art. I also wonder if this has something to do with the uncentred, anonymous artist figure, or the indeterminate and expansive role and function of artists at the time.

Learning through conversations

AFD participant Stephen Pusey suggests that political education did not only come from reading revolutionary literature and radical publications, but also from personal conversations in the 1970s, which involved, importantly, Brazilians, Argentineans, Cubans and Chileans who were living in exile in London.[23]

These individuals carried with them experiences of agitation and struggle against military junta, state violence, feudalism and imperialism.[24] In the 1970s, London itself was the library. Everyday conversations were a way to access first-hand political information. Pusey joined AFD as an art student at Saint Martins, and he later produced murals and engaged in community gardens in Covent Garden and Brixton, between 1977 and 1982. Beginning in May 1974, he was part of the core working committee to organise AFD's Chile festival at the RCA, together with David Medalla, Cecilia Vicuña, Guy Brett, John Dugger and Hugh Cave. He had been following the Chilean situation closely through the reports of the Brazilian exiles he lived with in Archway, North London.[25]

Ife Nii Owoo, whose work was shown at AFD and who was part of Poster Collective (later Poster-Film Collective), reflects similar formative experiences. She recalls her experiences after arriving in London in 1972 as an exchange student from the United States:

> I started to meet other students and young people living in London from Africa and the Caribbean. A few fellow Black American exchange students and I became regulars at the African Students' Union (called 'The Basement') at the University of London. I met members and leaders involved in African liberation movements in South Africa, Zimbabwe, Angola, Guinea-Bissau and Mozambique there. They would discuss politics and their home country for hours after meetings and lectures at the local pub. There were a lot of encounters and study groups with activists and freedom fighters in exile, along with interactions with local Black community activists. During this time, I was amazed at how much the civil rights and Black Power movement in America inspired the movement for Black people's civil rights in England. The solidarity was strong in the Black community. London was a cosmopolitan city where I met people worldwide.[26]

Nii Owoo became a member of the Brixton Black Women's Group, where participants read socialist and feminist literature together. After Nii Owoo left for Ghana, the UK-based activists Olive Morris, Gerlin Bean and Stella Dadzie, whom Nii Owoo had met at the Brixton study group and the African Students' Union, would become the key organisers of the Organisation of Women of Asian and African Descent (OWAAD).[27] Active from 1978 to 1982, OWAAD

23 Stephen Pusey, conversation with the author and David Morris, 2 May 2023.

24 This account of London being a hub for a diaspora of Latin American political refugees matches the observation of historian Eric Hobsbawm. See E. Hobsbawm, 'Third World', in *Interesting Times, A Twentieth-Century Life*, London: Penguin / Allen Lane, 2022, pp.376–79.

25 S. Pusey, conversation with the author and D. Morris, 2 May 2023.

26 Ife Nii Owoo, email correspondence with the author, 4–5 May 2023.

collaborated with Poster Collective in the late 1970s and was fundamental in placing the experience of Black and Asian women on the women's liberation agenda.[28] In such contexts, of study groups beyond art spaces, Nii Owoo built a life for herself as an artist – blurring the boundaries between art, daily life and collective political education.

The Cold War context partly explains the abundance of study groups and informal, collective political education that Nii Owoo experienced. Scholar Stephan Feuchtwang describes the situation in his elaboration of the origins of AREAS, which Terra was part of:

> In the 1960s, political economy could be a disguise-name for Marxism. Open scholarly interest in, let alone teaching about Marx, capitalism, and imperialism were forbidden by the Cold War conventions of the time, even though there were in fact a few anti-imperialist and communist full-time staff teaching at SOAS. In this curious situation we leftist staff, and a core of students in the Students' Union, formed groups both for the extra-curricular study of Marx and theories of imperialism, and for activities opposing US imperialism, in particular the bombing of Cambodia. Some of us formed the UK Association for Radical East Asian Studies (AREAS) in 1970, which was the more left-wing, sometimes openly socialist, equivalent to the Committee of Concerned Asian Scholars in the USA formed two years before.[29]

27 *Ibid.*

28 Natalie Thomlinson, *Race, Ethnicity and the Women's Movement in England, 1968–1993*, London: Springer, 2016, pp.88–91.

29 Stephan Feuchtwang, 'Negotiating Politics and Academia', *Journal of the British Association for Chinese Studies*, vol.7, July 2017, p.105.

The uncentred artist as technician and campaigner

Many of the political mobilisations in relation to AFD were loosely connected to informal groups sprung out of educational institutions in the 1960s and 1970s. Slade School of Fine Art was no exception. Jonathan Miles, one of the co-founders of Poster-Film Collective, begun at the Slade in 1971, recalls that the erasure of the individual artist was part of the thinking behind their group. The collective shared members with AFD, including Miles, Sylvia Stevens and Steve Sprung. Their screen-printed revolutionary posters were disseminated not as art objects but as agitprop materials for protests and political gatherings; in the 1980s they also began producing posters and teaching materials for schools. For Miles, the poster could emphasise political urgency through aesthetic decisions:

> The idea of gesture was all-important. The first gesture was to do with refusal, in this case to place politics before aesthetics. What went with the gesture was a logic of trying to establish a different apparatus and with it a mode of production. … The first real attempt to create a loop of production, distribution within a framing of a look, was a series of posters related to the anti-colonial struggles in the three Portuguese African states. They were composed of single photographic images with single slogans or identifications in relatively large-scale formats (A1) in batches of 500 produced in a single print run. In simple terms they made these struggles visible and were affirmations of the justice of the struggle. There was no name attached even though there was a simple name connected to this production: Poster Collective.[30]

30 Jonathan Miles's testimony in Christine Halsall (ed.), 'Reflections by members of the Poster Collective', in *'Art as a Mass Political Weapon': The Poster Collective 1972–82*, London: Chimera Publications, 2020, p.149.

Poster-Film Collective produced materials for a vast ecosystem of cultural, political and community organisations. They also ran workshops on practical printing techniques, so that organisations could produce their own materials – turning community members from 'users' into 'makers', enacting the Marxist theory of knowledge through practice. As a letter from their collaborators at

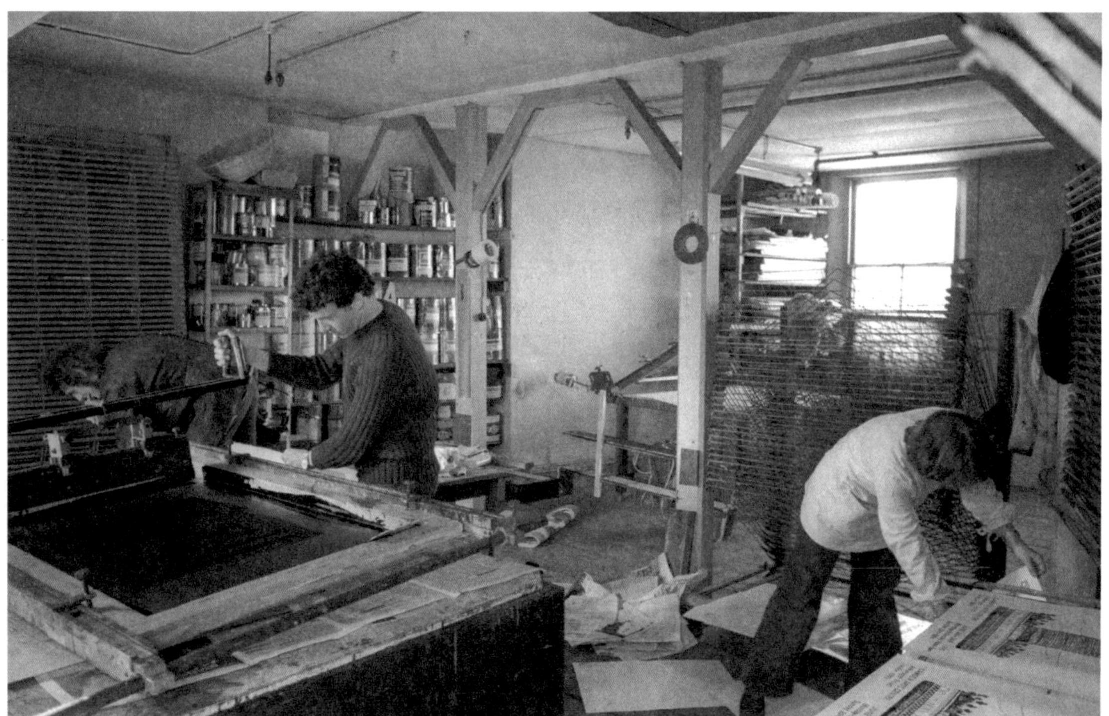

Poster-Film Collective's printing studio at Tolmers Square, London, 1970s

OWAAD highlights, in the 1970s and early 1980s these uncentred, anonymous artists provided an 'essential and invaluable community service'.[31] Nii Owoo also notes that 'as far as cultural training, I was learning by doing'. She does not shy away from calling herself a 'technician':

> I remember the colors of ink: red, black, and yellow. My fingernails were dirty looking from the ink, a large printing rack, squeegees on wall hooks, stacks of paper, the sound of vacuum sealing, mylar, a dark room, and the collaborative physical labor of printing an edition. Because of its collaborative nature, I could not say it was my work alone. Even though I could be considered a technician, I wanted our posters to be strong, beautiful, and hopeful.[32]

She highlights the collaborative process of creating posters in support of African liberation movements. Her poster that reads 'A for Africa', conceived in 1976 with Poster Collective and developed into the children's book *A is for Africa* (1993), is another example of information circulation for justice. She emphasises that the work provided an alternative to Eurocentric ideas in education: whereas 'A is for Apple' was a textbook term used by European publishers, children in Africa may never have experienced or seen an apple in Africa's own history and culture.[33]

The erasure of individual identity as an artist can also be traced in MacRitchie's campaigning work following her exit from AFD after the 'People of the World Learn from Indochina' festival in the summer of 1975. Thereafter she lived out her art by engaging directly in producing material for working class and feminist campaigns. Employed as a cleaner at the Royal Free Hospital in Hampstead, London, she joined the National Union of Public Employees (NUPE) trade union and became a shop steward. Her commitment to trade union and feminist activism transformed her artistic-political practice into organising and disseminating of information, which involved composing and designing newsletters for Royal Free Hospital workers and nursery workers against cuts in social services. Her October 1977 newsletter design for a spread with the bold slogan 'Defend the Occupations' was created to be used at demonstrations. Her 'Save the E.G.A.' poster, originally produced with Poster Collective, was featured in a photograph in a May 1977 newsletter as a demonstration tool on the picket line. The artist's figure became anonymous as her role

31 OWAAD coordinating committee letter to Poster Collective, 25 March 1979, archive of Mayday Room, London.

32 I. Nii Owoo, *op. cit.*

33 I. Nii Owoo, 'Introduction', in *A is for Africa: Looking at Africa through the Alphabet*, New Jersey: Africa World Press, 1992, n.p.

ALL OUT

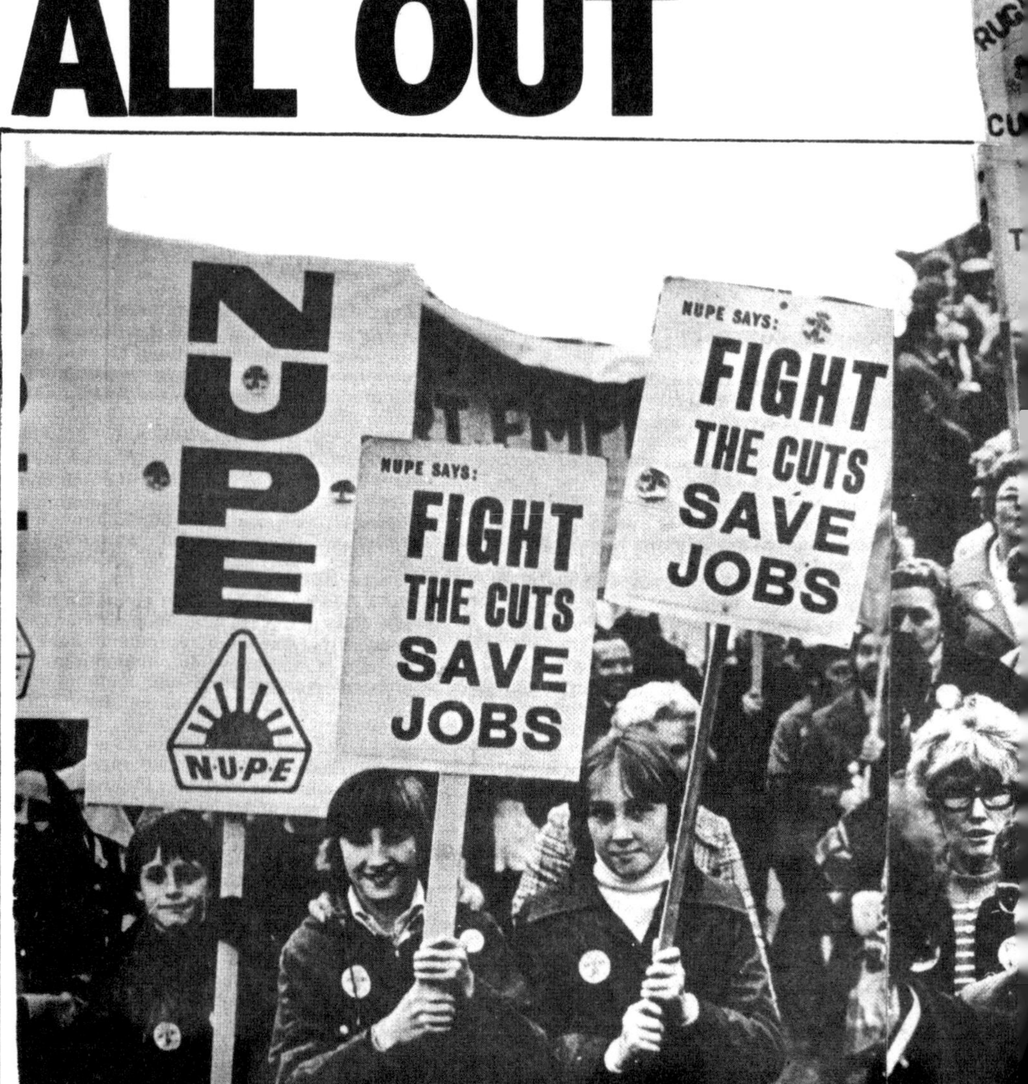

MAY 11 DEMONSTRATION AGAINST THE CUTS

NUPE has called for a protest march and lobby of Parliament against the cuts in social services on May 11. This is the culmination of a series of actions against the cuts on a national scale, and is fully supported by the Public Service unions and many others.

A meeting os all shop stewards of all unions in the Royal Free on April 11 voted to support the demo.

WHY SHOULD WE SUPPORT MAY 11?

OK, WE KNOW what a one day strike means - one less pay in the wage packet at the end of the week. But we have to think what the demonstration is for and that is to express our TOTAL OPPOSITION TO THE CUTS IN THE HEALTH SERVICE WHIC THREATEN ALL OUR JOBS AND COULD EVEN THREATEN OUR LIVES IF HOSPITAL FACILIT ARE DRASTICALLY CUT!

Spread from *The Royal Free Fight Back!* newsletter, produced by Lynn MacRitchie, 1977

MAY 11

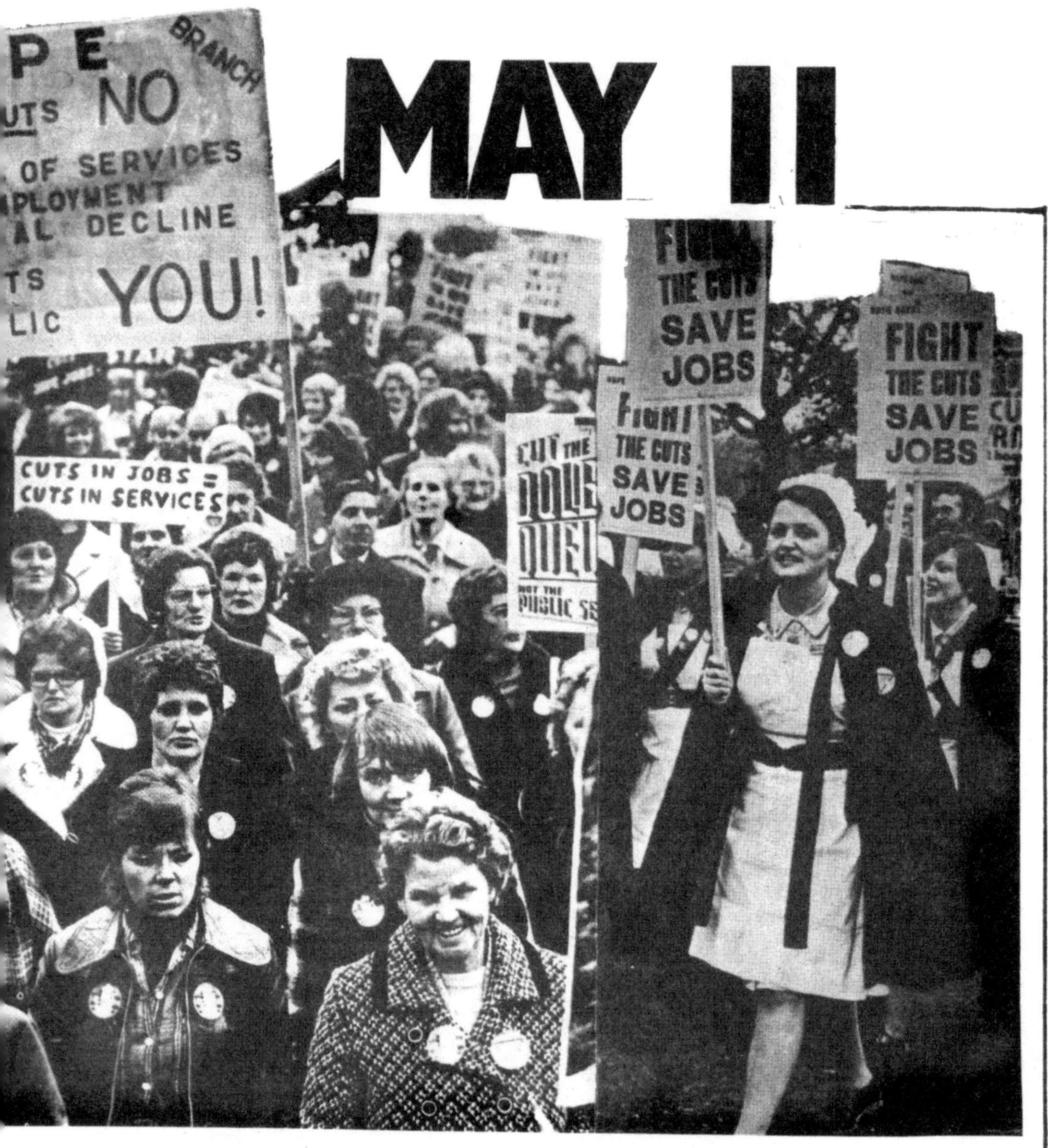

And it is not just a question of one days pay . . . if we as health service workers allow these cuts to go through, its we sho will suffer - for not only will we have lost our jobs, we'll have lost the National Health Service itself - that means the right to free and full medical care, regardless of wealth.

For the rich are not the ones who will suffer - they will be able to take advantage of the private hospitals which are already springing up all over the place - doctors wont suffer - they will be able to afford treatment privately. We've only had the Health Service since 1948, and many people can remember what it was like not to be able to afford medical treatment.

Nye Bevan, founder of the nhs, said 'No government that attempts to destroy the NHS can hope to command the support of the British people'. We have to make sure that the Labour Government doesn't do just that.'

ALL OUT MAY 11th!

a for africa

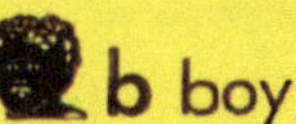
b boy

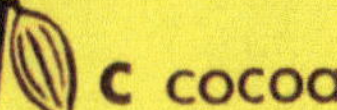
c cocoa

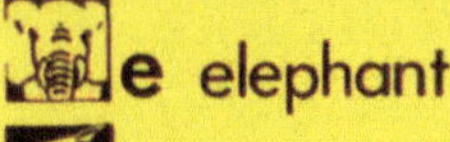
d drum

e elephant

f fish

g girl

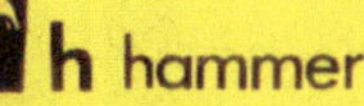
h hammer

i ink

j jug

k kerosene

l lorry

m maize

n nail

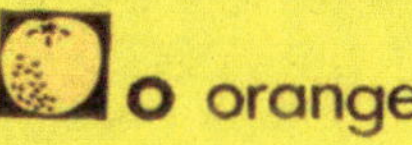
o orange

p peasants

q queue

r rifle

s saw

t tree

u unity

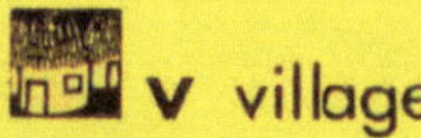
v village

w workers

x xylophone

y yam

z zebra

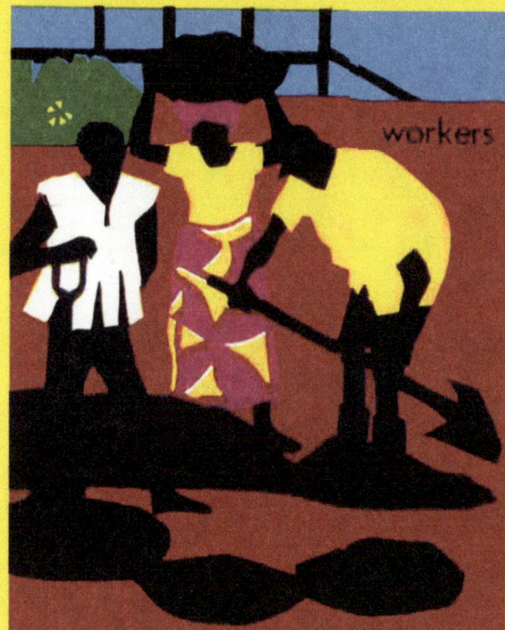

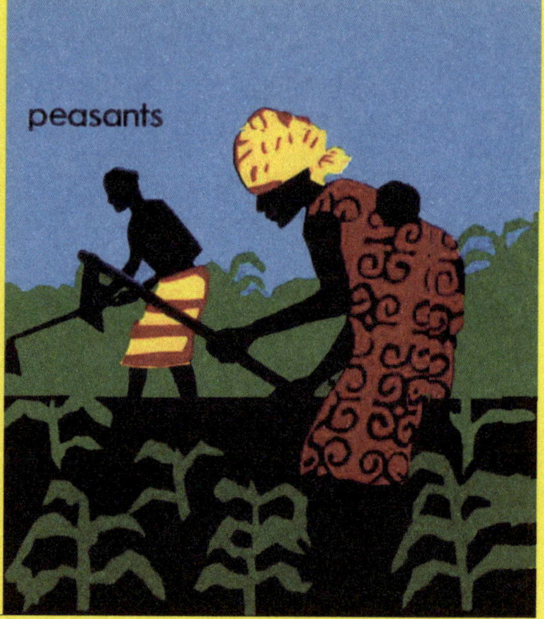

...FORGE SIMPLE WORDS THAT EVEN THE CHILDREN CAN UNDERSTAND...

poem: jorge rebelo

'A for Africa' poster, designed by Ife Nii Owoo and Poster-Film Collective, 1970s

and function as a technician and campaigner loomed larger, and as her actions and gestures translated ideas into forms of labour.

Conclusion: On precarious documents

The story of AFD is a backlit screen. It silhouettes artist-performers: their actions and gestures became of utmost importance in the moment. It is a frame that holds the possibility for spotlighting information and collective political education. As a projection, it prioritises the senses of the public. The viewing experience communicates a feature – the uncentred, *becoming anonymous* artist – expanding the role and function of the artist's figure into a cultural worker, poet, writer, reader, children's workshop facilitator, technician, cleaner and campaigner. It challenges the power and acceptability in the story of art and highlights the politics of representation through its precarious documents.

A special issue of the newsletter *Covent Garden Independent News*, released in December 1974 by Art Meeting Place, a venue where AFD activities were held prior to 143 Whitfield Street, invokes this uncentred, *becoming anonymous* artist and their expansive practice:

> There are in London a wide variety of artists' groups who are involved with the idea of meetings and get-togethers (perhaps as a kind of reaction against the Romantic idea of the lonely artist, painting away in his attic studio). There are different artists' groups involved with almost every possible kind of 'non-art' activity – women's liberation, philosophy, computers and technology, social change, politics, linguistics, trade unionism etc. etc. It became evident that there was no basic difference between these groups and other community organisations which are more general in scope – they all represent an attempt to break down the social barriers which are imposed by modern city life.[34]

The message urges us not only to consider AFD outside of institutional archives and beyond the story of art, but also to see contemporary exhibition-making and artistic practice from a historical perspective that breaks down divisions between the Global North and South, blurs art and non-art and destabilises other settled categories.[35]

34 Art Meeting Place, *Covent Garden Independent News*, no.132, 6 December 1974, archive of Lynn MacRitchie.

35 At the time of writing, ruangrupa's lumbung project for documenta 15 (2022) is one example of a major endeavour that demands such an approach.

A Museum for the People: On the Museo de la Solidaridad Salvador Allende

María José Lemaitre Mujica and Caroll Yasky

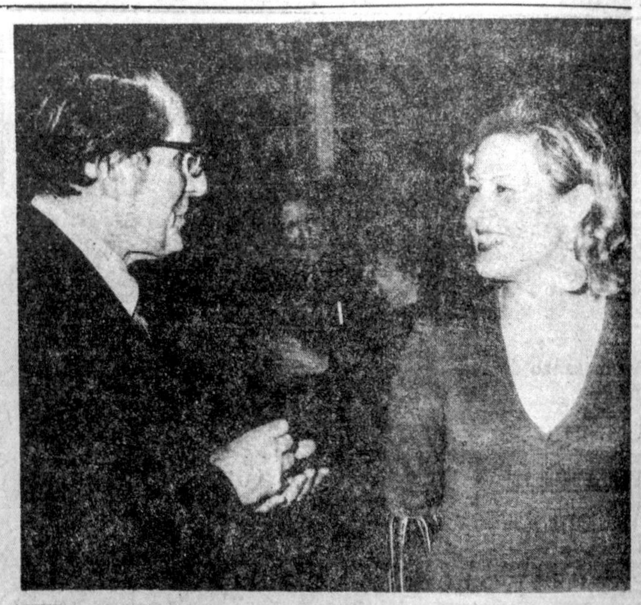

17-febrero-1973

ARTISTAS BRITANICOS DONAN OBRAS PARA UN NUEVO MUSEO EN CHILE

La señora Raquel de Bunster, esposa del Embajador chileno en Londres, departe con sir Roland Penrose durante la recepción ofrecida por esa Embajada para agradecer a los artistas británicos sus aportes al nuevo Museo de la Solidaridad, abierto en Santiago. La señora de Bunster, quien formuló el llamado, ha recibido ya ofrecimientos de pinturas y esculturas de parte de 25 artistas sobresalientes, entre los que figuran Graham Sutherland y el escultor Kenneth Armitage, cuyas obras son bien conocidas en América Latina. El Institute de Artes Contemporáneas, cuyo fundador es sir Roland Penrose, expondrá en su galería de arte las obras donadas por artistas británicos antes de que sean enviadas a Chile.—

'British artists donate works for a new museum in Chile', *El Siglo*, Santiago, 17 February 1973. In the photo, Roland Penrose (left) and Silvia Celis

MARÍA JOSÉ LEMAITRE MUJICA There are many relationships that link the Museo de la Solidaridad Salvador Allende (MSSA) and Artists for Democracy (AFD). These were established thanks to an affective, supportive and artistic network of people. Some of these names are more familiar: Roland Penrose was an important early link in the UK to the museum's founding director, Mário Pedrosa, for instance; and AFD members such as Guy Brett, John Dugger and Cecilia Vicuña would have ongoing connections to the museum. But there are other names that are important to highlight, such as Carmen Waugh, who collaborated with the museum in its earliest years, and became its director after the fall of the military government; Álvaro Bunster, Chile's ambassador to the UK during the administration of Salvador Allende; actress and theatre director Raquel Parot, who was married to Bunster and played a vital role in gathering the donations of UK-based artists for the Museo de la Solidaridad; Silvia Celis, who was the cultural attaché of the embassy at that time; and Alejandra Altamirano, who was key to establishing links between AFD and the museum in the early 1990s.

CAROLL YASKY The phrase 'London auction' was the beginning of our understanding of these relationships. In 2013, Cecilia Vicuña approached the museum in search of some of the works that were included at the auction AFD organised in 1974. At that time, we were in the process of framing the archive and putting together a catalogue of works from the period of political exile, as the Museo Internacional de la Resistencia Salvador Allende. A search of the inventories led us to the 'London auction' – but we discovered that this in fact held material from two distinct group of works. Vicuña's search led us to discover that materials from the AFD auction had been filed together with an earlier donation of works by British artists organised between 1972 and 1973 in support of the Allende government. And we would learn that there were many connections between the stories of these two London initiatives.

MJLM To understand this, we have to go back a little bit, to how the MSSA was formed.[1] The idea arose in 1971, in the context of 'Operación verdad' ('Operation Truth') – the political, social and cultural initiative that President Allende's government launched against a campaign of misinformation led by the national and

1 The museum has had three different names through its history: Museo de la Solidaridad (1971–73); Museo Internacional de la Resistencia Salvador Allende (MIRSA, 1975–90); and Museo de la Solidaridad Salvador Allende (MSSA, 1990 to present).

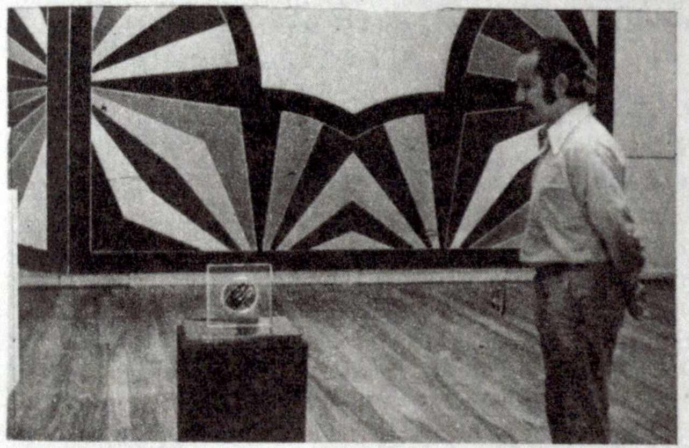

De todo hay en las 600 obras donadas a la muestra de solidaridad: cuadros, esculturas, posters, tapices

Ana Helfant,
'The solidarity brush',
Ercilla, Santiago,
2 May 1973

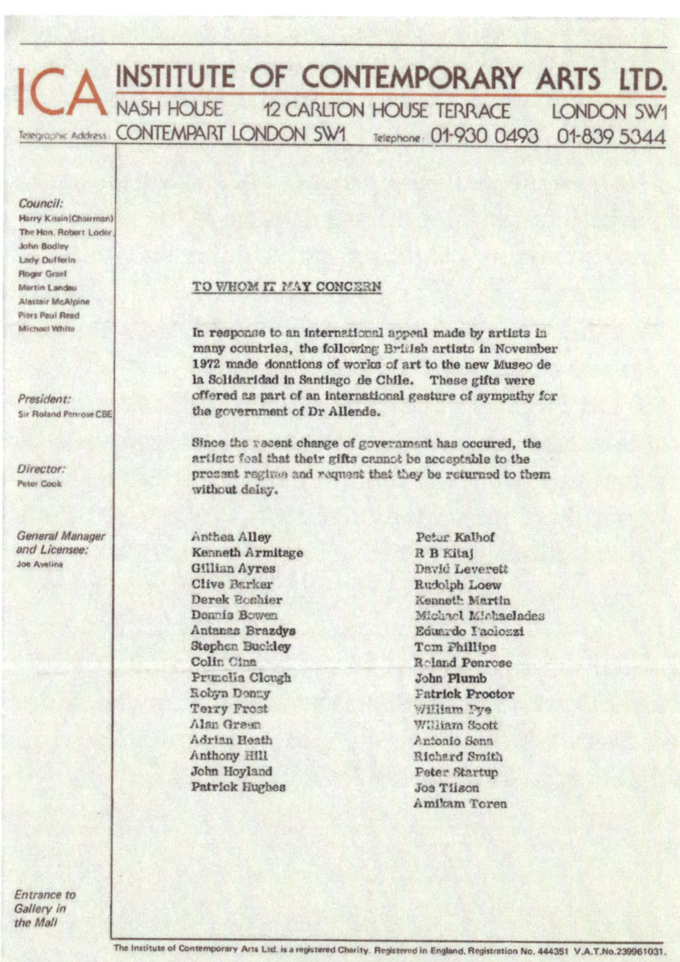

ICA INSTITUTE OF CONTEMPORARY ARTS LTD.
NASH HOUSE 12 CARLTON HOUSE TERRACE LONDON SW1
Telegraphic Address: CONTEMPART LONDON SW1 Telephone: 01-930 0493 01-839 5344

Council:
Harry Kissin (Chairman)
The Hon. Robert Loder
John Bodley
Lady Dufferin
Roger Graef
Martin Landau
Alastair McAlpine
Piers Paul Read
Michael White

President:
Sir Roland Penrose CBE

Director:
Peter Cook

General Manager and Licensee:
Joe Aveline

Entrance to Gallery in the Mall

TO WHOM IT MAY CONCERN

In response to an international appeal made by artists in many countries, the following British artists in November 1972 made donations of works of art to the new Museo de la Solidaridad in Santiago de Chile. These gifts were offered as part of an international gesture of sympathy for the government of Dr Allende.

Since the recent change of government has occured, the artists feel that their gifts cannot be acceptable to the present regime and request that they be returned to them without delay.

Anthea Alley
Kenneth Armitage
Gillian Ayres
Clive Barker
Derek Boshier
Dennis Bowen
Antanas Brazdys
Stephen Buckley
Colin Cina
Prunella Clough
Robyn Denny
Terry Frost
Alan Green
Adrian Heath
Anthony Hill
John Hoyland
Patrick Hughes
Peter Kalhof
R B Kitaj
David Leverett
Rudolph Loew
Kenneth Martin
Michael Michaelades
Eduardo Paolozzi
Tom Phillips
Roland Penrose
John Plumb
Patrick Proctor
William Pye
William Scott
Antonio Sena
Richard Smith
Peter Startup
Joe Tilson
Amikam Toren

The Institute of Contemporary Arts Ltd. is a registered Charity. Registered in England, Registration No. 444351 V.A.T.No.239961031.

Letter from UK artists requesting return of works donated to Museo de la Solidaridad Salvador Allende, October 1973

foreign press. Intellectuals, artists and journalists were invited to this meeting. The Chilean artist José Balmes, the Spanish art critic José María Moreno Galván and the Italian politician and artist Carlo Levi presented to Allende the idea to create an international art collection for the people of Chile. Allende was very supportive of this idea, and the project was entrusted to Mário Pedrosa as director. Pedrosa was an experienced man – an art critic, journalist and political organiser who was in Chile in exile from his native Brazil. Immediately he set up the International Committee of Artistic Solidarity with Chile, where internationally renowned intellectuals, critics and other experts participated as ambassadors in a call for works for the museum. The committee included Dore Ashton, Harald Szeemann, Eduard de Wilde, Jean Leymarie and many others. He listed Roland Penrose as the UK representative, and we recently discovered that Pedrosa also sent an invitation to Guy Brett to participate in the International Committee. The Embassy of Chile in London was actively participating in this project, and various initiatives happened in its support – most notably 'Chile Britain' (1973), an exhibition of donated works at the Institute of Contemporary Arts (ICA) in London. In a letter to President Allende, Penrose talks about how significant this was for the artists, who were invited 'for their talent, their originality and their belief in the importance of the role that the arts should play in society', to be part of the museum's project – an enthusiasm reflected by the many respondents to the museum's call around the world. 'Their gifts are a token of their sympathy for the revolutionary ideals of the Popular Government over which you preside.'[2]

2 Roland Penrose, letter to President Salvador Allende, 24 May 1973, Tate Library Archive.

CY All this happened during a very tense time. On 29 June in Chile, the attempted coup known as El Tanquetazo took place. It failed, but the political tension was building in Santiago and throughout Chile, anticipating what was about to happen with the September coup d'état. Shortly after that, the opening of the exhibition at the ICA took place, on 10 July, with donations from 43 artists – a considerable number. Amongst them were David Hockney, Bridget Riley, Denis Bowen and Henry Moore (relevant documents suggest Moore's work did not ultimately appear in the exhibition, although it was promised and his name is included in the exhibition catalogue). Hockney and Bowen were among the many artists who later donated works to AFD's auction in 1974.

MJLM When the coup hit, the works from the ICA exhibition were packed in crates at the Chilean Embassy in London, waiting to be shipped. Penrose contacted the artists, who subsequently signed a letter calling for the return of all donated works, on the grounds that they were gifted in support of Allende and 'cannot be acceptable to the present regime'. So began a long and tense process that lasted for six months. There is a very interesting letter from Prunella Clough, where she expresses her own ambivalence about the call to return the works: while not wanting the works to reach the military government, she emphasises that the donations were intended 'for the people'.[3] Ultimately Penrose would take responsibility for the selection as a whole, and these negotiations are the background for why the works did not reach Chile. The negotiations were not exempt from political discussions within the Chilean embassy and the new regime. They did not want the artworks to be returned to the artists, citing the fact that these were donations to the people of Chile – who they now claimed to represent.

3 Prunella Clough, letter to R. Penrose, 12 October 1973, Tate Library Archive (see facing page).

CY In the 1990s, the MSSA under Carmen Waugh's directorship began the project of regaining and gathering the museum's collection in Chile – based on the original calls by Pedrosa and the committee for Museo de la Solidaridad and the works gathered afterwards, during the exile period, when it was known as Museo Internacional de la Resistencia Salvador Allende. As part of that initiative it began to recover the donations from the British artists. With the support of Alejandra Altamirano, daughter of Silvia Celis, who was the cultural attaché of Chile during Unidad Popular (Popular Unity), and coincidentally the wife of Guy Brett, Waugh assumed this duty and recovered some of the ICA works donated for the people of Chile – plus Brett's donation of works from the AFD auction. Altogether almost 200 works were recovered.

MJLM Another important milestone that connected the museum with Artists for Democracy was the exhibition 'We Want People to Know the Truth: Patchwork Pictures from Chile', presented at the AIR Gallery, London in 1978 and later in several cities in the UK. It was an exhibition mainly organised by Brett, and alongside the 'patchwork pictures' – *arpilleras* produced by groups of women across Chile during the military dictatorship – it included works by John Dugger as well as photography, documentation and other objects – a set of 52 works in total.[4] The text on Dugger's banner,

4 See Josefina de la Maza and Carla Macchiavello, *Tejido social: Arte textil y compromiso político*, Santiago: Ediciones MSSA, 2019.

Letter from Prunella Clough to Roland Penrose, 12 October 1973

65 Moore Park Road
SW6 2HH

12 October 73

Dear Sir Roland,

Thanks for your letter about Chile.

Thinking about this I find myself a little out of sympathy with the letter to sign, as it stands; though I do see that in these awful circumstances, & with the things still here, there may be no practical alternative.

But my intentions, such as they were, - in joining with other artists, was to make a small gift to the people of Santiago and their museum. That it was also a gesture towards Allende's givernment goes without saying. So were it possible I would still be in favour of sending the work there, so long as the present deploable regime would not make political capital out of the situation.

However this is no doubt a minority view and your suggestion that the work should be returned to its owners may be the only thing possible. I am not much in favour of auctions which usually fetch so little, and would rather subscribe to a fund for Chilean artists it there was any likelyhood of this being actually realised.

With best wishes,

Yours sincerely,

Prunella Clough

below: John Dugger, *Nunca te entregues ni te apartes del camino* (*Never give up nor leave the trail*), 1978, sewn fabric stripes, 352 × 510 cm. Donated by the artist to Museo de la Solidaridad Salvador Allende

following pages: Documentation of John Dugger's *Nunca te entregues ni te apartes del camino* at AIR Gallery, London, 1978

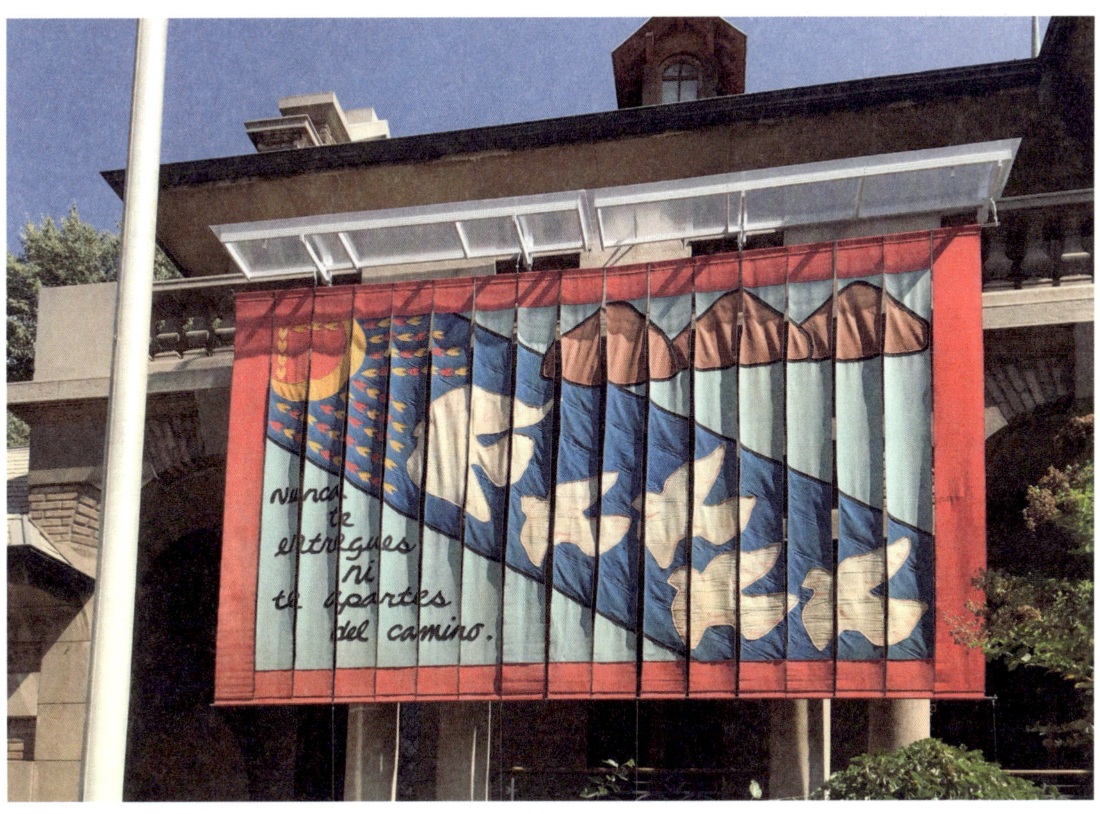

D44

"Patchwork Banner": based on no. 52 in the exhibiti[...]
photo taken at the peña on April 1st 1[...]

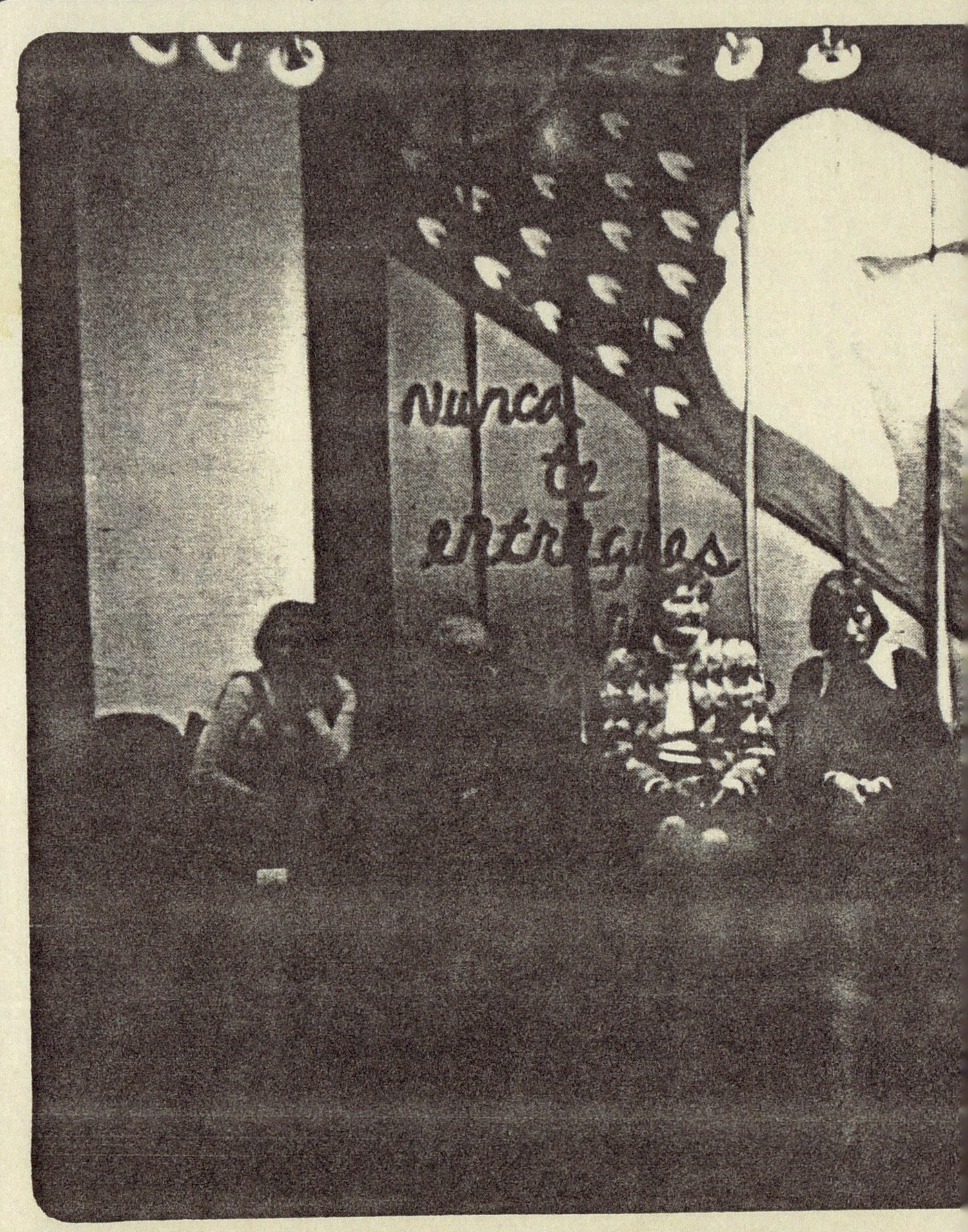

made by John Dugger of Banner Arts Project, London
R Gallery

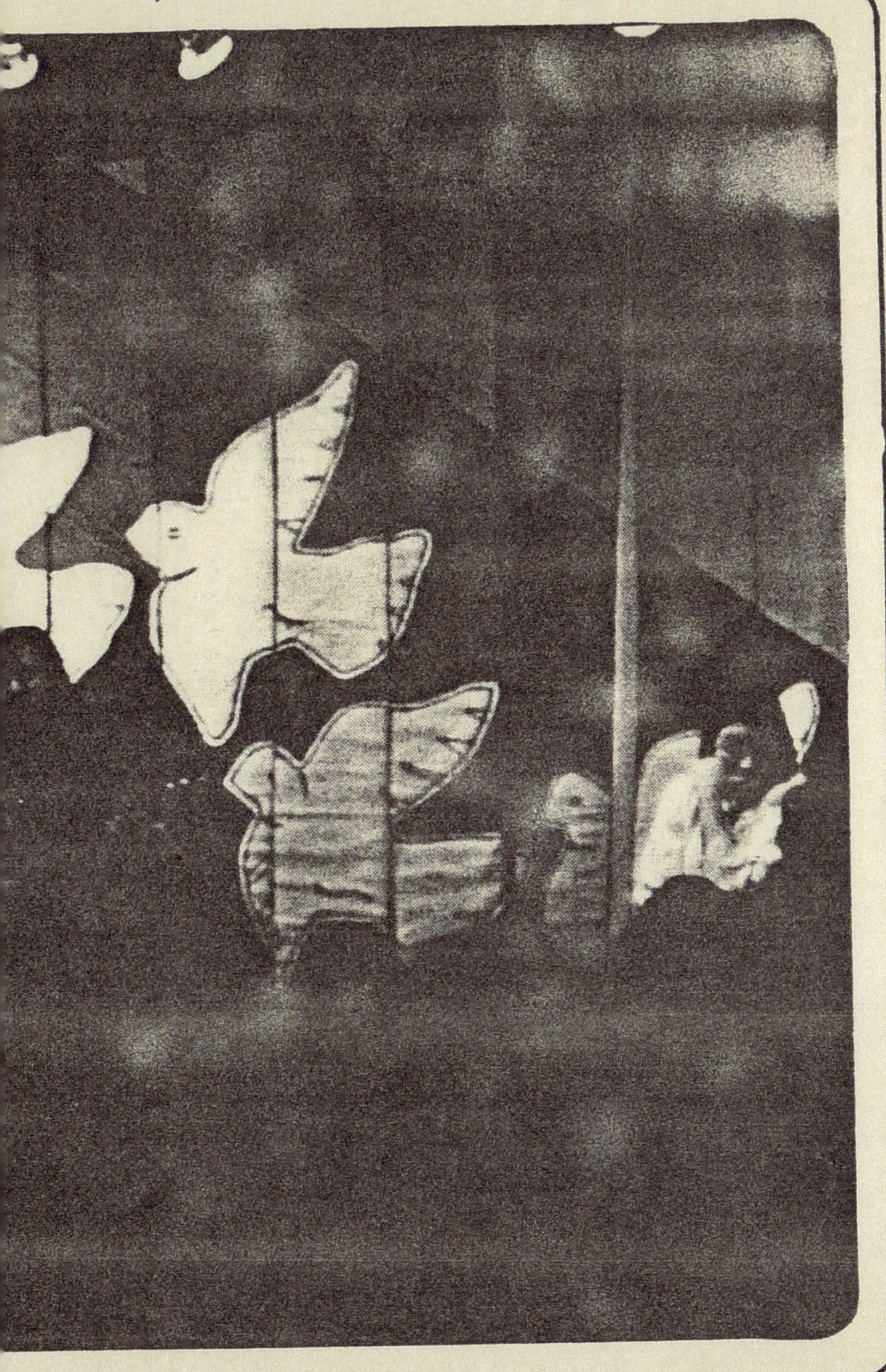

OBRAS DONADAS EN SOLIDARIDAD POR CHILE

No.	Artist	Country	Medium
108	CLAES OLDENBURG	USA	DRAWING
82	DEREK BOSHIER	UK	COLLAGE
265	DOM SYLVESTER HOUEDARD	UK	TYPE WRITER POEM
266	DOM SYLVESTER HOUEDARD	UK	TYPE WRITER POEM
110	DAVID LEVERETT	UK	ACRYLIC
264	RASHEED ARAEEN	PAKISTAN	PRINT
274	BERNARD AMIARD	FRANCE	OBJECT
3	M. CALLYANNIS	FRANCE	PRINT
253	PEDRO UHART	CHILE	PRINT
146	GAMARRA		PRINT
318	TOBAS	FRANCE	SMALL CLOTH
319	TOBAS	FRANCE	LARGE CLOTH
320	TOBAS	FRANCE	SHIRT
327	FORGAS	UK-FRANCE	PRINT
350	PETER MEYER	UK	ALBUM OF CALLIGRAPHY
351	MARIO MANRIQUEZ	CHILE	WATER COLOUR
11	BENGT BOCKMAN	SWEDEN	PRINT
310	DIRK LARSEN	UK	PRINT
296	JOHN PHILLIPS	PRINT	PRINT
237	HENRI JEAN	FRANCE	PRINT
253	PEDRO UHART	CHILE	PRINT
220	EDGARDO A. VIGO	ARGENTINA	PRINT
298	MERCEDES ESTEVES	ARGENTINA	PRINT
38	ALBRECHT D.	W. GERMANY	PRINT
142	PEPE MAYA	MEXICO	PRINT
30	WILLIAM FARLEY	USA	PRINT
244	ARESTIZABAL	CHILE	COLLAGE

List of works donated to Museo de la Solidaridad in solidarity with Chile, compiled by Alejandra Altamirano, 17 February 1992

View of the exhibition 'We Want People to Know the Truth: Patchwork Pictures from Chile', AIR Gallery, London, 1978

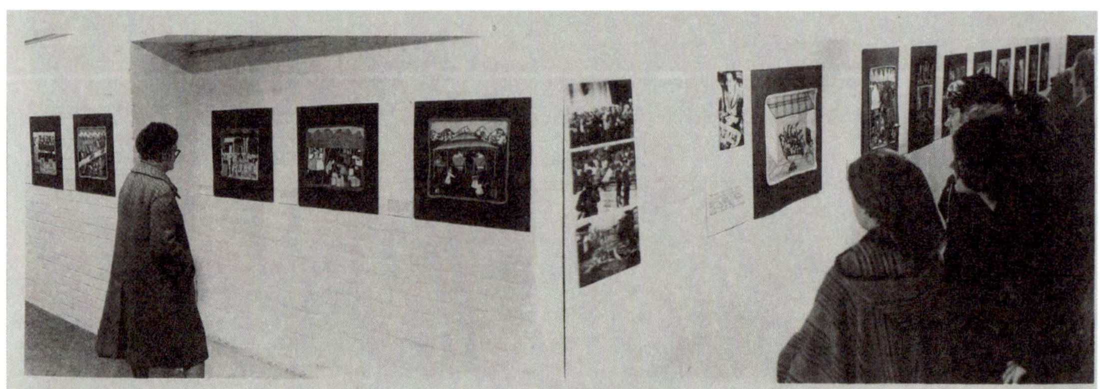

5 J. de la Maza, '"Nunca te entregues ni te apartes del camino": textiles de resistencia en la década de los setenta', *Historia 396*, vol.11, no.2, 2011.

'Nunca te entregues ni te apartes del camino' ('Never give up nor leave the trail'), is from the poem 'Palabras para Julia' ('Words for Julia') by the Spaniard José Agustín Goytisolo, which became a song of resistance for women and political prisoners during the Chilean dictatorship.[5]

CY Dugger was inspired by the *arpilleras* to create the banner, the second of three he dedicated to Chile. Commissioned by the Chile Solidarity Campaign, it was displayed at the Royal Albert Hall, at a concert with Quilapayún and Pete Seeger, as well as in 'We Want People to Know the Truth'. Many of the *arpilleras* were produced in sewing workshops established by the catholic solidarity organisation Vicaría de la Solidaridad. These workshops were a space of expression for women who had suffered the detention and disappearance of their children or family members, or had been torture victims themselves. The stories that emerged were a document of what was happening in Chile. A chain of solidarity was generated, to take the *arpilleras* out of Chile so that they could be sold abroad to support the resistance.[6]

6 Roberto Matta, who was part of the AFD Chile Festival and auction, donated works for this purpose. He was a close friend of Carmen Waugh and very interested in *arpilleras*; it is said that several of Waugh's and Matta's *arpilleras* were part of the 'We Want People to Know the Truth' exhibition. In 2018, along with twenty others, Guy Brett donated this collection of *arpilleras* to Tate, including the work that inspired John Dugger's banner.

MJLM A question we have been working on constantly, for several years now, is how we might develop the museum's political project, which is a legacy of the Allende era. Of course, we are no longer under a socialist government as such. At that time, artists from different parts of the world connected with this project, 'The Chilean Path to Socialism' – that is, a socialism that was also peaceful. This is also why it inspired so much hope in different parts of the world, and why the artists wanted to be part of this project. There are ongoing discussions of how to translate its founding commitment and collections in relation to present issues such as the environment, gender issues, migration and sexual liberation. We can see from the archive that the establishment and development of the museum was by no means easy. There were many complications and personal pains. Now the question is: How can we bring these histories to today's Chile, and not only today's Chile, but today's world?

CY I believe that in this sense there is a common denominator for all of us, including the artists: an awareness of wanting to work towards – although it sounds very utopian – a more just society, a better world. The collection also reflects the political dimension through aesthetic concerns, which was an important topic for early figures in its history such as Pedrosa and Dore Ashton. They talked about a politics of the senses, about awakening the senses of the people. This is something very important to us nowadays, since there are still many people in Santiago who do not visit the museum. We see the museum today as a space to discuss current political issues from the perspectives of art, creativity, action. For example, the 2019 protests in Chile made us reflect and pause. We stopped our programming and made the museum available for the public discussions that were going on at the time. Several assemblies were held. It was very enriching. In this regard, the political awareness of those of us who work at the museum is important.

MJLM What is mentioned a lot in the letters of the 1970s is 'a museum for the people of Chile'. In the current political context here – such as the recent protests and the social movement to change the constitution – we have also been questioning ourselves. It may be that there is no longer a single town in Chile that is composed of only the people of Chile. Different nations exist in it. We work a lot with our local community, our neighbourhood, which has resulted, for instance, in exhibitions such as 'Haciendo barrio' (2018) – in making this exhibition with us, a group of neighbours became important agents of the museum itself.[7] The museum we work in is not a white cube. It is a house from the 1920s that was refurbished and remodelled to function as a museum. It is not located at the heart of the city, nor in a cultural district, but in a neighbourhood on the periphery of downtown Santiago, near to the universities. It's diverse. So, all these relationships make the museum work on a smaller scale, with a more human project.

7 See 'Proyecto de investigación: Mirada de Barrio. Con los ojos en República,' Museo de la Solidaridad Salvador Allende website, 2017, available at https://www.mssa.cl/events/event/mirada-de-barrio-con-los-ojos-en-republica/.

CY We could say that the museum's infrastructure is the people and the collection. The interest in the museum continues and is contemporary – it is not only the museum of the previous era. It is always very important for us to account for our actions in the present.

MJLM We started by talking about the networks between particular people that led to the museum's founding. I believe that it is important that this collection of names will continue to grow, and be replaced, and be added to. We continue to investigate our own history, which is scattered throughout the world. This allows us to establish more situated projects on a bilateral basis, such as in Mexico and Cuba, as well as further research in the UK, Spain and France. We like to work in a network. It rewards us, it nourishes us, it enriches us.

Terry Frost, *Newlyn Rhythm III*, 1983, oil on canvas, 152.6 × 151.7 cm. Donated by the artist to Museo de la Solidaridad Salvador Allende

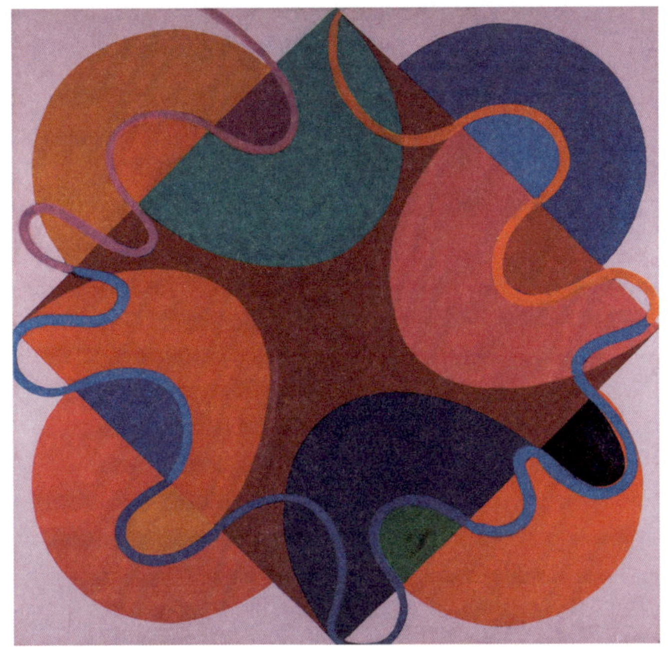

Derek Boshier, *Good Neighbor,* 1973, collage, 33 × 91.5 × 2 cm. AFD work donated by Alejandra Altamirano and Guy Brett to Museo de la Solidaridad Salvador Allende in 1993

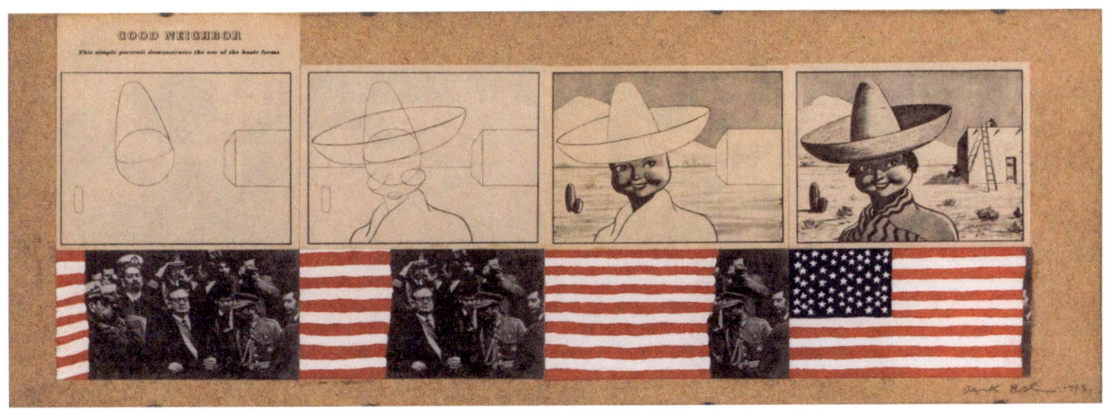

Opening at Museo de la Solidaridad Salvador Allende, 31 January 2020

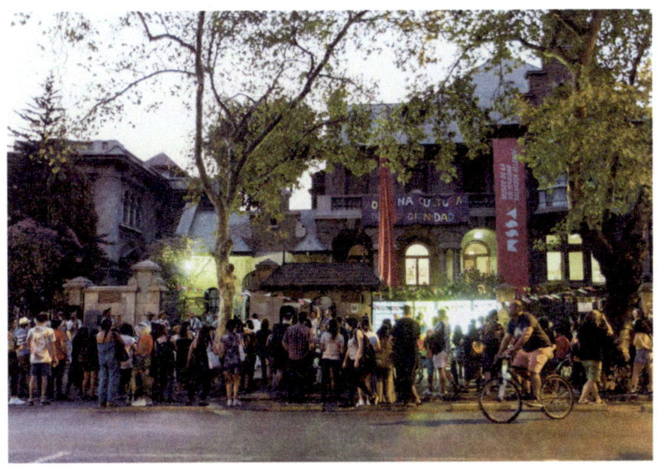

Following *Chile Vencerá*

Hannah Healey

Fifty years after the formation of Artists for Democracy (AFD), the artwork that has become emblematic of the group and its activities is the monumental banner *Chile Vencerá.* Made by founding member John Dugger in September 1974, *Chile Vencerá* declared AFD's support for the Chilean resistance – the cause selected as the focus of the group's initial activities at their founding meeting on 6 May 1974 at 3a Newport Place in Central London. The banner marked the one-year anniversary of the coup that had overthrown Chile's democratically elected Unidad Popular (Popular Unity) government, and led to the death of President Salvador Allende on 11 September 1973. The production of *Chile Vencerá* at the moment of AFD's formation illustrated the promise of the group at its inception in addressing international political causes, and the hopes of those early members and participants for an artistic-political practice of solidarity.

A photograph of the banner installed in Trafalgar Square in London in September 1974 has circulated in publications and displays more than any other image associated with AFD, and it is through this image that researchers have often come to work on the group. When I first encountered the image, it was not only Dugger's banner that struck me as remarkable, but its display alongside the banners of the British labour movement that were crowded around the base of the speakers' podium. In particular, a red banner with these words in white: 'MERSEYSIDE DOCKERS SHOP STEWARDS'. Having grown up in Merseyside, I have always been aware of the importance of the docks and the proud legacy of political action in the region. From my grandad, I grew up hearing stories about the dockers of Merseyside: 'working the welt' and the 'Cunard yanks'. Stories that exist somewhere apart from art history. When I came across the photograph of *Chile Vencerá* in Trafalgar Square, I was drawn into the story of AFD, and the artistic political project of solidarity that had brought Dugger – an artist from the United States living in London – together with a delegation of shop stewards representing the Merseyside dockers.

At the 1974 demonstration, *Chile Vencerá* contributed to a singularly important moment in the history of AFD and the politics of solidarity in the UK. In the two-year period following its initial appearance, however, *Chile Vencerá* continued to circulate in the international solidarity network, undertaking a prolonged journey through a number of locations, as listed in an October 1976 report written by Dugger for the Chile Solidarity Campaign.

While photographs exist that document some of these stops, archival material of others is as yet absent. This essay follows that journey and lingers at several stops in particular that have not been previously explored.

*

Measuring 7.3 metres high and 4.7 metres wide, the banner is comprised of a blue backing fabric cut into twenty vertical strips. Appliqued onto the backing and arranged across the strips are the words 'CHILE VENCERA' ('CHILE WILL PREVAIL') with red stars, below which ten figures represent the ten million people living in Chile in 1974.[1] The topmost figures include a medic; a musician holding aloft a guitar and a gun; and an education worker with an open book from which the words 'Chile lucha!' ('Chile fights!') spring. In the middle are two *campesinos*, or farmworkers, specifically a man tossing grain and a woman collecting eggs with a rifle on her back; a factory worker at a machine-tool lathe; and a foundry-worker pouring molten metal into ingots. Near the bottom, a fisherman pulls in a net and two miners extract copper ore. Scattered amongst the figures are twelve flowers, two fish, a butterfly, chicken and arrow shapes in orange, blue and yellow, representing earth, water and grain.[2] Dugger based the design on stories of life in Chile offered by the Chilean artist and poet Cecilia Vicuña, a co-founding member of AFD:

> I asked Cecilia Vicuña to give me a narrative of the life of Chile and how it was affected by the military junta. So one evening, among her fellow expatriates, after a meal of empanadas and mulled wine, she told me the story. As she spoke, I began to draw on a large piece of paper I had brought with me, which I had placed inside of the circle of her friends. And noting the figures – the men and women, the mountains and sea, the farms and factories, the common human activities and finally the spirit of sacrifice and rebirth, I made a sketch of Cecilia's poetic narrative – which while tragic, still held a 'forlorn hope' for her people and land.[3]

Before moving to London in September 1972, on a scholarship to the Slade School of Art, Vicuña had been a supporter of Allende and the Popular Unity government in Chile. As Pinochet's military junta began systematically targeting left-wing activists and sympathisers

1 John Dugger, 'Notes on the Big Chile Vencerá Banner', 1976, Chile Solidarity Campaign papers, People's History Museum, Manchester (CSC/12/1).

2 *Ibid.*

3 J. Dugger, 'A Festival for Democracy / Artists for Democracy 1974 / Making the Chile Vencera Banner', in *Artists for Democracy: El Archivo de Cecilia Vicuña*, Santiago: Museo de la Memoria y los Derechos Humanos, 2014.

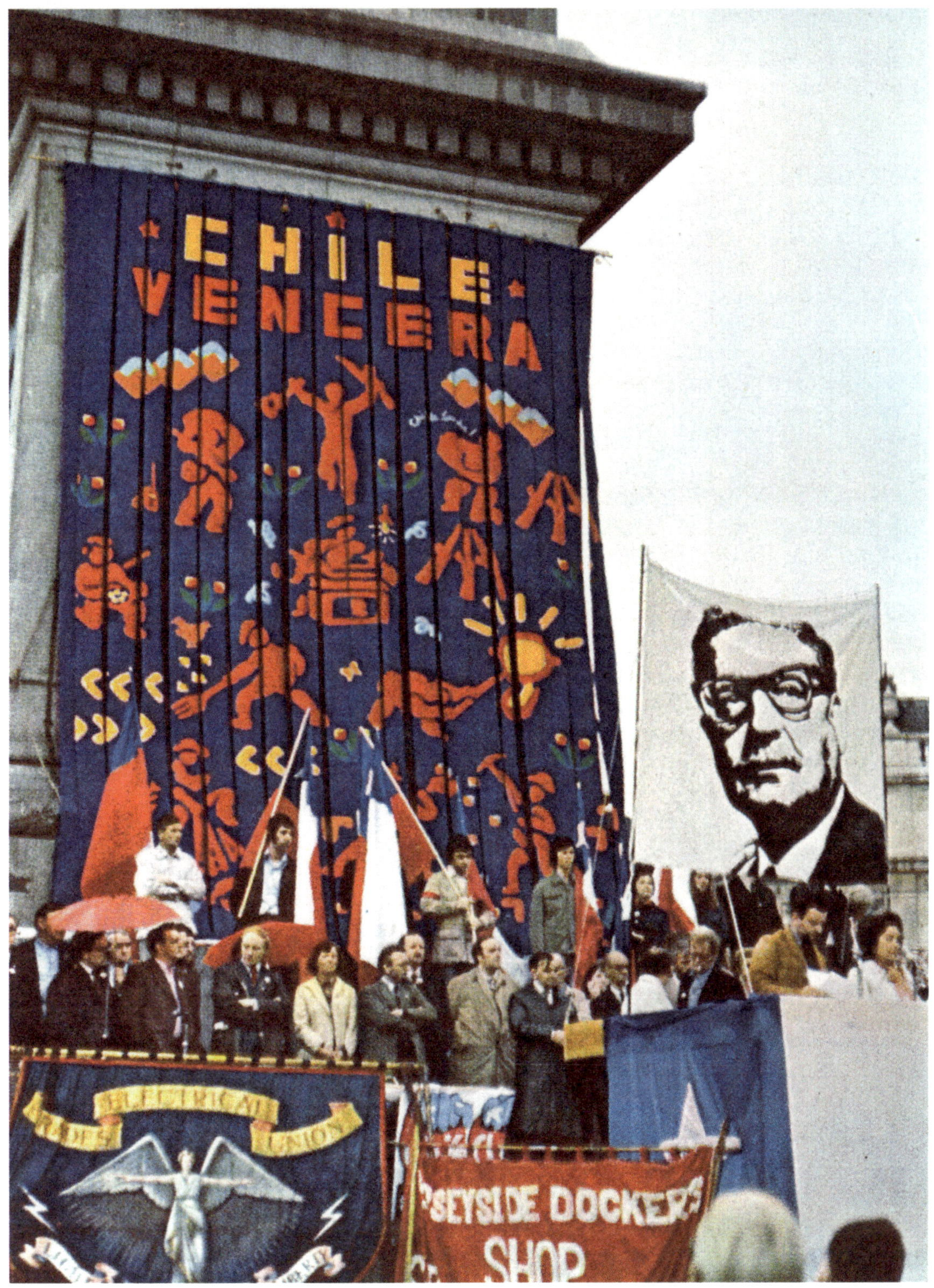

John Dugger's *Chile Vencerá* banner mounted on Nelson's Column in Trafalgar Square, London, 1974

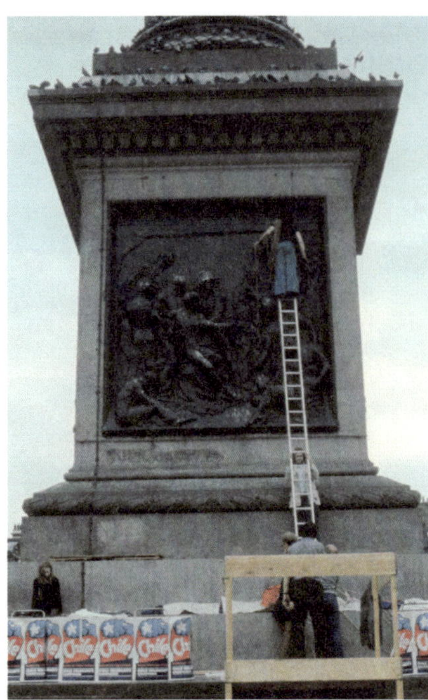

Peter Polish and others preparing for the installation of John Dugger's *Chile Vencerá* banner in Trafalgar Square, 1974

following the coup, she was unable to return to Chile and the cultural and political project she had been engaged in. In London, Vicuña became involved in the Chile Solidarity Campaign and drew attention to the situation in Chile within the London art scene. The stories she shared with Dugger represented an exiled young artist's vision of the hopeful country she had left behind, a vision behind which an emergent movement for solidarity was rallying.

The communal atmosphere in which the banner design was produced, as Vicuña and her Chilean guests shared their experiences, was invoked on a greater scale through the banner's production and installation, as Dugger drew on the resources, time and labour of volunteers. After developing the initial design, he presented a small-scale version of *Chile Vencerá* to the Chile Solidarity Campaign, who contributed £60 for its construction; support in kind followed from various sources.[4] Dugger's 1976 report records that Peter Townsend, editor of *Studio International*, volunteered space at the magazine's offices, where Dugger and volunteers made full-scale templates on paper to transfer onto canvas and cut out. On the evening of 11 September, they affixed the figures to the backing fabric and cut it into twenty strips. Over the next few days, a team of volunteers worked long hours in a studio space lent by 'Mr M.' to finish the banner in time for

4 *Ibid.*

its first public appearance at the Chile Solidarity Campaign's 15 September demonstration in Trafalgar Square, marking the one-year anniversary of the coup.[5] That morning, the strips were carried in backpacks to Trafalgar Square, where teacher Mavis Penn and construction worker and poet Vic Heath coordinated volunteers for the installation, and the banner was dramatically unveiled.[6]

Among the groups that travelled to London for the occasion were delegates from 34 unions, 35 trades councils and 19 shop stewards' committees; representatives from the International Socialists, the International Marxist Group, the Communist Party, constituent Labour Party groups and the Labour Party Young Socialists; and workers groups from Ireland, Spain, Portugal and Italy.[7] The 10,000-strong crowd assembled at Hyde Park before marching through central London and filing into Trafalgar Square to gather around a podium erected in front of Nelson's Column, where *Chile Vencerá* acted as an enormous, bright backdrop throughout the afternoon of speeches, music and rallying calls. Gazing up at the banner, the delegation from the Merseyside dockers shop stewards could see amongst the figures represented the miners and agricultural workers who produced the copper and food products that were the subject of the dockers' boycotting campaigns.[8] Teachers, musicians, poets and artists could see themselves represented in the cultural and education workers depicted. And delegates from the Rolls Royce factory in East Kilbride – who were thanked in a speech by the widow of President Salvador Allende, Madame Hortensia Bussi, for refusing to work on engines destined for Chilean military jets – could see themselves represented in the figure of the metalworker at the banner's centre.[9]

Dugger first adopted banner-making in his artistic practice in 1972, when he produced a banner for the *People's Participation Pavilion* at documenta 5 that read 'SOCIALIST ART THROUGH SOCIALIST REVOLUTION' below images of Marx, Engels, Lenin, Stalin and Mao.[10] The following year, John Gorman organised 'Banner Bright' at the Whitechapel Gallery in London, in a concerted effort to document, preserve and celebrate trade union banners. The exhibition traced the banners' origins in the nineteenth-century; their flourishing in the post-War period; and the subsequent decline of the practice in the 1960s, by which time many of the displayed examples were languishing in basements. Reflecting on this moment in 1986, Gorman described

5 J. Dugger, 'Notes on the Big Chile Vencerá Banner', *op. cit.*

6 *Ibid*. Dugger's 2014 account of the banner's installation in *Artists for Democracy*, *op. cit.*, notes that Peter Polish was 'a member of Red Rope the Climbing Club – who brought their ropes and carabineers for rigging the banner'. However, Red Rope was not formed until 1980. In a conversation with the author in March 2023, Polish could not recall how he came to be involved in installing the banner.

7 Ann Jones, *No Truck with the Chilean Junta!: Trade Union Internationalism, Australia and Britain, 1973–1980*, Canberra: ANU Press, 2014, pp.64–65.

8 Shirin Hirsch, 'A Quarrel of Limited Concern to the People of this Country'?: The British Labour Movement and Chile Solidarity', *Labour History Review*, vol.81, no.3, 2016, p.247.

9 An account of the blacking campaign by workers at the Rolls-Royce factory in East Kilbride can be found in *ibid.* It was also the subject of the 2018 documentary film *Nae Pasaran*, directed by Felipe Bustos Sierra.

10 The *People's Participation Pavilion* is discussed in the context of Dugger's practice in Courtney J. Martin, 'Collectivity, Temporality, and Festival Culture in John Dugger's Quasi-Architecture, 1970–1974', in Jo Applin, Catherine Spencer and Amy Tobin (ed.), *London Art Worlds: Mobile, Contingent, and Ephemeral Networks, 1960–1980*, University Park, PA: Penn State University Press, 2018, pp.94–114.

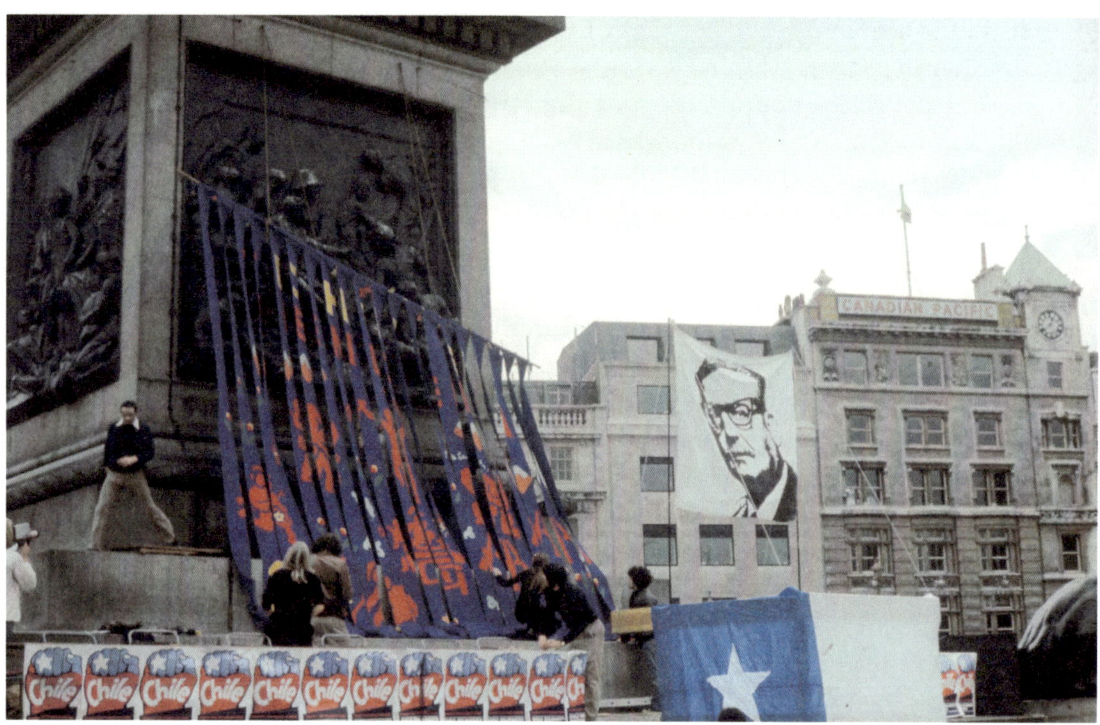

Rigging of *Chile Vencerá* banner on Nelson's Column in Trafalgar Square, 1974

how it had seemed that the practice of creating and carrying trade unions banners had declined 'to such an extent that we had reached the end of this peculiarly British form of working class culture'.[11] The 1970s however saw a re-emergence of the form for a new generation of trade unionists and artists. Replacing the allegory and optimism of post-War banners, with their images of 'well fed children nurtured on free milk and school dinners', a new iconography emerged as politically engaged artists brought new expressive forms to the increasing radicalism of the decade.[12] In the second edition of the 'Banner Bright' catalogue, Gorman referenced in particular the 'strip method for easy transportation developed by John Dugger'.[13] In the creation of strips banners such as *Chile Vencerá*, Dugger was influenced not only by the 'peculiarly British' tradition of trade union banners, but also by his experiences during a 1972 trip to China with a delegation from the Society for Anglo-Chinese Understanding, during which he observed Chinese scroll paintings cut into sections for ease of transportation.[14] Dugger's use of the strip-banner form in *Chile Vencerá* brought together his interest in and commitment to Maoist cultural thought and the context of the British labour movement that the banner was created to address.

11 John Gorman, *Banner Bright: An Illustrated History of Trade Union Banners*, Essex: Scorpion Publishing, 1986, p.9.

12 *Ibid.*, p.10.

13 *Ibid.*

14 John Walker, *Left Shift: Radical Art in 1970s Britain*, London: I.B. Tauris, 2002, p.204.

Following *Chile Vencerá*

While the banners held aloft by each delegation assembled in Trafalgar Square declared their representation of a particular political group, in *Chile Vencerá* Dugger used the form to instead present a marker of the collective identity of the solidarity movement, the individual strips of the banner brought together to produce a cohesive vision behind which the crowd was united. The monumental scale of *Chile Vencerá* dwarfed the delegations' banners, and the energy of its vivid colour, abstract forms and reactive strips, which moved as the wind passed through them, encapsulated and amplified the dynamism of the assembled crowd. Dugger described this effect in his 1976 report, writing that 'the power of mass-art is that it faces the people with a finished product on a scale and scope that reflects the people's collective energy and potential for united action'.[15] Depicted across the strips of *Chile Vencerá* and invoked throughout its production was the belief in the strength of solidarity as joint action. In its first appearance, the banner was displayed before a public audience of a size and political feeling rarely faced by a work of art, and it represented the hope and possibility of the moment: a visual and artistic show of force to match the political show of force of the day.

*

Following the demonstration, *Chile Vencerá* was installed in the Gulbenkian Hall at the Royal College of Art in London for the first public event organised by AFD: 'Arts Festival for Democracy in Chile', from 14 to 30 October 1974.[16]

*

Its next outing came the following year, on 11 September 1975. There was no public demonstration to mark the second anniversary of the coup, and *Chile Vencerá* was installed at a rally of the Labour Party National Executive Committee (NEC) in London. Photographs show the banner hung in front of the enormous organ in the Great Hall of the Methodist Central Hall, located in the governmental centre of the city facing Westminster Abbey.[17] Built in 1912 as part of the Methodist Church's project to establish venues for worship and discussion in major British cities, the building has acted as a de facto political venue for meetings and rallies across the political spectrum.[18] On 26 July 1945, Clement

15 J. Dugger, 'Notes on the Big Chile Vencerá Banner', *op. cit.*

16 An account of the Chile Festival can be found in the exhibition catalogue *Artists for Democracy*, *op. cit.* The publication is a key resource of information on the festival and the largely forgotten history of AFD. Both are the subject of this author's PhD research, currently being undertaken at the Courtauld Institute.

17 The venue is listed as 'Westminster Hall' in J. Dugger, 'Notes on the Big Chile Vencerá Banner', *op. cit.* Though Westminster Hall is a building within the parliamentary estate, photographs clearly show the rally took place in the Great Hall of the Methodist Central Hall, Westminster.

18 See Angela Connelly, 'Methodist Central Halls as Public Sacred Space' (2010), PhD thesis submitted to the University of Manchester.

Atlee joined the gathering of his party members in the hall following Labour's landslide election victory; on 30 October 1961, Martin Luther King Jr and Stuart Hall spoke at a 'Colour Prejudice Must Go' rally at the hall; and throughout the 1960s and 70s right-wing Conservative pressure group the Monday Club used the venue for events such as their 'Halt Immigration Now' meeting.[19]

Following Pinochet's coup, Chile became a flash issue in the UK that spoke to the political and social unrest of the moment. In September 1973, Edward Heath's Conservative government was besieged by unrest and seemingly poised to be succeeded by a Labour Party in which trade unions and the left were strong in influence. An election in February 1974, however, resulted in a hung parliament. A narrow victory for Harold Wilson's Labour followed in a second election held in October, with a majority of just three seats. To the British left, Allende's socialist project had represented a hope for a 'democratic road to socialism', and the overthrow of the Popular Unity government was decried as a violent affront to democracy. Labour General Secretary Ron Hayward described 'the crushing of the hopes of millions'; trade unions swiftly began to pressure successive governments to halt trade with Chile; and in 1974, frequent debates on the situation were held in the House of Commons.[20] The lamented hope Allende represented to the left corresponded to anxieties amongst the British right concerning the strength of trade unions and radical political groups within the UK. Reports published in *The Times* and *The Telegraph* positioned Pinochet's military coup as the inevitable – even desirable – response to the dangerously radical politics and damaging policies of Allende's presidency.[21] The right-wing press denounced advocates of the Chilean cause as communists, and *The Daily Express* made the sensationalist claim that there was an 'Allende Marxist' group within the Labour government.[22] Pinochet's restructuring of the economy and social provisions was of particular interest to some within the Conservative Party, as Chile became a testing ground for the economic policies that would inform Margaret Thatcher, who became the Conservative Party leader in February 1975.[23] Across the political spectrum, responses to Chile came to stand for the broader anxieties and divisions of British society.

The occasion of *Chile Vencerá*'s first public appearance, at the Chile Solidarity Campaign demonstration, had been a testament to the British labour movement's support for the Chilean cause. Yet despite the attendance of many constituency and Labour Party

19 *Ibid.*, p.154; Lisa Mason, 'The Development of the Monday Club and Its Contribution to the Conservative Party and the Modern British Right, 1961 to 1990', PhD thesis submitted to the University of Wolverhampton.

20 Quoted in Andy Beckett, *Pinochet in Piccadilly: Britain and Chile's Hidden History*, London: Faber & Faber, 2002, p.138.

21 'There is a limit to the ruin a country can be expected to tolerate. The circumstances were such that a reasonable military man could in good faith have thought it his constitutional duty to intervene', quoted in *ibid.*, p.139.

22 *Ibid.*, p.159.

23 *Ibid.*, pp.167–81.

Young Socialists delegations, the executive of the Labour Party had chosen not to officially sponsor the event due to concerns that doing so would distract from campaign efforts for the upcoming election.[24] Some party members had been allies of Allende during his presidency and following the coup became staunch advocates of the Chilean resistance, such as MP Judith Hart, who acted as the Labour Party's representative to the Chile Solidarity Campaign and sponsored AFD's 'Arts Festival for Democracy in Chile'. By 1975, however, the Chilean issue was positioned at the centre of party politics, as Hart described the NEC to be 'absolutely unanimous on Chile'.[25] At the Westminster Central Hall rally, Hortensia Bussi thanked the assembly. She identified the Labour Party and British trade unions as early and influential supporters of the international solidarity effort, and was photographed receiving a standing ovation with *Chile Vencerá* filling the space behind her.[26] In Trafalgar Square the previous year the banner had hung in the open air at a grass-roots public demonstration: sat in front of the grand organ of Westminster Central Hall, *Chile Vencerá* had arrived at the heart of the left-wing political establishment.

*

In November 1975, the banner was sent by sea freight to the United States.[27]

Its first appearance in the US was at a concert by the Chilean musical group Inti Illimani on 7 March 1976 at Glide Memorial Church, a focal point for countercultural activity and political organising in the marginalised Tenderloin district of San Francisco. Following the arrival of Reverend Cecil Williams in 1964, the church gave financial backing to the Black People's Free Store; provided a venue for a Black Panther Party breakfast programme; supported the United Farm Workers and the American Indian Movement (AIM); and was an important advocate for the gay liberation movement.[28] On 4 October 1973, Glide hosted one of the first public events to take place in the US in response to the Chilean coup: the 'Salvador Allende Memorial Poetry Reading – Pablo Neruda'. The reading was organised by Third World Communications, a collective of local poets and artists, to declare solidarity with the Chilean people.[29] At the event, poet Ismael Reed blended a eulogy to Neruda, whose suspicious death had just occurred in Chile on 23 September, and an indictment of US involvement in South America.[30]

24 A. Jones, *No Truck with the Chilean Junta!*, *op. cit.*, p.196.

25 Judith Hart, quoted in Michael D. Wilkinson, 'The Chile Solidarity Campaign and British Government Policy towards Chile, 1973–1990', *European Review of Latin American and Caribbean Studies*, no.52, June 1992, p.58.

26 Judith Cook, 'Two Years of the Generals', *Labour Weekly*, 19 September 1975, p.5.

27 J. Dugger, 'Notes on the Big Chile Vencerá Banner', *op. cit.*

28 See, for instance, 'The Black People's Free Store', *Venture*, August 1967, pp.2–3 and 10–11, available at https://www.glide.org/summer-of-love-flashback-the-black-peoples-free-store/; Ryan Lee Cartwright, 'Patient No More', *Journal of American History*, vol.103, no.22, June 2016, p.145; David Holly, 'Coming Out Under Jesus: Glide Memorial and the Struggle for Gay Civil Rights in San Francisco', *Clio's Scroll*, vol.14, no.2, Spring 2013, pp.48–67.

29 Tamara Lea Spira, 'From the Fringes of Empire: U.S. Third World Feminists in Solidarity with Chile', *nacla*, 2 October 2013, available at https://nacla.org/article/fringes-empire-us-third-world-feminists-solidarity-chile.

30 *Ibid.*

Co-organiser Alejandro Murguía recalled the church 'packed with angry people' on a night that ended with Chilean poet Fernando Alegría – formerly Allende's cultural attaché to the US – reading '¡Viva Chile Mierda!' (1964) to an enraptured audience.[31]

In the years since Reverend Williams's arrival, the space of Glide Memorial Church had undergone a transformation to reflect its new mission. Constructed in 1930, the building was designed by local architect James W. Plachek in a Mediterranean-revival style, with white walls and a light-filled open space. Tall stained-glass windows run down the length of one side of the nave, and a balcony holds additional seating above the pews of the main floor. Until 1967, the curved sanctuary space that congregants face held a 4.6-metre-tall crucifix. It was removed on 22 September by Williams, who believed it to be a symbol of pain and suffering and not an effective visual aid to his ministering.[32] In 1972, further changes were made to the interior as Glide's board brought in multimedia artist and self-trained architect Beverly Willis and gave her the directive to reshape the church into a multi-use space reflective of the building's transformation from a traditional house of worship to radical space that earnestly welcomed all.[33] She focussed on the space of the sanctuary and removed the structures that prescribed the interaction between preacher and congregation: the communion rail, altar and pulpit were replaced by a raised circular platform that opened up to the congregation with steps leading down to the nave. Willis also installed a two-way sound system that allowed the preacher to better hear the congregation, and a multimedia system which projected colours and images onto the white-walled sanctuary. Local photographer Bob Fitch's documentation of a dance group performing in 1972

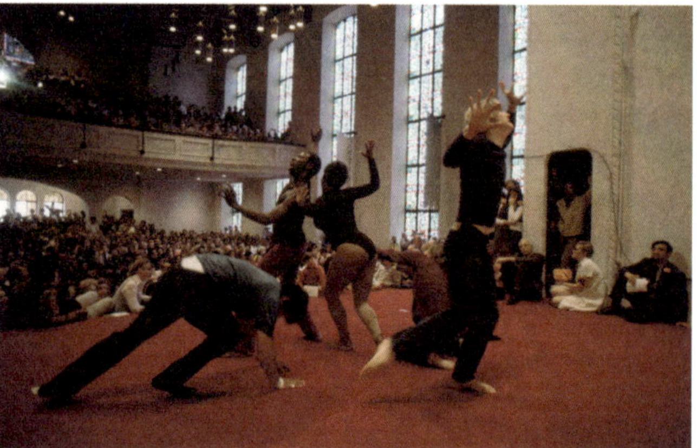

Dance performance at worship service, Glide Memorial Church, San Francisco, 1972

31 See Alejandro Murguía, 'Poetry and Solidarity in the Mission District', in *Ten Years That Shook the City: San Francisco 1968–1978* (ed. Chris Carlsson and Lisa Ruth Elliott), San Francisco: City Lights Foundation Books, 2011, p.63. A recording from the same night documents poet Ishmael Reed reading 'Poem delivered before an assembly of colored people at Glide Memorial Church, October 4th, 1973, and called to protest recent events in the Sovereign Republic of Chile', available at https://openspace.sfmoma.org/2016/10/for-mnemosyne/.

32 Cecil Williams, *I'm Alive!*, New York: Harper & Row, 1980, p.80.

33 For documentation of Willis's work, see 'Glide Church Renovations', Beverly Willis Archive, available at https://beverlywillis.com/architecture-project/0607/#pane2.

to a packed house shows how the church facilitated dynamic events and informal interactions, the sanctuary becoming a performance space with children and adults gathered on the steps up to and around the platform. By the time Inti Illimani and *Chile Vencerá* came to Glide in March 1976, the church was an enlivened space for spiritual, cultural and political communion.

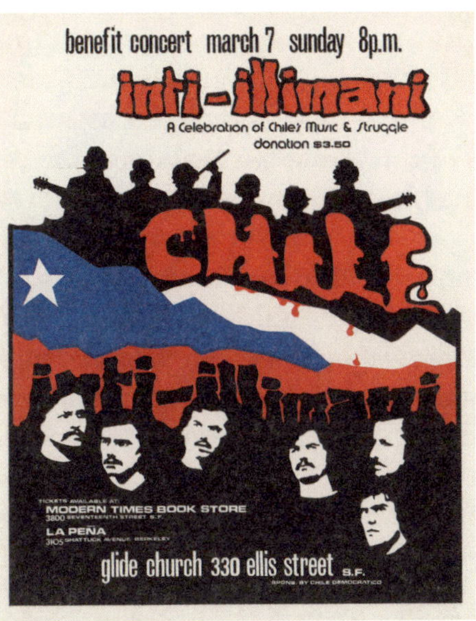

Poster for Inti Illimani's benefit concert 'Acelebration of Chile's music of struggle' at Glide Memorial Church, San Francisco, 1976

Music was central to Glide's new style, as Williams brought gospel, jazz and blues into Sunday services. In turn, Inti Illimani's performance brought the contemporary music of Chile to the church. The group was part of the Nueva canción music movement that had grown in Chile since the 1960s; during the 1970 presidential election, Inti Illimani were amongst many Nueva canción musicians that helped to mobilise support for Allende through performances at political events. In September 1973, the group was on tour in Europe, acting as cultural ambassadors for Allende's Popular Unity government.[34] Their absence from Chile when the coup occurred left them suddenly unable to return home; like Cecilia Vicuña, they instead witnessed the events of 11 September from abroad. In exile, they toured throughout Europe, the US, Mexico, Cuba and Vietnam, playing hundreds of concerts a year to raise awareness and funds for the Chilean resistance.[35] They undertook press engagements; met with local Chileans; and attended meetings with solidarity groups and trade unions to provide testimony to members. Inti Illimani's benefit concert

34 David Horn, 'Inti-Illimani', *Popular Music Special Issue:Prosecuting and Policing Rap*, vol.6, no.2, May 1987, p.241; J. Patrice McSherry, 'The Political Impact of Chilean New Song in Exile', *Latin American Perspectives: Democracy, Repression, and the Defense of Human Rights*, vol.44, no.5, September 2017, p.21.

35 A. Jones, *No Truck with the Chilean Junta!*, *op. cit.*, p.196; J.P. McSherry, 'The Political Impact of Chilean New Song in Exile', *op. cit.*, p.21.

at Glide was billed as 'A Celebration of Chile's Music and Struggle' and, held on the evening of 7 March 1976, tied into the church's wider programme of 'celebrations' – William's preferred term for Sunday services.[36]

Documentation of the performance cannot be found in Glide's archive, though *Chile Vencerá* was likely installed in the tall sanctuary space at the back of the platform. Inti Illimani had in fact performed in front of the banner at the 1974 Chile Solidarity Campaign demonstration in London, playing 'Venceremos' ('We will prevail') – the anthem of Allende's presidential campaign – as the delegates filed into Trafalgar Square.[37] Like Dugger's image of workers, the songs Inti Illimani performed represented the tragedy and lost promise of Allende's project, and the defiance of the Chilean resistance, embodying Williams's belief that bringing new forms of music to Glide could serve to 'reflect pain, hurt, devastation of the lives of people ... to express that suffering and yet that hope'.[38] Fundraising concerts were also an important means of catalysing support to the solidarity movement, as Nueva canción performances acted as a means of social and cultural communication that transgressed language barriers.[39] Audience members at Glide may not have been able to understand the Spanish lyrics, but they could understand the aesthetic and emotive force of Inti Illimani's defiant call to solidarity. As a visual support to the performance at Glide, *Chile Vencerá* strengthened the impact of the music, offering an imaginative bridge between the performers and audience.

When he removed the crucifix from the sanctuary of Glide, Reverend Williams told his congregation: 'I took down the cross because it kept getting in the way of the power of people.'[40] Standing several metres higher than the crucifix had, Dugger's monumental banner acted with Inti Illimani's swelling Nueva canción sound to fill that space, speaking to the power of people within and beyond the Chile solidarity movement who dedicated themselves to political, spiritual or cultural transformation.

*

The poster for Inti Illimani's performance at Glide advertised tickets for sale at Modern Times Bookstore in San Francisco and across the bay at La Peña Cultural Center in Berkeley, where the banner would appear next, in May 1976.

36 David Holly, 'Coming Out Under Jesus: Glide Memorial and the Struggle for Gay Civil Rights in San Francisco', *Clio's Scroll*, vol.14, no.2, Spring 2013, p.50.

37 Footage of Inti Illimani's performance is included in the video *Chile Lucha* (1974) by artist Mike Leggett, available at https://www.mikeleggett.com.au/projects/chile-lucha.

38 Cecil Williams in 'Guide My Feet', directed by Lulie Haddad, episode 3 of *This Far By Faith*, US broadcast on PBS, 2003, transcript available at https://www.pbs.org/thisfarbyfaith/about/episode_3.html.

39 See J.P. McSherry, 'The Political Impact of Chilean New Song in Exile', *op. cit.*

40 C. Williams, *I'm Alive*, *op. cit.*, p.80.

La Peña was formally established in June 1975 by Chileans residing in California along with American allies from the local community. Though the Chilean coup was the catalyst for its formation, La Peña, like Glide Memorial Church and AFD, engaged with a wide range of political causes, including the American Indian Movement, the Black Panther Party and the United Farm Workers, and opposed US intervention in Nicaragua and El Salvador.[41] In South Berkeley, opposite the Black Panther Party's national headquarters on Shattuck Avenue, the La Peña building offered a café and large open space for performances, workshops, exhibitions and meetings. As Pinochet utilised mass exile to eliminate an effective opposition within Chile, La Peña provided vital resources to displaced Chileans such as employment and education.[42] But the centre also carved out a vital space for exiles to engage with Chilean cultural and political activities, addressing the alienation of those now living in a country whose government enabled the oppressive regime they had fled. To do so, the centre evoked the Chilean *peñas* after which it was named.

Central to the Nueva canción movement, *peñas* were places where musicians gathered to perform and discuss life, art and the issues of the day over glasses of wine and plates of empanadas. Inti Illimani, for example, had formed through the *peña* of the Universidad Técnica del Estado in Santiago, where the members were students. These events had flourished during the Popular Unity years, as social spaces where culture and politics came together, and Allende underscored their significance when he declared that the Chilean socialist project would be a revolution 'with the flavour of red wine and empanadas'.[43] Later, as the apparatus of Pinochet's dictatorship dominated the public and social spheres, *peñas* became 'cultural refuges' in which the cultural memory of pre-coup Chile persisted.[44] Termed the *espacio peñero* by the scholar Sandra Molina, *peñas* provided safe spaces that functioned both physically and imaginatively, demonstrating the potential for cultural and political alternatives to emerge beyond the domain of the military junta and allowing a notion of resistance to emerge.[45] Through their activities, La Peña Cultural Center sought to reproduce this space within a building in Berkeley, California, and it was here that *Chile Vencerá* was displayed for the centre's May Day celebrations and an exhibition in June of 1976.[46]

While no archival material has yet been uncovered of the banner at La Peña, the notion of the *espacio peñero* can be brought

41 Patrick Hoge, 'La Peña turns 30 with a street fair / Small Chilean hangout gained national reputation', *SFGate*, 11 June 2005, available at https://www.sfgate.com/bayarea/article/BERKELEY-La-Pe-a-turns-30-with-a-street-fair-2513572.php#taboola-2.

42 The use of exile as a political tactic and the scale and consequences of mass exile pursued by Pinochet is discussed in Thomas C. Wright and Rody Oñate Zúñiga, 'Chilean Political Exile', *Latin American Perspectives*, vol.34, no.4, July 2007, pp.31–49.

43 'La nuestra se hará con sabor a vino tinto y empanadas.' Salvador Allende, senate log, 7 August 1963, quoted in Javiera Adones Soto and Claudio Pérez Silva, '"La revolución cubana se ha hecho con sabor a ron y gusto a 1964', *Revista electrónica de estudios latinoamericanos*, vol.20, no.79, 2022.

44 'Refugios culturales'; Sandra Molina, 'Las peñas folklóricas en Chile (1973–1986). El refugio cultural y político para la disidencia', *Aletheia*, vol.1, no.2, May 2011, p.3.

45 *Ibid.*, p.7.

46 J. Dugger, 'Notes on the Big Chile Vencerá Banner', *op. cit.*

into conversation with recent scholarship exploring the spatial function of trade union banners, to offer a way of understanding how *Chile Vencerá* functioned at the centre and the other sites it occupied. Since 2016, the project 'Banner Tales of Glasgow' has brought together academics, museum staff and trade unionists to co-produce knowledge of trade union banners through a process of 'participatory archiving'.[47] In oral histories, trade unionists describe how each banner was created at the outbreak of a labour dispute and employed to demarcate the picket line as a site for action. They recalled the emotional impact of arriving to their picket line, and seeing a banner sent by fellow trade unionists from a neighbouring factory to provide a physical manifestation of their support, when work prevented them from being present themselves. In these recollections, banners served to create and reinforce physical and imaginative spaces for protest and solidarity by articulating political action through material presence and visual acts of territorialisation.[48] *Chile Vencerá* likewise demarcated a space for political action in service of the Chilean cause, and as it travelled through the various sites on its journey it represented the solidarity of those across the international movement who could not be present at each event, but who sent with the banner their declaration of a shared resistance. The potency of the *espacio peñero* was evident in its ability to transgress national borders: to be constituted beyond the country of Chile, and indeed wherever those who sought to produce it found themselves. The strength of trade union banners, meanwhile, lay in their materiality, their ability to give physical presence to pledges of political support. At La Peña, and throughout its journey, *Chile Vencerá* drew on both of these notions. While the portability of the strip-banner form allowed it to more easily traverse geographic locations, its physical form gave materiality to its circulation through networks of solidarity involving people who gathered to protest, to decry, to communicate and to support.

Further invoking the notion of the Chilean *peña,* is the description Dugger gave of the evening on which the design for *Chile Vencerá* was conceived, in Vicuña's home in London: the sharing of wine and empanadas, and the discussion of life, culture and politics in Chile. In producing this space for communal social and cultural interaction, Vicuña, like the founders of La Peña, reproduced the *espacio peñero* from her position of exile as a means of creating community and affecting solidarity. Installed

47 J.M. Crossan, D.J. Featherstone, F. Hayes, H.M. Hughes, C. Jamieson and R. Leonard, 'Trade union banners and the construction of a working-class presence: Notes from two labour disputes in 1980s Glasgow and North Lanarkshire', *Area*, vol.48, no.3, September 2016, pp.357–65.

48 *Ibid.*, pp.358–59.

at La Peña, *Chile Vencerá* therefore not only contributed to the production of an *espacio peñero*, but in doing so returned to the imaginative space that engendered the production of this monumental yet mobile manifestation of solidarity.

49 J. Dugger, 'Notes on the Big Chile Vencerá Banner', *op. cit.*

50 See Martin Gostwick and Jim Tait, 'Widening anti-junta solidarity: BIG RALLIES BACK CHILE'S RESISTANCE', *Morning Star*, 13 September 1976.

*

Chile Vencerá returned to London by air cargo for the 1976 Chile Solidarity Campaign anniversary demonstration held in Trafalgar Square on Sunday 12 September.[49] The cover of the *Morning Star* the next day read 'Widening anti-junta solidarity: BIG RALLIES BACK CHILE'S RESISTANCE'.[50] The accompanying photograph showed Hortensia Bussi alongside Mike Gatehouse of the Chile Solidarity Campaign at the speakers' podium. Behind and above them, *Chile Vencerá* is just visible, its strips draping down once again over the base of Nelson's Column. This is the last appearance recorded in Dugger's 1976 report.

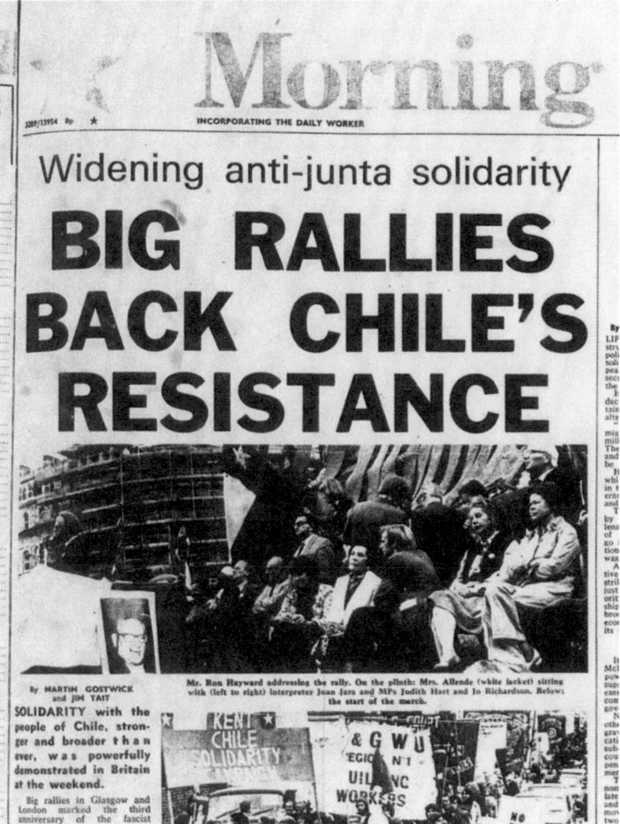

Morning

INCORPORATING THE DAILY WORKER

Widening anti-junta solidarity

BIG RALLIES BACK CHILE'S RESISTANCE

Mr. Ron Hayward addressing the rally. On the plinth: Mrs. Allende (white jacket) sitting with (left to right) interpreter Joan Jara and MPs Judith Hart and Jo Richardson. Below: the start of the march.

by MARTIN GOSTWICK and JIM TAIT

SOLIDARITY with the people of Chile, stronger and broader than ever, was powerfully demonstrated in Britain at the weekend.

Big rallies in Glasgow and London marked the third anniversary of the fascist

Newspaper clipping from *Morning Star*, 13 September 1976

With its return to Trafalgar Square, the banner came full circle; yet the object that appeared in London in 1976 should not be supposed to be the same one that had appeared in 1974. In its circulation through various sites of the Chilean solidarity network, the object underwent a process of accumulation – of geographic miles and meanings. Reflecting on its display in varied spaces brings a developing understanding of how the banner could function in public spaces as an object of solidarity:

At Trafalgar Square, *Chile Vencerá* first stood as a monument to the organisation of the grassroots British labour movement in service of the Chilean cause and a symbol of the collective political strength of the assembled crowds.

In the Great Hall of Westminster Central Hall, at a rally held by the Labour Party National Executive Committee and attended by representatives from across the party and affiliated organisations, the banner was amalgamated into the political establishment of the British left.

At Glide Memorial Church, it facilitated an experience of unity between performers and audience, while it also spoke to the radical project of a church whose mission and space was given over to political as well as spiritual communion.

At La Peña Cultural Center, it contributed to the production of a physical and imaginative space for solidarity that transgressed national borders and overcame the constraints of country, home and exile.

And finally, in its return to Trafalgar Square, it represented the continued commitment of the Chile solidarity movement in the UK, which would endure throughout successive governments and the many years of Pinochet's dictatorship.

The ways in which *Chile Vencerá* represented and manifested solidarity spoke to the potential of new and experimental art practices directed towards political concerns, and to the promise of AFD at the moment of the group's inception. It demonstrated the power of the convictions and imaginations of a group of artists to inspire others in the service of a political cause, and the ways in which an experimental art form was able to visualise, conceptualise and constitute bonds of solidarity. By the time of the banner's second appearance in Trafalgar Square, Artists for Democracy had itself undergone a transformation. The initial phase of the group was over, and Dugger and Vicuña were no longer members. *Chile Vencerá*, however, continues to encapsulate the energy and hope that allowed AFD to come together in May 1974, in the belief that art has something vital to offer to the practice of political solidarity.

As I finished writing this essay, I received news that John Dugger had passed away. I hope that this exploration of his *Chile Vencerá* banner goes some way to recognising the remarkable contribution he made to the history of political art.

Everything is suspended in thin air

Cường Minh Bá Phạm and George Clark

What is the sound of our group – of belonging – of not belonging?[1]

Pauline Oliveros

When families had questions, they called me, because they believed that I understood the UK system better than they did. They hoped that my English language and British contacts would magically right all wrongs, but most importantly, they trusted me. So when I moved to London after Thorney Island Reception Centre closed in 1982, there was an entire community that had come to depend on me for help dealing with daily life in the UK. People found where I was living in Hackney and would come to my flat asking for more help. This spontaneous gathering of Vietnamese families in my home became the birth place of the Vietnamese community in Hackney, officially founded on 25th November 1982.[2]

Vũ Khánh Thành

1 Pauline Oliveros, 'Deep Listening Meditations Egypt' (1999), in *Deep Listening: A Composer's Sound Practice*, Bloomington, IN: iUniverse, 2005, p.41.

2 Vũ Khánh Thành and Christina Puryear, *Catholic with Confucian Tendencies: The true story of the extreme adventures of a Vietnamese boat person*, London: self-published, 2016, p.161.

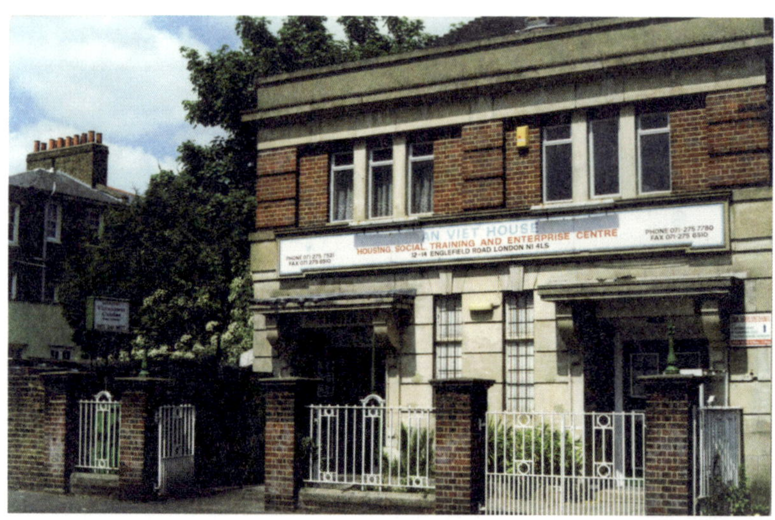

An Việt House, London, c.2003

Writing his memoirs, the late Vũ Khánh Thành outlined the informal origins of the An Việt Foundation (AVF), which he founded as a community centre for Vietnamese migrants trying to settle in the United Kingdom. AVF was a hub for Vietnamese families, providing support through housing, health outreach, community activities, festival celebrations and language classes. It also established the An Viet Housing Association to provide social housing for Vietnamese migrants, and housed the Southeast Asian Research Centre, also founded by Mr Vũ. The AVF closed in 2017 after Mr Vũ stepped down, and its materials are now looked after by the An Việt Archives, a voluntary organisation to which we both currently belong as members alongside Toan Vu, Tamsin Barber, Georgina Quach and Trà My Hickin.

When Cường first came to work with AVF in 2017, the building was already in a dilapidated state. Parts of the plumbing needed tending to and the overgrown garden had become a dumping ground. But it was the library Cường was drawn to most, an incredible and unexpected resource in the heart of Hackney. Its collection of books offered a diverse and at times idiosyncratic intellectual history of Vietnam and Southeast Asia, including a rich archive of documents, magazines, objects and photographs. Encounters with the collection opened the yearning to delve deeper. There were so many questions to explore.

A photograph was the first thing Cường asked Mr Vũ about. When was it taken? How did it come about? What's the story behind it? Mr Vũ replied that he did not remember. With his retirement and declining health, it became apparent that we were losing an important link to activating the documents and telling their stories.

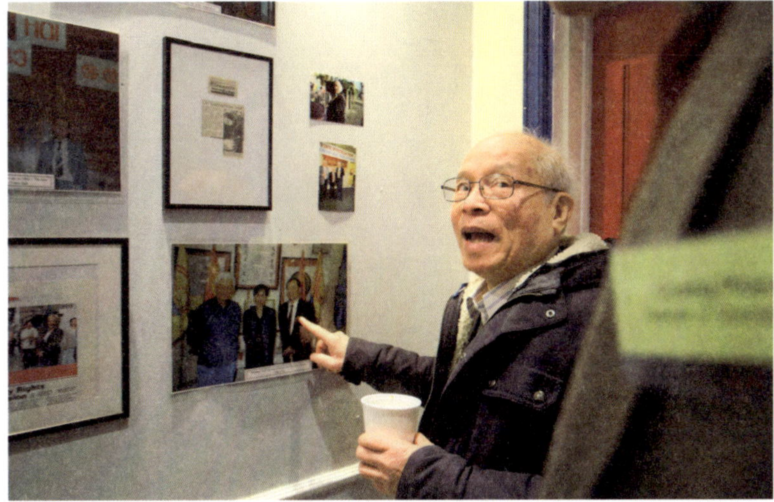

Vũ Khánh Thành pointing to a photo of Phạm Duy during Lunar New Year event at An Việt House, 2018

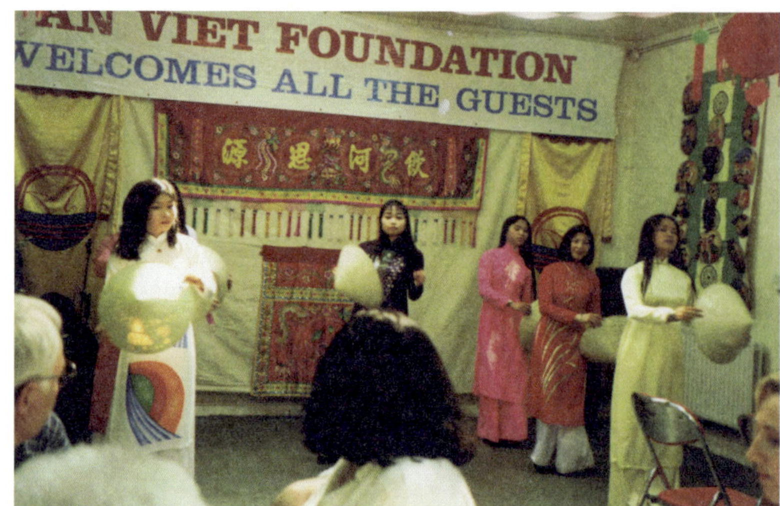

Performance
at An Việt House

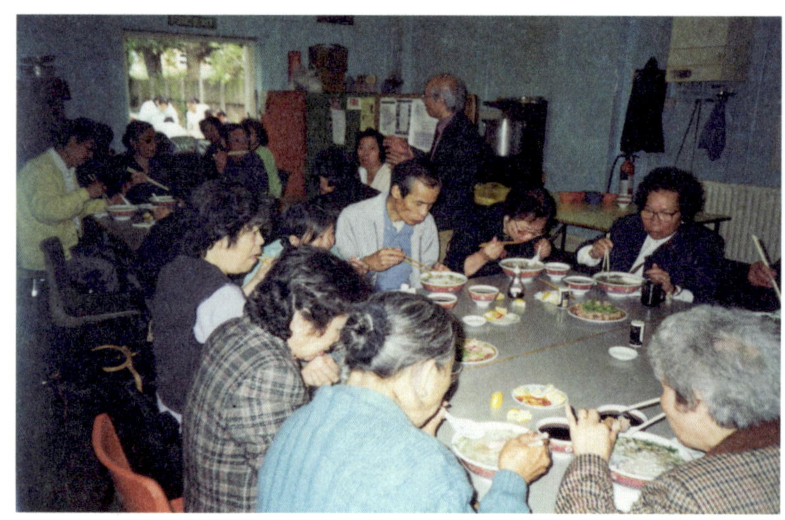

Luncheon club
at An Việt House

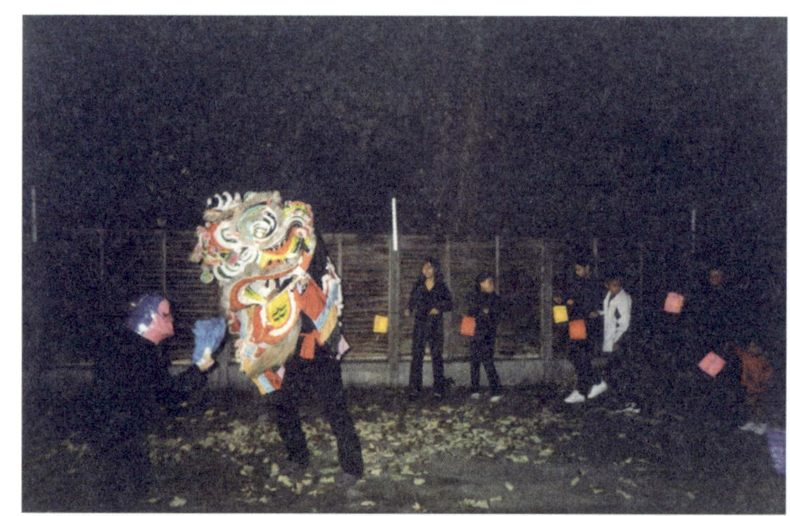

Ông Địa (Spirit of the Earth) and kỳ lân (Vietnamese Unicorn) during Tết Nguyên Đán (Lunar New Year) or Tết Trung Thu (Mid-Autumn Festival), in the An Việt garden

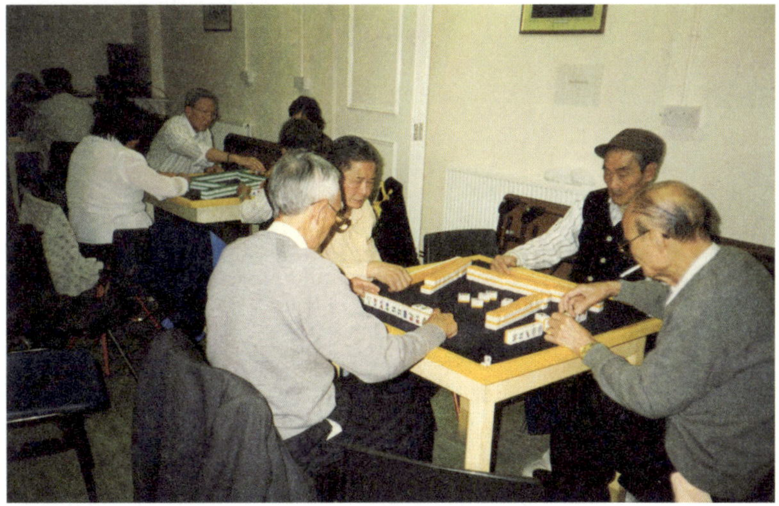

Mahjong club
at An Việt House

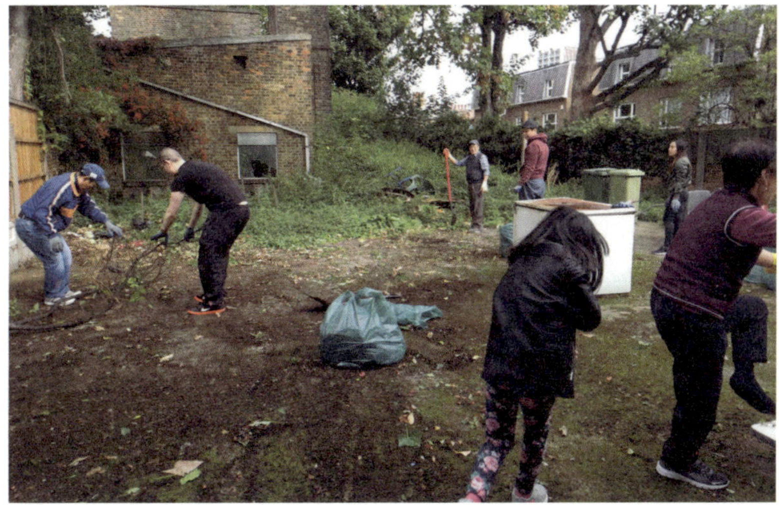

Community clean-up
at An Việt House, 2017

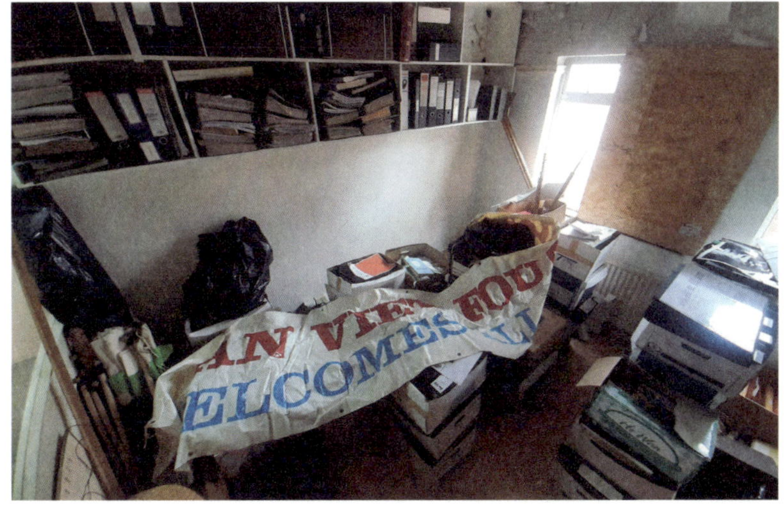

Materials saved for
An Viet Archives
including 'AN
VIET FOUNDATION
WELCOMES ALL
THE GUESTS' sign
discovered by builders
in attic of former
building on Englefield
Road, 2023

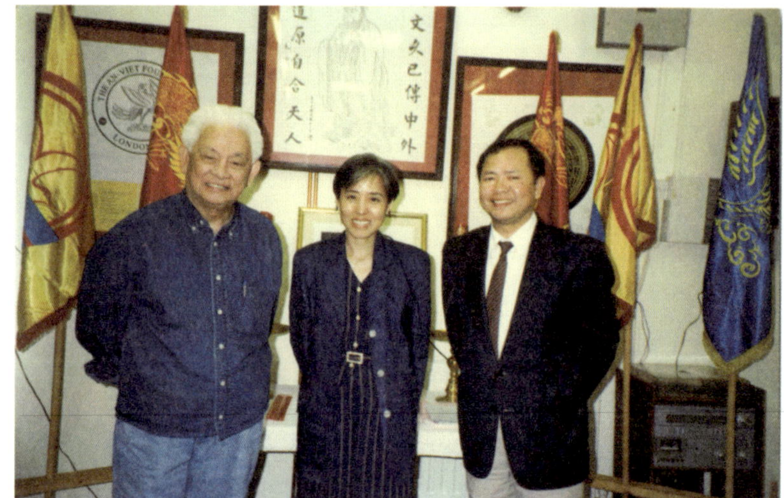

Phạm Duy (left) at An Việt House

The only thing we could do was to pull on the interesting threads, in search of more speculative ways of unlocking what has been left behind.

The photograph showed Phạm Duy, one of Vietnam's most famous musicians, with an An Việt logo behind him. Phạm Duy's and Vũ Khánh Thành's lives followed similar trajectories. Both were born in Hanoi; both became disillusioned with the Communist Party of the Democratic Republic of Vietnam (DRV); and both migrated to Saigon after the 1954 Geneva Conference split the country in two. When the American War ended, both migrated abroad: Phạm Duy to California, and Vũ Khánh Thành to the UK.

Following these biographical lines brought up questions about the parallel trajectories of the Vietnamese diaspora.

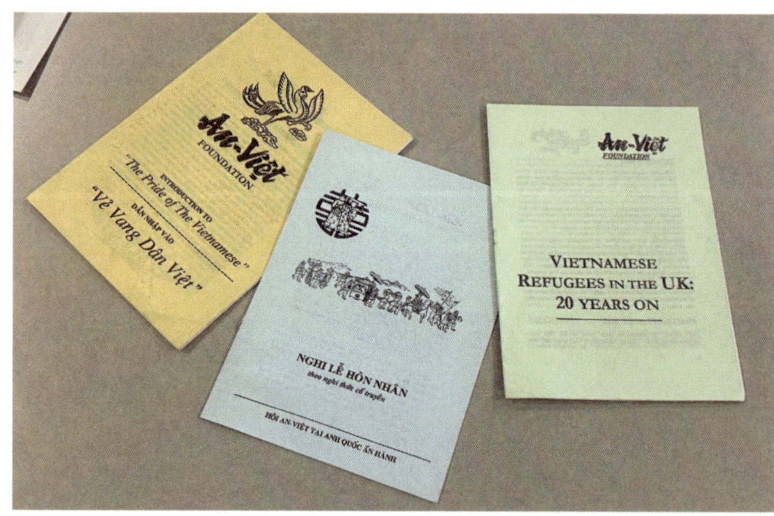

An Việt Foundation publications including *The Pride of The Vietnamese / Vẻ Vang Dân Việt* (1998)

As Trinh T. Minh-ha – who was born in Hanoi, studied music in Saigon, then migrated to the United States in 1970 – reflects:

> My past in Vietnam does not just belong to me. And since the Vietnamese communities, whether here in the U.S. or there in Vietnam, are not abstract entities, I can only speak while learning to keep silent, for the risk of jeopardizing someone's reputation and right to speech is always present. Suffice it to say that I come from a large family, in which three different political factions existed. These political tendencies were not always freely assumed, they were bound to circumstances as in the case of the family members who remained in Hanoi (where I was born) and those who were compelled to move to Saigon (where I grew up). The third faction comprised those involved with the National Liberation Front in the South.
>
> This is why the dualistic divide between pro- and anti-communists has always appeared to me as a simplistic product of the rivalry between (what once were) the two superpowers. It can never even come close to the complexity of the Vietnam reality.[3]

3 Trinh T. Minh-ha, in Nancy N. Chen, 'Speaking Nearby: A Conversation with Trinh T. Minh-ha', *Visual Anthropology Review*, vol.8, no.1, Spring 1982, p.83.

Cường's curiosity about the photograph came via the long reach of music and its multivalent reverberations. In particular, Phạm Duy's 'Đố Ai' and the 1960s version sung by Phương Dung. 'Đố Ai' was written by Phạm Duy in 1954 as a modern pop song that drew inspiration from the Vietnamese folk tradition of *ca dao*. The song uses poetic riddles to express romantic love. The Phương Dung version was produced by Y Vân and was released on the Sóng Nhạc

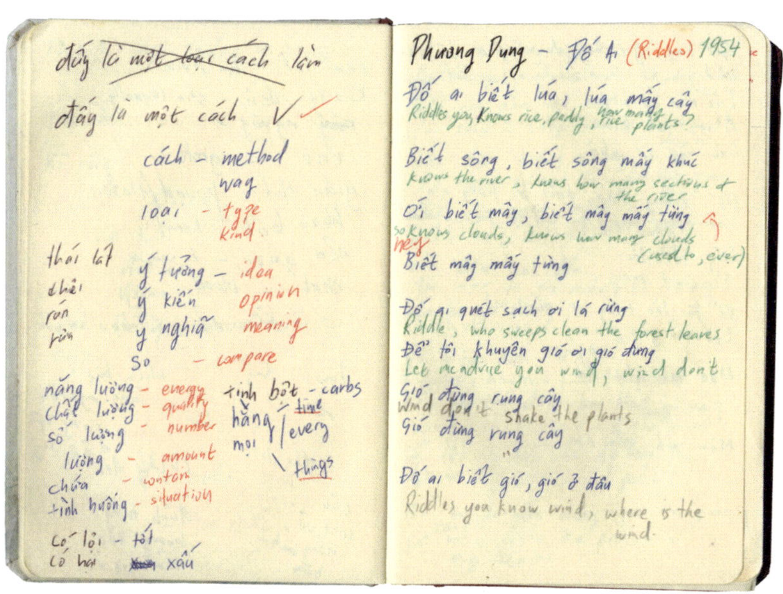

Cường Minh Bá Phạm's translation of the lyrics of Phạm Duy's 'Đố Ai' (1954), c.2014

label in 1967 and re-released on the Sublime Frequencies label in 2010. When Cường began re-encountering Vietnamese as an adult, he translated the song lyrics. 'Đố Ai' belongs to a rich era of Vietnamese music that has been obscured and sometimes forgotten. Songs from this era tell stories of war and love.

Music does not start when we hit play, nor does it end when we hit stop. There are things to be read beyond what's legible, to be heard beyond what can be heard, to be seen beyond what is visible. As Trinh T. Minh-ha reminds us: 'Music is neither sound nor silence. It is contained in each and encompasses both; invisible and intangible by nature, it is especially effective in bringing forth the tangible and the visible.'[4]

4 T.T. Minh-ha, 'Holes in the Sound Wall' (1985), in *When the Moon Waxes Red: Representation, Gender and Cultural Politics*, London: Routledge, 1991, p.203.

Precarious Solidarities: An Việt and Artists for Democracy

When we went to meet Wing Chan and David Morris at Afterall's office in London at King's Cross, accompanied by Cường's son Xuân An, we were not sure what to expect. Cường had suggested we walk and talk, as a way of getting his son to sleep. David and Wing said a walk was also a good way to see what gentrification had done to the local area and economy. We spent about an hour walking, talking and interacting with the local environment as we thought about our work with two fragmented and precarious archives, of the An Việt Foundation and Artists for Democracy (AFD). It was a cold and rainy November day.

Once Xuân An had dozed off, we gathered in a corner of the Lethaby Gallery at Central Saint Martins as Wing and David shared some of the research they had gathered. One of the documents really sprung out at us: a review by Annabel Nicolson of a performance by David Toop and Paul Burwell ahead of AFD's

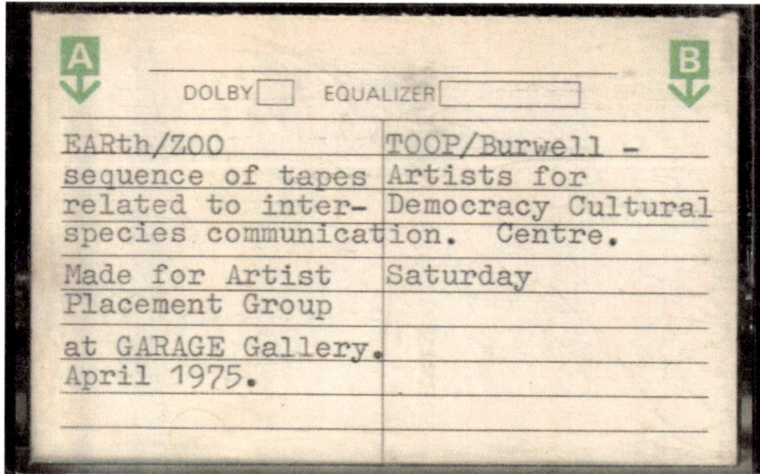

Cassette tape liner notes for David Toop's recording of his performance with Paul Burwell at Artists for Democracy, 1975

arts festival 'People of the World Learn From Indochina, Homage to Ho Chi Minh and the Victory of the Indochinese Peoples' in 1975. We were particularly intrigued the concluding lines:

> Very physical sounds occupy the performance and David taps quietly on the silver parts of a white flute. He also did a strange breathing into the flute causing sounds to transform. Everything is suspended in thin air. They pack up, sliding flutes into cloth bags as if they were fishing rods and someone asks where they learnt Vietnamese music.[5]

Their performance for voice, strings, flute and slides was dedicated to the 'distinguished scholar of Vietnamese music' Trần Văn Khê and introduced by a quote from the poem 'Jiu Ge / The Nine Songs / 九歌' in the collection *Chu Ci / Songs of the South*, attributed to Qu Yuan. Trần Văn Khê was a musicologist, writer, teacher and performer of traditional music who wrote the influential publication *La musique viêtnamienne traditionnelle*, published in 1962 in Paris, where he worked as a professor at the Sorbonne. Here again, via Trinh T. Minh-ha, we find more entangled trajectories:

> While in Paris [...] one of the happy encounters I made was with noted Vietnamese scholar and musician Trần Văn Khê, who continues until today to shuttle to and fro between France and Vietnam for his research, and with whom I studied ethnomusicology. That's the part that I got the most out of in Paris. So you go to Paris, finally to learn ethnomusicology with a Vietnamese (*laughter*).[6]

AFD's festival for Vietnam in the summer of 1975 included many well-known songs, listed in the programme as poems, and used by the DRV to promote the war effort. One song that stands out is 'Giải phóng Miền nam' ('Liberate the South'). Written in the style of a march, this was the official anthem of the National Liberation Front (NLF, colloquially known as the Viet Cong). It encouraged comrades to

> Rise up, [heroic people of the South!]
> Rise and face the tempest of our revolution!
> We pledge our lives to save our country,
> And we'll fight to the very end.
> Forward, advance, with swords and guns in hand.

5 Annabel Nicolson, 'Paul Burwell and David Toop at Artists For Democracy', *MUSICS*, no.5, 1975.

6 N.N. Chen, 'Speaking Nearby', *op. cit.*, p.84.

Songs such as 'Giải phóng Miền nam' were adopted by anti-war protest movements around the world, in many different versions and translations. Turning to his record collection, Cường found versions of this song in Swedish and German and in compilations across Europe and Latin America. We wondered how a track like this was able to proliferate? We started following some of the routes of dissemination of these records, to map how experimental musicians in London might have learned about Vietnamese music.

One record that could account for the transmission of some of these songs to London is an EP released in 1970 that features 'Quốc ca Việt Nam' ('Vietnamese National Anthem'). Composed by Văn Cao in 1944 and titled 'Tiến Quân Ca' ('The Marching Song'), the national anthem of the DRV would become, as of 1976, also the national anthem of the unified Socialist Republic of Vietnam. On the same EP is 'Giải phóng Miền nam' ('Liberating the South'), the anthem of the NLF. Turning the record over we can see that it was published by Dihavina (Đĩa Hát Việt Nam), a state label of DRV before reunification in 1975. Although based in Hanoi, much of their vinyl was pressed in the former Czechoslovakia, Hungary and elsewhere in the USSR. Cường's Vietnamese tutor, Dương Thu Hương (not the dissident author), told us that these songs were played at public events and via public speaker systems across

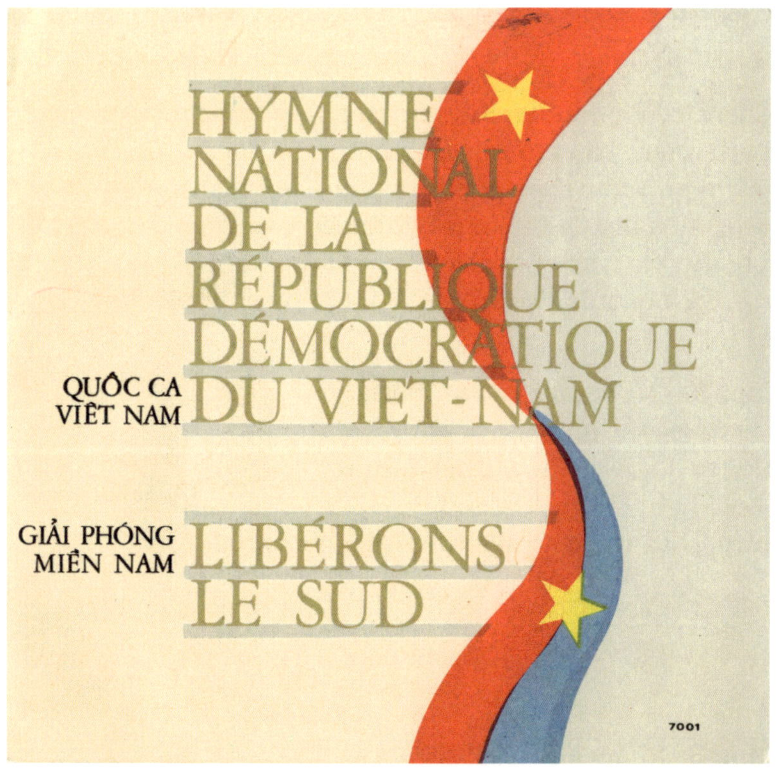

From the record collection of Cường Minh Bá Phạm

Vietnam (*loa phường*). Therefore, the general Vietnamese public did not really buy them. Much of the music they released was known as *nhạc đỏ* (red music), a genre developed in early twentieth century with socialist and anti-imperialist lyrics combined with elements of Western classical music. On the album's cover, 'Quốc ca Việt Nam' is placed at the top and superimposed on the DRV flag, which features a yellow star on a red background. 'Giải phóng Miền nam' appears on top of the NLF flag, which features a yellow star on a blue and red background. Suggesting a strong political symbiosis, the flags are conjoined in the shape of an S, the geographical shape of modern Vietnam.

Trần Văn Khê's *Musique Du Viet-Nam*, released by Disques Bam in 1959, features two rather different sets of recordings. The A side features studio recordings of traditional songs interpreted by Trần Văn Khê with Mai Thu and Mme Mong Trung, while the B side features field recordings made in 1955 in Vietnam amongst Jarai, Maa, Bahnar and Dié peoples. The recordings were supported by the Centre d'Etude des Musiques Orientales (Center for the Study of Oriental Music) at the École des hautes etudes en sciences sociales (School for Advanced Studies in the Social Sciences) in Paris. Elsewhere other clues could be found in Cường's collection. Some records feature handwritten diacritics added to the printed text. These are records that lived internationally. A message is written on the cover of one: 'Paris 25-12-61, Men Tang chau KIM-ANH. TonTon' ('Paris 25-12-61, lovingly gifted to my niece/nephew Kim-Anh, from Uncle').[7] A gift, given on Christmas Day in Paris. On another, a postage stamp is stuck to the sleeve, evidence that the record's packaging was used as an envelope. Who sent it? Why send it?

In April 1975, when the DRV troops rolled into Saigon, one of the first things they did was to take control of Saigon Radio to make a special broadcast. Listeners heard Trịnh Công Sơn, a well-known pacifist singer-songwriter, singing a famous song preaching unity: 'Nối vòng tay lớn' ('To connect hands in a big circle'). As we extend our search, we see how the revolutionary songs of Vietnam spread. We are led to the Chilean record *Por Vietnam* by Quilapayún, a folk group that went into exile in France following the military coup. In 1968, the Communist Youth Party of Chile pressed 1,000 copies of the album to raise funds for Quilapayún's travel to the International Youth Festival in Bulgaria. The record unexpectedly sold out, and in response, La Jota,

7 *TonTon* here is the French word for 'uncle', which suggests a blood tie. Whereas in Vietnamese there are two words for uncle, *bác* and *chú*, which can instead refer to quasi-family and are used as pronouns.

the communist youth group, created Discoteca del Cantar Popular (DICAP), a socially conscious record label that grew in just five years from a 4,000-record operation in 1968 to pressing over 240,000 records in 1973. As we move further, we find the record *England's Vietnam: Irish Songs of Resistance: Sung by The Men of No Property*, released on Folkways Records in 1977.

From AFD's Jun Terra we also hear how songs for Vietnam travelled to the Philippines, via the United States, to be sung at demonstrations; how he composed new protest songs in Tagalog based on revolutionary songs from China, as part of his involvement in the cultural bureau of the communist youth organisation Kabataang Makabayan; and how these songs circulated in the Philippines and beyond.

> In order to have lively, snappy marching songs for the demos I composed four songs. Makibaka, Linyang Pangmasa, Ang Masa and Magbangon ka Aking Bayan. [...] The first three songs became popular as they were easy to sing. The last one, Magbangon ka Aking Bayan, structured more like a traditional song with an introductory slow, lyrical section and a rousing second section part, did not catch on. A solidarity group in Oakland, California made a recording of the first three songs sung by a chorus and accompanied by a rondelle. The group sent me a copy of the record (LP) sometime between 1972–74, which I lost in my moving around in Europe.[8]

Thinking about how the protest songs for Vietnam are connected to the An Việt Foundation, we can see immediately that these are inherently all creations of conflict at different degrees of proximity; or, to draw on scholar Lisa Lowe, they reflect different intimacies across continents. They put us in mind of Edward Said's description of exile as 'irremediably secular and unbearably historical ... like death but without death's ultimate mercy, it has torn millions of people from the nourishment of tradition, family and geography.'[9] What is distinct about these types of dissemination is that they have all created means of community and gathering that sit outside of the reach of the state.

Revisiting the cassette recording of his performance with Paul Burwell at the AFD space in 1975, David Toop reflected: 'When I came to listen to the tape I found that it had seriously deteriorated. Listening to it feels like eavesdropping on history, the act of listening accelerating the sense of temporal distance, decay, loss,

8 Jun Terra, correspondence with David Morris and Wing Chan, 28 April 2023.

9 Edward Said, 'Reflections on Exile', in *Reflections on Exile: And Other Literary and Cultural Essays*, London: Granta Books, 2001, p.174.

facing page: Selections from the record collection of Cường Minh Bá Phạm

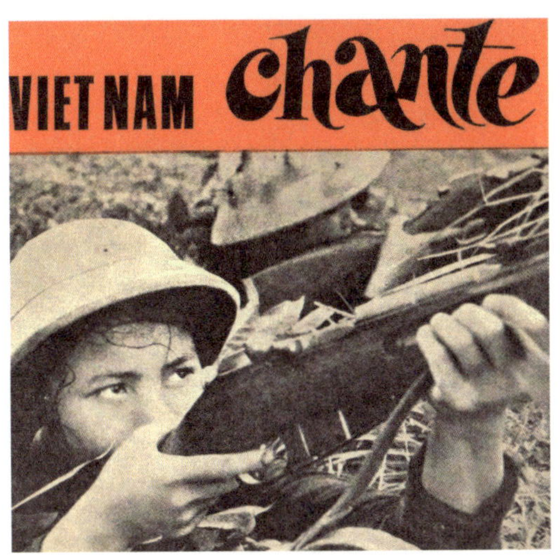
VIET NAM chante

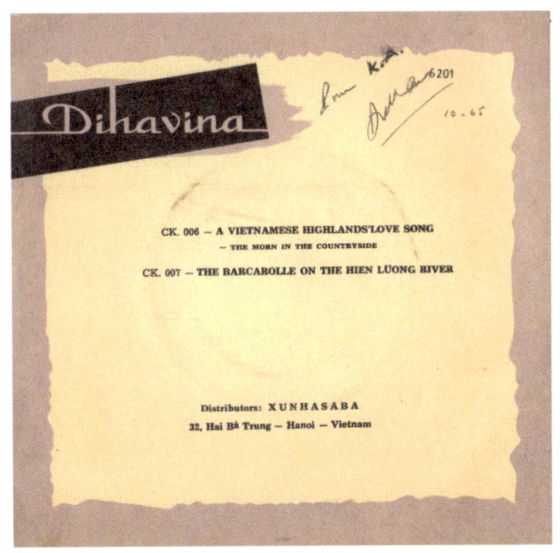
Dihavina
CK. 006 – A VIETNAMESE HIGHLANDS'LOVE SONG
– THE MORN IN THE COUNTRYSIDE
CK. 007 – THE BARCAROLLE ON THE HIEN LÜONG RIVER
Distributors: XUNHASABA
32, Hai Bà Trung – Hanoi – Vietnam

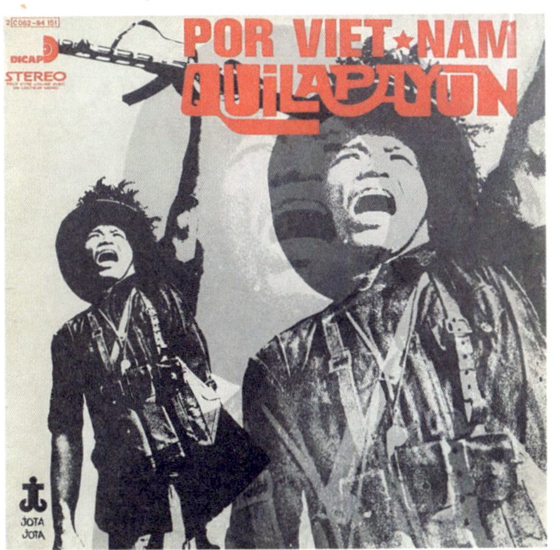
POR VIET★NAM
QUILAPAYUN
DICAP
STEREO
JOTA JOTA

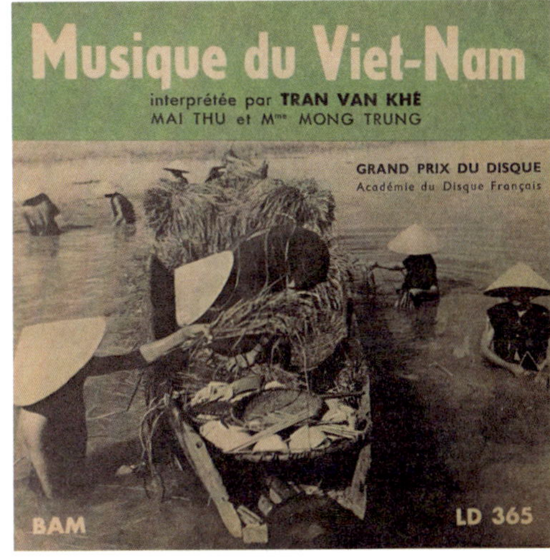
Musique du Viet-Nam
interprétée par TRAN VAN KHÊ
MAI THU et Mme MONG TRUNG
GRAND PRIX DU DISQUE
Académie du Disque Français
BAM
LD 365

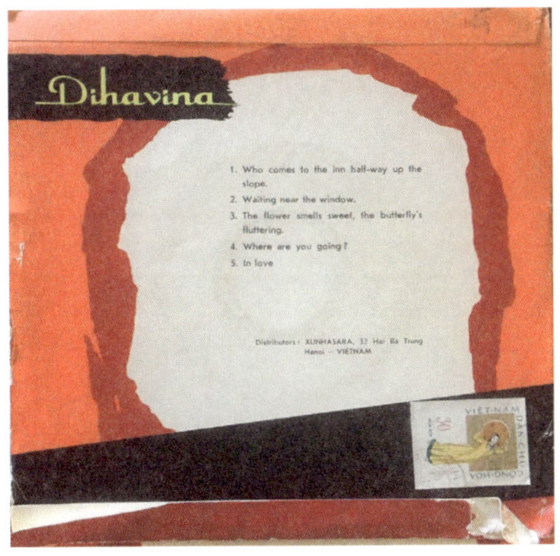
Dihavina
1. Who comes to the inn half-way up the slope.
2. Waiting near the window.
3. The flower smells sweet, the butterfly's fluttering.
4. Where are you going?
5. In love
Distributors: XUNHASABA, 32 Hai Ba Trung
Hanoi – VIETNAM

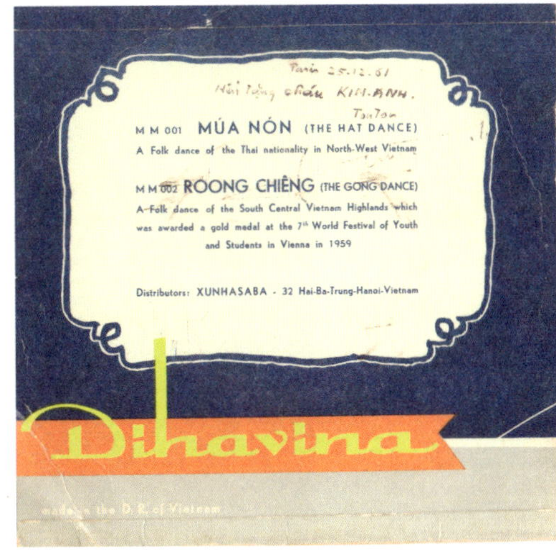
MM 001 MÚA NÓN (THE HAT DANCE)
A Folk dance of the Thai nationality in North-West Vietnam
MM 002 ROONG CHIÊNG (THE GONG DANCE)
A Folk dance of the South Central Vietnam Highlands which was awarded a gold medal at the 7th World Festival of Youth and Students in Vienna in 1959
Distributors: XUNHASABA - 32 Hai-Ba-Trung-Hanoi-Vietnam
Dihavina

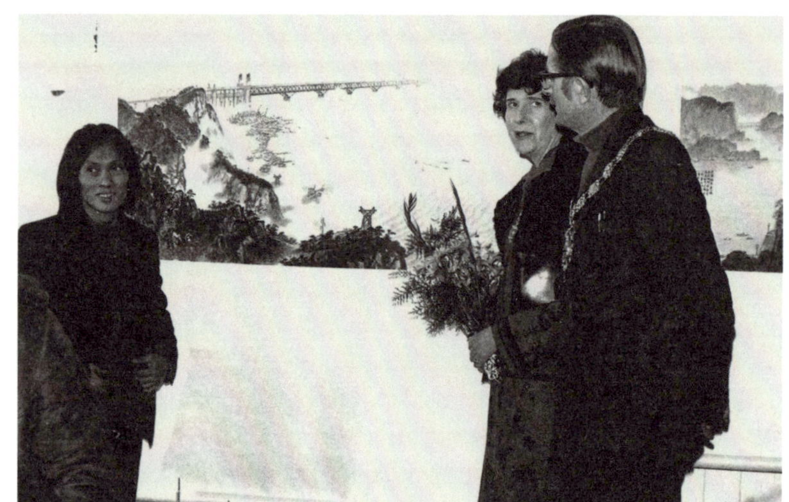

David Medalla with the Lord Mayor of Westminster at Artists for Democracy's 'China Show', 143 Whitfield Street, 1976

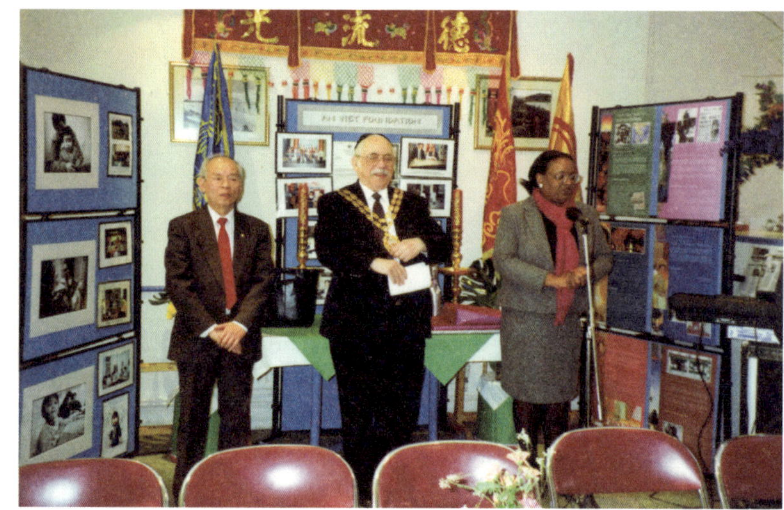

Joe Lobenstein, Mayor of Hackney (1997–2001), with Vũ Khánh Thành (left) and Diane Abbott, Member of Parliament for Hackney, at An Việt Foundation

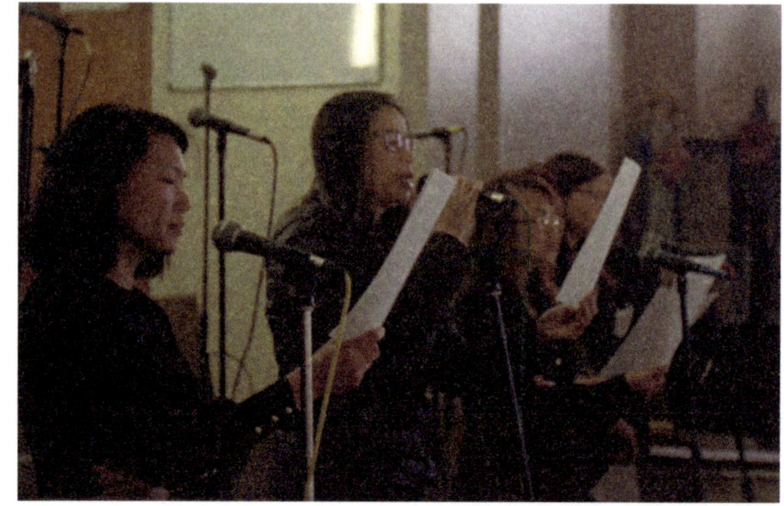

Graduates from the An Việt Training for Nails course closed their shops to sing at the funeral for Vũ khánh Thành at Vietnamese Church London in Poplar, 12 May 2022

eventual erasure.'[10] When we asked how he came to know Vietnamese music, he outlined the various channels at the time – from his work as manager of the record department at the bookseller Dillons on Malet Street, around the corner from AFD, to how Paul and he became fellows of the Royal Anthropological Society, to a rare 1972 concert by Trần Văn Khê's son Trần Quang Hải, organised by Jane Jenkins at the Horniman Museum in Southeast London. These elements informed the improvised music he was making with Burwell; but, more than this, the spaces of AFD and other organisations of the time allowed for many types of dialogue and exploration of what Trần Quang Hải advocated as a 'trans-global improvisation'. Spaces such as AFD allowed artistic groups to 'become a recognisable community and to connect to other recognisable communities'. Reflecting on the continued importance of space in the hostile environment of contemporary London, Toop referred back to Cafe Oto in Hackney, where we met in early June 2023 to hold our conversation – not ten minutes' walk from the former AVF building. 'If this place disappeared, the whole scene changes dramatically for the worse. Everything gets atomised. People lose. So much comes from the social stuff,' Toop said.

As we follow the intersection of various individuals and communities through these entangled and unfolding histories, the many stories still to be unearthed and told, we come back again to the types of communion enabled through song and the importance of the linkages the sonic enables, which reverberate across space and time. As we think about this, we are brought back to asking: What is the sound of a group? What are the sounds left behind, and what sounds can be brought with us?

10 David Toop, correspondence with D. Morris, 6 November 2022.

Listen to the soundtrack compiled by Cường Minh Bá Phạm:
www.mixcloud.com/Phambinho/everything-is-suspended-in-thin-air

'We are going to win': On Artists for Democracy and the 1970s Conjuncture[1]

Vijay Prashad

1 This text is based on Vijay Prashad's conversation with David Morris and Wing Chan on 25 March 2023 for the purposes of this publication.

Coming together in this project, Artists for Democracy (AFD), we see a clash between two of the great social processes of the twentieth century. One of the great social processes is, of course, the decolonisation wave, which started in the 1940s and is continuing. The 1970s was a decade of great contestation. It's not that people lived feeling like 'these are the last years of our aspirations', that these are the last years of decolonisation. After all, in '74, there's the Carnation Revolution, and the Portuguese colonies in Africa are liberated. Amílcar Cabral's dream, even though he'd been assassinated, comes to fruition. In 1975, the Americans have to flee from Vietnam. At that time, people thought, 'We are going to win' – the Vietnamese are going to win, the Palestinians are going to win, the people in Southern Rhodesia are going to win, Kenneth Kaunda is going to come to power. In that period, they actually thought, 'We're going to win, everywhere.'

This is why the coup in Chile is so significant – it's a coup against the Third World, openly backed by the United States, at a time when all these victories were getting ready to happen. In the mid-1960s, three coups take place in very quick succession – Brazil, Indonesia and Ghana, in '64, '65 and '66. But by then a new momentum sets in – and now we get to the second great social process, which is the uprisings of 1968. Remember that '68 was a global uprising – not just in art colleges in the UK, in Columbia University in New York and so on. In Pakistan, the student rebellion brought down the government – that never happened in the UK! So the second great social process is '68. There were great student rebellions in Mexico, in Brazil, across the world. And the coups that had happened in Brazil, Indonesia and Ghana allowed for a sober assessment that the decolonisation process was in danger of being crushed. I think the 1968 uprising also produced amnesia for what had happened before, which is why the '73 coup in Chile evoked such a response from people around the world. There was no such uproar, no such wave of solidarity for Indonesia in '65, or for Ghana in '66. I mean, Ghana was a British colony. Why didn't London explode with rage at the coup in Ghana? This didn't happen for Brazil, Indonesia or Ghana. And Chile is a tiny country by comparison. In my opinion, the reason Chile in '73 produced such a response has a lot to do with the jubilation of the generation of '68. So there were these two great social processes that come together, the decolonisation process and then the post-'68 sensibility – a bit of hippie, a bit of radical adventurism, a bit of great sincerity toward people who are struggling around the world – and it's these two processes that generate this moment, the moment of Artists for Democracy, 1974 to 1977.

Regarding the sociology of the time, these are generations of people who are not allowing their lives to become fully commodified. An interesting feature of this seam of revolutionary art – let's call it – is that it's about ideas. Take Chile as an example. It's interesting that AFD started with that cause. Because art was crucial, all over the place during the Popular Unity government led by President Salvador Allende. So somebody like Cecilia Vicuña, she's arriving in London, she has her politics and she wants to say something. Her poetry is very powerful and beautiful – to me, she's like the parallel of Raúl Zurita, who operated in the Americas. Post-'68, there are new artistic vocabularies, which you can see in the work of the Organization of Solidarity with the People of Asia, Africa and Latin America [OSPAAAL], founded in Havana after the first Tricontinental Conference in 1966. A kind of psychedelic revolutionary portraiture emerges, displacing the earlier social realism. You see this in Santiago Álvarez's film *79 primaveras* (*79 Springtimes of Ho Chi Minh*, 1969). Or the amazing poster art and mural art from Chile that is then exported through the Chilean solidarity movement. I think there's a great underestimation of the role of the Third World in breakthroughs in poster and mural aesthetics, and what this then does to the use of colour in the advanced industrial countries. The context also helps us understand the kind of urgency in the art, and the forms of artistry that develop from this sense of urgency. That skill is learned in practice – a lot of people who are getting involved in this struggle find out that they are artists, one way or the other. And this sensibility among revolutionary artists continues. These projects don't die away with neoliberalism.

It's interesting to consider the name 'Artists for Democracy'. If you read Ho Chi Minh in the 1960s and 70s, for instance, he uses a phrase that would be quaint today: the 'camp of peace'. He says, 'The camp of peace is expanding.' What he means is socialism – the socialist camp is the camp of peace. And the capitalist camp is a camp of war. I still find this to be a really good description of reality, frankly. But let's look at the use of the word 'peace'. It sounds so anachronistic today. Now consider 'democracy'. The United States invested a lot in this term, especially from the 1990s onwards. They create a National Endowment for Democracy in 1983, a government-funded entity, and they start 'promoting democracy' around the world. They divide the world into 'authoritarian' and 'democratic' countries. So 'democracy' refers to any country where there's an election and where the elected government is pro-US. 'Democracy' is quite an ordinary word, you know, it's not such a grand word. And it's given too much meaning by the United States – they invest too much meaning in it, because it's a complicated process of democracy. In a sense, they take it away from humanity.

Before the United States' big project of reinscribing the term 'democracy' with this kind of strange meaning, it was a contested word – people were contesting the idea and the practice of democracy. The word was being used politically, because even in the 1960s and 70s, the West was saying that the Eastern Bloc was not democratic. But the term more commonly used was 'freedom'. So you have the CIA-funded Congress for Cultural Freedom, an 'artists for freedom' initiative, if you like. At this time it is very unlikely that a group of the left will use the term 'freedom' so loosely, because it had such a density of meaning – it meant somehow the free West, whereas the rest of the world had no freedom. But at this time the term 'democracy' was a term of contest – there was a coup in Chile in September 1973 against the democratically elected government of Salvador Allende. So to be 'for democracy', clearly, is to protest the military coup. At the time, the majority of these anti-democratic overthrows were conducted by the West. Hungary and Czechoslovakia are the two examples of Soviet intervention, but the bulk happened with Western backing – Iran, Guatemala, Congo, Argentina, El Salvador, Indonesia, Brazil, Ghana, Pakistan… The list goes on. So when a group says, 'We are artists for democracy', what they mean is, 'We are artists against coup d'état' – or maybe, 'artists against imperialism' – much more than, say, 'artists for socialism'. They were more united in terms of what they were against, rather than what they were for – which is a limitation of 'united front' platforms. Why didn't this group call themselves 'artists against imperialism'? They made a very good tactical decision, I would guess. It would have been an error at the time to say 'artists against imperialism' or 'artists for socialism' – I would have argued against it. 'Artists for democracy' I would have argued for. Why? Because it's the perfect united front vehicle. It's not a sectarian grouping. I mean, I don't know any of them in terms of their specific personalities or affiliations. But the term certainly seems historically accurate.

AFD's identification as 'cultural workers' also deserves consideration. It reflects a greater sense of proletarian consciousness. It's often forgotten that the '68 generation was not just students, it was also workers – you've got all the trade union struggles. And by the 1970s in the UK there are strikes upon strikes taking place; those governments of the late 1960s and early 70s were struggling to manage capitalism. Labour as it is moved rightward, in a way, after the General Strike of '26. In the 1970s the Labour left was pretty strong. But still they struggle – why? Because there was cascading working-class struggle with strikes upon strikes upon strikes, which is difficult to control and manage. That's what it was like in that period, in the late 60s up to the oil shock of '73. So there was a kind of proletarian consciousness. It's no surprise that they would use the term 'cultural workers' rather than 'artists'. Also, it's likely that many of them were only beginning to discover that they might be artists.

The term 'artist' in the West is a curious term. It comes with all kinds of bourgeois trappings – that you have to go to art school, that you have a gallery showing, that you have a kind of individual perspective. It's you and your soul and, you know, the genius. And there is a way in which the term 'artist' is subordinated to – a kind of traditional institutionalizing of your practice. Whereas, looking at the stickers that AFD produced, for example... The technology at the time of actually making stickers was not that difficult, because you could actually buy the paper. I think sticker paper comes in the 60s, mass-produced, among other technologies that allow this kind of 'guerrilla art', as some people used to call it. I don't think it's guerilla art. I just think it's public art. And that decommodification or anti-commodification art continues, with young people using the many various forms of public expression that have emerged online, making memes and so on. And if 'artist' means a proscenium, a gallery show, we might consider this alternative approach as a kind of street theatre performance. In India, it's called Nukkad Natak, corner theatre, the theatre of the corner. It's different from the proscenium, with a different consciousness of the craft. The term 'international' is also interesting in 'international cultural workers'. It may just be accurate, because there are so many exiles, from the US, from Chile, from Philippines – here, there, everywhere. But maybe also they were indicating 'international' as a perspective. It's just a description of reality, since there were people from all over, and their perspective was international.

Some of the structural features you can't replicate. The fact that the AFD group moved into a squat, for instance, is an important difference between then and now. Neoliberalism really stole this possibility. Squatting has become harder, given municipal control over property. In London, the wretched Metropolitan Police will be on you in a minute. So the actual structure of creating a group is, in a sense, taken away from younger people. In fact, young people often don't have places to meet in most parts of the world. Because meeting places are commodified. There's no community centre, you know. It changes a little bit about the institutional practice of these groups of cultural workers. So now your practice has to change. Cities have become hard for people to do the kind of art that could have been done in earlier times. I think we need to register that. That's why I think a lot of young people have taken to online spaces. Because it's harder to do it in many cities around the world.

The idea of festival was very common in the left culture, very common around the world. In Chile, there is the *peña*, a kind of gathering where you have a tent and you bring a bunch of people in – say, artists – and it's like a circus almost. You'd play music and you'd have, like, an ensemble show. It comes through Violeta Parra and the Parra family, who absorbed the idea from older, Indigenous forms. And this was taken up by the young artists of the Popular Unity government. They would hold these in cafés, of course – they would play in left wing cafés in Santiago, in Valparaíso and so on. But these kinds of things were happening in many places. The Soviets had festivals all over the world – the World Festival of Youth and Students, connected with the World Federation of Democratic Youth. The tenth was in East Berlin, in 1973. And there were also regional ones, and so on. Anyway, the point of the festival is a very key idea. Of course, there are music festivals as well. But what was different about the left festivals was they were not just about music. They were about visual art. They were about political speeches. They were about political education workshops, artistic workshops. It had a circus feel to it. There's a lot of things happening, you know. Now, obviously, like at Woodstock, there were a lot of things happening, but it was mainly the stage. And you are mainly a spectator, watching the stage.

What's interesting in these left festivals is not about being a spectator. You went to listen to small workshops, you signed petitions, you could go and start making posters – there's a lot of participatory activity. And I think that comes to us as an inheritance from the left. It is very important that it was not just procedural activity, in other words. And I know that in Chile, that was very much there – getting people to participate.

It was around this time that Augusto Boal, the great dramaturge, coined the term 'spect-actor'. He says that we don't want to create a spectacle for spectators, we want to create 'spect-actors', where you come to watch but you perform in a way, you have to be a part of it. And I think these festivals are designed around spectactors. As they say, in Spanish, *mas o menos*, because it's not always the case ... But looking at this project [*Eskimo Carver*, 1977, by David Medalla[2]], is a great example of this spect-actor idea. This is not like a workshop. This is the art itself. And you get to do it and make it. I'm hugely sympathetic to this kind of practice. Because I think it's interesting to involve people, so they feel they are also participants in history. So much of bourgeois institutionalisation is about making you feel like you're a bystander. This actually changes your approach.

Looking at photographs from the 'People of the World Learn From Indochina'[3] festival/exhibition – what's the difference between this and a standard gallery installation? So I walk into this room – obviously, the picture does no justice to it – and I am transported, just for a second, to Vietnam and to a little revolutionary camp. And that small sensation of the extraordinary comes into me. In fact, isn't that the purpose of an installation? It's to, for a moment, give you a feeling of being somewhere else. So this is pretty extraordinary in that sense. I can't imagine being an eighteen-year-old walking into this room. Extraordinary. And in that sense, I would just say, picking up on the pedagogical aspect, that the pedagogy is also emotional. It's not just what you read on the wall, right? There is the battle of ideas, but then there's the battle of emotions. And the battle of emotions is often neglected in our thinking. There's a pedagogy of emotion, which is very, very important. The pedagogy of emotion I've always felt is the purpose of something like this. It should transport you.

2 David Medalla's *Eskimo Carver*, presented at 143 Whitfield Street, 1–30 May 1977. See the AFD archive section in this volume, pp.286–91.

3 'People of the World Learn from Indochina, Homage to Ho Chi Minh and the Victory of The Indochinese Peoples', 143 Whitfield Street, 13 July – 9 August 1975. See the AFD archive section in this volume, pp.214–24.

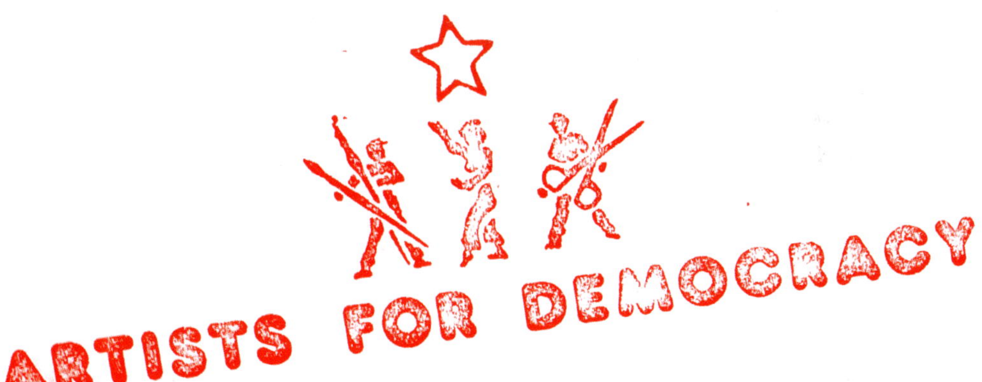
ARTISTS FOR DEMOCRACY

VOICES FROM ARTISTS FOR DEMOCRACY

Artists for Democracy is a story of many. Gathered in this section are perspectives from a number of its participants, including Rasheed Araeen, Conrad Atkinson, Anne Bean, Guy Brett, Virgil Calaguian, Hugh Cave, Stephen Cripps, John Dugger, Rose English, Charles Hustwick, Tina Keane, Roberta Kravitz, Lynn MacRitchie, Kathleen McCreery, David Medalla, Jonathan Miles, Ife Nii Owoo, Nii Kwate Owoo, Nick Payne, Stephen Pusey, Saleem Arif Quadri, Steve Sprung, Sylvia Stevens, Jun Terra, Anna Thew, Giles Thomas, Cecilia Vicuña

Interviews with participants for publication in the present book were conducted between 2021 and 2023. These are supplemented with previously published material from various sources (see pp.328–29).

‘Arts Festival for Democracy in Chile’, Royal College of Art, 14–30 October 1974

Artists for Democracy space opens at 143 Whitfield Street, January 1975

'Inaugural Show', 31 January – 6 February 1975
Tina Keane, ‘Conversation Future Tense’, 7–17 February 1975
Lynn MacRitchie, ‘The World in a Grain of Sand’, 2–19 March 1975
Guy Brett, ‘Fruits of the Earth in Decorative Art’, 2–19 March 1975
Rasheed Araeen, ‘Works 1959–1975’, 23 March – 9 April 1975
Peter Cross, ‘Net’, 23 March – 9 April 1975
‘Victory to People's War’, 6 May – 1 June 1975
‘Living Words, Living Images: Festival of Progressive Poetry and Art’, 8 June – 10 July 1975
Bertha Husband, ‘Murals, Images of Women’, 8 June – 10 July 1975
‘People of the World Learn from Indochina, Homage to Ho Chi Minh and the Victory of the Indochinese Peoples’, 13 July – 9 August 1975
John Heartfield, posters and photomontages, December 1975
‘China Show’, 8 February – 7 March 1976
Virgil Calaguian, Hugh Cave and Stephen Cripps, 26 March – 25 April 1976
Stephen Cripps, 26 March – 23 May 1976
Giles Thomas, June 1976
Virgil Calaguian and Steve Oxley, ‘On Meat & Metaphysics, of mice & men’, 13 June – 12 July 1976
‘The End of an Era: Hand in Life and Art’, 25 July – 25 September 1976
London Calling Arts Festival, various venues, 7–27 September 1976
‘American Indian Movement 1976 Exhibition’, 25 September 1976 – 25 January 1977
Caroline Tisdall, ‘Joseph Beuys’ Coyote’, April–May 1977
David Medalla, ‘Eskimo Carver’, 1–30 May 1977
‘Vernacular Art in Camden', 12 June – 7 August 1977
Anne Cloudsley, ‘Women of Sudan Omdurman’, 10 July – 7 August 1977
‘Final Show’, 3 July – 6 August 1977

Any account of Artists for Democracy is bound to be partial. The above list includes only the known exhibitions and festivals organised by the group between 1974 and 1977; the pages that follow gather fragments from these and the many other events, performances, meetings and activities that took place under the banner of AFD.

Artists for Democracy formed in London in the spring of 1974. Its founding document – signed by Guy Brett, Hugh Cave, John Dugger, David Medalla, Stephen Pusey and Cecilia Vicuña – states its intention as ‘a broad front organisation of artists, art critics, art historians and other cultural workers including art students, film-makers, graphic designers and others, with the expressed aim of giving real and active support to liberation struggles all over the world, particularly in the Third World countries of Asia, Africa and Latin America’. Roles were formalised: Medalla as chairman; Brett as secretary; Vicuña and Dugger as festival coordinators.

Artists for Democracy [AFD] aimed to combine this participatory philosophy of art and organisation with actual support, 'material and cultural', to 'liberation struggles throughout the world'. ... We were aware of the activities of groups in the US such as Art Workers Coalition, Artists Meeting for Cultural Change, groups in which black, Hispanic and native American artists were represented (AMCC produced the memorable *Anti-catalogue* for the exhibit of the Rockefeller Collection in 1977, exposing the official catalogue's cultural, race and class bias). AFD had a turbulent history. Some artists left to form new groups of their own, such as the Poster Collective (Jonathan Miles, Sylvia Stevens, Steve Sprung). But it seems to me that, in its three-year existence, AFD played two roles; it was one of the few artists' groups to concern itself with the relationship between the First and Third Worlds and to demonstrate the indivisibility of cultural and political questions in that relationship ... [a]nd AFD provided young artists of different nationalities with a space for early experiments in what later flourished as the movements of performance, installation and video (these included essays into autobiography and identity, such as the Irish artist Sonia Knox's performance *Echoes of the Earth*, Tina Keane's *Shadow Woman*, Bertha Husband's *Doors*, [David] Medalla's series *Reciprokal Didactiks* with Oriol de Quadras and Nick Payne, the Italian artist Gennaro Telero's *Performance*, etc.). In the late 1970s there was a kind of interchange between artists at the main foci for experiment: Gallery House, AFD, Acme, Mayfair Illuminations. As an outcome or accompaniment of all these complex currents, life vitalised art in new structures of the 'real'. In the activist 70s, the social sciences (political science, sociology, anthropology, psychology, linguistics) interested artists in the way the physical sciences had in the kinetic 60s. Works that stay in my memory are 'life materials' configured, illuminated, by investigative, participatory or deconstructive frameworks.

Guy Brett

We were at the beginning of the Do-It-Yourself era. In terms of study, I was in a *Kapital* reading group, a Freud reading group, so we worked hard. We took our politics extremely seriously on every level. We did it for real in the real world, as feminists, trade unionists, activists of all kinds, but we also wanted to learn. There seemed to be so much to learn. That's one of the things that I was relieved to find when I arrived in London – I was instantly included in all manner of critical discussions at a very high level, which I was thrilled by and very keen to contribute to. This kind of self-learning and constant discussion was important. You didn't sit on your own and do your project, you did it with your friends, with your colleagues or your comrades, because it was important. We wanted to understand, wanted to base our politics on something solid, such as personal experience and activism – now people call it activism, in those days it would be called political activism, that's a crucial distinction in the use of language, because that would involve taking part in demonstrations, learning, and learning from doing.

Lynn MacRitchie

AFD, as its name makes clear, was a group of artists animated by the practice of democracy in its broadest sense, as applied to art, politics and life in general. It was never a 'collective project' or a choir singing from the same hymn book. That would have been the end of autonomy, diversity, of multifacetedness, of [the] inventiveness upon which art thrives. Every member had his/her own, individual set of ideas that criss-crossed, met at some points, contradicted, intertwined, opposed one another, etc. There were no assigned 'roles', at least not in a bureaucratically structured way, when preparing for shows or even festivals. Everything was hands-on and members helped in their own time and in their own way.

Jun Terra

ARTS FESTIVAL for CHILEAN RESISTANCE

ganised by Artists for Democracy

at the ROYAL COLLEGE of ART

Kensington Gore SW7

OCT 14 to NOV 1

USIC · DANCE · THEATRE · FOOD · BOOKS

· CHILD ... 'S EVENTS · INTERNATIONAL

ENTS · MIME · POSTERS

HE FESTIVAL —

SOLIDARITY

Conrad [Atkinson] made this invitation [to a discussion at his show 'Work, Wages and Prices', Institute of Contemporary Arts (ICA), 1974]. I found an article in *The Guardian* written by Caroline Tisdall, published in April '74. And there is a photo where I am there in the group. And the situation was this: They were speaking about wages and how much artists should get from the galleries. And I was in the audience, I was just one of maybe sixty to eighty artists, there was a big crowd there. And suddenly, I stood up, and I said, 'Excuse me, I'm going to change the subject. There's a military coup in Chile, artists are being persecuted. What are we going to do about that?' And that was the catalyst. So also in the audience, maybe five or six lines behind me, were sitting three people. And these were Guy Brett, David Medalla and John Dugger. So they sent a little note to me, saying, 'Let's meet outside.' And that's how AFD began.

Cecilia Vicuña

It was part of an intensely political period in London and the arts. There was much criticism from the right of my exhibition ['Strike at Brannans'] at the ICA in 1972 saying art and politics should remain separate. Artists for Democracy invited me as the first honorary member at my solo exhibition discussion in 'Work, Wages and Prices' about Art and Politics, where I think [Cecilia Vicuña] and John Dugger and David Medalla connected first. Then what Artists for Democracy did was to introduce another element; (women and working class issues had already been developed by '74/'75) the revolutionary politics of South America, and in a sense prompted the Artists Union to march in the Chile Solidarity Campaign. ... [Dugger's] banner was painted in my house in Peckham. Also I think it was [Vicuña] who said at the time about the art and politics debate, 'it doesn't make sense for art not to reflect politics', or words to that effect. So Artists For Democracy reinforced that international dimension. ... We were outraged at the coup and Allende was a great inspiration to us, especially the photos of him on the steps of the Government building with a gun. The meaning of the event was like many other events in the early seventies, it was to internationalise our ideologies and reinforce many of our beliefs forged in the sixties.

Conrad Atkinson

With the sounds of the two great wings of the marching columns of demonstrators, coming in from the East by the Strand and down from the North via Charing Cross Road – their chanted slogans ringing through the streets – we laid out the numbered strips, laced them together with the top-rope, attached the rigging line and then Peter [Polish] mounted the ladder and fed the two rigging lines through the two large eyebolts already affixed to the face of the plinth. Then with two teams of dock workers grabbing the rigging lines, we hoisted the first monumental strip-banner, *Chile Vencerá*, up into the air and onto the face of Nelson's Column and made it secure. We had done it! And just at that moment, the demonstration arrived in two great waves filling the historic Trafalgar Square – carrying with them their traditional Trades Union banners, Labour Party banners, Student Union and Chile campaign banners along with the many home-made banners and flags made by the passionate supporters of a new and democratic Chile! It was a very moving sight – and an experience I shall never forget. The feat accomplished, the long hours now forgotten in the pride of having done our job as artists, held as we were to a tight and demanding deadline, the participation of so many helpers and well-wishers, and most of all, the reception by the crowd of demonstrators – who saw in this colourful rendering of Cecilia [Vicuña]'s narrative, the story of struggle and hope with which they could identify – a colourful standard to hold the attention of the world, so that for this day and this moment, we might not forget the great effort and passion of a whole nation in its darkest hour. With this one artwork, we showed how AFD must be taken seriously – and it brought in that many more artists to our cause as well as the notables and VIPs to endorse our cause and our project.

John Dugger

ARTS FESTIVAL FOR DEMOCRACY IN CHILE
organised by
ARTISTS FOR DEMOCRACY
at the Royal College of Art, London

14 October - 30 October 1974
open daily (except Sunday) 10 am to 9 pm

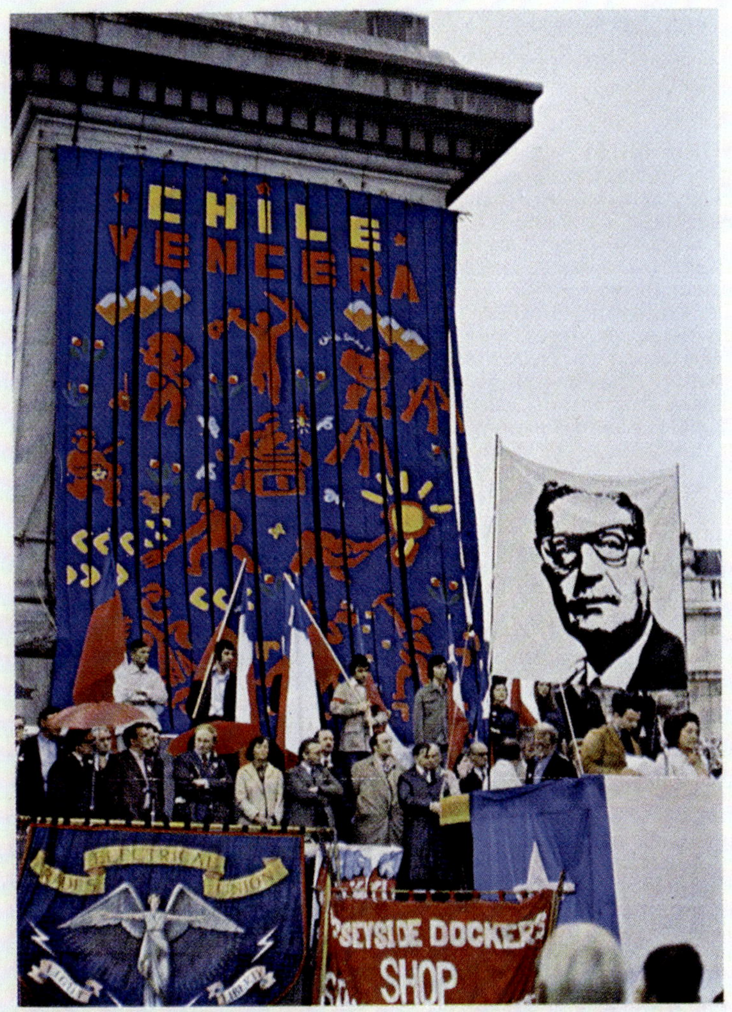

Señora Salvador Allende speaking before a mass rally in support of Chilean resistance, Trafalgar Square, London, 15 September 1974. Organised by the British Joint Labour Movement and the Chile Solidarity Campaign. In the foreground are trade union banners and in the background *Chile Vencera* banner by John Dugger of AFD

FESTIVAL SPONSORS

Señora Hortensia Bussi de Allende, Judith Hart MP, Professsor Alvaro Bunster, Harald Edelstam, Leo Abse MP, Joan Lestor MP, Professor Maurice Wilkins FRS, Sir Roland Penrose, Joris Ivens, Mary McCarthy, Constance Cummings, Joseph Losey, Peter Townsend, Edward Wright, David Sylvester, George Melly, Chile Solidarity Campaign, National Union of Students.

CULTURAL WORKERS PARTICIPATING IN THE FESTIVAL (partial list)

Adamus, AGOR-MMBA, Aijalaksoo, Albrecht D., Alley, Amiard, Atelier Lautaro, Ballet Popular Chilena, Bannerjee, Barker, Beke, Bertholo, Peter Blackman, P. Scott Blackman, Bockman, Bollar, Braden, Brett, Bruce, Calles, Caraballo, Caro, Castillo, Castro, Chen, Chissano, Christo, Cinema Action, Ciotti, Clark, Clegg, Tom Cohen, Cooke, Cortázar, Coxhead, Cummings, Libba Davies, M. Davies, del Renzio, Dewata, Donagh, Dorfman, Dugger, Eatherley, Elias, Ellin, el Razzaz, Farley, Firestone, Hervé Fischer, Fisher, Folklore Chilena, Forest, Fraire, Eric Fried, Getino, Giner, Ginsberg, Glusberg, Godard, Gonzalez, Graham, Grigg, Grogan, Guerrilla Art Action Group, Grupo de Teatro Lautaro des Volktheaters Rostock (DDR), Grupo de Trece CAYC, Gustavsson, Hartel, Vic Heath, Hendricks, Debbi Hess, Hiller, Hockney, Houédard (dsh), Howell, Hunter-Henderson, Huntley, Husband, Hussein, Immendorf, Ivens, Jayasuriya, Jones, Keane, Kennedy, Kessel, Kitaj, Kim, Knox, Kwate, Lange, Lansley, Larsen, Lee, Lek, Leggett, Lijn, Liss, Litten, Lewis, Lewitt, Limited Dance Company, Lundstrom, Donnie MacRitchie, Lynn MacRitchie, McCarthy, Manriquez, Marker, Masoero, Massip, Matsinhe, N. May, Pepe Maya, Medalla, Miles, Adrian Mitchell, Mumprecht, Muel, Hayden Murphy, Namboodiri, Nayar, Neizvetzny, Nerkner, Nightingale, Ogaz, Claes Oldenburg, Meret Oppenheim, Padín, Pearce, Pechter, Penn, Pipsi, Ponte, Potter, Prado de Caravalho, Janice Punchard, Puppet Tree, Pusey, Pye, Qabb'im, Qoakka, Rabbit Press, Rajendra, Reedy, Redfern, Red Star Puppet Theatre, Rickword, Rodriguez, Roberts, Robichet, Rosen, Andrew Salkey, Salt, Sanjines, Schwartz, Scott, Sembene, Sharkey, Sky Jacker, John Smith, Pippa Smith, Peter Smith, M. Snow, Solanas, Sosa, Sprung, Staeck, Sylvia Stevens, Stockholm Academy of Art Film Collective, Stojevic, Strausberg, Strauss, Sung Wen-Shih, Terra, Third World Troubadours, Tobas, Toche, Tozzi, Pedro Uhart, UHURU Arts Group, Ultvedt, U Maung, van Geluwe, Vicuña, Vidal, Waley, Wieland, Woolston, Wright, Xhan Duc, Yhap, Zabala, Zarate, Zorilla, Amaral, Aristia, Ariztizabal, Azocar, BBKA-Dutch Art Workers League, Batti Mamzelle, Boshiek, Bowen, Caboo, Campbell, Mario Castro, Centro Documentazione Cinema e Lotta di Classe, Chabot, Cueco, Cliff, Couzzyn, Cruz-Diez, Dooley, Dominguez, Ferreira, Fleury, Forgas, Fromanger, Gray, Grupo de la Joven Pintura, Grupo Malassi, Punita Gupta, Hammond, Hidden, Jarrett, Kiki, Kyrlitsias, Latil, Le Parc, Leverett, Martin, Martinoyo, Mesac, Miguel, Morel, Morteyrol, Parre, Percival, Perez Roma, Phillips, Pignon, Polychronopoulos, Rumers, Takako Saito, Searle, Dorothee Selz, Salona, Sotelo, J. R. Soto, T. Thomas, Tisserand, Valentiner, Vigo, Vylbrief Zamora, Zanartu, and many others.

Please note: this list is necessarily incomplete as it was compiled three weeks before the festival opening. A complete list of participants will be included in THE BOOK OF THE CHILE FESTIVAL which ARTISTS FOR DEMOCRACY will publish shortly after the festival ends. The book will cost £5 per copy (plus a small charge for packing & postage). If you wish to buy a copy of THE BOOK OF THE CHILE FESTIVAL, please write to: BM-ARTISTS FOR DEMOCRACY, David Medalla, London WCIV 6XX and send us your cheque or postal money order for £5.25p.

David Medalla, chairman,
Cecilia Vicuña and John Dugger, festival coordinators,
Guy Brett, secretary, and all the members of
ARTISTS FOR DEMOCRACY
warmly invite

....

and friends
to the opening night of the
ARTS FESTIVAL FOR DEMOCRACY IN CHILE
on Monday 14 October 1974 at 6.30 pm
at The Hall of the Royal College of Art, Kensington Gore, London SW7 2EU
RSVP BM-Artists for Democracy, London WC1V 6XX

OPENING NIGHT PROGRAMME

Invocation on conga drums by Caboo of Trinidad

1. Mavis Penn will introduce David Medalla who will speak on behalf of Artists for Democracy.
2. Colin Grigg will introduce Cecilia Vicuña who will read a declaration by Chilean cultural workers.
3. Guy Brett will introduce Professor Alvaro Bunster who will speak on behalf of the London Committee for Human Rights in Chile.
4. Steve Sprung will introduce Brian Nicholson, chairman of the Chile Solidarity Campaign, who will speak on the British working people's solidarity with the Chilean people.
5. Ann Hodges will introduce Peter Blackman who will read selections from his poem *Song for All Men.*
6. Rob Hunter-Henderson will introduce Constance Cummings who will read two poems from *Canto general* by Pablo Nerudá: *'Los muertos de la plaza'* ('The Dead in the Square') and *'El pueblo victorioso'* ('The people victorious'), and a poem by Victor Jara: *Te recuerdo, Amanda* ('I remember you, Amanda').
7. Tina Keane will introduce a performance of Victor Jara's *Te recuerdo, Amanda* by the Red Star Shadow Puppet Theatre. Director: Jun Terra.
8. Lynn MacRitchie, John Dugger and Catharine Waley will announce the events in the festival and will read messages of support and solidarity with the Chilean people in their heroic fight against fascism.
9. Pippa Smith will introduce Libba Davies who will read three poems by Violeta Parra: *La carta* ('The letter'), *Me gustan los estudiantes* ('I like the students'), and *Gracias a la vida* ('Thanks to life').
10. Sylvia Stevens will introduce a performance of Violeta Parra's *Gracias a la vida* ('Thanks to life') by Martha Grogan (dancer), Peter Smith (guitar), and Simon Steyne (flute).
11. Jonathan Miles will introduce 7-year-old Accabre Huntley who will read her poems in support of the Chilean resistance.
12. Steve Pusey will introduce 75-year-old Andrew Kim who will perform rhythmic movements with illuminated Chinese clubs to the song *Todos juntos* ('All together') composed and sung by Los Jaivas musical group of Chile.
13. Mass-singing by Artists for Democracy and the audience of the Chilean revolutionary song *El pueblo unido jamas sera vencido:* 'The people united can never be defeated'.
14. Mitch Davies will introduce the film *Chilean September* made in 1973-74 by the French film-makers Bruno Muel and Theo Robichet.

I have faith in Chile and its destiny. Other Chileans will overcome these dark and bitter moments when treachery reigns. You must know that sooner rather than later, there will again open up broad avenues of poplars along which worthy men and women will walk to build a new society. Long live Chile! Long live the people! Long live the workers!
President Salvador Allende of Chile
11 September 1973

By your example we shall grow.
We shall be a multitude upon this earth.
Our energy will be an ocean's infinity.
Today's prisons will be tomorrow's victory.
Pablo Neruda

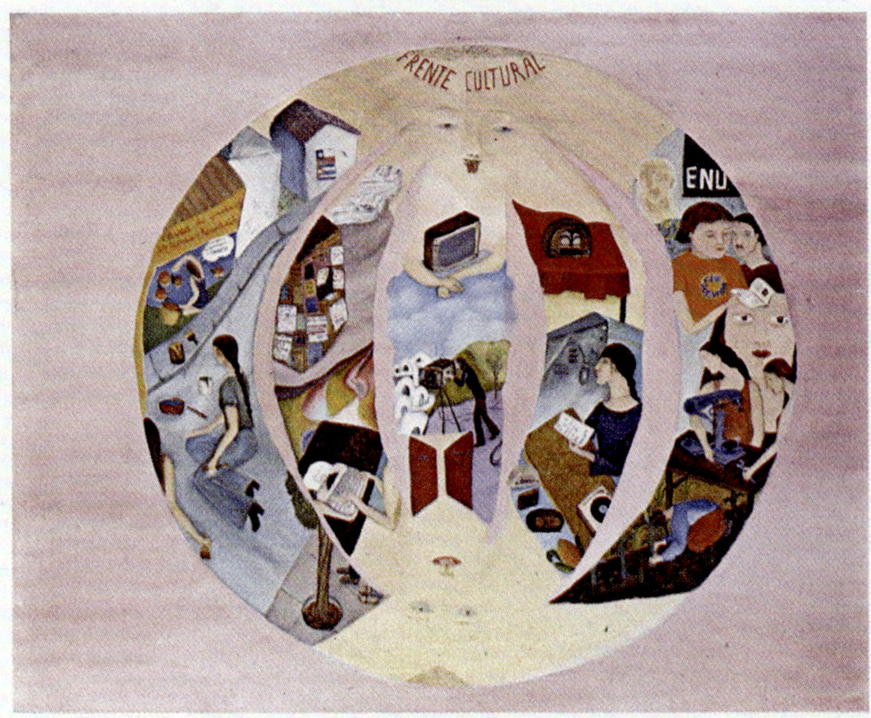

Cultural Front of the Popular Unity Government
oil on canvas, May 1973, by Cecilia Vicuña.

SOME IMPORTANT DATES OF THE FESTIVAL

Tuesday 15 October at 7 pm: the Chilean writer Ariel Dorfman will speak at a Symposium on Cultural Imperialism and Latin American art and culture.
Friday 18 October at 7 pm: Symposium on Art and Culture in Asia. In the chair: Lek of Kampuchea and Jun Terra of the Philippines.
Friday 25 October at 7 pm: Symposium on Art and Culture in Africa and the Black culture of the Caribbean. In the chair: Lester Lewis.
Saturday 26 October is Poetry Day. Saturdays are also children's days.
Monday 21 October at 6.30 pm: Symposium on Third World culture will be held at the Architectural Association, 34-36 Bedford Square, London WC1, as part of the Arts Festival for Democracy in Chile organised by Artists for Democracy.
The auction sale of art works in the exhibition will be held on Wednesday 30 October 1974 at 8 pm, inside The Hall of the Royal College of Art, Kensington Gore, SW7 2EU.

The minute I arrived in London, I realised in one second that everything that I thought about Europe was 'fake news' – as you would say today – that Europe was in the past, and that we in South America were the vital present and the future. So I immediately turned to the realisation that the revolution that we were creating in Chile was *la papa* – meaning 'the potato', which means the real thing. ... At the time we had the most active correspondence between lots of poets around mostly Latin America, some of them in the US, and very few in Europe, as I can recall – but in Latin America, we had that. So I immediately start writing to people, saying, 'Don't come to Europe! This is not really that we imagined. The place to be is Latin America.' So I never undid my suitcase, waiting to go back to Chile. ... Once the coup happened, immediately they began murdering my friends. So I was forced to seek political refuge in the UK, because I was a public figure in Chile; at age 23, I already had a TV programme reaching the entire nation. That's the kind of universe that Chile was. I had two one-woman exhibitions at the National Museum of Fine Arts, where it was all about the celebration of socialism. So if I were to return, I'd be [killed] you know. But at the time the British govern-ment was conservative and would not allow any of the Chilean students to stay in England. So I had to be defended in a trial against the Home Office by this extraordinary organisation of lawyers that defended refugees – and they won my case by presenting my book *Sabor a Mí* as proof of the fact that I would be killed, which was the first book to come after the coup, not even two months after September '73.

[...]

The London that I encountered, arriving ... was a London filled with refugees of persecuted lands. I made friends practically instantly with refugees from Africa, Czech refugees, where the revolution had been crushed, with Greek people, and people from different countries of Latin America that were crushed before us, the Brazilians, the Argentinians, the Uruguayans ... and also I met, for example, in the Slade school – immediately, who were my friends – the Irish, the Galicians ... you know, I didn't really have English friends as much as the invaded ones from the UK itself. So there was this community of exiled artists and poets and musicians. And we immediately had a common feeling for each other. ... And as soon as the military coup occurred, I entered into a relationship with the Chilean Solidarity Campaign, which was also very international. And part of that was the British unions. ... So this crossing, of artists and unionists and workers and people from different countries, was fluid back then, because that is the way London was.

Cecilia Vicuña

The energy generated by the intent was a powerful magnet. Believing in possibility is contagious! In the space of a few months, the initial small group succeeded in creating an organization and bringing to fruition an unprecedented collective achievement: a great impetus for Chile and other liberation movements. The focus was on creating a big art festival and an auction of artworks donated to help restore democracy in Chile. But in the process, a space of conversation and mutual apprenticeship was created that brought together artists from Africa, Asia, Europe, and the Americas in a multifaceted conglomerate, which also included representatives of the Committee for Solidarity with Chile, trade unions, the student union, and the Chilean opposition to the military junta. And this network was woven in an era before the Internet, by means of a modest letter we sent to the four corners of the world. The response was immediate. We received artworks, letters, and telegrams of support. Volunteers became increasingly numerous, and we ended up with a floating group several dozen strong. Artists from other regions began to propose local satellite exhibitions that extended AFD's call. The enthusiasm and the desire to participate in a global mobilization were palpable.

Cecilia Vicuña

I first encountered John Dugger and David Medalla when they gave a lecture about the work of Lygia Clark at Saint Martins School of Art, which I attended from 1970–75. I clearly recall John coming to me in the auditorium with these long acoustic tubes. I was later introduced to them – probably in 1974, by Steve Sprung, a fellow student (who went on to become an activist film maker with Cinema Action) and attended soirees at their residence in Newport Place and on one occasion, Guy Brett's large flat in Holborn. It was at one of these meetings at Newport Place, with John, David, Guy, Cecilia Vicuña and Hugh Cave (a student from the Slade and long-time friend) that we founded AFD. We discussed Chile and I proposed that the first major project of AFD should be a collective art project about Chile and this was seconded by John. This really just coincided with everyone's interest; there was full agreement. I had been sharing a residence with young Brazilian exiles in Archway and prior to that a Chilean. So I had been following events in Chile through a weekly bulletin my flatmates provided me from the International Coffee Organization. Much of what I read was not reported fully in the mainstream news. During this period at Saint Martins I also designed and made many screen-printed posters about what had happened in Chile and attempted to inform and solicit support from the students – but, incredible as it may seem now, other than Steve Sprung and a few others, my approach was met with general disinterest, disdain and the expression that it was not relevant to their lives.

The organization of the festival proceeded at a whirlwind pace and included many more artists and activists including Mavis Penn, Tina Keane, Lynn MacRitchie, Jonathan Miles, Sylvia Stevens, Steve Sprung and many others. Artists from all over the world donated their work for exhibition and auction. Among these were David Hockney, Claes Oldenberg, Conrad Atkinson and Roberto Matta. Matta signed a canvas on the floor of the gallery in front of myself, John and Cecilia. Needless to say, I was in awe and speechless. His work was later displayed in the upper gallery overlooking the hall. The centre of the gallery was occupied by John, David and Cecilia. John's large banner, which had previously been displayed in Trafalgar Square, hung on the main wall in front of which was an installation by Cecilia. David constructed a large bubble machine which frothed to one side. My six-by-eight-foot painting of Salvador Allende and Pablo Neruda hung at the entrance to the exhibition. Andrew 'Pop' Kim gave a performance with clubs in front of the work. The festival was a phenomenal and pivotal event organized in the space of six months by a loosely affiliated group of artists. At the core of this whirlwind was the contradiction of the personal relationship between John, David and Cecilia, which was also responsible for its eventual fracture. Radiating out of this was the network of artists and the influence of Guy Brett's society connections. It was something that could only be possible during that short period in London when passion and motivation ruled over bureaucracy.

Stephen Pusey

Peinture

Le Chili à Londres

Un festival international est organisé à Londres au Royal College of Art (Kensington Gore) par le mouvement des Artists for Democracy (A.F.D.) pour soutenir le peuple chilien dans sa lutte contre le fascisme.

Le groupe Treco d'Argentine, des peintres français et latino-américains, établis à Paris, ont envoyé leurs œuvres ; des artistes venus de diverses villes d'Allemagne sont venus à Londres pour peindre une fresque sur le lieu même du festival, et des messages de solidarité ont été envoyés par des mouvements de résistance d'Afrique et d'Asie.

Les organisateurs du festival recueillent des dons pour les envoyer au Front anti-fasciste de Rome. Une vente aux enchères aura lieu le 30 octobre.

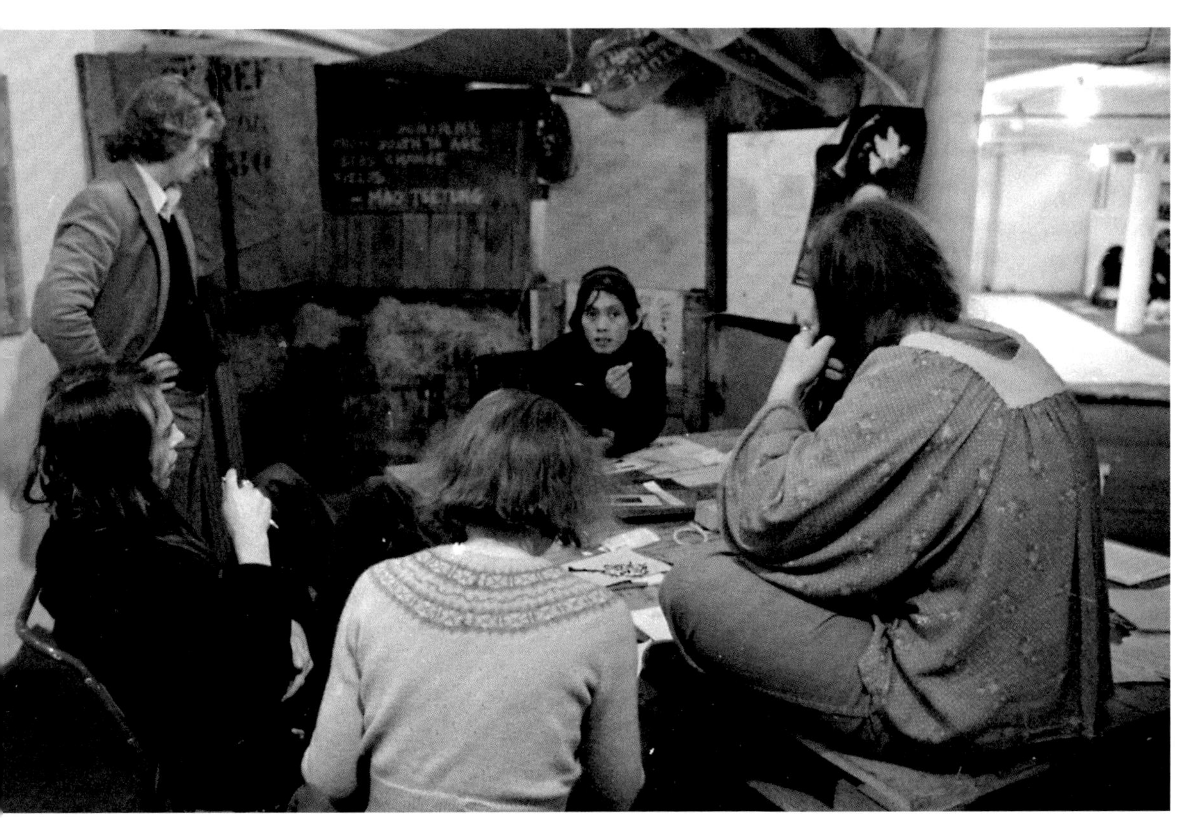

David Medalla (centre) and others at 'Arts Festival for Democracy in Chile', Royal College of Art, October 1974

INTERNATIONAL ARTS FEST
FOR THE CHILEAN RESISTA
at the RCA and AMP

INTERNATIONAL ARTS FESTIVAL
FOR CHILEAN RESISTANCE

14th-30th October, open every day except Sunday, from 10am-9pm.

EVENTS & PERFORMANCES AT THE
ROYAL COLLEGE OF ART
Kensington Gore
(unless otherwise stated)

An auction sale of art works will be held at the RCA on the last day of the festival: Wednesday 30th October at 8pm.

MONDAY 14th
7pm Opening night ceremonies.

TUESDAY 15th
5pm Event - Grant B.Cooke
5.30pm Film-"Hour of the Furnaces"
7.30pm Poetry reading - Andrew Salkey
8pm Symposium on Latin-American Art and Culture, Ariel Dorfman speaks on Cultural Repression

WEDNESDAY 16th
2pm Video event - Mike Leggett
5.30pm Film - "Campamento"
7.30pm Discussion - Cultural work in Chile
8pm Indian Classical Music - Punita Gupta

THURSDAY 17th
2-4pm Discussion - conducted by women's groups
4pm Dance - Limited Dance Company, Sally Potter and Jackie Lansley
5.30pm Film - "Attica"
6.30pm Poems - Jeni Couzyn
7pm Discussion - Women in the arts
8pm Indian Classical Music - Punita Gupta

FRIDAY 18th
2-5pm Discussion - Art and Society with particular reference to repression of cultural workers in La America and other part the world.
5.30pm Film - "People and the Guns"
7pm Cecil Rajendra and the Third World Troubadour
7.30pm Red Star Shadow Puppet Theatre: Jun Terra
7.45pm Symposium on Asian and Middle-East Art and Culture - led by Lek H Tan (Cambodia) and Jun Terra (Philippines)

SATURDAY 19th
2pm Agor MMba dance/mime c
5.30pm Film - "What is Democra
6.30pm Discussion - Democratic and Popular Culture le David Medalla and AFD

SUNDAY 20th
5.30pm Cartoons and art films followed by an open discussion at the Art Meeting Place

MONDAY 21st
2pm Event - Dirk Larsen Participation event-Pa
3pm Dance events - various dance groups
7pm Discussion on films an film making led by St Sprung, Mick May, Mitc Davies

TUESDAY 22nd
2pm Projection event - Sus Hiller
5.30pm Films by English film-makers
7pm Discussion on Community Arts led by Colin Grig and Mavis Penn

WEDNESDAY 23rd

2pm Video - Fred Forest
Art Film - "The Astronaut" by Lennart Gustavsson
Video - Dirk Larsen

4pm Dance events

5.30pm Films - Cinema Action and Berwick St.Collective

7pm Discussion - The artists in Capitalist and Socialist societies led by Jorg Immendorf (Germany)

THURSDAY 24th

4pm Dance events

5.30pm Film - "Chile, the Reckoning"

7pm Discussion - The past and present in Chile led by Cecilia Vicuna

FRIDAY 25th

4pm Ballet Chileno

5.30pm Film - "When Bullets begin to Flower"

7pm Red Star Shadow Puppet Theatre: Jun Terra

7.15pm Symposium - African and Caribbean Art and Culture led by Lester Lewis

8pm Uhuru Arts Group

SATURDAY 26th

2pm Art film - "The Secret Life of Guillaume Apollinaire by Per Olof Ultvedt

4pm Performance - Folklore Chileno

5.30pm Film - "When the People Awake"

7pm Ballet Chileno

8pm Discussion -"Lessons of the Chilean Struggle" led by representatives of the Chile Anti-Fascist Front

SUNDAY 27th

5.30pm Art Film - Liliane Lijn
Cartoons and Art Films

7.30pm Folklore Chileno

MONDAY 28th

2pm Event - Tina Keane

5.30pm Films - Chippenham House

3pm Event-Video - David Medalla

TUESDAY 29th

2pm Event - Mathematics of Liberation by S.Nambodiri

5.30pm Film - "China", a film in progress by John Dugger

7pm Symposium on Experimental Forms of Art led by David Medalla, John Dugger, Guy Brett and AFD

WEDNESDAY 30th

5.30pm Aparcoa - Chilean Folk Group
Lautaro - Chilean Theatre Group
Martha Grogan - Dance
Red Star Shadow Puppet Theatre: Jun Terra

8pm Auction Sale

note: October 26th is poetry reading day. There will be poetry reading throughout the day.
Jazz groups of various idioms will be performing during the 3 weeks of the festival.
There will be children's workshops 3 times a week during the day.

INTERNATIONAL ARTS FESTIVAL
FOR CHILEAN RESISTANCE
organised by
Artists for Democracy 14-30 Oct.
at ART MEETING PLACE

The following artists will show their work at the Art Meeting Place during the festival:

Su Braden - Info Banners
Americo Castilla (Argentinian Artist) - glass event
Bill Lundberg - fire event
Chilean Artisans
Sally Pollitzer - paintings
Lord Milford - paintings
Liliane Lijn - films
Joyce Wieland - films
Michael Snow - films

The Chilean Folklore and other performance groups will be at AMP during the festival. Films by collectives and various film groups will also be shown.

FOR MORE INFORMATION ABOUT THESE & OTHER EVENTS, PERFORMANCES, FILMS, AND ARTISTS AT AMP DURING THE FESTIVAL PLEASE RING 580 6181

This is not a complete list - it will be growing with the festival

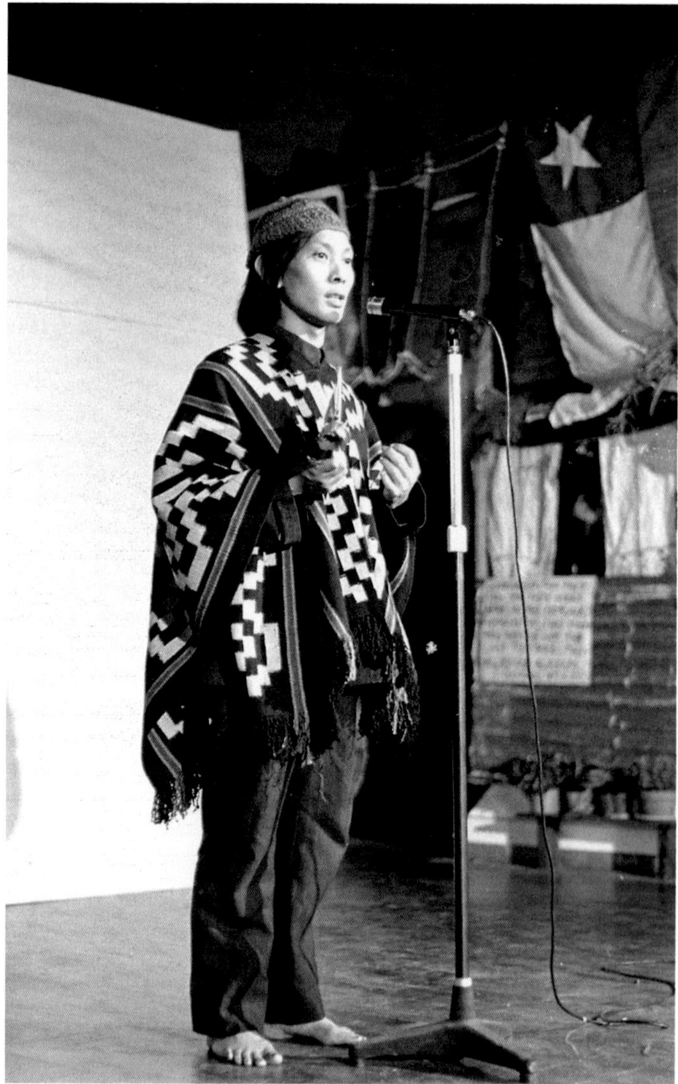

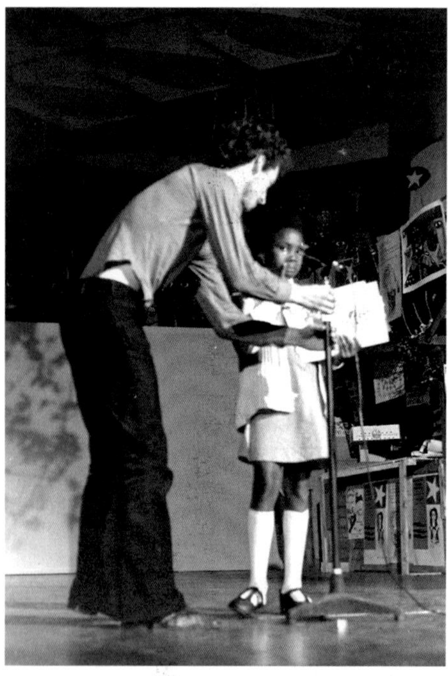

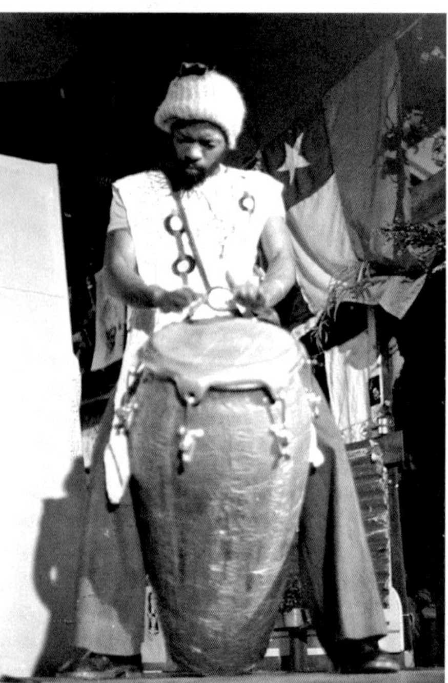

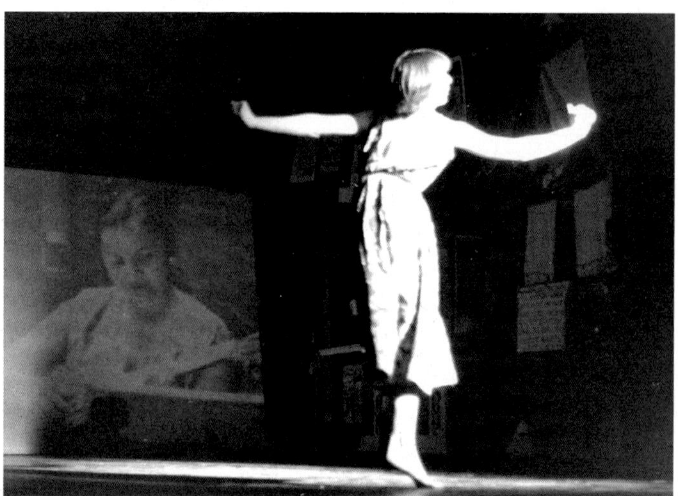

'Arts Festival for Democracy in Chile' opening night (from top): Opening remarks by David Medalla; poetry reading by Accabre Huntley (right), with Jonathan Miles; conga invocation by Caboo; dance performance by Martha Grogan, to a recording of Violeta Parra. Royal College of Art, October 1974.

The Chilean exhibition had both known and unknown artists doing painting, installations, banners, film, etc. with an attitude of 'by any format necessary'. Hence the exhibition exuded a strong sense of energy and stimulated discussion between the visitor and the artist. The venue became an integrated meeting place representing both an aesthetic and political experience. I liked this way of working. In the States I had been involved in the anti-war movement but art and politics always seemed in different boxes, here they had the opportunity to merge.

I met Steve Sprung and Jonathan Miles during this exhibition. Jonathan had been working with Christine Halsall and Ife [Nii Owoo] ... doing silkscreen posters. I had a studio at Tolmers Square and they needed a place to work and it was a good match. I became involved and others joined at different points including Annie Grove White, Andy Darley, Steve Sprung, Dave Fox, Jude Rayner, and Nancy Schiesari formed the core. Others were part of the [Poster] Collective for a short time – Peter Cross, Bernadette Brittain and Martin Walker. Some of us still did exhibitions at AFD.

Sylvia Stevens

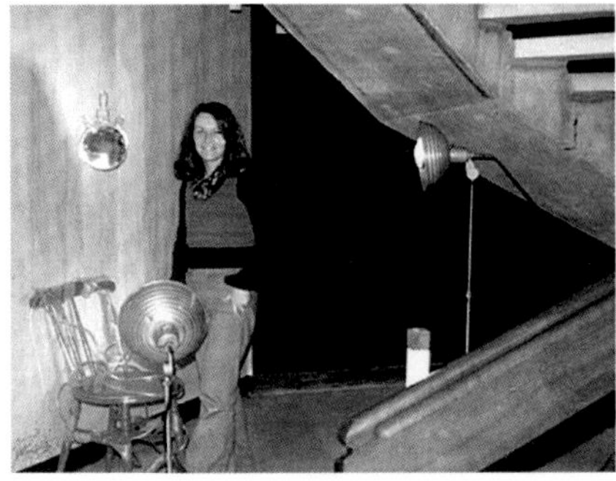

At the Royal College of Art I was in a show, the Chilean show that Guy Brett and David Medalla had put together, called 'Artists for Democracy'. I made an installation using poetry, mirrors, a chair and a blackboard with a poem on it. *Under the Stairs* it was called. It was a political piece, about being incarcerated in prison.

Tina Keane

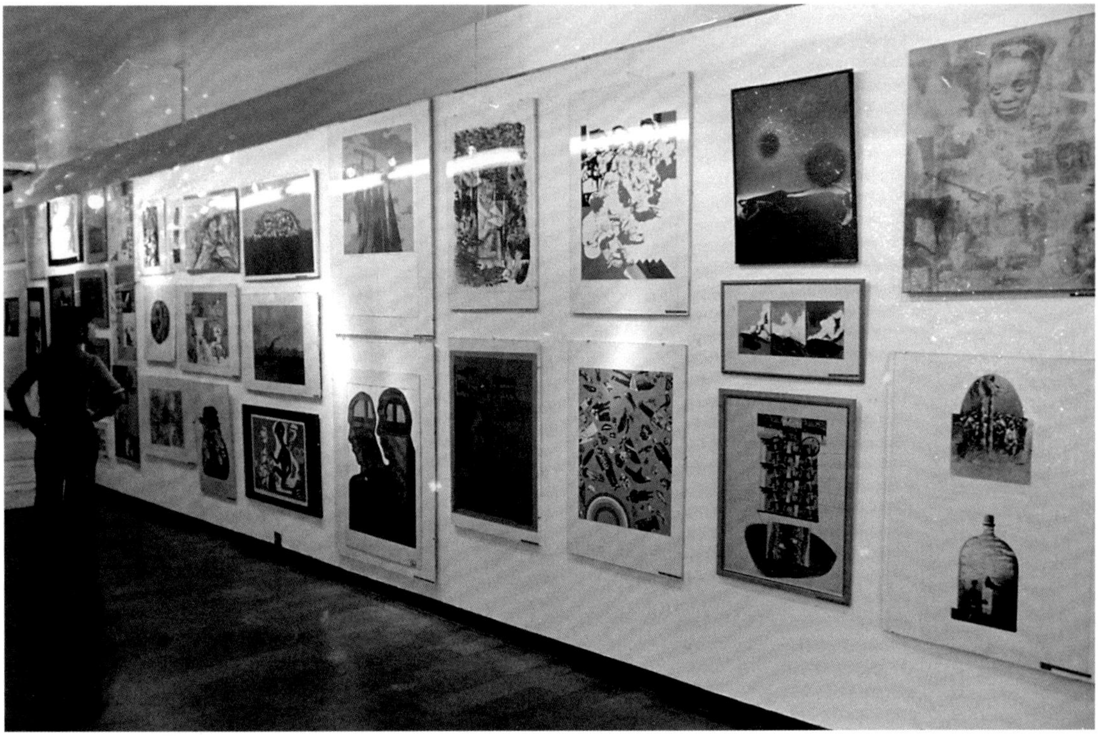

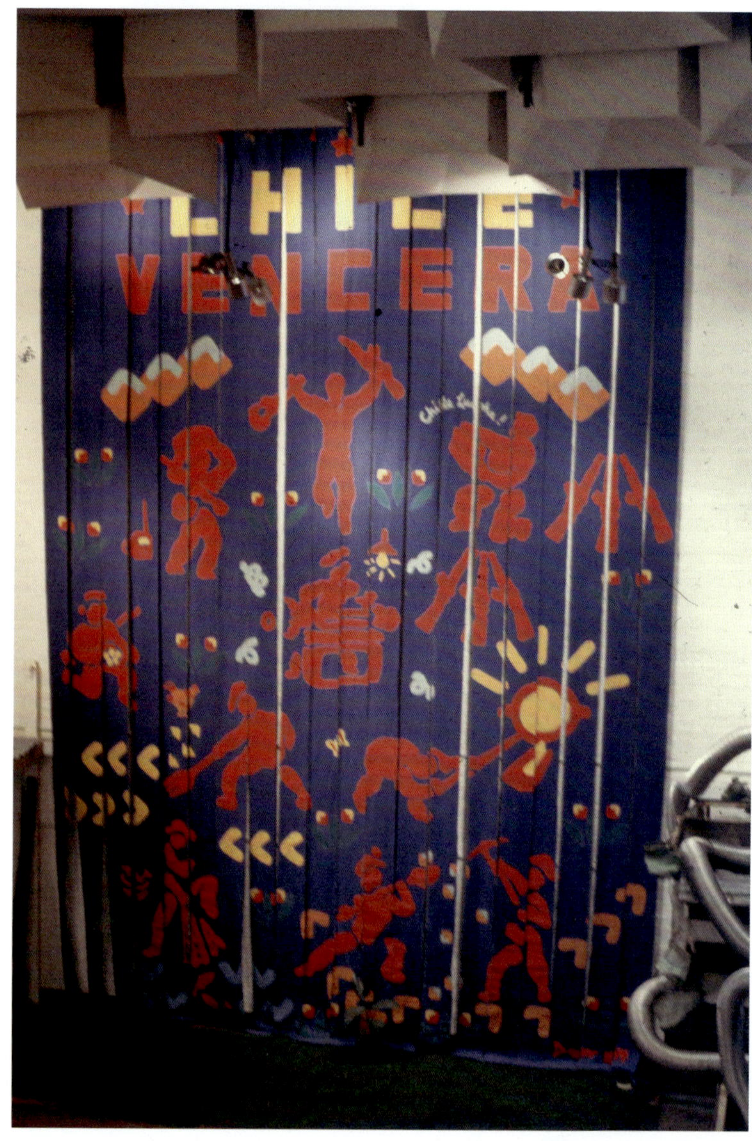

above: John Dugger's *Chile Vencerá*; facing page: *Bubble Machine* installation by David Medalla. 'Arts Festival for Democracy in Chile', Royal College of Art, October 1974

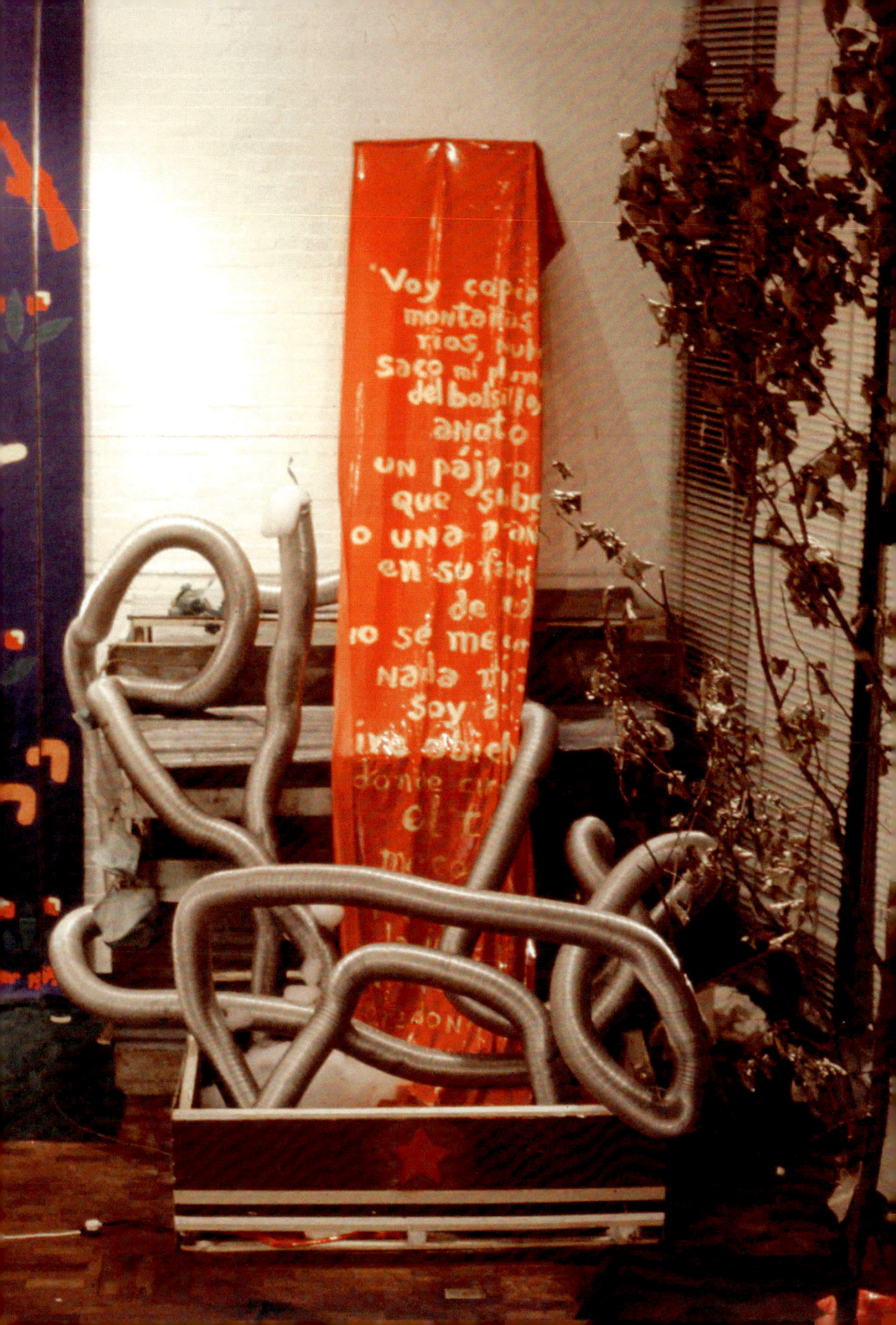
"Voy
montañas
ríos,
saco mi
del bolsillo
anoto
un
que
o una
en su
de
lo sé
nada
soy
el

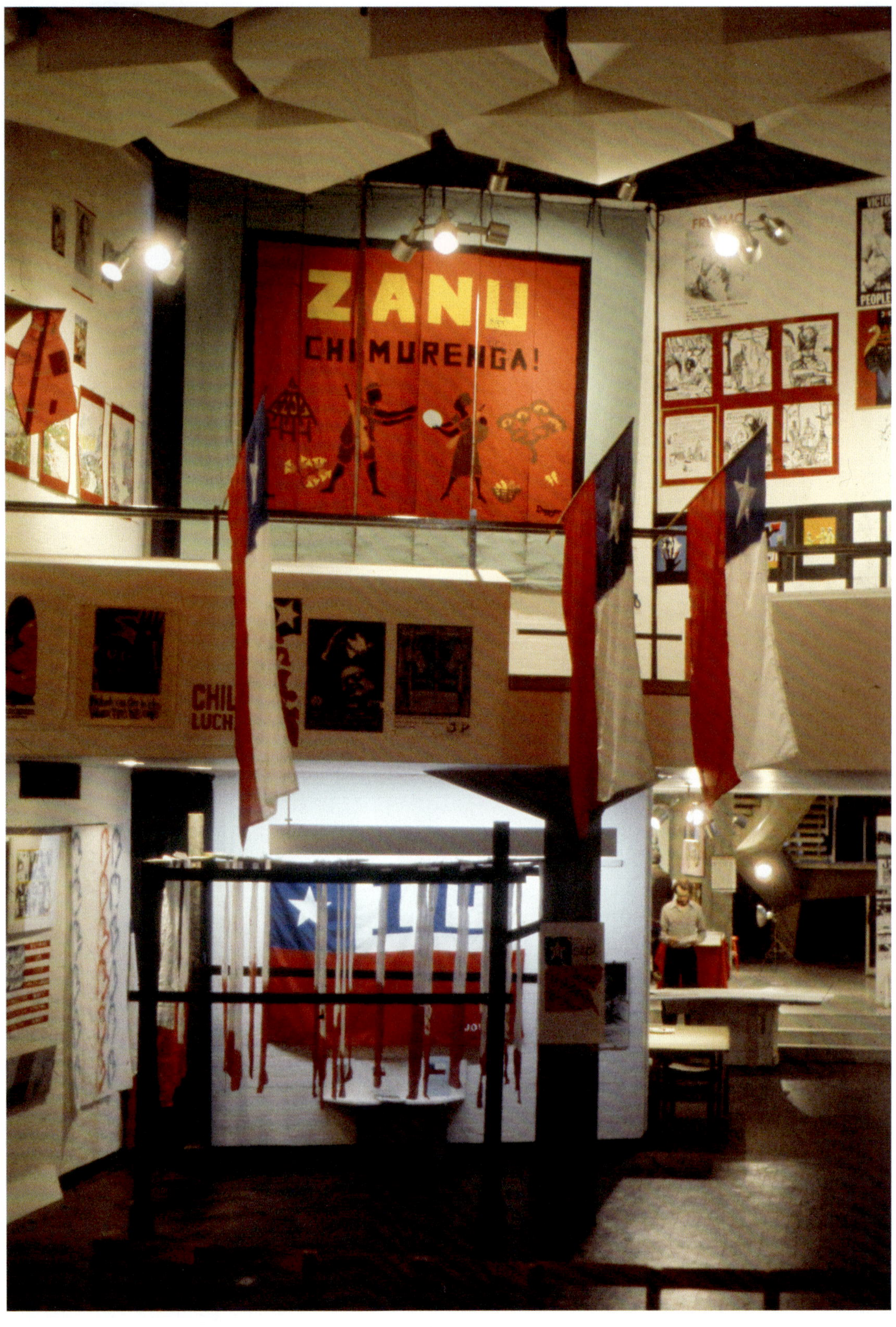

‘Arts Festival for Democracy in Chile’, Royal College of Art, October 1974

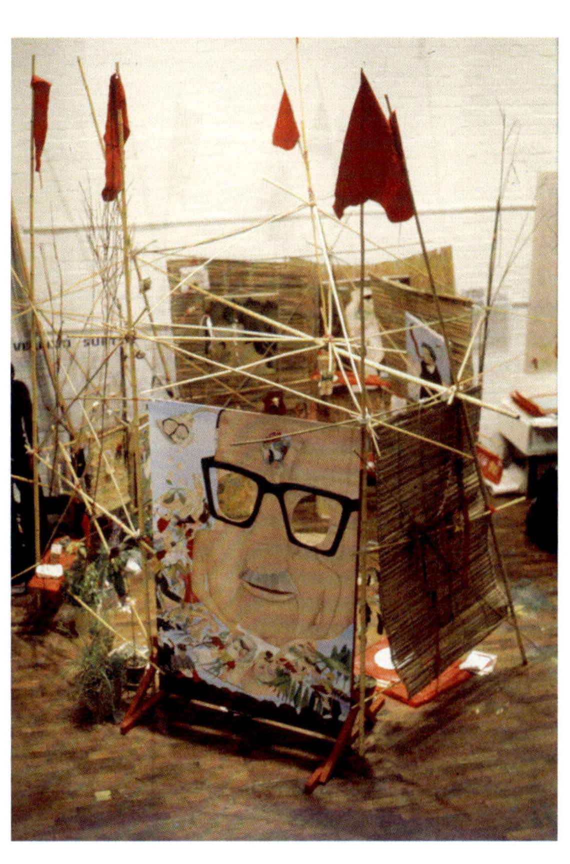

above: Cecilia Vicuña, *La Ruca Abstracta*;
following pages: Lynn MacRitchie (left) next to one of the *campamentos*.
'Arts Festival for Democracy in Chile', Royal College of Art, October 1974

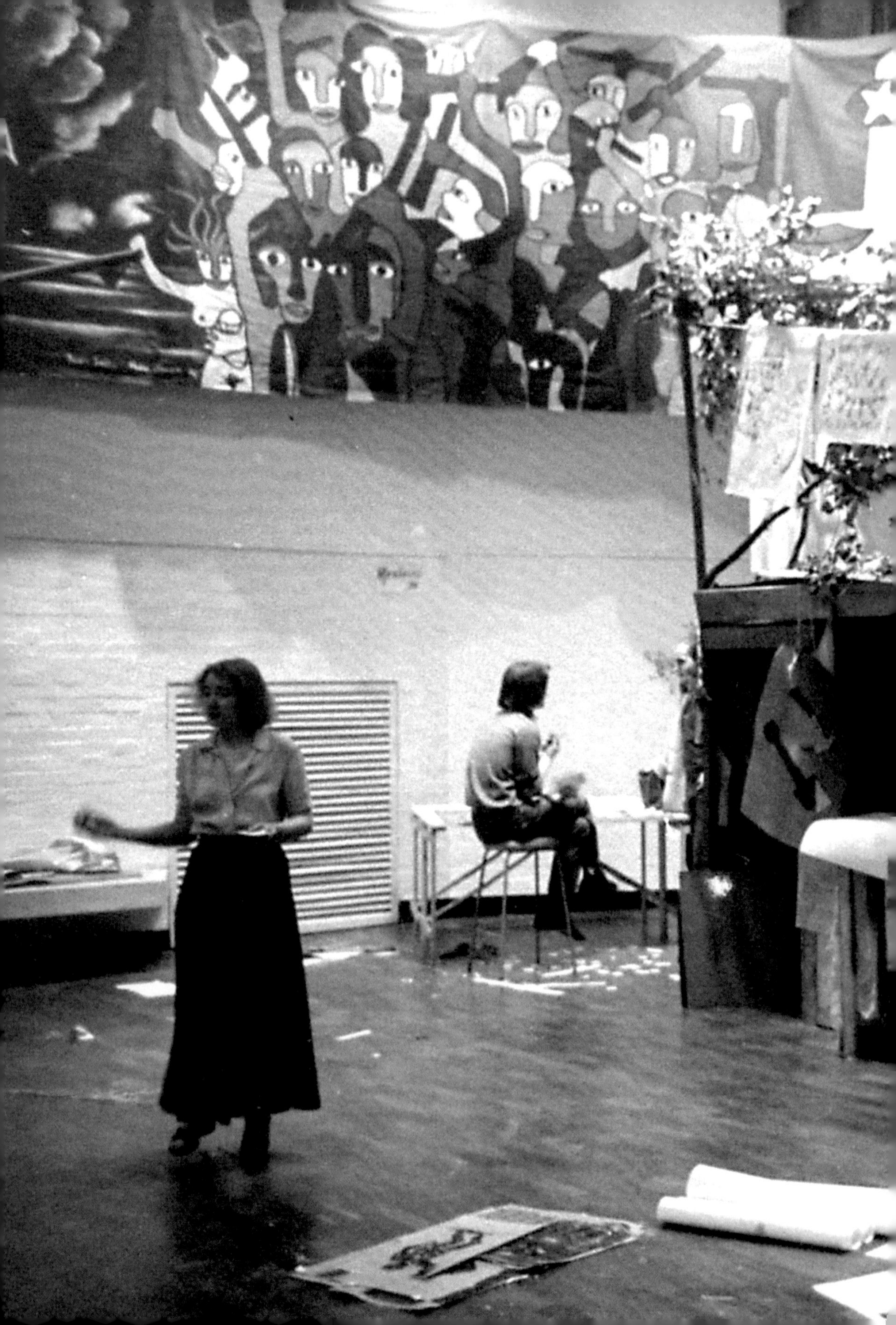

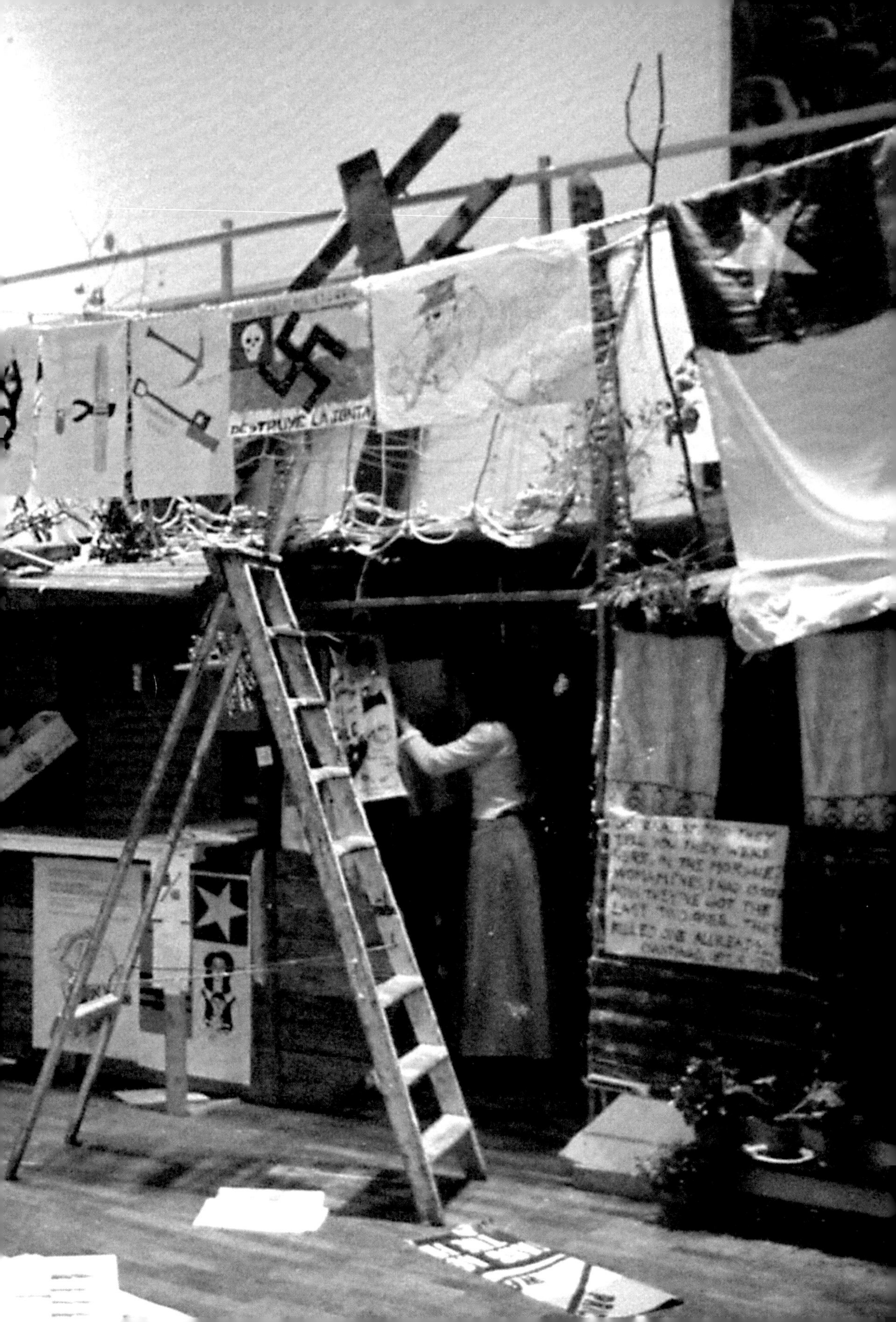
DESTRUYE LA JUNTA

For the AFD's Arts Festival in Support of Chilean Democracy, we recreated the *campamentos* during Allende's time, before the Americans bombed his La Moneda palace. The *campamentos* were centres set up by people all over Chile where they democratically evolved new ways of doing things socially, politically and culturally. The artists were centrally involved in these *campamentos*, where they experimented in various forms of art and education which involved the masses. Each member of the AFD set up a *campamento* where the audience, the guests, could participate in various forms of art either as initiators or participants in the art activities happening in the *campamento*. In my *campamento* there was a puppet workshop for groups of school kids, where they learned how to cut out puppets, manipulate them and perform stories they made up with the puppets. There was also a workshop for movement – for basic mime and dance.

Jun Terra

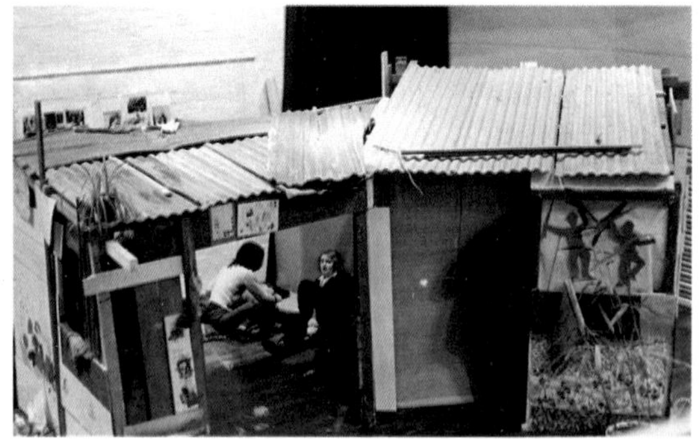

We each built our own contribution – you can see Jun [Terra]'s (where he and I are sitting) in the picture, he rehearsed his shadow puppets there. Cecilia [Vicuña] built a little hut in which she hung her paintings. I made a rope bridge, which was hung between some of the structures but doesn't seem to be in any of the photos. I loved the *campamento/favela*: it was such a great idea, such fun to make, but also so very serious – it was, after all, how many people actually lived in Chile. It was also the best spot to hang out, chatting and getting to know each other as we put the little structures together – everyone helping everyone else with tools and labour. We scavenged the materials from the streets – London still had old bomb sites and empty lots in those days, surrounded by corrugated iron, which we 'liberated', with lots of random bits of wood, wire, etc. just there for the taking.

Lynn MacRitchie

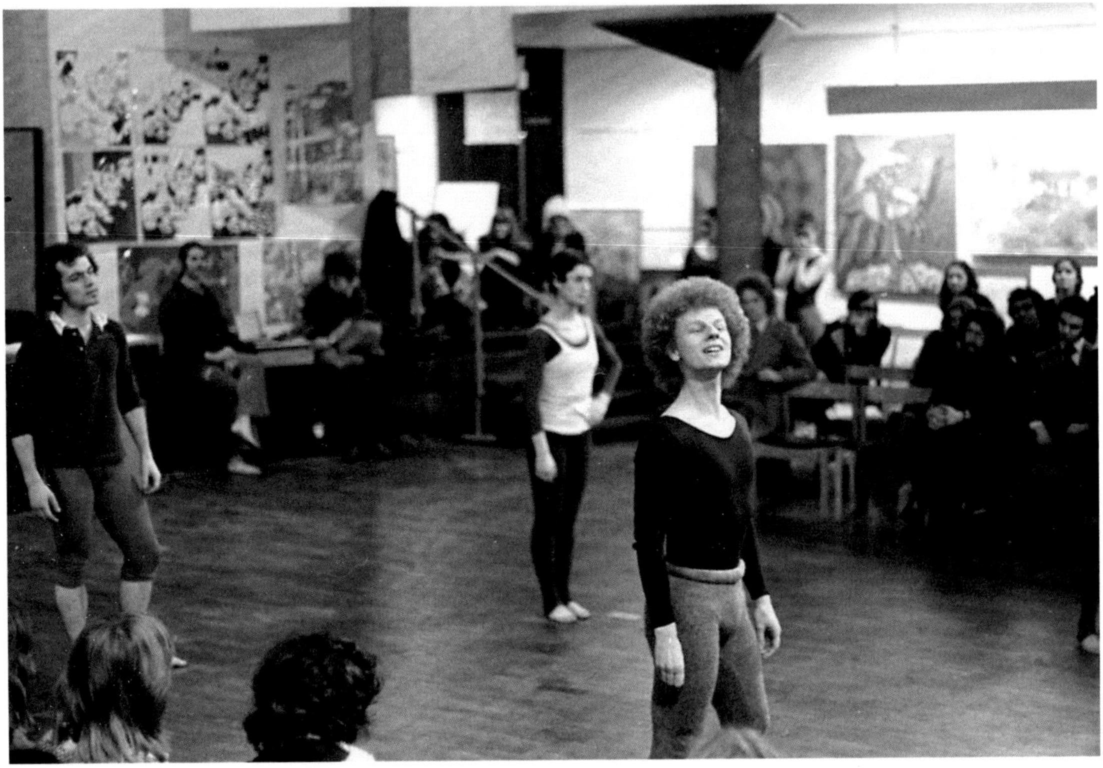

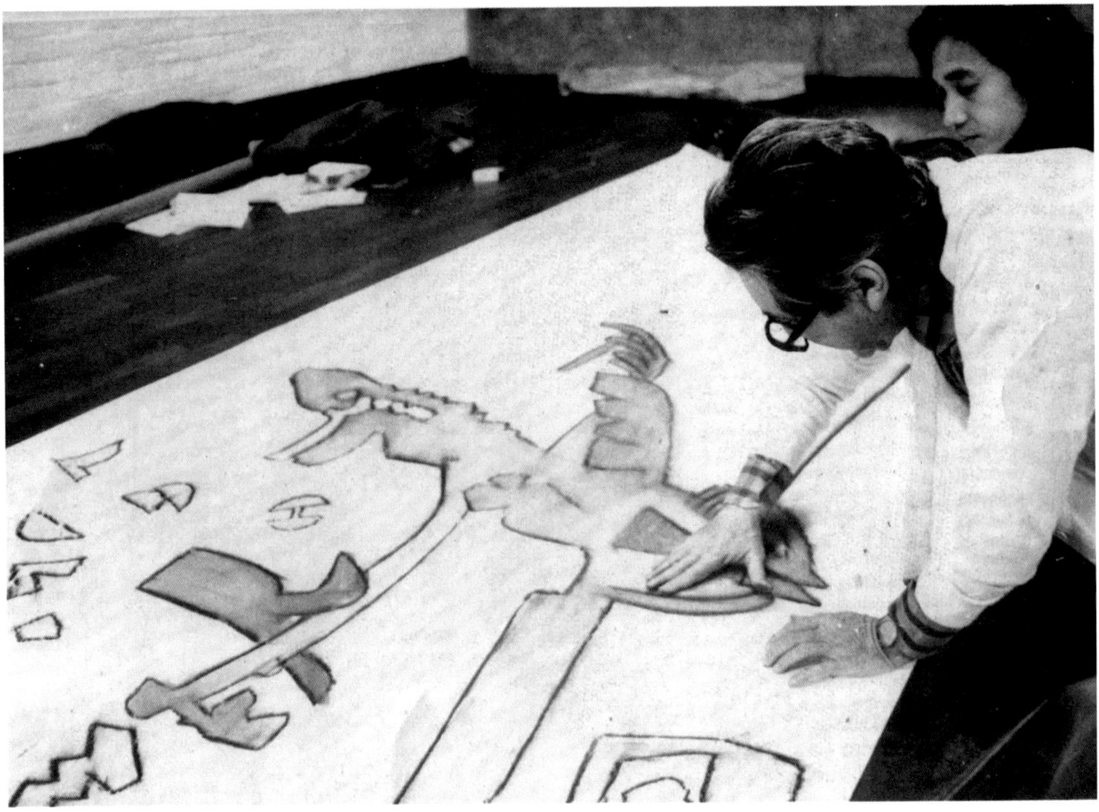

top: Dance group performance; bottom: Roberto Matta drawing, with Jun Terra (right).
'Arts Festival for Democracy in Chile', Royal College of Art, October 1974

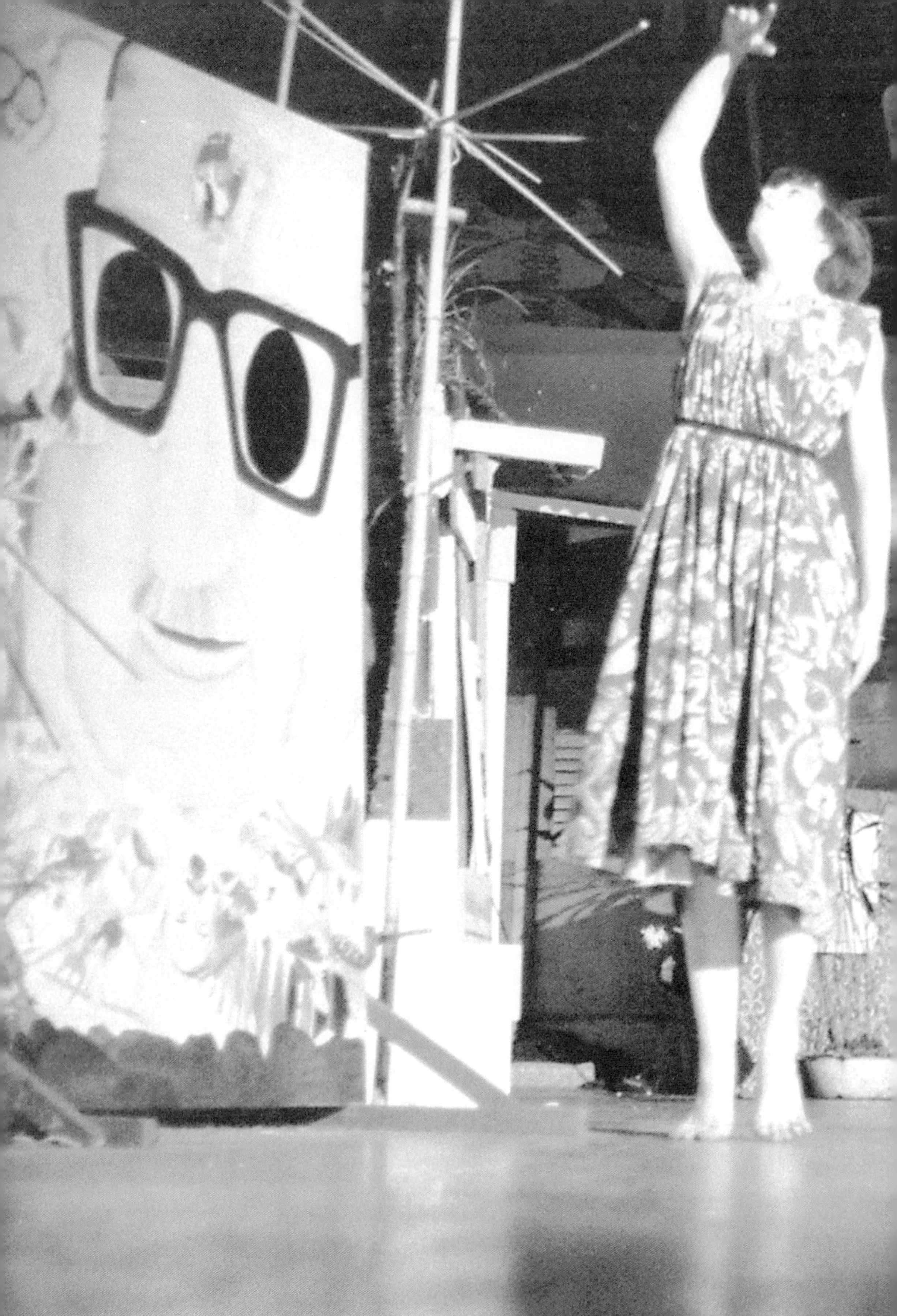

ORGANIZED DREAMING / Cecilia Vicuña, Santiago, December 2013
(Translated by Christopher Winks)

"What I have called the imaginary eras and super-nature, form an intertwining of germ, act, and potency."
"Every poesis is an act of participation in this excess."
José Lezama Lima

Organizing dreams   fantasy & imagination

imagine   sending forth
your imagination
like an arrow
with a needle and a
thread at the tip
(which)
discovers and organizes
weaves and reveals
swiftly advances
reaches destiny
hits the mark exactly · heart's
marrow.
1974

I contemplate the weave of my thoughts, the discontinuous warp of my writings from 1974 and my vision of today, and I see a coherence, a co-inheritance, that contains and exceeds me, that comes from before and continues after me.

I wrote: "we are forming Artists for Democracy (AFD) to educate artists on how to create work in the service of the people" (1974).

Today, this phrase would not be possible, the meaning of the words "people" and "service" have disappeared, erased by the language of corporations and "free trade" installed in Chile by the military coup of 1963.

I wrote: "Revolution is art and art revolution."

Today, revolution is a soft drink1 and art serves the market.

The distance between a word and its meaning is the space of transformation. The distance between action and dream, the separation that dis-empowers speaker and listener.

The London poet William Rowe, on a visit to Santiago, said yesterday: the challenge is to restore meaning to words, and this overturning is only possible in a communal poetic act, through the vulnerability of the poet who does not fear ridicule.

"E-duc-ate" in the sense of liberating the duct of a current, the desire that moves us toward the good, was our wish.

To seek together "the love that gathers" in the words of the mbyá-guaraní.
To educate desire,
to make it conscious is to see its light!

"to desire" is to shine,
from the Latin desiderare, sidus,
the star of con-sideration, the sidereal.

Where did the absurd yet relevant idea of "educating artists" come from?

It came from the depths of a sea, from the body memory of an immense social movement that had risen up in Chile from the beginning of time, in the wars of liberation of the peoples of the south against foreign domination. Perhaps it came from before then, from the collective ritual practices in which peoples attacked by cataclysms asked for (and ask for) a guiding light that would allow them to survive, in ceremonies dedicated to the transformation of individual consciousness into collective consciousness.

"The Mapuches do not have a concept of music because music is life itself... In the fiesta, when all the musicians play together, it is an absolute and simultaneous expression of freedom, of a freedom grounded in individuality. There is complete independence. All the musicians are playing at once, but there is no conductor. Each is the conductor of himself and yet there is no chaos, because there is respect and everyone is listening. All are ONE instrument. All of them are being ONE individual."
José Pérez de Arce, in La música mapuche

In his testimony on Artists for Democracy, Conrad Atkinson says that AFD's contribution was to bring to European consciousness the revolutionary politics of South America, which in my reading is the participatory meaning of a collective dreaming-acting that transforms society.

To dream on a cosmic scale is the cultural inheritance of the Americas, the dwelling of the "dangerous dreamers" forever persecuted.

"Executions, mutilations, rapes, such was the conquest of America. Massacres, murders, amputations of hands and feet, wounds cured with boiling oil...such crimes appear to be the product of a disturbed mind. But these were daily occurrences in the battles."
Antonio Espino, "La conquista de América"
http://www.elconfidencial.com/cultura/2013-10-12/ejecuciones-mutilaciones-violaciones-asi-fue-la-conquista-de-america_40390/

The first priority of the military coup in Chile was to kill the capacity to dream, establishing a vision of the world that glorified power and ridiculed dreaming and its potential. The result was that today's neo-colonial Chilean society values neither Salvador Allende nor the Unidad Popular. However, the never-recognized continuity between the rituals of Chile's First Nations peoples and the social movement that brought Allende to power is reborn in every student demonstration, in every mass protest where the mestizo people take to the streets.

Paulina Varas exclaimed upon first encountering the AFD documents:

"AFD's language in 1974 was completely untimely. In Chile, It was impossible to talk about democracy. It was the moment of the initial terror. Here people still believed that Pinochet would give power to the ex-president Eduardo Frei Montalva. People still didn't know about the disappeared. Exile on a large scale hadn't yet occurred. People still thought there could be a fight. They were killing people and we knew nothing about it. There was complete obscurantism. Everything changed in the 80s: they discovered the furnaces of Lonquén. That made it public that the disappeared could have been murdered" (conversation with Cecilia, April 5, 2012).

(And that was just the beginning: in the Museo de la Memoria y los Derechos Humanos in Santiago de Chile, a "map of tortures" is displayed, showing 14,000 torture centers distributed throughout the country, where, between 1963 and 1989, they electrocuted the genitals of men, women, and young people arbitrarily chosen in order to establish collective terror.)

José Lezama Lima wrote that a people attains its "imaginary era" when it incarnates an image, and Chile did this in 1970 by democratically electing Salvador Allende and undertaking a non-violent battle for justice. This image radiated a new beauty throughout the earth, and the military coup that destroyed it was felt in the world as an attack not against Chile, but against a fundamental human aspiration: the right to create a joyful and free society, a participatory democracy, yet to be realized on earth.

Photo: the human ocean

Artists for Democracy emerged as a response of artistic solidarity in the face of the loss of the Chilean dream, but its intention went further: it sought to apply the example of a people that had generated new forms of collective participation. I am thinking of the resonance of the agrarian reform and the Cybersyn project, a cybernetic system of national administration managed by the workers in order to guarantee their autonomy and democratic decision-making power. It was a practical utopia that was being fully realized until the moment of the coup.

Once, I heard a Mapuche peasant say that in Chile there was a light, a pillán[2] that emerged from the volcanoes. A force that recent history has tried to cover over, turning Chile into a champion of the market and the cult of greed imposed by the military coup.

"We are shining," said the striking workers.
"There is a great light in our lives" (José María Arguedas).

The light of the world's revolutionary movements inspired AFD, which for a moment echoed the imaginary fibers of the interrupted search.

If before AFD, other Latin American artists like Lygia Clark and Hélio Oiticica had inspired Europe by creating forms of participatory art centered on the interaction of bodies, the Chilean experience offered a further possibility: to think of a social movement that changes the order of the world as an "artwork" or a form of participatory art on a large scale.

(I remember that when I presented this idea in my lecture at the ICA on May 11, 1973, the British Council cancelled my grant, which they only restored when some members of the Council went on hunger strike in my support.)

AFD's revolutionary attempt was to dream on the scale of the Americas by reversing the colonial order of the art world, where the metropolis dictates the aesthetic language the colonies must follow. It offered an alternative model of creativity generated from South America and the Third World (a name that has fallen into disuse), where revolutionary politics and experimental art merge with ease.

The energy generated by the intent was a powerful magnet. Believing in possibility is contagious! In the space of a few months, the initial small group succeeded in creating an organization and bringing to fruition an unprecedented collective achievement: a great impetus for Chile and other liberation movements. The focus was on creating a big art festival and an auction of artworks donated to help restore democracy in Chile. But in the process, a space of conversation and mutual apprenticeship was created that brought together artists from Africa, Asia, Europe, and the Americas in a multifaceted conglomerate, which also included representatives of the Committee for Solidarity with Chile, trade unions, the student union, and the Chilean opposition to the military junta.

And this network was woven in an era before the Internet, by means of a modest letter we sent to the four corners of the world. The response was immediate. We received artworks, letters, and telegrams of support. Volunteers became increasingly numerous, and we ended up with a floating group several dozen strong. Artists from other regions began to propose local satellite exhibitions that extended AFD's call. The enthusiasm and the desire to participate in a global mobilization were palpable.

We worked in precarious conditions, using public telephones and living letters, friends who carried messages. We didn't have any funds or official support, but we sought the legitimacy granted by letters of support from great figures of the art world like Joris Ivens, Mary McCarthy, and Sir Roland Penrose, along with various members of the British Parliament who were opposed to the UK's official support for the Chilean military junta.

The Arts Festival for Democracy in Chile at the Royal College of Art was a beautiful and chaotic event, a true mix of political and experimental art. Roberto Matta came to work with us and created a monumental drawing in situ. Other artists did installations and performances in the campamento, or encampment inspired by the Chilean shantytowns we created. The whole festival was a large participatory event with many people taking part in the intense debates.

AFD flourished as a disorganized organization open to all, but at halfway point authoritarian voices began to emerge within the group. As a result, the founding group divided into two factions with different political and human orientations, and the energy and desire to sustain a passionate effort to help Chile began to dissipate. The auction of the donated artworks we had planned as the closing event did not have the expected results. It only produced aprox. £300, while the much larger value of the unsold art was diverted. (Later on there was a second auction of which I was not part. See John Dugger testimonial and Guy Brett's interview.)

After the festival, the internal discord intensified and David Medalla, one of the founders, moved to revoke AFD's public commitment to support the united front of The Chilean resistance and, instead, to redirect the funds to the MIR, (Movimiento de Izquierda Revolucionaria). There was a rushed vote. The other founding members, Guy Brett, John Dugger, and I opposed this decision. We asked that the previously adopted commitment be honored, but our voice was silenced, and Medalla's proposal carried. John Dugger and I came under attack and we were forced to withdraw from AFD.

"Hatred is forked love" say the mbyá-guaraní.

The movement's energy and beauty had been destroyed. The organization and the living web of relationships that had made our collective action of 1974 possible, was no longer in place. Unfounded accusations followed this post-auction decision, and a wave of shame and grief engulfed the project and its history. A veil covered the original ideals and intentions of AFD and even today, questions remain regarding the fate of the donated artworks. (See text by the Museo de la Solidaridad Salvador Allende).

Hearing this story, Paulina Varas said: It was a "second coup".

Several months after the auction, David Medalla, opened an art space in London, an alternative gallery he named "Artists for Democracy." It had great success, but only lasted until 1977. The irony of the story is that this gallery was to be remembered in London as the only AFD, while the original AFD organization and the Festival were forgotten. In retrospect, the exhibition space created by the second AFD on Whitfield St. was a different animal. However 'radical', it was aligned with the changing times where art exists in a niche that does not threaten the system.

The poet Carlyle Reedy, who participated in the original AFD and continues to work in London, observed that in the mid-1970s a cultural change took place. The art market grew in power, art turned into a business and artists and curators, critics and art writers, moved to seek personal prestige to insure their survival in the new academic and institutional system. The idealism of the social struggles that inspired so many artists in the 60s and 70s began to seem a failed and irrelevant idea.

The failure of the original AFD is its greatest beauty, as failure seeds the birthing of new forms. Forty years on the dream of justice flowers again in protest movements across the globe and the story of AFD returns to its place of origin in Chile, where the power of collective dreaming, "the love that gathers", now re-emerges in the student movement rising up against profit, to demand a more just society, a return to the communal language of debate and democratic participation.

Today it is of the utmost urgency to recover the memory of the lost dream. The system of unbridled exploitation that the coup established in Chile has now spread throughout the Earth and an outraged humanity is rising up, because what is at stake is no longer just the freedom of a people, but the continuity of life and human civilization threatened by imminent social and ecological catastrophe.

The demolition of participatory democracy in Chile on September 11, 1973 was the beginning of a worldwide repressive wave against democratic rights, which has now reached even the centers of hegemonic power in the northern hemisphere, which spy on and persecute their own citizens, as Edward Snowden has shown.

And September 11, 2001, marked the moment in which the system succeeded in justifying the repression of global civil rights on grounds of "security."

An inescapable symmetry arises like a prayer from these two "elevens."

In this context, the effaced memory of Artists for Democracy rises up like a call: If in 1974, artists mobilized on behalf of Chile, it is now necessary to mobilize on behalf of the planet and its species, on behalf of all the Earth's cultures and peoples.

AFD's dissolution is an axis of reflection, a mirror to observe the force that destroys the "love that brings the community together."
The idea they wanted to kill was the desire for unión.
AFD's history re-emerges today to make manifest the search for a language that enables us to comm-unicate, to discover a

new way of connecting individual consciousness to the communal and viceversa.
A question for participatory democracy must be posed, to con-template, to see together the way in which the possibility of achieving a common consciousness, a pivot between worlds, is obscured, covered over, and effaced.
Only on this basis, starting from this question, will we succeed in turning back the power of greed that is destroying the planet and threatening the continuity of the human species.
Only by acting collectively as a species in search of the common good will we awaken to another reality, to an art that expresses the innate desire for justice and beauty within being.

1 http://www.amazon.com/Red-Cola-Revolution-Bottles-16-5-Pound/dp/B005NYx4M4
2 Pillán: (Mapuche) Le word "pillán" "is the mystical union of the spirit with the soul (püllü + am = pillán); Ziley Mora Penroz, Filosofía Mapuche (Editorial Kushe: 2011).

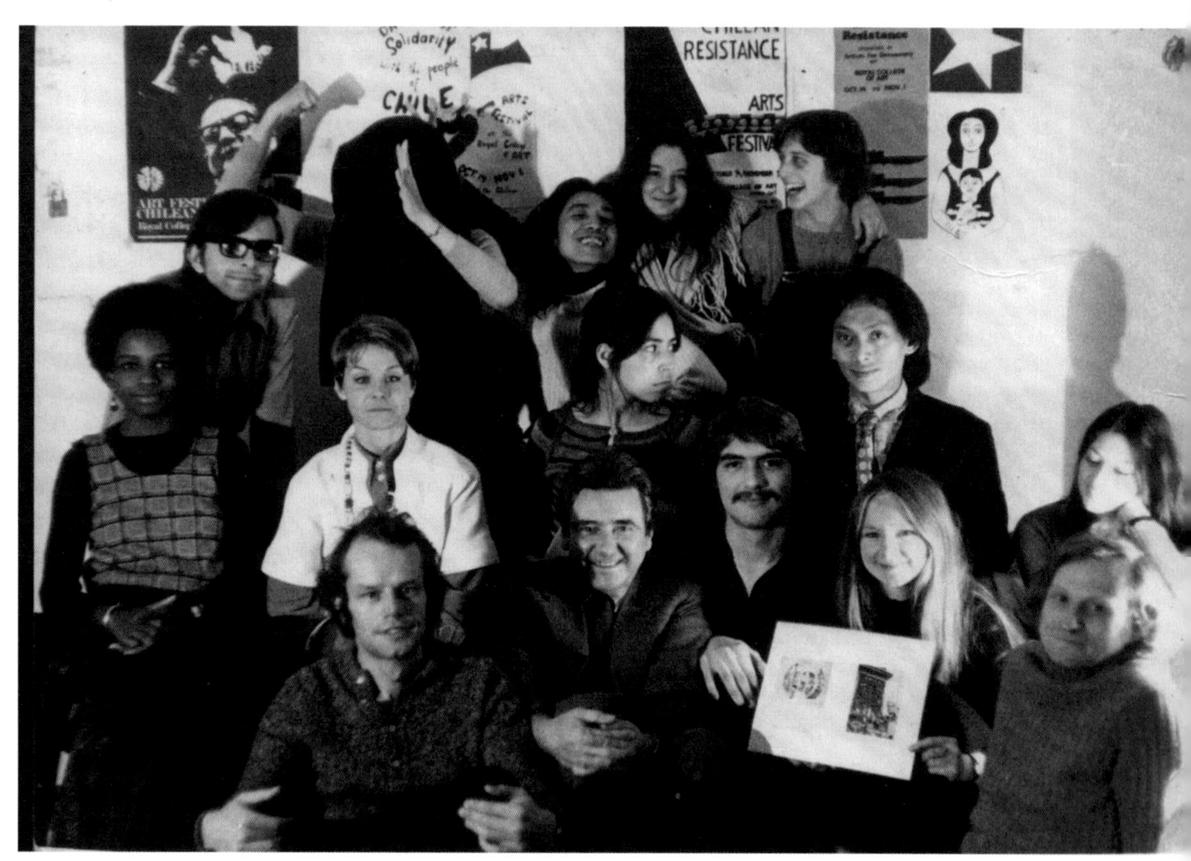
Solidarity
CHILE
RESISTANCE
ARTS
Resistance

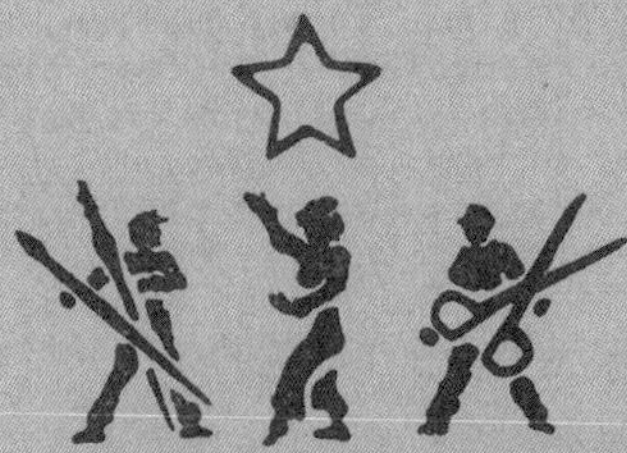

ARTISTS FOR DEMOCRACY

c/o STUDIO INTERNATIONAL, 14 West Central Street, London WC1A 1JH

Dear____________________,

Greetings. On behalf of ARTISTS FOR DEMOCRACY we would like to thank you for your participation in the INTERNATIONAL ARTS FESTIVAL FOR CHILEAN RESISTANCE. So far the response to our festival is tremendous. Many artists from all parts of the world continue to send us materials, art works, documentation, messages of support and statements of solidarity with the heroic Chilean people in their just fight against brutal fascism.

We would have liked to write individually to every artist participating in this festival but as we in ARTISTS FOR DEMOCRACY have to do all the organisational work ourselves (plus the fact that we have veritably no funds, except for the small sums that come out of our own pockets and the donations of progressive sympathetic persons), we have decided to send you this circular to inform you of the progress of our organisation so far.

The INTERNATIONAL ARTS FESTIVAL FOR CHILEAN RESISTANCE will open at the Royal College of Art, Kensington Gore, London, on Monday October 14, 1974, at 8 p.m. The programme for that evening will include an opening speech by Professor Alvaro Bunster, former Ambassador of Chile to the United Kingdom during the Popular Unity government of the late President Salvador Allende, and now London chairman of the Chilean Committee for Human Rights of the Chile Anti-fascist Front in Rome. Musical, theatrical, dance performances and other events will also be held on that evening, with brief talks on the aims and purposes of the festival and of ARTISTS FOR DEMOCRACY. ★ And readings of poems by Pablo Neruda, Violeta Parra, Victor Jara.

So far the following events have been scheduled for the duration of the festival:

Tuesday October 15 at 6:30 p.m.: Symposium on Cultural Imperialism and Latin American art and culture. In the chair: Ariel Dorfmann of Chile.

Wednesday October 16th at 6:30 p.m.: Cultural Work in Chile during the Popular Unity government. In the chair: Cecilia Vicuna of Chile.

Thursday October 17 at 6:30 p.m.: Progressive Women and the Arts: a discussion. In the chair: Tina Keane, Rob Henderson and Sonia Knox.

Friday October 18 at 6:30 p.m.: Symposium on Art and Culture in Asia and the Middle East. In the chair: Lek of Cambodia and Jun Terra of the Philippines.

Saturday October 19 at 6:30 p.m.: Popular and democratic culture: a discussion. In the chair: David Medalla, chairman of Artists for Democracy.

Monday October 21 at 6:30 p.m.: A discussion on films to be led by Steve Sprung of Cinema Action, Mitch Davies of the Royal College of Art Film School, ' Nick May of the National Film School,

Tuesday October 22 at 6:30 p.m.: A discussion on poster-making and the role of the poster in revolutionary struggles, to be led by John and Pippa Smith of Rabbit Press, and Jonathan Miles of Artists Liberation Front.

Wednesday October 23 at 6:30 p.m.: A discussion on the role of the progressive artist in capitalist and socialist societies: a discussion to be led by Jorg Immendorf of Germany.

Thursday October 24 at 6:30 p.m.: The Situation, Past and Present, in Chile: a teach-in, to be conducted by Chilean artists in exile.
Friday October 25 at 6:30 p.m.: A Symposium on Art and Culture in Africa and the Black Culture of the Caribbean. In the chair: Lester Lewis.
Saturday October 26 at 6:30 p.m.: Lessons of the C hilean struggle: a discussion to be led by representatives of the Chile Anti-fascist Front in Rome.
Monday October 28 at 6:30 p.m.: The Artist and the Community: a discussion to be led by Mavis Penn and Colin Grigg of Artists for Democracy.
Tuesday October 29 at 6:30 p.m.: An open forum on current artistic movements with the participation of all the artists in the festival.
Wednesday October 30 at 6:30 p.m.: Experimental forms of art: a discussion to be led by John Dugger of Artists for Democracy.

The auction sale will be held on Thursday October 31st, 1974, at 8 p.m. If you have any friends in Britain whom you would like to come to both the exhibition and the auction sale, and to participate in the festival, please let us know their names and addresses and we shall send them invitations. Better still (and this also saves us valuable money for extra postage) , when you next write to them, do tell them about the festival and encourage them to come. We welcome all the support we can get from all progressive people.

We have decided to make the festival itself an on-going continuous creative process. For this reason, and because we are really low on funds, we have decided <u>not</u> to publish an expensive glossy catalogue in advance of the festival. Instead , at the exhibition, we shall display all relevant information and documentation about the artists participating. So, if you have further documentation to send us, please do so, and we will include them in the exhibition. At the exhibition itself there will be three wall newspapers: one will explain the situation in Chile during the Popular Unity government and the events in Chile during the coup of September 11, 1973 and events in Chile today. The second wall newspaper will be for people coming to the festival to put their comments, criticisms of the exhibition as a whole and of the individual works on view. The third wall newspaper will contain all statements of support and solidarity with the Chilean people in their fight against fascism. If you belong to any cultural group or political party in your country that support the Chilean people's struggle, we suggest asking your group or party to send a telegram of greetings to Artists for Democracy, c/o Studio International, 14 West Central street, London WC1A 1JH, England, stating your group or party's support and solidarity with the Chilean people in their fight against fascism.

For the third wall-newspaper, David Medalla suggested putting up translations in all the languages of the world:a sentence from the last statement of President Salvador Allende shortly before he was assassinated by fascist troops at the La Moneda Palace in Santiago de Chile on September 11, 1973, and a stanza from a beautiful poem by the late poet Pablo Neruda. On a separate piece of paper (enclosed) you will find the statement and the fragment of poetry in Spanish and in English translation. If you and your friends know other languages apart from Spanish and English, please send us translations of these texts and we shall put them up in the exhibition.

The texts by Allende and Neruda we shall also print in the book of the festival which we will publish after the festival ends. This book will contain all relevant information about the festival, illustrations of the events and of the works on show, texts of the discussions, and general data which will serve as guidelines to all progressive and democratic loving artists in the world. We are now asking for financial contributions to make this book a reality, and we hope that the book itself will be a work of art.

This is all for now. We shall write again soon. Meanwhile, many many thanks for your cooperation and support. With all best wishes,

Yours in friendship,

David Medalla
Chairman, AFD

Cecilia Vicuna · John Dugger
Festival coordinators

Guy Brett
Secretary, AFD

ARTISTS FOR DEMOCRACY

TIME AND DATE OF HANDING-IN OF THIS SLIP: ______________________

ADVANCE BIDDING SLIP : AUCTION SALE OF ART WORKS
ARTS FESTIVAL FOR CHILEAN RESISTANCE
ORGANISED BY ARTISTS FOR DEMOCRACY
AT THE ROYAL COLLEGE OF ART LONDON OCTOBER 14 – 30, 1974

DATE OF AUCTION SALE: WEDNESDAY, OCTOBER 30, 1974
TIME: 8 p.m. precisely.
PLACE: The Hall, Royal College of Art, Kensington Gore, London SW7.

Note: this is an advance bidding slip to enable prospective buyers to bid for the art works on sale at the festival in advance of the auction sale on Wednesday, October 30, 1974. The works on sale are by international artists and cultural workers. Half the proceeds of the auction sale will go to the Chile Anti-Fascist Front in Rome, Italy. The other half will go to tho participating artists, or, in some cases, as specifically stated by individual artists, to ARTISTS FOR DEMOCRACY to cover the costs of mounting the arts festival.

To: BM – ARTISTS FOR DEMOCRACY
LONDON WC1V 6XX

I wish to bid for the following lot(s) with corresponding sum(s):

LOT NO.	ARTIST/TITLE OF ART WORK	THE SUM I WILL PAY

Signed ______________________

YOUR NAME (IN BLOCK LETTERS) ______________________

ADDRESS ______________________

______________________ TEL. NO. ____________

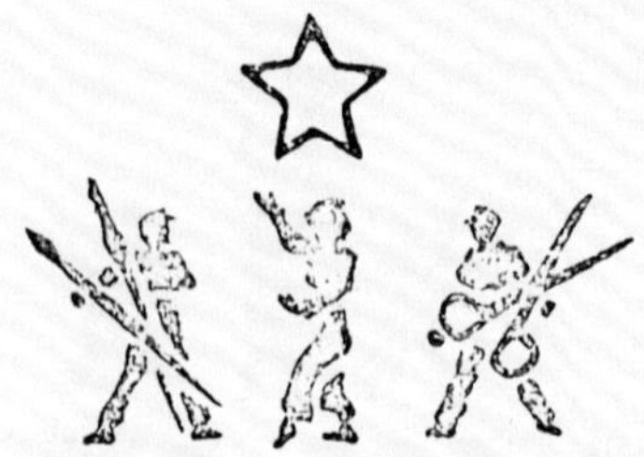

ARTISTS FOR DEMOCRACY

c/o STUDIO INTERNATIONAL, 14 West Central Street, London WC1A 1JH

THE AIMS OF ARTISTS FOR DEMOCRACY
and some suggestions for our organisation,
with proposals for immediate and long-range tasks

Document drafted by David Medalla and presented to an AFD general meeting on Tuesday, 26 November 1974, in London, for general discussio[n] by all AFD members.

On 6 May 1974, a group of progressive international cultural workers gathered in London and formed ARTISTS FOR DEMOCRACY.

The basic aims of our organisation are three-fold and inter-linked:

1) To give moral, cultural and financial support to genuine liberation movements all over the world;

2) To propagate democratic culture everywhere and to encourage all forms of progressive experimental art and cultural work:

3) To explore and develop concrete ways of integrating our varied artistic theories and practices with the struggle for emancipation of the international working class.

ARTISTS FOR DEMOCRACY is a broad artistic front organisation of international cultural workers who support fully all three inter-linked aims mentioned above. These basic aims are the main principles of our organisation and motivate all our cultural activities.

Thus, the word "broad" in "broad artistic front" is interpreted by us purely in relation to the wide range of artistic practices and cultural activities in which organisationally we engage , and covers the entire spectrum of artistic expression and production in the world, traditional and new, with the distinct emphasis on the new, i.e., the experimental.

Politically speaking, the word "broad" in "broad artistic front" is interpreted by ARTISTS FOR DEMOCRACY in the light of the correct revolutionary thesis that,

> "in the world today,
> nations want independence,
> the masses want liberation,
> and people want revolution".

We in ARTISTS FOR DEMOCRACY recognise that imperialism (which LENIN called the "highest stage of capitalism"), which is now in its death-throes, is the main enemy of the world's masses.

We in ARTISTS FOR DEMOCRACY stand firmly on the side of the masses in their heroic march along the revolutionary road to genuine interna[tional] socialism.

The auction was disappointing. I was surprised that the works of these major artists did not sell for larger sums – but it was not professionally managed. There was confusion and acrimony when it came to deciding to whom the funds should go. I do not think all of us had been party to a prior decision of sending the funds to the European anti-fascist organization [Chile Democrático]. It had been my understanding that the proceeds would go to the MIR [Revolutionary Left Movement], the only identifiable resistance to the Junta, so when David declared that a vote should be taken on this I agreed as did Jonathan Miles and others. It is quite possible – likely – that we were being duped by David who was probably aware of the prior decision and was using this reversal to go against John and Cecilia. Following this, some of us – John, David, Jonathan and myself – returned to Newport Place where there had been a fire. There were suspicions as to the cause. This seemed to be the juncture for the initial breakup of AFD.

One night I was walking up Whitfield Street, past number 143. I peered through the large window at the front of the space and on a whim climbed over the tall fence at the side of the building on the adjacent property and into an alley that led to the back of the building from which I was able to enter easily. I went from floor to floor and was impressed at how pristine the space was. I left the building and visited David who was living in a squat near Tottenham Court Road with his new partner. I related what I had discovered and my belief that it would make a great arts center as well as accommodation for a few of us. (Of course, there was self-interest, too – I needed a place to live.) David was very negative but I kept insisting so he sent his partner back with me to the building. He was then convinced of the feasibility of the venture and on a January morning, a group of us in a flatbed truck loaded with spring beds and mattresses and driven by a very nervous Guy Brett turned up at the front of 143 Whitfield Street. I, Jonathan and David's partner broke off the lock on the front door and took possession of the property. So AFD was reborn.

Stephen Pusey

Squatting was the thing to do at the time. There was a serious lack of housing – we couldn't afford to pay for our own spaces in London, so we decided to squat an empty building for greater use, not only for ourselves but for others. So we set up AFD, after the big, big show of Chile at RCA. Some of the AFD members squatted off the Drummond Street, but it was only one floor and we were all together there. We thought there must be some spaces around. We looked and there were empty buildings on Whitfield Street.

[...]

All kinds of people came to AFD, from the gallery-goer types, to the street children in the neighbourhood, to waiters in the restaurant. They were curious about their neighbours. So there were local audiences, artists and the elites, all kinds of people who came.

Jun Terra

I may be wrong, but I believe I had the first exhibition in the ground-floor space – of a series of Social Realist paintings I was doing at the time. This preceded my first mural a couple of years later in Earlham Street, in 1977, which was a product of my involvement with the Covent Garden Community, where I both lived and had my studio. Local residents, community workers and neighbours were portrayed. By this time I had long moved on from AFD. I painted a number of murals from 1977 to 1982, but the two largest ones were the Covent Garden mural and the Brixton mural in Stockwell Park Road [1982]. … These were formative years for many of us.

Stephen Pusey

143 Whitfield Street was not only an exhibition space, we (myself, David Medalla and Virgil Calaguian) lived on the top two floors. The gallery occupied the first two floors. There was a constant flow of artists, young and old, and visitors to the gallery, some of them staying overnight or for a few days. When the property was repossessed, members of the AFD went their own ways, but there was never any formal end to the organisation. The members, although dispersed around the world, are carrying on with the lessons of their experience, whether briefly or sustained, with the AFD. Some maintain contact with one another. Some are still active in other 'democratic' ventures.

Jun Terra

We had set up AFD in 1975 and I did the first show. We put on film shows and Dave Medalla was waving the red flag. We had amazing shows there, film shows, performances. Alice Hughes would come and do things there. That's how I first met her, she was at Chelsea, a student of Dave Medalla. We had linked up with the art schools in some way and found that we all knew each other somewhere on the line. It was of course the politics of AFD. My gallery became AFD, there were some very interesting installations there.

[…]

I think I'm a political artist. I have always been political but I'm just naturally political, but I don't allow my politics to change the aesthetics of my work. My work would actually speak for itself. I work on many, many different levels. I work with the idea of beauty, movement, light and colour; all the things that I've always loved as an artist and as a painter. But I love that a conceptual side is how you can weave different ideas of notions through the work, but also that the work doesn't actually say with neon lights: 'I am political.'

Tina Keane

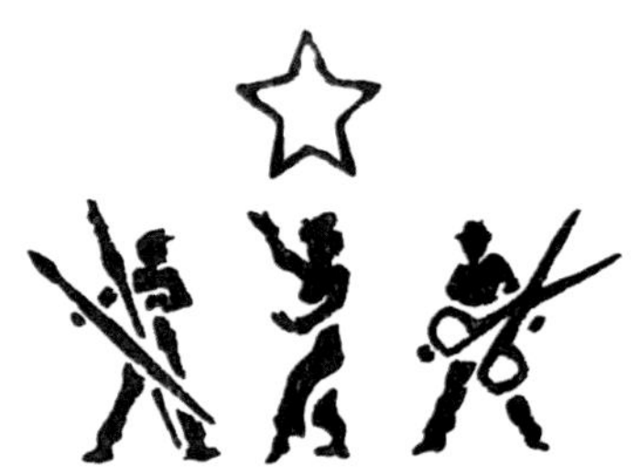

ARTISTS FOR DEMOCRACY

Cultural Centre 143 Whitfield St. London W1P 5RY

INAUGURAL SHOW

FRIDAY 31 JAN. – THURSDAY 6 FEB.
1975

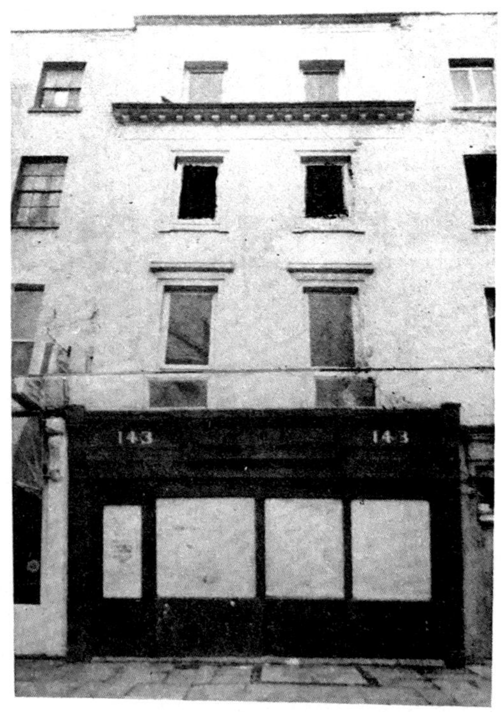

SUNDAY 9 FEBRUARY ONWARDS

WORKS IN PROGRESS

Continuous exhibit of current work projects by members of AFD

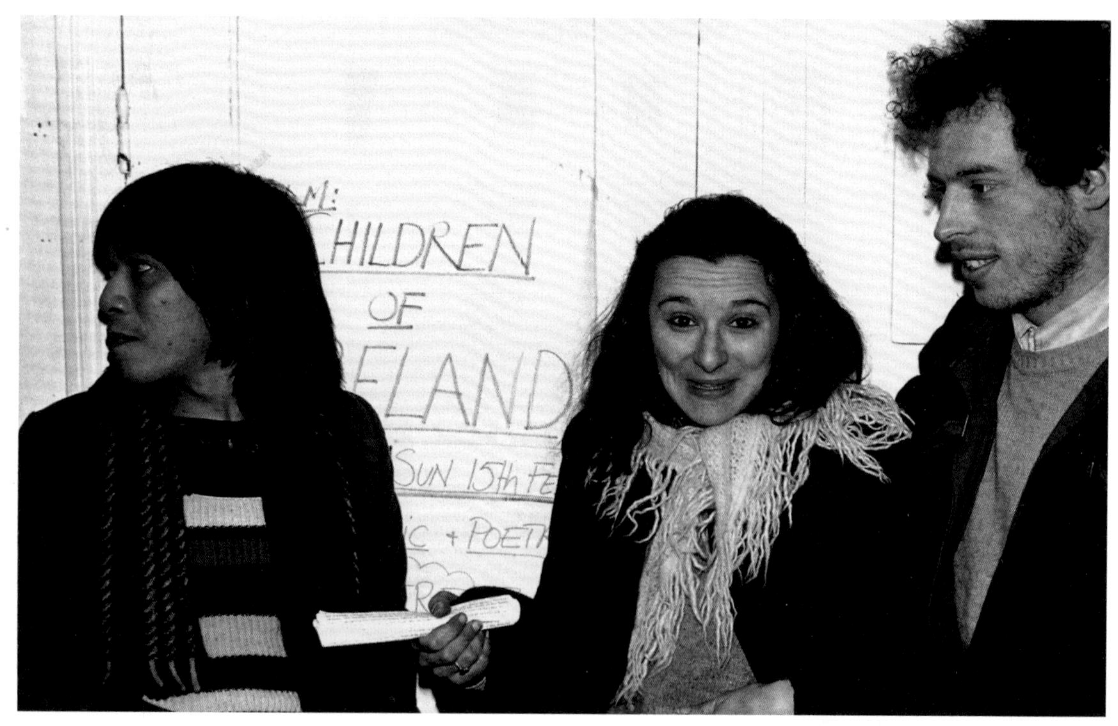

Virgil Calaguian, Sylvia Stevens and Jonathan Miles

ARTISTS FOR DEMOCRACY
143 Whitfield St. W.1. (by Warren St. Tube)
presents from March 2 to March 19

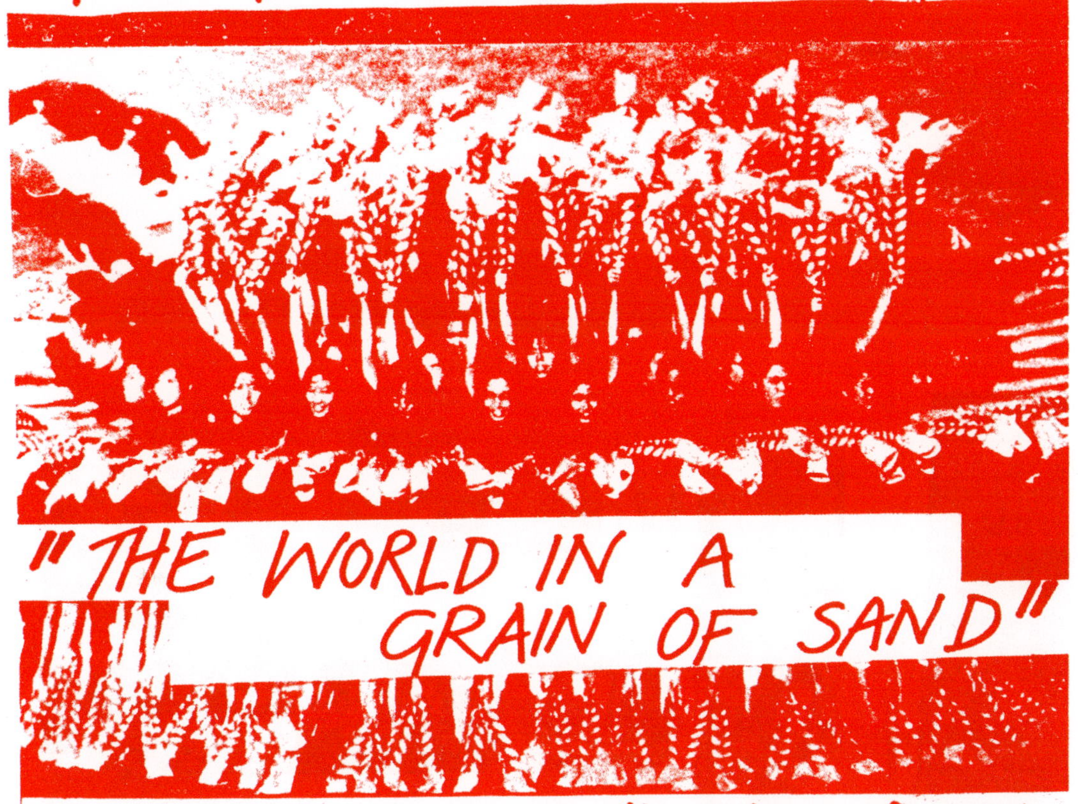

An investigation into the agricultural bases of social organisation with – Participational Enviroment by Lynn McRitchie; "Fruits of the Earth in Decorative Art" a photographic exhibition compiled by Guy Brett.

March 7. 8·00 p.m. a discussion "The Food Machine" with representatives from BSRS, World Medicine + others.

March 9. 8·00 p.m. premiere "Bread" a film by David Glynn.

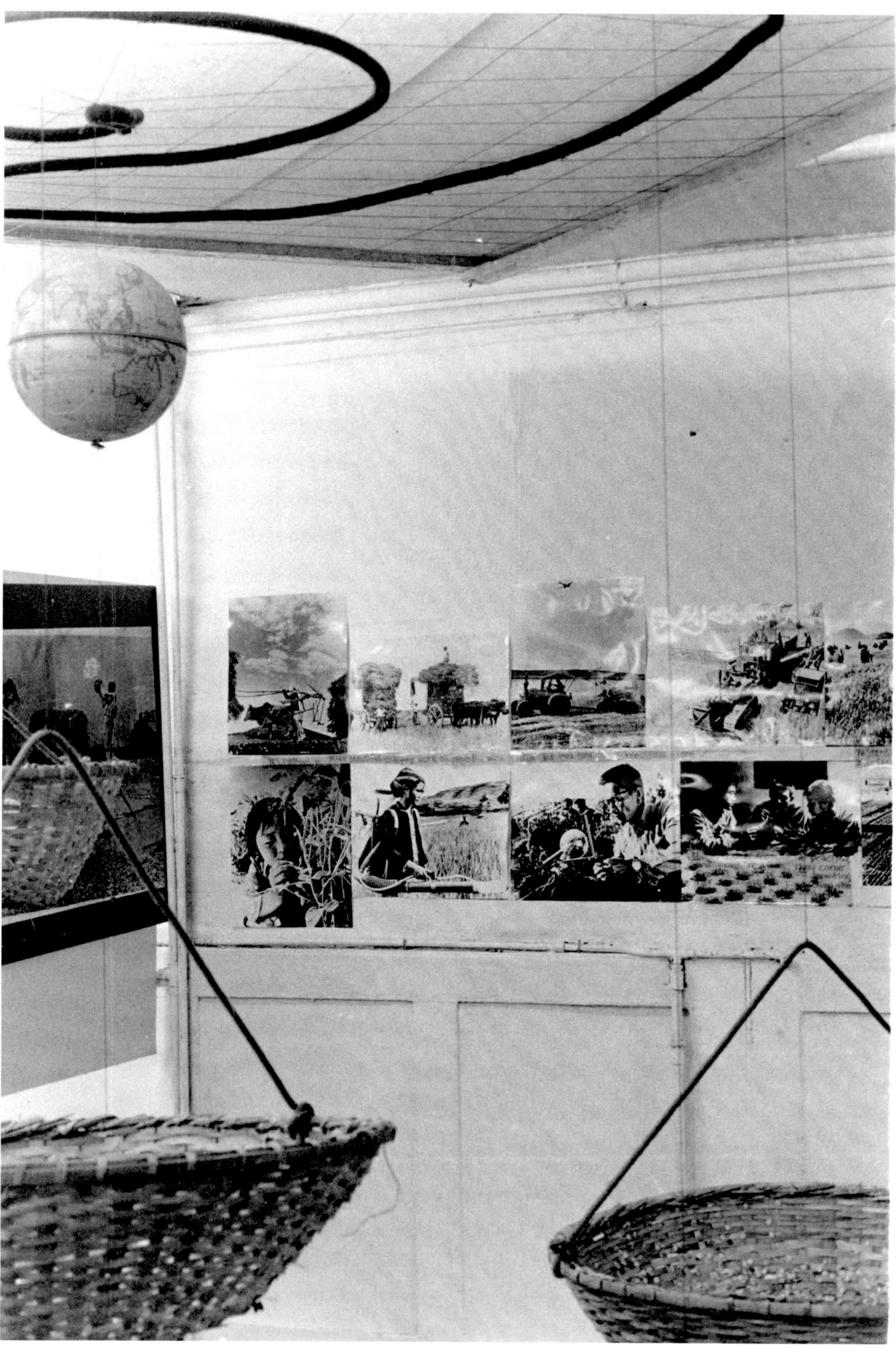

Lynn MacRitchie's 'The World in a Grain of Sand', 143 Whitfield Street, March 1975

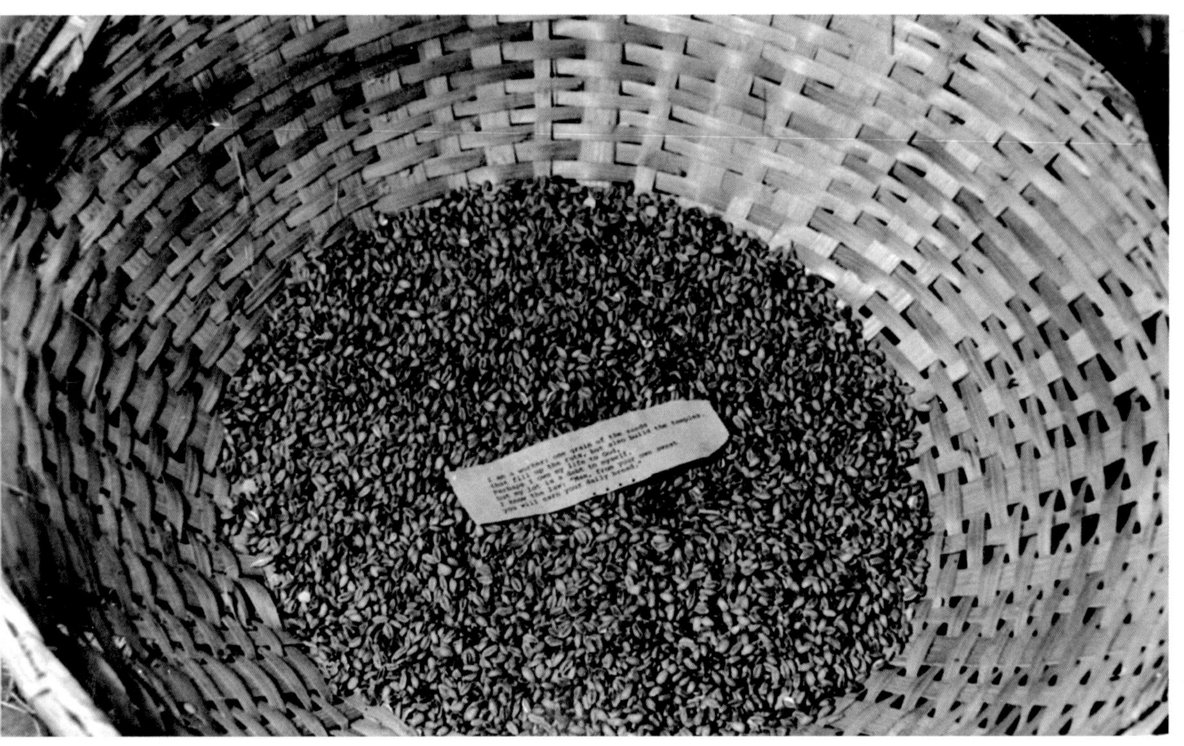

A screen was hung in the doorway, made of double strips of clear plastic containing photographs cut from travel brochures. Visitors had to push their way through the screen (i.e. through the world of illusion!) to enter the installation. Inside, a further set of screens, made from torn-up newsprint paper stitched together and hung on canes, made a maze-like interior which visitors walked through. At the heart of the installation, an arrangement of baskets filled with wheat grain or with small pink paper discs punched from pages of the *Financial Times* was suspended from a yellow cloth panel with a globe of the world hanging at the centre of a blue rope spiral. Visitors could sift through the grain or paper discs to reveal texts about the relation between labour, politics and production. On the walls, photographs showed images of sowing, tending and harvesting grain from China, India and Russia and images of bread and bread-making – the staff of life.

Lynn MacRitchie

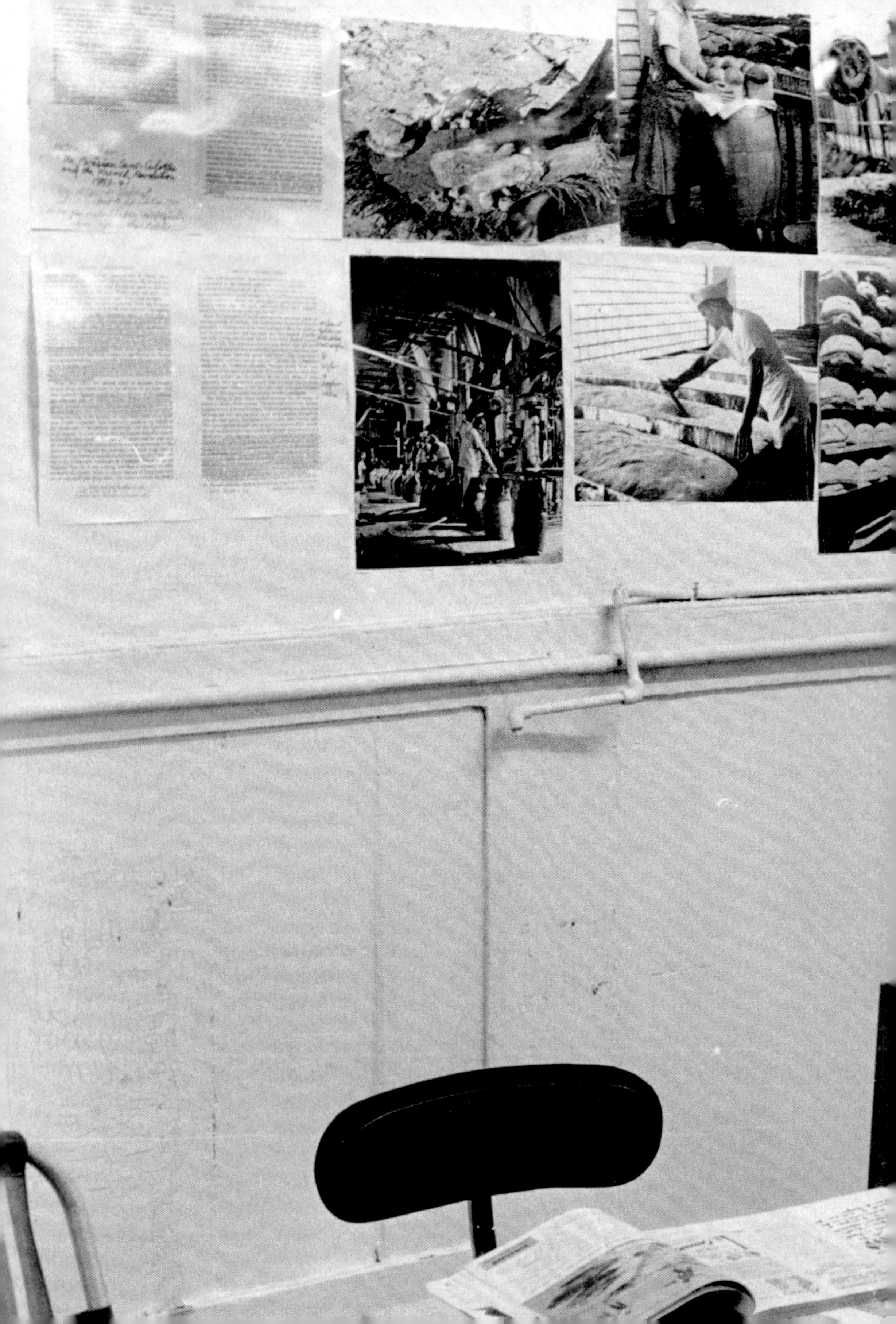

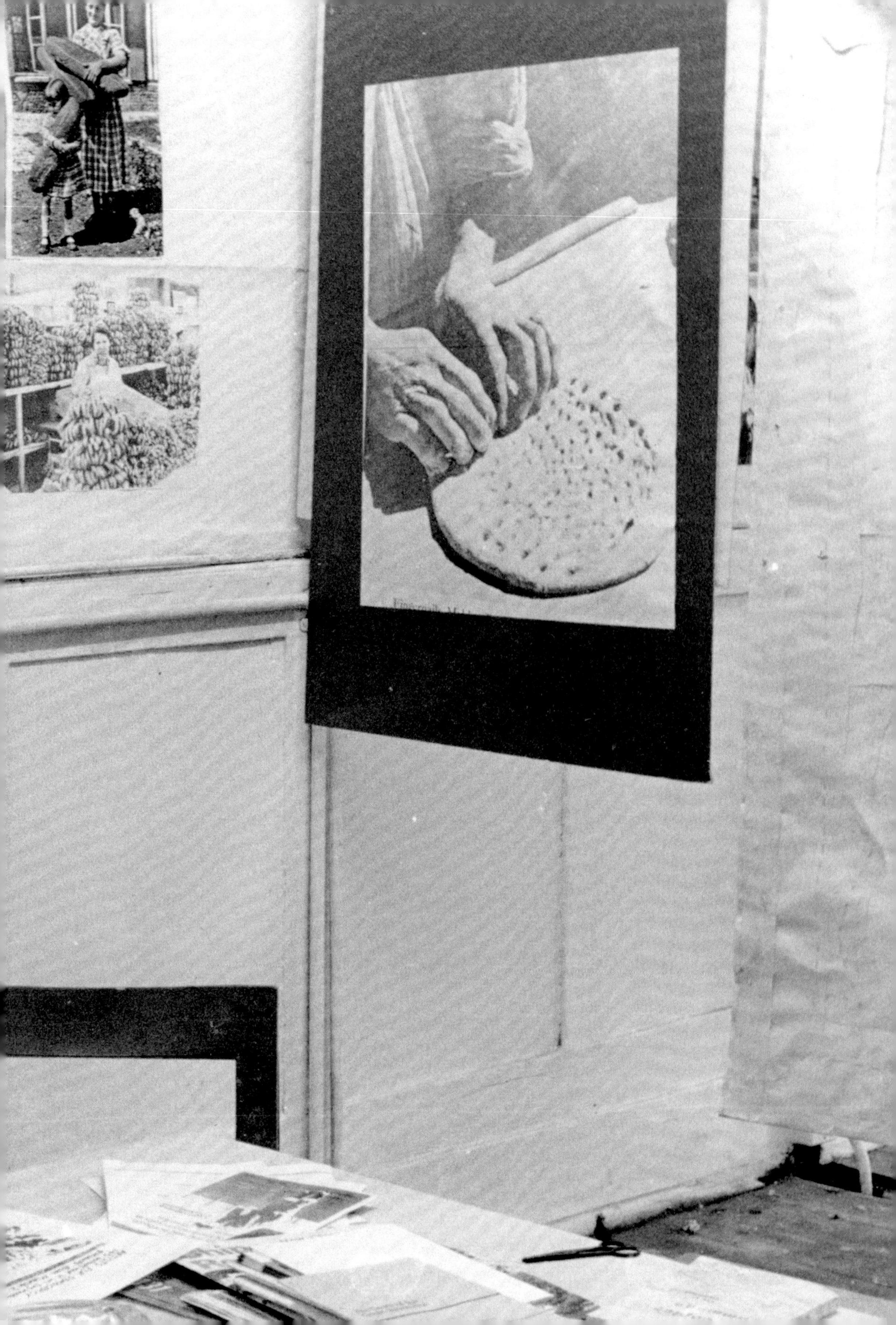

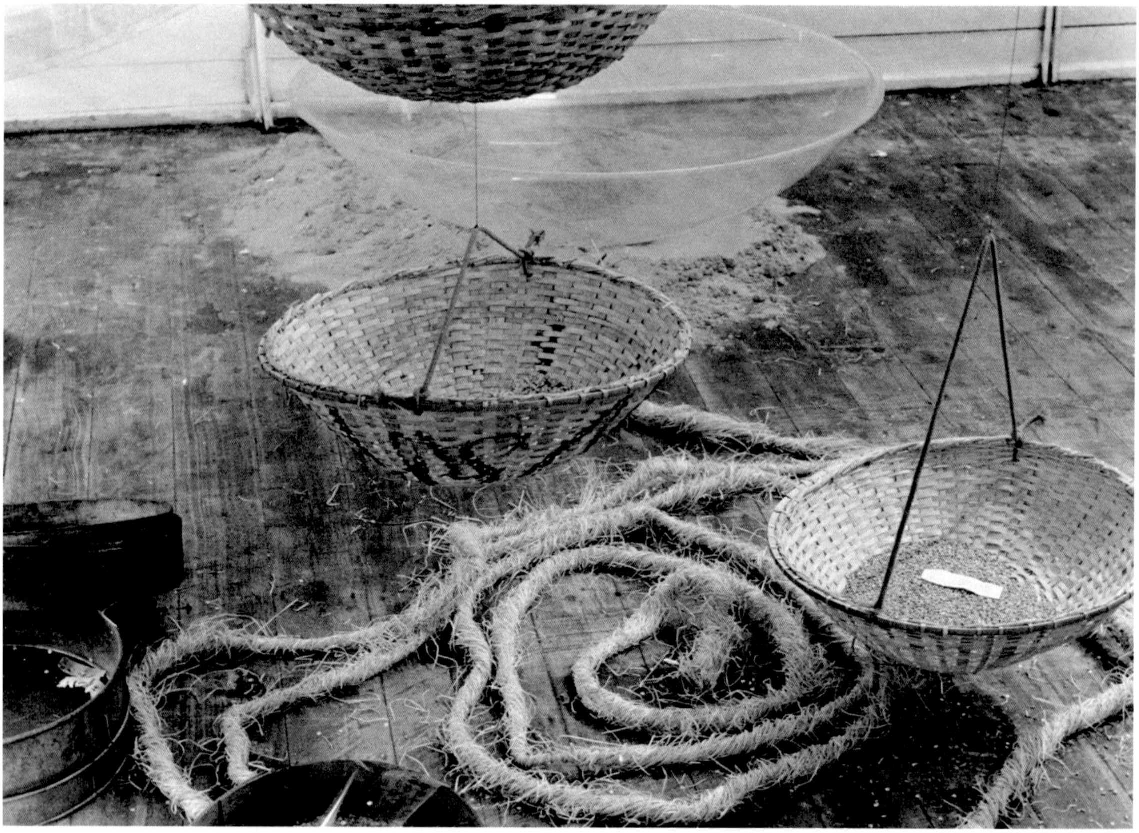

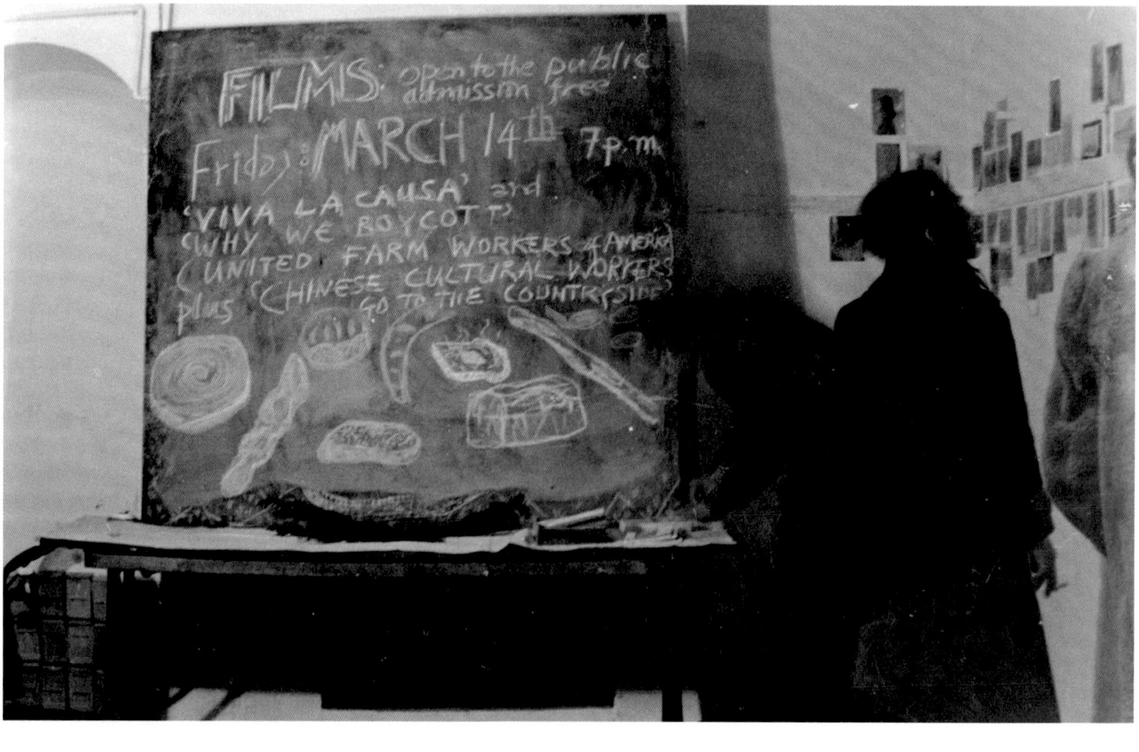

Lynn MacRitchie's 'The World in a Grain of Sand', 143 Whitfield Street, March 1975

Squatter-artists with a social purpose

Galleries

OPPOSITE a boarded-up demolition site in among the oriental groceries and restaurants near Warren Street, **Artists for Democracy** have set up a London cultural centre. It's at 143 Whitfield Street, W1, in a large decaying house, where they've been squatting for about a month, using the ground floor ex-restaurant for exhibitions and the rooms above for workrooms and offices.

Some members live here too, manning the exhibitions on a rota. They're hoping to stay long enough to make a creative impression on "fellow cultural workers and progressive organisations," and to this end they welcome visitors from noon till midnight, especially on Mondays when at 7 pm they hold discussions on works on show and in progress.

AFD are a casual group of about 20 artists who share similar ideas about art and society. They first acted as a group last year in initiating the international Arts Festival for Chilean Resistance, donating their time and artist power for months.

Their "fledgling organisation" now has three aims: to give moral, cultural and financial support to genuine liberation movements; to propagate democratic culture and at the same time encourage progressive experimental art; to integrate artistic practice with the struggles of the international working class and oppressed people everywhere for emancipation.

"Our spectrum is from vague democrat to Maoist," said the publicity man, Jun Terra, himself an experienced Maoist painter. Their chairman is also a Maoist, David Medalla, a well-known artist whose warmly humanist inventions I have reviewed from time to time.

Their secretary is Guy Brett, an art critic for *The Times* till last month, when they gave him the push because of divergent views (thereby causing an important correspondence in *The Guardian* on journalistic freedom and editorial responsibility).

AFD decide collectively what activities to support and what art to show, giving priority to their own members but also inviting internationally famous artists, in every case considering quality and social content. A good practice. But I would not like to be the vague democrat committed to some of the opinions of the consensus. "Oppressed people," for instance, rightly include women in many parts of the world, but "genuine liberation movements" cover only ZANU, and not ZAPU, in relation to Zimbabwe/Rhodesia.

That said, let me unreservedly recommend the current exhibition which runs to March 19. Not being permanent works of art like paintings, these transient cultural experiences don't last long and vary considerably. But if you catch it in time I think you'll find this particular show beautiful and full of ideas, reaching out with feeling and meaning through structures and pictures.

I wish its title was not such a clumsy mouthful: "*The World in a Grain of Sand* — an investigation into the agricultural bases of social organisation with participational environment by Lynn McRitchie; and *Fruits of the Earth in Decorative Art* — a photographic exhibition compiled by Guy Brett." Extending the show, a film, *Bread* by David Glynn, was given its premiere this week, and there are to be discussions on *The Food Machine* with scientists involved in Social Responsibility in Science.

So what do you actually see? Pushing through a curtain of transparent plastic bags, each containing a coloured advertisement for a trip to some far-off place, you find yourself in a symbolic far-off place — a miniature rice-terrace constructed inside a large paper tent. From outside, slides project pictures of cultivation on to one translucent wall, while from above inverted perspex domes hang at eye and knee level, each filled with grain from which you can fish out buried poems or comments.

But the grains are not uniform: some are husked rice or wheat, others are punched-out grain-size circles of the pink *Financial Times*. Newspaper cuttings on food costs, gluts, shortages, and photographs of Chinese prints of food products hang on another wall.

Guy Brett's photographs are a subsidiary exhibit, showing plant-forms used in popular decorative art from every continent throughout the centuries, in hand-blocked cotton curtains from Java or seventeenth-century plaster-work from England. "All people's art," said the artist on duty. I thought of Gandhi's "If village art dies, India dies."

Thus the common theme is the gap between product and process, consumer and producer, commercial glamour and natural beauty. The imagery makes us re-see our wrapped loaf as the end-product of real wheat grown in a field by real workers, processed by other real workers, and sold to us as a convenience food. And package tours to exotic places are another aspect of the same selling technique, feeding our dreams but keeping us out of contact with the Real Venice, Bali or South Africa.

When I got home I looked up Mao's thoughts on art, and found three which seem relevant to AFD. *1940:* "Prepare the ground ideologically before the revolution is ripe." *1942:* "Works of art which lack artistic quality have no force, however progressive they are politically." *1944:* "An army without culture is a dull-witted army, and a dull-witted army cannot defeat the enemy."

Margaret Richards

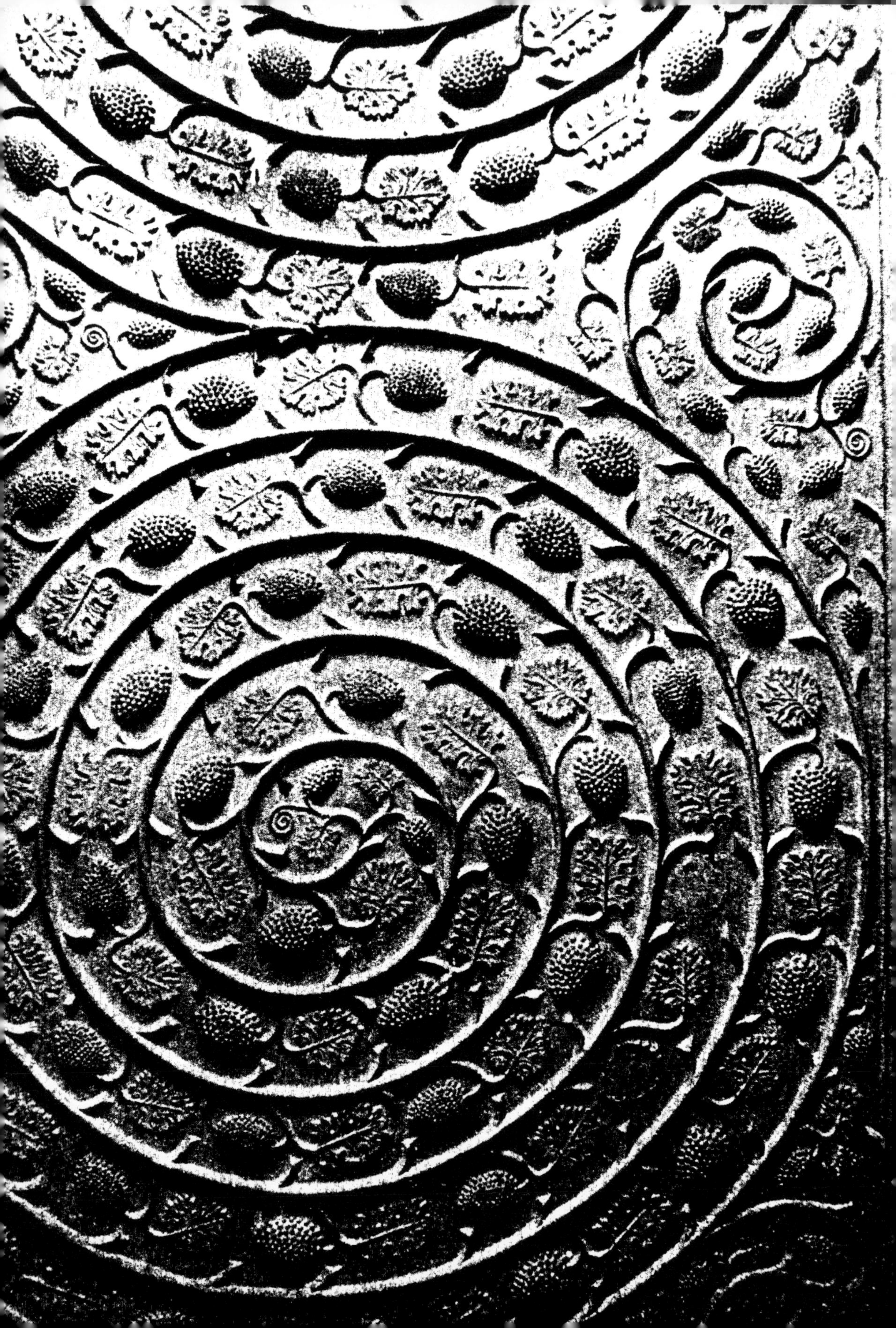

Agriculture, Field, Decoration

Good tidings: sea fruitful, wave-washed strand, smiling woods; witchcraft flees, orchards blossom, cornfields ripen, bees swarm, a cheerful world, peace and plenty, happy summer.[1]

Everything evolves, it is the cycle of nature:
After the rainy days, the fine weather comes.
In an instant, the whole world shakes off its damp clothes,
Thousands of li of mountains unfurl their brocade carpet.
Under the warm sun and the clean wind, the flowers smile,
In the big trees with branches washed clean, the birds make chorus.
Warmth fills the heart of man and life reawakens.
Bitterness now makes way for happiness.
This is how nature wills it.[2]

The old Irish chant, surviving from the days before written poetry, expresses the desire, common to all peoples, for a world of beauty and plenty. Ho Chi Minh's poem, written in prison in 1942–43, is also about a great renewal of nature and man. In it he refers to the mountains unfurling their 'brocade carpet'. To link the brocade carpet and the mountains covered in flowers is more than just a figure of speech. There is a real connection. A piece of decorative art such as a carpet is normally given a low status in the hierarchy of art, at least in the West. It is hardly considered to have any subject matter, to have any meaning. In fact the persistent theme of decorative art, common to many different epochs and cultures, is this same desire for fruitfulness and abundance. I've tried to bring this out in this selection of photographs.

All over the world decorative art is marked by its density, its repetition, its close-packed richness of pattern and colour. This gives it its force as a visual metaphor for fertility and growth. Perhaps decorative art came into existence with the invention of agriculture after the 'period of hunting and gathering'. Certainly, apart from its subject matter, there is a similarity between many of its techniques – weaving, embroidering, quilting, plastering, painting – and the slow and patient techniques of agriculture, which though undramatic and even toilsome and monotonous, can produce such radiant results.

There could be other connections too between decoration and the invention of agriculture. The cave paintings of the paleolithic hunters have a fluid composition and run in every direction over the cave walls. With decoration appears a sense of planned order and the building up of composition. Perhaps this is a reflection of the orderly work necessary in cultivation compared with the free-ranging hunt; and also of the new consciousness of limits and boundaries that must have come with the domestication, the penning-in, of wild animals. Looking at the results of their scientific work upon nature – for example, the slow breeding of wild grasses into more and more healthy, plump and regular strains of wheat – may also have led

Guy Brett, 'Agriculture, Field, Decoration'
(originally published in French as 'Terre fertile. Champ, agriculture, décoration', *Macu*

people to give decorative art its almost invariable optimism. Has anyone seen a decoration of faded or withered plants, or thin and mangy animals? Or of forms that could be described as drooping or exhausted? The keynote of decoration is energy.

Geographical differences are one of the things often reflected in decorative art: compare for example the impenetrable tropical luxuriance of Javanese batik designs with Scandinavian folk art, sparse and chaste like snow crystals. English Elizabethan embroidery makes one think of meadows, banks, countryside, a natural garden. The designs of some Maori canoe paddles are like a graphic transcription of the eddies and waves of the ocean. Many Peruvian patterns are sturdy and rough, a counterpart to their fields terraced on the sides of inhospitable mountains. In Persian designs, especially the carpets, the conditions governing the local agriculture, in this case the vital irrigation channels, seem to have filtered into decoration, into the stems and branches which meander through the patterns exploding here and there into flowers.

Some decoration is highly realistic in the sense of differentiating precise species of plants, animals, insects, fishes, etc., but a flower in decoration is never a *particular* flower, localized in time or space, shown in a particular light, blemished or individualized in any way. The joyful effect of objects in decorative art is closely linked with this lack of uniqueness: pattern and rhythm fuse the particular in the general, emphasizing the mass. The development is not towards locating objects and giving them substance (as it was in Western painting after the discovery of perspective). On the contrary, there is a continual tendency to dismantle and recombine the components of natural objects, especially flowers, almost as if they were the atoms of chemical compounds.

The natural object is used as a basis for formal changes, either towards simplification or towards elaboration. The varieties of development are apparently never-ending. (Observing loom-weaving, for example, we can see the fantastic elaboration of flower-like designs compatible with the linear technique of weaving – a technique of depositing one straight line after another to build up the image, not unlike the lines on a television screen.) This formal elaboration is another metaphor for the human capacity for working changes upon nature. The whole sense of poetry and lyricism is bound up with it, which is why the 'celebration' of nature in decorative art is also the joy of knowing it, understanding it and working upon it. Decorative art revolves around the contradiction between the wilderness and the garden.

This has been an art produced by ordinary people. Clothes and other objects have been decorated by tribal peoples and peasant societies for their own use. But even in work carried out by artisans for the nobility, for the Church, or for a foreign conqueror, the decoration is very often the democratic element, the one element that scoffs at the illusion of private property among the riches of the earth. (In Mexican baroque churches, for example, covering the walls with masses of local fruits and flowers in plaster was a means by which Indian craftsmen, forced to work for the Spanish, resisted and kept their cultural identity.) An investigation of the practice of decorative art in different societies would indeed reveal many conflicts. Embroidery has sometimes been seen by the women who made it, not as a pleasure, but as part

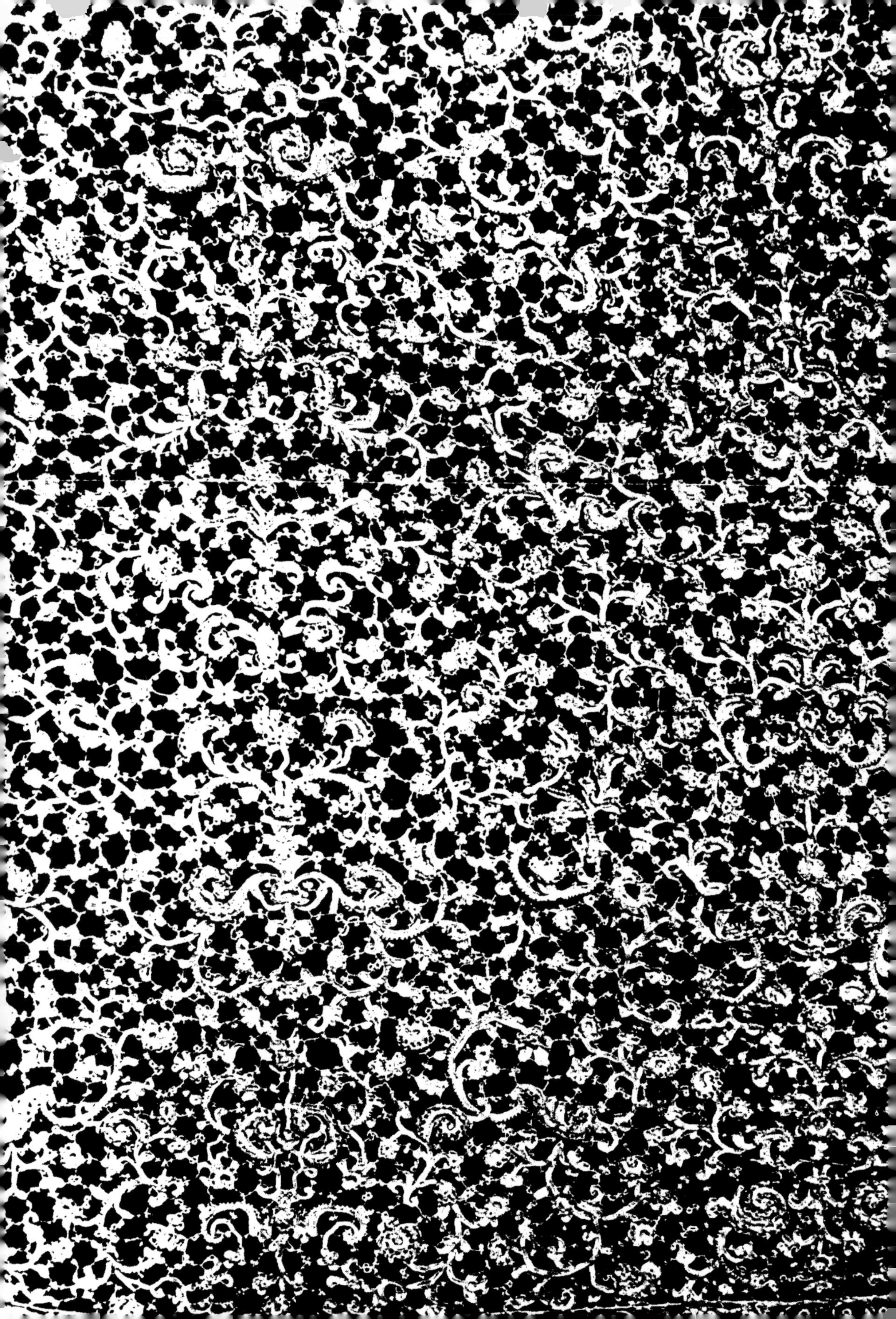

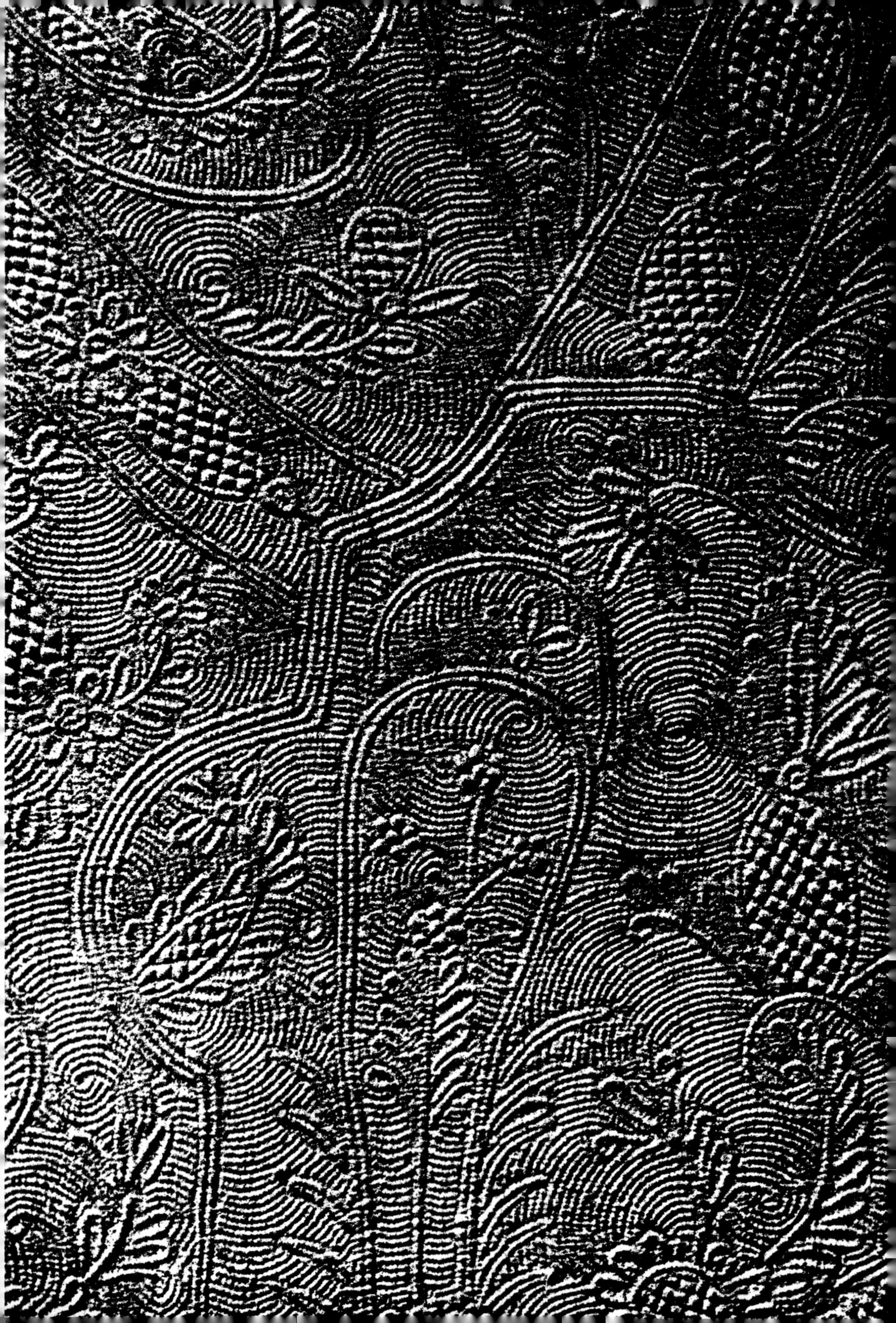

of their oppression, a kind of mindless work to keep them docilely at home. To separate good from bad in the activity then becomes a political issue.

What is the future of these art forms? Do they all belong to the past? Or to 'primitive' peoples who today are dying out or whose lives and culture are being corrupted by modern civilization? Some people believe that the loving attitude to nature and one's work which they see among 'primitive' peoples must disappear under industrialism, and is 'on the wane' today all over the world. But the people themselves are proving the contrary in their liberation movements. Nobody could miss the spirit in the 1970s paintings by peasants in the Chinese communes (such as Huhsien) which show their cultivation in such enthusiastic detail. The old abundance metaphor of decorative art – repetition, order, profusion – comes to life again in these paintings.

If decoration reflects an agricultural life, it also arises organically out of certain techniques of production. A bricklayer produces a pattern on the end wall of a house by inserting coloured or glazed bricks at certain points. The wall then displays his skill. The whole activity of bricklaying is enhanced, poeticized. But in industrial production so often all that relates to technical skill, ingenuity and imagination is hidden from sight. The intricacies of machinery and electronics, however, have an extraordinary visual fascination; they too show people working on nature, and a correspondence with traditional decoration appears. The little metallic ribbons of electric circuitry echo the branches in a Persian carpet which echo the conduits of irrigation: a lively energy flows through each. But in the modern world this is hidden. Many modern artists and poets – people like Walt Whitman, Bertholt Brecht, Fernand Leger, El Lissitsky – have advocated showing and enjoying modern technical processes as they really are.

What, then, are they hidden by? Usually by some form of cover or casing which has been designed to the dictates of 'taste'. The notion of taste is ambiguous and hard to come to terms with. But a brilliant observation by Walter Benjamin succeeds in distancing us from it so we can see it more clearly. He links the development of taste with the predominance of commodity production over any other kind of production. As a consequence of the manufacture of products as commodities for the market, 'people become less and less aware of the conditions of their production – not only the social conditions in the form of exploitation, but of the technical conditions as well'.[3] To make up for this, and to mask his lack of expertness, 'taste' becomes more and more important for the buyer. And the manufacturer, in turn, plays on taste because it is often a convenient means of disguising bad quality. Evidently, only when the reasons for these petty deceptions are removed can humankind's technique regain a sensuous, an entertaining, a magnificent relation with the 'fruitful earth'.

First published in *Macula*, Paris, no. 1, 1976.

1. *Old Irish Mantic poem 'chanted by a prophet as an augury of a good season'. Quoted in George Thomson,* Marxism and Poetry, *London: Lawrence and Wishart, 1945.*
2. *Ho Chi Minh, from* The Prison Diary of Ho Chi Minh, *trans. Aileen Palmer, New York: Bantam Books, 1971.*
3. *Walter Benjamin,* Charles Baudelaire: A Lyric Poet in the Era of High Capitalism, *London: New Left Books, 1973, pp. 104–5.*

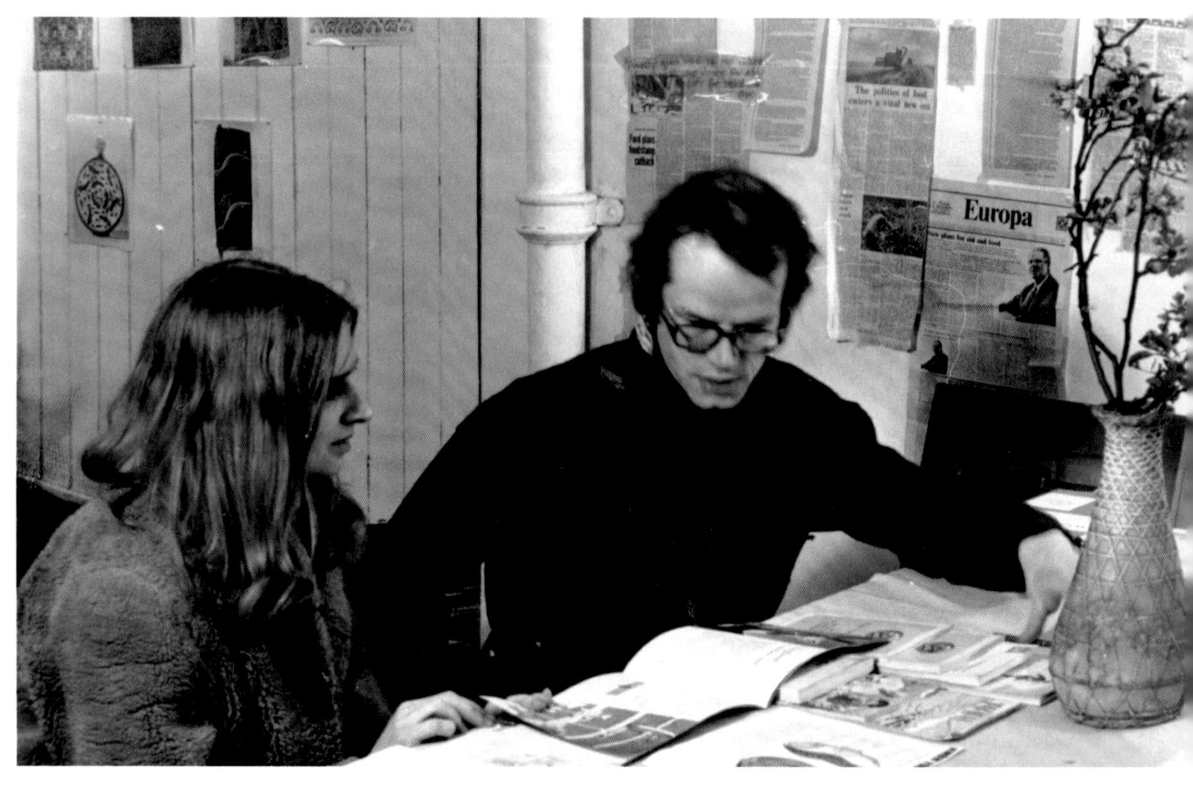

ARTISTS FOR DEMOCRACY in London

by Caroline Tisdall

ARTISTS FOR DEMOCRACY is the name of the latest platform for London's radical artists. It's a gallery-cum-meeting place run in a cooperative way and on a tight budget, and looks as if it could last until the demolisher's ball hits the rest of the Tandoori belt of Whitfield Street. The emphasis of the gallery is em, ..atically third world, and the aim is to try to combine that kind of interest with progressive art forms, discussions, and poetry readings. Exhibitions to date have included participational environments, an investigation into the relationship between social organisation and forms of agriculture, and a photo-documentation display by Guy Brett tracing the theme of the fruits of the earth.

The current exhibition presents the work of a Pakistani artist, Rasheed Araeen, who has in the past been justifiably vociferous in his condemnation of the lack of thought given to the position of the third world artist in western discussions of art. His own work started with paintings that depicted the movement of fire, and shifted to movement itself, the use of fire and water, in environmental works with which he hoped to involve people more directly.

More recently he has been working with collage: the juxtaposition of pieces of information to give a message or provide a new context. Here the problem is, that the ground is almost too well-trodden to be effective: the placing together of Kenneth Clark's Civilisation with Churchill and his tommy gun over a background of world violence and hunger is the kind of callous coexistence often criticised in the colour supplements.

Artists for Democracy, 143 Whitfield Street W1 until April 9.

Guy Brett with unidentified individual at 'Fruits of the Earth in Decorative Art', 143 Whitfield Street, March 1975

RASHEED ARAEEN

AN ARTIST FROM THE THIRD WORLD SHOWING A SELECTION OF HIS WORKS (1959–75), SPATIOSTRUCTURES, DOCUMENTATION OF ENVIRONMENTAL EVENTS, COLLAGES AND SLIDE SHOW.

PETER CROSS

AN INSTALLATION WITH NOTES

OPENING MARCH 23 AT 5 PM
12 TO 8 DAILY
MARCH 23 TO APRIL 9
POETRY READING BY NAZARETH MARCH 23 AT 7 PM

ARTISTS FOR DEMOCRACY

CULTURAL CENTRE 143 WHITFIELD ST. LONDON W1

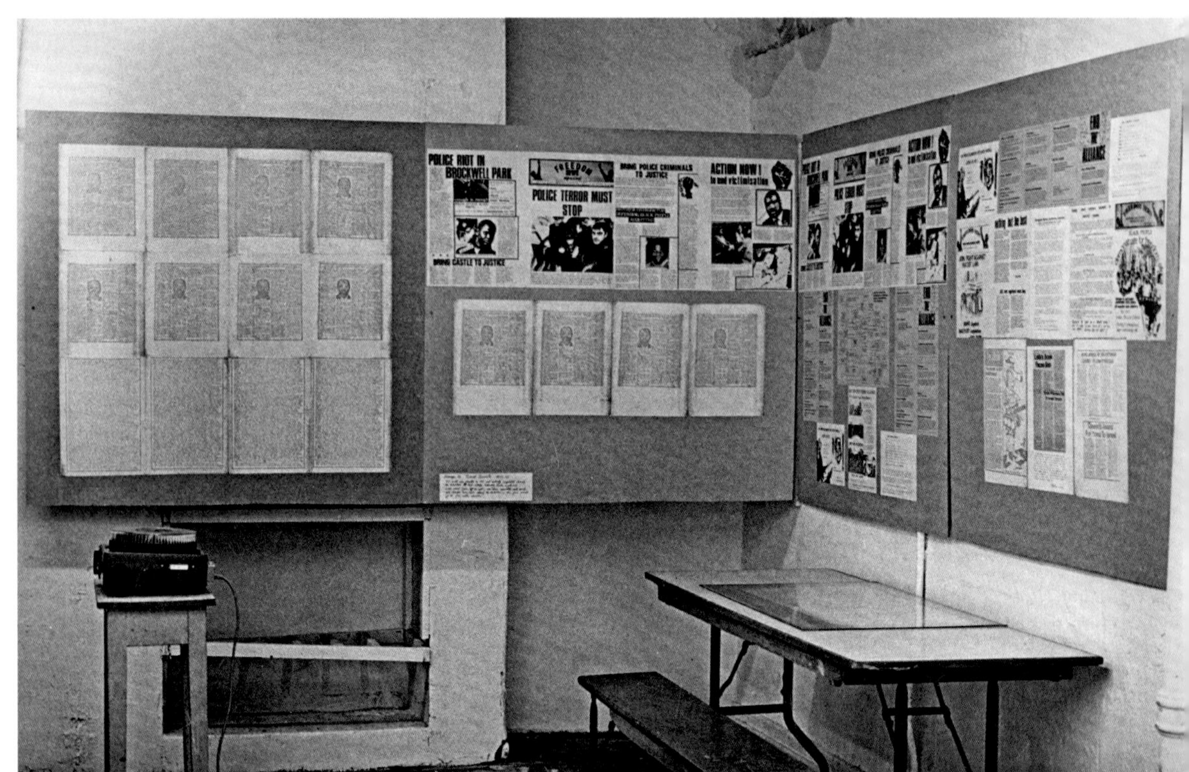

This group was founded by a group of artists and led by David Medalla; they were involved in working-class struggles in the early 70s, and then turned to art activities in support of anti-racist and anti-imperialist struggles worldwide. After successfully organising an art festival against the brutality of Pinochet's military regime in Chile, at the Royal College of Art in 1974, they established a squat for events, meetings. ... I joined the collective on the invitation of Medalla, and held my first exhibition there. AFD had no money and the Sunday gatherings needed some kind of refreshment. So, I decided to cook food. People would bring their own drinks and I provided 'curry 'n' rice' for a small sum of money.

Rasheed Araeen

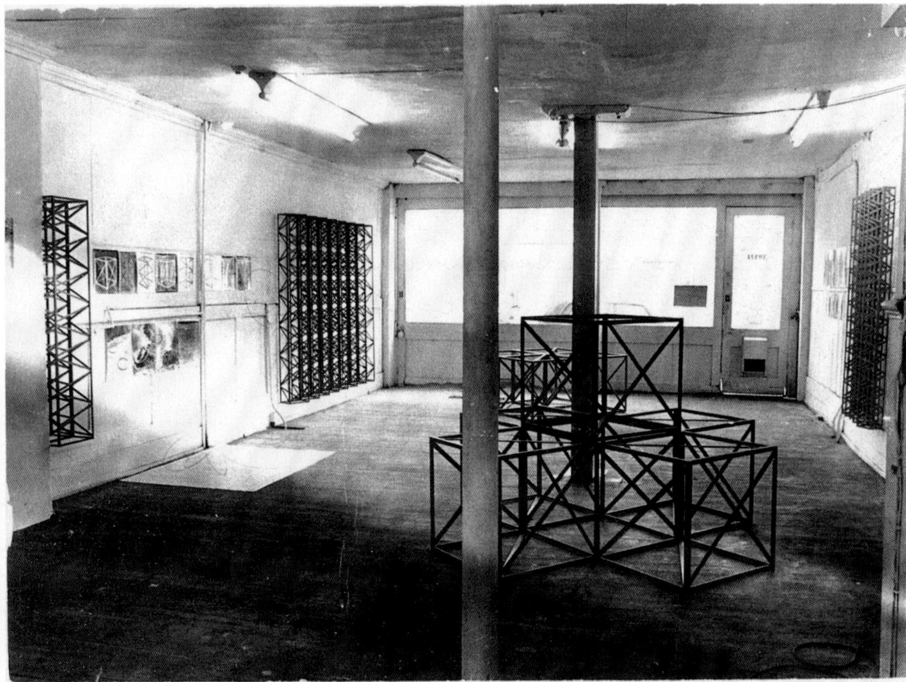

Left: Lal 1971–75 Right: Sharbati 1973 (incomplete)

Centre: Nine 1968–75 Installations: Artists for Democracy 1975

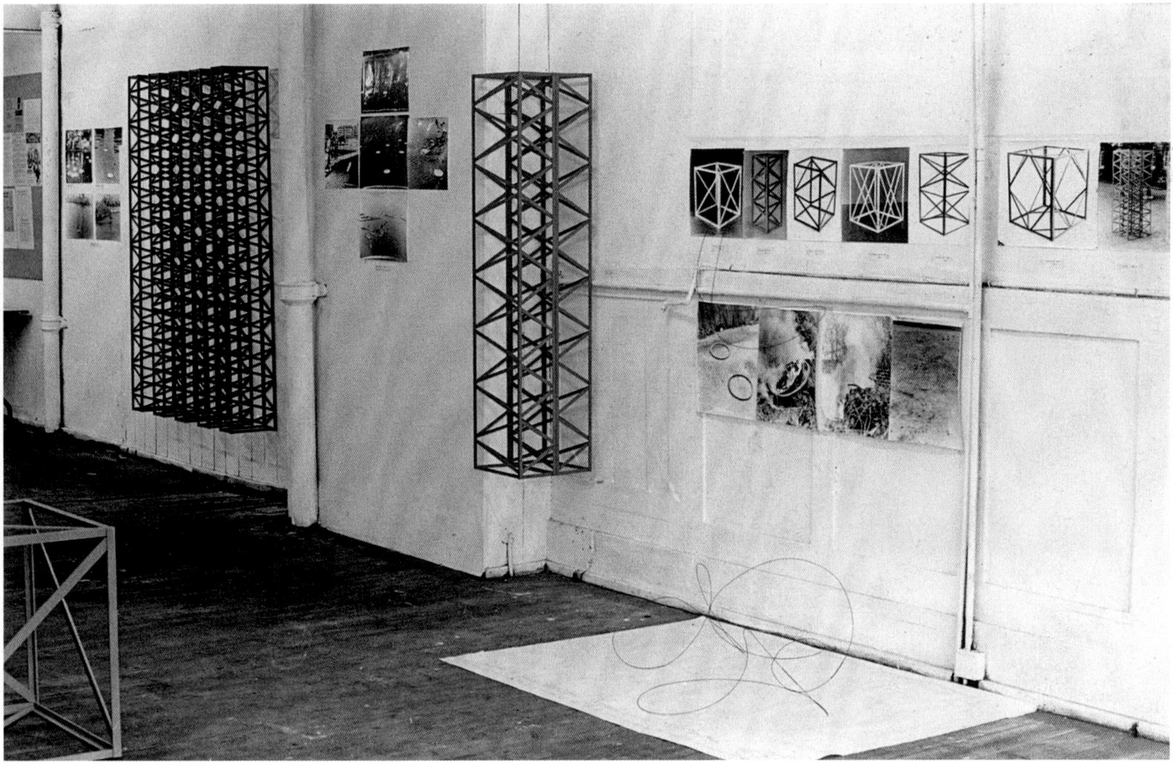

above and facing page: Rasheed Araeen's 'Works 1959–75', 143 Whitfield Street, March–April 1975

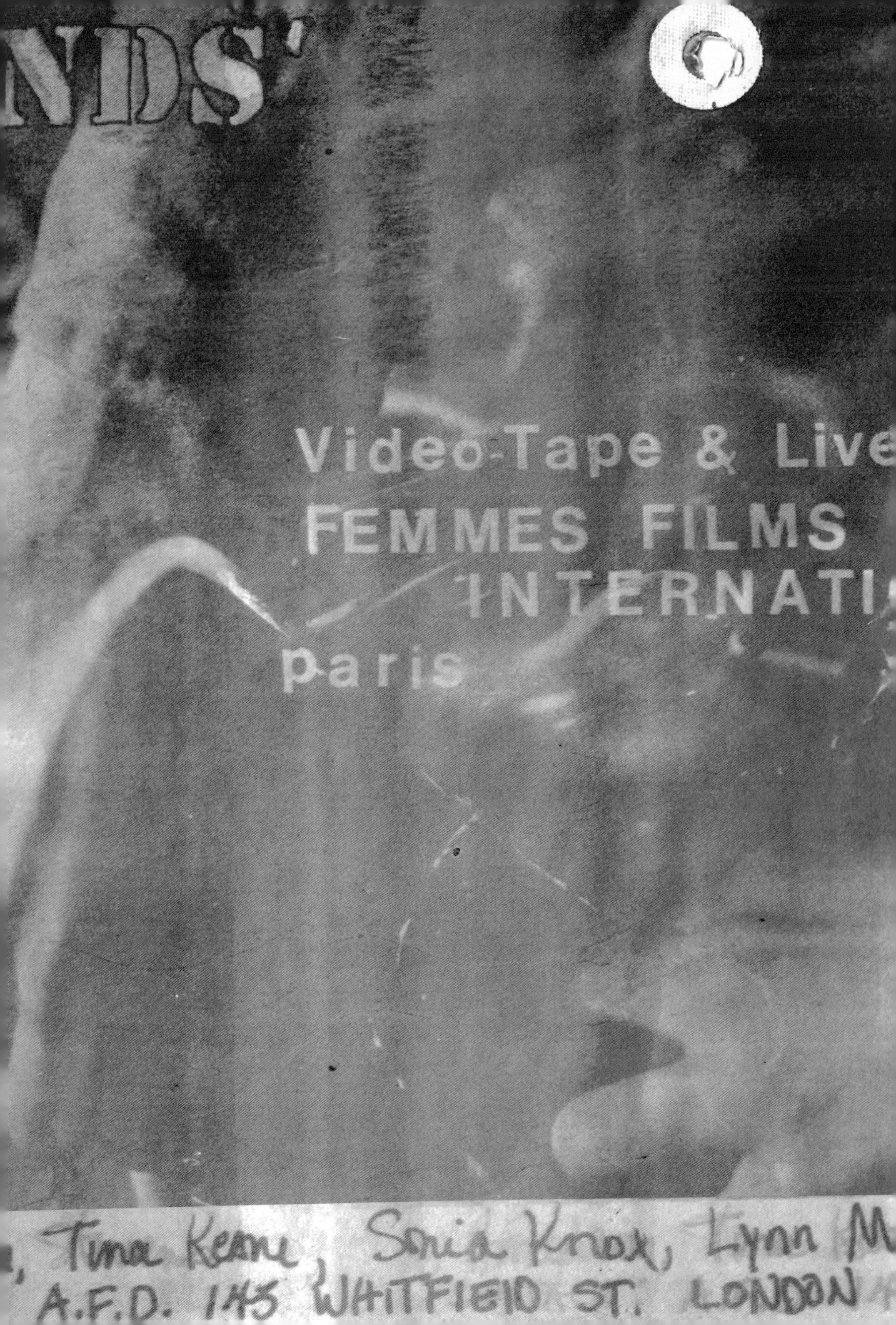

NDS'

Video-Tape & Live
FEMMES FILMS
INTERNATI
paris

, Tina Keane, Sonia Knox, Lynn M
A.F.D. 143 WHITFIELD ST. LONDON

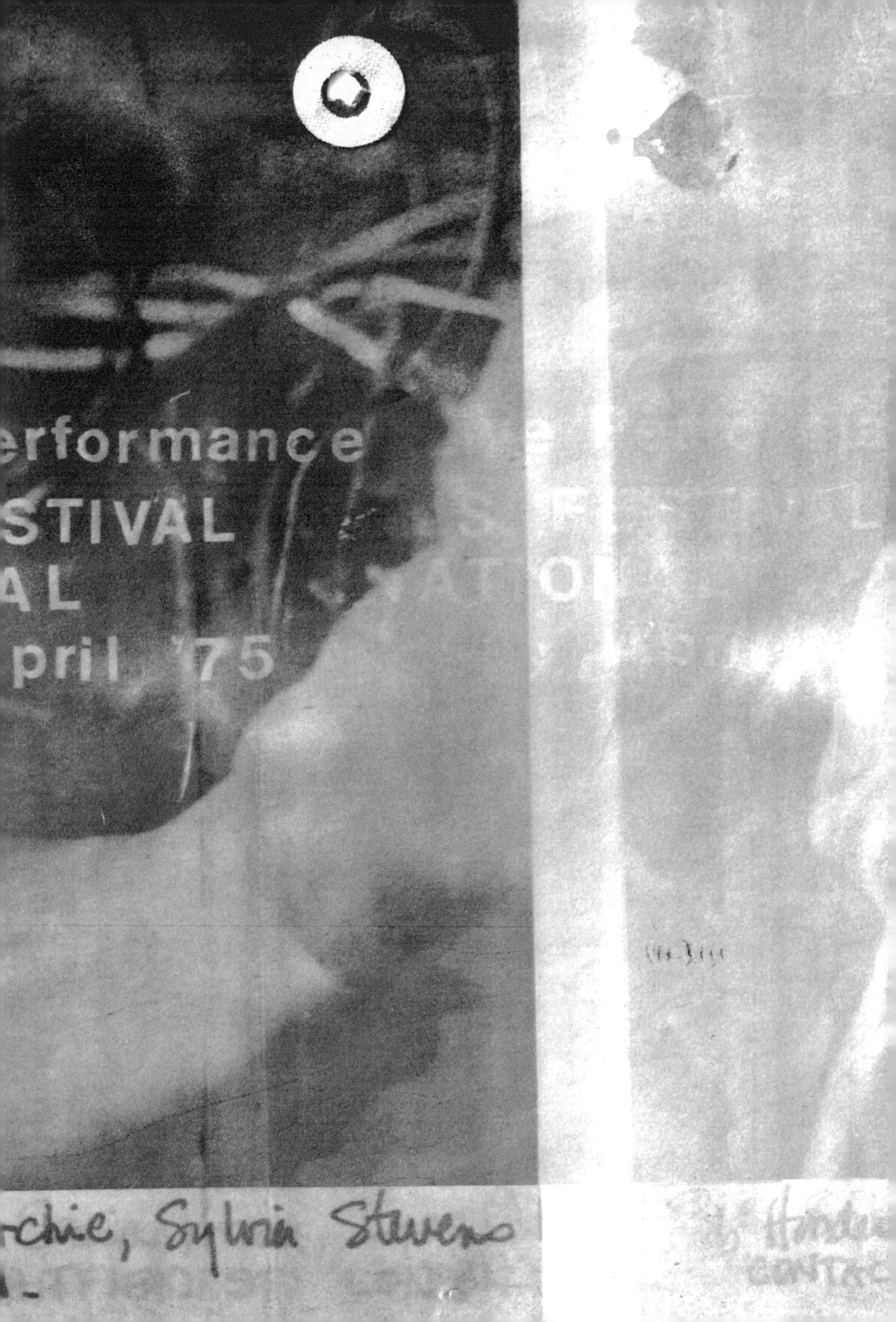

erformance
STIVAL
AL
pril '75

rchie, Sylvia Stevens

London in the 1970s was a cultural network, a counterculture growing up. I met Nii Kwate Owoo through Cinema Action. We had all these theatre groups, film groups, poster groups, all these different projects – AFD was a project, they all overlapped, but they overlapped as a network. It's not hierarchical, more like a network of differences. [...] The reason I started making a lot of posters was because of the Portuguese colonial struggles. Amílcar Cabral came to London and gave a speech. He called it 'Our people are our mountains', because an expert on guerrilla war said that you can't fight a guerrilla war without mountains, you need mountains to survive guerrilla warfare. Guinea-Bissau didn't have mountains, so Cabral said 'Our people are our mountains'. That resonated with me, so I went to see the committees for Mozambique, Angola, Guinea-Bissau and did some posters. Guerrilla fighters from Mozambique came to London, so you could meet people who were engaged in struggles actually in London. There was a surge of not just colonial struggles but a way of connecting those struggles with domestic struggles. There was vast inflation in the 1970s. London was breaking down. It was depopulating to a large extent. It gave an opportunity to draw new lines.

Jonathan Miles

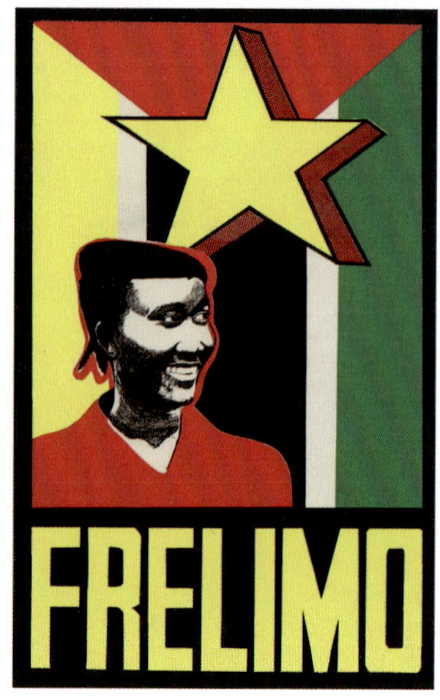

We had to do a lot with very little resources back in the day. There was no grants available and we had to use our own resources to activate projects. The contribution of Cinema Action was significant for my development as a film-maker, in terms of setting the political orientation of my films. Cinema Action made it possible for *You Hide Me* [1970] to be made, because they provided all the post-production facilities for free. ... *You Hide Me* was shot in a day, from 9am to 5pm. We had to rush to the basement of British Museum. There were so many things. Sometimes we had to put our camera aside and [we] opened the boxes and touched these incredibly rare works of art. People asked me, 'Why is the content of the commentary of *You Hide Me* so contemporary, that it deals with a situation as if it were happening yesterday?' I said while I was there, the commentary just wrote itself. When I opened the boxes and touched the art, the whole script unravelled in my system.

Nii Kwate Owoo

Victory to People's War

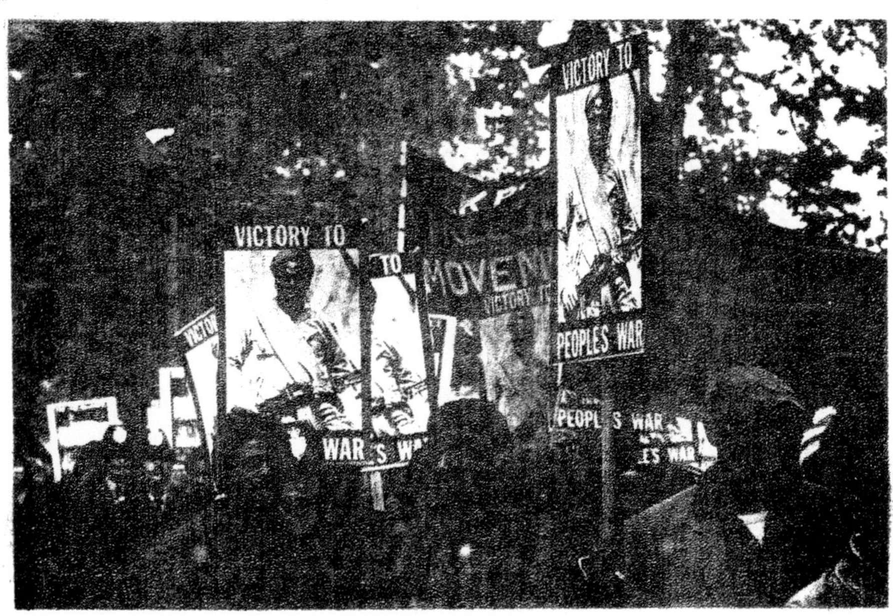

AN EXHIBITION OF POSTERS IN SUPPORT OF LIBERATION MOVEMENTS
MAY 6 to JUNE 1 1975
143 Whitfield St.(NR. Warren St.tube)
open weekdays 1pm to 6pm

SUNDAY)-MAY 25	4:00pm	Exhibition of photograhs on Colonial Invasion into Southern Africa
	6:45pm	video Jonathan Miles
	7:30pm	Irish Film-Discussion
FRIDAY-MAY 30	4:00pm	slide show "Liberation Movements in Southern Africa" Ifriqiyah Films Collective
	7:30pm	Symposium on the Role of Arts,film etc. in the African Revolution: Chairman Walata Culture in the Zimbabwean Liberation Movement
	9:00pm	"You Hide Me" a film on cultural imperialism in Africa by Ifriqiyah Films Collective-Discussion
SATURDAY-MAY31	4:00pm	slides of Cuban Posters
	4:30pm	slides on Political posters
	5:00pm	Symposium on uses posters,film etc. in agitation and propaganda: Chair people Ife and Jonathan exploitation of women by bourgeois media/ sterotypes use to degrade and exploit Blacks.
SUNDAY -JUNE 1	7:30	Miner's Film Cinema Action-Discussion

'Victory to People's War', showing posters produced by Poster-Film Collective alongside a programme of talks, screenings and discussions including films by Cinema Action and the Ifriqiyah Films collective, both of whom shared members with Poster-Film Collective. Several members of Poster-Film Collective met for the first time at AFD's Chile Festival; they were based at the Keskidee Centre during 1974 to 1975, before moving to a squat on Tolmers Square, London.

COMMENTARY

You Hide Me

1. This is the basement of the British Museum.
2. This is where they keep their vast collections of African Art, tools, furniture, Musical Instruments and clothes.
3. We are going to have a look at what they have in their collections. (P) Similar collections can be found in museums in all former colonial powers in Europe and America.
4. The main part of these collections was acquired during the period of Colonial rule.
5. The objects were brought back to Europe by officers, tradesmen, missionaries and the colonial specialists called ethnographers.
6. On the whole the collections represent the looting of a conquering army (P).
7. When a British expeditionary force sacked the city of Benin in 1897, they took with them more than 3,000 pieces of Art.
8. Many of them are still locked away and kept in these boxes and plastic bags in these rooms. (P)
9. Ethnographers were sent to the colonies to collect any kind of Art or objects made by the Africans.
10. The Europeans never brought with them their own works of art to Africa. (P) No European artist at that time seemed to have gone to Africa to learn about African Art.
11. Why did the colonizers bring back to Europe a stool of a chief, statueof a chief, a statue used for worship, an ancestor's image a pipe with tobacco still in it, a comb, a vessel used to contain food.
12. During the long period of the European slave trade in Africa there was little interest in African Art. (P)
    The Europeans began collecting art objects when their presence changed from slave trading to direct colonial administration.
13. The colonizers established regimes in Africa to suit the particular role the colonies played in their own economies.
14. The colonizers attitude to African civilization stem's from this basic aim.

15. **To establish their rule in the colonies, they made an all out attack on African civilization, social structure, religion, language and art.**

16. **In cultural and social affairs a particular tactic was employed by the colonizers. Certain types of cultural and social life were encouraged but only after they had been reduced to a stage where they could be controlled.**

17. **After the power of the Kings and chiefs had been broken, some were reinstated by the colonial administration to be used by them.**

18. **After an all out attack on African religion some ceremonies were allowed to continue in order to present an African façade.**

19. **This is the tactic of destroying a civilization from within, like the tactics of brainwashing. The tactic was to destroy the civilization they found, (P) to brainwash Africans into believing that their own civilization is inferior whiles at the same time insisting on preserving an African façade in the countries they ruled.**

20. **What was the purpose of the ethnographic collections in Europe?**

21. **These ethnographic collections were displayed in such a way as to establish a cultural hierarchy.**

22. **Greek Roman Egyptian and Assyrian objects were given prominent places in their museums, whereas objects from Africa where crammed into small rooms or hidden away.**

23. **The purpose of the ethnographic collections was to establish for the white man, which is the higher civilization and which are the primitive ones. (P)**

24. **The ethnographic collections were used in the ideology of colonialism, which talks about backward races and primitive civilizations.**

25. **This is why the colonizers bothered to collect and preserve material from a civilization they set about to destroy.**

26. **The colonizers did not collect this material in order to study, understand and appreciate the civilization they encountered.**

27. **The colonizers did not try to understand African civilization but dismissed what they saw as something that was of no intrinsic value.**

28. **The material they collected in Africa was used as propagandamaterial against Africans and people of African descent.**

29. **Now that they have discovered that this material speaks for Africa, they cling on to it and try once more to use it to their own advantage.**

30. **African countries had achieved independence, the former colonial powers changed their tone when they talk about African civilization.**

31. **Not long ago they talk about the colonized as backward races with primitive civilizations.**

32. **Now they talk about the masterpieces of African Art. (P)**
Not long ago they lectured to Africans about European civilizations. Now they talk about Benin bronzes and Ife sculptures.

33. **Not long ago it was fashionable to suppose that before the Europeans came Africa had no history. Now African history is taught in Europe and America.**

34. **Not long ago creative activity among the colonized was looked upon with suspicion.**

35. **And now exhibitions of contemporary African Art are arranged in Europe and America.**

36. **Suddenly the former colonial powers have changed their tone.**

37. **However their change of tone and their rehabilitation of African Art are suspect.**

38. **First they destroy a civilization and condemn it as primitive and non human. Then they rehabilitate aspects of it as examples of a high civilization.**

39. **They refuse to understand African Civilization, then present themselves as the experts on the subject and decide which are the masterpieces of African Art. Which is now becoming a very profitable business in Europe and America.**

40. **The European attitude of today resembles the attitude of the colonizers who decided which customs and traditions should be allowed to continue.**

41. **Because Europe and America have the most important collections of objects from Africa, they can feed back to Africa a certain image of what is traditional African Art.**

42. **Today the advanced industrial countries need an African middle class that is orientated towards the west. The image of African art that they feed back to Africa is meant for the African middle class.**

43. And they find it necessary to distinguish between Africans the higher and the lower classes. The image of African art that they feed back to Africa is meant for the African middle class.

44. The western theorist and so called experts on African society depend on what kind of African society the advanced industrial countries need. (P)

45. They hardly say how these objects were acquired, from whom or what they gave in return. They never say how many objects were burnt by their missionaries and destroyed by their armies.

46. They know that museums in Africa have very little to show of their past. They say that the material is more easily accessible in Europe, but accessible to whom???

47. Many books on African art are now being published in Europe and America but these books can not replace the material that is now being kept outside Africa.

48. Why should Africans including African Artists only be able to read about their own works of art in books published by white people.

49. How can independent African governments explain to the generation that is now growing up that they cant see their own cultural heritage in their own countries

50. We the people of Africa and of African descent DEMAND that our works of art which embodies our History, our civilization, our religion and our culture,

Should immediately and unconditionally be returned to us!!!

Nii Kwate Owoo, voice-over script for *You Hide Me*, c.1970

Through *You Hide Me* [1970], I brought together an African-American, Ife, and a Caribbean cultural activist called Mitch Holder, and this led to the creation of Ifriqiyah Films, the first Black film collective in this country. We did a lot of very interesting documentaries on the experience of Black people in this country. We have an archive of about thirteen films which we were never able to marry print. We felt the existing news archives, like Visnews, were very much in the British Movietone tradition, and did not really give a correct representation of the sentiments of Africans and African-Caribbeans. We used to take a double-headed projector into the community and show the edited version of the films. We established a direct link between making films and showing them in the community.

Nii Kwate Owoo

I came to London and Europe as an exchange [student in 1972–73]. I started to meet other students and young people living in London from Africa and the Caribbean. A few fellow Black American exchange students and I became regulars at the (African Students Union) (called 'The Basement') at the University of London. I met members and leaders involved in African liberation movements in South Africa, Zimbabwe, Angola, Guinea-Bissau and Mozambique there. They would discuss politics and their home country for hours after meetings and lectures at the local pub. It was there I met Nii Kwate Owoo. And we began a long-term personal and working relationship. ... We shared a common bond to use art as a tool to liberate our people. During this time, I was amazed at how much the civil rights and Black Power movement in America inspired the movement for Black people's civil rights in England. The solidarity was strong in the Black community. My second trip to London was from 1974–76. I received an artist residency at the Keskidee Centre to work with Ifriqiyah Films and teach media to Caribbean youth at the centre. My work with Ifriqiyah consisted of fundraising, working production with video cameras, lighting and creating storyboard concepts. ... We (Ifriqiyah Films, Kwate, myself, Mitch Holder and various students who would work with us) began working with AFD. I remember a great event, the great hall at the Royal College of Art. I remember meetings and discussions with David Medalla and AFD. We (Kwate and I) had our own study groups with African Students from Zimbabwe, Ethiopia and South Africa and a collective of anti-racist educators in London. We also did community engagement with youth in the local schools; this work led us to create 'A is for Africa'. This work in primary schools focusses on reaching young children to help them to demystify racial stereotypes. We were learning from each other, collectively and individually. We worked and studied with various collectives to design an anti-racist curriculum.

[...]

I learned how to make photo stencils with the Poster Collective; as far as AFD, they were more of a solidarity [group] with their expressions of kinetic art. Our work was more into agitprop, and I began to continue my exploration of aesthetics, questioning capitalist conceptions of art for art's sake. At this time, I also had a young son, and so my time was limited. Many times I worked in my home studio alone and would share my ideas and sketches with the collective, and then the work would change often, this collaborative process of going back and forth until we all agreed on the final design. ... It is unclear when it hit me that I was doing cultural work. The collaborative nature of the work and how vital culture preservation, uncovering a history or history lost or hidden. As I talked in school and worked on concepts meant to demystify racial stereotypes for me, I saw this artistic work differently; because of its collaborative nature, I could not say it was my work alone. Even though I could be considered a technician, I wanted our posters to be strong, beautiful and hopeful.

Ife Nii Owoo

FRELIMO

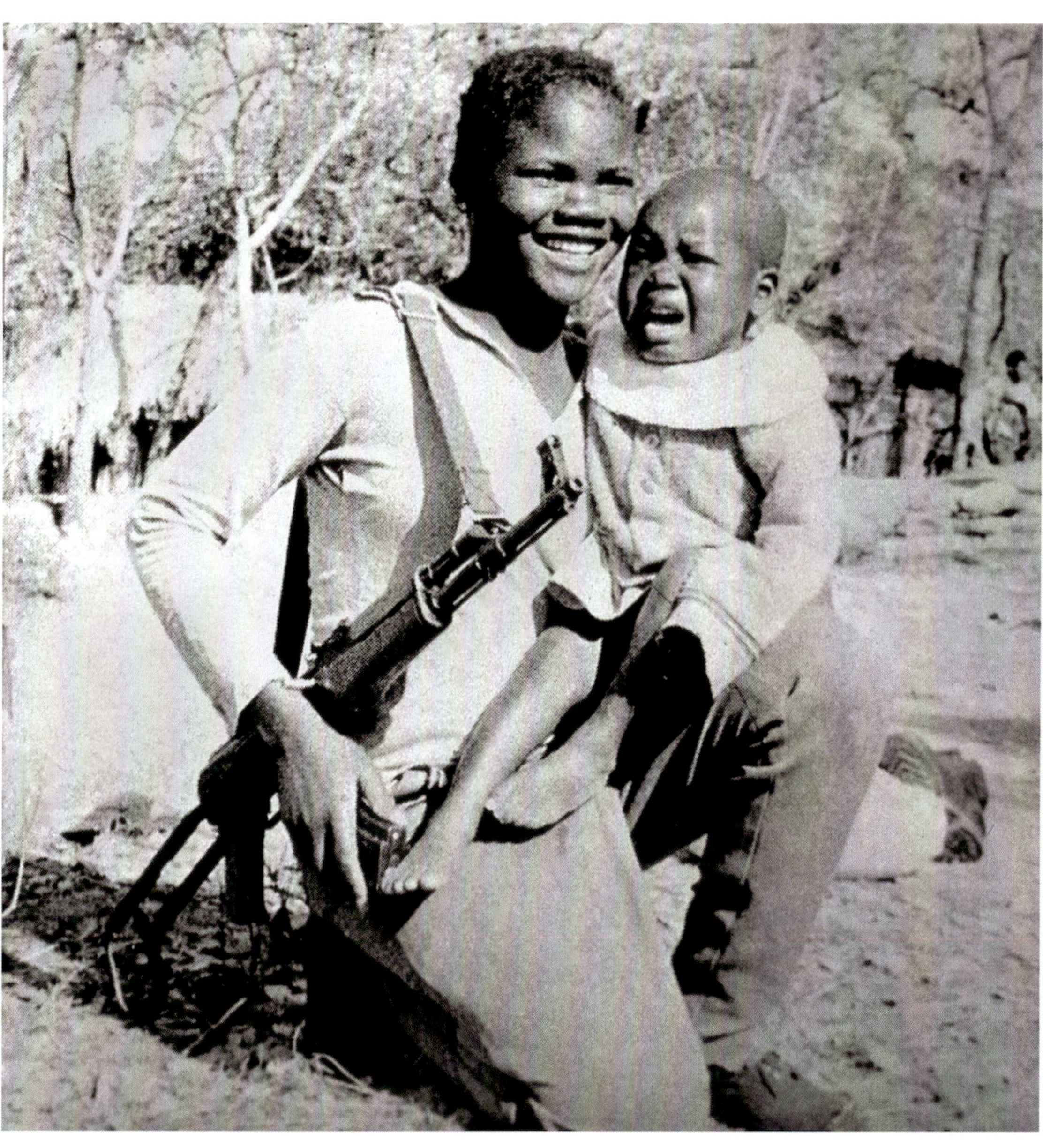

**THE ANTIDOTE TO CURE COLONIALISM
IS ARMED REVOLUTION
THAT IS THE ONLY WAY
TO WIN TOTAL INDEPENDENCE**

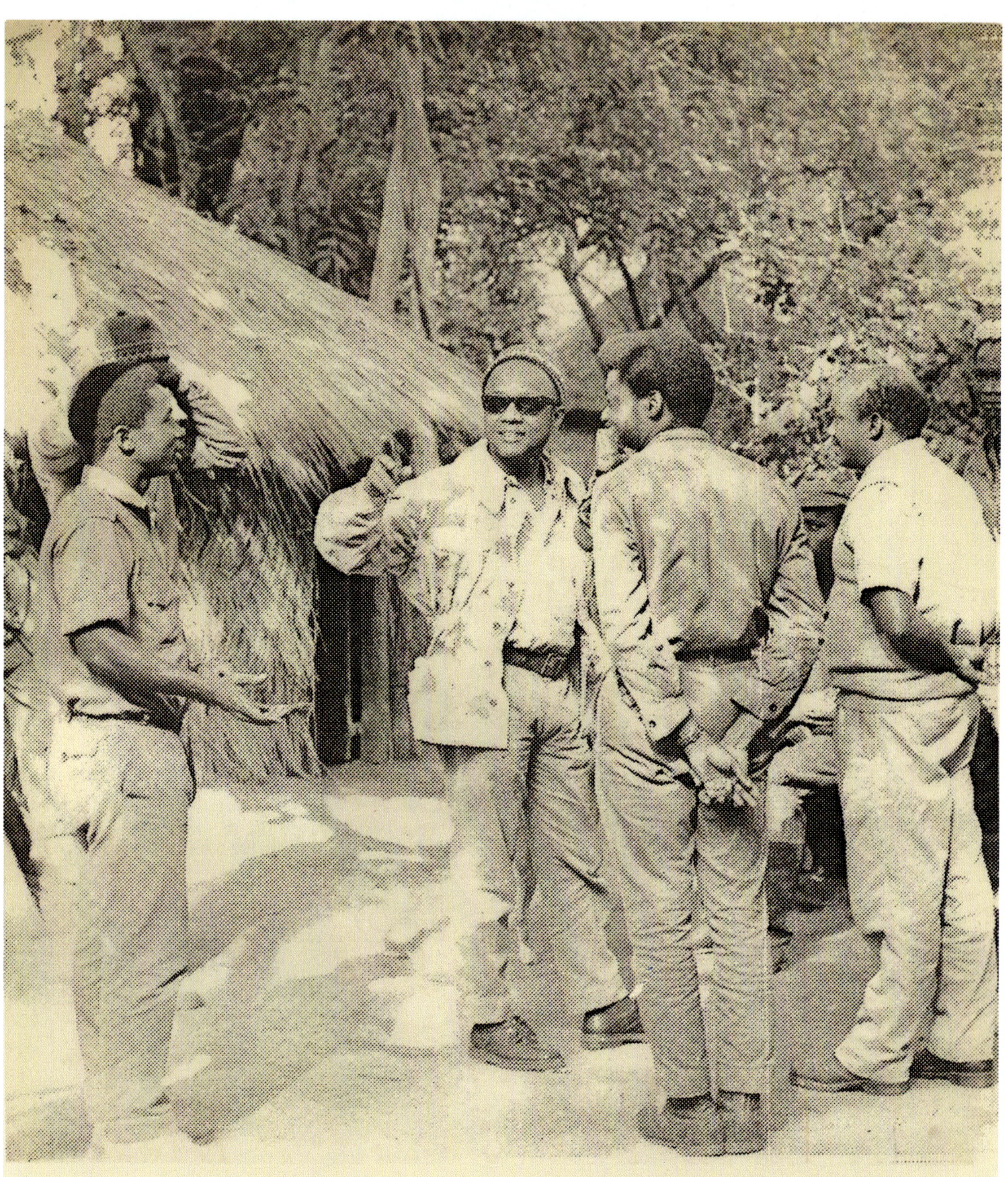

They will continue to perpetuate crimes against our people, they will make more attempts at destroying our Party and our struggle. But all in vain. For no crime, no force, no manoeuvre in word or deed of all the criminal Portuguese colonial aggressors will be able to stop the march of history, the irreversible march of our own African people of Guinea and the Cape Verde Islands towards their independence.

AMILCAR CABRAL

How do you see the role of the artist?

In most respects we have rejected the traditional cultural role of the artist. Fundamentally the artist's role within capitalist society is not really one of creating illusions *about* the class, but rather has become structurally an illusion *of* the class. The artist is a kind of emblem of freedom, someone who is *negatively* free to do anything in the name of art. The adoption of a preconceived, historically constructed, model (in the avant-garde tradition) moves against any radical rupture with the existing state of things. But at the same time, the manner in which an alternative practice is constructed and developed constitutes a problematic. There is no easy answer; the question can only be resolved over a protracted period and in conjunction with the unfolding of class struggle.

Who do you see as your 'audience'?

As a group we hold together an apparatus of production which lends itself to be used to give a form of voice to those in struggle. At the same time the posters, slide shows, film shows, themselves create a basis for struggle. The question of audience is difficult in the sense that we have very little empirical information on, say, how the posters eventually get used. Our posters are distributed through many different sources – bookshops, meetings, demonstrations, groups. Also, there are many people who have large selections of posters for showing in exhibition form. Probably the majority of this form of display is abroad. Although the more politically structured showing and use of posters is important we also feel that the availability of posters for people to put up, either in their home or in the workplace, is also vital.

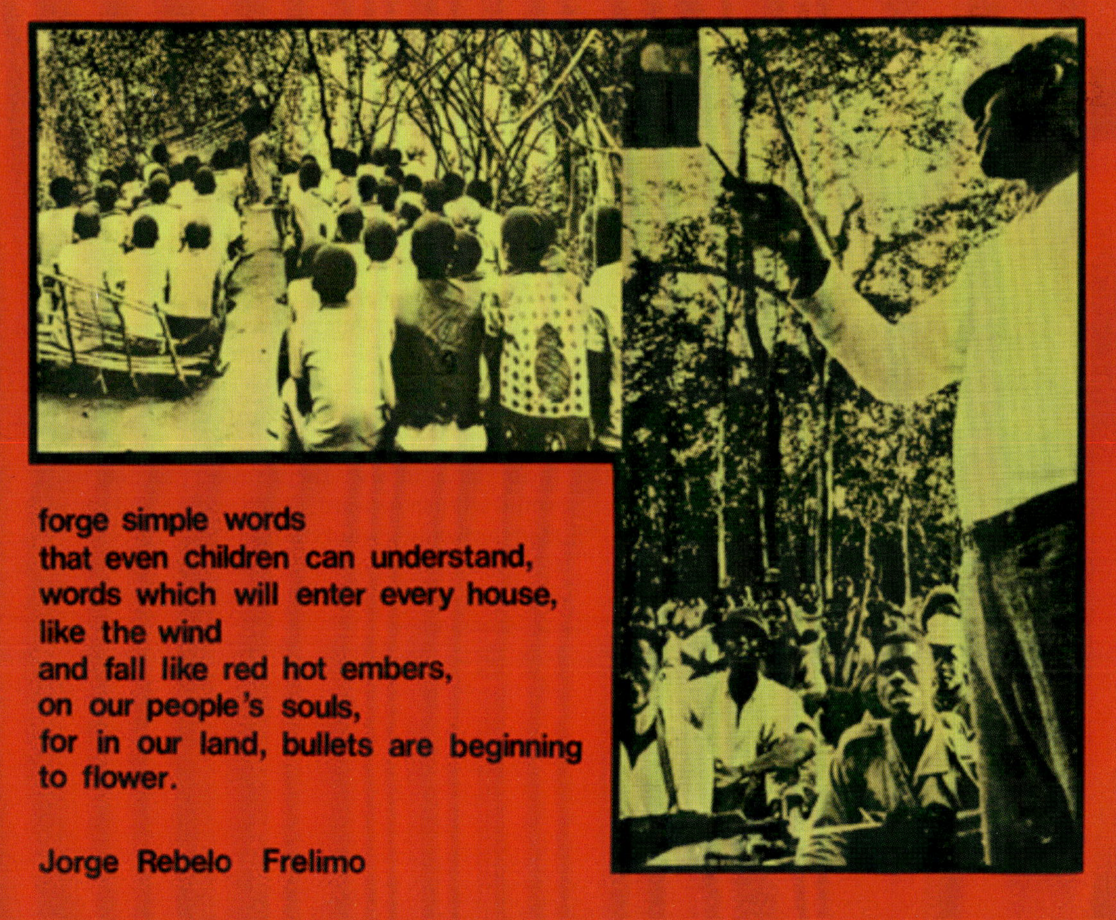

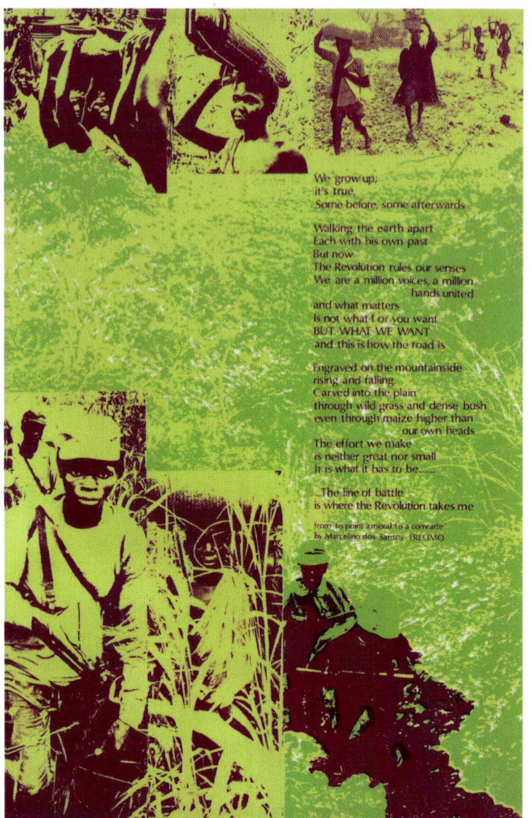

I joined the Poster Collective in 1976, although I'd known many of the people involved for some time, through various activities and organisations happening on the radical edge of art/politics in London. These were mostly concerned with challenging cultural elitism and the sanctity of the White Cube Gallery – AFD being one, where I'd first met Jonathan Miles and Sylvia Stevens – a loose association of artists and Art College students that put on exhibitions in a squat in [Whitfield Street] and organised surreal demonstrations (we were budding artists after all) at various locations, such as the Tate Gallery and Sotheby's Auction House. ... I had already been involved in a practice not dissimilar to the Poster Collective, having been part of the Cinema Action political film collective, that had its roots in screening films, filled with working class voices, that were not aimed for TV release but shown for discussion back in the communities where they originated.

The demonstrations at the Tate were quite surreal. It was to do with the idea that they were the gatekeepers of everything, and they had things stored and hidden away all the time, and against the idea of that 'establishment art'. And the idea of bringing a bit of surreality to it all. And the sense that they couldn't eject us – we would say 'we're just trying to look at things'. The [demonstration] at Sotheby's was particular. This was motivated by David Medalla and the fact that someone seemed to have stolen a work that he owned, a work by another famous artist [Jesus-Rafael Soto]. It was down as 'provenance of David Medalla' but someone else was selling it. And it was to protest the idea in general of people stealing works of art, from Third World people. This was the very first modern art sale at Sotheby's, people like Mick Jagger were there. We were at the back ... and when they came to this item we would all rush forward, which we did, and David Medalla would go and confront them, which he did. At which point all the security appeared and there was a big melee and confusion.

Steve Sprung

VICTORY TO

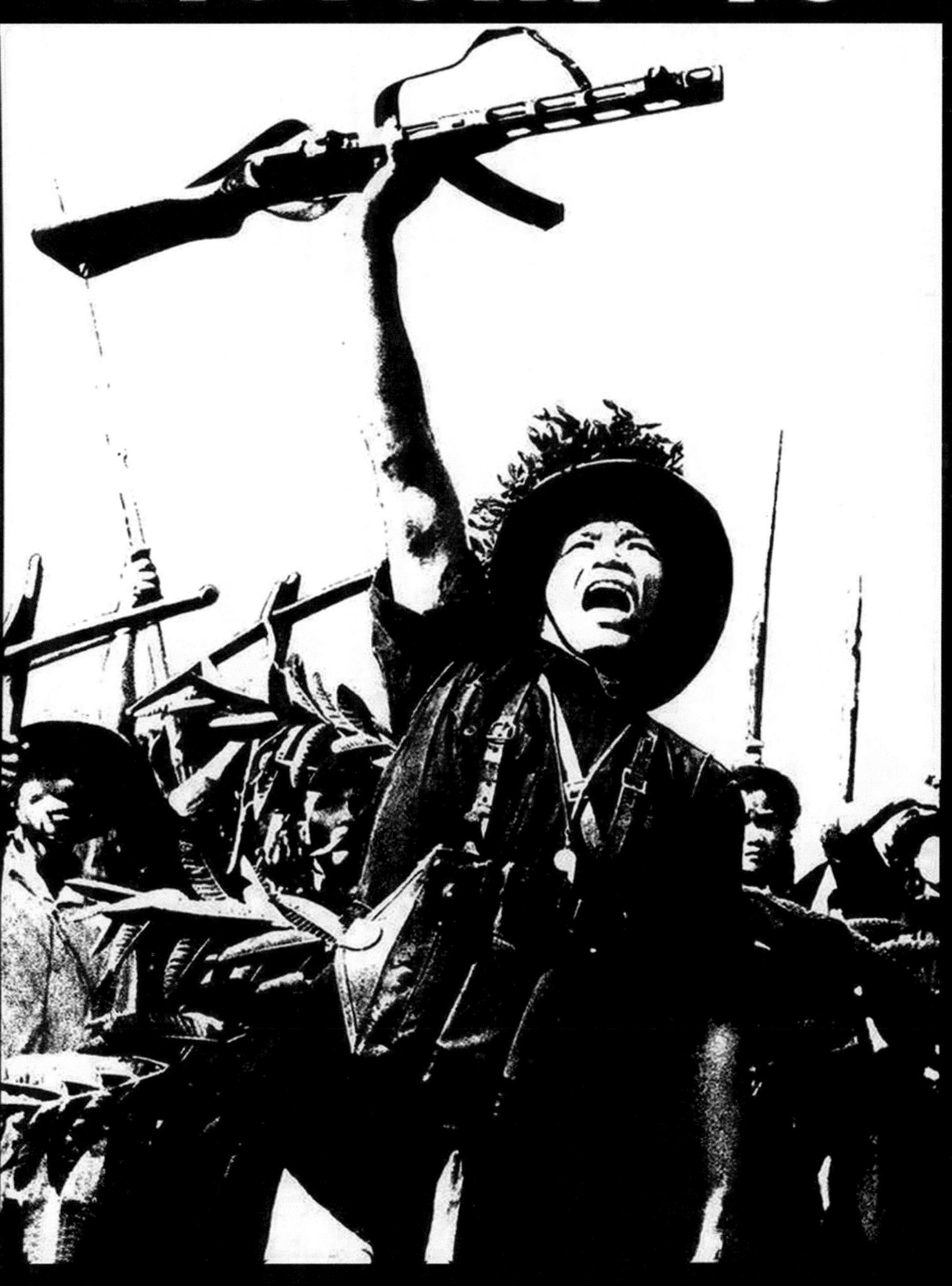

PEOPLE´S WAR

VICTORY TO

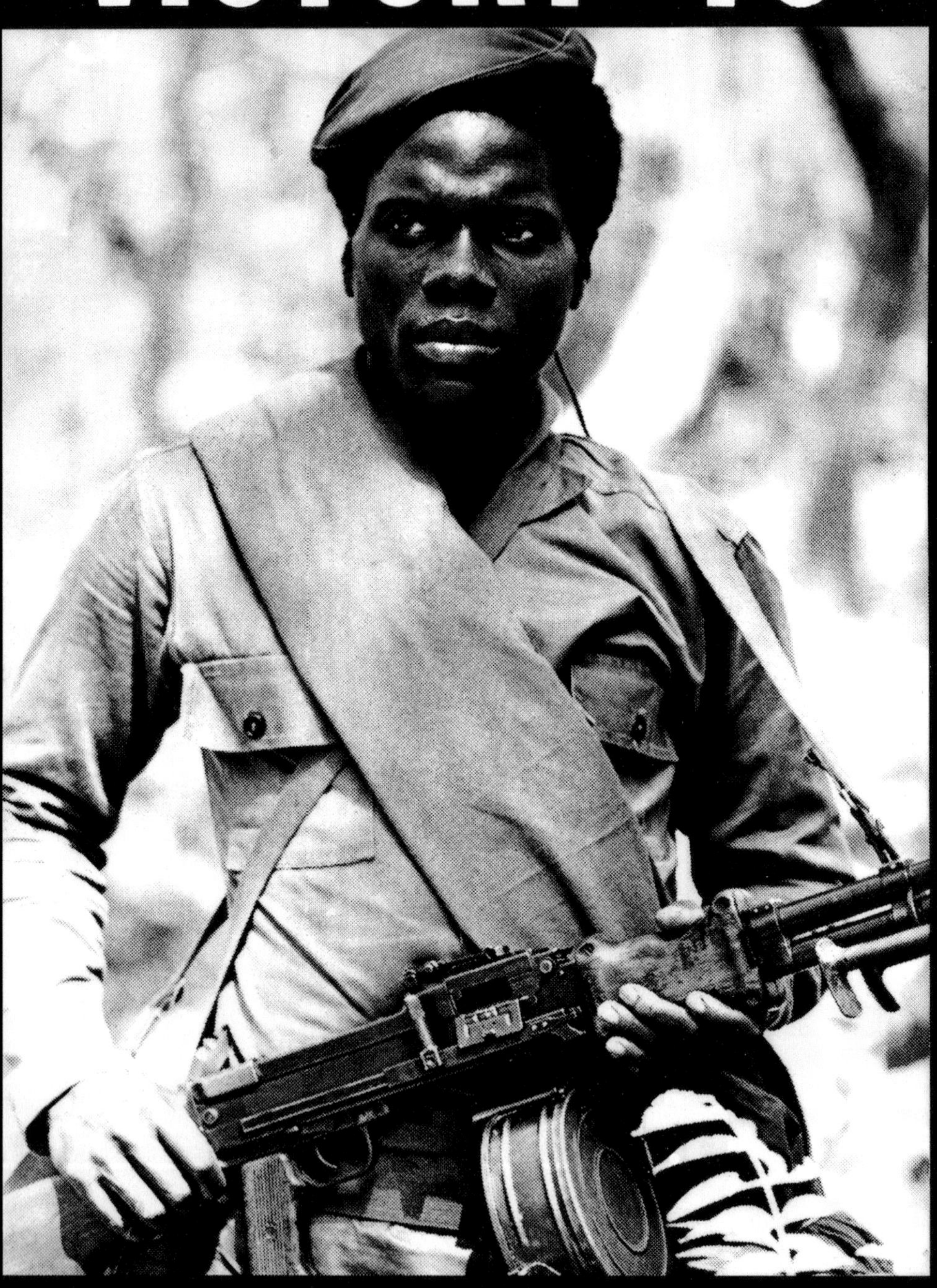

PEOPLE´S WAR

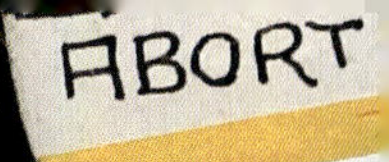

ROLE of ART and LITERATURE
in Society and Revolution

OPEN DISCUSSION

Speaker, David Medalla

SUNDAY, June 30, 1975, 3 pm

143 Whitfield Street, W.1.
(near Warren St. tube)

-- All Welcome --

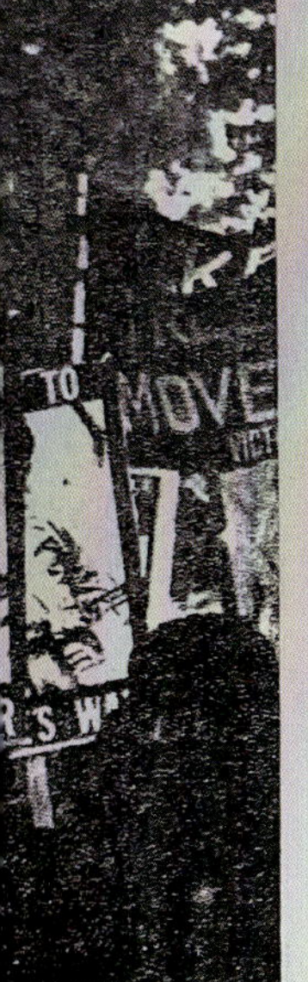

Dear Comrade,

As decided by our meeting on June 1st, 1975, the first of our monthly discussions in the second half of this year will be on "The Role of Art and Literature in Society and Revolution."

Comrade David Medalla, a revolutionary artist from the Phillipines, will be the opening speaker. We shall appreciate if you could invite other friends interested in the revolutionary struggle of the people against imperialism.

As agreed previously, concrete arrangements for holding regular weekly study classes in:

1) Revolutionary theory
2) Monthly forum and
3) Concrete cultural projects

will also be discussed.

Looking forward to seeing you,

Yours fraternally,

A. Manchanda

(A. MANCHANDA)
General Secretary,

INDO-CHINA PEOPLE's SOLIDARITY FRONT

Telephone:
01-485-3609

58, Lisburne Road,
London,
NW3 2 NR.

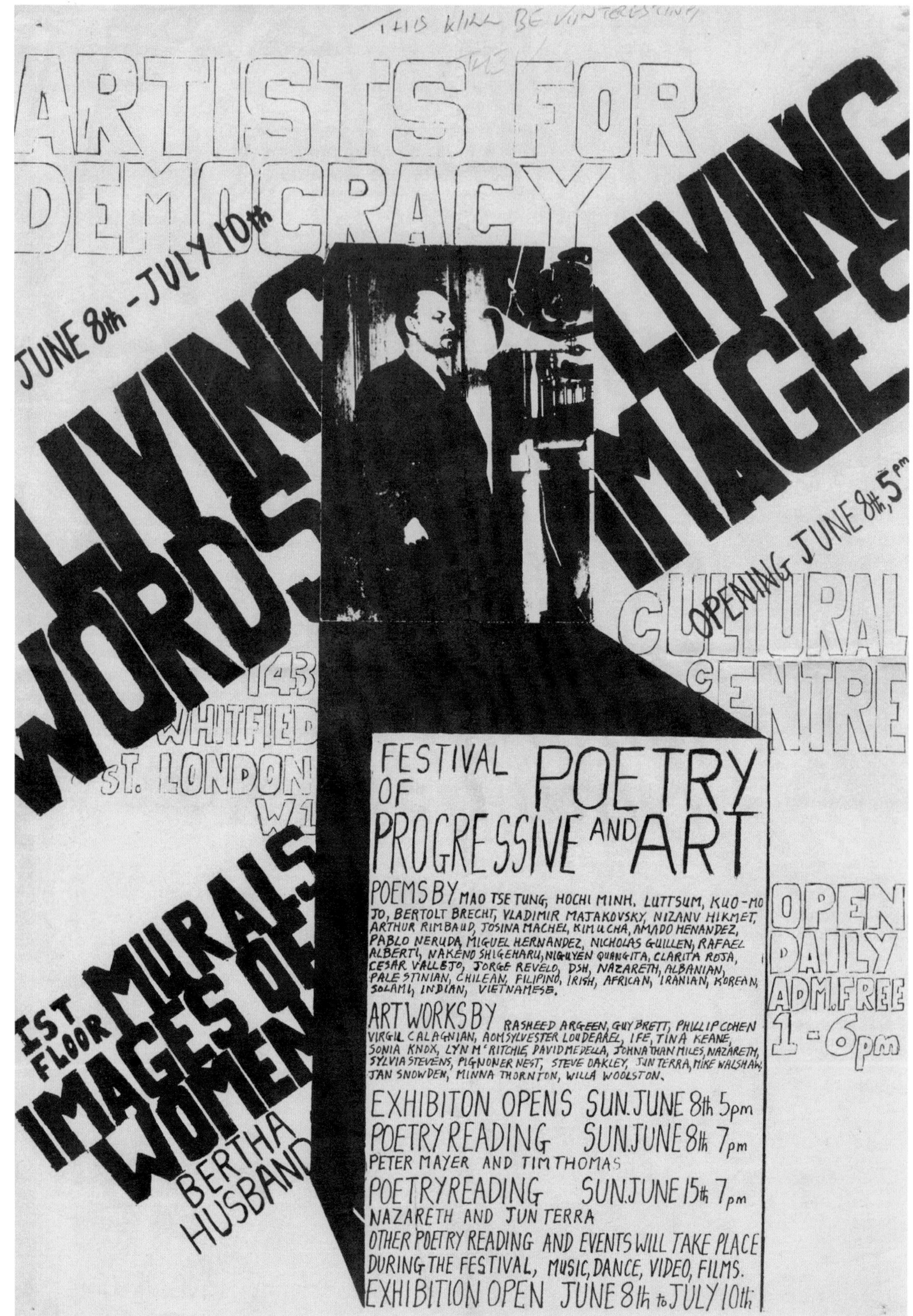

THIS WILL BE V INTERESTING
ARTISTS FOR DEMOCRACY
JUNE 8th - JULY 10th
LIVING WORDS
LIVING IMAGES
OPENING JUNE 8th, 5pm
CULTURAL CENTRE
143 WHITFIED ST. LONDON W1
1ST FLOOR
MURALS
IMAGES OF WOMEN
BERTHA HUSBAND
FESTIVAL OF PROGRESSIVE POETRY AND ART
POEMS BY MAO TSE TUNG, HOCHI MINH, LUTTSUM, KUO-MO JO, BERTOLT BRECHT, VLADIMIR MAJAKOVSKY, NIZANV HIKMET, ARTHUR RIMBAUD, JOSINA MACHEL, KIM U CHA, AMADO HENANDEZ, PABLO NERUDA, MIGUEL HERNANDEZ, NICHOLAS GUILLEN, RAFAEL ALBERTI, NAKENO SHIGEHARU, NIGUYEN QUANGITA, CLARITA ROJA, CESAR VALLEJO, JORGE REVELO, DSH, NAZARETH, ALBANIAN, PALESTINIAN, CHILEAN, FILIPINO, IRISH, AFRICAN, IRANIAN, KOREAN, SOLAMI, INDIAN, VIETNAMESE.
ARTWORKS BY RASHEED ARGEEN, GUY BRETT, PHILLIP COHEN VIRGIL CALAGNIAN, AOM SYLVESTER LOUDEAREL, IFE, TINA KEANE, SONIA KNOX, LYN M'RITCHIE, DAVID MEDELLA, JOHNATHAN MILES, NAZARETH, SYLVIA STEVENS, PIGNONER NEST, STEVE OAKLEY, JUN TERRA, MIKE WALSHAW, JAN SNOWDEN, MINNA THORNTON, WILLA WOOLSTON.
EXHIBITON OPENS SUN. JUNE 8th 5pm
POETRY READING SUN. JUNE 8th 7pm
PETER MAYER AND TIM THOMAS
POETRY READING SUN. JUNE 15th 7pm
NAZARETH AND JUN TERRA
OTHER POETRY READING AND EVENTS WILL TAKE PLACE DURING THE FESTIVAL, MUSIC, DANCE, VIDEO, FILMS.
EXHIBITION OPEN JUNE 8th to JULY 10th
OPEN DAILY
ADM. FREE
1 - 6pm

One of the poets was H.O. Nazareth. We knew him as Naz, and in those days he worked as a night telephone operator – a good job for aspiring poets and artists, since they could do their own work during the day. ... Poetry was quite a thing in London at the time, as I recall. David Medalla loved poetry and knew a lot about it, as did Jun Terra. Lu Hsun was a favourite and his shadow-puppet play was based on a Lu Hsun story. ... Bertha Husband did an installation going up the staircase and into the upper floor – smallish panels with stylised figures of women, I seem to remember. She was a lovely person and an excellent artist. She went to America and continued as a radical artist there.

Lynn MacRitchie

In hindsight much of this can be understood as a crisis of temporality, the accumulation of capital within an industrial framework was imploding, the regulatory structures of the state no longer cohered, a mood of revolt was sweeping the Third World and the stress lines relating to all of this striated minds and bodies. The tension of the near future was everywhere in evidence: a drama played out in everyday news. The issue was how to live within this drama. What was dramatic about London in the early seventies was the extent that it appeared to be rotting as a city. High inflation (25% in 1975) meant that developers as being economically unviable abandoned vast amounts of property and this in turn lead to large-scale squatting. This was coupled with massive unemployment giving rise to a drop-out culture affecting all strata of society. This gave rise to the sense of 'no future'. This period might be seen as representing the trapped nerve of capitalism.

Jonathan Miles

GALLERY

SUNDAY 6 JULY

Reading by poets from India/BanglaDesh - 7.oo - 8.oopm

. . . .

david toop: "In his fish-scale house, dragon-scale hall, Portico of purple-shell, in his red palace, What is the Spirit doing, down in the water?"

voice/strings/flutes/slides

dedicated to distinguished scholar of Vietnamese music - Tran Van Khe

\+

film: "SHELL HAT"

paul burwell: " . . . riverrun, past Eve and Adam's, FROM SWERVE OF SHORE TO BEND OF BAY, brings us by a commodius vicus of re-circulation back to "the kit" and Environs."

\+

other pieces . . . .

. . . .

ARTISTS FOR DEMOCRACY GALLERY 143, Whitfield Street, W1.

Sunday evening from 7.oo Admission free

PERFORMANCE AT ARTISTS FOR DEMOCRACY

THE PIECE MUST CONTAIN.

6/7/75 PERFORMANCE STARTED BY THE BURNING OF the envelope and its contents. "THE PIECE MUST CONTAIN"

THEN "THE MEMORY OF THE FREEZING SEA"

THEN "STRING & PERCUSSION PIECE"

THEN RIVERRUN PAST EVE & ADAMS, FROM SWERVE OF SHORE TO BEND OF BAY, BRINGS US BY A COMMODIUS VICUS OF RE-CIRCULATION BACK TO THE KIT & ENVIRONS.

THEN 1/3 (LATERAL SEGMENT) OF 'STRING TRIO FOR SIX INSTRUMENTS'.

THEN "PIECE FOR BASS DRUM & CHINESE DRUM" (PERHAPS IT COULD BE CALLED "HOLINESS DANCE"

IT IS GOING TO TAKE ME A COUPLE OF PERFORMANCES TO GET ~~THE~~ COMPLETELY COMFORTABLE ABOUT PLAYING SOLO. ~~[illegible]~~

THURS 19 JUNE

TO COLLEGE TO PICK UP MORE INSTRUMENTS

FRI [illegible] [illegible] OVAL: SET UP + 2 MORE CHORDS (SOFT) + Δ MARITIME ~~[illegible]~~

FRI 20 JUNE PERFORMANCE WITH KEITH, MARIE & SALLY

SAT 21 JUNE DITTO

WED JULY 2ND 1975 TITLE GIVEN TO TRUMPETS/DRUMS/GONGS/ DRUMS/FIDDLE/GONGS/VOICE PIECE:

"THE MEMORY OF THE FREEZING SEA"

NEWHAVEN JULY 14

"washed ashore on a lonely island in the sea"

above: Paul Burwell's notes on 'performance at Artists For Democracy', 1975; facing page: Annabel Nicolson's article 'Paul Burwell and David Toop at Artists' For Democracy', *MUSICS*, August/September 1975

Paul Burwell and David Toop at Artists' For Democracy   143 Whitfield St.N.W.I.

In the morning Paul was listening to Gaelic long psalms.We also heard some Mongolian music,that day or the day before.In the afternoon we met a man in Harrow who makes mediaeval instruments.

Paul arrived at AFD and looked around.David came later,talking about a record by La Monte Young and Marion Zazeela.He said that if you move around,even a little,while listening to it the sound alters.If you sit still while someone else is moving around the sound still alters.

Hearing this in between the words of a conversation with Petal we join our conversations together and set off for a drink.In front of Petal's house is a roof with a dent in it and someone appears at Petal's window,summoning him We can only see the person because there is a dent in this other roof.

After a drink Paul and David walk round the corner to AFD where one or two people are studying the blackboards and notices out on the street.Inside a large man is setting out short rows of chairs.Paul and David lay out instruments on the carpet,percussion and flutes.I take this photo.Four people are watching.

Sounds don't add up after the event. One or two stay in the mind such as Paul playing an appache fiddle.He works with each moment,allowing a lot of space around it.When he crosses the room to close the door,footsteps, The space is as thoroughly keyed up now as if he had stretched piano wires all through it.Very physical sounds occupy the performance and David taps quietly on the silver parts of a white flute.He also did a strange breathing into the flute causing sounds to transform.Everything is suspended in thin air.They packup,sliding flutes into cloth bags as if they were fishing rods and someone asks where they learnt Vietnamese music.

David Medalla and friends arrive clapping loudly.

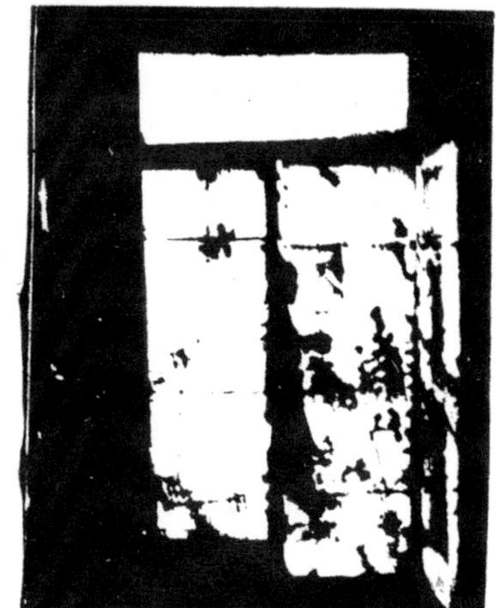

People of the World Learn from INDOCHINA

Homage to Ho Chi Minh And the Victory of The Indochinese Peoples

ARTS FESTIVAL

13th. JULY – 9th. AUGUST 1975

Artists For Democracy

143 Whitfield St. London W.I.

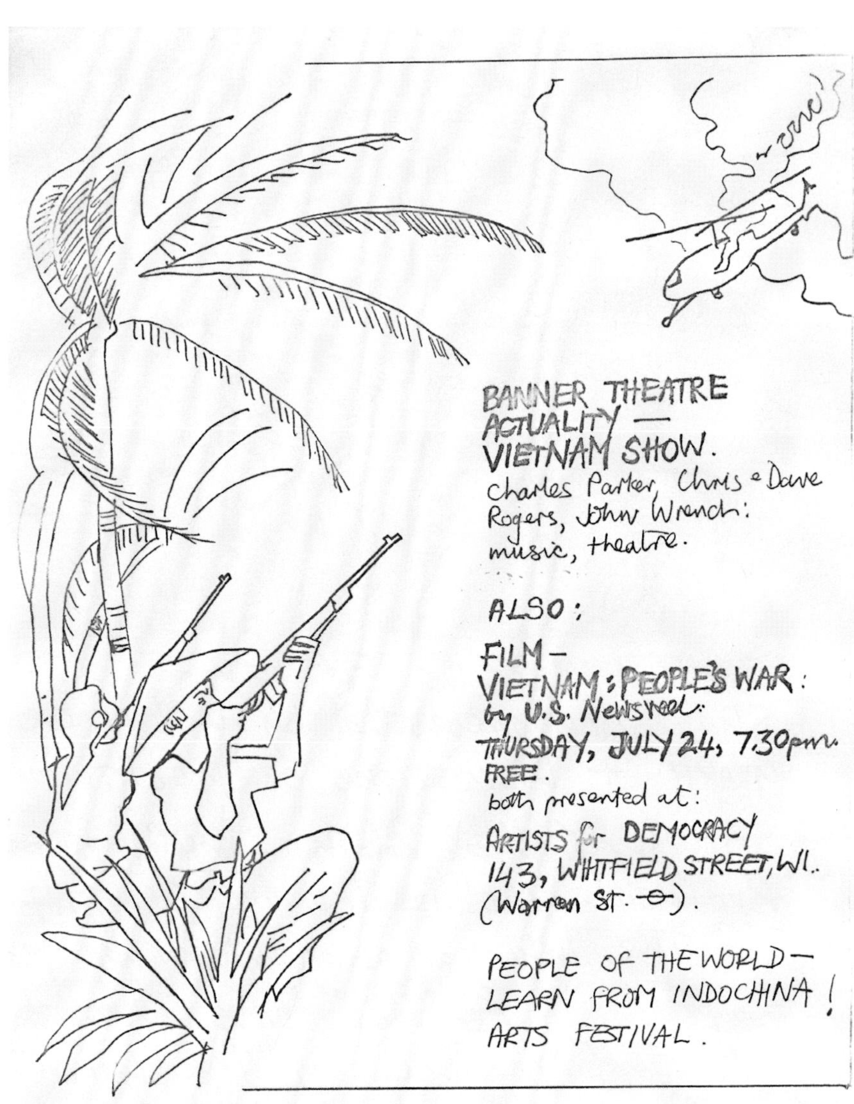
BANNER THEATRE
ACTUALITY —
VIETNAM SHOW.
Charles Parker, Chris & Dave
Rogers, John Wrench:
music, theatre.
ALSO:
FILM —
VIETNAM: PEOPLE'S WAR:
by U.S. Newsreel.
THURSDAY, JULY 24, 7.30pm.
FREE.
both presented at:
ARTISTS for DEMOCRACY
143, WHITFIELD STREET, W1.
(Warren St. ⊖).
PEOPLE OF THE WORLD —
LEARN FROM INDOCHINA!
ARTS FESTIVAL.

"PEOPLE OF THE WORLD LEARN FROM INDOCHINA"
ARTS FESTIVAL

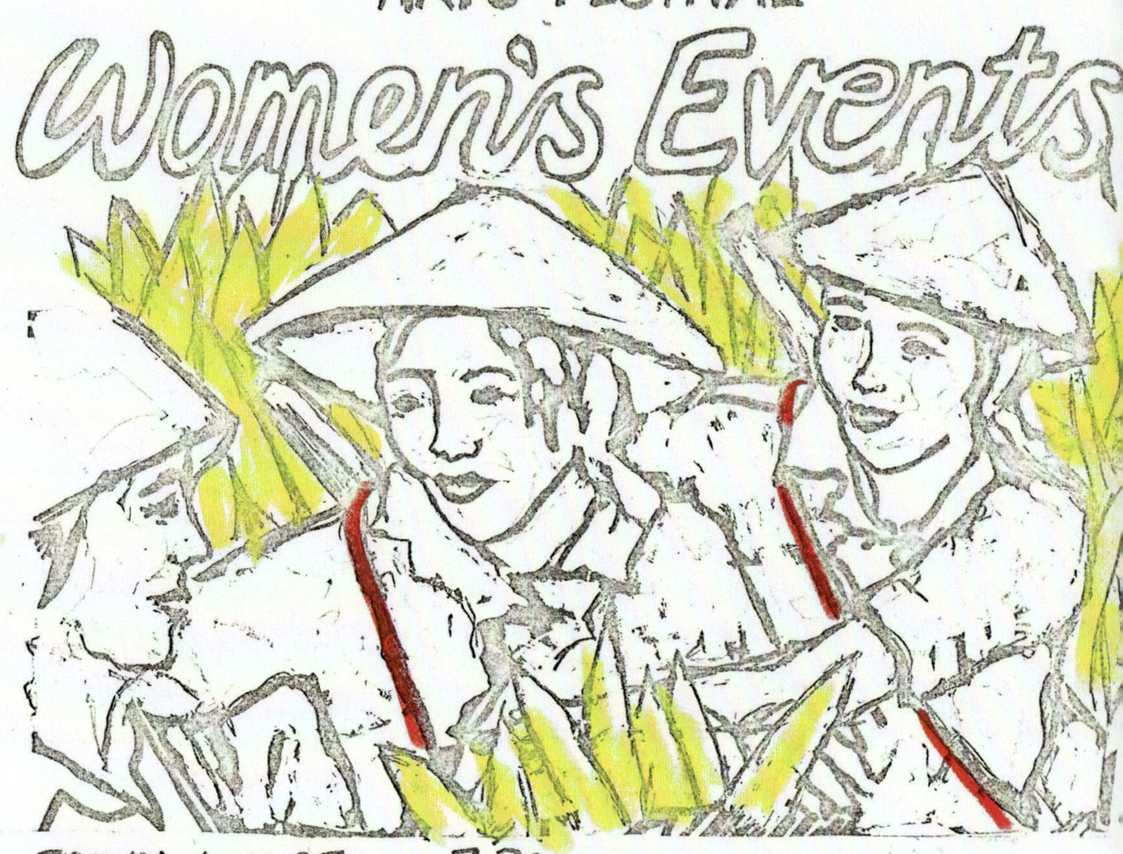

FRIDAY JULY 25th. 7·30 p.m. –
Slide Show presented by the Women in Indochina Group + Discussions on prostitution in Vietnam.

SATURDAY JULY 26th. 8·00 p.m. –
Broadside Mobile Theatre Group, present :-
"The International Women's Year Show"

SATURDAY AUGUST 9th. Throughout the Day –
A performance by the Limited Dance Co. (Jacky Lansley, Sally Potter + others)...
... concerning women in Ireland.

at:- A.F.D. 143 WHITFIELD ST. W.I. (Warren St. Tube

Down by the Salley Gardens was a site-specific collaborative performance presented for one night only in the area immediately outside the AFD building in Whitfield Street. The collaborators and performers were myself, Jacky Lansley, Sally Potter, Judith Katz, Siddhartha Shivtansani and Sylvia Stevens. We were invited to make the performance by David Medalla in connection with an exhibition and events programme about Ireland taking place at AFD. The title of the performance was taken from the poem by William Butler Yeats – 'Down by the Salley Gardens / An Old Song Re-Sung'. In the performance we referenced aspects of Irish history including the Irish Potato Famine – also known as 'the Great Hunger'. Although I do not have any documentation of the performance in my archive and I do not remember every detail of what we all did, certain images remain indelible in my memory.

We assembled an atmospheric set from detritus that we found in the area around AFD on the day of the performance, including an old sofa and a standard lamp. These were placed near an open brazier of burning wood and provided the only light in the evening darkness of the street. I accompanied Sally Potter on my violin as she sang the song 'Down by the Salley Gardens'. I sat on the sofa in the firelight dressed in black mourning dress and spoke softly to a young boy, as if I were his widowed mother telling him of the sudden death of his father. Others were in situ in adjacent buildings – including Sylvia Stevens, located on the top floor of a warehouse from which she threw a cascading torrent of cold water and potato peelings – her arms spot-lit in the flood of light in the open warehouse loading platform.

It was an exciting summer for open-air site-specific performance in London in 1975: Sally, Jacky and I, along with Judith and Sylvia, had also created the performance *Park Cafeteria* in the Serpentine Gallery in Kensington Gardens, referencing the communal past of the building itself. It is possible that David invited us because of this performance, but without doubt we were thrilled to hear afterwards that he had thought highly of *Down by the Salley Gardens*.

Rose English

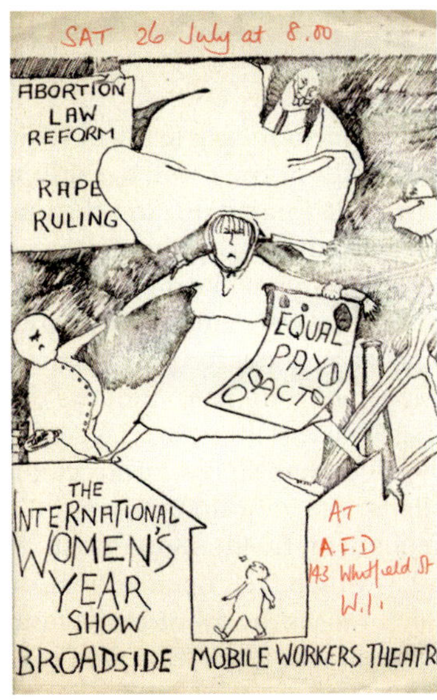

The United Nations declared 1975 International Women's Year. Broadside Theatre responded by producing 'The International Women's Year Show', our contribution to the struggle for equal rights. We used a mix of satire and drama to inform our audiences about what women were up against in the UK and worldwide, from Japan to Chile to South Africa. We also highlighted women's activism and achievements. To maintain flexibility and topicality, we combined cabaret with living newspaper and documentary/verbatim theatre, adding new material or re-writing as situations changed. In sketches and songs, using quotes from the press, placards, letters and narration, we addressed issues such as rape, abortion, equal pay and nurseries. Following performances, we facilitated lively discussions with our audiences where they could share their views and experiences, raise problems in their communities, colleges or workplaces, and suggest solutions. Not all the invitations came from women's organisations. We might be at Newham Women's Action Group or a benefit for a women's refuge in Stevenage one night, and the next at a General and Municipal Workers' Union's course for shop stewards with an audience of 27, only four of them women, or at a Labour club in Bolton for unionised Littlewoods shop workers.

Kathleen McCreery

One of my abiding memories of living in Whitfield Street, apart from the art we created, exhibited, participated in, collaborated on, and the many artists from around the world who came and went, has to do with our dear cat Ming Khai. We named her after a Vietnamese war heroine. The Vietnam war was about to end with the last American evacuated from the roof of the US Embassy. Ming Khai was literally prised out of the mouth of a dog when she was a street kitten by David Medalla. She grew up to become a self assured, independent, freedom-loving cat. She used my window which I left open as her door. Very convenient, too, as the ovens of the tandoori restaurants next door to us were located in their backyards. Ming Khai was so devoted to David that she came back regularly with tandoori chicken legs or breasts, freshly roasted, from the restaurants next door and dropped them on David's lap, or his chest, if he was asleep! Whether she was given the pieces by the restaurant cooks or she stole them, we did not know, but she did not eat them and instead offered the still-warm chicken pieces to David. She got pregnant one day and gave birth to a few kittens in one corner of David's room. As soon as they were strong enough to be able to crawl, she put them one by one on David's bed, as if to present them to him and to all of us.

Jun Terra

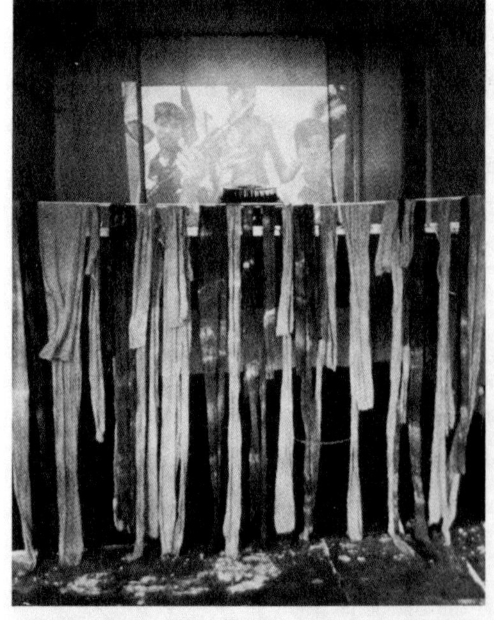

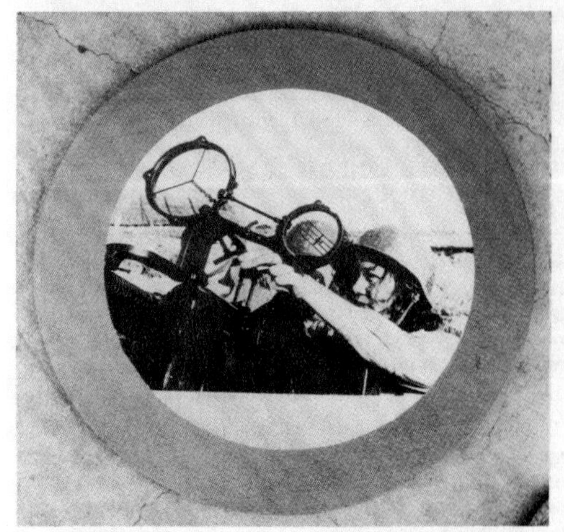

Artists for Democracy,
143 Whitfield Street,
London W1P 5KY, England.

23rd May, 1975

Dear

Warm greetings.

We write on behalf of Artists for Democracy, an organisation of international progressive and revolutionary artists based in London, and founded a year ago. Last October 1974, we organised an international arts festival in support of the Chilean Resistance. One of our activities this year is another arts festival with the theme: Homage to Ho Chi Minh and the great victory of the Indochinese people against U.S imperialist aggression.

The festival in homage to the Vietnamese revolution will be held from July 15 to August 31, 1975, at our cultural centre; 143 Whitfield Street, London, W1P 5 KY. The festival will comprise an exhibition which will be prepared by our members, to draw lessons from the Indochinese struggle, plus films, talks, discussions, poetry reading, musical, dance and video performances, and other events.

For this festival we are organising a comprehensive documentation on various forms of agitprop and street theatre organised by progressive and revolutionary forces all over the world in support of the Indochinese struggle. We therefore are writing to you to request for any relevant documentation that you may have regarding this particular subject; we would appreciate relevant contributions pertaining to any theatrical event that you may have participated in, performed or produced (as an individual or as a group), including photographs, coleur slides and films of such an event, also documentation such as scripts (if any), programme notes, manifestoes, clippings, and the lessons you have drawn from your activities. If you wish to make other contributions vis-a-vis the theme of our arts festival, we would be very glad to accept them.

We hope that you will cooperate with us in this happy endeavour

SOLIDARITY WITH THE VIETNAMESE PEOPLE

Yours fraternally,

Sylvia Stevens and Sonia Knox

facing page: Rasheed Araeen's *Holes in Earth* at 'People of the World Learn from Indochina, Homage to Ho Chi Minh and the Victory of the Indochinese Peoples', 143 Whitfield Street, July–August 1975

* * * ARTISTS FOR DEMOCRACY * * *

143 WHITFIELD STREET, LONDON W1P 5RY, ENGLAND

PEOPLE OF THE WORLD LEARN FROM INDOCHINA!

HOMAGE TO HO CHI MINH

AND THE VICTORY OF THE INDOCHINESE PEOPLE

an international festival of the arts organised by
Artists for Democracy

13 JULY - 10 AUGUST 1975
daily: 1 - 6 p.m. Admission free.

OPENING NIGHT PROGRAMME: SUNDAY, 13th JULY 1975

1. Opening remarks by David Medalla, Chairman of Artists for Democracy.

2. Poems by International Poets Celebrating Indochina's Victory and the Just Struggles of the World's People, including poems by Portilla de la Luz (Cuba), Marcelino dos Santos (Mozambique), A. Hallawani (Sudan), Said Abou-L-Hosn (Syria), Lee Ying (China), Ewan MacColl (England), Abdo Othman (The Arab Republic of the Yemen), Jose Maria Sison (Philippines), and the Red Star Singers (USA). Readers: Virgil Calaguian, Mahmoud Jamal, Nazareth, and Sylvia Stevens.

3. Poems by Vietnamese Poets of our time:
   We Will Liberate the South by Huynh Minh Sieng.
   Uncle's Verses by Ngoc Khuyen.
   Marching Troops by Hong Thao.
   A Hundred Mountain Ranges by Hanh Can.
   Girl from Hue by Vu Duong.
   Confidences to the Perfume River by Tran Ngoc Xuong.
   My Native Land, Quang Binh! by Hoang Van.
   Van Troi, Your Words Will Echo Through the Centuries by Vu Thanh.
   The March of Liberation by Luu Nguyen and Long Hung.

4. VIETNAM VICTORIOUS! part three of a three-part d[...]
   collectively created by David Medalla, Virgil [...]
   and Jun Terra of AFD and the International Co[...]
   Freedom in the Philippines. Incorporated in t[...]
   drama are kinetic sculptures and light works; [...]
   The Path Which Led Me to Leninism by Presiden[...]
   Thirteen Poems from The Prison Diary of UNCLE [...]
   excerpt from the poem TET Song of Spring 68 b[...]
   HAIL LIBERATION FIGHTER!
   Songs; Ngon den dung gac ('The Lighthouse Whos[...]
   Shall Never Be Extinguished'); and
   Tieng ho tren dong ruong tham canh ('Song of [...]
   Rice').

5. Talk on the Problems of Reconstruction in Vietnam [...]
   LE CHAN of the Embassy of the Democratic Repub[...]

6. Film from Viet-Nam: THE LIBERATION OF HUE AND DANA[...]

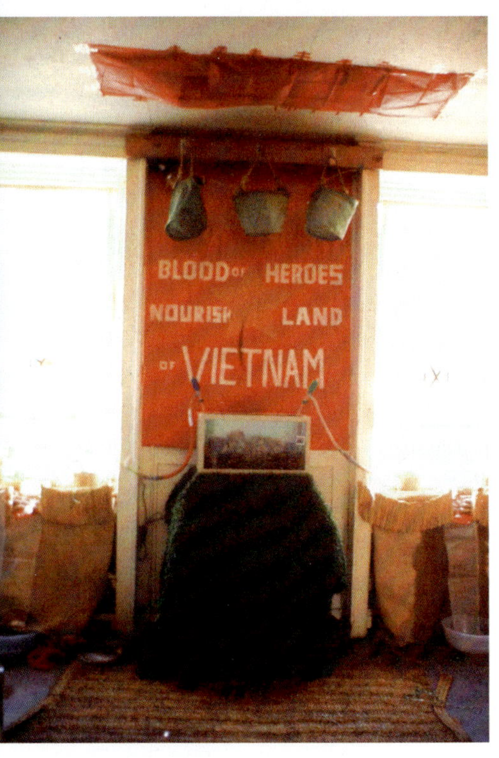

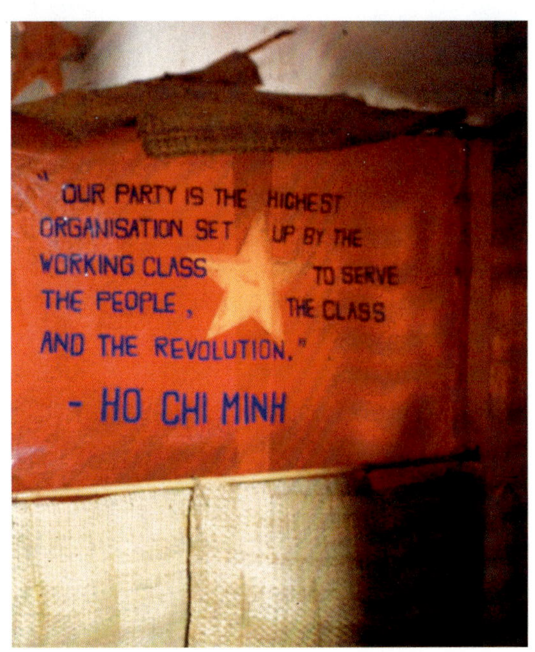

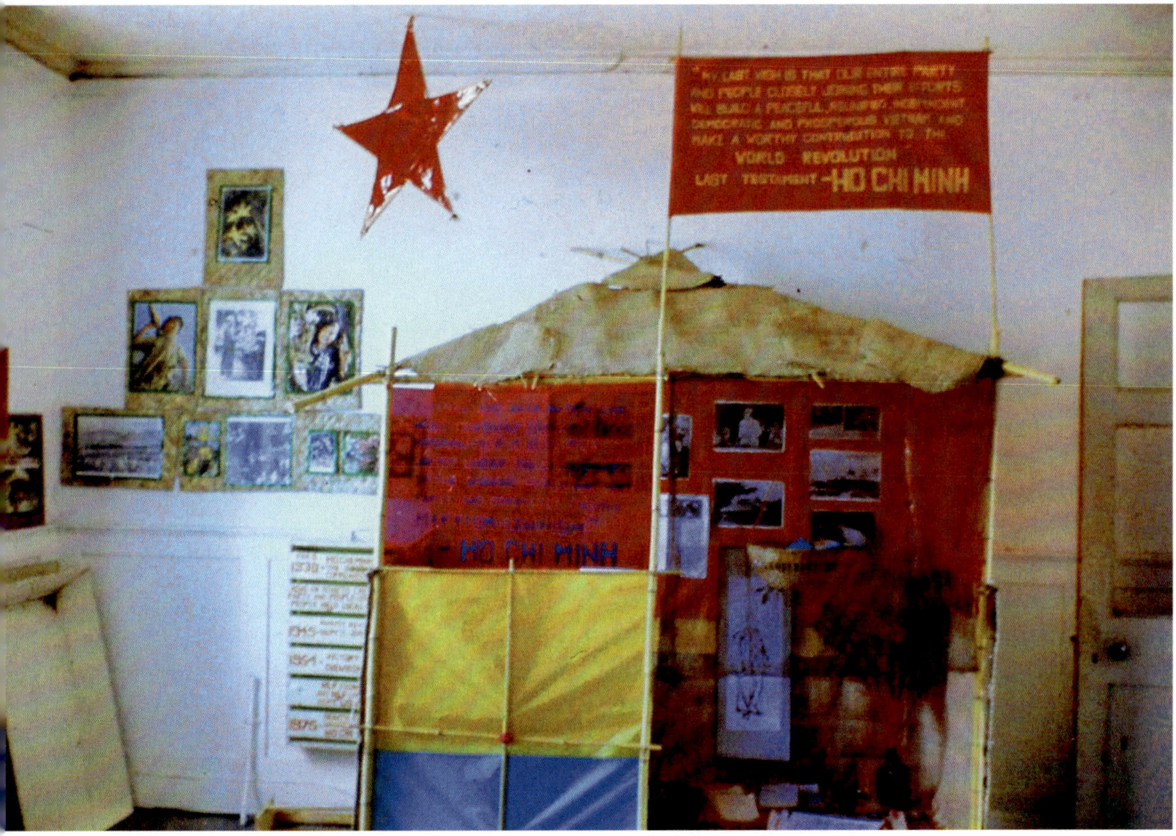

above: 'People of the World Learn from Indochina, Homage to Ho Chi Minh and the Victory of the Indochinese Peoples', 143 Whitfield Street, July–August 1975. following pages: Lynn MacRitchie and Sylvia Stevens

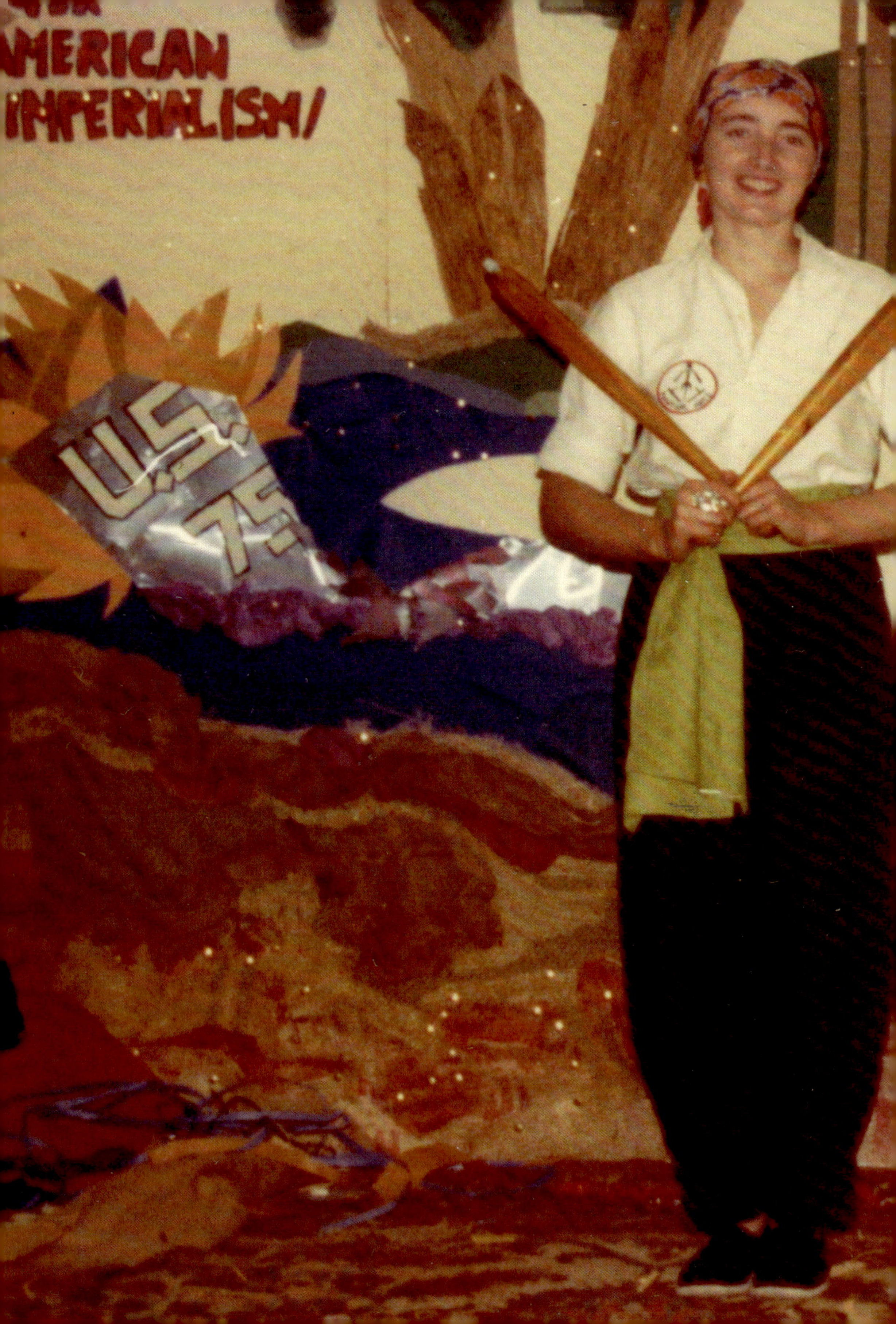
AMERICAN
IMPERIALISM/
U.S.
75

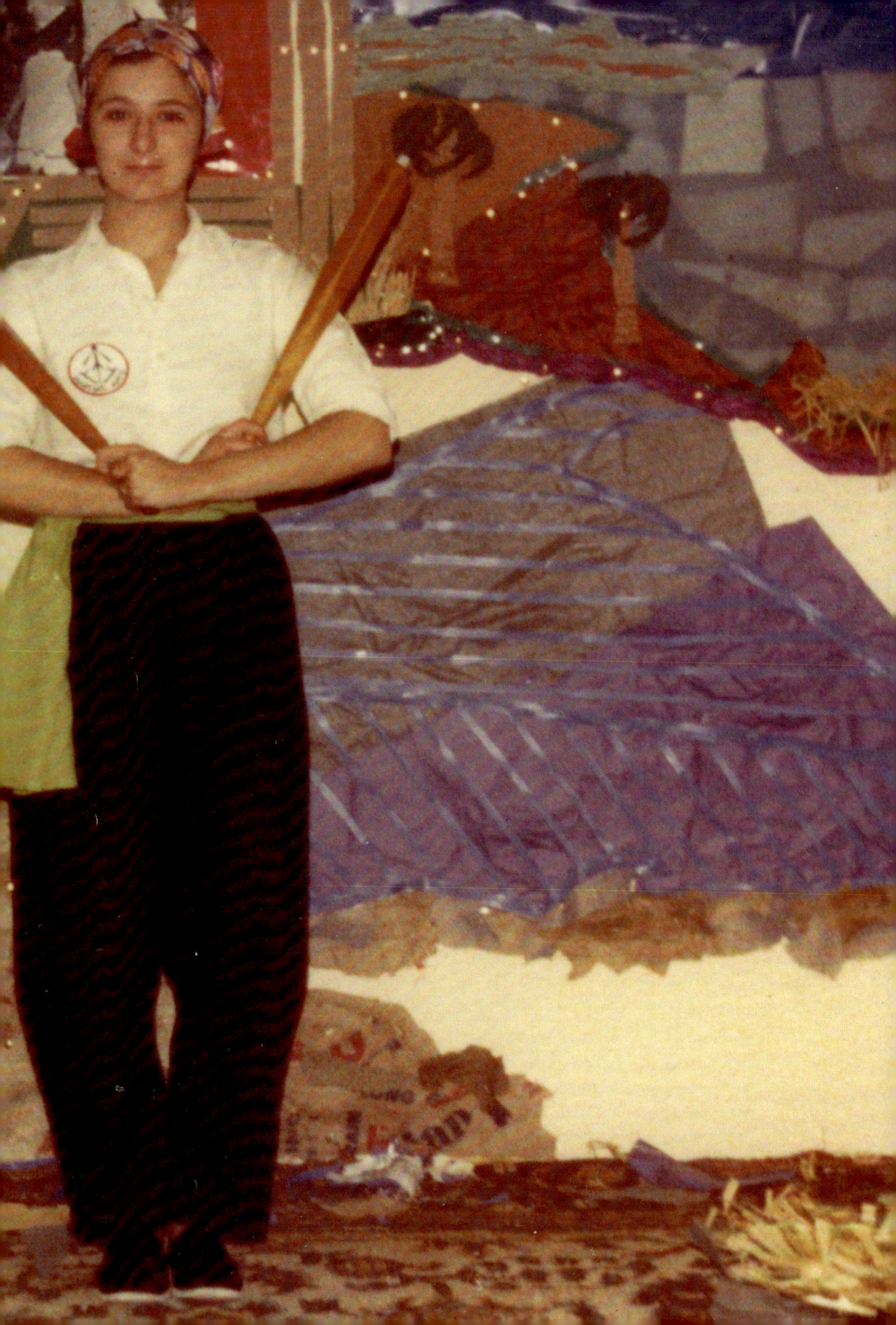

One of the most extraordinary things about AFD was how internationalist it was at that point in time. That was the London art world in the 1970s, the size of a postage stamp. It was small, it was grey, it was miserable, but there were these astonishing people who had wide perspectives on the world. There weren't many of us, but what I can see has happened over all these decades is that that little place in Whitfield Street had so much energy and that energy has rippled out into the world.

Lynn MacRitchie

the Thirties.

Hence it is with certain reservations that one approaches an exhibition like that which forms part of the Vietnam Victory Festival at Artists for Democracy, 143 Whitfield Street, W1 (with evening events, until August 31). None of the artists who have contributed to this celebration is Vietnamese and probably none has been to Vietnam, although several of them are from other parts of the Far East. Yet the intensity of television and newspaper coverage of Vietnam was such that it was possible for anyone in the world to judge what was happening.

The exhibition consists of a series of environments made of simple, often waste, materials, to symbolize the reconstruction of the country after the end of the war, photographs and photomontages and anti-Vietnam war posters from various countries. Some of the works, like *The Life of Ho Chi Minh*, display a kind of knowing *faux naiveté*. The best, because the most imaginative and controlled, are a photomural and an environment with "photo-discs" inspired by the one-man air-raid shelters of Vietnam (which perhaps more than anything else stick in one's mind from films and photographs as symbols of the courage and resilient ingenuity of the Vietnamese). These two works are by Rasheed Araeen who is from Pakistan but has worked in England for some years (one of his brightly painted constructions was shown at the John Moores Liverpool exhibition several years ago). Also effective, because simple and straightforward, are Bertha Husband's window murals on perspex, *Women in Vietnam*.

Other works look very like those made for the Chile Festival at the Royal College of Art last autumn, which is not surprising as many of the artists are the same. The trouble with many of them is that the construction of simple, symbolic, peasant-like structures and the juxtaposition of waste materials with photographs and slogans is not really enough to make significant statements of political and artistic import.

For unless charged with imagination and sensibility such works contribute neither to art nor to political awareness.

TRIỂN LÃM NHÂN DÂN THẾ GIỚI HỌC TẬP NHÂN DÂN ĐÔNG DƯƠNG VÀ TỎ LÒNG THÀNH KÍNH ĐỐI VỚI CHỦ TỊCH HỒ CHÍ MINH TẠI ANH

Theo tin từ Luân Đôn, một cuộc triển lãm kéo dài một tháng do Hội nghệ sĩ vì dân chủ của Anh tổ chức và mang tên *Nhân dân thế giới học tập nhân dân Đông Dương và tỏ lòng thành kính đối với Chủ tịch Hồ Chí Minh*, đã khai mạc ngày 13-7 vừa qua

Phát biểu ý kiến tại lễ khai mạc có gần 200 người dự, ông Đê-vít Mê-đan-la Chủ tịch Hội nghệ sĩ vì dân chủ gửi lời chúc mừng nhiệt liệt đến nhân dân Việt Nam anh hùng, nêu rõ ý nghĩa và vị trí to lớn của cuộc chiến đấu chống đế quốc xâm lược của nhân dân Việt Nam trong hơn 30 năm qua để giành độc lập và tự do

Ông nhấn mạnh ý nghĩa quốc tế hết sức quan trọng của chiến thắng lịch sử của quân và dân Việt Nam, đánh bại tên đế quốc Mỹ đầu sỏ và bọn bù nhìn tay sai của chúng.

Ông kêu gọi nhân dân Anh đẩy mạnh hơn nữa phong trào ủng hộ nhân dân Việt Nam trong công cuộc hàn gắn vết thương chiến tranh, xây dựng lại đất nước.

Tiếp đó, các nghệ sĩ đã trình bày một số bài thơ của Hồ Chủ tịch, của nhà thơ Tố Hữu và một số nhà thơ Việt Nam khác cùng với một số bài thơ của các tác giả thế giới ca ngợi cuộc chiến đấu kiên cường anh dũng của nhân dân Việt Nam. Hai bộ phim tài liệu *Đà Nẵng ngày đầu giải phóng* và *79 mùa xuân* và bộ phim đèn chiếu minh họa bài của Hồ Chủ tịch *Con đường dẫn tôi đến chủ nghĩa Lê-nin* chiếu tại buổi lễ khai mạc được người xem nhiệt liệt hoan nghênh.

Working People No 9. Sept/oct '75. p.13.

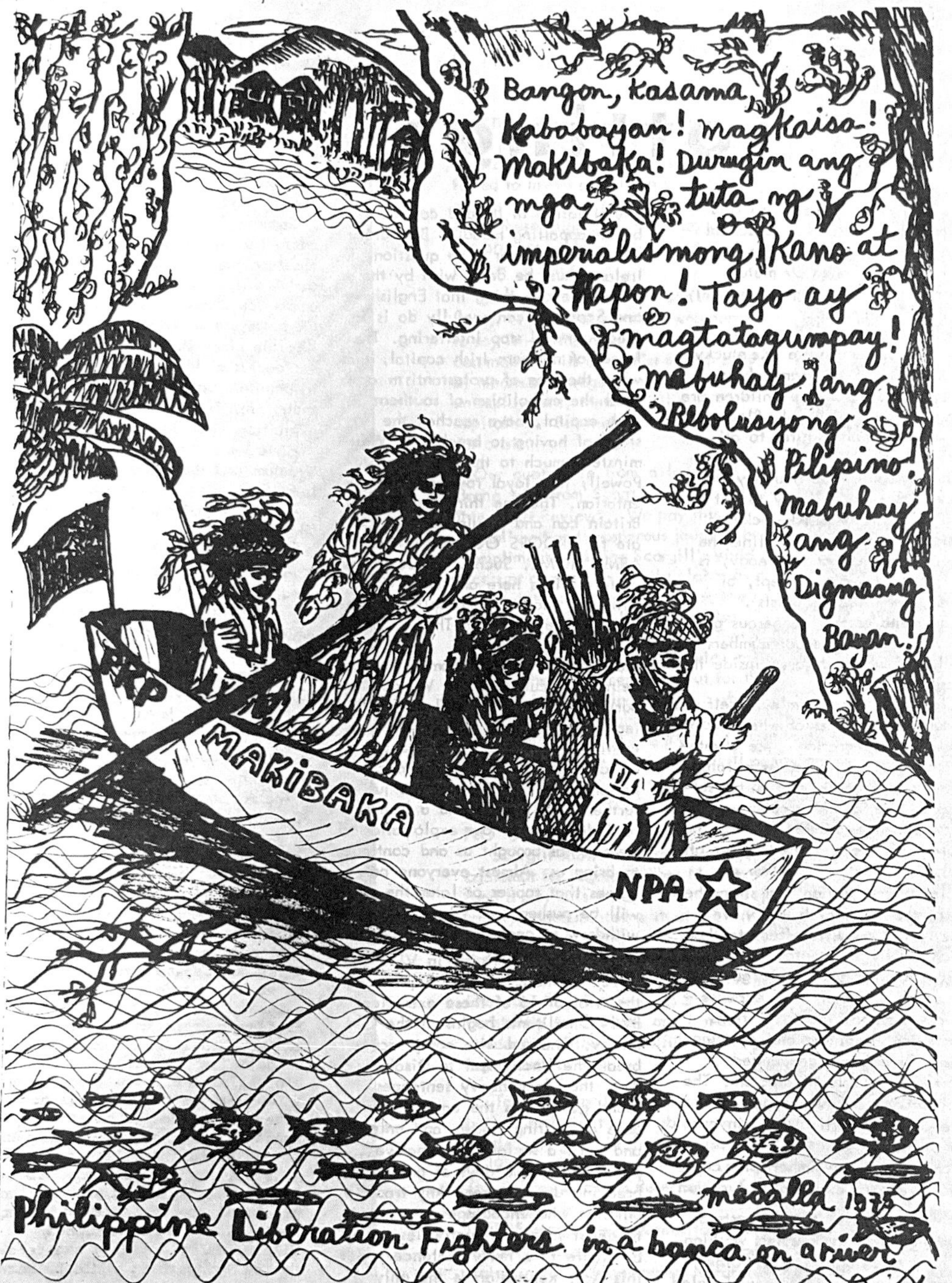

Ink Drawing by David Medalla, chairman of the International Committee for Freedom in the Philippines - Philippine Solidarity Campaign.

The inscription on the rock is in Tagalog-Pilipino, and reads (in translation): "Arise, comrades, compatriots! Dare to struggle! Smash the puppets of American and Japanese imperialism! We shall win! Victory to the Philippine Revolution! Long live People's War!"

The banca is a wooden boat carved out a single tree trunk and is a popular riverine and maritime transport in the Philippines. Written on the banca are the word [cont. on p. 8]

pto.

t U

ed

d

Where would you expe
children being escortec
under armed guard? A
their bodies scanned b
detectors - the kind no
at airports - for guns?
Belfast?

Boston and Louisvill
are just two of the m
cities in the US where
being 'bussed' to scho
all-white schools; whi
black schools.

That the kids - part
black kids - are unlik
yond the rows of blac
'national guardsmen' v
streets, bayonets at t
obvious to anyone - e
course, the 'integrati

The name of this da
'Racial balance' - equal nu
black and white children ir
classroom.

Classroom 'separatism' is
product of centuries of whi
Classroom 'integration', the
racism of white liberals wh
to see that there is no 'wh
ution to the 'black' proble

There are lessons for us
ticularly in view of the cu
empts to strengthen the la
'racial discrimination' - a
ing of the law which will
exactly the opposite effect
which is allegedly intende

By making black people
the courts - at their own e
the new Jenkins' 'race rel
commission' is aiding and
racism. It must be denounc

There is no 'black' probl
problem is in our own impe
society. More particularly,
own attitudes.

Capitalism - now imperia
italism - cannot exist witho
which alone serves the inte
the ruling class by keeping
people divided against eac
No amount of 'buses' or ne
'race relations commissions'
rid of imperialism. How th
they be expected to get ri
racism? Much less, change
itudes. For, finally, racism
disappear until our racist a
disappear.

cont. from p.13 "M a k i b a k a" ("Dare to struggle" -- a quotation from Chairman Mao -- and a popular slogan of the Filipino revolutionary masses) and the initials "PKP" (Partidong Kommunista ng Pilipinas -- the Communist Party of the Philippines), and "NPA" - New People's Army, the armed might of the Communist Party of the Philippines (Marxist-Leninist), comprising at present 50,000 regular men and women soldiers. Since 1968, the Filipino New People's Army, under the dashing command of Commander Dante, has won victory after victory over the puppet-troops of Ferdinand Marcos, the stooge of American and Japanese imperialism. At present, the Communist Party of the Philippines is consolidating liberated areas in the north and south, and has extended guerilla warfare to more than fifty per cent of the Philippines.

The chairman of the Communist Party of the Philippines, Amado Guerrero, wrote in a poem dedicated to the heroic Vietnamese people: "C o m m a n d e v e r y i n c h o f n a t u r e w i t h g e n i u s". The Filipino artist David Medalla has conveyed this directive in his drawing. The Philippines is famous for its volcanoes, mountains, dense forests and thick tropical jungles, terrains suitable for guerilla warfare. The Philippine rivers are famous for their rapids. Of all known species of fresh- and salt-water fish in the world, over sixty per cent are found in the Philippines, which is composed of over 7,100 islands. The fish in Medalla's drawing refer to another quotation from Chairman Mao: "G u e r r i l l a s s h o u l d l i v e a n d m o v e a m o n g t h e p e o p l e l i k e f i s h i n t h e w a t e r".

David Medalla is the chairman of Artists for Democracy, a broad-front organisation of progressive international cultural workers, founded in London on 6 May 1974. Artists for Democracy organised the highly successful international Arts Festival for Chilean Resistance held last year, and more recently, at their cultural centre at 143 Whitfield Street, London, W1p 5RY (near Warren Street tube station) the highly successful arts festival celebrating the glorious victory of the Indochinese people. Artists for Democracy are currently showing films from China at their cultural centre, 143 Whitfield Street, W1, every Sunday at 7 p.m. (until the end of October), open to the public, admission free.

s to
ely
of
ie
men
to
he
that
ag-

Vest-
Mr
am-

agit-
THE
can
em
tever
rs of

are
(Lab-
sold-
to
mbs
x-
st a
ner
on of
inues
ow
army
present
hav-

am?
ber,
ary
Old
y to
ction'
if
crisis
ess
is
strike-
es
er
ill
nder

can

Bailey,
ber,
led-

The 'control units' press conference (see p.5) was held at the Artists for Democracy, who are currently being threatened with eviction from their Whitfield St. premises. Already the landlord's 'heavies' have been round to try and force them out before the court has had time to hear the injunction taken out against the landlord.

Camden Council is being petitioned to take out a compulsary purchase order on the premises which, should the Artists be thrown out, may stand empty for several years, as before. Or be mysteriously gutted by fire like the premises next door.

'Peoples of the world, learn from Indochina', urged the Artists through their latest Vietnamese anniversary exhibition, just ended.

Have we not much to learn? From Vietnam and the 'third world'? Not least from our own mistakes.

As a WP reader points out elsewhere in this issue:

'We need a grass roots army of poets, writers, songsters, actors, (and) cartoonists' to wage war on the cynicism and demoralisation which is holding back the development of a socialist movement here in England.

Only with a vision of the future is it possible to transform the present.

But transform the present we must if there is to be any future at all worth working for.

The Artists are part of that army of poets we m u s t build.

• • •

The acute phase, the real crisis for British capitalism is now
near ... ite
a few ... lly
be sm ... em-
selve
Profe ... tates-
man w ... that
he pa ... n for
his c ... gins
to wo ... ot
after ... tly
pract ... r an
actua ... eet
this ... t is
on pr ... y on
pract ... lson/
Heale
Wilso ... e de-
feate ... more
accur
milli ... ough
by Jo ... ur-
ther ... not
reall ... need
to be ... move-
ment ... truc-
cont.

Meetings

THE SOCIALIST PARTY AND REVOLUTION — NO COMPROMISE Saturday January 17, 7.30pm, at 52 Clapham High Street, London SW4 (5 minutes Clapham North Tube). Questions, discussion. All welcome. The Socialist Party of Great Britain.

LABOUR PARTY Local Government Conference. Militant/Tribune meeting. Fight Cuts! Fight Unemployment! Implement the Manifesto! Hear: Joan Maynard MP, Emlyn Williams (President South Wales NUM), Terry Burns (Cardiff South East Labour Party — in personal capacity), Steve James (EEPTU Shop Steward British Rail). Odd Fellows Hall, Newport Road, Cardiff. Friday January 23 at 7.30pm.

COMMITTEE to Defend Czechoslovak Socialists, Bertrand Russell Peace Foundation Seminar at Essex University, Saturday, January 24, 11am: John Saville — 'What is socialist democracy? Sunday, January 25, 11am: Stan Newens MP — Socialism, detente and the British Labour movement. Registration £1 to 49a Tabley Road, London N7. Some accommodation free. Apply with SAE.

ALBANIA
SOCIALISM IN EUROPE
Talk: History of the Party of Labour

Sunday, January 18, at 7 pm.

At: Artists for Democracy, 143 Whitefield Street, Near Warren Street Tube.

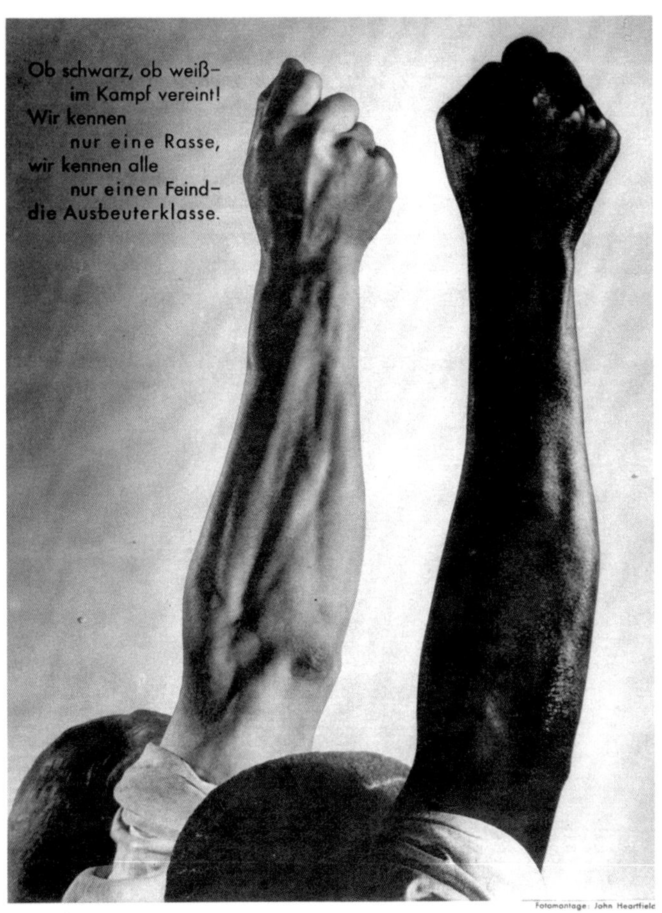

Photomontage was a collage technique much used in the Twenties, when it virtually became a cliché. But John Heartfield made it into a powerful political weapon more effective in its time than drawn caricature. An impressive portfolio of poster-sized versions of these montages has recently been published in East Germany where Heartfield spent the last years of his life, after 12 as a refugee in Britain. (John Heartfield: 33 Fotomontagen, VEB Verlag der Kunst, Dresden.) These can be seen displayed on the walls at Artists for Democracy, 143 Whitfield Street, W.1. The selection includes most of Heartfield's best-known works, but there are some omissions which no doubt reflect the political viewpoint of the DDR, like the brilliant montage of Goebbels as a valet standing on a chair to fit Hitler out with Karl Marx's beard.

John Heartfield, *Ob schwarz, ob weiß– im Kampf vereint!* (*Black or White – United in the Fight*, 1931). An exhibition of prints by Heartfield is held at 143 Whitfield Street in late 1975. During the show, Guy Brett gives a lecture on Bertolt Brecht's ideas on art.

Before I met David, m ny artists whom I spoke to during my travels in ·sia, & Europe referred to Medalla s "the enfant terrible of the interna avant-garde". I was therefore pleasantly uprised, when I encountered Medalla for the first

INTERVIEW WITH DAVID MEDALLA

by D vid Lee

time, to discover th t, in spite of his tremendo artistic achievements, achieved t very young age, for w he has gained the admiration of many international art critics and artis David is truly unassuming, warm nd gentle.

My impression of David Medalla is of a young man, alert, sensitive and naturally friendly. He immerses himself thoroughly in the cultures of the world's peoples, and participates enthusi stically in the struggles of the world's masses for liberation. "The emancipation of humankind is, for me, more important than person l f me or glory", Med lla remarked to me. This is not just empt rhetoric, for David Medalla has lw ys sought to integrate his artistic theories & ctivities with revolutionary social practice.

I interviewed David on December 7, 1975, in his room on the top floor of 143 Whitfield street, London W1. This is the house occupied by Artists for Democracy. Downst irs w s an exhibition of posters nd photomontages by the great Germ n anti-fascist artist of the thirties John He rtfield. The ceiling of D vid's room h d parti lly collapsed. The building, which was early Georgi architecture, w s empty for more th n two ye rs before Artists for Democra moved in nd converted it into London's only cultur l centre for progressi nd Left-wing artists. In the summer of 1975, Artists for Democr cy org nised a festival of art nd politics celebr ting the historic victory of the Indochinese people against imperi lism cultur l groups nd organisations supporting liber tion movements all ove the world p rticip ted in. The festival w s given an enthusiastic notice by NHAN DHAN, the offici l newspaper of the Democr tic Republic of Vietn m. AFD's Vietn m Victory Festiv l, which was lso in homage to Ho Chi Minh, w s followed by smaller festiv l of socialist films, m inly from the People's Republic of Chin . D vid nd his comr des in rtists for Democr cy worked indef tig bly m ke both festiv ls gre t success.

D vid's small room gave an impression of creative ch os, th t is to s y, the ch from which creativity springs. There were books everywhere, magazines & paper spilling from three sets of bookcases and shelves. On one bookc se there w two fine Shihw n pottery figurines, of PLA soldier nd wom n militi member, from Fush n City, Kwantung Province, Chin . On the w lls of the room were pinned posters, colour photographs, watercolours & drawings, includin a silk embroidered h nging inscribed with the words of Mao Tsetung's "The Fairy Cave at Mount Lush n", a l rge paper-cut of the writer Lu pingpong bat inscribed with the names of the Chinese table-tennis te m which came to England on December 1971.

D vid also showed me a carved wooden spear of the Dogon tribe of Afric . He expl ined th t the spe r was both symbolic and utilit rian: it served to tell time and seasonal changes. I observed also a sm electric digit l clock in D vid's room. In the centre of the room there hu a small naked electric light bulb, propped up from the ceiling by patte of coloured plastic t pes like n Americ n Indi n design. David said that the t pes were put together by his friend Philip, a young merican interested in homeop thy nd her medicine.

When I talked to him, he was preparing n article on the Phi

Each of my 3 interview with David l sted sever l hours. We s t on his bed improvised from an old m ttress upon three wicker laundry b skets. From time to David got up to make tea, answer the doorbell (a const nt stre m visitors is a daily occurence in David's life), nd feed his three kitten

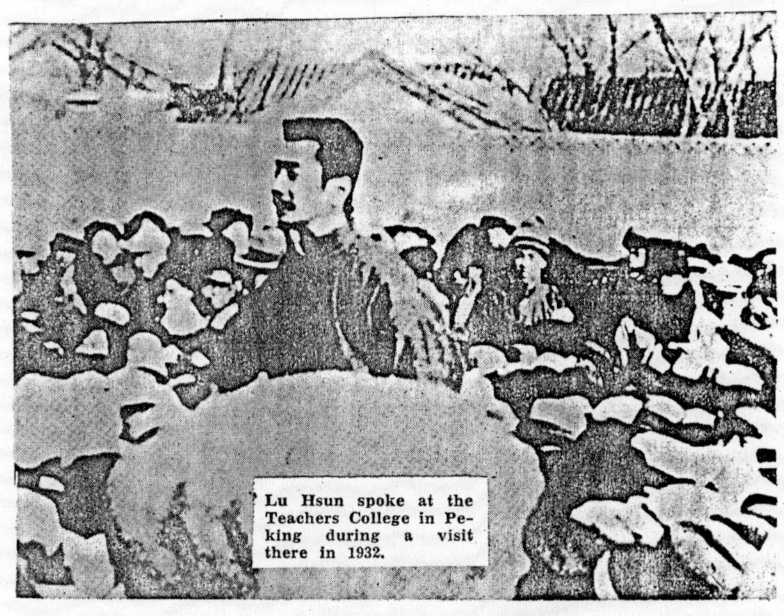

* LU HSUN's "WILD GRASS" *

David Medalla, Chairman of ARTISTS FOR DEMOCRACY, cordially invite

and friends, to a performance of an experimental dance-drama based on LU HSUN's prose-poems "Wild Grass" by the AMNESIA INTERNATIONAL DANCE COMPANY (Artistic Director: Virgil Calaguian), on Sunday, March 7th, 1976, at 7 p.m., at AFD's FITZROVIA CULTURAL CENTRE, 143 Whitfield street, London W1P 5RY. Near Warren street tube station.

RSVP: The Secretary, AFD, 143 Whitfield street, London W1P 5RY.

'China Show', 143 Whitfield Street, February–March 1976. Described as an 'exhibition of contemporary Chinese watercolour woodcuts by China's leading artists, papercuts, reproductions of peasants' wall paintings, and black & white and colour photographs.' It is organised in cooperation with the Cultural Section of the Chinese Embassy and Society for Anglo-Chinese Understanding. A related film programme, organised by Phillip Cohen, Hok Thye, Law Long and David Medalla, is presented at various venues in London.

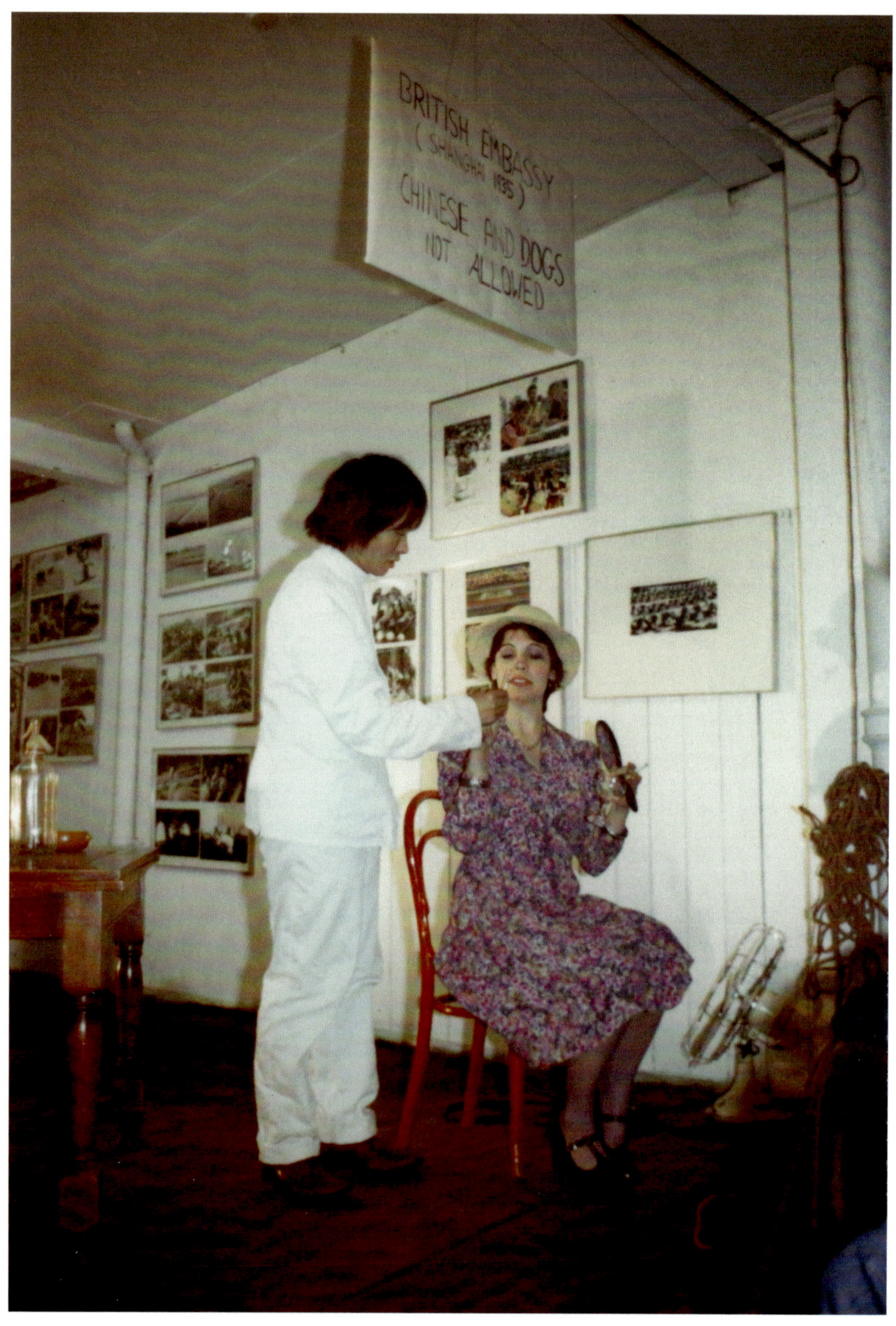

David Medalla as Ah Q and Harriet Clark as Lady Harriet.
Wild Grass **performance at 'China Show', 143 Whitfield Street, March 1976**

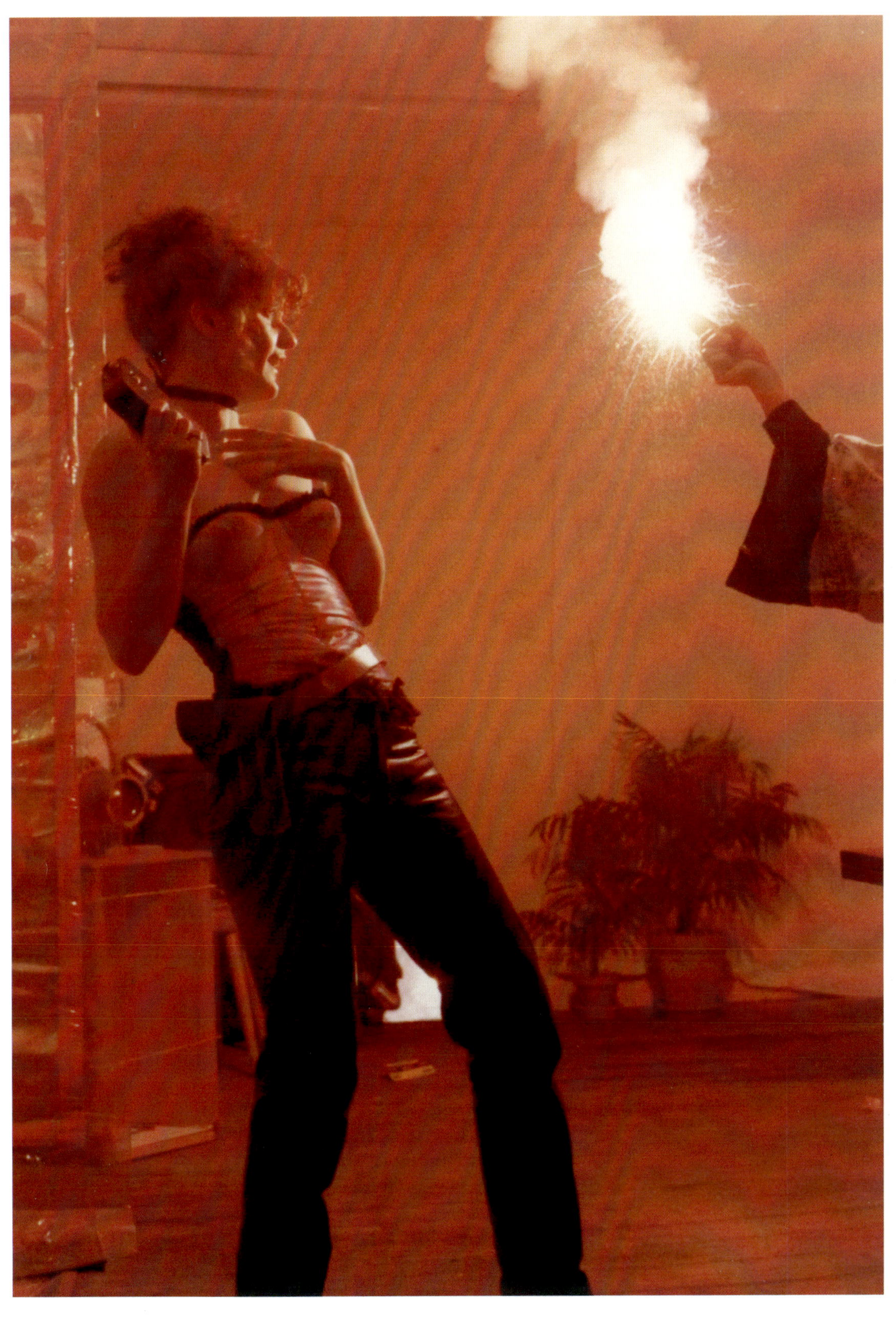

Jane England as Miss Liberty. *Wild Grass* performance at 'China Show', 143 Whitfield Street, March 1976

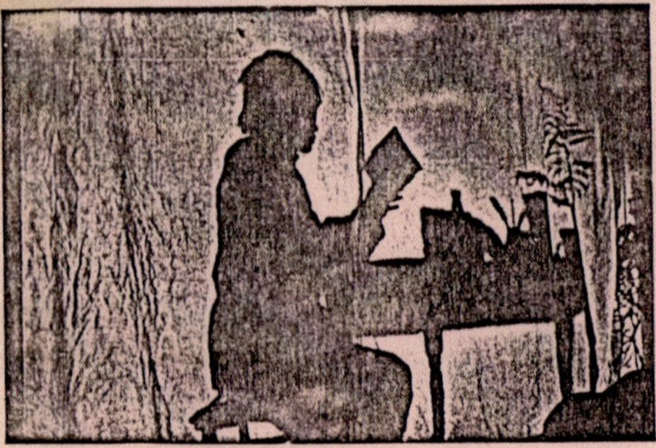

David Medalla as Lu Hsun

Lu Hsun's WILD GRASS

an experimental dance-drama by the
AMNESIA INTERNATIONAL DANCE COMPANY

Repeat performance by public demand
Wednesday, March 24th 1976, at 8:00 pm

at

ARTISTS FOR DEMOCRACY
FITZROVIA CULTURAL CENTRE
143 Whitfield St. W.1, near Warren St.

Wild Grass

Lu Hsun

CAST

Beancurd	Alan Fleming
Sally Bentley	Long
Guy Brett	David Medalla
Virgil Calaguian	Steve Oxley
Harriet Clark	Nicholas Payne
K. Chattergee	Cid Reyes
Steve Cripps	Jun Terra
Jane England	Hok Thye

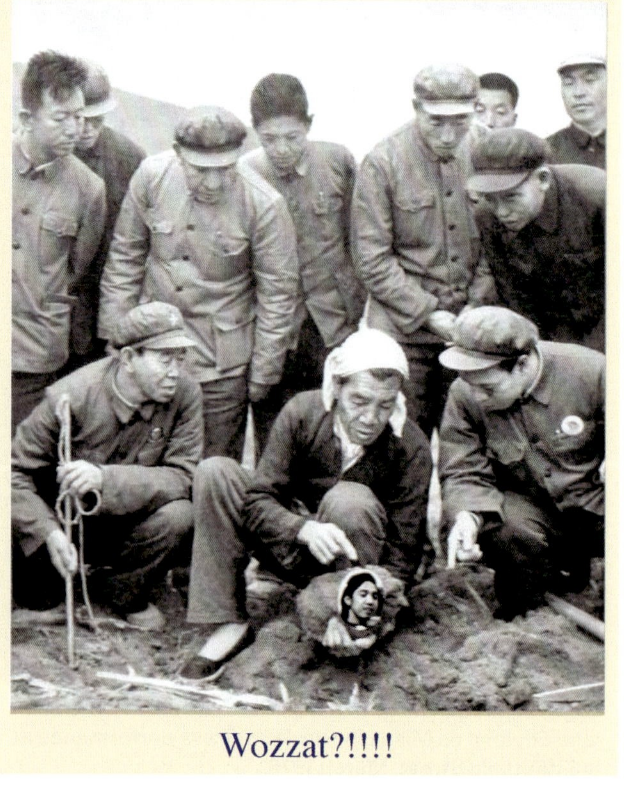

Wozzat?!!!!

The venue in Whitfield Street changed its name to the innocuous-sounding Fitzrovia Cultural Centre. It broadened out as an experimental centre open to any progressive proposal and was not inhibited by bureaucratic procedures, 9 to 5 hours or stylistic preferences: an attractive proposition in a city which can impose a depressing isolation on artists and their publics. The most incongruous diversity of events ensued. One night there might be a meeting of an exiled Third World opposition group that ended in furious faction-fighting. Another night, there might be a luxurious champagne opening for a young artist. (This in fact happened only once. Two tables laden with food and drink were the gift of the staff at Boodle's Club to Giles Thomas, who was working in the club on a temporary job to support his painting.) All this was typical of [David] Medalla's 'cacophony of voices'. In particular, early experimenters in performance and video, in artist/audience dialogue, in the exploration of self and identity, congregated at Whitfield Street...

Guy Brett

A big printed version of this image pasted on a wooden backing was shown as a light, quirky piece during the 'China Show' at AFD where we exhibited beautiful painting scrolls and prints given (some were lent) by the Chinese Embassy which was then located at Portland Street near Regent's Park. Members of AFD were invited to some of the public events of the Embassy.

Earlier on, before ALF (Artists Liberation Front) became AFD, when we were living at Newport Place in Chinatown we used to make collages of images of the Cultural Revolution. We had a rich mine of images of China of the period from books, magazines and posters, souvenirs and knick-knacks of the revolution from our next-door-neighbour bookshop owned by Tang. He was so generous, we could get what we wanted from his shop on a 'buy now, pay later' basis. He often cancelled our debt. Thanks to Tang, we were able to follow the many twists and turns of the events in China, especially the Cultural Revolution and the debates within the Chinese Communist Party that led to momentous changes in the government and eventually the country. The debate was spurred by an article entitled 'Evening chats at Yenshan'.

The picture of me in drag, it is one of the many performances members of the AFD and other groups and individuals did. ... Cid Reyes was one of the 'actors' in this performance about spies and counter-spies set in Vienna [and] devised by David Medalla. I was an anti-communist spy preparing to dance with the main character to Jack Buchanan's (a popular post-War singer) laconic singing of 'Goodnight Vienna, a city of a million melodies'. The scene with myself and Reyes together was a meeting of 'old' and 'new' China. The narrative is not a straightforward one but is carried along by accidents – for instance, when my toupee fell on the floor while I was dancing the tango with another character, we stirred the narrative into another path.

Jun Terra

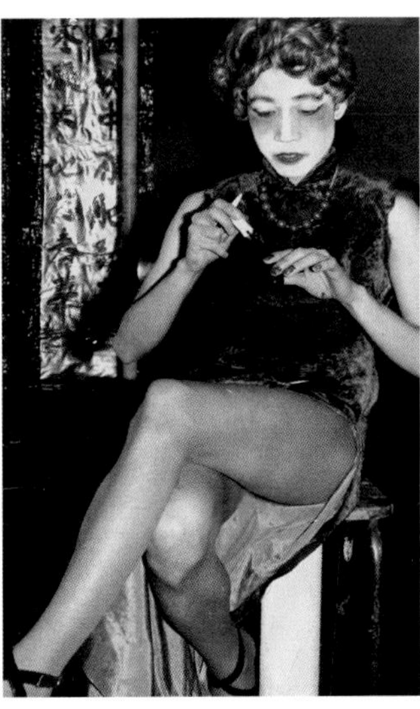

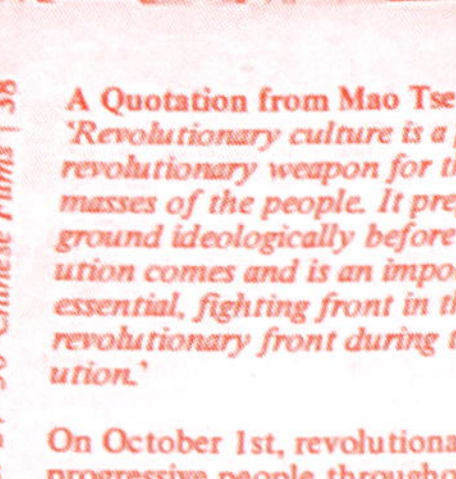

CHINESE FILMS

In this article artist David Medalla introduces the films to be shown in the Festival of Chinese Films to be shown at the Baker Street, Brixton, Notting Hill, and Hampstead Classics starting on September 26, add also by the Friends of China at various venues from September 21.

A Quotation from Mao Tsetung
'Revolutionary culture is a powerful revolutionary weapon for the broad masses of the people. It prepares the ground ideologically before the revolution comes and is an important, indeed essential, fighting front in the general revolutionary front during the revolution.'

On October 1st, revolutionary and progressive people throughout the world will celebrate the 22nd anniversary of the founding of the People's Republic of China. Various Marxist-Leninist groups in Britain are planning public meetings and celebrations to mark this occasion.

Friends of China and the **Society for Anglo-Chinese Understanding** (SACU), two cultural organisations independent of one another, are organising showings in London of recent films from the People's Republic. British audiences will have the opportunity of seeing the latest developments in the cultural front in Red China since the Great Proletarian Cultural Revolution, initiated and led by Chairman Mao, which unfolded in the mid-sixties.

Friends of China will show the following films:
China's 3 Nuclear Tests (documentary), at 236 Westbourne Park Road, London W.11 (Ladbroke Grove Tube), on Thursday, Sept. 23, at 7:30 p.m.;
'Mine Warfare' (feature film), at Camden Studios, Camden Street, London N.W.1. (Camden Town Tube), on Sunday, Sept. 26, at 7:00 p.m.

Public discussions on China's foreign policy and socialist life in the People's Republic today will be held in conjunction with the showings of the above-mentioned films.

On a more comprehensive scale is the **Festival of Chinese Films** which is being organised by SACU. The festival will be held in four of London's Classic Cinemas (Baker Street, Brixton, Notting Hill and Hampstead) starting on Sept. 26 and ending on October 9th. There will be a different and continuously changing programme in each Classic Cinema, and I suggest consulting Time Out's cinema listings for the schedules of performances.

The SACU-organised Festival will feature three full-length films in colour: the modern ballet **'Red Detachment of Women'** (which the Chinese government entered at this year's Venice Film Festival), and cinematic transcriptions (with English sub-titles) of two new Peking operas.
'Taking Tiger Mountain by Strategy' and **'The Red Lantern'** (with English sub-titles).
In addition two documentary films will also be shown—one on the building of **'The Red Flag Canal'** and the other on the construction of **'The Nanking Bridge,'** plus two shorts in colour for children, **'Cock Crows at Midnight'** (a puppet film) and **'Heroic Sisters of the Grassland'** (a very beautiful animated cartoon).

The technical level of these new Chinese films (colour photography, sound registration and editing) is generally very high and on the whole shows a marked improvement on films made before the Cultural Revolution. There are no tricks of photography used for cheap thrills; all technical innovations have been introduced discreetly, primarily to aid the flow of the stories in all films. One innovation is the consistent use of the camera to make deliberately the villains in the stories (landlords, bandits, capitalists and oppressors) appear physically stunted and insignificant by shooting them from certain strategic angles, such as a bird's eye view, and in a murky light symbolic of the devious minds of all reactionaries.

All these films, incidentally, were made collectively, not only by the workers of the different Chinese film studios, but also with the active cooperation of the masses in China: workers, peasants, soldiers of the People's Liberation Army, Communist Party cadres, and revolutionary youth (the Red Guards). The technical improvements in film-making are a reflection of the revolutionary changes in the performing arts in China undertaken since 1964 (two years before the Cultural Revolution was announced) under the leadership and personal guidance of Chiang Ching, Chairman Mao's wife and herself a former stage and film actress.

The changes in the cultural front were aimed at creating new art forms which, though preserving and improving the best elements of traditional literature and theatre, will (by portraying the heroic struggles of the masses) serve to consolidate the dictatorship of the proletariat over the hated and despised bourgeoisie.

The new films and operas of China all portray proletarian heroes (such as the railway worker Li Yu-ho in **'The Red Lantern'**; the Communist Party representative Hung Chang-ching and peasant girl Wu Ching-hua in **'Red Detachment of Women'**; and PLA scout-platoon leader Yang Tzu-jung in **'Taking Tiger Mountain by Strategy'**) whose stirring deeds combine revolutionary realism with revolutionary romanticism. They are portrayed 'on a higher plane, more intense, more concentrated, more typical, nearer the ideal and therefore more universal than actual everyday life'.

Although idealised, the stories are all based on actual events that took place during the struggle for liberation of the Chinese masses, under the leadership of Mao Tsetung and the Communist Party of China.

The themes of the stories are solidly based on Marxism-Leninism-Mao Tsetung Thought. To the uncommitted. all this may sound dry and empty propaganda, but in actual fact, the stories are full of lively and fast action, and the films (comprehensible to young and old) are immensely entertaining.

The film **'Mine Warfare'** is about People's War: it shows the ingenuous methods evolved by the people's militia in the villages in making explosives from stones, iron nails, hair, charcoal, saltpetre and sulphur, to defeat the Japanese invaders during the War of Resistance Against Japan (1937-45).

The films **'Taking Tiger Mountain by Strategy'** and **'Red Detachment of Women'** show clearly the 'fish-in-water' relationship of the soldiers of the People's Liberation Army among the Chinese masses, which accounted in great part for the success of the Communist Party in China. **'Red Detachment of Women'** shows the successful blending of traditional Chinese dancing and music with Western ballet and music.

There is a mass skiing dance in the 9th scene of **'Taking Tiger Mountain by Strategy,'** when the combined forces of the PLA and the People's Militia of Chiapi Valley attack the bandits' stronghold in Tiger Mountain in a raging blizzard, which is a wonderful example of modern choreography in contemporary Chinese theatre. The finale of this film, and also the finales of the two other feature films in the SACU-organised Festival (**'Red Detachment of Women'** and **'The Red Lantern'**), feature amazing displays of the famous acrobatics of Peking opera, remoulded to express new political content and adapted to include the use of modern weapons in hand-to-hand combat such as rifles and bayonets, pistols and hand grenades, without in the least becoming incongruous. I predict that the acro-

batics will be the m
of these new Pekin
Communist Chines
will doubtless inspi
The elements w
appear difficult to
Western audiences
forms of Peking op
opera-singing is an
non-Chinese; in tin
constant exposure,
like Chinese cooki
popular with non-
especially as the n
opera has been sh
Incidentally Weste
already been intro
traditional Chines
The level of act
of a high calibre. I
the revolutionary
emotionally high-
Red Lantern' mak
operas credible (u
classical operas) a
being banal, senti
(unlike Hollywoo
The new Pekin
and the films base
success in China.
because they port
deeds and aspirati
can serve as a suit
actually witnessin
live—but until tha
those of us in the
provide fairly acc
for ourselves the
artistic front in C
Cultural Revoluti
In the case of
on the building o
and **'The Nanking**
unfamiliar with n
valuable insights
People's Republi
films record the
Chinese people,
strength and wis
engineering won
living proofs (am
of Chairman Ma
that 'the masses
power'.

Note: both **Frien**
Society for Angl
ing (SACU) welc
SACU's address:
London W1P 5D
secretary: Betty
of **Friends Of Ch**
Lanes, London
C. McKinnon. T
films discussed i
the public.

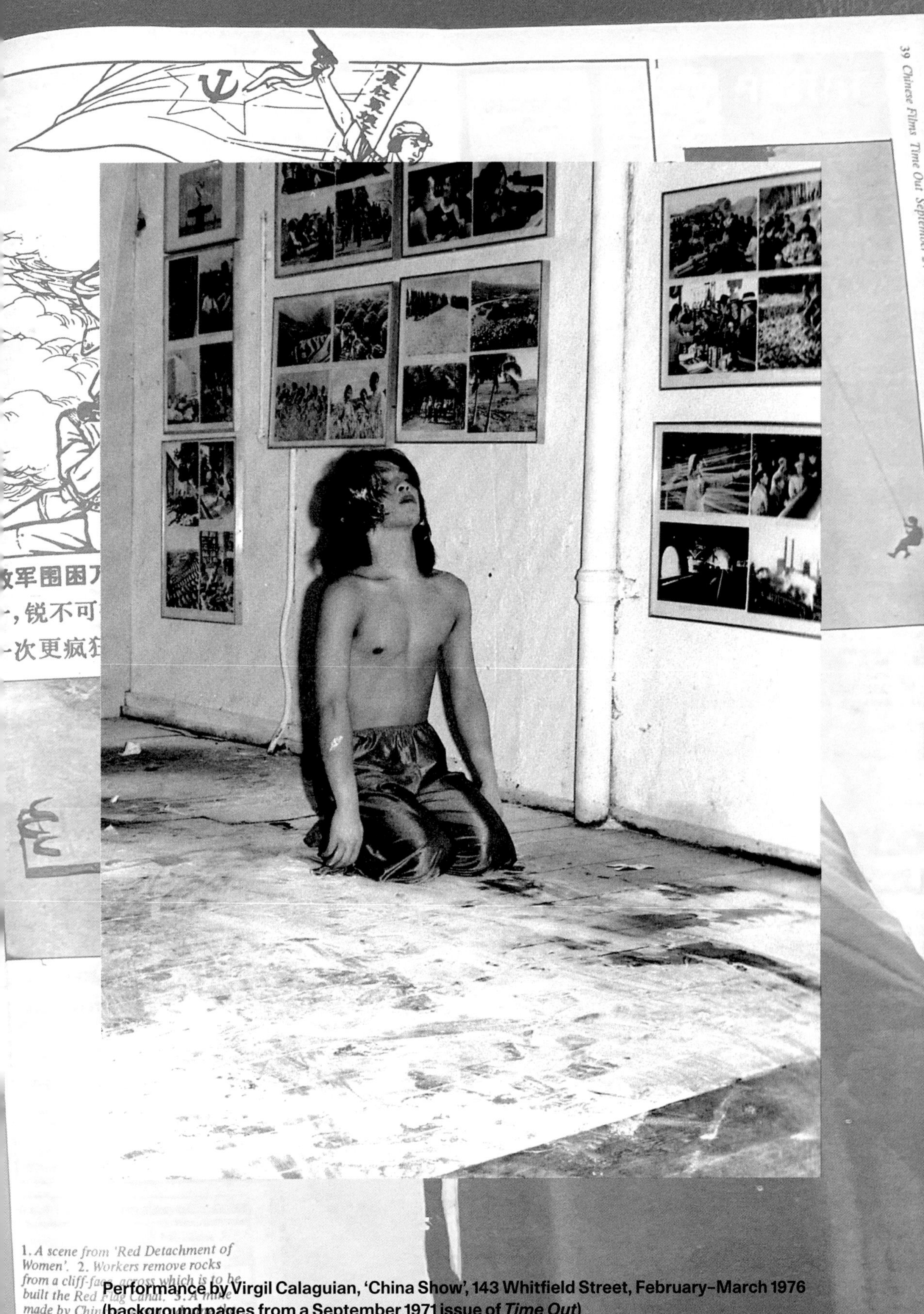

Performance by Virgil Calaguian, 'China Show', 143 Whitfield Street, February–March 1976 (background pages from a September 1971 issue of *Time Out*)

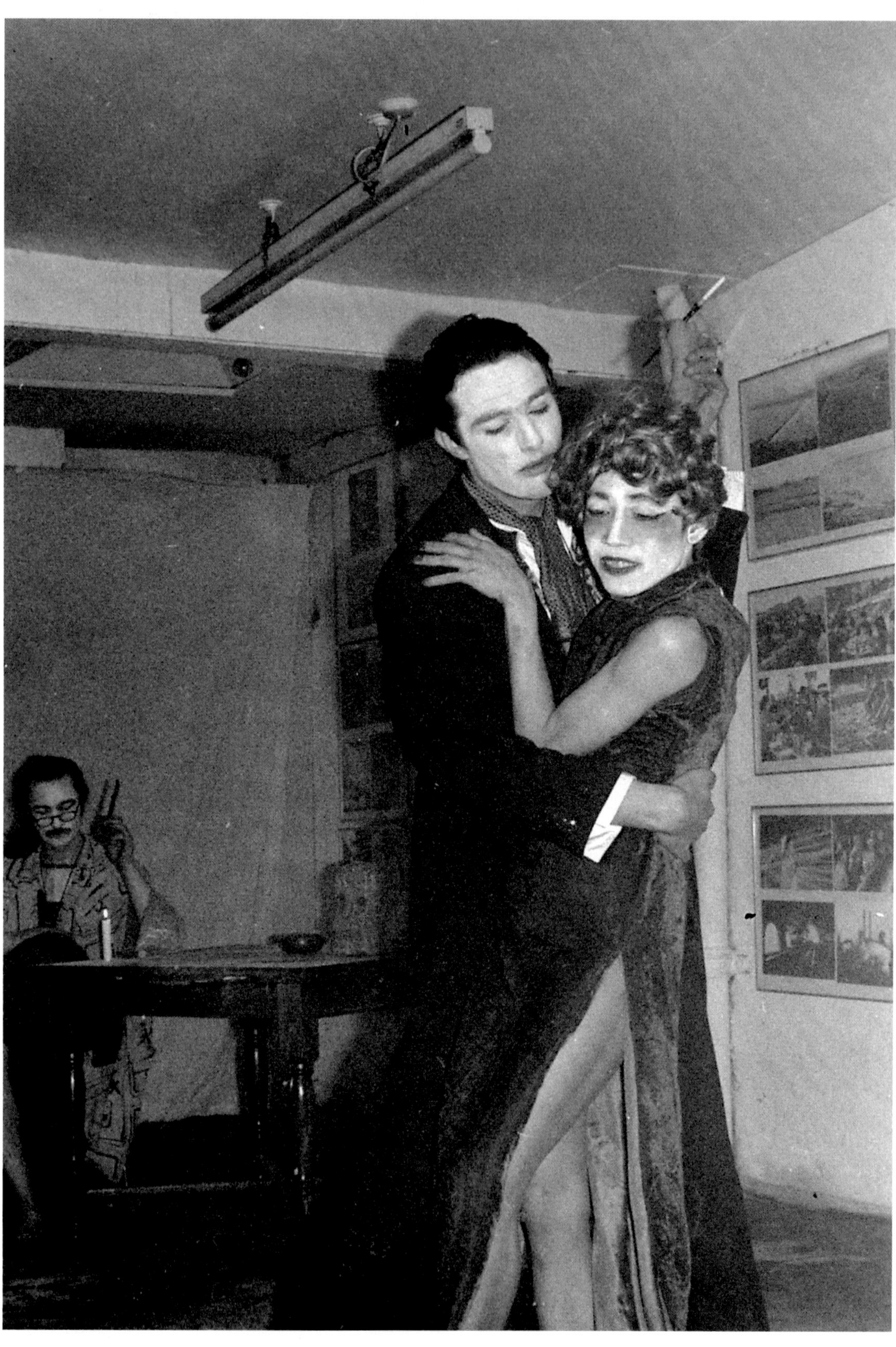

Alan Fleming and Jun Terra performing, with Nick Payne behind, at 'China Show', 143 Whitfield Street, February–March 1976

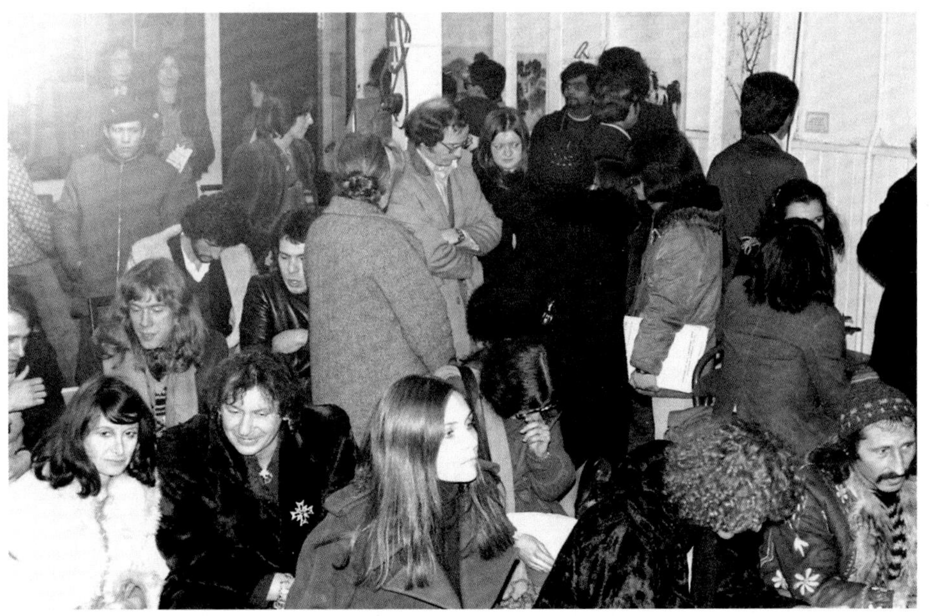

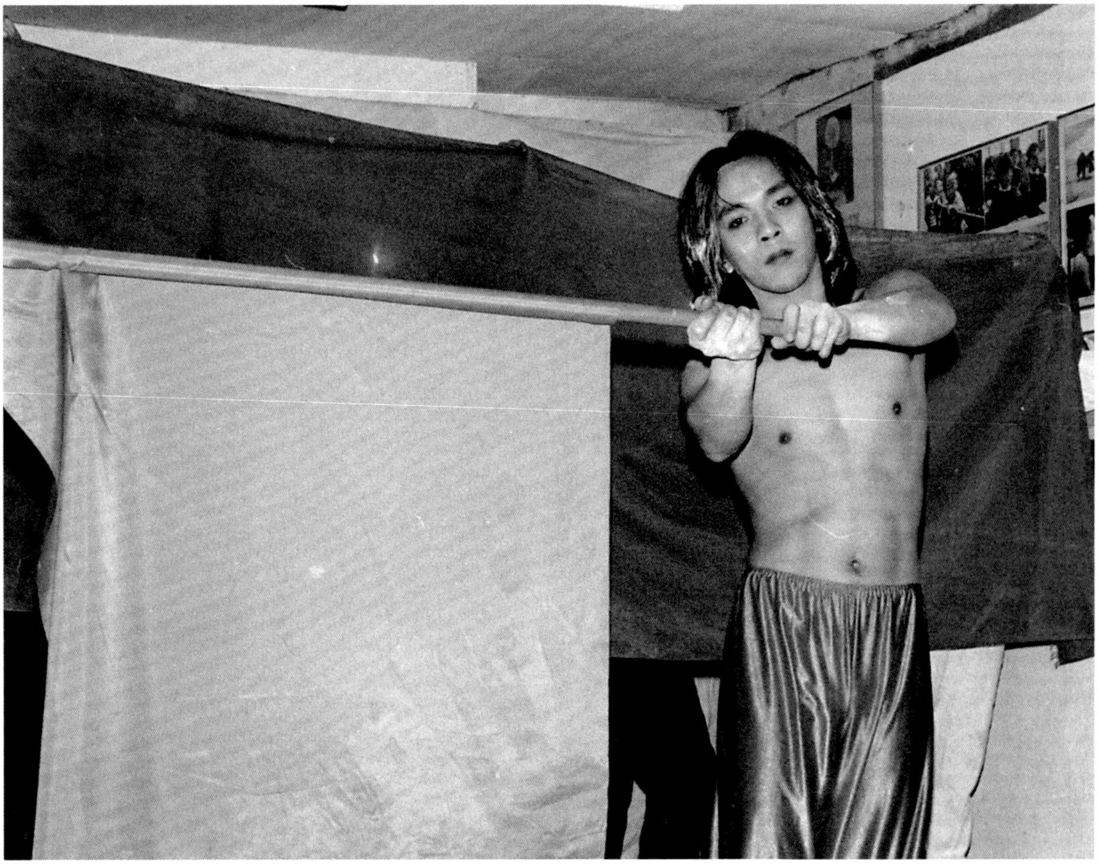

'China Show' opening, and performance by Virgil Calaguian, 143 Whitfield Street, February–March 1976

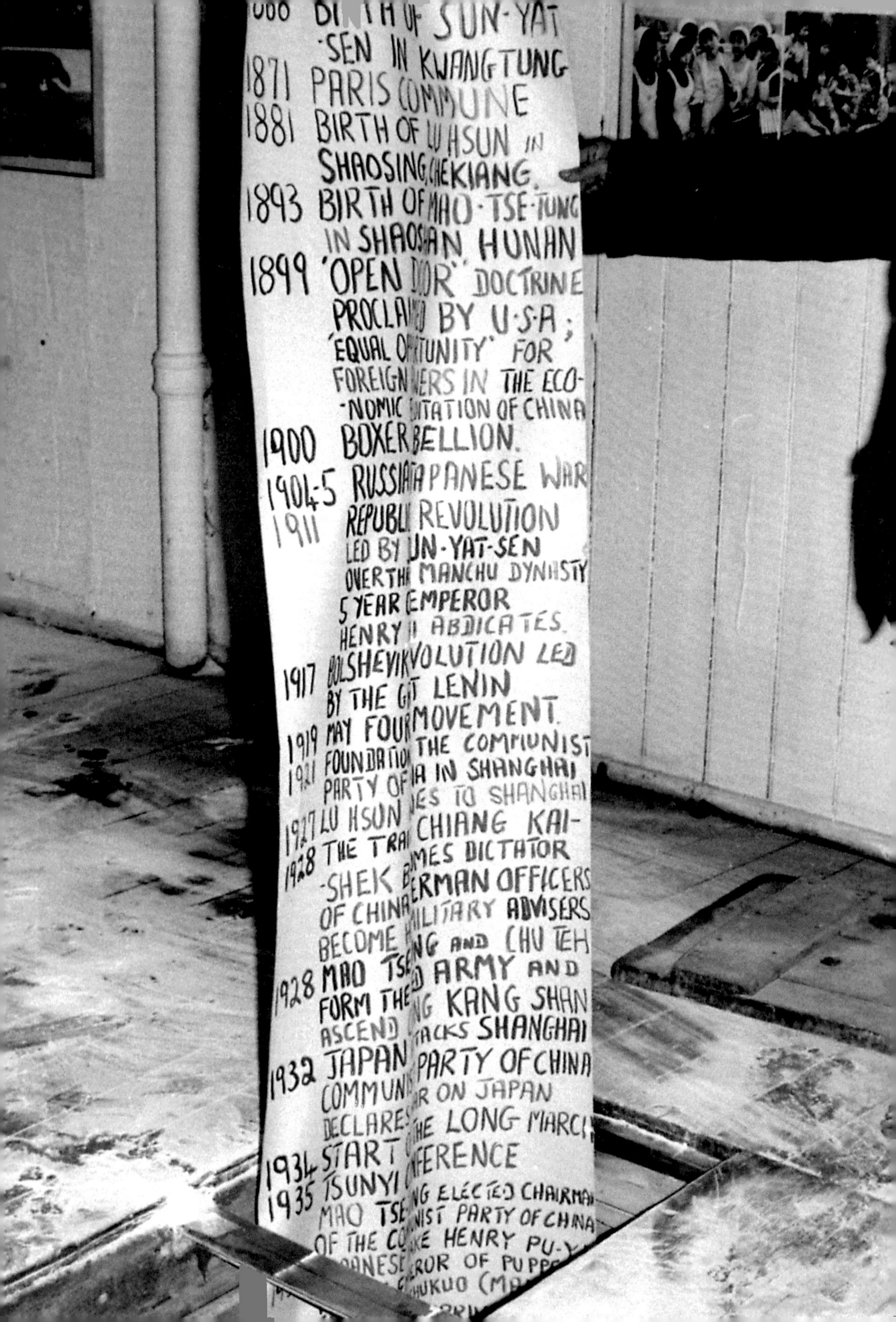

1866 BIRTH OF SUN-YAT
-SEN IN KWANGTUNG
1871 PARIS COMMUNE
1881 BIRTH OF LU HSUN IN
SHAOSING, CHEKIANG.
1893 BIRTH OF MAO-TSE-TUNG
IN SHAOSHAN HUNAN
1899 "OPEN DOOR" DOCTRINE
PROCLAIMED BY U.S.A;
"EQUAL OPPORTUNITY" FOR
FOREIGNERS IN THE ECO-
-NOMIC EXPLOITATION OF CHINA
1900 BOXER REBELLION.
1904-5 RUSSIAN JAPANESE WAR
1911 REPUBLI REVOLUTION
LED BY SUN-YAT-SEN
OVERTHR MANCHU DYNASTY
5 YEAR EMPEROR
HENRY II ABDICATES.
1917 BOLSHEVIK REVOLUTION LED
BY THE GT LENIN
1919 MAY FOUR MOVEMENT.
1921 FOUNDATION THE COMMUNIST
PARTY OF CHINA IN SHANGHAI
1927 LU HSUN MOVES TO SHANGHAI
1928 THE TRAI CHIANG KAI-
-SHEK BECOMES DICTATOR
OF CHINA GERMAN OFFICERS
BECOME MILITARY ADVISERS
1928 MAO TSE-TUNG AND CHU TEH
FORM THE RED ARMY AND
ASCEND CHING KANG SHAN
1932 JAPAN ATTACKS SHANGHAI
COMMUNIST PARTY OF CHINA
DECLARES WAR ON JAPAN
1934 START OF THE LONG-MARCH
1935 TSUNYI CONFERENCE
MAO TSE-TUNG ELECTED CHAIRMAN
OF THE COMMUNIST PARTY OF CHINA
JAPANESE MAKE HENRY PU-Y
EMPEROR OF PUPPE
MANCHUKUO (MA

Artists for Democracy (143, Whitfield Street, W1) are showing contemporary Chinese watercolour woodcuts. These are printed from many blocks so that at first sight they look like paintings. The style is traditional but into the delicately rendered landscapes the artists have inserted pylons striding through the wooded hills, or an artificial reservoir in the mountains. Sometimes these record something already achieved, like the huge bridge across the Yang-Tse at Nanking, sometimes schemes not yet carried out. The effect is curious and charming, but not much more than that.

They are far less exciting than the peasant paintings excellently reproduced in a book which has just become available in English, *Peasant Paintings from Huhsien County* (Foreign Languages Press, Peking £1.60). These include many of the pictures which created such enormous interest in Paris when they were shown in the Musée Galliera as an invited part of the *Bienale des Jeunes* this autumn.

It is hoped that many of these images of vitality and abundance will be shown in the very large contemporary Chinese exhibition which the Arts Council is now in the preliminary stages of planning for the Hayward Gallery, possibly for the latter half of 1977.

TIMOR MEETINGS

FRETILIN, the Front for National Liberation in East Timor, has hit back hard against the Indonesian troops since their full-scale invasion last December. Latest news is that for the first time, fighting against the troops has started in Dili, the capital. An army convoy was ambushed, a tank destroyed and a large amount of weaponry and electronic equipment captured.

The 30,000 troops, the warships, napalm and chemical defoliants and planes which the Indonesian regime is using against the people of East Timor have not been able to crush the liberation movement. FRETILIN has re-established radio broadcasting and is now in control of 80 per cent of the country.

In Australia, support for FRETILIN is very strong. The ACTU (Australian TUC) has passed a motion condemning the invasion, and the waterside workers are blacking trade with Indonesia. On 18 March international protests took place throughout Australia and Europe, including a picket on the Indonesian Embassy in London.

The British Campaign for an Independent East Timor is holding a public meeting in London on Friday 23 April at 7.30pm at Friends Meeting House, Euston Road, London N.1. There will be a slide-show on East Timor and a film on Indonesian prisoners, plus speakers from BCIET and an MP. On both Friday and Saturday, 23/24 April there will be an exhibition and film-show beginning at 10am showing in depth the situation in East Timor, the policies of FRETILIN and the nature of the Indonesian regime at Artists for Democracy, 143 Whitfield St, London W.1.

facing page: Scroll by David Medalla, 'China Show', 143 Whitfield Street, February–March 1976

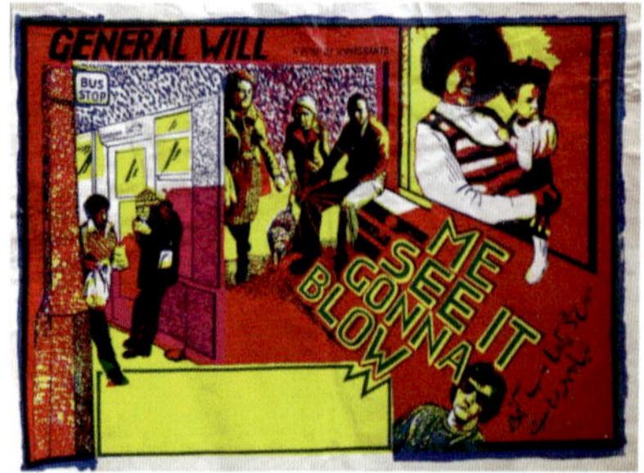

ME SEE IT GONNA BLOW

"Her Brittanic Majesty's Principle Secretary of State for Home Affairs Requests and Requires in the name of Her Majesty all those whom it may concern to allow the bearer to pass freely without let or hindrance and afford the bearer such assistance and protection as may be necessary except......"

A group of immigrants tell a story to show what is going down on the dark side.

امیگرینٹ لوگوں کا ایک گروپ آپ لوگوں
کو ایک کہانی بتانا چاہتا ہے جو کہ یہ دکھانے
کی کوشش کریگی کہ اندھیرے کے پیچھے ہمارے
ساتھ کیا ہو رہا ہے۔

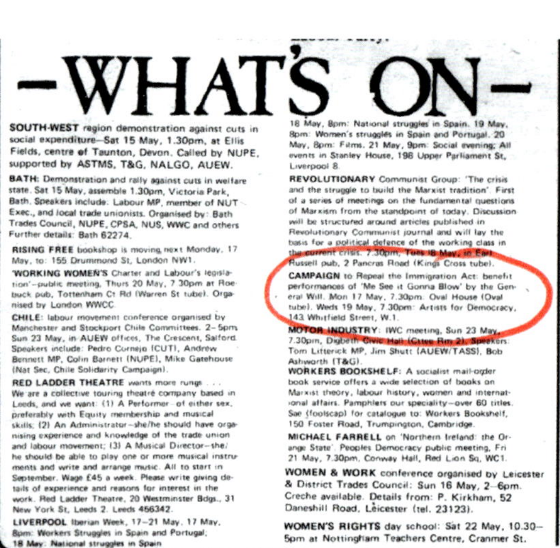

–WHAT'S ON–

SOUTH-WEST region demonstration against cuts in social expenditure—Sat 15 May, 1.30pm, at Ellis Fields, centre of Taunton, Devon. Called by NUPE, supported by ASTMS, T&G, NALGO, AUEW.

BATH: Demonstration and rally against cuts in welfare state. Sat 15 May, assemble 1.30pm, Victoria Park, Bath. Speakers include: Labour MP, member of NUT Exec., and local trade unionists. Organised by: Bath Trades Council, NUPE, CPSA, NUS, WWC and others Further details: Bath 62274.

RISING FREE bookshop is moving next Monday, 17 May, to: 155 Drummond St, London NW1.

'WORKING WOMEN'S Charter and Labour's legislation'—public meeting, Thurs 20 May, 7.30pm at Roebuck pub, Tottenham Ct Rd (Warren St tube). Organised by London WWCC.

CHILE: labour movement conference organised by Manchester and Stockport Chile Committees. 2–5pm Sun 23 May, in AUEW offices, The Crescent, Salford. Speakers include: Pedro Cornejo (CUT), Andrew Bennett MP, Colin Barnett (NUPE), Mike Gatehouse (Nat Sec, Chile Solidarity Campaign).

RED LADDER THEATRE wants more rungs . . . We are a collective touring theatre company based in Leeds, and we want: (1) A Performer—of either sex, preferably with Equity membership and musical skills; (2) An Administrator—she/he should have organising experience and knowledge of the trade union and labour movement; (3) A Musical Director—she/he should be able to play one or more musical instruments and write and arrange music. All to start in September. Wage £45 a week. Please write giving details of experience and reasons for interest in the work. Red Ladder Theatre, 20 Westminster Bdgs., 31 New York St, Leeds 2. Leeds 456342.

LIVERPOOL Iberian Week, 17–21 May. 17 May, 8pm: Workers Struggles in Spain and Portugal; 18 May: National struggles in Spain 18 May, 8pm: National struggles in Spain. 19 May, 8pm: Women's struggles in Spain and Portugal. 20 May, 8pm: Films. 21 May, 9pm: Social evening; All events in Stanley House, 198 Upper Parliament St, Liverpool 8.

REVOLUTIONARY Communist Group: 'The crisis and the struggle to build the Marxist tradition'. First of a series of meetings on the fundamental questions of Marxism from the standpoint of today. Discussion will be structured around articles published in Revolutionary Communist journal and will lay the basis for a political defence of the working class in the current crisis. 7.30pm, Tues 18 May, in Earl Russell pub, 2 Pancras Road (Kings Cross tube).

CAMPAIGN to Repeal the Immigration Act: benefit performances of 'Me See it Gonna Blow' by the General Will. Mon 17 May, 7.30pm: Oval House (Oval tube). Weds 19 May, 7.30pm: Artists for Democracy, 143 Whitfield Street, W.1.

MOTOR INDUSTRY: IWC meeting, Sun 23 May, 7.30pm, Digbeth Civic Hall (Cttee Rm 2). Speakers: Tom Litterick MP, Jim Shutt (AUEW/TASS), Bob Ashworth (T&G).

WORKERS BOOKSHELF: A socialist mail-order book service offers a wide selection of books on Marxist theory, labour history, women and international affairs. Pamphlets our speciality—over 60 titles. Sae (foolscap) for catalogue to: Workers Bookshelf, 150 Foster Road, Trumpington, Cambridge.

MICHAEL FARRELL on 'Northern Ireland: the Orange State'. Peoples Democracy public meeting, Fri 21 May, 7.30pm, Conway Hall, Red Lion Sq, WC1.

WOMEN & WORK conference organised by Leicester & District Trades Council: Sun 16 May, 2–6pm. Creche available. Details from: P. Kirkham, 52 Daneshill Road, Leicester (tel. 23123).

WOMEN'S RIGHTS day school: Sat 22 May, 10.30–5pm at Nottingham Teachers Centre, Cranmer St.

The General Will Theatre Company's 'Me See it Gonna Blow', 'a show written, produced, performed and sung by a group of immigrants', benefit performance at AFD for the Campaign to Repeal the Immigration Act, 143 Whitfield Street, 19 May 1976.

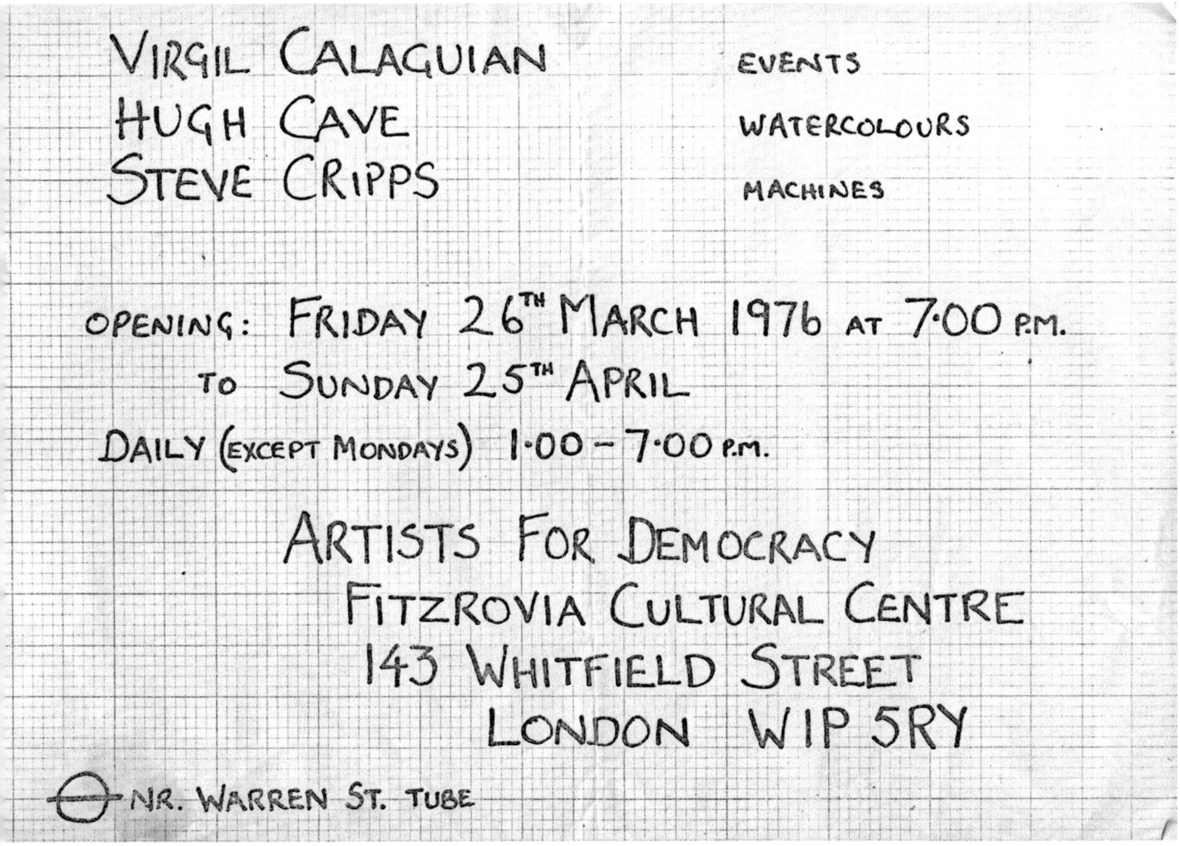

VIRGIL CALAGUIAN EVENTS
HUGH CAVE WATERCOLOURS
STEVE CRIPPS MACHINES

OPENING: FRIDAY 26TH MARCH 1976 AT 7·00 P.M.
TO SUNDAY 25TH APRIL
DAILY (EXCEPT MONDAYS) 1·00 – 7·00 P.M.

ARTISTS FOR DEMOCRACY
FITZROVIA CULTURAL CENTRE
143 WHITFIELD STREET
LONDON W1P 5RY

NR. WARREN ST. TUBE

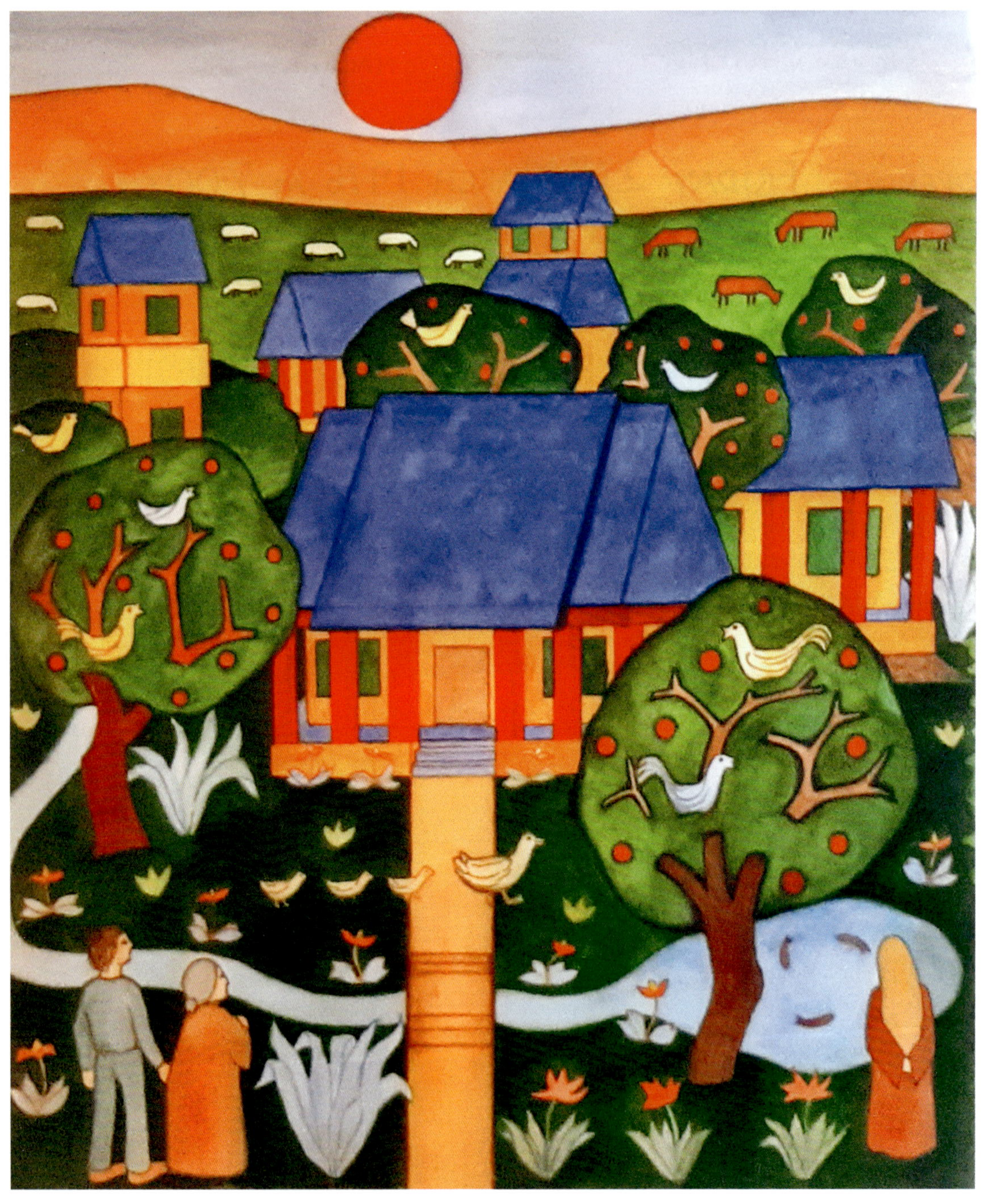

Hugh Cave, *The Piece of Chuang Brocade: A Taoist Tale*, shown at 143 Whitfield Street, March–April 1976

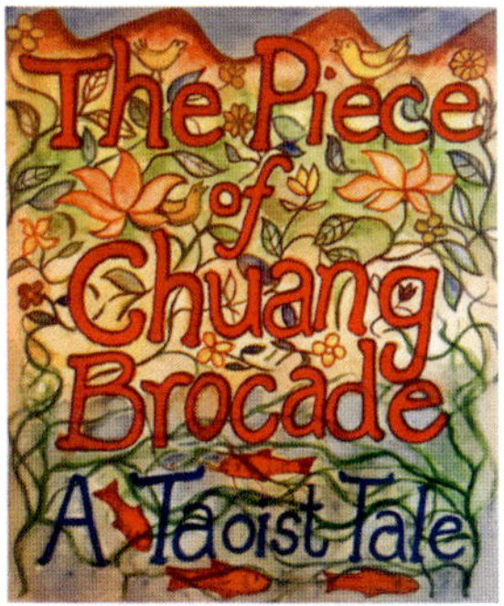

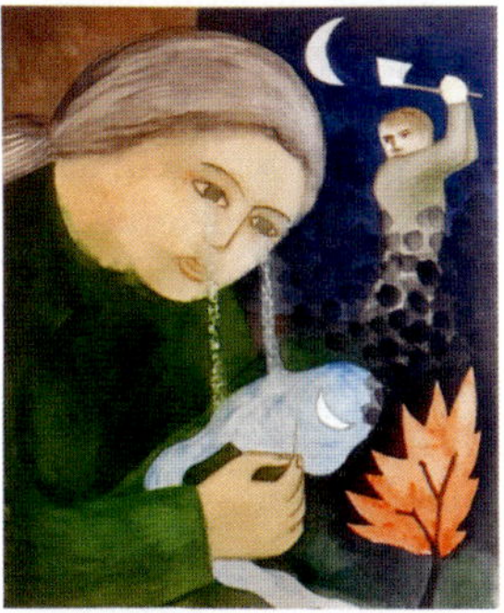

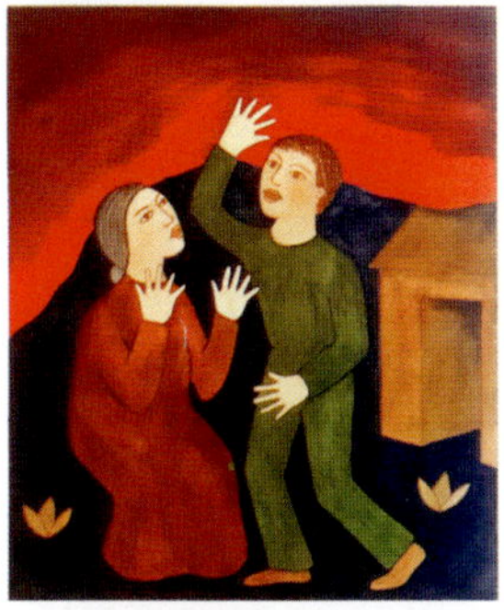

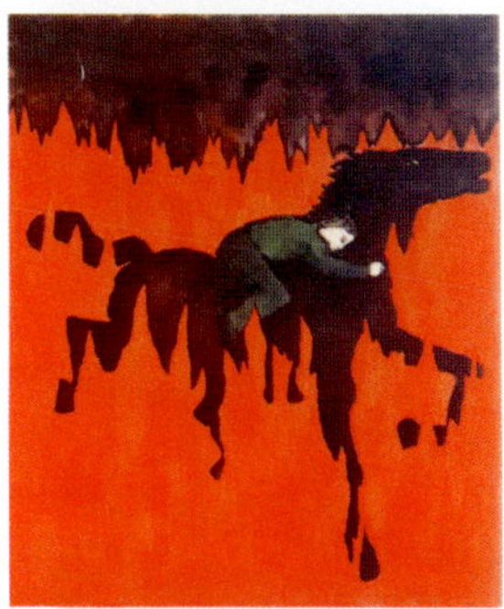

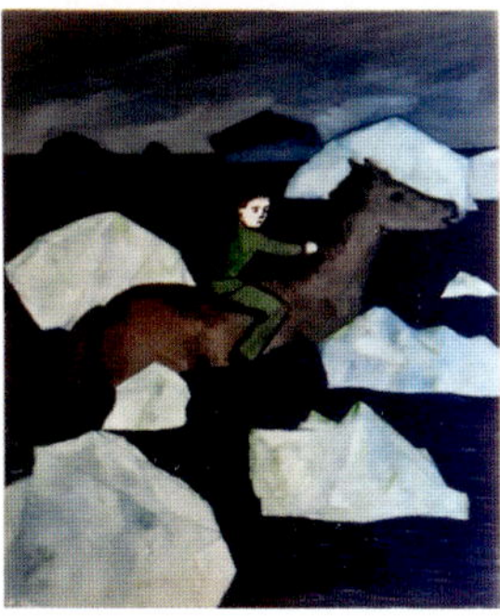

My relationship with AFD began with John Dugger and David Medalla, who I'd met in the early 1970s (when they were working as the Artists Liberation Front). As a young art student, fairly naive on the whole, John and David represented a rather exotic lifestyle, living in a rather chaotic cramped one-room apartment in Soho on the edge of Chinatown. The place was filled to bursting with books, art-works of all kinds, plus their own belongings. On top of this, it was a meeting place for many people, with lively discussions about art and politics going on every evening. Needless to say I was drawn to this rich environment although I could never quite get into the heavy Maoist propaganda which was very much in vogue at the time. China was held up to be a shining example of how humans could live harmoniously together. Which of course as we all now know was a bit of an ideal-istic dream. However, I was always a supporter of social justice, perhaps as a natural outcome of the spiritual studies that I was absorbed in. I was passionate about the Indian philosopher Jiddu Krisnamurti and his excruciatingly difficult dis-courses made me feel that the inner journey was really the only way to go. But, being a true Gemini, able to balance all kinds of different interests and somehow connect them up and having a great fondness for those two guys, I wanted to be part of their movement and to help in any small way. David had a very charismatic personality and was a very talented artist, pushing boundaries and creating new ideas; I think he was some kind of child prodigy and it fascinated me that he chose to live this humble life and maintain his inner freedom, rather than get sucked into the capitalist-run 'art world'.

[…]

The watercolours would have been a series of illustrations I did for a Taoist short story. The idea for this came from David, who was then my tutor at the Slade School of Fine Art. I remember chatting with him one day and saying how I was having a problem deciding what to include in my graduation exhibition. He put me on the right track by suggesting that I illustrate a piece of literature that I found inspiring. The piece I chose was a symbolic Taoist short story called 'The Chuang Brocade'. During the period mentioned I was in India but it's possible that David had obtained my water-colours from my then-partner in my absence, and, communication being what it was in those days, they may have gone ahead without asking me.

Hugh Cave

I've been doing a series of tapes of just distinctive sounds like Battersea Dogs Home or Heathrow Airport, cars at Brands Hatch as well and so on, cutting the sound away from the environment and then reusing the stroke sound having been recorded as, say, like with the jets, using that in a very sort of straight way, like using the jet as a drone and the different pitches and tones and timbre from the dogs, sort of cutting through and joining which is on that machine over there. Which is amplified at one point in the revolution so that the drone of the jets, which changes very slightly in places, that's going through a regular beat or the dogs, which are changing all the time – that's sort of just on one change of the dogs when it's going across the microphones amplified, so one tape which is at one certain point being quite a variable, and the other tapes remain almost the same except for the jets speed up and taxi up the runway, so there's a small change in the jet tape [which] is in fact very big in total because a lots been going on before and sort of I've changed that. While the dogs are sort of changing all the time. And the same with the tape of Brands Hatch and motor racing, it's looking at the sound of engines and how the pitch and sound change when you change gear or start up, or slow down to go round a corner, which side of the exhaust pipes you are facing it changes a lot of the balancing off the grandstand and [...] any commentary going on about the race, sort of fits in with the sound almost like the excitement of a voice, it's [...] backed up as well by the excitement of the changing of the pitch of the engine.

[...]

[The swing seat is] just perhaps more of a social context, or something, where the swing seat, as a piece of garden furniture which is association where somebody is just like sitting in the sun, in a quiet suburban back garden while on the top, like perched on the top like birds or sort of trees... So the shapes which are related to the garden or growing things, but on the shapes are stuff that perhaps you don't want to hear when you're sitting on a swing seat like the car horns and this wheel running round the glass and the clicking of the programme switch and the vibrating of that eccentric fan which shakes the whole thing.

[...]

I tend to collage a lot, with the tapes that I've made and I still do lots of taping, in cars or in the tube and for a very long time, play the whole tape through, I do decide which bits I want to take out and [...] collage, but I think of the sounds also in an environmental way as to partly what sort of feelings they have and also if you do tape off, tape from the street. There's this strong association thing with it, which I partly want to get away from because I think the association thing is very limited in fact, a sort of limited way of approaching something. In a way to take out sounds that you hear all the time and to reappraise them, put them into [...] a more ordered format of experimentation, whatever, and I also play percussion, gongs, with tapes going as well, pre-recorded tapes. And again it's where the thing [...] you playing in a sort of theatrical situation, dance or to someone reciting a poem, or [...] going into kind of street theatre and things which I haven't actually done yet. I'm in the middle of making a sound machine, a kind of 'Hurdy Gurdy' to take onto street corners and play – which is again perhaps getting back into the mechanical with the sound.

Stephen Cripps

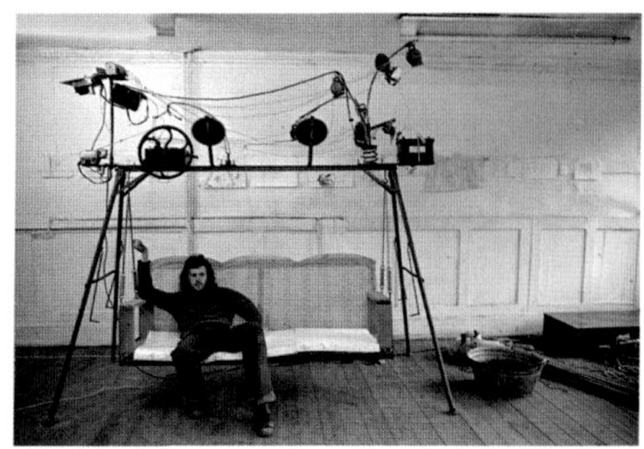

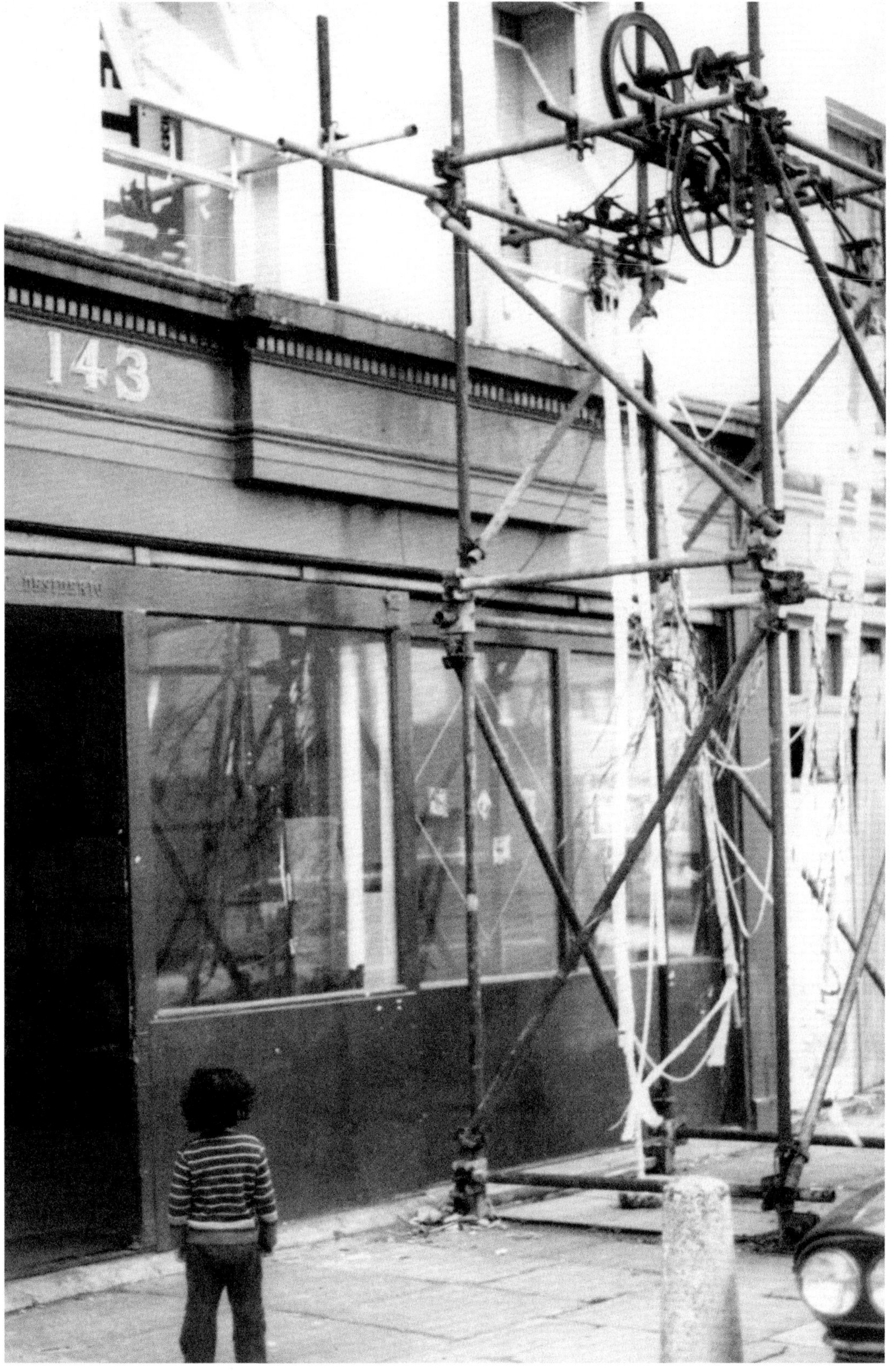

facing page: Stephen Cripps with his work *Garden Swing* at his exhibition at 143 Whitfield Street, March–May 1976; above: View from outside 143 Whitfield Street; following pages: Installation views with Cripps and Paul Burwell

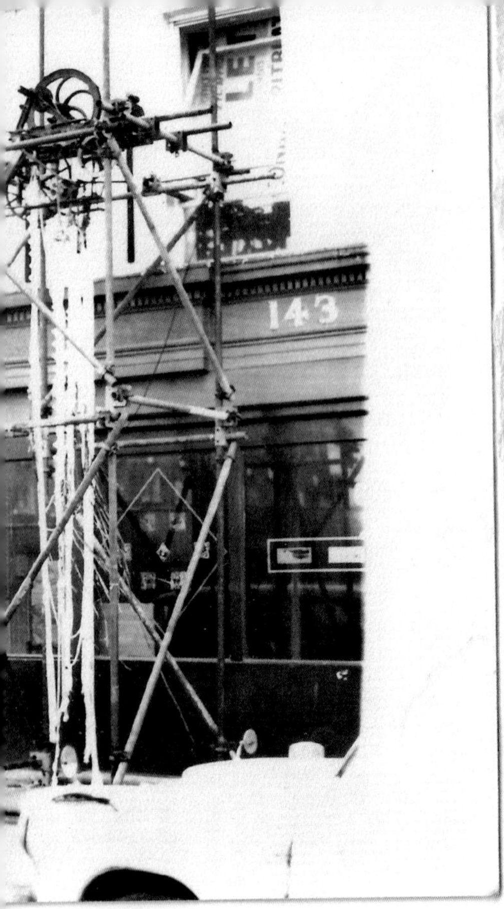

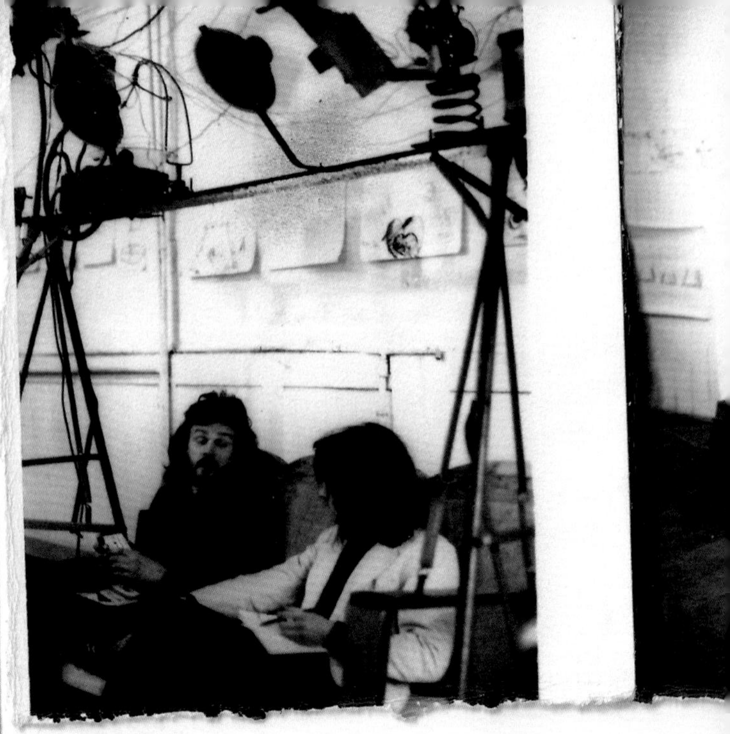

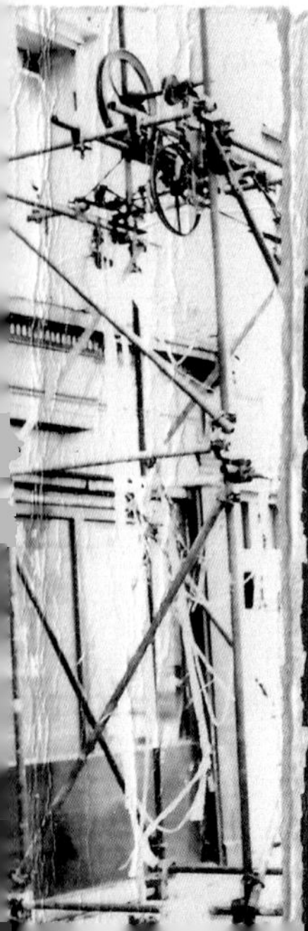

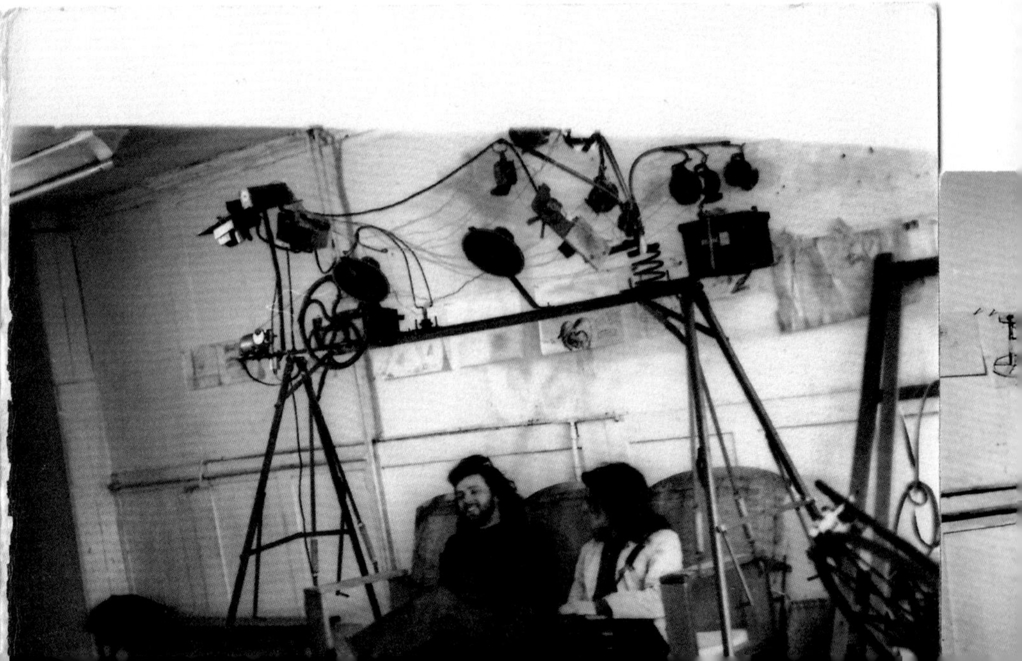

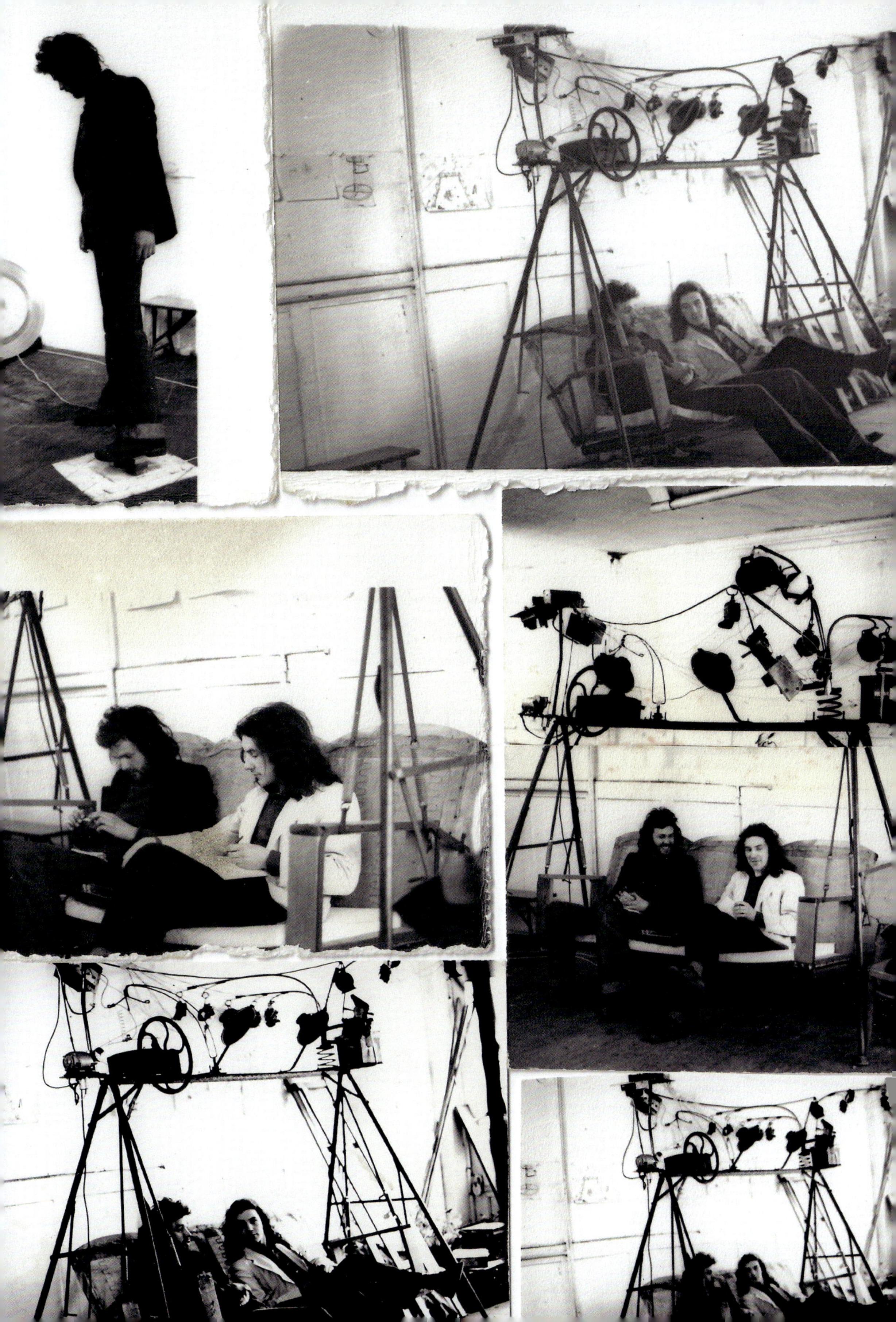

DAVID MEDALLA
Chairman

NICHOLAS PAYNE
Gallery Manager

24th May 1976

Dear

Groetings.

ARTISTS FOR DEMOCRACY cordially invite you and your friends to the following events:

Exhibition of new paintings and drawings by the young English artist GILES THOMAS daily (except Monday) 1 to 7 p.m. until 5th June 1976.

Lecture and slides show by the English art critic GUY BRETT on the constructivist reliefs, articulated sculptures, participatory environments and events by the Brazilian artist LYGIA CLARK, pioneer of participation art and artist-in-residence at the Sorbonne University, Paris, on Sunday, 30th May, 1976, at 7 p.m.

ECHOIC by TINA KEANE, video event and performance, on Sunday, 13th June, 1976, at 8 p.m.

Evening of super-8 and 16 mm. colour/sound films by various film-makers living in the Borough of Camden, including the premieres of films by two American film-makers GEORGE ISHERWOOD ("Maya", an animated cartoon) and WARD SELLARS ("Padma", a documentary), on Saturday, 5th June, 1976, at 7 p.m. This evening coincides with the annual FITZROVIA FESTIVAL.

The next exhibition at AFD FITZROVIA CULTURAL CENTRE will be a show of drawings, watercolours, paintings, photographs, art works and environments by the London-based Filipino artist VIRGIL CALAGUIAN. The show, entitled "On Meat & Metaphysics, of mice & men",, opens on Sunday, 13th June, 1976, at 7 p.m. Concurrently there will be a show of photos by STEVE OXLEY.

ARTISTS FOR DEMOCRACY have been invited to participate in the First LONDON CALLING ARTS FESTIVAL this summer. DANCE CONSORT, AIRLINES, MIRAGE and other dance and theatre companies will give performances at AFD FITZROVIA CULTURAL CENTRE in the near future.

ARTISTS FOR DEMOCRACY will also conduct free art lessons for members of the community. We welcome suggestions and new ideas. All our events are open to the public, admission free.

With best wishes,

Yours sincerely,

David Medalla

I consider AFD as a David Medalla artwork. The name started as a typical David joke. Historically the context was the Iranian Revolution and the building was a squat occupied by radical Iranian students. David wanted to use the space but the students said it wasn't political and they only wanted political interests in the building. David responded by saying we are 'artists for democracy' and they were accepted. That's the story I got from David at least. His amusement centred around the naivety of the students. Of course, he was a profoundly committed Marxist and in fact subversive political actors from the Philippines were occasionally present. I was member of AFD from around 1976 and later The Synoptic Realists. I was a mature student at Chelsea School of Art. David gave talks and seminars in the art history department, that's where I met him. In a strange loop I had seen his work at Signals gallery (there is a whole story) around 1963? And hadn't thought about him much until we met at Chelsea. Chelsea was a little dull at the time and David opened an alternative route in my last year. I was already living in squats in London and engaged in counter-culture life, so [I] was aware of the Exploding Galaxy, Arts Labs, etc. Being in David's company I received a real education politically. I have family feelings about AFD and occasionally bump into someone from that experience. ... It definitely set me on a path which I pursue to this day, central to this, in spite of all the art, events and fun, are values.

Giles Thomas

rose
summer, like a leaf,
the vulva
and the two sides also
conscious

is it

crossed to intersect the point
the eyes in
mirror
yama
afraid of it.

/ /

A... Perthen, musician
William Bryan, musician

Programme: *Poems – by H.Diamant-Drew...*
collection 'It's been Winter lo...
by Shelley and modern poets.

Dances – danced by Hadassa...
to music by Chopin, Vivaldi, ...
song 'The song of the birds' d...
Pablo Casals.

Music – Bach:Suite No.2, De...
especially composed by JUDI...

New Work, written by Allen S...
dance and percussion.

Echoic

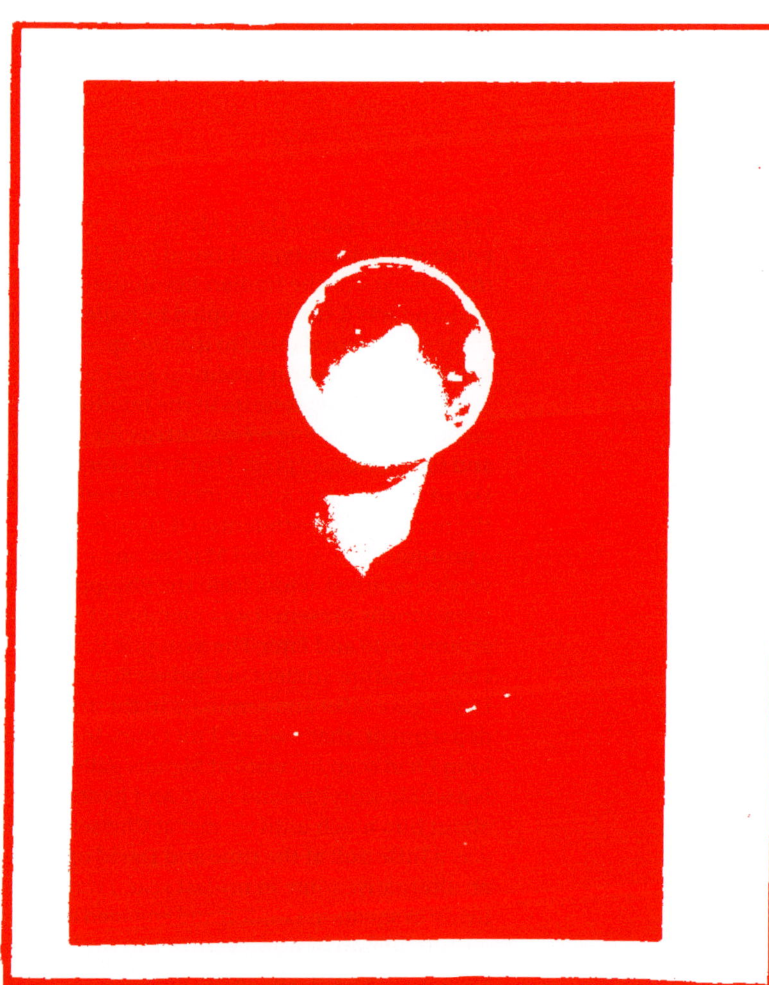

Sounds and
Pictures Reflect

...a mystical & religious significance.

The way women appeared in boureois European painting has been as titillating objects to be consumed by the male spectator and buyer (see John Berger's book "Ways of seeing" for further information about how this is, & has been, done).

Women are now beginning to break through all false distinctions & barriers made between arts & crafts, sacral & profane — all hierarchical values. It is only we who can do this as we have nothing to lose, no status to maintain, divisions to keep or power-relationships to protect.

We must recreate a society where every person can develop the creative potential within themselves — everyone is born, dreams & dies — & can express it in our immediate environment as well as in individual & collective ways. ———

Obviously the precondition for this is an economic revolution.

Monica Sjoo — Bristol aug 1976.

Tina Keane

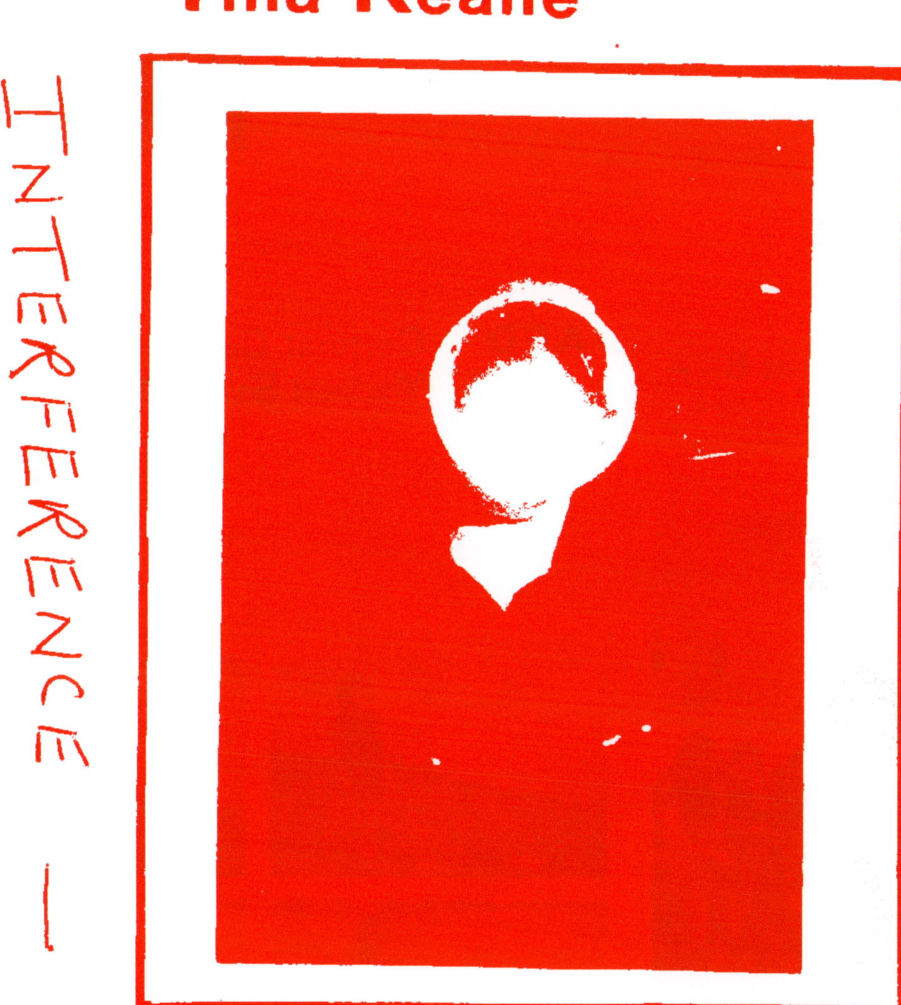

INTERFERENCE — Lightning Flash

Echoic

by Tina Keane

INTERFERENCE —
Lightning Flash

Sounds Echo

Pictures Reflect

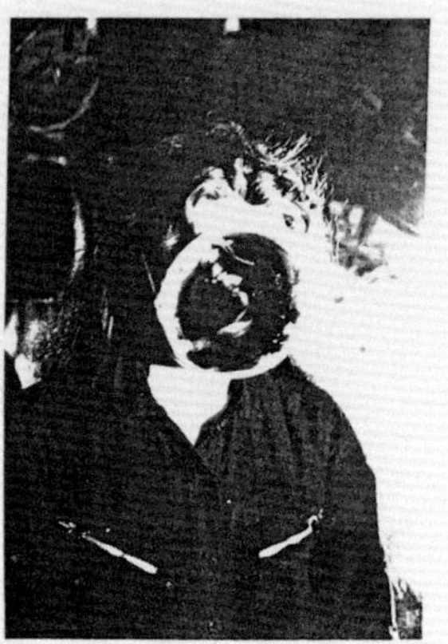

13th. June at 8p.m. AFD Cultural Centre
143 Whitfield St. W.1.

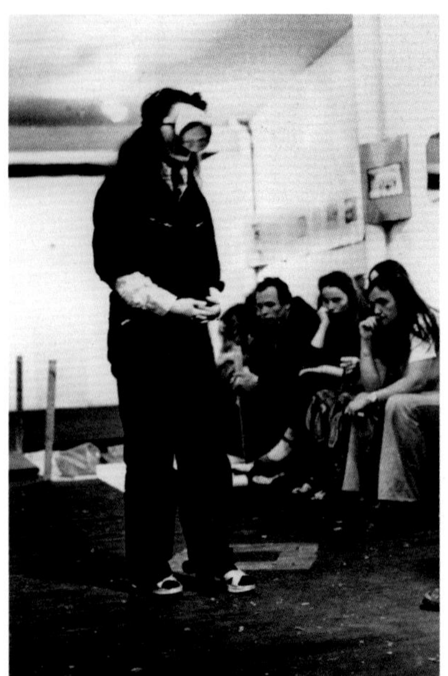

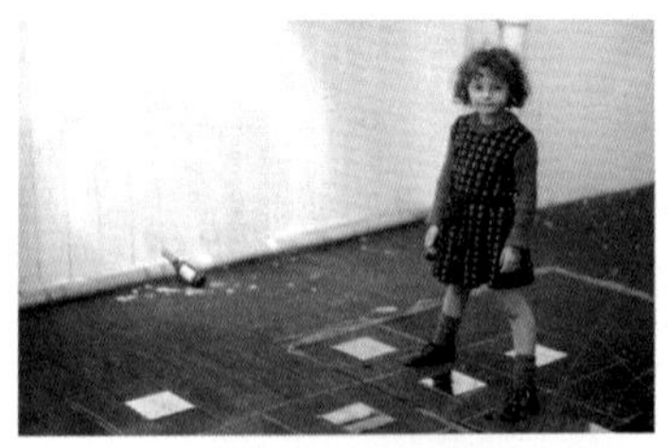

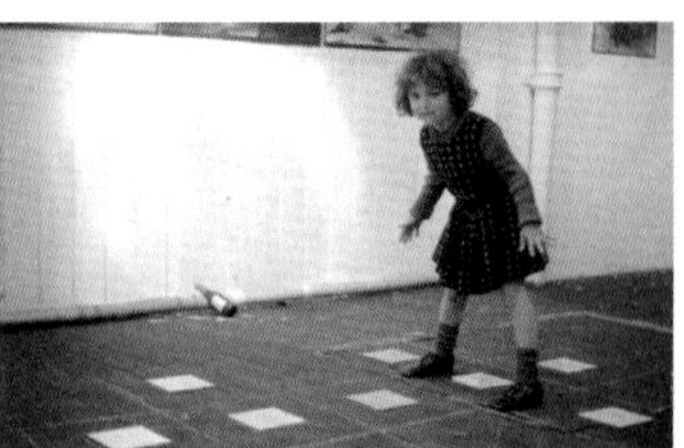

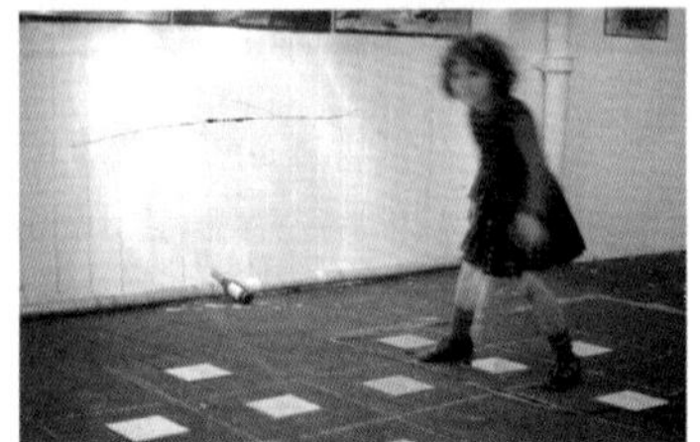

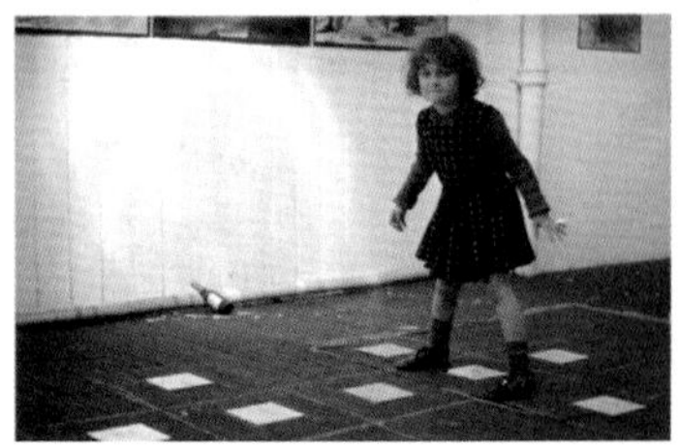

Tina Keane performances at 143 Whitfield Street: *Echoic*, 17 September 1976 and 13 June 1977; *Shadow Woman*, a 'performance with my daughter Emily', 1977

Emily I remember the one when I had to skip up and down the hopscotch in front of an audience while you put down mirrors, which were saying a poem and afterwards you sat down behind a screen and said a different poem out of a book and I was trying to get behind the screen too, but I couldn't because a projector was shining onto the screen, so I couldn't get past, and while I was trying to get behind the screen too, you was still reading the writing poem, so everybody thought that I was supposed to be waiting near the screen.

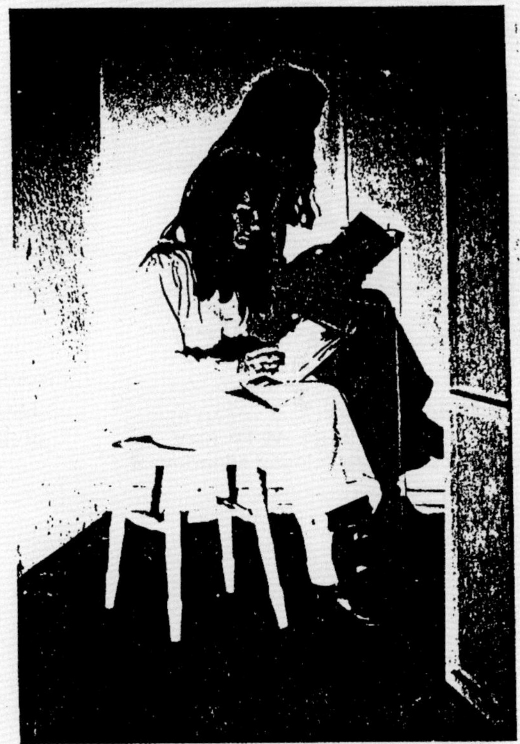

'Shadow Woman' A.F.D. London 1977.

Tina Oh yes; that was 'Shadow Women'. You were only six then, and you laughed at me trying to do the hopscotch, because I couldn't do it, and we decided you should do it instead. The poem was written on mirrors,

'The Shadow of my daughter,
becomes the shadow of my life.
As I will become the shadow of hers,
as my mother
grandmother and
great grandmother.'

which slowly covered the numbers on the hopscotch and restricted your movement. The 'Waiting' poem was by Faith Wilding, about women waiting from the time their born, till the time they die.

Emily What did it mean ?

Tina That we must break-away, not from being women, but the restrictions of being a women.

Tina Keane, *Conversation with my daughter*, 1979

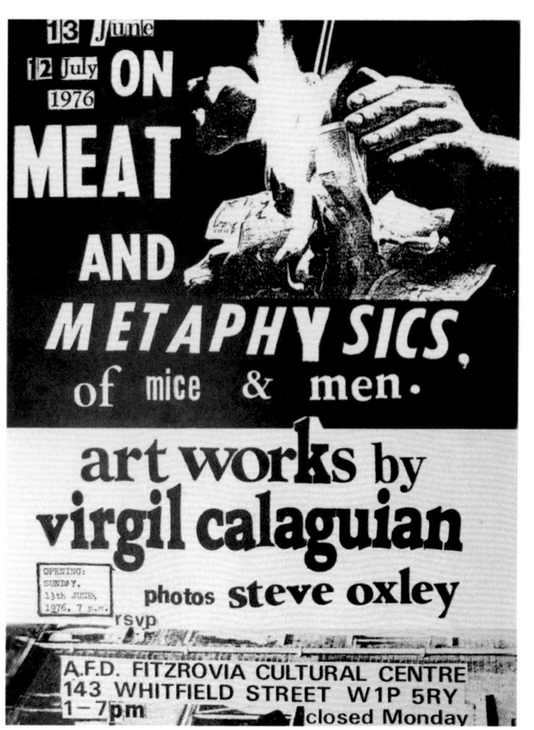

This is a participative installation that was part of my multimedia show at AFD Fitzrovia Cultural Centre, 'Of Meat and Metaphysics', which featured an array of thought-provoking visual works, installations, photographs, and performance events. The below image is from a set of monochome photographs taken by Peter (aka Steve) Oxley showing myself in different sites in London, serving as variations on the theme of the artist as the art object, and hence commodity, which is the underlying concept of performance art.

Steve Oxley investigated the alienation of people from objects in the West, particularly his native England. One of the ironies of England is that, although it is an advanced consumer society, people are actually forbidden to touch or handle commodities before purchase most of the time. Steve has done a series of photographs of actual examples of this a fruit stall, a furniture shop, a department store, etc. – and presented them under a glass case, on top of which is a fitting 'Do Not Touch' sign that comes from one of the shops.

Virgil Calaguian

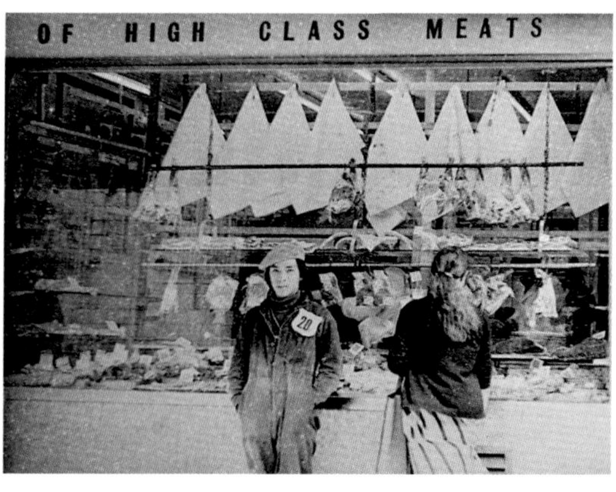

facing page: Virgil Calaguian, *The Elusive Essence of Becoming (For Mayakovsky, My Fellow Cloud in Trousers)*, 143 Whitfield Street, June–July 1976

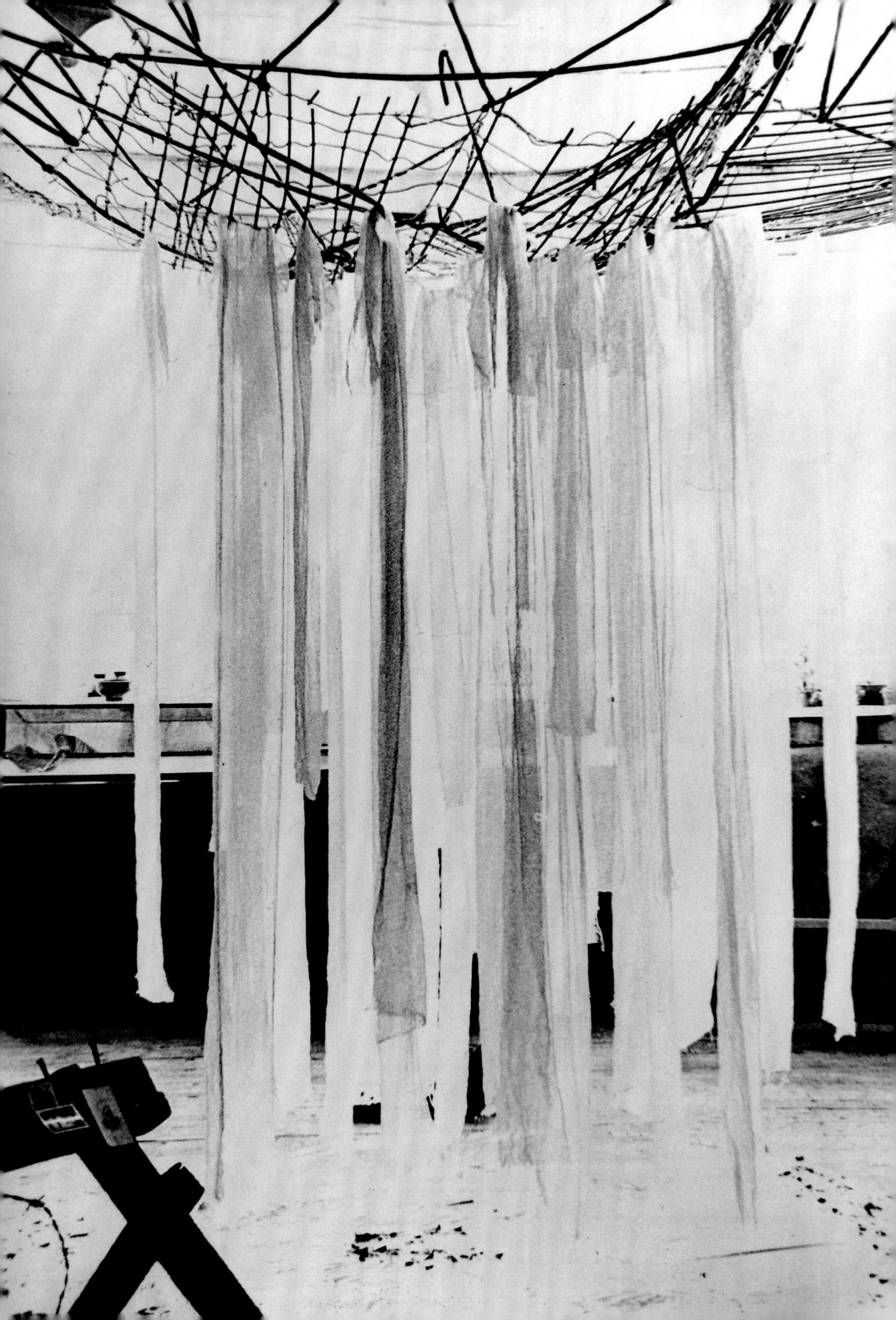

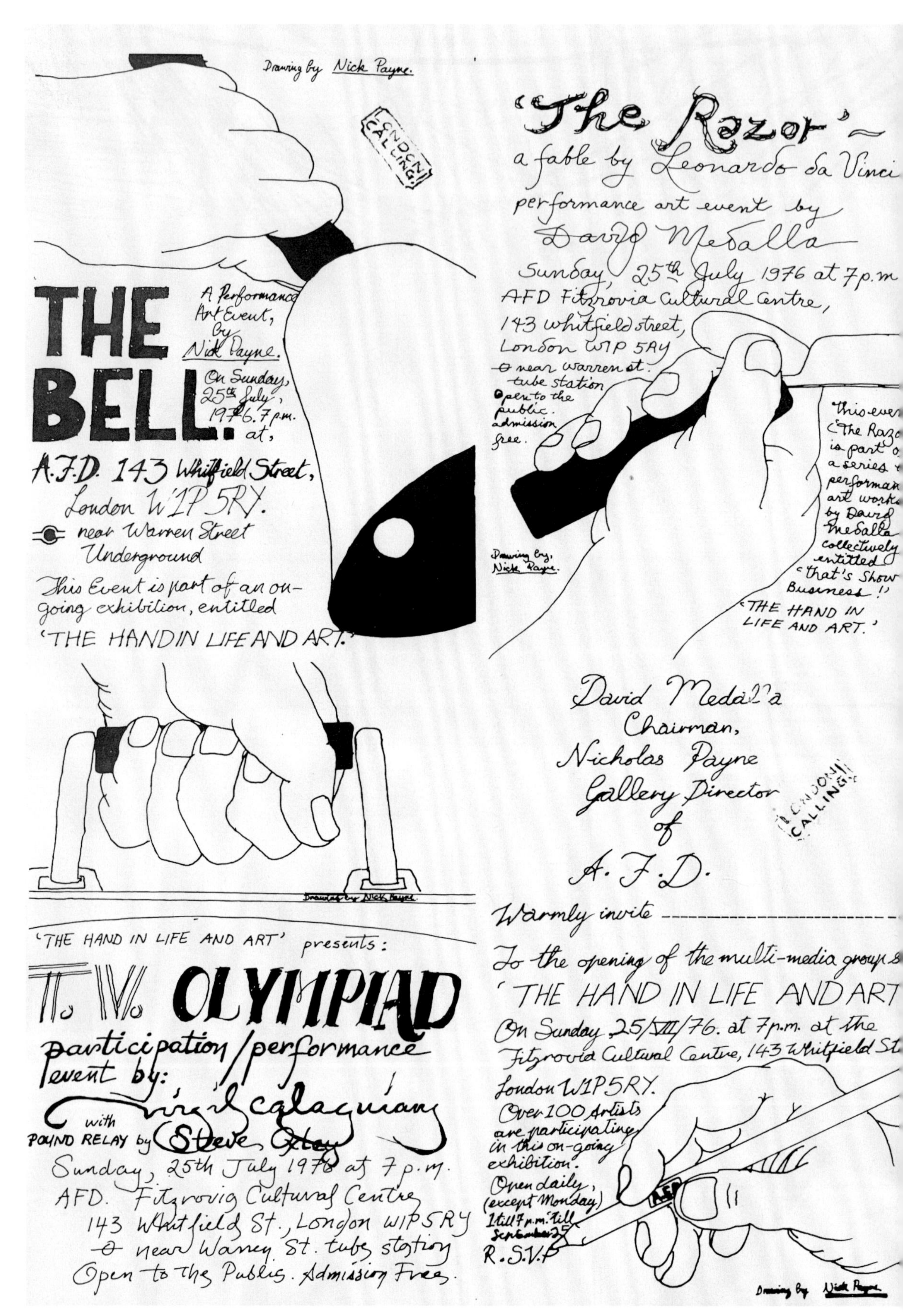

Drawing by Nick Payne.
LONDON CALLING
THE BELL.
A Performance Art Event, by Nick Payne.
On Sunday, 25th July, 1976. 7 p.m. at,
A.F.D. 143 Whitfield Street,
London W1P 5RY.
near Warren Street Underground
This Event is part of an on-going exhibition, entitled
'THE HAND IN LIFE AND ART.'
'The Razor' –
a fable by Leonardo da Vinci
performance art event by
David Medalla
Sunday, 25th July 1976 at 7 p.m
AFD Fitzrovia Cultural Centre,
143 Whitfield street,
London W1P 5AY
near Warren st. tube station
Open to the public. admission free.
This event 'The Razor' is part of a series of performance art works by David Medalla collectively entitled 'that's Show Business!'
'THE HAND IN LIFE AND ART.'
Drawing by, Nick Payne.
David Medalla
Chairman,
Nicholas Payne
Gallery Director
of
A.F.D.
LONDON CALLING
Warmly invite
To the opening of the multi-media group s
'THE HAND IN LIFE AND ART
On Sunday, 25/VII/76. at 7 p.m. at the
Fitzrovia Cultural Centre, 143 Whitfield St
London W1P 5RY.
Over 100 Artists are participating in this on-going exhibition.
Open daily, (except Monday) 1 till 7 p.m. till September
R.S.V.P.
AFD
Drawing by Nick Payne
'THE HAND IN LIFE AND ART' presents:
T.V. OLYMPIAD
participation/performance
event by:
Virgil Calaguian
with
POUND RELAY by Steve Ozley
Sunday, 25th July 1976 at 7 p.m.
AFD. Fitzrovia Cultural Centre
143 Whitfield St., London W1P 5RY
near Warren St. tube station
Open to the Public. Admission Free.

Occasionally, we had fundraising events like jumble sales on Sundays, or Rasheed [Araeen] would sell curry; the money would then be used to hire projectors to show avant-garde films. Philip Cohen was in charge of our adventurous film program. ... I was totally in favour of showing women artists at AFD, and it was also the time when feminism started in England. They were Tina Keane, Carlyle Reedy, Sonia Knox, Bertha Husband, and many other women artists. Although Susan Hiller and some others never showed there, they hung around, which meant that they met each other and got mutual support. It was so easy for an artist to be isolated and twice as easy for women artists to be isolated in London. The city was very scattered, and transport, postage stamps, and telephones were expensive. To be working on a project and to know that other people were working in the same direction was very good. If anything else, that was the best thing AFD offered; it gave a sense of community, which you don't find in many of the art centres today because they were only nine-to-five places.

At AFD, you could go in at three in the morning and say you'd like to show your video or do an installation. Because it was four floors and there was lots of space, we would say go ahead, show your films or do your theatrical piece. I would ask if anyone would come to see it, and the artist would say 'I have lots of friends'. So, at two in the morning, you would have these shows going on.

One time, I came back early in the morning from a trip to Paris and I couldn't understand why AFD was packed and totally silent. I thought it must have been a mime piece.

It turned out that the Royal Society for the Deaf was performing for its members. Then, political groups would use it too, like the group of Iranians who said they would do their Iranian festivities. The whole thing broke up and they ended up killing each other. I could not figure out which group was which: the Ayatollah's, the Shah's, or the Marxist Iranians. I ended up calling the police.

Then one time, we had a Basque group that gave beautiful performances and they used (the place) for meetings also. I forgot about them until many years later. I entered Spain and the border police put me in jail. I told them I was a guest of a Barcelona family, but they said that my name was on their computer. I told them that I wasn't Basque and just to search me, I wasn't smuggling guns or drugs. They initially would not tell me what I did, and it was only after they confirmed my passport with Madrid that they said some Basque terrorists had used my name!

[...]

We played host to the Sacred Flute, an amazing group from Bahia, Brazil, that practiced macumba and actually had sacrifices. They could not find a goat so they sacrificed a chicken, shaved this girl, then de-virginised her in the full moon and amid all their singing. We had the neighbours calling in the police. The Bahians were true macumba practitioners who had come from the Edinburgh Festival and got stuck in London after their promoters disappeared with their money. We put them up for a month at the Fitzrovia Cultural Centre.

[...]

If somebody came and he or she had the feeling that he or she could take over the entire space or a section of it, I would say go ahead, do it. I wouldn't say send me your proposal with twelve slides and all that rubbish. The thing was, if a person had enough guts to say that, he must have something to say. Because some people didn't have anything to say, they just made fools of themselves. This taught people who came and saw them to be a little bit more wary about using free space. But the most important thing was the element of surprise.

David Medalla

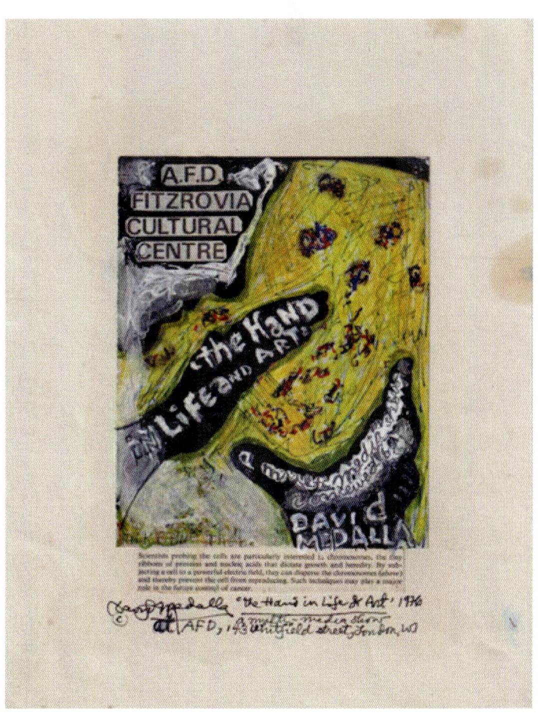

... I was just starting out in the glorious 70s. As director of Artists for Democracy I dived in at the deep end. The Fitzrovia Cultural Centre was obviously a political as well as an artistic centre, but the results of all its activity had a far greater impact on the art world than on the world in general, the political world. To me, the 70s weren't all that bleak, or if they were I was too busy to notice. I had my first one man show, contributed to and organised a great many group shows and attended a great many forums and symposia on and about the arts, one of which I recall being the somewhat drunken discussion concerning the eventual fate of *Studio International* itself, whether it should be sold, funded or forgotten. I gave an impassioned speech about the function of a prestigious and glossy art mag with an international distribution, and its invaluable use as a piece of advertising copy for London as art dealing centre of the world rather than its supposed function as an organ of free speech for creators of art, that is, until the late Barbara Raise grabbed the seat of my pants and yanked me back into my seat growling about how I should be less honest in front of all these people or I'd ruin my career. Ho hum. As I said, I enjoyed the 70s, pushing art critics onto pieces of cardboard on the floor and drawing around them, painting the road surface and pulling endless rabbits out of my revelations about the Fibonacci series. The 70s put me on the map...

Nick Payne

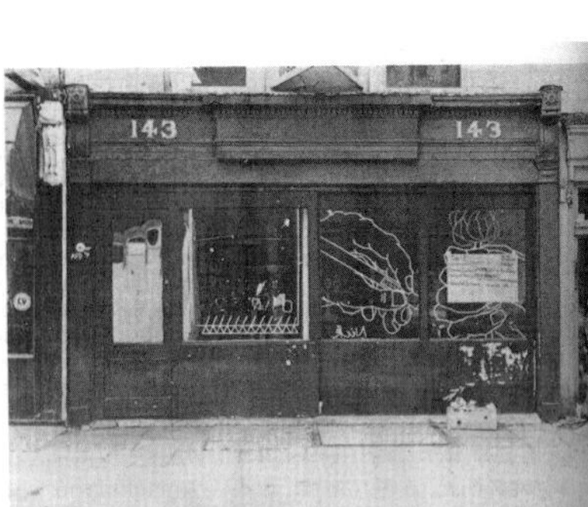

Nick Payne. *The End of an era – hand in life and art.* The window of the Fitzrovia Cultural Centre of Artists for Democracy at 143 Whitfield Street, London W1, 1976.

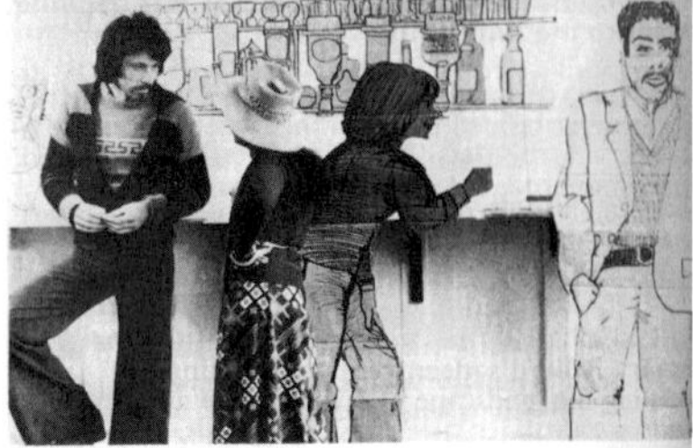

Nick Payne. *Cardboard bar*, felt pen and wood, 1976.

individuality is concerned. a symbol is a living picture. whenever something inward happens you have to use outward symbols. rationally we have denied and denied what is not materially real: but rituals and symbols come always back again. the connection with symbols is basic to human character and they are the corresponding points with another reality. my subjective, psychic reality is as real as a taperecorder is real in the objective reality.

the mind is a training in symbols, nothing else ..... and we conceive of it through metaphors, pictures or (as jung calls them) archetypes.
so as these objects belong to this state of mind, they also are to be understood as an essay to transcend the symbol, to go beyond, as you do when you want to reach the state of NO – MIND.
then the end of the mind is the end of the symbol.
then the end of the mind is the end of the symbol.
then the end of the mind is the end of the symbol.
clear light samadhi good night ...

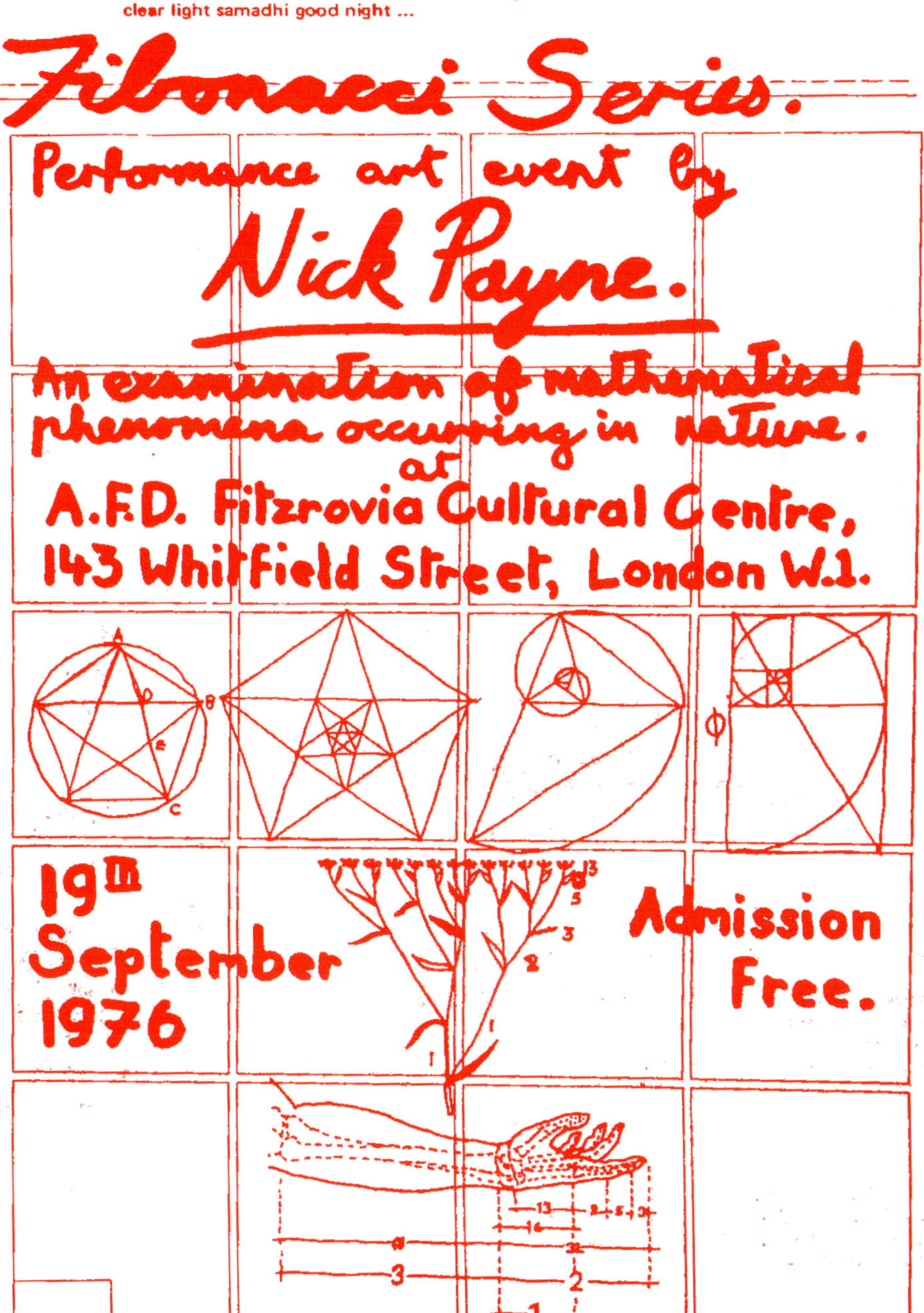

SEPTEMBER **PROGRAMME** 1976

DATE	VENUE	EVENT
Monday	Basement 7.30pm	Preparations — all artists welcome
Tuesday 14th	Basement 7.30pm	AMP presents PERFORMANCE ABOUT FLIGHT by Bruno Demattio & Kevin Costello. PUBLIC CONVENIENCE by John Blandy & Paul Sibbering. PERFORMANCE by Tom Puckey & Dirk Larsen.
Wednesday 15th	Basement 7.30pm	AMP presents Poetry and Dance with *The London Cello Ensemble*. Finnan MacCollum & Talcott Belbin in *Quarehawk.*
Thursday 16th	Basement 7.30pm	THE TING: THEATRE OF MISTAKES— *Scenes at a Table.*
Friday 17th	Basement 7.30pm	PERFORMANCE by Reindeer Werk (UK). SPACEBOX by Uli Trepte (Germany). Synthesised music & dance by Linda Jaime Lavender of Jupithor's Child (USA). ECHOIC by Tina Keane. Jan Swidzinski and other Polish artists.
Saturday 18th	Basement 5pm	FILM. *Children of Ireland, Maya-Maya* (with Sarah Child) & *How Letters Came to China* by George Isherwood (8mm). *The Last Days of Richard Nixon* by Mick Kidd (8mm). VIDEO PRESENTATION by Bruno Demattio. A DIALOGUE by Peter Lloyd Jones & Michael Upton. "A thing that moves acquires as much space as it loses" (Leonardo da Vinci)
Sunday 19th	AFD 8pm	*Tatlin at the funeral of Malevitch* by David Medalla. *Fibonacci Series* by Nick Payne.
Monday 20th	Acme Gallery 8pm	TONE PLACE SEMINAR by Dom Sylvester Houedard, poet from Prinknash Abbey, Glos.
Tuesday 21st	Acme 8pm	TONE PLACE SEMINAR by Monica Sjoo, Swedish artist resident in Bristol.
Wednesday 22nd	Acme 7.30pm	TONE PLACE SEMINAR by Paul Buck, poet from Hebden Bridge, West Yorks. *holding thorn. does. culture. : a series/were/the root/*
	Basement 9pm	READINGS. Anthony Barnett, Paul Buck, Anthony Howell, John Sharkey, John Welch. m.c. David Coxhead. This event has been organised in conjuntion with the London Poetry Secretariat (Poets in Public plus the Greater London Arts Association)
Thursday 23rd	Acme 1pm	PERFORMANCE by Virgil Calaguian. *The Stone and Paper Orchestra.*
	Acme 8pm	TONE PLACE SEMINAR by Carlyle Reedy, poet of the theatre.
	Basement 8.30pm	CONCERT. Paul Burwell — solo percussion. Evan Parker — solo saxophones. Hugh Davies — solo electronics.
Friday 24th	Acme 1pm	PERFORMANCE by Nick Payne. *Bourgeois Bondage.*
	Acme 8pm	TONE PLACE SEMINAR by David Medalla. *THUNDEROUS APPLAUSE — 3 years work.*
	Basement 8.30pm	CONCERT. Steve Beresford — solo piano. Duo: Frank Perry — percussion & David Toop — flutes.
Saturday 25th	Acme 8pm	TONE PLACE.SEMINAR by Marc Camille Chaimowicz. *Walking the circle.*
	Basement 8pm 9.30pm	RENOIR — Impressionistic Rock Group followed by............. CABARET BAL. *Was the Cafe Voltaire an Existentialist Wetdream?* ....late night dress party £1.
Sunday 26th	Basement 5pm	OPEN DISCUSSION. *Is the Artist Responsible for his/her Destiny.*
	Acme 8pm	PERFORMANCE by Rose Finn Kelcey.
Monday 27th	Acme 8pm	PERFORMANCE by Rose Finn Kelcey.

ADMISSION 50p per evening (includes admission to both Acme Gallery and the Basement)

LONDON CALLING 1976 Festival organised by Artists For Democracy, Art Meeting Place, London Musicians Collective, The Art Room, Tone Place. Coordinated by John Sharkey 57 Endell St. London WC2

Supported by the Arts Council of Great Britain and the Greater London Arts Association.

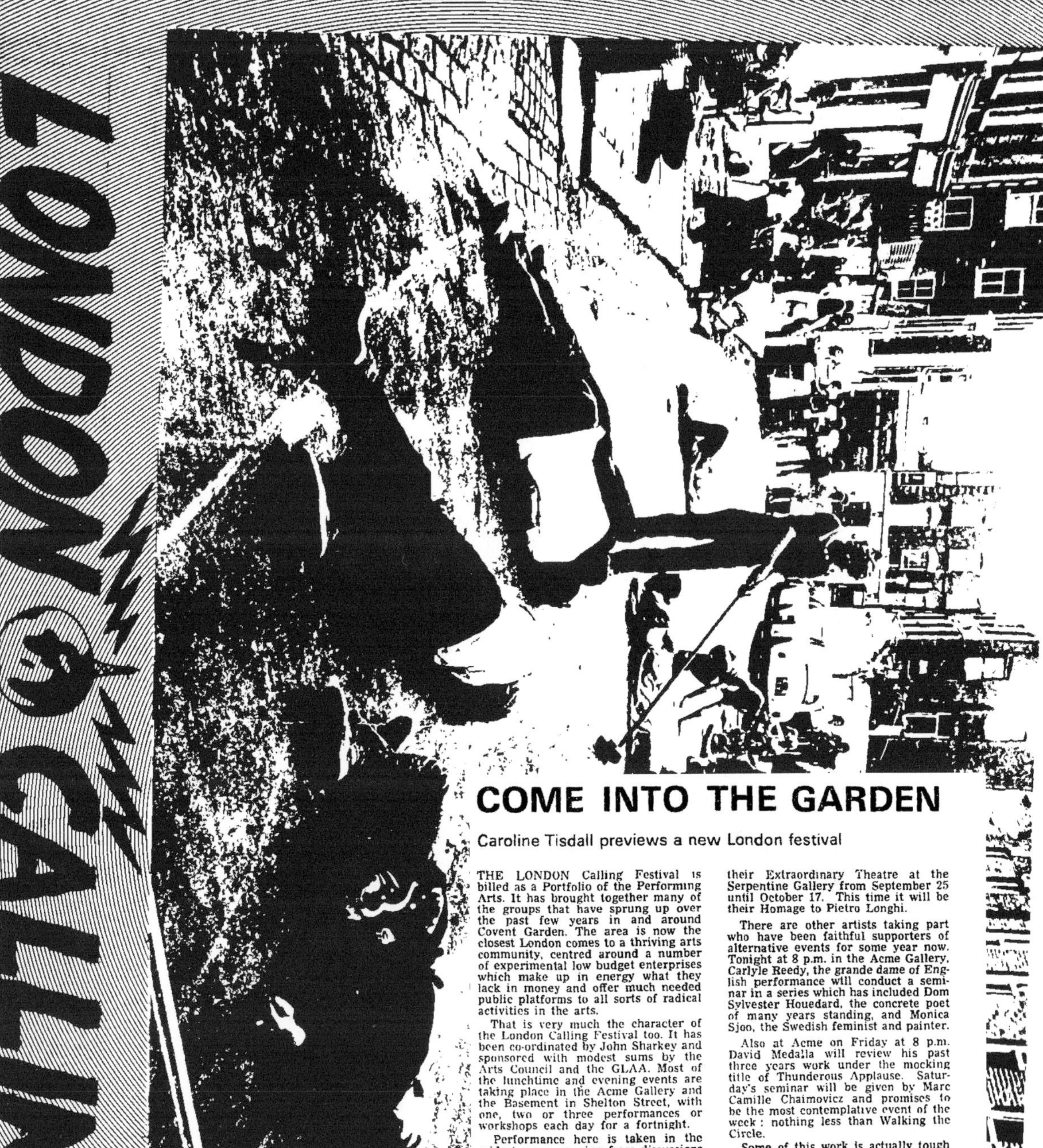

LONDON IS CALLING!

COME INTO THE GARDEN

Caroline Tisdall previews a new London festival

THE LONDON Calling Festival is billed as a Portfolio of the Performing Arts. It has brought together many of the groups that have sprung up over the past few years in and around Covent Garden. The area is now the closest London comes to a thriving arts community, centred around a number of experimental low budget enterprises which make up in energy what they lack in money and offer much needed public platforms to all sorts of radical activities in the arts.

That is very much the character of the London Calling Festival too. It has been co-ordinated by John Sharkey and sponsored with modest sums by the Arts Council and the GLAA. Most of the lunchtime and evening events are taking place in the Acme Gallery and the Basement in Shelton Street, with one, two or three performances or workshops each day for a fortnight.

Performance here is taken in the widest sense, ranging from discussions and seminars to concerts, poetry readings, films, theatre, dance and performance as an art form. For the wider public who may still not know about them, this is a good chance to sample the activities of Artists for Democracy, the Arts Meeting Place, the London Musicians Collective, the Art Room and Tone Place.

It is an occasion too to meet a new generation of artists bearing exotic names so different from the straight-up-and-down nitty-gritty of the welded metal boys: Reindeer Werk, Finnan MacCollum, Rose Finn Kelcey who will be performing at Acme on Sunday and Monday at 8 pm and The Ting: Theatre of Mistakes (the name is taken from the old Norse word meaning an unarmed meeting as used is the Icelandic Viking parliament — a term which Hitler too attempted to revise . . .).

The Ting will also be performing their Extraordinary Theatre at the Serpentine Gallery from September 25 until October 17. This time it will be their Homage to Pietro Longhi.

There are other artists taking part who have been faithful supporters of alternative events for some year now. Tonight at 8 p.m. in the Acme Gallery, Carlyle Reedy, the grande dame of English performance will conduct a seminar in a series which has included Dom Sylvester Houedard, the concrete poet of many years standing, and Monica Sjoo, the Swedish feminist and painter.

Also at Acme on Friday at 8 p.m. David Medalla will review his past three years work under the mocking title of Thunderous Applause. Saturday's seminar will be given by Marc Camille Chaimovicz and promises to be the most contemplative event of the week: nothing less than Walking the Circle.

Some of this work is actually tough and far more rigorous than the old let-it-all-hang-out sloppiness of the sixties. If the festival proves anything it is that there is a wealth of thinking going on among those whose art is not generally seen as "accepted art." It certainly represents a stage on from the theoretical dryness of English conceptual art, a fresh move to find a means of expression for theory without throwing intuition overboard.

John Sharkey is right to emphasise the need for discussion as this art develops and London Calling should help people to find common interests as much as the Tone Place seminars he organised last year. Hopefuly the result will be a greater move towards the kind of outward looking collective art that is impossible in the commercial gallery and the traditional set up.

London Calling at the Acme Gallery and the Basement, Shelton Street until September 27.

artist John Heartfield, organised by Trudi Glap and Paul Overy, art critic of *The Times*.

In early spring of 1976, ARTISTS FOR DEMOCRACY organised, in cooperation with the Cultural Section of the Embassy of the People's Republic of China and SACU (the Society for Anglo-Chinese Understanding) a magnificent exhibition of contemporary Chinese watercolour woodcuts by China's leading artists, papercuts, reproductions of peasants' wall paintings, and black & white and colour photographs. This show was opened by the then Mayor and Mayoress of Camden Councillor & Mrs Bernard Taylor, Councillor David Offenbach and by the late Lord Bradwell (the Rt.Hon. Tom Driberg). Concurrently with this show, there was a festival of films from China organised by Phillip Cohen, Hok Thye, Law Long and David Medalla, and films made in China by Western film-makers including the late Dr.Joshua Horn, Felix Greene, Mary Britain and Caroline John. It was also during this show that the premiere was held of *Wild Grass*, an experimental-dance-drama inspired by the writings of Lu Hsun, presented by the Amnesia International Dance Co., artistic director: Virgil Calaguian. Another memorable evening was a demonstration of illuminated clubs swinging by Andrew Kim ('Pop'), a 76-year old Chinese herbalist, and his pupils Peter Fisher and Sylvia Stevens.

The many cultural events held at AFD's Fitzrovia Cultural Centre include events by Tina Keane, a lecture on volcanoes in Iceland by the English painter Keith Grant, musical concerts by David Toop, Paul Burwell, and the talking drums

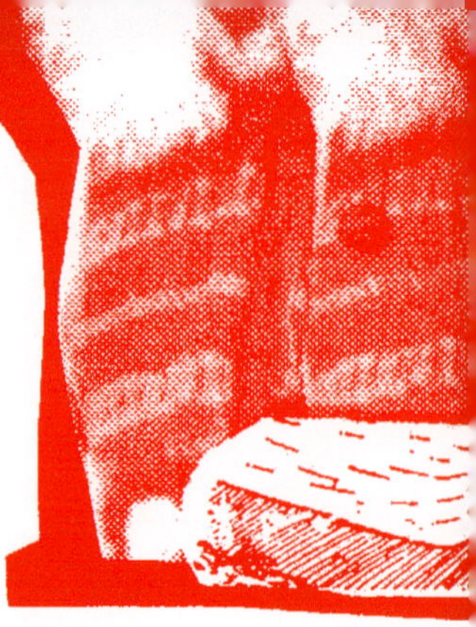

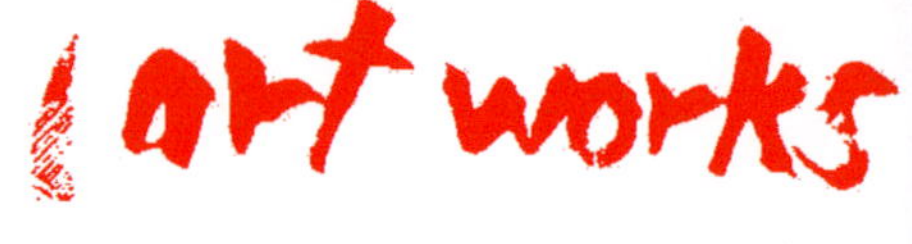

the R's wipers

homage to RABELAIS

a performance art event by VIRGIL CALAGUIAN & STEVE OXLEY, in conjunction with the "London Calling" arts festival...8:00 pm,25th July, 1976 at the AFD Fitzrovia Cultural Centre, 143 Whitfield Street, London, W1P 5RY (near Warren Street underground station)

ADMISSION FREE

LONDON CALLING - a portfolio of the performing arts. 1976 Festival organized by Artists for Democracy, Artists Meeting Place, London Musicians Collective, The Art Room, Tone Place. Co-ordinated by John Sharkey. Sponsored by the Arts Council of Great Britain & Greater London Arts Assn.

calaguian ~ oxley

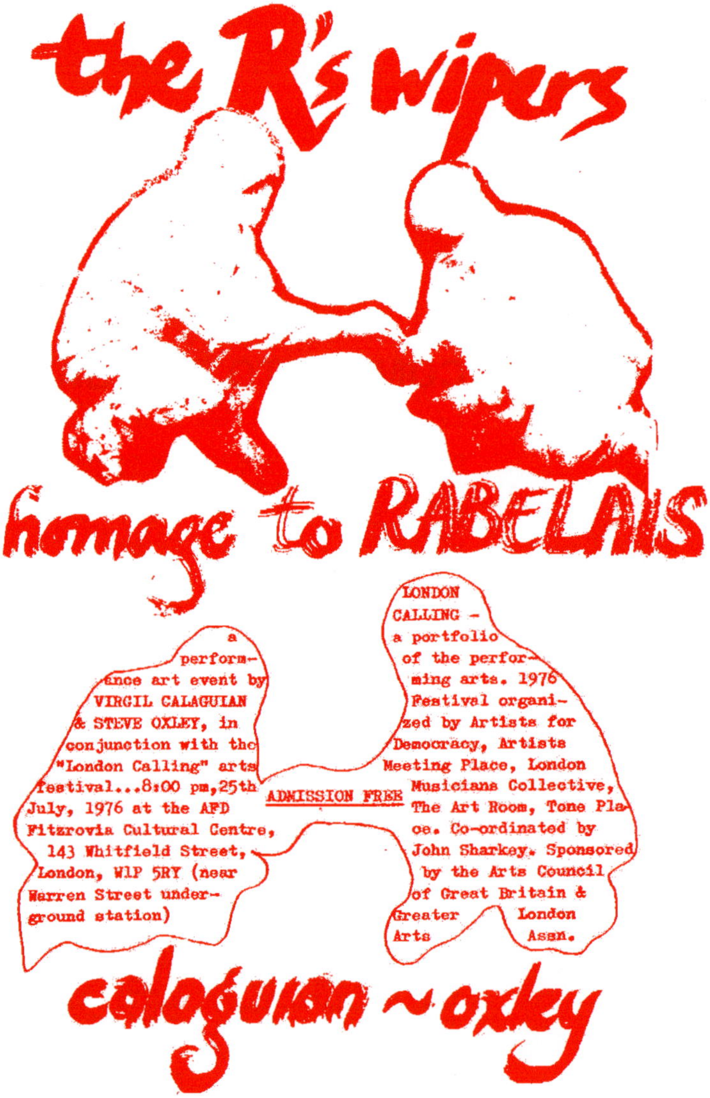

TONE
workshop
professior
musicians
their worl
The centr
held in co
within a c
peer-grou
genuinely
individual
The 12 *19*
means get
drawings
to explore
language,
ritual and
Sound an
those ever
and it is h
can be pu
This will h
of the arti
others a w
of the idea
this form

Typeset by Brea

For 'London Calling', Peter (aka Steve) Oxley and I presented *The R's Wipers: Homage to Rabelais*. Wearing gas masks and something uncannily prescient of the PPE worn by front-liners during the terrifying early days of the COVID pandemic (the Black Death of our time), Peter emerged from underneath the trapdoor on the floor of AFD Fitzrovia Cultural Center, while he, joined by myself, recited disjointed fragments from Rabelais' books. Peter represented Gargantua; while I impersonated Pantagruel. On the walls of the gallery were projected images of alienation and loneliness in present-day Western society. From inside the open trapdoor, Peter and I pulled out all kinds of objects found in the piles of rubbish left out on the streets of London, the wanton waste of the twin evils of capitalism and consumerism.

[...]

My article 'Performance art – it lives and breathes' was featured in an art and literary publication in Manila, prior to the performance art event *Sharawadgy* staged by Peter and I on 23 and 24 June 1977 at Sining Kamalig, the leading independent art venue at the time. *Sharawadgy* introduced performance art to the Philippines with a seminal multimedia event featuring live musicians, a shadow play, multiple slideshows, and a fusion of Eastern and Western theatrical techniques. In the event, Peter sat motionless in the centre of a circle of fire while reciting and chanting passages from the lives and works of thinkers, writers, revolutionaries, mystics, and other historical figures, ranging from Shakespeare, Milton, Thomas Aquinas, Francis of Assisi, Tolstoy, Dante, Heloise and Abelard, Emperor Hadrian, Oscar Wilde, Jose Rizal, Gandhi, to Mao Tse-Tung, along with current events such as American raids dropping Agent Orange on helpless Vietnamese and Cambodian villagers, while onstage I performed a slow, silent shadow play projected onto a giant screen. The fires around Peter were created with burning plastic strips that dripped into trays of water, presaging some fifty years earlier today's huge global environmental problem posed by plastic waste.

Virgil Calaguian

London Calling
London Calling was a good idea. Sub-headed 'a portfolio of the Performing Arts', it was organised by a number of artist-run organisations and mushroomed spasmodically throughout last summer. September was the turn of the Covent Garden area, and the Artists Meeting Place and Tone Place organised the final programme. Lasting two weeks, it was the biggest and the busiest of the series. Neither Tone place nor AMP has a home suitable for large audiences, so they co-opted The Basement (the usual home of the local youth club) and the Acme Gallery. Each was responsible for one week of activity. Given the nature of a festival intended to focus on interaction and discussion as much as on the actual work, it is impractical and inappropriate to review in depth any specific presentation. Rather, here are brief notes on the live work featured, in running order.

Tom Puckey and Dirk Larsen are Reindeer Werk (see this column, Sept/Oct issue). They work in a self-defined area called 'behaviourism' and argue that '. . . a tramp is someone to emulate. His swaying stance alone is a sufficient action. It is enough that he is there, "being", rather than involving himself directly with an activity in order to resolve a situation . . .' Their piece consisted of Puckey and Larsen quietly, and at first almost unnoticably, concentrating on one simple action akin to a nervous tick, like repeatedly twitching one arm or emulating a disabled walk, and with much concentration building up a rhythm on that behaviour and its developments. By pushing the threshold of control and the boundaries of what is acceptable as 'sane,' they were able to build an intense piece that was paradoxically formal and disciplined. Perhaps they found an energy within their actions that took them beyond both contol and rationality, into an automatic mental/physical state that was self-regulating. It is disarming to see them wander in dressed in their street clothes and with no equipment or preparation whatever begin, just like that. Once the audience had overcome the obvious aspects of the 'crippled and the mad' elements of their grimaces, references and movements, they appeared intent on experiencing a piece that seemed to end only at the point of exhaustion. But assuming they travel beyond the rational to another state, the questions of whether they could take the audience with them remained unresolved.

Tina Keane presented a short piece called ***Echoic***, seen before at AFD (Artists for Democracy). She appeared anonymously dressed in a boiler-suit, her face concealed by a circular mirror. All we could assume from the flowing hair and a monologue, presumably from a concealed tape recorder, was that it was a woman. The soundtrack was a collage of sounds, whisperings and dislocated words and was rather unclear. She wandered tentatively (her eyes covered) within the audience, reaching close to those at the front so they could catch a reflection of themselves in the mirror. The concept of cross-identification with the audience through the device of the mirror at head level was not, however, open to development in a crowded basement where most of the audience were to her physically out of reach.

A Dialogue by Peter Lloyd-Jones and Michael Upton was a balanced piece. (Beginning late, and therefore witnessed by few people, it was fittingly quiet and discreet). Taking the form of a demonstration, Upton, working to a time clock, would arrange a red ribbon or two red sticks in various configurations on the red floor and afterwards retire. Lloyd-Jones would then configurate sheets of paper, upon which he arranged knives, brushes, a mirror and some clothes pegs, and also retire. Upton would return and work with the light from a cine projector, and so on. His gestures and comments tended to be 'modernist' and ethereal. Lloyd-Jones' were 'classical' and territorial. These two diverse approaches resulted, through equal involvement and understanding, in a harmonious joint work. The dialogue was mute and the silence positive. The specific decisions tended towards pretentiousness and obscurantism but the overall approach to the relationship was lyrical, and it was moving to see two men working well and so understandingly together.

Virgil Calaguian presented ***The Stone and Paper Orchestra.*** Beginning with a story of his youth in the Phillippines, he then gave a demonstration of the stone, paper and scissors hand-game with the assistance of a local lad. After a relaxed attempt at inducing audience involvement in noise-making with the use of various waste materials, he meandered on to a sketch which involved him walking on with a suitcase, talking of 'opening his mind to find shattered illusions,' of dreams and of his experiences on arriving in England. He then gave a varied slide presentation and, via a sketch about the ominous bourgeois force and the burial of remnants in a box then nailed down and rejected, he finished to the sound of cardboard drums and slides of Red China.

Carlyle Reedy discussed 'potential,' the poet's role of delineating the void, the peak of perfection occurring within mutuality enterprises, the command of the intuitive process and establishing anarchy as a criteria. She demonstrated sleep and, with a regal presence, her ease in summoning ghosts. With her experience as poet and artist and her natural dialogue, she held her audience spellbound and brought some magic into one of the few successful seminars.

David Medalla presented ***Thunderous Applause.*** Although he had originally planned a talk on three years' work, he staged instead a mixed-media piece based on a discussion between Tatlin and Malevich. Medalla is the architect of AFD, and the mastermind of their house style of The East is Red-influenced poetic narrative work. His piece included dancing, chanting in Russian and basic symbolic usage of simple materials, ***eg*** a torchlight to simulate moonlight. Later green light transformed to blue light which, with good fortune, occurred simultaneously with thunder and the blue flash of lightning outside to produce from the audience . . . thunderous applause. The piece ended, as often, with slides of Red China. AFD productions tend towards an informal style that oscillates from the embarrassingly amateur to stunning moments which usually benefit from an oriental sense of pace and timing. Medalla, on this occasion, was in good form and rightly enjoyed his role of celebrity for that one night.

Performance by Rose Finn-Kelcey was a tableau inside the Acme Gallery which was visible to the audience from outside on the street. The display consisted of some big tree branches, herself and two magpies in cages. Internal sound was relayed outside through a loudspeaker. Having let the birds out of the cages, she attempted to set up relationships between them, their food, glittering trinkets and herself, slowly, over two hours.

Tina Keane finished the programme with ***Epilogue***, a procession from The Basement to the Acme Gallery which she led, a mirror fixed to her back. Mirroring the movement of the audience from both venues, this impromptu piece was more effective than her first and ended poignantly with Keane reading a short text from ***Towards a New Expression*** by the Italian artist Suzanne Santoro, on the need for women to discover new ways of seeing and doing.

There were also performances from Paul Buck, Nick Payne, The Ting (see below) and myself as well as poetry readings, seminars, concerts, some film and a cabaret.

London Calling was co-ordinated by John Sharkey as a development of last year's seminars. But, partly because of its ambitiousness and size, it was in many ways less successful. The breadth of activities covered meant arbitrary programming and a gruelling marathonian demand on the audience. To make any attempt at continuity demanded large parts of each day for a fortnight and this inevitably produced a small core of 'the faithful', somewhat counter-productive to the intention of the festival. It is indicative that a general discussion planned for the last day was, through poor attendance, abandoned. Perhaps the audience was by then exhausted. Generally the intimacy, intensity, and high level of discussion of last year was missing. Maybe a few intensive days, or two evenings per week, is a more productive structure, and bigger is not necessarily better.

Marc Camille Chaimowicz, review of 'London Calling', *Studio International*, January/February 1977

What is performance art? I have been asked that question continuously since I arrived from London in February. It happened when I walked into the 'MANILA office (hence this article); it happened when I went to see Ray Albano, the gallery director of the Cultural Center; it happened when I was introduced to Eva Toledo, on whose invitation Steve Oxley, an English friend who's also visiting in Manila, and I shall be introducing performance art to the Philippines at Sining Kamalig in about a month's time; it has happened whenever I've met fellow artists; it is still happening whenever I see old friends or make new ones.

The performing arts are perhaps one of man's earliest achievements, next to language, of which they are a natural extension. Poetry and song are a purer or embellished form of everyday language, and dance is the same with regard to human movement. Early forms of these performing arts were not even written; they were simply handed down from one generation to another by word of mouth. Even the most primitive tribes, who might neither read nor write, invariably possess a tradition of poetry, song and dance. They are also usually rich in rituals, a form of performing arts and something they readily resort to in order to externalize the mysteries of life, nature and the universe.

However, performance art, as it is known and practised in the West today, differs from the traditional performing arts in that it seeks to strike a synthesis between the visual arts and the performing arts. Thus, it can touch on any art form, from poetry and music to painting and sculpture, and employ any medium, from theatre to films and video.

Guy Brett, the English art critic, in an article on some of my performances, compares the development of performance art to the evolution of self portraits by Western artists. He points out a parallel between the performance artist today and Courbet's painting (self-portrait) "The Artist in His Studio." Self-portraits by artists from the Renaissance until Courbet concentrate on the artists in their physical entity: they confront the spectator with the artist's physicality, emphasized perhaps by a hat, an object in the hand, the manner of dress, etc.

On the other hand, in Courbet's seminal work "The Artist in His Studio," he places himself in the center of the picture beside a nude woman (art herself?), while to one side are artists, writers, intellectuals and to the other, workers and peasants. It no longer stresses the artist's physical being; instead, it portrays him in his relationships with society as the observer and observed, passive and active, a meeting point between art and science, manual and intellectual labor, labor and leisure, etc.

Let me add to that. It is very interesting that Courbet chose the studio, especially when you consider its significance in the development of the Western artist. Before the Renaissance there was practically no distinction between craftsmen and artists in Europe. We have, for instance, very little record of individual artists who executed the magnificent sculptures and stained glass windows we encounter in Gothic cathedrals. It is only with the coming of the Renaissance that the artist began distinguishing himself from the craftsman, eventually breaking away from the collective guilds of the latter in order to set up his own studio. And whereas the craftsmen carried on their work mostly in the decorative arts, the artist now turned his attention to other matters, among which was the question of his individuality. It was in the studio that the Western artist began asserting his individuality as an artist, and it was in the studio that Courbet chose to portray the artist in his relationships.

Artists and craftsmen in the Middle Ages produced artworks on specific commissions - for a church, a palace, a bishop, a lord, etc. In the Renaissance, although the artist still depended heavily on the patronage of church and state, he started looking at more personal interests – philosophy, the sciences, the rediscovered Greek and Roman antiquities – and gradually drew away from being solely in the employ of Church and State. He was no longer content to produce artworks only on commission from a king, a bishop, a prince or a lord; instead he even began creating works for himself, among which was his self-portrait. It is at this stage in the history of the West that art turned from being produced only for a specific "market" (the patron or customer) into a commodity to be sold on the open market.

Getting back to performance art, we can distinguish two types of performance artists on the same basis of distinction that Guy Brett makes of self-portraiture in the West. To one group belong those who focus on themselves in their physical or psychological make-up and to another those who explore themselves in their physical, spiritual and social relationships.

I doubt that anybody can tell you exactly when it started, but performance art is the most discussed art phenomenon in the West today. It seems that every artist is now contemplating on putting on a performance or two, if not thinking of being a performance artist altogether. Somebody once compared it to the Sixties when artists tried to crash into the pop world or the early days of Hollywood when people fought for stardom.

I certainly sensed that sort of feeling in "London Calling," a recent festival of performance art in London. There was a sort of tension in the air as to who was invited to participate and who was not. However, it was a healthy, friendly feeling of competition that eventually became a joyful celebration towards the end of the festival in an evening called "Cabaret Voltaire." Everybody performed that night.

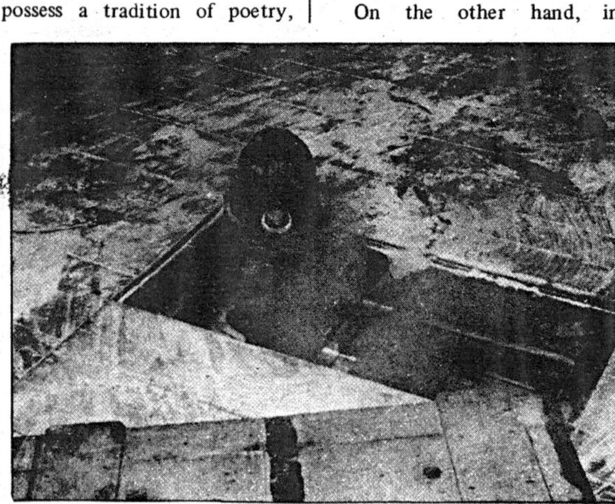

Coming out of a trap door.

Virgil Calaguian, 'Performance art – it breathes and grows' *Manila*, May 1977

"London Calling" was the first festival of performance art in England. Coordinated by John Sharkey, who was at one time the director of the Institute of Contemporary Arts in London, it ran for about a fortnight and included among its participants Dom Sylvester Houedard, a Benedictine monk rated by many to be the foremost concrete poet in Britain; the Filipino artist David Medalla, a pioneer of kinetic art and founder of the Exploding Galaxy, a group of artists in the '60's who may be considered forerunners of performance art; the American artist Carlyle Reedy, whom Caroline Tisdall, the art critic of the Guardian, called "the grand dame of performance art"; Nick Payne, the "angry" conceptualist; Tina Keane and Rose Finn Kelcey, the former working distinctively with mirrors and the latter singularly in an environment with magpies; the avant-garde musicians David Toop and Paul Burwell.

For the festival Steve Oxley and I presented "The R's Wipers: Homage to Rabelais," in which we explored the relationship between people and objects, especially with regard to sensation. Briefly, the performance happens in an unlit gallery, with the only light coming from an open trap door on the floor. There are four performers gathered around the trap door. Two of them speak the lines from a typically Rabelaisian skit, while the other two pull out from the trap door an incredible array of objects as each one is mentioned in the dialogue. The latter also play around with the textures, shapes and uses of the objects, sometimes coming up with something very far removed from their original purpose. The objects are passed on to the audience, who themselves experiment with them.

In an earlier work (June, 1976), a conceptual piece, Steve Oxley investigated the alienation of people from objects in the West, particularly his native England. One of the ironies of England is that, although it is an advanced consumer society, people are actually forbidden to touch or handle commodities before purchase most of the time. Steve has done a series of photographs of actual examples of this a fruit stall, a furniture shop, a department store, etc. - and presented them under a glass case, on top of which is a fitting "Do Not Touch" sign that comes from one of the shops.

Later on in the festival I employed a similar theme as the framework of a participation/ performance piece I did at the Acme Gallery entitled "The Stone and Paper Orchestra."

"The Stone and Paper Orchestra" was conceived in the winter of 1974. I was then going through an extraordinary time of linguistic discovery, constantly awakening to the actual experience of things that before then I had known only from books. It was as if words were assuming flesh and blood.

The idea for an environmental and participatory artwork based on that experience cropped up in my mind every now and then, but it was not until the autumn of 1976 that I presented it as "The Stone and Paper Orchestra," having evolved it meanwhile into a participation performance piece.

"The Stone and Paper Orchestra" is a highly personal work in the sense that it is structured along the line of development my person has taken in the last three years. However, it is also a search for the social origins of my personal impulses, relationships, etc., so that in the end it is more about society than myself. This is the

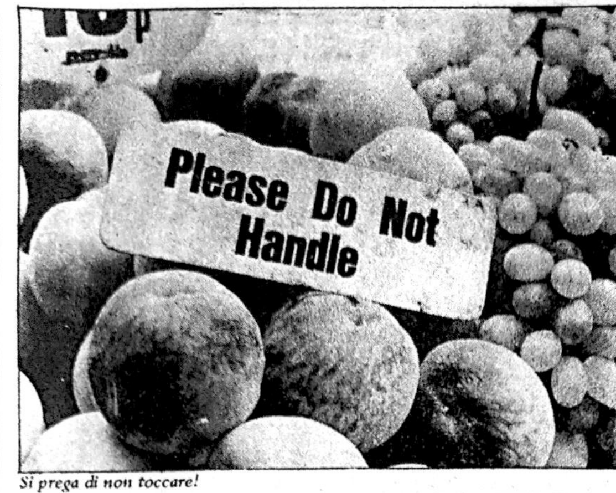

Si prega di non toccare!

case with most of my work – I present myself in juxtaposition with my audience in particular and society in general.

The performance begins in total darkness. Then a door slowly opens; light comes in, casting my giant shadow across the performance area. It is the opening of the subconscious. You feel yourself breathing. The door is closed, again slowly. You hear footsteps. The center of the performance area is slowly lit, until I am standing there alone and barefoot, clutching a suitcase in my hand. It is a feeling of vastness and being opening the suitcase with me. When it is at last open, together we find only ashes. These I slowly scatter on the floor. Then I put a foot on a square mirror, also on the floor, bend down and wash my foot in its reflection. Finally, I lie down on the ashes. This is the beginning of a journey through broken dreams, shattered illusions, crumbling images, vanishing mirages which my audience and I take until I regain equilibrium in a synthesis between past and present, my personal and social beings.

One of the reasons why I have come back to the Philippines is to look at my roots after having been away for approximately eight years. I have come back particularly to be with my family with whom I have not lived since I was eleven years old, having entered a seminary at that age. My eight years abroad have taken me through the different cultures of practically the whole of Southeast Asia, certain parts of Europe and England, where I have lived for the last four years or so. I wish to rid myself of any romantic illusions I may have about my childhood here and come to a proper assessment of my sense of values as a Filipino.

As a Filipino I feel naturally close to performance art. Our culture, after all, has never been tied up to art objects in museums, monuments of heavy permanence or institutions that act as guardians of rigid tradition. Perhaps it is because of our climate. Perhaps it is because of the nature of our people. Perhaps it is because of the way our history has been. But the fact is that our culture has been very much joined to our lives - our immediate needs, daily problems, common joys and as such it is often spontaneous, sometimes ephemeral and largely practical. Perhaps this is why I have always found what people do more interesting than what they make.

I look to my parents and family as the origins of my being a performance artist. As children we were always encouraged to try a hand at all sorts of things and coaxed to sing, dance, play the piano, recite poetry, etc. at the slightest pretext. I also remember early "environments" we used to create from blankets, pillows and other everyday objects in which we played out our fantasies. There was no television and very little radio and cinema to distract us. We had to put on our own entertainment. In retrospect, all these were exercises in self-expression.

As a performance artist, I see a very thin line dividing life from performance, in the same way that I believe that the audience is as much a part of a performance as the performer. This is why I find theaters in general very restrictive. They are too impersonal. They presume that on the one hand is the performer and on the other the audience. I always make it a point in my performances to try to break down this traditional barrier between the performer and the audience.

When I, as the founder and director of Amnesia International Dance Company, was invited to the Stedelijk Museum in Amsterdam in February, 1976, we in fact "forgot" to make the scheduled appearance. I devised an "auto-theater" piece, instead, and sent a set of guidelines and minimal props for the audience to stage their own performance. In that particular case the audience themselves were the performers.

If the theater is intimate I find it helps a lot to be with the audience before the start of the performance – be at the door to greet them, talk to them and for, say, three or four minutes, together contemplate the performance area. I want to feel that I am doing a performance for more than just a mass of nameless shadows, each one clutching a ticket, quietly seated in their chairs in order to consume my act. I want to be one with my audience. I want to be a mirror on which the audience can see themselves as much as I would want them to be a mirror on which I can see myself. Finally, I want society to be reflected in my performance with each person in the audience seeing himself or herself in that reflection.

I also find that theatricality can be predictable and less effective in the context of a theater than in such everyday places like a train, a bus, a square, a street, a marketplace or wonder it if were for real or not. The tension is greater and the bite therefore sharper.

Two propositions of mine for the theater are The Theater of the Abandoned Houses and The Theater of the Trees. The former is more suited for London, where, because of some strange thing called speculation, landlords make more money keeping their property empty than occupied, ~~and~~ there are approximately 100,000 vacant houses. The Theater of the Abandoned Houses would be a group of performers who would go from one part of the city to another and do performances around and possibly inside these empty houses, many of which are in such a state of decay that would be very powerful and evocative for a theater piece. It would also call attention to the need of artists for space to work in. I could initiate the Theater of the Trees here. All it entails is a clump of trees, preferably mature and strong, and heavy-duty ropes to make rope bridges from one tree to another, rather like a giant cat's cradle.

The performances would take place in the trees, with the rope bridges enabling the performers to go from one tree to another, while the audience can lie on the ground to watch the multiple apparitions.

I would like my audience to continue, either physically or mentally, what I initiate at my performances even when they have left the performance area – into the streets, their homes, their officers, etc. – and I believe that it helps to make the audience wonder during the actual performance whether what they are witnessing is a performance or life itself. I consider it important to make clear to the audience that what is taking place in a performance may at that very instant be happening outside, that there is a continuity from the past to that instant to the future, that the spectator is not seated in a vacuum called a theater but on the stage of life itself.

Lastly, performance art should be organic. It should breathe. It should be able to expand and contract depending on time, space and the people involved. It should have a structure that can swim in and out of different currents of vibrations that time, space and people jointly generate. It should be such a master of its own structure that it can go right or left, backward or forward, accommodate changes, deliberate and accidental, go from one variation to another and, like a sonata by Beethoven, thematically end on the note it began. ●

WE ARE THE EXPATRIATES OF A FUTURE WORLD

large & small stones inside a spherical (netting) structure

one end of the strings is attached to a stone the other end to a a hammer

the glass panes are gradually darkened by the smoke from lit candles inside the glass environmental installation

WE EXPATRIATES FUTURE WORLD

Medalla 1976, AFD, London, 143 Whitfield Street

Installation Environment for 'Tatlin at the Funeral of Malevitch

when the hammers are used to make constructions out of the squares of wood, the glass panes break: the letters made of optical fibre then appear

Drawing for David Medalla's *Tatlin at the Funeral of Malevitch*, a 'mass propulsion' first performed at 143 Whitfield Street, 19 September 1976

EXHIBITION

"THE U.S. Government's treatment of Indian people amounts to a scandal bigger and more severe than Watergate" state the American Indian Movement and they point out that "On the Pine Ridge Reservation since 1973 (when the much publicised occupation of Wounded Knee took place) 300 A.I.M. members or sympathisers have met violent deaths."

To show Londoners that Indians are not "picturesque feathered savages," A.I.M. have organised an exhibition opening on Saturday at 8 p.m. at the Fitzrovia Cultural Centre, 143 Whitfield Street, W.1.

The exhibition will include photographs together with background stories on the activities of A.I.M. over the last few years, posters, literature and music and will be open every day (except Mondays) from 1 p.m. to 7 p.m. until October 25. Admission is free.

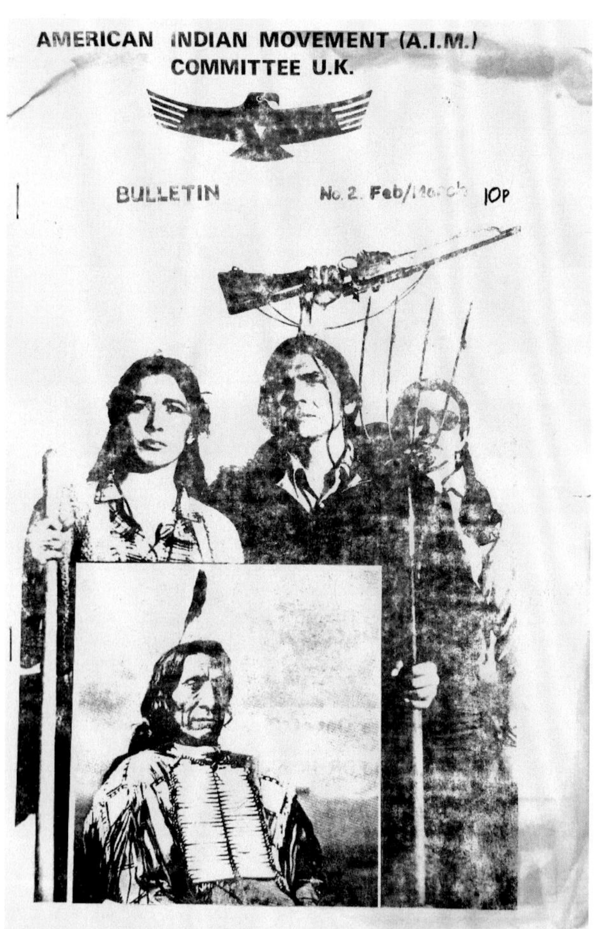

'American Indian Movement 1976 Exhibition', 143 Whitfield Street, September 1976 – January 1977. A document circulated by the American Indian Movement (AIM) Committee UK states that the exhibition would include: 'PHOTO BLOW-UPS showing the true situation of the Native American and showing the work of the American Indian Movement. POSTERS designed and produced by Native People, about their struggle. POSTERS by young American Artists living in London relating to the AIM struggle. ARTWORK by Native Artists. POETRY by Native people interpreted by London Calligraphers. INFORMATIVE GRAPHICS giving the stories behind photographs, captions etc. DISPLAY by the Artists for Democracy, showing the exploitation of the American Indians.'

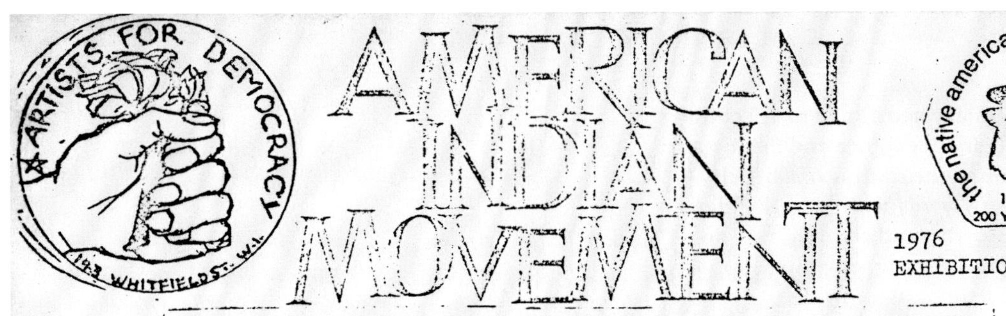

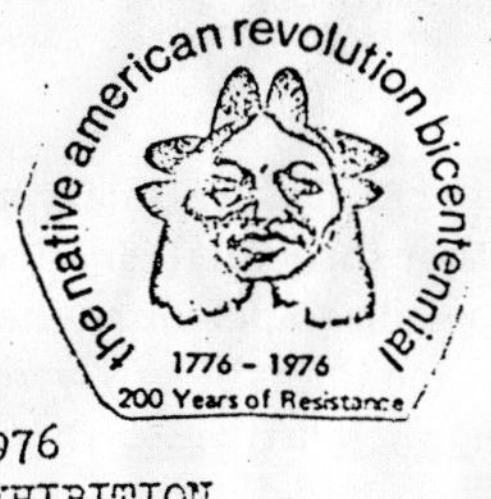

1976
EXHIBITION

"I lived here 77 years. This whole reservation was in total darkness. And somewhere, these young men started the American Indian Movement. And they came to our reservation and they turned that light on inside. And its getting bigger - now we can see things" - an Oglala elder.

AFD FITZROVIA CULTURAL CENTRE
143 Whitfield street, London W1P 5RY
near Warren street tube station

SUNDAY, OCTOBER 3rd, 1976, at 8 p.m.
Slides show and talk on the history and development of the AMERICAN INDIAN MOVEMENT

Speaker: TERRY LEWIS of A.I.M. (U.K. Committee)

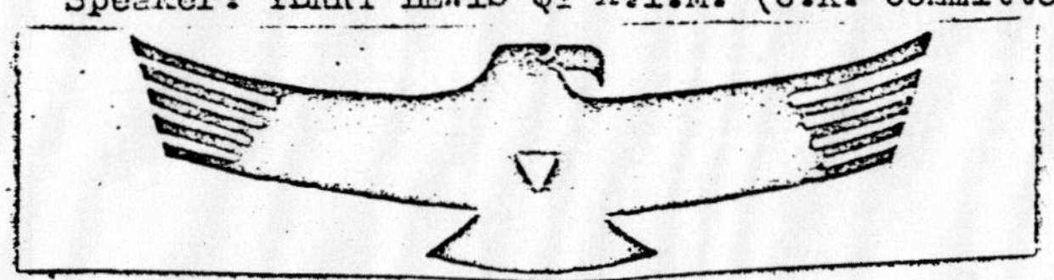

ARTISTS FOR DEMOCRACY present
"AIM STRAIGHT, STAND TALL!"
a dance-drama in support of the just struggle of the heroic American Indian People for Liberation

Written and narrated by David Medalla,
Collectively evolved and performed by
Nick Payne, Virgil Calaguian, Charles Hustwick, Gary O'Donnell, Mick Demny, Law Hok Long, Hok Thye, with Rose Finn-Kelcey as Earth Mother/Lightning Woman and Royce Ullah as Thunder Child.
Poems by American Indian poets set to music by Paul Burwell. Tensile teepees by Nick Payne.
Elemental sculptures by Virgil Calaguian.
Spatiostructures by Rasheed Araeen.
Rainbow arrows by David Medalla.
The title of this dance-drama is from the song "Starwalker, for the American Indian Movement", by Buffy Sainte Marie.

Admission: 50 p. to benefit A.I.M.

Exhibition coordinator: Veronica Chapman.

With grateful acknowledgement to AKWESASNE NOTES.

If the Exploding Galaxy had aimed to affect the public through their appearance and behaviour – person-to-person in the routine of a big city – the members of AFD were inspired by the idea that their artistic work could actually have an effect on historical events by providing support for liberation movements worldwide.

[...]

A notable example of AFD's public role was the organisation of an exhibition in solidarity with the American Indian Movement in 1976, documenting the political, legal and community struggles of Native Americans in the USA. It also featured poems, paintings and other artwork. It was planned to coincide with the Hayward Gallery's prestigious 'Sacred Circles', in which a collection of some of the finest Native American artefacts belonging to museums and collectors were used, with wholly unconscious but bitter irony, to boost the celebrations of the Bicentennial of the establishment of the USA. At the time, AFD was the only artists' group in London to rise above the national context to concern itself with the relationship between First and Third Worlds, and to show the indivisibility of culture and politics in that relationship.

Guy Brett

['Sacred Circles'] was quite a beautiful show, you know, with all the artefacts of the American Indians, although not one American Indian was involved with that show! While that show was going on we also had a show – in fact I think our show opened earlier than their show! – that was the American Indian Movement show, which for most people had more meaning than the 'Sacred Circles' show, in other words – or the 'Sacred Circles' show only gained meaning when people came here to the AIM show.

David Medalla

"SOVEREIGNTY – LIBERATION – INTERNATIONAL TREATY LAW"

AMERICAN INDIAN MOVEMENT (A.I.M.) COMMITTEE U.K.

National Organiser - Terry Lewis.

Chairman - Fredda Shepherd.

Treasurer - Beryl Lewis.

London Organiser - Nicky Chapman

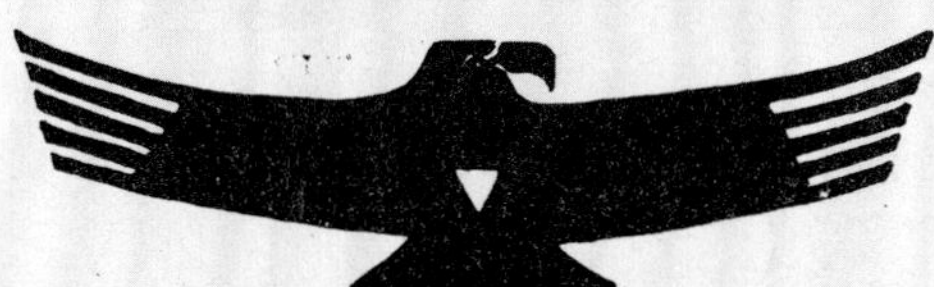

6, Woodland Road, Northfield, Birmingham, B31 2HS., Telephone: 021 476 7003

Dear Friend,

We are organising an exhibition to be entitled:

THE AMERICAN INDIAN MOVEMENT 1976 EXHIBITION

Starting September 25th 1976 and running for one month at a Cultural Centre in London W. 1. After this showing we plan to take the exhibition to other parts of Great Britain.

The exhibition will show the true situation in the United States today, of the struggle by the American Indian Movement / Native American Nations for Sovereignty and self - determination.

It will show the lengths that the U. S. has gone to to prevent the people from achieving their aims, from achieving what is in fact theirs by right, proven by 371 Treaties, still in existence although ruthlessly violated.

It will also show the spirit of the American Indian People, still alive today despite everything, still following the true Indian Way and still producing beautiful poetry and artwork.

The American Indian Movement will not stop trying to achieve victory until the Treaties have been honoured and their people have been freed. Bullets, bombs and false criminal charges will not prevent the American Indian Movement from continuing and we believe that this exhibition will help to bring International Awareness and Solidarity to their aid.

It will involve the purchasing of display units and materials to show our exhibits to their full advantage and will need an extensive publicity campaign.

Therefore we need a large sum of money and we ask all friends to help us by sending donations to enable us to finance this exhibition.

Thank you.

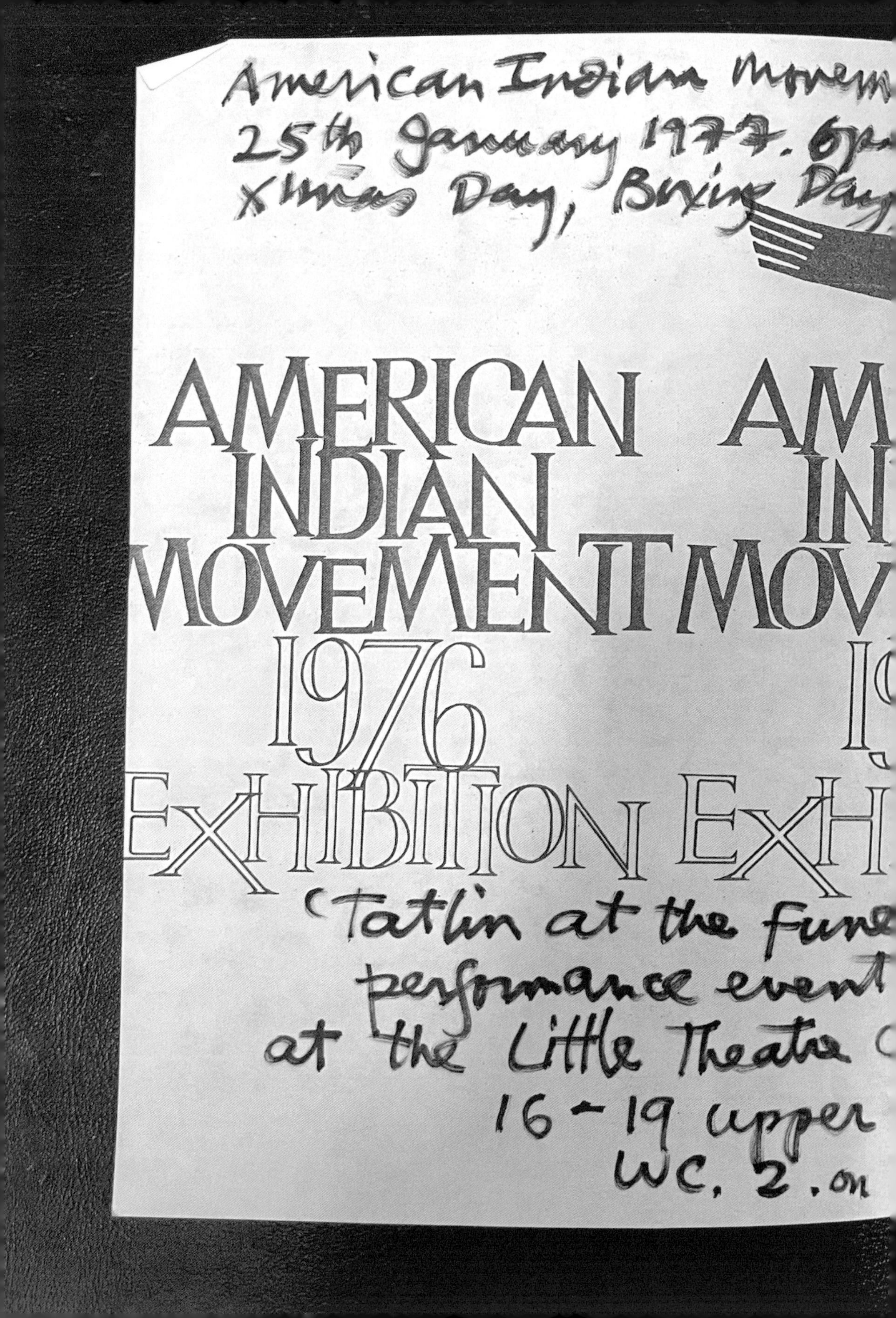

American Indian Movem
25th January 1977. 6p
Xmas Day, Boxing Day

AMERICAN AM
INDIAN IN
MOVEMENT MOV
1976 19
EXHIBITION EXH

'Tatlin at the Fune
performance event
at the Little Theatre C
16 – 19 upper
WC. 2. on

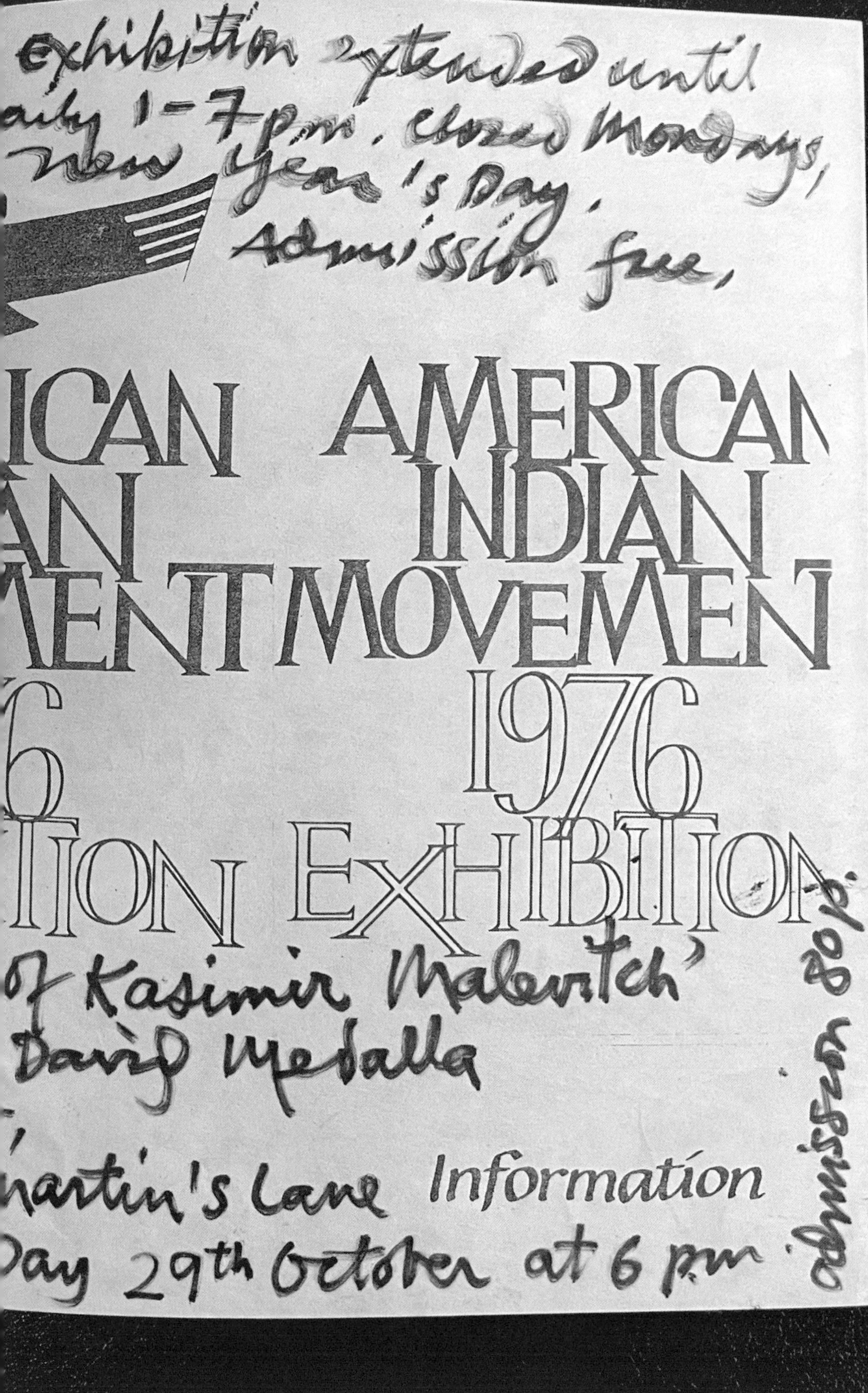

exhibition extended until
aily 1-7 p.m. closed Mondays,
New Year's Day.
Admission free.

ICAN AMERICAN
AN INDIAN
ENT MOVEMEN
6 1976
TION EXHIBITION

of Kasimir Malevitch'
David Medalla

artin's Lane Information
Day 29th October at 6 p.m.

admission 80p.

AFD 19.12.76

Theatre Group AIM
presentation of how the West was won –
very funny girl who played the white
squaw – parody of back to nature
was good. Miss Selfridge Indian
look – comment on the consumption
of the society by the dominant
culture. Taking of the blanket –
good line – what a beautiful
banket – you shouldn't be using it;
it should be in a museum.
Boy with Canadian lumberjacket
reciting 10 ~~little~~ green bottles type
poem, lisp, Americo-german accent.
Film – used word play very well
BISON – BUY SOME. Bison → ham
burger. Prop of metal conduit
tube as feed for the hamburgers
one of many link motifs going through
the pieces.
Pantomime spirit suitably seasonal

Lenya. Admission £1. p.m. Admission £1, £1·50, £2.

LUNCHTIME TOMORROW

THE American Indian Movement exhibition has been so successful that it is being extended to mid-January. AIM was founded in 1968 at Stillwater Prison, Minnesota, to help the American Indians in their struggle for liberation and self-determination. Exhibition at the Artists For Democracy Fitzrovia Cultural Centre, 143 Whitfield Street (Warren Street Tube), explains all. Open daily, 1 p.m.-7 p.m. Admission free.

Charles Hustwick's 19 December 1976 diary page, with notes on a performance at 'American Indian Movement 1976 Exhibition', 143 Whitfield Street, September 1976 – January 1977

THE TIMES TUESDAY OCTOBER 12 1976

THE ARTS

The indigenous Americans

Paul Overy

It is ironic that the enormous bicentennial exhibition at the Hayward Gallery should be devoted to the art and artifacts of the American Indians. The year of the bicentenary of American Independence is also the centenary of the defeat by the Sioux of General Custer at Little Bighorn in June, 1876. This defeat, the news of which reached Washington on July 5, the day after the nation's centennial celebrations, provoked a colossal retaliation against the Plains Indians which eventually culminated in the massacre of 200 men, women and children by United States soldiers at Wounded Knee in 1890. It was the death-blow to the Indians' hope for an independent way of life.

The humiliation and denial of the rights of the original inhabitants of the United States did not end there. The wrongs that were done to the red man by the white man in the past and earlier centuries are not glossed over in the exhibition, and moving quotations from speeches and writings by Indians are printed on the screens at the Hayward. A more complete collection can be found in *Touch the Earth*, compiled by T. C. McLuhan with photographs by Edward Curtis (Abacus, £1.25), which is on sale at the Hayward bookstall.

But there is no hint in the exhibition or catalogue of the continuing plight of the surviving Indians today, although something of its enormity can be gleaned from another publication on sale in the foyer, the Minority Rights Group Report, *The Original Americans: US Indians*. A more urgent and committed revelation of the state of the American Indians today is contained in a small but eloquent exhibition at The Fitzrovia Cultural Centre (143 Whitfield Street) organized by AIM, the American Indian Movement, the militant Indian group which played a big part in the occupation of Wounded Knee in 1973.

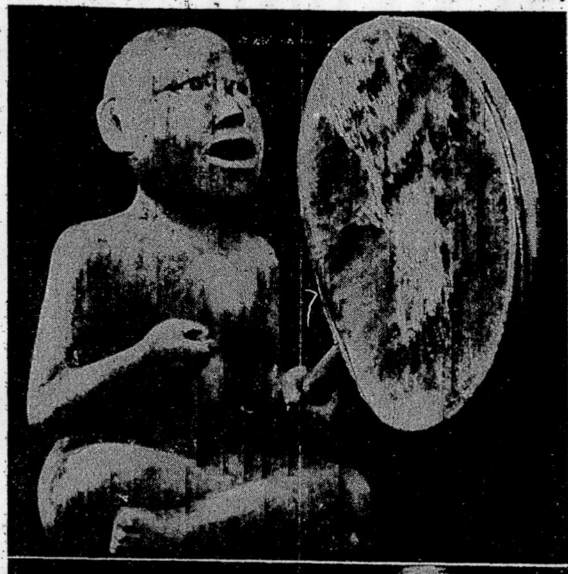

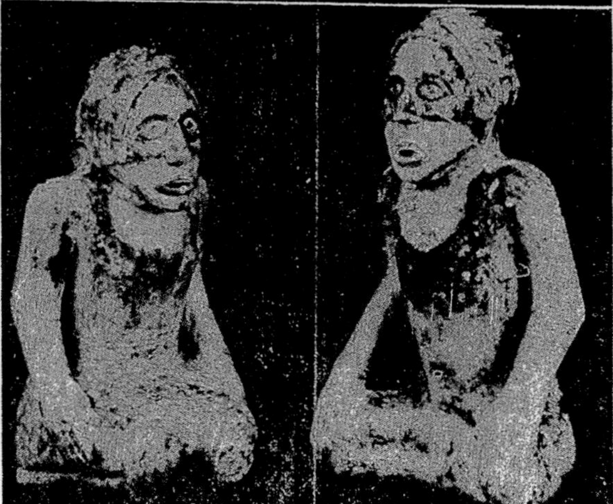

Pair of figures c 1400-1500 (painted marble, Georgia, Etorah) and, top, nineteenth-century Eskimo figure sculpture (Alaska)

THE CONTRAST could not be more revealing.

At the **Hayward Gallery**, a lavish exhibition of **Two Thousand Years of North American Indian Art** has been mounted as part of the interminable American Bicentennial celebrations, under the joint patronage of the Duke of Edinburgh and Nelson Rockefeller backed up by a shoal of all-white Anglo-American Volunteer Committees.

But at **Artists for Democracy**, a small, decaying gallery in 143 Whitfield Street, W1, the present-day descendants of the men and women whose work is fêted on the South Bank have scraped together an angry polemic called the **American Indian Movement 1976 Exhibition.**

The Hayward survey has assembled, with diligent scholarship and a flair for showmanship, almost 700 exhibits, most of which are illustrated in a catalogue containing an American museum director's patronising statement that "Perhaps we are still a little shocked at having to admit what fine sculptors, designers, and craftsmen native American artists were and are."

Whereas the Whitfield Street show's collection of duplicated protest leaflets, photographs and drawings, all dominated by a picture of an Indian imprisoned behind the bar-like stripes of an up-ended American flag, is dedicated to the AIM's beliefs that "The U.S. government's treatment of Indian people amounts to a scandal bigger and more severe than Watergate."

SACRED CIRCLES: 2,000 YEARS OF NORTH AMERICAN INDIAN ART

Hayward Gallery, 7 October—16 January

Reviewed by Susan Hiller

The 700 objects in this exhibition include many of the finest Native American artefacts—that is, the objects most highly valued by their original owners and makers, and by white anthropologists, curators and collectors. Materials have been gathered from a wide range of sources; many have never before been publicly displayed, or have been available only in small or geographically isolated collections. The exhibition, organised in celebration of the American Bicentennial, has been given extensive publicity. There is a detailed, well-illustrated and documented catalogue, prepared by Ralph T. Coe, the Curatorial Director. Surely such efforts ought to be, and deserve to be, taken seriously.

For 400 years, from 1513 until the beginning of this century, Europeans and Native Americans fought a series of wars to determine the ownership of what is now the United States. The struggle of the Native Americans was of great importance in the creation of the US, and 'was in many ways the anvil upon which Anglo-American character was forged . . . In 1787, Benjamin Franklin wrote, "During the course of a long life . . . it has appeared to me that almost every war between the Indians and whites has been occasioned by some injustice of the latter towards the former.' By the end of the 18th century a number of European-Americans had come to share this viewpoint; however, the forces that drove the newcomers westward were too great to be stemmed or made less harsh by the sentiments of a small intelligentsia. The average Anglo-American had already become a restless, ambitious, aggressive person—and nothing could stand between him and his dream of wealth.[1]

From the Anglo-American point of view, then, all the items in this exhibition document the success of the sustained attempt to destroy the native societies in the US, and the exhibition itself is a gauge of the degree of that destruction. For the basic fact of the matter is that 'we' now have in 'our' possession a multitude of important Native American objects, whose display by 'us' commemorates our decimation of the makers, our destruction of their history, our appropriation of their lands, and our attempted obliteration of the 'sense' of their cultures over a period of more than 200 years.

It would have been educational, as well as provided badly needed 'context', if the exhibition had attempted to make us aware of the interactions between the objects displayed and our own history; but instead, there has been an effort to empathize with the Native American world view. Passing reference to the tragic consequences for the Native Americans of the original white invasion of their territories, and the subsequent efforts of the whites to subjugate and exterminate them, show how tightly the exhibition is caught in a mass of contradictions stemming from its initial conception as a suitable event to celebrate the Bicentennial. For example: the catalogue reminds us that, while 1976 is the 200th anniversary of the American Declaration of Independence, it is also the 100th anniversary of the defeat of Custer by the Sioux at the Battle of Little Big Horn. All this does, though, is to situate the 'Indian problem' firmly in the historic past. Possibly 'we' need to be reminded that not all the Native Americans are dead, and many are still fighting: 'The Wounded Knee Occupation (1973) and The Trail of Broken Treaties (1972) were carried out by the American Indian Movement in order to draw public attention to the problems of Indians generally . . . One of the . . . demonstrators said: "The myth has been perpetuated that we don't exist anymore—that's the hardest thing we have to fight against." '[2]

For information about contemporary Native American struggles, legal, social, and political, the exhibition organised by the American Indian Movement (AIM) at Artists for Democracy, 143 Whitfield Street, London W1, to coincide with the Hayward show, also needed to be visited.

Certainly, the ostensibly well-meaning references in the 'Sacred Circles' catalogue to the Native tragedy never indicate that the oppression, struggle, and heartache are contemporary. Neither the brief excerpts from a few well-known 19th-century Native American speeches scattered through the exhibition proper, nor the remarks in the free handout reminding us that 'the dominant feature of the history of North American Indian culture has been the crushing effect of the white man's determination to suppress and remove the native population,' bring the reality of the situation *now* into focus. For nowhere in the 'Sacred Circles' exhibition—and this is crucial—will you find any sense of how the Anglo-American viewpoint formed in the early years of Native-white confrontation, and crystallized over the centuries, continues to influence the present-day Anglo treatment of Native Americans, as well as 'American' attitudes towards indigenous population in *eg* Korea and Vietnam. The reason you will not find any sense of this, is that the exhibition has been organised within the same terms of reference.

Looking at the bloodstained trophies and souvenirs, immaculately dry-cleaned and antiseptically isolated in the Hayward Gallery, not a trace of their original existence as

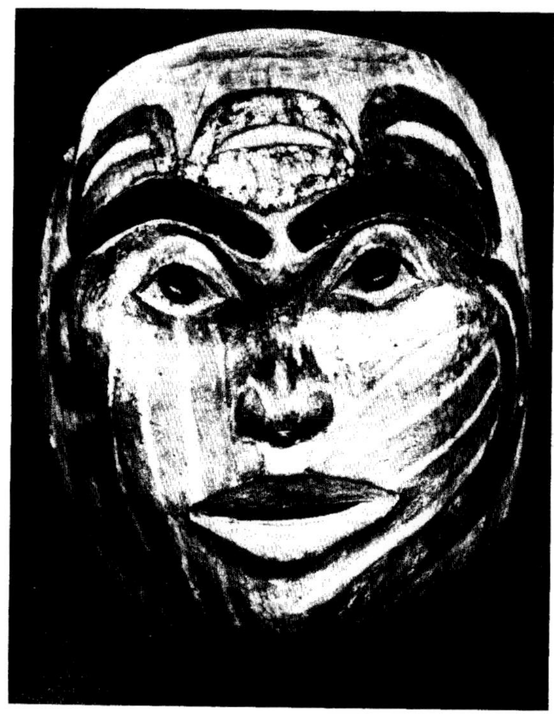

Mask. Early 19th century, Northwest Coast, Haida

things that work comes across. And, of course, no effort has been made to record the near-accomplishment of genocide in the presentation of the objects, although Coe's catalogue is highly informative on this point. Only a slight re-emphasis would have been needed in order to be able to read the material for its historical implications: 1. *The passage of effective territorial control from native to white hands is signified by the change of ownership of valuable symbolic objects.* Catalogue entry no. 52, Powhatan's Mantle: Powhatan was the great chief who united the Algonquin tribes of Virginia, and whose daughter Pocahantus married John Smith. Forty-nine years after the first white settlers had arrived, this mantle was mentioned in an inventory of the Tradescent family, who were 'Virginia landowners.' By that time, the Native Americans, at first welcoming, had risen twice in rebellion and attempted to destroy the white settlements. Defeated, they 'declined' in numbers.[3] So possession of this mantle by a white family at a certain date indicates when the takeover of Indian possessions, lands, etc, was complete in that area of the country.

2. *The making of treaties with the Native Americans was considered purely gestural by the whites.* This is indicated by catalogue entry no. 53, wampum belt, Iroquois: '. . . a wampum belt served as a gift, also as a binding symbol of an agreement . . . and they were of the highest importance as documentary evidence of such pacts.' This belt was 'collected' by the Duke of York's secretary in 1700. Seemingly, the document was considered of aesthetic or curiosity value only, not as legal evidence of an agreement. It is now in the British Museum.

Wampum belt, Delaware, *c.* 1700: is associated with the treaty regulating Delaware-White relations in Pennsylvania under William Penn. It shows two figures of equal size holdings hands, and was preserved by Native Americans long after the treaty ceased to be honoured, until passing somehow (we're not told how) to the Royal Ontario Museum; the belts kept by the Penn family are in the Museum of the American Indian.

3. *War booty, spoils, and trophies were frequently captured by whites.* The catalogue limits mention of this custom to instances connected with the history of specific 'art' objects: catalogue no. 67 is a 19th-century Seminole sash, a relic of the Florida Indian Wars, taken by Lt. John H. Hill 'from Gouchataminchas, Nuctilage Hammock, March 10, 1840.'

Catalogue no. 430, carved wooden spoon: now in the Smithsonian. It was 'captured by the Second Nebraska Cavalry from the Sioux, September 3, 1863.'

Frequently the trophies consisted of scalps, fingers, and 'men, women, and children's privates'.[4]

4. *If not associated in some way with violence, Native American objects now in 'our' possession indicate degrees of economic insecurity and stages of cultural collapse which are the direct result of white domination.* Catalogue no. 646, Navajo silver and turquoise bracelet: 'Note the simplicity and restraint of this late 1930s "pawn" bracelet. Pawn bracelets were put into pawn at the trading post for cash; unredeemed jewelry enters the trade.'

Page 126: '. . . Chief Mathews (Weah) of the Haida . . . pointed to a depression in the ground where his father's totem pole (today at Oxford University) once stood: "It is customary for the nephews of a Chief to keep him supplied with halibut, but do you think this is done any more for me? Not one piece! They want to go to the movies . . ."'

Catalogue nos. 469 and 471, medicine bundles: Medicine bundles, 'owned by societies, villages, and doctors were at the very core of Indian religious mystique; they only found their way outside the Indian world when the last owner disposed of it. These are all owned by private collectors.

But the catalogue avoids structuring the information in this way. Instead, a typical entry reads: '431, Warbonnet, c. 1880 AD, Northern Plains, Oglala Sioux, buckskin, feathers, tradecloth, 2.18 M total length, lent by C.F. Taylor Collection, Hastings.

Warbonnets had a highly symbolic meaning. Traditionally, each feather represented a brave exploit, not necessarily of the warrior, but of the tribe itself. A warbonnet may also represent the council fire, each feather signifying a member of the council with the horsehair tips being the scalplocks of each warrior. The central plume represents the owner of the bonnet. The feathers are from the Golden Eagle, the sidedrops are ermine, the front band is of seed beads on hide. This bonnet belonged to Cinte Mazzo (Iron Tail, 1847-1916). He worked for Buffalo Bill's Rodeo for many years.'

Symbolical, material, and biographical 'facts' are given, and are seen as comparable descriptive levels which define the object. The historical significance of 'our' possession of the bonnet is ignored. Such a description creates the illusion that the meaning of the object has been fully illuminated, and helps to assimilate it into the white tradition of ownership while alienating it from the ongoing traditions and struggles of contemporary Native Americans.

The effulgent prose of the catalogue text and exhibition labels, which try to give us the 'Indian' point of view, fail utterly to convey anything more than a liberal-romantic-formalist interest in noble savages and their artefacts. The sincerity of statements like 'One cannot separate Native American clothing from either wearing, sewing, ceremony, or medicine power,' surely has to be judged in relation to the display of articles of clothing as discrete items praised for their 'craftsmanship'. Value judgements based on contemporary sensibility and an ethnocentric aesthetic pervade the text, with words like 'subtlety', 'delicacy', 'refinement', 'ruggedness', 'latent humanism' (the archaeological Hopewell culture), 'eccentric and macabre' (Temple Mound culture), and sentences like 'The deer was evidently worshipped as an animal of great beauty' (Key Largo culture). They must surely raise doubts about whether the stated aim of the exhibition, 'to provide bases for cross-cultural comparison', could conceivably have been realised, given such an obvious naiveté about personal preferences, projections, and culture-bound traditions of presentation.

Or perhaps none of this is naive at all, but rather part of the process of voiding the objects of meaning? A sort of cultural-imperialist pretence of taking the other side's viewpoint? 'Shifting psychic associations led to corresponding interweaving of association and content in design, until in the process, the exact meaning became lost . . .' Is this merely naive ethnocentrism? For surely the 'meaning' was not lost to the people who made and used the items; it is lost to us because it isn't ours. And anyway, if we are really to take 'Sacred Circles' seriously as an art exhibition, if it's really real *art* (using the word the way the show does), then what is an exact meaning, anyhow? Why not investigate the aesthetics of the makers to find out, instead of omitting any reference to their sometimes-recorded judgements?[5]

A further comment on the means taken to void the objects in the exhibition of significance: the private is made public, the sacred is profaned, at the same time that homage is paid to the mystical world-view of the Native Americans. When it comes to display, no respect is shown for the others' viewpoint. Plains shields, for instance, bearing cryptic designs representing the original owner's personal dream or vision, motifs that functioned as mnemonic devices for recreating that heightened awareness, were never uncovered except just before battle, when the owner would contemplate his shield in order to enter into communion with the sacred once again. Recapturing a sense of himself as a spiritual, and therefore invulnerable, being, he overcame fear. Such shields are nakedly displayed without their covers in this exhibition, showing not only that the organisers don't accept their efficacy as *things that work*, but that they have no sensitivity toward the Native American mode of display (with painted covers).

It is obvious, then, that although 'Sacred Circles' represents a massive effort of organisation, it is at the service of a one-sided and consequently distorted historical perspective. This is what it celebrates.

The point of view throughout the exhibition is that of the collector, and the sensitivity and respect that are said to permeate it, are the sensitivity and respect toward *objects* of the curator. For the exhibition also celebrates 'our' success in absorbing the creative energies of the Native Americans into the mainstream of our commerce. As the catalogue (p.14) states: 'The Indian relic market of yesterday has become a sophisticated art market today. We admire collectors like J.D. Dyer at Fort Reno, Nevada, Morley Reed Gotschall of Philadelphia, William E. Clafflin of Boston, who preserved many treasures that might otherwise have disappeared from the record . . . In the last years, all of these objects, once considered homespun and of only marginal local interest, have begun to be collected as avidly as any other art. While this is sad for the old-time Indian buff, it signifies the advancement of American Indian art to the status it deserves.'

The degree to which this point of view is not only accepted, but celebrated, is suggested by the availability on the Hayward's lobby table at the private view of Sotheby's card advertising 'A Sale of American Indian and Pre-Columbian art to coincide with the exhibition of American Indian art opening at the Hayward Gallery, London, on 7th October.'

The ethnocentric aesthetic judgements mentioned earlier can be seen as a means of validating the current increase in market value of these objects. The caption of catalogue no. 452, painted and carved wooden bowl, says: 'Its quality is denoted by the thin painted rim line and the subtle way the heads are stepped upon the rim. Collected in 1768, this bowl was autioned at Sotheby's April 29th, 1974, number 128.'

Personally, I don't find this relegation of cultural artefacts to the category 'art' as distasteful on economic as on *moral* grounds. The ability to treat indescribably sad facts with a false objectivity, which seeks to avoid both condemnations and pathos, must be seen as an instance of the brutalization of our psyches resulting from the perpetuation of attitudes more than 200 years old. So, if buying and selling the objects concerned is the only way we can express a bewildered sense that there is some inherent value in them, it could be argued that this implies a functional necessity to integrate the symbols of these 'others' into the mainstream of our culture after having destroyed their social relevance. Buying and selling are apparently the only way we can perform such a ceremony of integration.

This exhibition, then, is really about using 'art' to cover up some historical truths; about using aesthetic judgements as a way of avoiding moral judgements; about professing admiration for spiritual values while manifesting only materialist ones; about admiring the 'work' while ignoring the meanings; about voiding symbols of their complexity by eliminating their context; and about valuing art objects more than societies.

To say that the purpose of the exhibition is 'that this art should at last be properly regarded for the sake of a better understanding among peoples' (catalogue, p.13), is, at the very least, an inadequate way to render justice to the peoples whose works are represented.

1 J.D. Forbes, ed., *The Indian in America's Past*, Prentice-Hall 1965, pp.35-40.

2 James Wilson, *The Original American: U.S. Indians*, Minority Rights Group Report no. 31, London 1976, p.24.

3 John R. Swanton, *The Indian Tribes of North America*, Smithsonian Inst. Bull. Amer. Ethnol. no 145, Washington 1953.

4 'The Sand Creek Massacre,' Testimony of 1st Lt. Cramer, in Frobes, *op. cit.*, p.47.

5 See Ruth Bunzel, *The Pueblo Potter*, 1929, reissued Dover, NY 1972; of any of Frances Densmore's studies of Native American music.

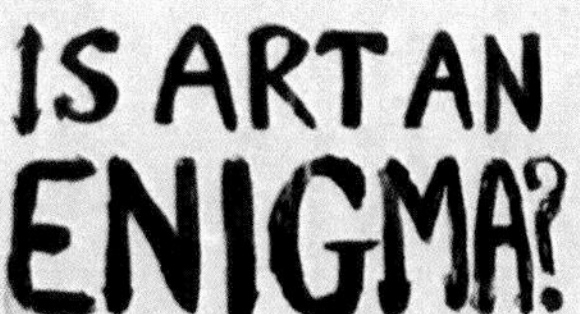
IS ART AN
ENIGMA?
Johannes
of Delft
evolved BY
DAVID MEDALLA,
PETER CROSS,
VIRGIL CALAGUIAN,
STEVE OXLEY,

4 for VIRGIL

The following 4 articles deal with Virgil Calaguian's 4 performances in December 1976 at:
Artists for Democracy (Fitzrovia Cultural Centre)
Film Makers' Co-op
Women's Free Arts Alliance
Little Theatre Club

by

1. *Guy Brett*
2. *Robert Tai*
3. *Emmanuel Cooper*
4. *Robbie Kravitz*

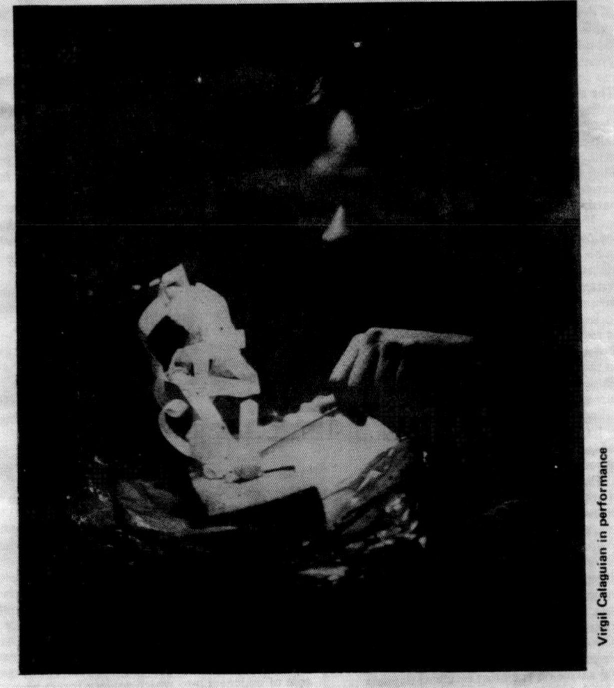

Virgil Calaguian in performance

Virgil has used what was already implicit in the picture to show the truth of the situation. In his performances Virgil also uses advertisements and exposes them so that we can see certain truths about ourselves and our environment.

In the first of his four recent performances he constructed an environment from trash found on the streets (discarded consumer goods) on the decaying ground floor of AFD at Whitfield Street. Around this environment he burned strips of polythene hanging from the ceiling, which dripped into and were reflected by trays of water. In the center, an armchair and two television sets, one facing the audience without screen – in its place a mirror.

Slides were projected from three carousels set around the room, one behind the structure, another beside it and the third onto a golden torso set on a pedestal. A tape recording of street and cafe sounds was also played.

On the torso in one sequence Virgil was shown, photographed in a boiler suit and wearing a meat price. He was standing outside banks, supermarkets, employment bureaux and various other places in London.

On the wall most easily visible he showed slides of his collages: naked Italian women giving advice on the most efficient depilation, a baby dwarfed by a silver dollar, company directors surrounding a colleague in a bath with a rubber duck, defecation without mess or smell, fashions – one under a heading 'meet our £39 suit'. A high society dinner: in which the activity of eating that could be a means of sensual and social development is buried beneath etiquette and plastic charm. In all the collages Virgil brought out the essence of the advertisements with minimal adjustment, either visual or verbal, to the originals, as in 'meet our £39 suit' in which he simply blacked out the model's face and hands.

The advertisements all played on biological and emotional needs which they offered to satisfy. Placed in a correct perspective they were revealed to be hollow and meaningless.

The third projector showed news photos of the suffering that supports this world where even emotions are portrayed as easily handled with deodorants, mouthwashes and after-shave lotions. (The most potent image from his fourth performance was Virgil eating a dinner of tickertape, which he later slowly vomited. The tickertape is biologically unacceptable.)

Unlike the work of many artists, Virgil's does not require the audience to forget itself or 'external' reality – to be passive before some egotist. All of the objects and pictures that Virgil uses are either familiar or easily accessible to his audience. He does not place himself apart from or above his audience. Instead, in an atmosphere of intense space and silence he invites us to see, hear, smell, feel and taste his arguments. He asks us to consider ourselves in the context of the intrinsic relations of objects and environments, and hence their sensual worth, and to recognize that genuine sensuality is in our body and it its functions and not in the antiseptic and cardboard images that media is constantly presenting us.

Robert Tai
27 Kyverdale Road
Stoke Newington London N16

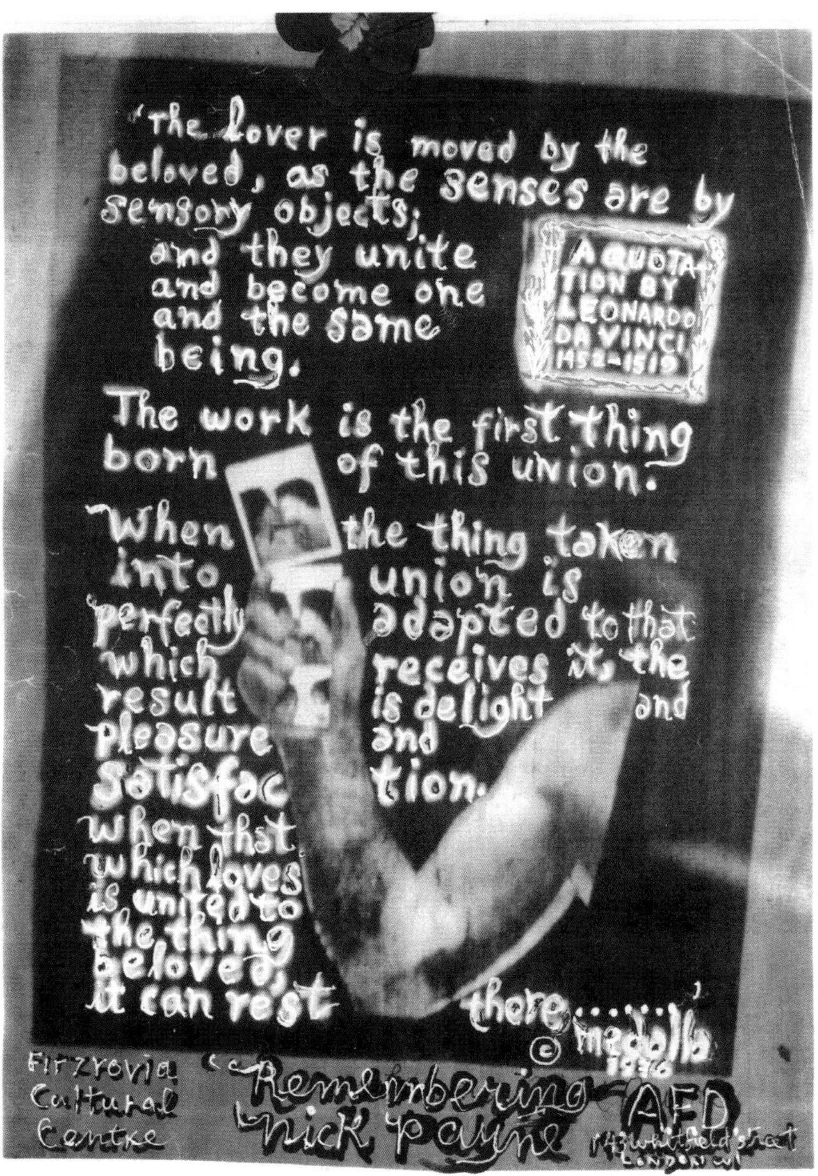

POETRY

AN ENGLISH minimal artist talks to a garage mechanic in a pub—an exchange made more confusing because the dialogue is in poetry and songs.

Nick Payne and singer Rob Collins take part in this "performance art event" on Sunday at 7.30 p.m. at the Artists for Democracy Fitzrovia Cultural Centre, 143 Whitfield Street, W.1.

Admission is free and there will probably be a party afterwards so you can bring your own drink and food.

ART

DIALOGUE Between Stomach and Conscience is not specifically aimed at vegetarians and fatties—it's a "performance art event" by young artist Nick Haynes and everyone is welcome to see his act on Sunday at 2.30 p.m. at the Fitzrovia Cultural Centre, 143 Whitfield Street, W.1. Admission free.

Actually, I hate galleries. I don't know if that's what you'd call a 'stand', but it's a deep feeling. I go to see shows sometimes, and what depresses me is that whatever the supposed stance of the gallery, whatever point the artist is trying to make, they all fall into the mould or trap of trying to emulate the ritziest capitalist gallery or galleries around, which is absolutely fatal, *n'est-ce pas*? I mean the whole ritual of arranging it all a year in advance, having some failed art student mincing around trying to get all the stuff 'hung' or 'arranged' artistically, getting another one to design a poster and invitation card, then employing some poor drudge to send all the private view invites off to all the right people ... eurgh! Then, of course, we have 'The Opening', usually a horrendous parody of a society party with everyone trying to out chic one another and scrambling to get to know the right people ... Okay, it's what's known around here as the 'Bond Street Syndrome', and I'm sure it's very successful in the right context, which is purely and simply to sell the product to the richies and coerce the critics into writing it up in the Daily Brainwasher so the plebs'll have something to think of as 'culture'. Art dealing and speculating must revolve around the very summit of the capitalist mountain. Well, I'm sure in theory it's very good for the balance of payments and all that, but I've got a feeling a lot of the money made by dealers and their pet artists doesn't stay in this country for very long. So why do the public-funded galleries have to copy all that? Museums of art, like the National or the Tate, they're fine as museums – they don't really purport to produce anything but dust and art historians. But the so-called 'progressive' or 'experimental' galleries, well, they're just carrying on the tradition. Look at the Hayward, what I often hear referred to as 'that giant concrete bunker', it must have been doomed from the start. All that ethnic stuff, Tantra, Islamic, Amerind. Very nice for the parties of school kids, I'm sure, but much better for the people who deal in it. Somehow, the British Rail mentality of most of our nationalised industries has crept into state-subsidised art too. ... It's not often I hear it suggested to me by any of my friends, be they artists, bus conductors, teachers or whatever, that we meet each other in such and such a gallery. They're just not very good places to meet up in. I can only suggest this: that every artist, whether politically committed or just sensitive and daring, should get together with their party, or their friends, and start their own 'galleries', or, better still, take over some of the existing ones. Advertise your studio as a gallery and just show your own work, utilise some of this empty space in London. Take a risk, experiment, make galleries that don't need white walls, lighting on rails and electric typewriters, make galleries that *do* produce art, that are good places to meet friends in.

ARTISTS OF THE WORLD UNITE, YOU'VE NOTHING TO LOSE BUT YOUR DEALERS.

Try selling each other's work, or buying it, if you need the money. Put 'Gallery Director' in your passport and try and live up to it. I have, it's fun!

Nick Payne

ibitions & events at the
tzrovia Cultural Centre
e sponsored by Friends of AFD
d, in part, by GLAA *
e Greater London Arts Association.

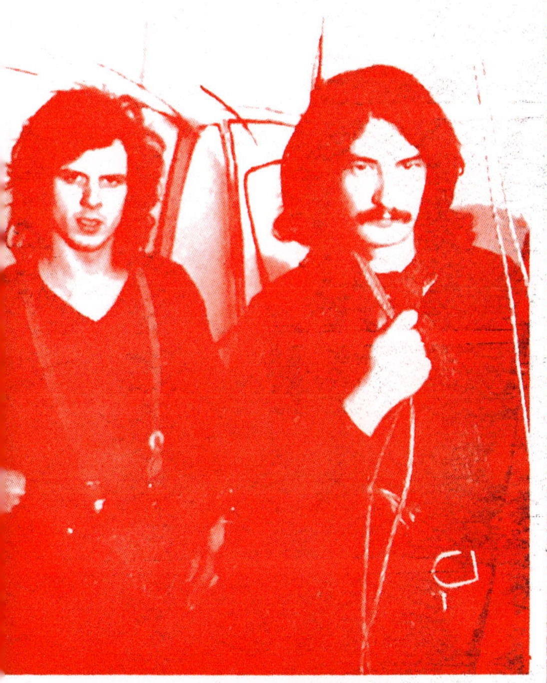

MECHANICKS

a performance art event
written and performed by

NICK PAYNE

with guitar music especially
composed and played by

ROB COLLINS

Sunday, April 17th, 1977, at 8 p.m.

"DREAMBOXES"

video event & environment by

MORRIE CRAMER

assisted by

JEFF RUBIN

Sunday, April 17th, 1977, at 7 p.

th grateful acknowledgement
the Arts Council of Great Britain
r the loan of video equipment

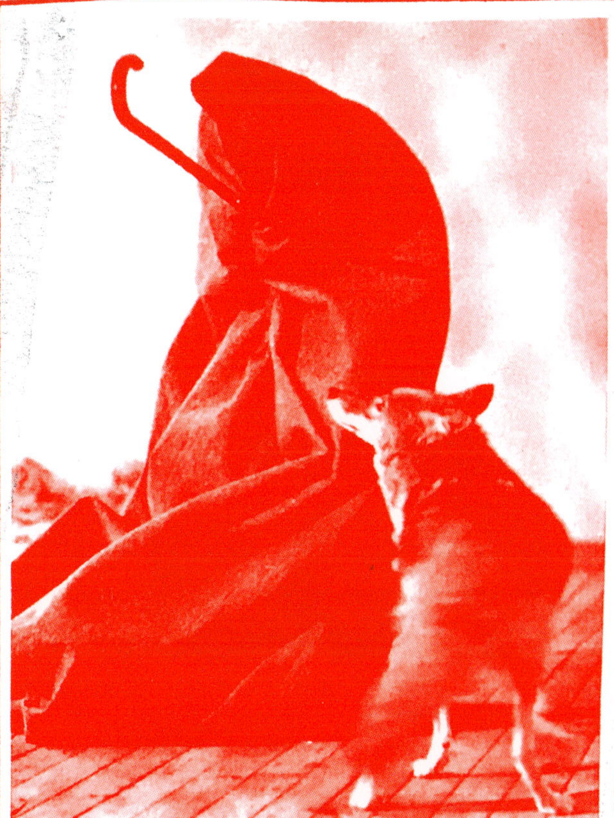

COYOTE

JOSEPH BEUYS

photographs by

CAROLINE TISDALL

CAROLINE TISDALL, art
critic of The Guardian,
will give a talk with slides
on JOSEPH BEUYS' "COYOTE"
on Sunday, April 24th, 1977,
at 8 p.m. Admission free.

"COYOTE" show by
BEUYS and TISDALL
closes on May 31st. 1977.

Gallery open Tuesday-Sunday,
1 to 6 p.m. Admission free.
Nearest tube: Warren street.

armly thank AIM, UMA (Holland), poets Edgell Rickword, Arthur Clegg, dsh, film-maker Joris
Clark, Matta, Claes Oldenburg, Christo, Kenneth Noland, Sol LeWitt, Lourdes Castro, Susan

RTISTS FOR DEMOCRACY **FITZROV**

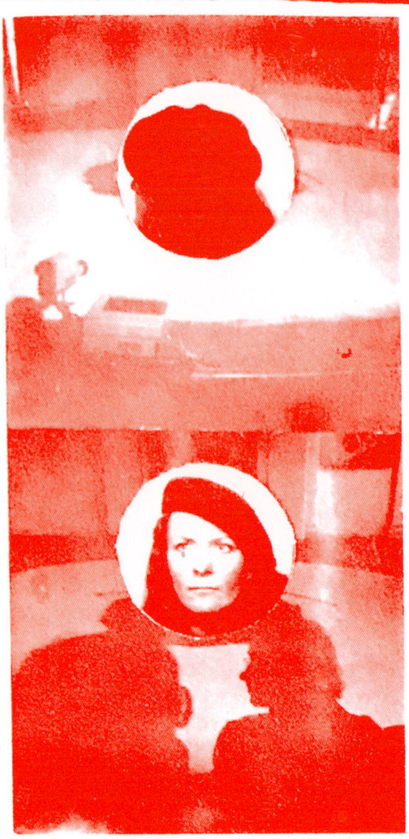

SHADOW WOMAN

live event with film by

TINA KEANE

Sunday, April 24th, 1977, at 9 p.m.

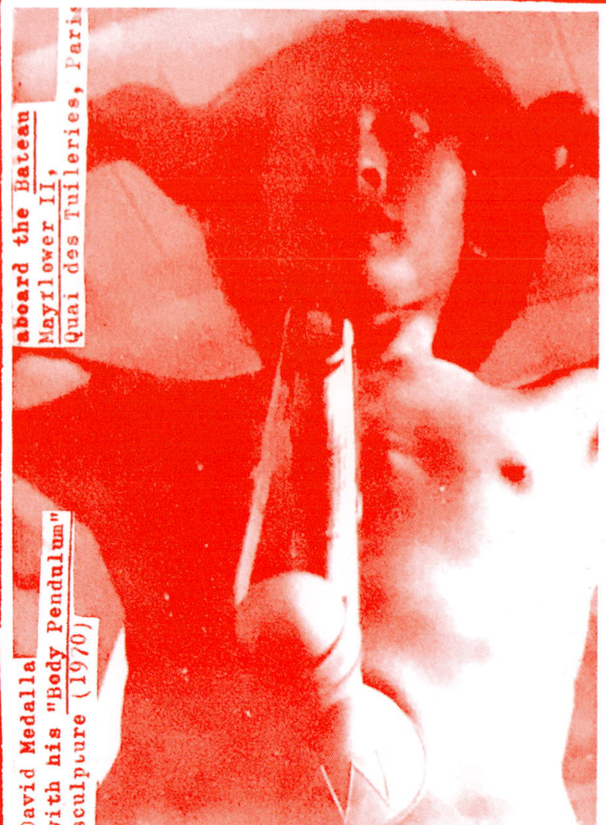

'Eskimo carver'

new works (1977), video,
drawings, paintings, events,
by **DAVID MEDALLA**

opens Sunday, May First 1977 at 8 p.m.,
closes on June 7th, 1977.

"Popular Art Forms
and
Modern Artists"

a lecture & slides show
by **GUY BRETT**

Sunday, May First 1977, at 7 p.m.

"VERNACULAR ART IN CAMDEN",
a mixed show featuring new art works, performance events, video, films, photos, books, and poems by Rasheed Araeen, Su Borrow, Virgil Calaguian, Ray Childerstone, Harriet Clarke, Philip Cohen, Robert Curwen, Tom Dragičević, Ian Findlay, Peter Fisher, Andrew Forrest, Lel Green, dom sylvester houédard (dsh), Charles Hustwick, George Isherwood, Atilio Lopez, Steve Oxley, Carlyle Reedy, Susan Romer, Rod Shepherd, Aro Soriano, Jun Terra, Giles Thomas, Steve Thorn, and other artists, opens on Sunday, June 12th, 1977, at 8 p.m.

Ivens, writers Mary McCarthy, Julio Cortazar, artists Sonia Delaunay, Meret Oppenheim,
Hiller, Joyce Weiland, Takis, Les Levine, Rene Bertholo, Paul Pechter, Pedro Uhart &
others for their support

A CULTURAL CENTRE 143 Whitfield St. London W1P 5RY

I do not have an image of my 'Eskimo Carver' contribution to the AFD exhibition although David Medalla once long ago showed me a photo of it alongside several other carver contributions and I wonder now if it could have been a knife-shaped piece of ice that was continuously replaced or melted back into its own knife-shaped mould as a tiny performance or did it simply drip down the wall and disappear or was it an objet trouvé a beachcombing perhaps a walrus tooth a ravaged horn or bone fragment or could I have wrapped a knife in written-out quotations from Raymond Carver as a Carver collage with words pulsating together 'I could hear my heart beating. I could hear everyone's heart. I could hear the human noise we sat there making, not one of us moving, not even when the room went dark' 'And what did you want? To call myself beloved, to feel myself beloved on the earth' 'That's all we have, finally, the words, and they had better be the right ones' 'A little autobiography and a lot of imagination are best'

Anne Bean

['Eskimo Carver'] is my only show here really, where I'm showing something deliberately, just on my own – and I even chose the least amount of space, compared to say the Joseph Beuys downstairs because – I'm not afraid of being accused of being egotistical or narcissistic or doing things only for myself – that doesn't really worry me – the thing is – my main interest in AFD, apart from the fact that upstairs is where I live, which is the basic interest, not being able to afford rent – is really to provide some space for people to come in and out – I feel once they can grasp that – I don't believe in say putting it down in words and then – they can grasp it, that they can grasp it, you know.

David Medalla

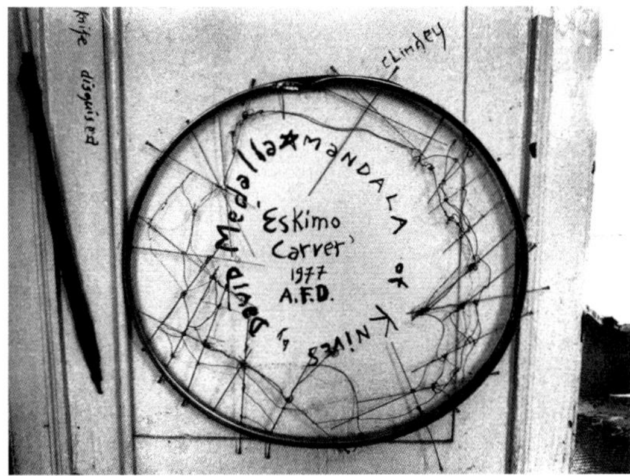

David Medalla, *Eskimo Carver* (detail), 143 Whitfield Street, May 1977

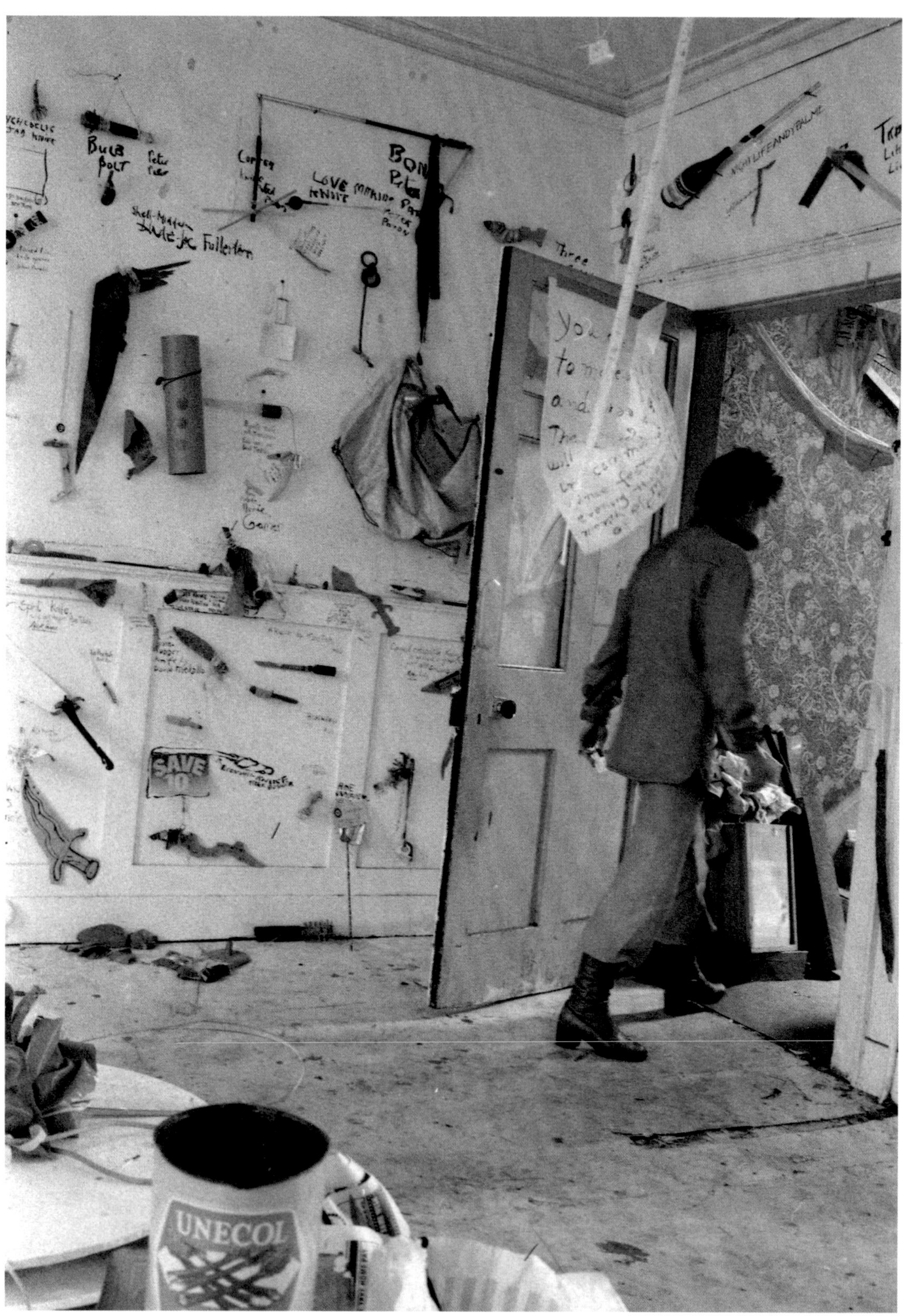

David Medalla, *Eskimo Carver*, 143 Whitfield Street, May 1977

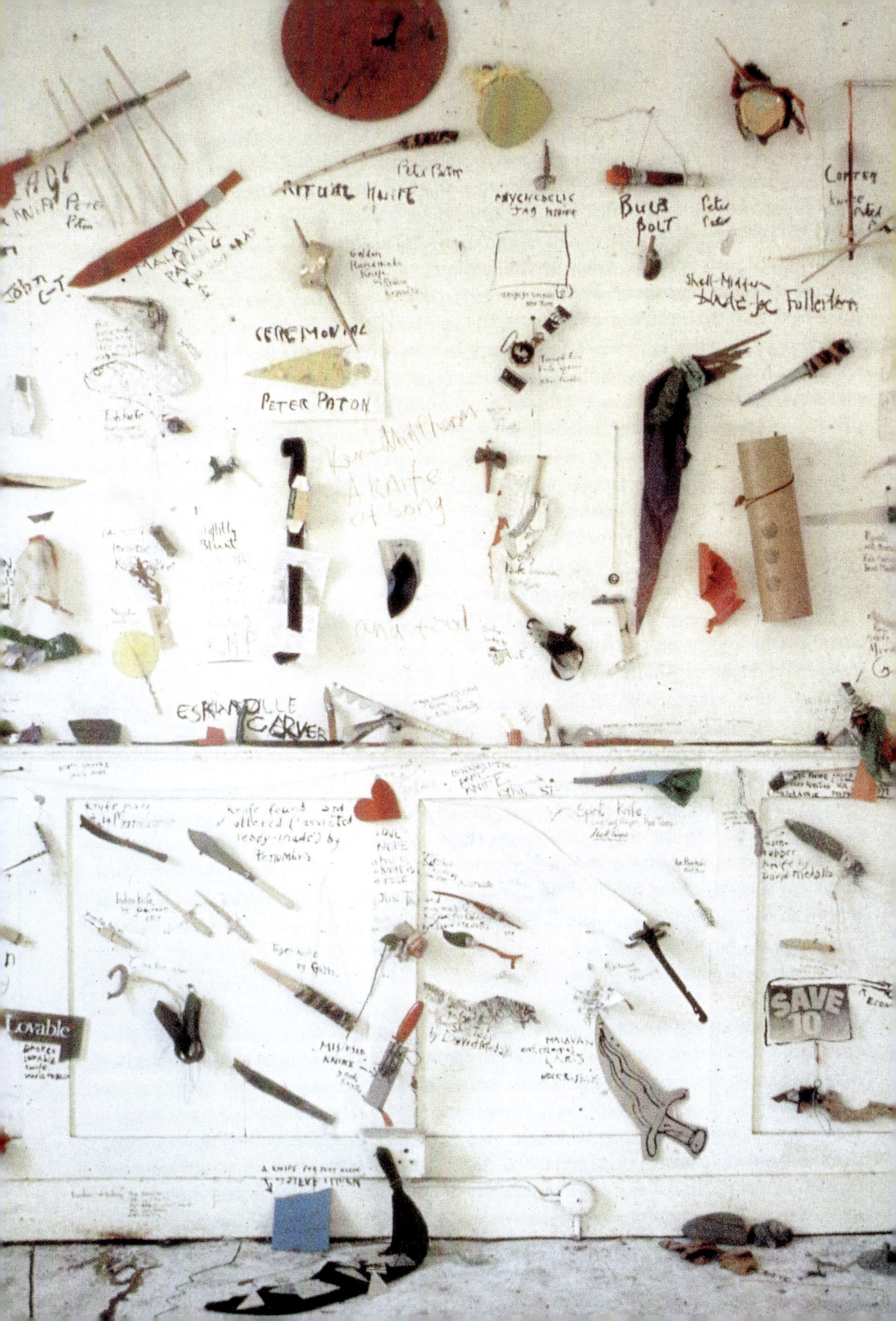

RITUAL KNIFE
Peter Paton
PSYCHEDELIC JAG KNIFE
BULB BOLT
Peter Paton
MALAYAN
Shell-Midden blade-Joe Fullerton
CEREMONIAL
PETER PATON
A knife of song
and tool
CARVER
Knife found and altered ("assisted ready-made") by
LOVE KNIFE
Sport Knife
Tiger knife
MISSILE KNIFE
MALAYAN
SAVE 10
Lovable

[David Medalla's 'Eskimo Carver'] consisted of several elements. There was an exhibition of his drawings and transcriptions of Eskimo poetry, and a performance, *Alaska Pipeline*, in which the British tabloid newspapers' glorification of pioneering pipe-layers combined with a racist denigration of the Inuit, effectively condemned itself. The third part was an invitation to visitors to make knives out of non-perishable garbage which had been collected in the neighbourhood and piled in a corner. The ambience opened people's minds in a certain way. The Inuit people have given some of the most succinct and eloquent descriptions that exist of the mixture of desire, anxiety and pleasure which is present in the human urge to compose poems and songs. They traditionally have a democratic, non-professional practice of creating them. As the collection of knives built up, everyone, including the artist, was astonished by the variety of people's contributions. They ranged from very functional-looking knives to remarkable kinds of fantasy. Medalla always stressed that his propositions were easy to enter. ... 'Eskimo Carver' could be said to have anticipated the wave of sculpture made from the scavenging and re-presentation of waste during the 1980s by a younger generation of ecologically-minded artists. For Medalla, however, the problems of consumerism and commodity production could not be illuminated by the mere creation by the artist of a new object, since they were bound up in the relationship between the artist and the public. ... At the same time, 'Eskimo Carver' was a kind of critico-poetic parody of the workings of ethnographic museums. And therefore it linked one part of the system, the context of contemporary art, with another part, the context of ethnographic art, and the image made by ethnographic museums of 'other cultures'.

Guy Brett

People can walk in and out of my situations. ... [T]hey are dependent on each person falling back on his or her own resources. ... [Their aim is] to infuse people with a certain kind of enthusiasm, to trust their own capacities to be creators. ... Artistic propositions are really just processes. ... [P]eople can be in them like oceans or seas, you can just sort of swim in them.

[...]

You cannot say that one knife is better than another. It is really a show – or a concept if you like – that effectively destroys the idea of the unique art object. ... If you put such a proposition in a public place, literally it's an endless proposition, there is no end to people coming in and making knives. I could easily inundate, say, the Tate Gallery.

David Medalla

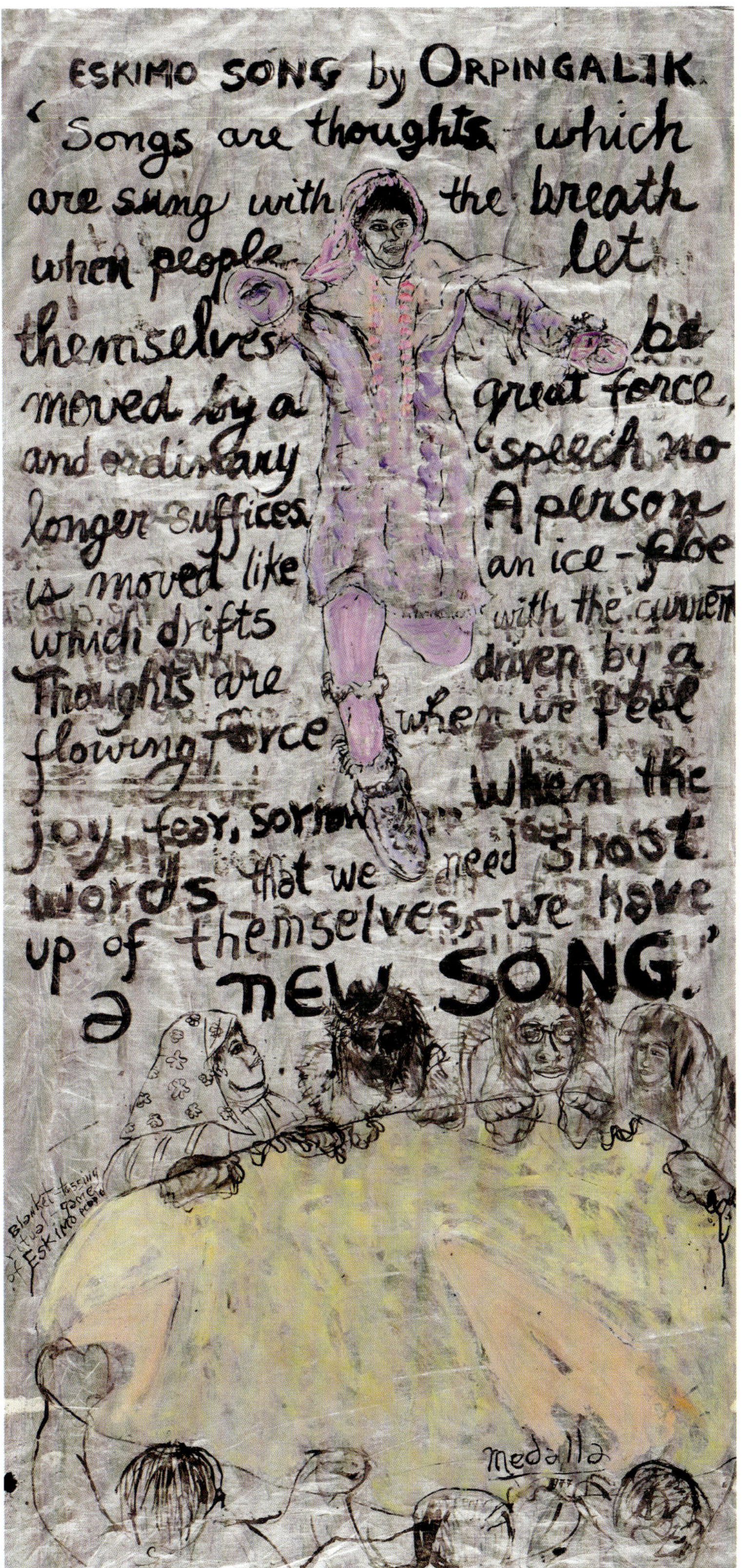

POETRY

IF YOU feel like making knives and drums from bits and pieces collected from dustbins around Whitfield Street then head over to the Artists for Democracy Fitzrovia Cultural Centre, 143 Whitfield Street, W.1 on Sunday at 8. David Medalla has devised this curious entertainment which he describes as a "performance art work inspired initially by beautiful Eskimo poems." Admission free but it's a good idea to take food and drink.

David Medalla, *Eskimo Carver (Eskimo Song by Orpingalik)*

DAVID MEDALLA
in conversation with Brandon Taylor

The French critic Pierre Restany, ideologue of *nouveau realisme* and friend of Tinguely, Christo and Yves Klein, once described David Medalla as "the marginal artist *par excellence*". Today, having figured prominently as painter, sculptor, earth artist, kinetic artist, happenings artist, gallery manager (at Signals, London, and at the Lisson), and teacher of art, Phillipine-born David Medalla now works from the centre he and Nick Payne direct at 143 Whitfield Street, London, otherwise known as the Fitzrovia Cultural Centre or Artists For Democracy. AFD has been going through a bad patch financially, as anyone can see who visits the now almost derelict building in Whitfield Street. But whether or not Whitfield Street survives the property-speculator, Medalla's work will continue, this time in the fields of performance art, environmental art, and what he calls participation-production art. He seems extraordinarily resilient to changes of fortune (both artistic and monetary), and may well justify many people's conviction that he is one of the most consistently under-rated artists now working in London.

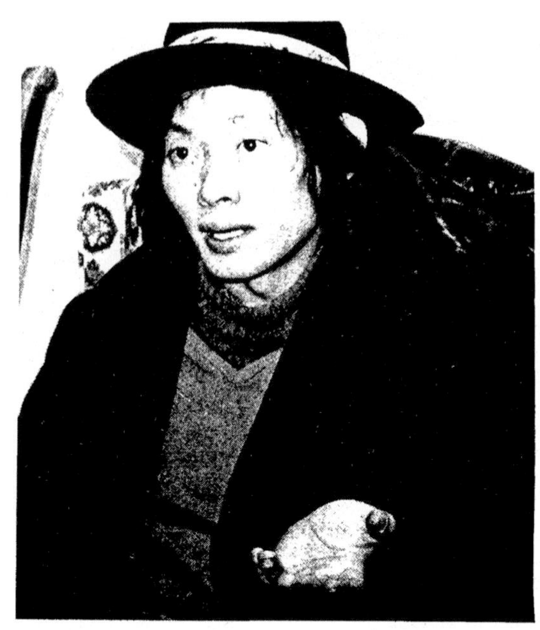

I was interested to discover whether he was still a marginal artist. I was also interested in learning something of his new performances, which English audiences know next to nothing about. We began by talking about the long-forgotten history of performance art. "It goes back to Shamanism, which itself is a kind of performance" he said. When I replied that Shamanism was not performance at all, so much as a form of ritual, he became insistent. "No, Shamans were *never* ritualists. They were not priests. Shamans were diametrically opposed to the priesthood. Priests appropriated certain gestures and incantations from Shamanism, and distorted them in order to bring about various material and spiritual results. Unlike the priests, the Shamans did not exist to reinforce an existing system of beliefs, but questioned the very existence of any such system. In performance art today there are a few priests, admittedly. But I'm certainly on the Shamanistic side."

I had always taken it for granted that the parentage of performance art in the twentieth century consisted of happenings, in the 1950's and 1960's, of Dada events and the early Futurist 'evenings' organised by Marinetti. What kind of happenings had Medalla been involved in, in the last ten years? He preferred to call them dance dramas. "One dance drama which I really enjoyed was in Trafalgar Square in 1967. It was during the Thang Loi Festival in support of the Vietnamese people's struggle against American aggression. I used the story of Chuang-Tzu's butterfly dream. In his dream he was a butterfly; but when he woke up he could not tell whether or not he was a butterfly dreaming he was a man. I used the idea of Chuang-Tzu waking up in a landscape that had been bombed by napalm. I was trying to put across the idea that one type of culture, specifically South-Eastern Asian culture, was really something that affirmed life, and that the American killers were destroying it. I also tried to put forward the idea that the lovers and creators of truth and beauty ultimately are the victors in any struggle. The drama took place in one of the fountains in Trafalgar Square. There were about twenty-five thousand people there. I was dressed like a puppet, and an identical figure, a life-size puppet, moved round the fountain on the other side. It was very dramatic and moving, as people who were there will tell you."

You often hear people ask why artists took to happenings and events in the early 1960s – but the more interesting question was why happenings and events had been appropriated as an expressive vehicle by *visual* artists particularly. "I don't know the full answer to that" Medalla said. "In the thirties there was a strong link between visual artists and the theatre. People like Heartfield, Moholy-Nagy, and George Grosz all did work in conjunction with people in the theatre. And early in the century the Russian pioneers of modern art such as Tatlin, Malevich, El Lissitsky and Popova all worked for the theatre. And then there was Diaghilev – a dynamo of the arts. We have no connection like that today. And in any case people in the commercial theatre are mostly interested in making careers. One very good thing about performance art, by the way, whether it is successful or unsuccessful, is that it challenges the isolation of the artist. Some artists are totally isolated from other fellow beings when they make their art. Obviously there is a necessity now for artists to get together, and to work together. In the past, you did this by spending time in cafes. In fact most events were done in cafes. But now cafes of that kind, such as the Cabaret Voltaire in Zurich or the Cafe Pittoresque in Moscow, don't exist.

"When people ask me about performance art I always say that its present condition is symptomatic of a kind of new unification of the arts. You have this occuring at certain historical stages. The most significant was the Baroque era. Baroque is something unified; we understand it to include Bernini and Bach as well as Caravaggio, Rembrandt, Vermeer, Velasquez and Rubens, the five great Baroque painters. Historically the Baroque came about because of the expansion of Europe into America and the consolidation of centralised monarchical rule in the European nation states. Artistically it represented the release of a lot of energies, and the exploration of certain definite themes, certain definite areas of experience". Was something like this taking place again, I asked? He thought it was. "Even the rather romantic concepts of fifteen years ago, like Buckminster Fuller's and Marshall McLuhan's concept of the global village – it was rather naive, but it was near the point. Take this tape-recorder. It is a tool that you not only find in a place like this in Dalston, but also in the jungles of Columbia. And the camera, flashing there. There is one in this room, and there is one also flashing on the moon. The electronic age is definitely for real. And alongside it there has been a breakdown of every kind of social structure. You could see this beginning in the May events in Paris in 1968, and in the flower power movements in America and England, and the hard rock movement that was beginning to appear here, as well as the tropicalia movement in Brazil – even the cultural revolution in China. If you look at the external forms of these phenomena, you will of course see nothing in common between them, between a batallion of Red Guards rushing up and down writing Dazibad (that is wall-newspapers) in Tien An Men and Peking, and groups of youngsters dancing at Hyde Park Corner saying we must legalise pot. But the essence is the same. It is the desire of people to be truly free beings. The movement of the Red Guards was liberating, just as rock music is liberating. It is important to remember that we are on the same planet as the people of China."

We passed on to the subject of Medalla's own performances. People are often struck by the elaborate underlying structure of these works, which, though often unplanned, allows the same theme or set of relationships to emerge again and again, altered and transposed, as in a fugue. I particularly wanted to know about the structure of the performance which involved Tatlin and Malevich. "In this piece I became very interested in the idea of obliteration", Medalla explained. "One specific image that inspired me was a photograph of women working in Brazil in a computer factory. We are taught that in the bifurcation of the sexes, man implanted the seed in the woman. The woman is the receptor. Here you had a group of women. They're not pregnant, or waiting to be impregnated. They are working in a factory, which is a contradiction of what was supposed to be their biological role, which was to create and nourish life. You see I believe in the saying: women hold one half of heaven. But here they had to do one specific motion, perhaps glue together two pieces of a micro-circuit. They are doing it for eight hours a day, for the greater part of their lives, and in return for meagre wages. Our sensory faculties are supposed to have developed over thousands of years, and yet at the end of that process a great majority of people have to obliterate 99 per cent of what is presented to their senses. I found this paradoxical and disturbing, that a small section of humanity, the international monopoly capitalists, could invent such madness. So this theme of obliteration is really one of the elements of the Tatlin and Malevich piece. On the other hand there is an autobiographical element too, because there was a period in my life when I was discovering love again, and relating to another person; and at the same time I became aware of how two people who love one another can have contradictions that obliterate each other's thoughts and feelings. I did not see Tatlin and Malevich as lovers, but I saw them as ideological and cosmic complimentaries. In fact in the end I saw Tatlin as the sun, as a solar being, and Malevich as the moon, as a lunar being. The famous quarrel they had I interpreted as an eclipse. Two kinds of minds, both creative, put in opposition at an important historical juncture, the moment of the Bolshevik revolution. Malevich's work was always lunar; the first suprematist canvases of his were for Victory Over the Sun. And Tatlin's last work was called The Moon On Stage. You see, underneath all the apparently random things that I do there is a very mandala-like sructure. It is difficult to describe. You have to see the work for yourself."

He explained that another theme in most of his work was that of democracy. "I've always believed in Lenin's concept of the democratic and socialist elements in all people's cultures; but I've always interpreted this concept in a way that conflicts with my friends of the far left. What I mean by democratic is . . . there are certain things that we all share. You see, you may have a higher income than me, but if we have to cross the road we both have to use our eyes. The same with eating. The Buddha said that the only sickness that can never be cured is hunger. Even in New York restaurants where very 'sophisticated' people eat ants, or caterpillars, they are still eating and trying to cure their hunger." I asked for an example of how this democratic element appeared in his art, and he chose the example of a performance that took place on Parliament Hill, "many years ago", called Questions of King Milinda. "This performance was based on a classic Buddhist text which is the most brilliant synthesis of Ionian Greek dialects and Indian psychology. What happened was that the hundreds of people who came to Parliament Hill were formed into a big human body which then walked around the hill! Some people were part of the brain, some were part of the hands, some were part of the legs. If you were in the toes you would not be able to see the shoulders, the body was so large. The kids who were running around trying to make trouble and pull the thing apart we decided to incorporate as fleas and lice in the hair of the head. Then five people forming one of the hands held a gigantic comb, so that the kids would be combed out of the hair! It was really incredible. This took place every Sunday from May until October, and each week we would think of a new action for the body, scratching itself, or clapping hands. I remember that clapping was very difficult to synchronise, because the two hands kept missing each other!"

I suggested that the democratic and socialist element appeared in this work in three ways: as something that was enjoyable, as something that people actually wanted to do, and as something that involved everybody. He agreed. The multi-human body became a symbol as well as a literal depiction of how individuals ought to be related to each other. "People were free to choose a different part of the collective body each time we enacted the piece".

It was time to talk about Medalla's new work, some of which had already been performed in January this year, in Paris. "I work simultaneously on two or four or even eight pieces" he explained. "At this stage in my development I find that I am synthesising my researches of the last fifteen years. For example my large environmental sculpture of 1975 called The Mountain, which is a factory for people to make tiny mountains, was a development of other earlier artworks such as my project of 1964 for monumental bread-making machines (I hope to show the drawings and maquettes for this work at the Food Show which Roger

Malbert is organising this summer at Kettle's Yard in Cambridge), the project of 1966 for a peelable village, or my participation-production work of 1973 entitled Porcelain Wedding. But even in my new work . . . if one is looking for a major theme in all the disparate things I do, you find it has always been the problem of culture. Culture is what unifies people, but what also divides them. That is the paradox. Perhaps I have been able to see this because I have moved about so much from one culture to another". Not freely, he wanted to stress, but at least he had been able to move.

I asked how this concern with the idea of culture was expressed in his new work called A La Recherche Des Cinq Inconnus. "It's a series of five performances about five people who lived at some moments of their enigmatic lives in Paris. The inconnus . . . they were people who, when they were alive and living in Paris, were relatively unknown. They were enigmatic persons". Were they contemporaries? Who were the five? "No, not all of them were contemporaries. Lautreamont and Rimbaud lived in Paris at approximately the same time. But the other three, Ho Chi Minh, Franz Fanon and Tatlin, they were obviously not all contemporaries. Lautreamont was in Paris just before the Paris Commune. There is a theory, which I rather subscribe to, that he was in fact killed by the secret police because of his dealings with communists and anarchists."

I had no idea I was going to use five people. In fact this came about in a strange way. I was visiting a fortune teller in Montmartre and I was a bit early, so I went down to the Place Clichy to watch a striptease show. It was really geared to the immigrant workers who are now living in that part of Paris. There happened to be five strippers in the show, and I was amazed by them. They were very beautiful. I was in a sort of daze after having seen them. But I was still early to see the fortune teller, and I wandered around Abbesses and came into a fish shop. It was snowing, and the shop was brightly lit up. I began talking to the manager of the shop and his assistant, and asked hin whether I could do a small experiment with the fish. First of all I asked him the names of the fish, and he gave a very systematic list of what he had for sale. I was looking at the eyes of those fish and trying to communicate with them, you know! Their forms had evolved over very long periods of time. They had all adapted to different conditions in the sea, but they had now been brought out of the sea and put in boxes for people to buy. I realised next that different people came to buy the different types of fish. The wife of the fishmonger introduced me to the customers as they came in. They were mostly women who told me what their husbands did for a living. They all pursued specialised occupations; one was an architect, another was a laywer, a third was a clerk, a fourth worked in the metro, and so on. So here was a mirror image of what happens in the sea, in the lives that people were living around Abbesses. The differences in their tastes, also, was a cultural thing, an adaptation to conditions. Some cannot bear to eat oysters, some save all their money to have a lobster . . ."

But what, I interrupted, did this have to do with the five inconnus? "Well, the sea came into Lautreamont's poetry, and he is also very much concerned with taste. But more importantly, the inconnus came eventually to symbolise for me the five senses of man. Marx wrote that the development of the senses is the history of mankind. Tatlin symbolises the tactile, Franz Fanon the olfactory, Lautreamont the sense of taste, Rimbaud the auditory, and Ho Chi Minh the visual, because Ho worked in Paris as a photographer for tourists, and also made fake Chinese antiquities, to fool the foolish eye. Again, you would really have to see the performances to appreciate how these themes fit together."

Medalla's latest performance work? "The next one I want to do will be entitled The Pictorial Biographies of Mozart and Medalla. It's been germinating in my mind for some time. It started like this. I owe a lot of people a lot of money just at the moment. Mainly I owe money to companies and banks. I had the idea that if I owe money to the electricity board, there should be Zeus coming and hitting me with a thunderbolt, as in a Greek comedy! Nepture would come from the water board, and so on. There is a passage in Marx's Introduction to Political Economy which I remember, where he says that the old Greek gods and goddesses do not compare to the new gods and goddesses of the industrial age. The Roman goddess Fama is feeble compared to Printing House Square. Mercury, who is on the Interflora design, was never as quick as telegraph wires. Then I was very interested in Mozart's music for the freemasons. He was a freemason, and his death, as an inconnu, really, may well have been due to some freemasons who did him in because he used some of their secret music for The Magic Flute. This is only one of the stories about Mozart's death – but at the end of his life no one really knew what was happening to him. There was also his friendship with Doctor Mesmer, which will come into this work. Doctor Mesmer was a precursor both of psychiatrists and advertising men, who today have a symbiotic relationship with one another."

"I don't yet know the form of this event. But when I read this pictorial biography of Mozart, and how he couldn't pay his bills, it seemed so similar to my relationship with the Water Board and the Gas Board and the other boards. There are various parallels. The event will be a kind of exploration of why certain people, especially artists and working people, cannot pay their bills. The explanation cannot be metaphysical. Debts are not made in heaven.

(photos by Jackie Gaff)

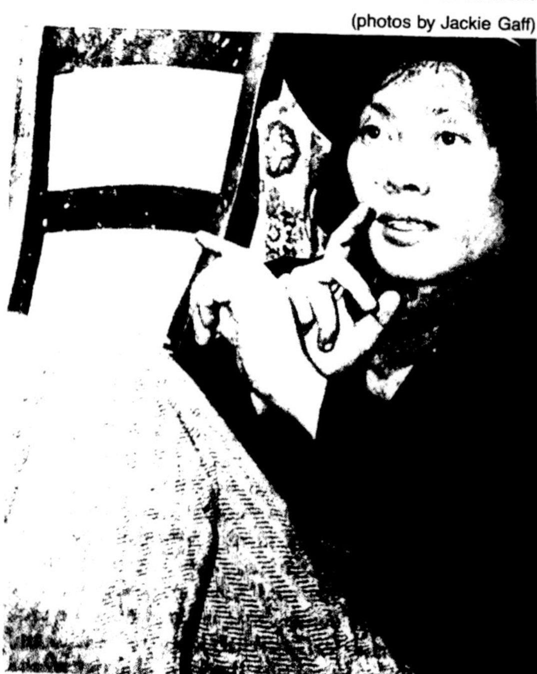

And after all, artists are on the whole reasonable people, not parasites on society as they are often portrayed by hack journalists."

Something that has always interested me is how performance art differs from the theatre. Why are performances not repeated night after night, as in a theatrical run? "It's a question of demand, really" he said "there is nothing about a performance that makes it unrepeatable". What was the ideal place to do a performance? Trafalgar Square? "Anywhere is an ideal place. What is an ideal place to make love? I've made love going up an elevator in the Empire State Building, which is just as ideal as a beautiful room". I explained that I was thinking more about the audience than about the room where the performance took place. I pointed out that if you go to the ACME Gallery or Butler's Wharf you see performance artists doing performances in front of other performance artists, or other artists of some kind. No one else seemed to go to these places. "I don't mind that" he countered. "That is irrelevant, really. We are seeing the early stages of this phase in the history of performance art. Don't forget that the people who looked at Cubist paintings were other Cubist painters, to begin with."

I reminded him that he had once told me that he wanted AFD to be a local centre."Well, it has been to some extent. The problem is that there is no coherent local life in that area. You find that people who live there work elsewhere, and people who work there live elsewhere. In any case we have had a variety of shows. There was the American Indian Movement show, which people came from all over England and Wales and Scotland as well as Europe to see, and on the other hand we have done events there which are only likely to attract certain local people, such as puppet-plays for children and concerts for old-age pensioners."

I ended by asking him what kind of work would be put on at AFD in the future. Was it going to be democratic? Or revolutionary? "I am not prepared to die for a mere career in the bourgeois art world" he said, "as Gina Pane who eats razor blades or Rudolf Schwarzkogler who castrated his penis. I think that's extreme. I don't believe bourgeois art is important enough to justify that. I believe in experimentation, but I always ask myself the question *for whom*? whenever I create anything. We will try to be revolutionary, yes. Otherwise there is no point in doing art."

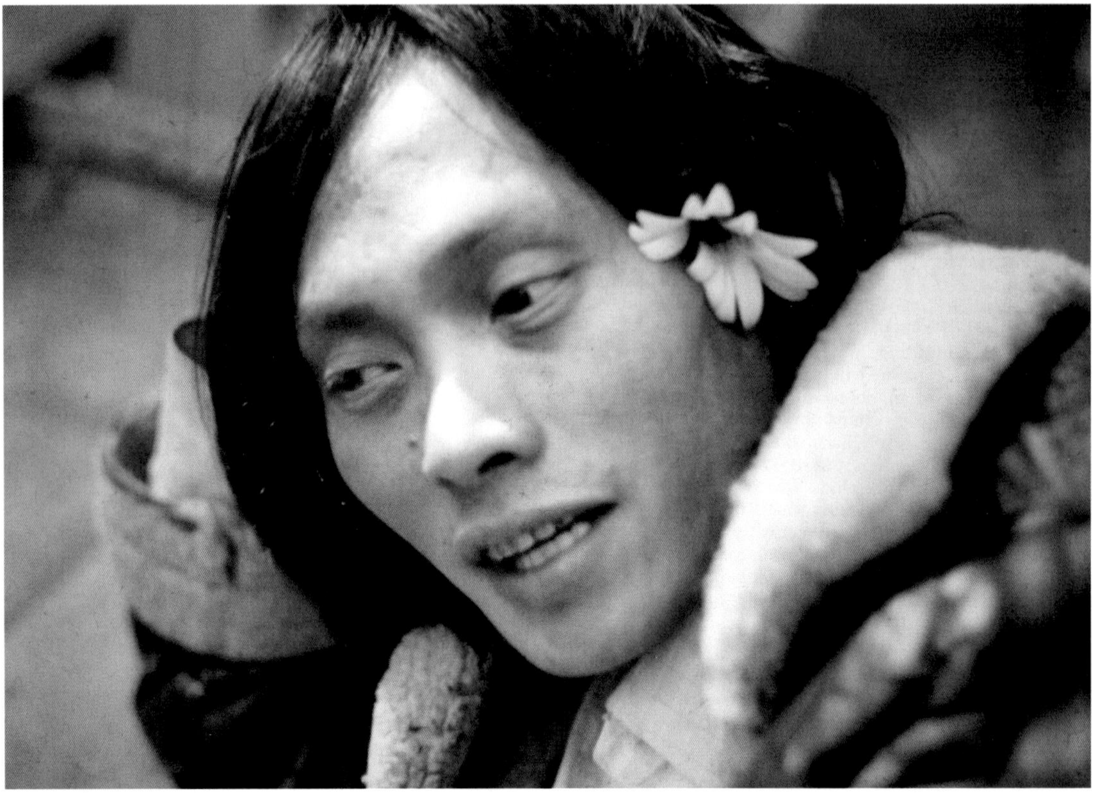

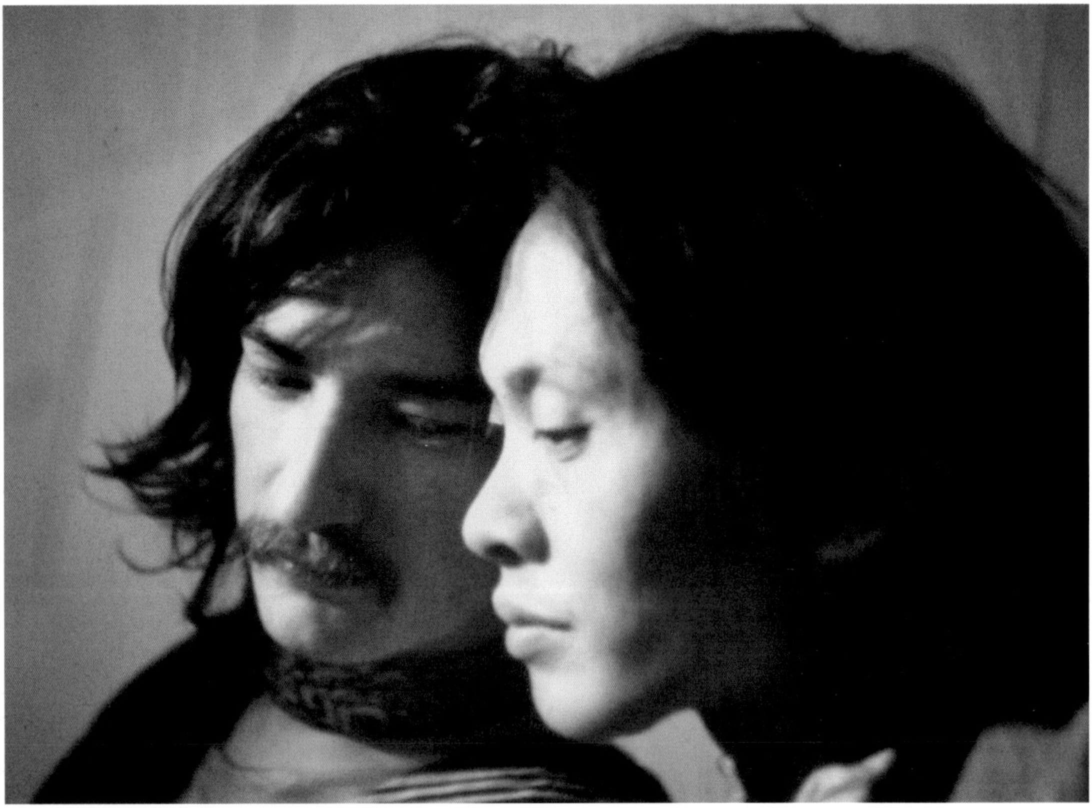

David Medalla and Nick Payne

Sweeping Gestures was a last minute addition to one of the AFD shows. It consisted of a man, smiling, waving his arms and blowing kisses in a manner recognisably camp as he moved slowly winding his way through the assembled audience. A second performer emerged in another part of the room working his way slowly amongst the audience, earnestly sweeping the floor, moving people out of his way if necessary. The first character was Trevor Thomas and the second character was myself. Trevor Thomas was a leading light in the Campaign for Homosexual Equality in Bedford (where he lived at the time), and the father of artist Giles Thomas. A visual juxtaposition of a gay liberation vibe with a reminder of the reality of working lives trapped in class struggle, it was an open-ended schemata that left the audience to construct meaning for themselves, arousing both seriousness, perplexity and amusement. David [Medalla] would incorporate artists and others into the open days arranged around the exhibitions. So the dates for an exhibition, 'Vernacular Art in Camden' for example, would be set and printed on the flyers or handwritten invitations, and usually a weekend or a Sunday would have a suite of associated events. Events could range between lecture-style presentations, open discussions, a film, a performance, or other live 'events'. One could find oneself incorporated into the flow at the drop of a hat. Such was *Sweeping Gestures*, an unrehearsed, improvised – and in David's terminology – an impromptu performance happening.

We didn't really think of it in these terms, but AFD was a queer space, at least to me – and I know through experience, to many others too. That needs to be put into a context that the people coming to AFD manifestations, events, exhibitions, whatever, were taken from a much wider demographic of age, gender and diversity. People were drawn in from surrounding shops and service providers as well as varied occupational groups, visiting political and socio/political/artworld groups and practising artists and speakers. My connection to AFD was as much personal as it was to the artistic proposition that the Fitzrovia Cultural Centre was. I was also searching for a life in which to continue to work as an artist and find a way of remaining in London, and at the same time pass through the experience of youth, of love, of friendships. Spending time at AFD was the perfect fit, and it was David that spotted me as an outsider and invited me in. I became fascinated by the conversations, the discussions, the laughter, the satire, the wit, the constant talk of artists and where 'art history' was in the present tense. It was more the fact that David and friends (Jun Terra and Virgil Calaguian) lived a life of freedom, of freedoms many globally could not live. AFD never consciously aligned itself to the many sectional groups emerging in these years such as the Gay Liberation Front, the Campaign for Homosexual Equality, or even the Sisters of Perpetual Indulgence. But the background was a London ten years on from the passing of the laws which decriminalised homosexuality between adults over 21. This liberalisation still had a way to go to remove further inequalities – the position of the Isle of Man, the age of consent, civil partnership and so forth still not yet recognised.

I get the idea that all the last exhibitions at AFD were in fact a rolling sequence that did not really separate out into distinct exhibitions as we think of them in the gallery world. 'Informal' would be to understate its improvisatory nature. Things would be put up and taken down, or put up somewhere different. *Eskimo Carver* grew and grew eventually replacing anything else that was there hitherto, maybe including my own early *Trans-Apparent* pieces (but to be honest I don't fully remember).

Charles Hustwick

I was absolutely thrilled when David Medalla booked me a Sunday afternoon slot at AFD to present a performance. I was by nature and habit a performer. Having tried unsuccessfully to get into RADA (Royal Academy of Dramatic Art), I happened to meet philosopher G.A. Cohen – Jerry – at a party and he persuaded me to join his philosophy department at University College London. Knowing that he had another life as a stand-up comedian/impersonator, I thought it would be fun to ask him to join me and do something comical. The brief for the AFD event was totally open. Thus I would be Myra Braggee, TV interviewer, and he would be Karl Marx, who has come back to life in 1977. The scene is set.

I asked him questions such as 'How has Soho changed since you were last there?' He answered in the voice of Groucho Marx (having conveniently brought a Groucho moustache with him), exclaiming 'We didn't have the girls! All serious politics happened in Soho then, though life was lived very freely, no structure to day or night, and lots of drinking. Still I managed to write Das Kapital there, how I don't know! I'm sorry my ideas didn't work out' 'What surprised you the most?' 'Going to the moon – I would never have dreamt that was possible.' Stuff like that. Jerry hijacked the whole performance, but never mind. He gave a very funny lecture on Karl Marx with lots of jokes and impersonations. I was the 'straight man'. We reprised the performance a couple of years later at the ICA.

Roberta Kravitz

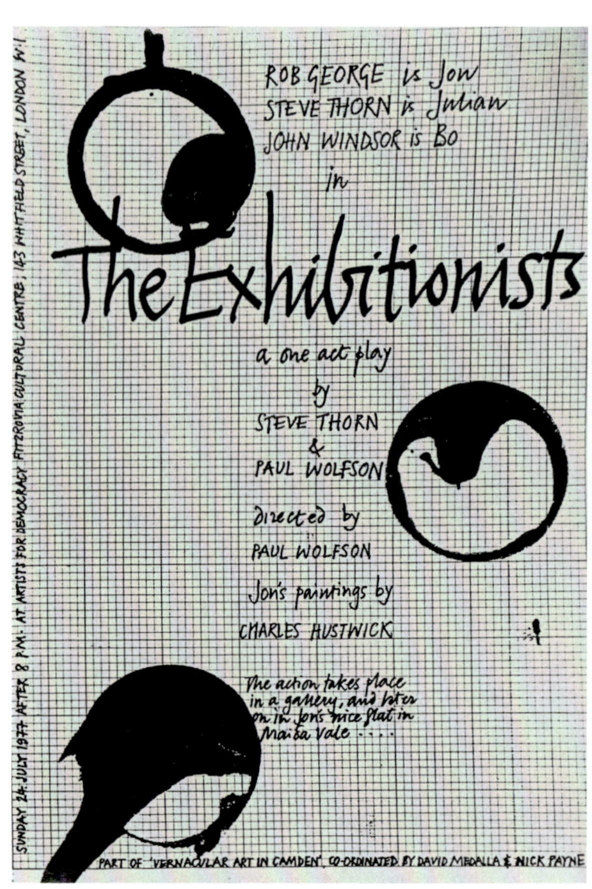

I remember David [Medalla] saying something to the effect that the title 'Vernacular Art in Camden' was as an ironic riposte to some Arts Council or Tate Gallery exhibition that was scheduled around the same time. It's stuck in my mind that the exhibition was celebrating the Bloomsbury Group. (I got the feeling he didn't rate them particularly, which is not my opinion exactly, their art could be weak or derivative but their rebellion against Victorian values, pioneering of modernism in Britain, and their free-thinking and acting out in their sexual/social relations were all innovative.) 'The Bloomsbury Group' sounds grand; 'Vernacular Art in Camden' stresses the indigenous, the local. I think that was the idea behind the title.

Charles Hustwick

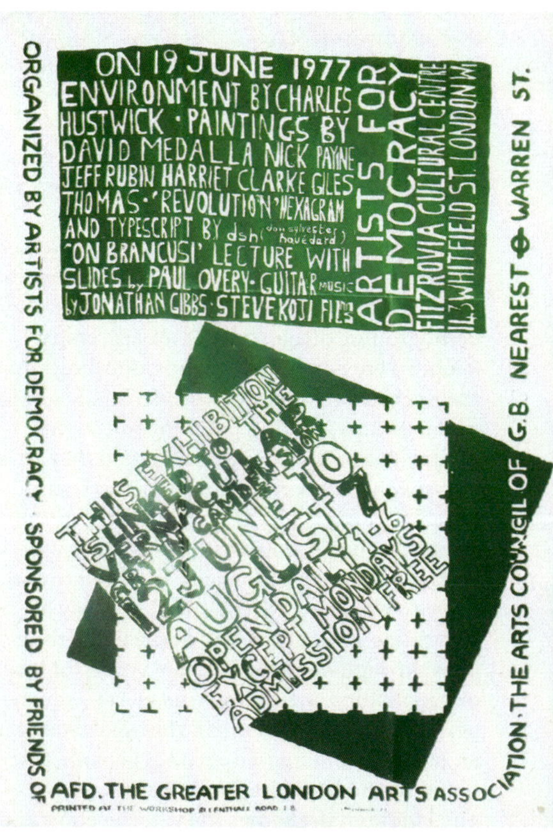

A.F.D.

may present 'art' as part of its whole function as gallery, community centre, space for whatever is needed, but the space seems part of the community – by operating in that space one becomes a part of that community. During the times I've been present at both venues the audience has reflected this difference. The audience at Acme has consisted to a greater extent of artists/performers, and at A.F.D. of the local community. A.F.D. has an atmosphere of beginnings/trying out, Acme of presentation of matured work. Both places could be seen as complementary parts of the same system with A.F.D. functioning as a workshop, Acme as a presentation centre.

Sheer Madness are a newly formed group working in the political/community field. Under the direction of George Isherwood they presented a barrage of songs, film, slides, drama and a puppet show relating to the Spanish Civil War. In terms of communication they were highly effective, working at such a fast pace, with so much imput that one's interest could not fail to be aroused. The puppet show and final short drama from Lorca were so funny that I almost forgot the political content.

Stephen Cripps performed at Acme, and also at the end of the evening at A.F.D. At Acme he was in the lower gallery. The space was full of all manner of equipment – ancient projectors, film screens, a row of gongs, a large speaker cabinet, a string of small unboxed speakers on the floor, and many devices whose function wasn't apparent until they blew, spun or burnt. An image of a garden and a space-suited man were projected until the screens were consumed by flames. A wheeled turntable moved slowly across the floor, the turning wheels causing the record to play. Firecrackers behind the gongs caused echoing explosions. A fire extinguisher revolved under the power of its own emissions. Some of the devices failed to work (which unfortunately gave the piece too great an air of comedy) and the audience was somewhat effected by smoke. This problem did not exist at A.F.D. as the performance took place in the open air. A long black painted flag hung from two uprights above a brocade drape. Everything was consumed by fire, the flag burning with a magnesium flare. Snaking tubes behind belched orange smoke as Stephen ignited and directed the conflagration. The pieces had an ephemeral majesty that is difficult to convey as all is cause and effect, creation and destruction.

from Suzy Adderley, '"Five Days in July" performances at Acme, and at AFD', *Artscribe*, September 1977

official complaint about police violence. Mr Chris Ball, London area organiser of APEX, alleged that one of the organisers of the strike, Mr John Patel, aged 23, had been repeatedly hit by a policeman who called him a "Paki bastard."

"PAKI BASTARD"
(Portrait of the artist as a black person)
a live event with slides and sound by
RASHEED ARAEEN

"Paki Bastard" is the 2nd part of the trilogy (art events) which was conceived in 1976-77 as part of **Preliminary Notes for a BLACK MANIFESTO** published in **Black Phoenix** No.1 and which deals with the relationship between the Third World and the West. "Paki Bastard", first performed on July 31 1977 at the ARTISTS FOR DEMOCRACY, London, specifically reflects upon the predicament of black people in Britain; showing also how a black artist, uprooted from his original environment in the Third World and rejected by white society in the West, eventually comes to terms and identifies with the reality of his people. The 1st and 3rd parts, called "Noble Savage" and "Blood Sausages" respectively, will, it is hoped, be performed later this year.

N O T E

The following 6 photographs is a selection from 50 sequences. The text is not exactly the interpretation of the images here, but contains some of the thoughts that went into the making of the work. And although it contains autobiographical references, it would be wrong to read it at personal level.

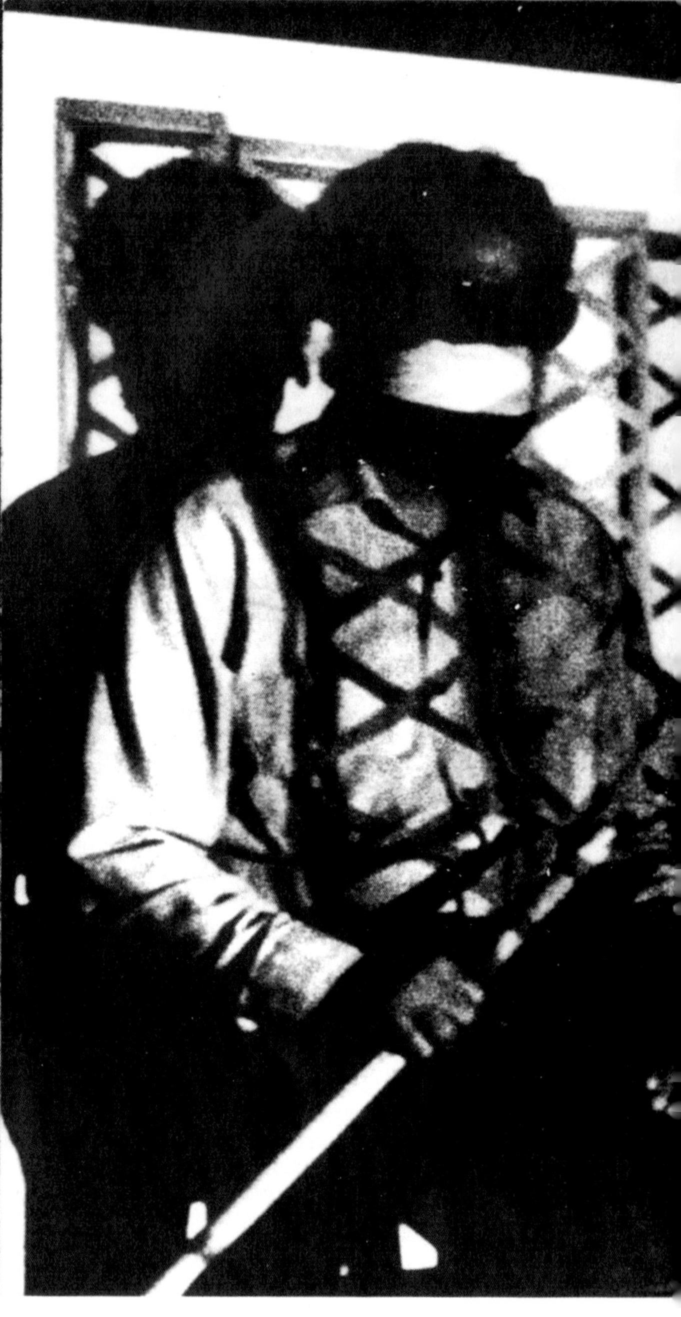

He sits there facing a slide projector, blind and gagged, holding a broom that defines h role in the contemporary world. In the background is the flute sound he made some time a when he was very depressed. (He can't play 'music'.) The projector projects on him the image of one of his earlier works, the purpose being to create an artistic identity whic is used throughout the piece in various manners. It also alludes, at a different level, the mythical space, which is elevated, privileged and universalised, and in which the art of the bourgeois world ends up cocooned and incarcerated. It is the mythical space withi which the bourgeois 'freedom of artistic expression' manifests, and which is inversely p portional to the real space at the bottom of the hierarchical pyramid. The black, Third World, person thus remains outside this space confronted with reality.

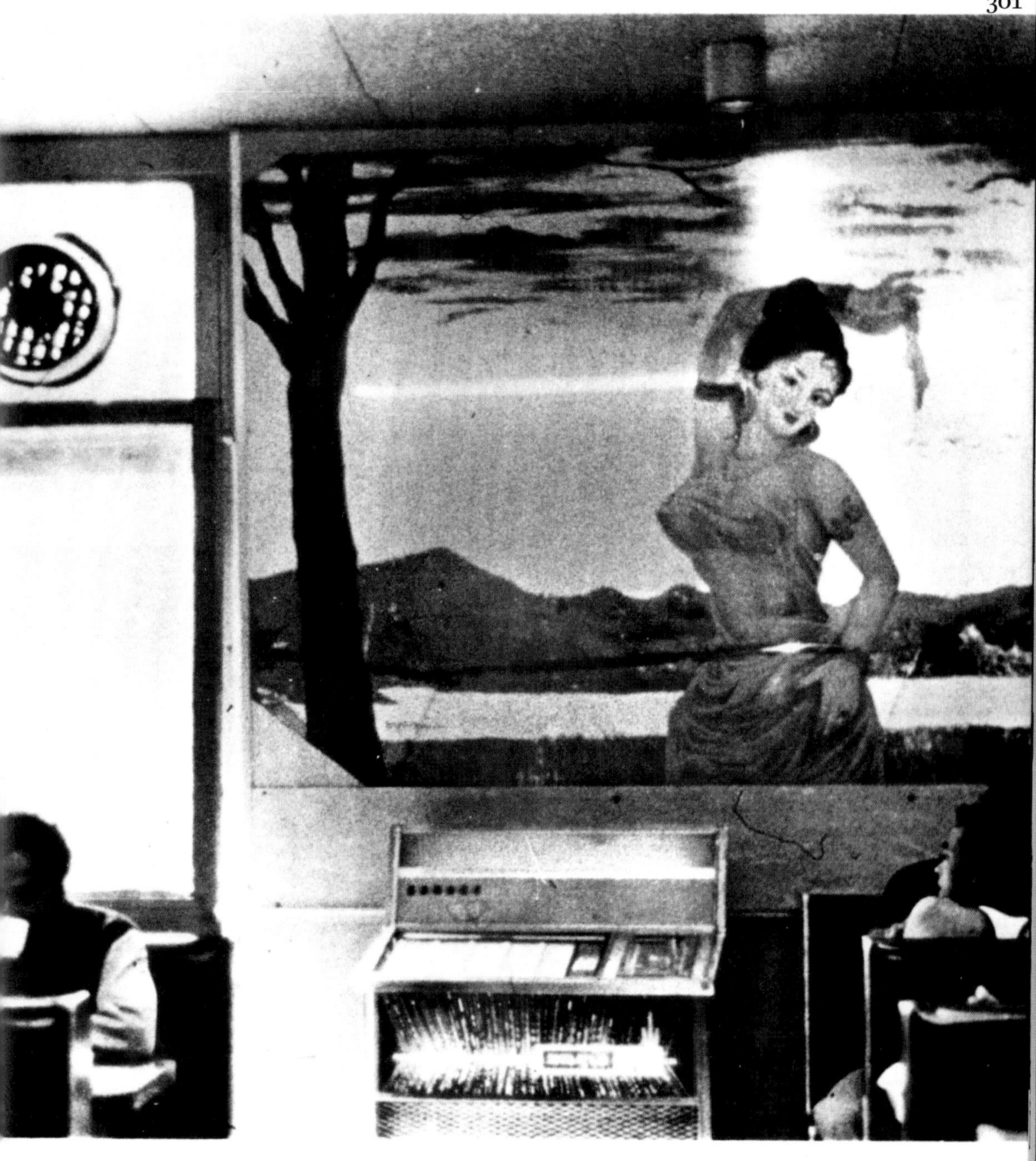

Sitting alone in a café in Brick Lane, he listens to the sexy, jazzy, romantic, sugary, vulgar, ... Indian film songs that pour out continuously from a jukebox. He is overtaken by nostalgia... He thinks of the time, his youth, when he himself secretly entertained the thoughts of becoming a film hero... He remembers his friends with whom he went to school/ university, with whom he spent long evenings sitting in cafés and quite often talking about what was new from the West - literature, art, films, etc. How they all longed for the free and bohemian life in Paris, London, New York,... He thinks of his mother, father, brothers and sisters, who are still waiting for his return. They thought that their eldest son, their eldest brother, would one day be a successful engineer - after all he did complete his graduation. He would have been the pride of the family! But he had the crazy idea

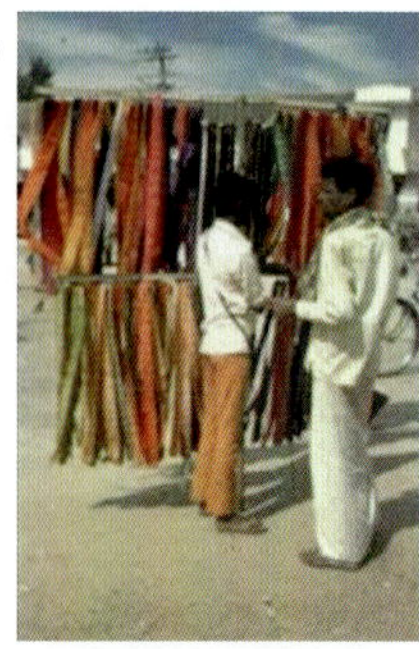

My association with AFD was very brief. It just so happened I was at the right place at the time with various artist friends who were members of AFD, hence my invitation to share images of my travels from India. It must have been a show of images taken during my travels in India in 1975–76. This was my first in-depth self-discovery of my 'Cultural Heritage'. I travelled for nearly one year (two days short, due to my return ticket date). It was a very profound realisation of my 'Cultural "Heritage"' that is India in all its 'Multiple Cultural Glory'. It still astonishes me that I managed to extend that travel for twelve months. Rasheed [Araeen]'s performance and my slide show were very educational to me personally.

Saleem Arif Quadri

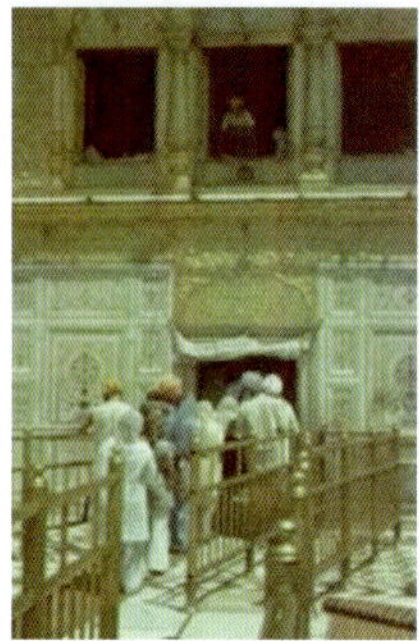

At A.F.D. the first piece was a performance by Rasheed Araeen, *Paki Bastard*. Announced by the performer as neither political, nor political art, and only violent because his life contains violence, the performance allowed the facts to speak for themselves. It used film, slides and action to express the apparent unwillingness of the police to protect the Asian community from violence. Examples given were of a man stabbed by a white boy being asked to drop charges to protect community relations, and of a policeman on duty at Grunwick calling a picket a "paki bastard" as he beat him. There was some trouble with slide/sound co-ordination, and some obscure imagery, but the expression was clear. The problem of racial disharmony, and the role of the police is well known. The problem lies in the minds of the community and can only be solved on a community level. The next event at A.F.D. was a show of slides of India taken by Saleem Arif. By giving us a greater understanding of the origins and customs of another race, this kind of activity might go further towards solving racial tensions than that of the previous piece, which displayed a high degree of alienation.

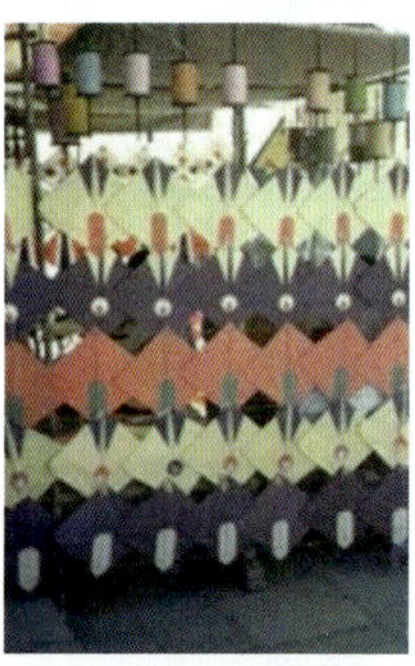

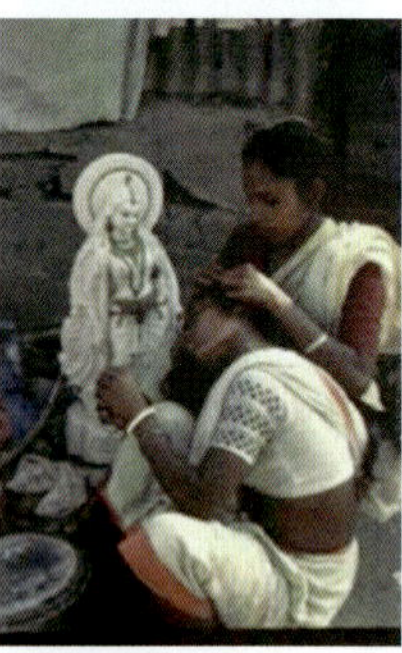

Ms Adderley is probably right in saying that my work has "displayed a high degree of alienation", but the way she has put it amounts to its condemnation. She should have first looked at the society which creates alienation and particularly the one she has detected in my work. It has become a fashionable thing, amongst some liberal and 'Marxist' circles, to talk about alienation and denounce those who have become the victims of it, as if an individual *alone* is responsible for this 'despicable' predicament.

The recognition of the causes of alienation and their elimination is, of course, imperative, if an individual must integrate into society. But to ignore the problematics of alienation-integration is as bad as the bourgeois mystification of alienation. To believe that one can mechanically get rid of one's alienation without/before a radical change, or a process of change taking place, in society is to deny its relationship with the material world.

To conclude, Adderley's failure to see my work in its right perspective is due to her own failure or incapacity to penetrate a complex work at its different levels, and it was also, perhaps, due to her own attitude and prejudices. Although this is not untypical of many of our art critics today who often fail to respond to a new and original work, only a hack journalist could have confused the function of an art activity with that of the showing of slides about India.

Rasheed Araeen

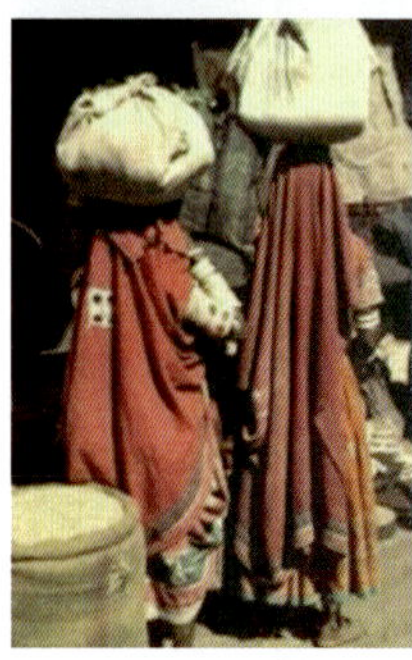

Saleem Arif Quadri, slides shown at 143 Whitfield Street, 31 July 1977

Preliminary Notes for a BLACK MANIFESTO

Rasheed Araeen

Introduction

The problems of contemporary art in the Third World today are part of its socio-economic and political predicaments, resulting from colonialism and its present relationship with the West. We must therefore go beyond formal and aesthetic considerations and look into the historical factors which influenced or suppressed artistic developments in the last few centuries, as well as those forces which are today predominant, in the Third World.

By Third World we mean Asia, Africa, Latin America, and the Caribbean. But we *must* also include in it all those non-European peoples (whom we shall collectively call 'blacks' or 'black people') who now live in various Western countries and find themselves in a similar predicament to that of the actual Third World.

What concerns us here specifically is the situation of contemporary visual art in the Third World. But we cannot meaningfully deal with the problems of visual art alone isolated from the cultural context. What affects culture as a whole is also reflected in art activity.

A cursory glance at the Third World today shows that, even after years of 'independence', its contemporary cultures in general and the visual arts in particular remain what could be described as the stagnant *backwaters* of Western developments or what Paulo Freire[1] calls the 'culture of silence' of the masses.

There does exist, however, an increasing awareness of the situation and efforts are being made to confront the problems. We must therefore look into how this problematic situation is actually being dealt with. **How are Third World people trying to enter the modern era or/and create their own contemporary history? If their voice is muted or not heard at all, what are the underlying causes? And what are the actual alternatives open to them?**

The awareness that the Third World must now find a direction which is different from that imposed on it by the West has been growing; and, in fact, organised attempts pointing towards this goal have recently been made. But these efforts[2] have either remained confined within different regions or lacked a clear (ideological) perspective. They have not therefore made any unifying impact on the overall situation or offered a real challenge to those forces which have been responsible for the present predicament of its art and culture. This is partly due to the lack of *direct* communication of ideas between the Third World countries; and the problem has been further compounded by the extremely oppressive political situation in many Third World countries today—and which is, in most cases, the legacy of colonialism or/and the result of Western imperialist domination.

Although there does exist an opposition to imperialism and questions are being asked about the growing domination of Western culture, the general situation *in practice* remains West-oriented. That is, even when there is a strong tendency among many Afro-Asian countries to maintain the continuity of their own traditions, resulting in the preservation and revival of old forms—particularly their reintroduction in contemporary works, the actual result or its underlying criterion often tends to conform to the standards created in the West. This could be explained by the fact that it is not unusual today for many Afro-Asian countries to seek advice from the so-called Western experts of Oriental/African Art in understanding their own traditional past and to depend on the guidance from the West for contemporary developments.

And therefore Third World artists today are *in general* accepting the 'supremacy' of Western developments in the contemporary field by following whatever styles are developed or produced in the major art centres of the West. This not only uproots them from the reality of their own culture and history, but leads them into an alienated situation which cannot question the domination of foreign values, thereby also denying them any opportunity to develop their art indigenously.

This is not, of course, due to what many Western critics would have us believe. As Edward Lucie-Smith has put it: "In places such as India and Japan, traditional culture between the wars was already in a state of decay; it was natural therefore that artists in those countries should try and rebuild upon the European and American model."[3]

It is typical of many (if not most) Western critics not to see things in the correct historical perspective. Mr Lucie-Smith has very cleverly tried to conceal the actual truth. He might have impressed his own lot, but he cannot fool us. Who does not know that Western colonialism in India—and for that matter in the whole Third World—was directly responsible for what he himself calls 'a state of decay' of traditional culture? And then he has the arrogance to suggest that it should be *natural* for the people, who have been subjected to the traumatic experience of colonialism, to rebuild their future on the model created by those who once were, and still are, their oppressors. This is no more than an attempt to keep the Third World people perpetually under Western domination so that apologists like Lucie-Smith may continue enjoying their international privileges granted by the system they unashamedly serve.

It is essential not to fall into the pitfalls of the Western attitude that tends to disguise the truth. On the one hand, Western interpretation of human history is often extremely biased against non-European peoples and their achievements; and on the other, while ignoring the real dynamics of historical developments, it lays a great emphasis on the *individual* achievements of Western men supposedly struggling against all odds. The fact is that socio-economic and political forces play a fundamental role in moulding, nourishing, supporting, and sustaining all human productive and creative activities, both physically and psychologically.

This brings us face to face with the question of the developments of our own socio-economic and political institutions. The question here really is: what actually happened to these institutions, and why did they fail to play an historical role in providing support to the indigenous developments of arts in the Third World in the colonial period of the last few centuries? The answer to this is, of course, well-known but not widely and fully acknowledged, particularly in the West, for reasons which we hope would become more clear by the end of this manifesto.

Contrary to what we are often told by the West, the colonial era was one of the most exploitative and oppressive periods in human history; and its legacies are still with us today as part of neo-colonialism. This was the period when the West preached **human liberty, equality,** and **fraternity.** But at the same time, it was the very same West which, in brutal and blatant violation of basic human dignity and in contradiction to its own presumed human values, actually enslaved and subjugated the majority of the world's population and plundered its resources for the West's interest alone. The wealth it thus acquired helped the West develop its various institutions. This development was in fact achieved at the expense of ignoring, if not actually suppressing, the historical developments of indigenous institutions. And on top of this, it had the audacity to perpetrate lies about the 'primitiveness' of indigenous Third World peoples whom, as most Western people still believe, the West *only* wanted to 'civilize'.

The truth of the matter is, whether one likes it or not, that the actual aim of colonialism was to merely appropriate other peoples' wealth and resources, by hook or by crook, as a result of which the West was able to become what it is today. As Frantz Fanon has rightly said: **"This European opulence is literally scandalous, for it has been founded on slavery, it has been nourished with the blood of slaves and it comes directly from the soil and from the subsoil of that under-developed world. The well-being and the progress of Europe have been built up with the sweat and the dead bodies of Negroes, Arabs, Indians, and the yellow races.** *We have decided not to overlook this any longer.*"[4] (italics added).

While the West flourished during colonialism, Western art also flourished along with the emergence of its various institutions. The historical developments of Western art of the modern era took place not because of the mental 'superiority' of Western artists (as is commonly believed in the West), but due to the advantage they had by being placed within the complex totality of developing forces of an historical process. And this was made possible to a large extent with the material resources from the Third World. While the historical process in the West provided Western artists with necessary incentives or driving force for their creativity, colonialism suppressed the developments of indigenous art and culture in the Third World by preventing the historical development of the productive forces of its peoples.

For this reason the history of Western art over the last few centuries also becomes an issue here; not only for the fact that its developments took place at the cost of Third World people, but more essentially because of the West's assertion today that its history must be accepted as the mainstream of human developments and that in the light of this all human achievements must be seen. THE ESTABLISHMENT OF EUROPEAN CIVILIZATION AS THE MAINSTREAM IS ONE OF THE MOST CATASTROPHIC DEVELOPMENTS THAT HAVE TAKEN PLACE IN HUMAN HISTORY, DESTROYING OR SUPPRESSING OTHER CULTURES AND CIVILIZATIONS. And today this European MAINSTREAM is used to measure the achievements of the peoples whose very historical developments were suppressed by it. It is therefore not a surprise that the West either ignores other peoples' contributions to human knowledge or history, or it allocates them an inferior status determined by an attitude that sees all non-European phenomena as ahistorical.

This is, of course, a fundamental feature of the dominant ideology that perceives the world in terms of its different parts arranged in a hierarchical order, so that this system serves the interests of those who control it from the top. As such, the West sees the rest of the world as its own appendage and expects all the world resources, natural as well as human, to serve the interests of Western civilization alone. THIS WESTERN PERCEPTION OF THE WORLD HAS REDUCED TODAY THE WHOLE WORLD INTO A 'GLOBAL VILLAGE' WITH A VULGARLY AFFLUENT WEST AT ITS CENTRE SURROUNDED BY STARVING PEOPLE WITH BEGGING BOWLS IN THEIR HANDS.

Moral double standards, arrogance, hypocrisy, and racism are some of the manifestations of the ideology which maintains that Western people alone have a civilized existence and that they should constantly maintain and protect this even at the expense of denying other peoples their humanity. WHILE EUROPEANS ARE HAILED AS PATRIOTS, FREEDOM FIGHTERS AND HEROES, OTHERS ARE DENOUNCED AS BLOODTHIRSTY TERRORISTS. The various attempts of some pseudo-scientists to prove the 'superiority' of the white race, is also part of the same apparatus which deliberately perpetuates lies about non-European peoples. And these attempts to give scientific respectability to racism only reveals the hideous designs of those who are an integral part of the Western imperialist domination of the world today.

The present state of affairs in the Third World is not the result of the 'natural laziness' or 'a lack of imagination' of its peoples, as we are often told by the West, neither is it the legacy of the devastation of some oriental 'barbarian'. It is in fact the direct consequence of the colonial pillage by the 'civilized' West whose pretentious claims to all humanity have now turned out to be no more than a mask to hide its pathologically excessive greed and which has today reached dangerous proportions. The Western obsession for more and more material wealth (mostly in the form of consumer goods), which in the West is euphemistically called 'a higher standard of living', cannot be perpetually fulfilled without further exploitation and appropriation by the West of resources *which are not its own resources.* These resources actually belong to Third World peoples who themselves should now utilize them to fulfil their own needs, by developing their own productive forces and rebuilding their own socio-economic, political, educational, cultural, and artistic institutions *which must be free from foreign domination.*

Against this historical background, therefore, we must place the present predicaments of our art and culture. We must recognise that as long as we allow the West (and for that matter anybody else), willingly or unwillingly, to dominate our lives, we will only be exploited. As long as our physical and mental resources are under its direct or indirect control, our development will either be suppressed or used for the benefit of the West alone, its art and culture, and its civilization. In other words, **we must free ourselves from foreign domination before we can create our own contemporary art and culture.**

But this does not mean that we have no option open to us at present or that we cannot carry on an art activity. Of course, if we continue accepting the general situation today which demands our subservience to the West we are doomed as a people. On the other hand, we can and must stand on our feet and oppose those alien values, as well as our own, which obstruct radical change by preventing the development of internal dynamism of our people; and in the process of confronting these values we can and shall discover new art forms that will authentically reflect our own reality today. However, before we proceed further to look into possible alternatives, we must examine here the various aspects of those forces which are holding us back.

The Third World Today

One of the important features of colonialism was and is to violently suppress the indigenous culture of the colonized country and then impose its own cultural values on the colonial people. In many instances, colonialism imposed an actual ban on native cultural practices, taking away by force from the people their cultural artifacts. The loot was then transferred to the West. As a result, most of the Third World heritage is today either hidden away stored in the basement lockers of Western museums[5] or insolently displayed in their glass cases as part of the evidence of the West's pride and precious possessions. AFTER EXTERMINATING MILLIONS OF PEOPLE AND THEN LOOTING THEIR BELONGINGS, THE WEST TODAY HAS THE AUDACITY TO CALL ITSELF THE PROTECTOR OF THE ARTISTIC AND CULTURAL HERITAGE OF THE WORLD.

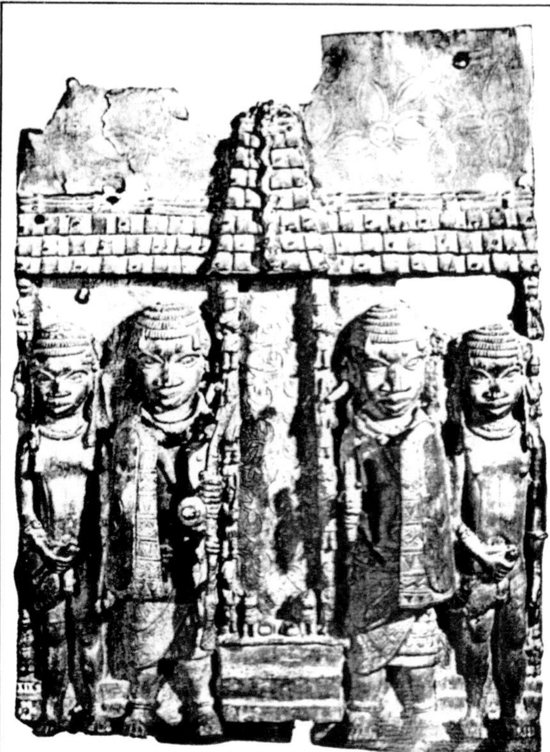

Benin Bronze, The British Museum, London

"The deplorable state of most Benin work is due to the fact that it was eventually plundered by the British when, in 1897, they sacked and burnt the city. In some of the pieces part of the bronze has melted; in others there are gashes caused by their being torn roughly from their places. These, and the burnt ivories, are the mute record of the city's rape."

Boris de Rachewitz, *Introduction to AFRICAN ART*

At the same time, colonialism created and creates a native bourgeoisie by giving some of the native population Western colonial education, and by awarding them some socio-economic privileges and a share in political power. In turn, this native class, to quote Amilcar Cabral, "assimilates the colonizer's mentality, considers itself culturally superior to its own people and ignores or looks down upon their cultural values."[6]

With the coming to power of *this* native bourgeoisie, after 'independence'. colonialism is only replaced by neo-colonialism; which in fact is a general phenomenon in the Third World today. One of the most important characteristics of neo-colonialism is the perpetuation of Western imperialist domination in the 'decolonized' countries through Western cultural penetration, against which the native bourgeoisie cannot and does not act as a shield. On the contrary, its own lifestyle facilitates further propagation of Western values, which openly relegate the indigenous cultural life. In effect, it virtually becomes an instrument through which Western culture is projected as civilized and progressive vis-à-vis the 'primitive' and 'backward' native culture.

It is therefore no surprise that, immediately, after the Second World War, Western imperialism under the leadership of its most powerful country, the US, unleashed an unprecedented cultural propaganda in the major cities of the Third World, particularly in Asia and Africa, through its control of mass media (films, TV, glossy publications, etc.). The whole purpose of this propaganda, which constantly assaulted people's senses with alien images of the values of Western life, was to inflict their minds with the illusions of a better life (in the West) and to lure them into believing that they could also possess this life, if only they would abandon their own values; thereby making them develop a sense of their own inferiority. The aim of the cultural aggression, in fact, has always been to make the dominated people totally abandon their own values and accept the projected superiority of imperialist culture, turning them into passive objects of Western domination, since, as Amilcar Cabral has pointed out, "with strong indigenous cultural life, foreign domination cannot be sure of its own perpetuation".[7]

At a time when people were trying to recover from their colonial past and were looking forward to a new future free from foreign domination, this new onslaught from the West not only caused a further loss of national cultural identity among the native bourgeoisie, who thus fell in love with 'Babylon' called AMERIKA; it also disturbed, if not shattered, the sense of direction among the urban 'intelligentsia' who could have otherwise played a positive role in the post-colonial reconstruction of the country. The native bourgeoisie who was supposed to offer a new direction, leading to a better and prosperous life which it had promised to *all* its people during their anti-colonial struggle, instead became an instrument of an accelerated superficial change whose main driving force has been to turn the major native cities into centres of native bourgeois life *based on vulgar imitations of the West.* It set in motion a process whose consequences can be seen today in the Third World cities. A skyscraper rising from/above poverty-stricken shantytowns has become a symbol of 'progress'.

One only has to cast a glance to see the absurdity of present developments in most Third World countries based on the Western prescriptions. Instead of improving the land and waterworks to produce more basic and essential food, either the land is used to produce exportable commodities or the peasants are recruited into the factories where, for example, motor cycles, blue jeans, platform shoes, etc., are assembled/manufactured mainly for the teenage kids of the affluent urban classes. Instead of improving livestock to increase milk production, Coca-Cola factories are set up everywhere. Instead of creating an incentive for the fishermen to catch more fish and providing them with better boats and equipments, the sea-shore is transformed into a holiday resort for the native, as well as international, leisure class and the inhabitants of the surrounding villages are turned into waiters, domestic servants and entertainers. Consequently some Third World cities have become exotic brothels for globe-trotters.

The basic priority, the development of an indigenous economic infrastructure serving the basic needs and interests of all the people, has been virtually ignored. Instead, the country's wealth has been appropriated by the few, through trickery, deceit and bureaucratic corruption, and spent mostly on the importation or production of Western consumer goods and sophisticated military hardware which cannot, of course, fill the hungry bellies of the masses. It simply maintains the Westernized lifestyle of small native elites and their political power.

Any human development which is based on foreign values—unless these values are absorbed through a critical process as part of the indigenous development—disturbs and suppresses the imagination and creativity of people, thereby destroying any incentive for the creation and development of new and original ideas. Instead, it perpetrates/perpetuates imitation, submission and apathy, which in fact characterizes native bourgeois life today. The native bourgeoisie thus ends up trapped in its milieu protecting its selfish interests, incapable of providing any leadership or support for the positive and progressive forces of the people. Instead the people are fed with illusions, vulgar fantasies, religious fatalism, and populist slogans; all this leading to a life pattern which becomes insensitive to its own environment. And if all this is not enough to keep the people contented and/or silent, they are mercilessly put down by the sophisticated oppressive state machinery on which the native ruling classes end up spending most of the country's wealth.

It is therefore clear that the native bourgeoisie, which virtually becomes an agent of imperialist domination, cannot and does not protect the real interests of the people. It gives almost a free hand to the multinational foreign companies which not only exploit the people indiscriminately but cause great damage to indigenous cultural life. The following example, which is typical as well as topical, illustrates how an apparently innocent commercial operation persuades people to abandon their own cultural values and take up Western ways in the hope of improving their life, whereas the actual result is a disaster, economically as well as culturally.

In most parts of the Third World, even today, breast-feeding is not only a common traditional practice, but also an important part of its socio-economic reality. And it cannot be replaced by any other method without a real change, *brought about by the conscious efforts of the people themselves,* in the economic forces, creating a socio-cultural environment in which acts like bottle-feeding and its various implications are fully grasped by the masses. An imposition of bottle-feeding on the other hand, particularly through an aggressive cultural propaganda (euphemistically called 'commercial ads'), would in the present Third World environment naturally create dangerous health hazards and without giving much economic benefit. To say that the Western companies do not understand this simple act, would amount to calling them idiots, which they are not. They couldn't care less as long

'Sadat, oh Sadat, you dress in the latest fashion while we sleep 12 to a room'

—Cairo demonstrators' slogan

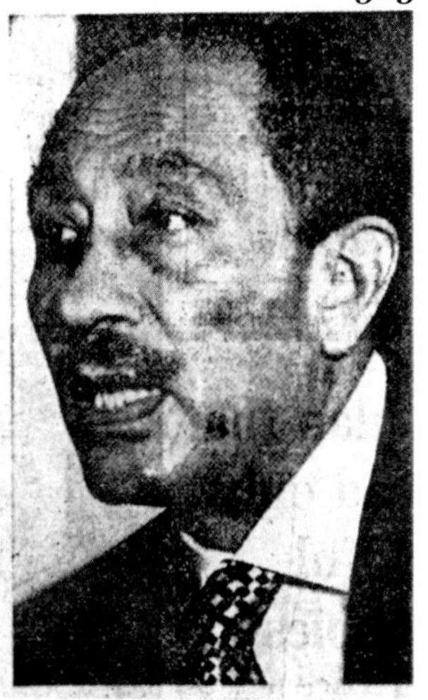

from *The Sunday Times*, 23.1.1977

as they make money. If their actions cause malnutrition among children, poverty and starvation, and even deaths, they do not consider it their moral or human responsibility.

It is well known now how Western baby-food producers have been persuading the women in the Third World into giving up their *traditional* breast-feeding in favour of *modern* bottle-feeding, simply to sell their products. In the hope that it would help their children grow better (as suggested by the ads), many poor women switched on to bottle-feeding, even when they did not lack their own milk. It not only deprived them of their hard-earned small income which they had to spend to buy the manufactured baby-milk, it also caused malnutrition and a disease, unknown before, among these children. As a result, many of them died.

The debate here is not about the merits or demerits of breast-feeding or bottle-feeding. Neither is it the question of a 'failure' of the women in the Third World to grasp the new reality of bottle-feeding. It would be very easy, of course, to accuse these women of a 'lack of awareness' of the problems of hygiene in bottle-feeding, but would anybody blame the mothers of the Thalidomide children for their lack of scientific knowledge?

The issue here really is the immorality of the whole money-making operations of the multinational companies in their total disregard of human life. Their aggressive commercial and cultural propaganda deceives people into believing that they can buy a better life by purchasing consumer products (which do not contribute to their welfare but only further their poverty), and undermines people's cultural values which would otherwise protect them from such vicious traps.

The paradoxical situation in which the native bourgeoisie finds itself after 'independence', must also be recognised. On the one hand, its own lifestyle betrays its acceptance of the supremacy of Western cultural values. On the other, it cannot totally ignore the national aspirations of the people and their own culture. A resurgence of interest in indigenous art and cultural activities therefore occurs. But this development, which in most cases is manipulated by the native bourgeoisie to consolidate its political power by making it part of its populist demagogy, often fails to go beyond the level of mere entertainment or a reminder of the past glories.

The exuberant colourful tribal dances at Nairobi Airport, Kenya, welcoming the arrivals of international celebrities, is an interesting example of the manipulation of indigenous culture by a native bourgeoisie *which prides itself on dressing up in European three-piece striped suits even on hot days.*

This is not to say that indigenous national art and culture should not play any role in international affairs. International diplomatic relations alone cannot provide a real dynamic for the historical development of national art and culture in the Third World. In fact, if this becomes the only basis for the preservation or continuation of indigenous art and cultural activities—as is the fact in most cases, the result is their degeneration into an exotic entertainment for those whose actual allegiance lies with foreign culture.

Although the wearing of indigenous dress does not necessarily reflect a genuine commitment to the development of national culture today, in view of the fact that indigenous dress is still an essential part of the masses in the Third World, the European dress of the native ruling classes can only project their separateness from the masses, if not an elevated status whose roots are embedded in European soil.

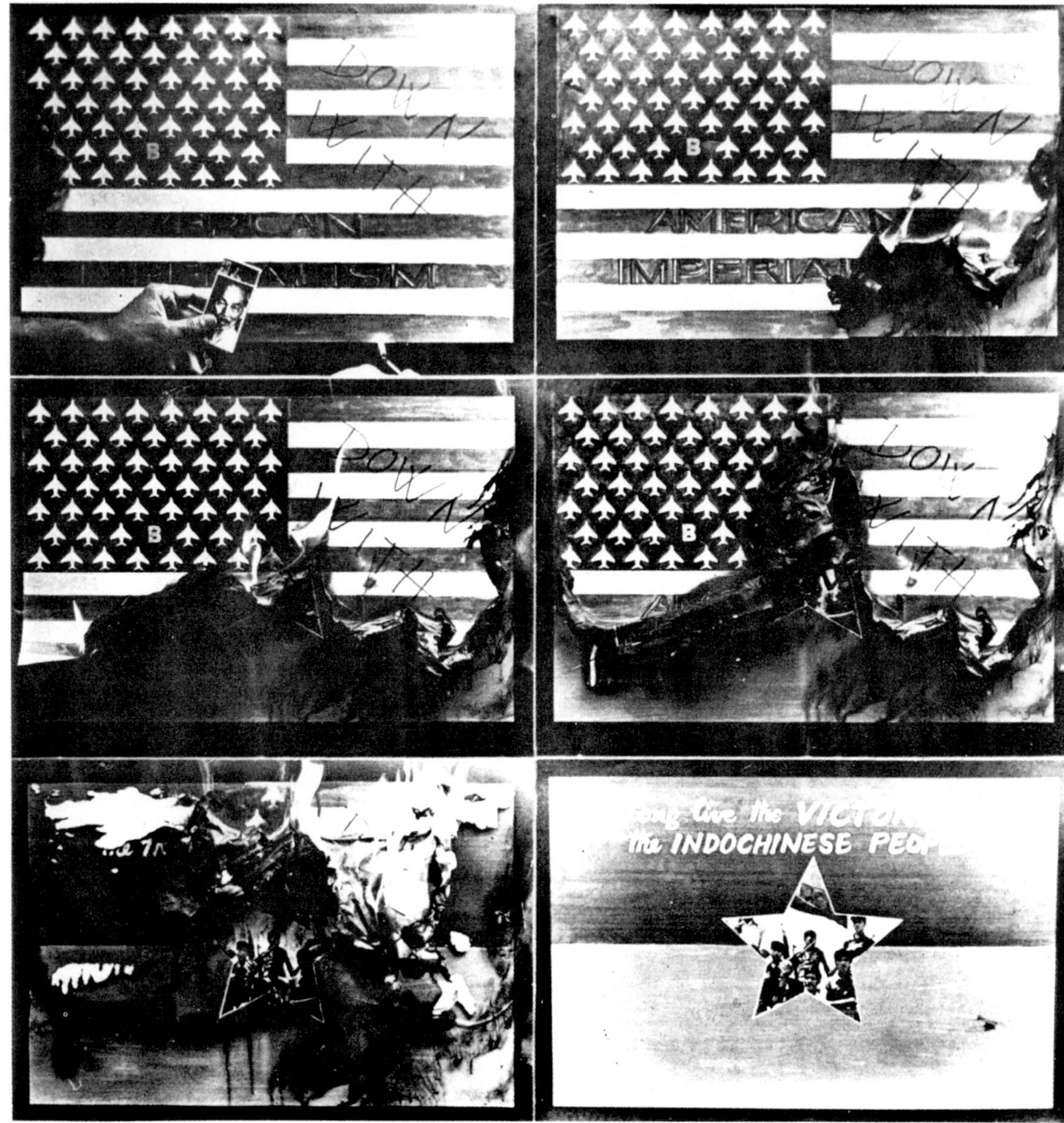

RASHEED ARAEEN *Fire* (6 of 30 or so photo-amal'aags) 1975

What is important now is not WHAT WE WERE IN THE PAST, but WHAT WE ARE TODAY. Whether we live in our own countries of origin or in the West, neither a mechanistic revival of our traditional forms nor a trailing behind on the paths formed by the so-called historical styles of Western art can offer us a positive direction. While rejecting both these options, but still finding ourselves surrounded and dominated by the forces which either demand our return to ethnic traditions or make us accept the hegemony of Western developments, WE HAVE NO CHOICE BUT TO OPPOSE THEM BOTH; AND OUT OF THIS CONFRONTATION WILL EMERGE NEW FORMS THAT TRULY REFLECT OUR PARTICULARITY IN THE WORLD TODAY.

We are no longer *national* entities, in the literal sense of the word. The problems facing us today are not necessarily of national dimensions or characteristics. They are in fact the consequences of the dominating forces *internationally* unleashed by the West. Our efforts, while containing individual/national elements, must therefore transcend both individual and national boundaries to reflect upon the international aspect of our predicaments and to come to terms with a situation that demands solidarity amongst all the peoples who are struggling against the same enemy.

The Third World must evolve its own independent identity, which cannot be, of course, homogeneous. But in its formal diversities, it must embody and express its underlying unity based onthe common historical past and the present reality of 'underdevelopment', also reflecting its *unified* opposition to Western domination. From the problematic situation of the Third World MUST EMERGE AN INTERNATIONAL MOVEMENT, WHICH IS DIFFERENT FROM AND IN OPPOSITION TO WESTERN ART. This would, of course, require the development of our own *international* platform, or communication/gallery network through which we could exchange our ideas directly without Western intermediaries/interference, creating historic links between the peoples whose emergence can offer a new hope to all mankind.

While coming to terms with the modern technological age and our own contemporary reality, which must involve A SEARCH FOR NEW METHODS AND FORMS beyond the narrow/obsolete concept of art based on the Western tradition of purity of painting/sculpture or craftsmanship—and the content of which must be oriented towards our own cultural situation, we must avoid the pitfalls of the stylistic sectarianism which has been one of the hallmarks of the Western avant-garde.

The struggle between different styles for so-called historical primacy is one of the characteristics, if not *the* dynamic, of contemporary art in the West, perpetrating aggressive competition between individuals for recognition. No wonder that the dominant ideology lays so much emphasis on the identity of **the individual** through one's work; which is actually realized by turning a particular style/form into a precious pedestal on which its innovator, the artist, must stand, maintaining the consistent position for the identification to be established. The recognition thus achieved not only gives a tremendous boost to the artist's inflated ego—a result of alienation, it also provides one with especial material benefits and social privileges. A formal style which must be the function of a content thus becomes content itself, thereby leading the artist into a formalist cocoon in which he/she is perpetually trapped, isolated from the grasp of an actual and changing reality outside.

The Western avant garde is, however, nearly reaching the end of its bourgeois cul-de-sac. On the one hand there is a wild talk about *the end of art*—as if art cannot exist or flourish outside bourgeois art history! On the other, the new 'radicals', in their last and desperate attempts to keep clinging to Art History by perpetuating the so-called evolution of historical styles, are even grabbing whatever material or forms they can get hold of from their flirtation with Marxism, class struggle, the predicament of dominated people, etc., manipulating them only to perpetrate a new formalism. The radical polemics/rhetoric of most Western artists, however, is not applicable to Third World conditions.

We ourselves do not need to look for any material outside our own existential reality, which is in fact part of our peoples' predicaments. We do not have any art-historical axe to grind. We have no art-historical pedestal to stand on and defend bourgeois values or preach sermons about beauty and aesthetics, nor shall we indulge in the futile activity of *art for art's sake*. Our history is in fact the history of the pillage and plundering by colonialism. We must grasp *this* truth and turn it into a weapon of our cultural struggle. FROM CENTURIES OF OPPRESSED EXISTENCE, FROM THE WILDERNESS OF COLONIALISM, THE THIRD WORLD MUST NOW EMERGE, LIKE A BLACK PHOENIX RISING FROM WHITE ASHES.

"... it is necessary to totally destroy, to break, to reduce to ash all aspects of colonial state in our country in order to make everything possible for our people."
– AMILCAR CABRAL

It does not follow from this that we must cut off ourselves from the activities of our Western contemporaries, particularly those who are also aware of their role in society and are aiming at the radical change. Since many of us live in the West, we must avoid isolation and separatism which is no recipe for the positive development of a society in which all people, irrespective of race and colour, must interrelate. But in the present situation it is very difficult. *So long as* Western people speak from their privileged positions and with their usual paternalistic attitude and arrogance, there is no possibility whatsoever for the development of a real dialogue between THEM and US.

The development of a true international platform/movement, from/to which all cultures could make their unique contributions, is not only possible but desirable in the long run. But if this is to serve the true interests of all peoples rather than become another instrument of selfish Western interests, it must be based on the clear rejection of Western art history as *the* mainstream. The subjective conditions of the affluent Western society—particularly when these conditions have been ahcieved at the expense of the majority of the people in the world, cannot offer a truly international perspective.

The concept of individual geniuses as *the* creators, looking down on the rest of the people as being incapable of an art or a creative activity, is another aspect of the dominant ideology. The present relationship between an individual as a *creator* and the people as mere *consumers* must therefore be questioned. What we could instead do as art/cultural workers in the present transition, before a new society emerges in which art and culture shall be collectively developed and created, is to *initiate* activity which is then taken up *critically* by people; and the eventual development or completion of the work must depend on their actual participation/contribution.

It ought to be made clear that this work is not meant to be an objective analysis. It is *mainly* a personal statement by A THIRD WORLD MAN who, as a result of being uprooted by cultural imperialism from his Asian environment, was sucked into the Western World where he has spent a considerable part of his life in pursuit of freedom of artistic expression in what he has now come to realize is A WHITE MAN'S WORLD. The experience of living in the West has led him to *black consciousness* and to the awareness that HIS REAL PLACE IS IN THE THIRD WORLD. This is an attempt now on his part to re-examine his relationship with the West, and redefine his artistic role in the cultural context of his people, whether they live in their own countries or in the West.

A Third World Praxis

No recipes or prescriptions are being offered here. We must not believe in ready-made solutions. Art cannot be developed by a set of rules but only through an evolving life-process that generates new ideas at every stage of its transformation. Therefore the suggestions here are not meant to be taken as canons to be followed, or guidelines for the production of art. They may in fact trap us, if followed mechanistically, into a dogmatic/formalistic situation stifling our imagination and energies.

Nevertheless, it is hoped these notes will initiate a discussion from which may emerge a clearer picture, providing us with a starting-point in a direction towards a new dynamism which helps us liberate our energies and awaken us from our present lethargic generality. The success of this will, of course, depend on the imaginative and creative response from the Third World people, particularly black people, who may also be thinking in the same way but have not yet come forward or did not have an opportunity to express their ideas.

Cultural imperialism cannot be dealt with by making appeals to its liberal conscience or pretended humanity. So long as we look to others for the solutions of our own problems—and no matter how much noise we make—we will only be ignored or pushed around. We must *ourselves* take a concrete step. These notes are therefore being offered as A PRELUDE to A WORK whose realization and completion depends on *all of us together*, including our Western comrades.

The conceptual structure of *THE PROPOSED WORK* can therefore be laid down in the following order: INITIATIVE/writing of this prelude; CONTACT WITH PEOPLE through its publication; PARTICIPATION by people in the form of their critical intervention; UNIFICATION of all the material thus created by being published together as a completed work (ARTBOOK). RE-CONTACT; return of the completed work to the participants; PROPAGATION/general distribution of the work; and so on . . . .

Would you therefore send your contributions, in the form of WORDS and IMAGES relating to the cultural problems of the Third World. Keeping in mind that the aim of the work is the DENUNCIATION OF AND CONFRONTATION WITH IMPERIALIST CULTURE and THE SYSTEM that perpetuates international domination. Your contributions may also include constructive criticism of the work. The visual IMAGES may be produced, for example, by collective actions (events etc.) against the cultural strongholds of the system, and by documenting them photographically. The decision how to act or what to contribute, however, entirely lies with you.

The material thus received, comprising of statements/criticism/photographic documentation, will, it is hoped, be published (depending on the availability of publisher or money) as a completed BLACK MANIFESTO, and the copies sent to the participants, who must also send their names and addresses: c/o *Black Phoenix*

(London, 1975-76)

---

1. For Paulo Freire's works see *Pedagogy of the Oppressed* and *Cultural Action for Freedom*, both published by Penguin, London.
2. Although the activities of *CAYC, Buenos Aires, Argentina*, have been confined to Latin American situation and those of *Artists for Democracy, London*, tend to centre around particular political issues, they both are worth mentioning here. *FESTAC '77* was in fact the most important and spectacular event of 'Black Arts' which took place in Lagos, Nigeria, in January/February 1977.
3. Edward Lucie-Smith, *Movements in Art Since 1945*, Thames & Hudson, London; paperback p.17.
4. Frantz Fanon, *The Wretched of the Earth*, Penguin, London; p.76.
5. A short film *You Hide Me* by Ghanaian film-maker Kwate Nee Owoo (Ifriqiyah Films, London), has thrown some light on the storage of thousands of artifacts in the basement lockers of the British Museum. In addition, there are about two million artifacts, looted mostly from the Third World, being stored in a warehouse, Shoreditch, London, and to which the public in general has no access.
6. Amilcar Cabral, *Return to Source*, Modern Reader, New York/London; p.45.
7. Ibid.; p.39.
8. Herbert Read, *A Concise History of Modern Painting*, Thames & Hudson, London. Revised edition; paperback p.8.
9. For the predicament of migrant workers in Europe, see *A Seventh Man* by John Berger/Jean Mohr, Penguin Books, London.

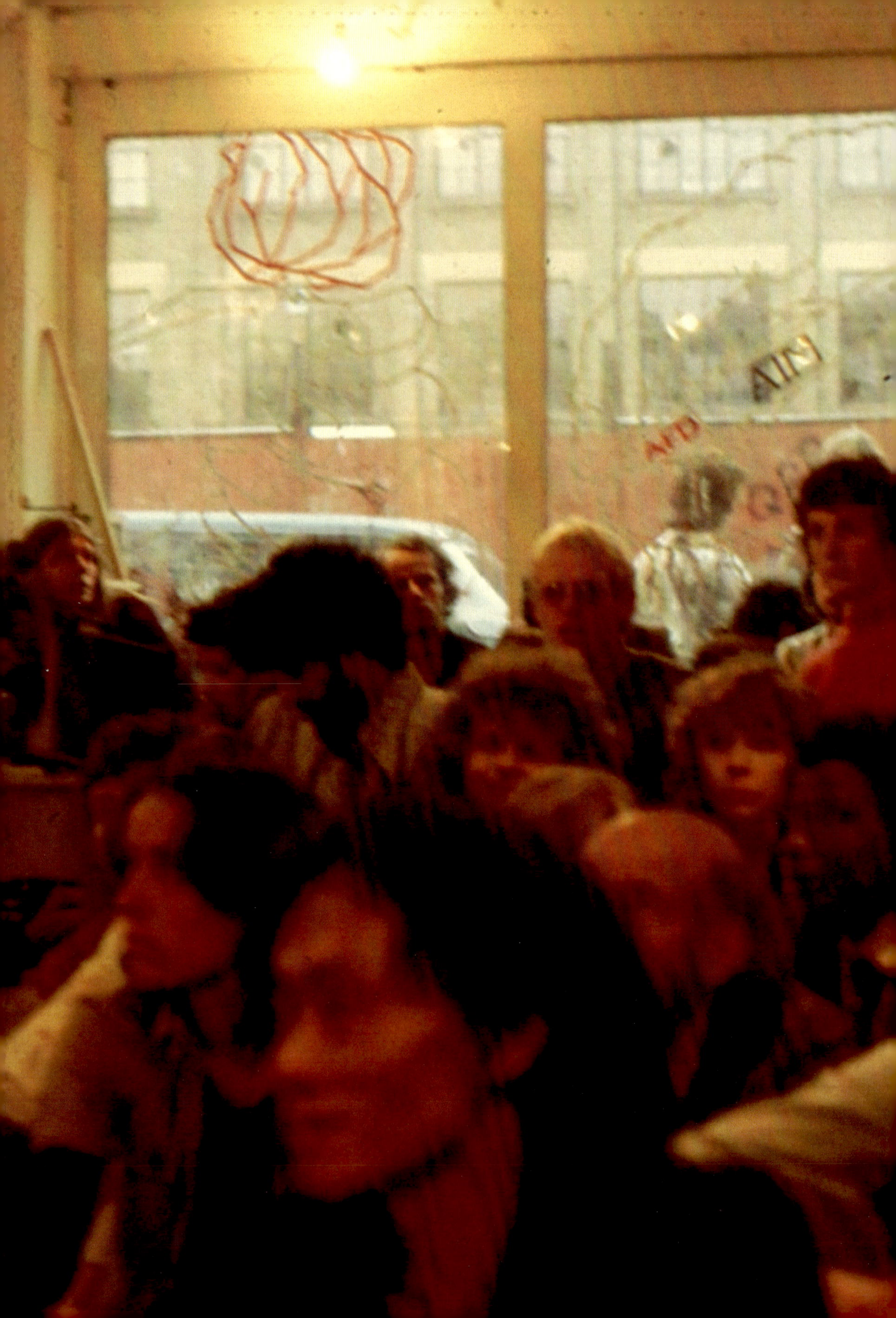

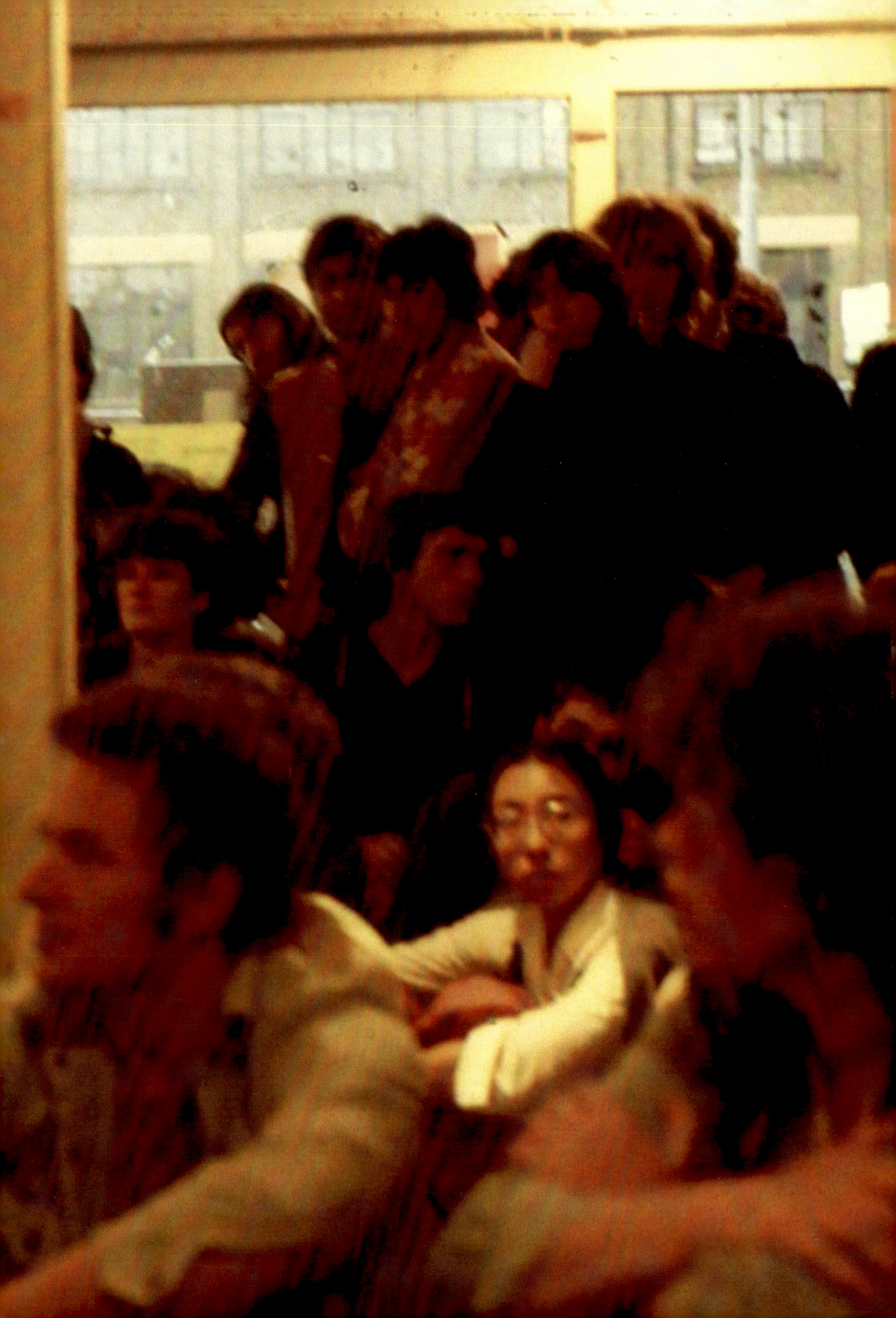

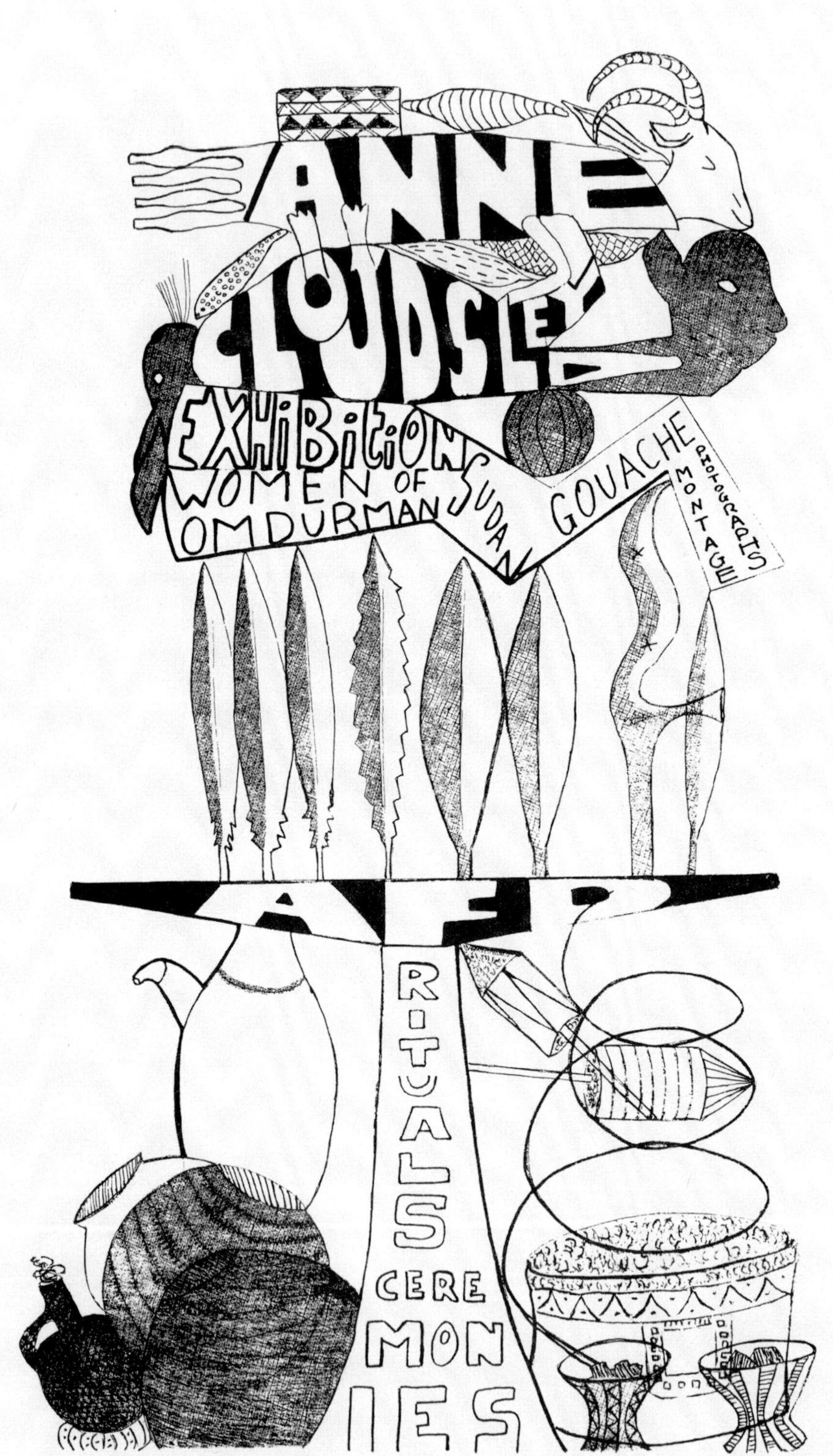

JULY 10 to AUGUST 7
OPEN DAILY EXCEPT MONDAYS 1–6 SUN 1–9 pm
NEAREST ⊖ WARREN ST
ANNE CLOUDSLEY
EXHIBITION
WOMEN OF OMDURMAN SUDAN
GOUACHE
PHOTOGRAPHS MONTAGE
AFD
RITUALS
CEREMONIES
ARTISTS FOR DEMOCRACY
FITZROVIA CULTURAL CENTRE
143 WHITFIELD ST W1

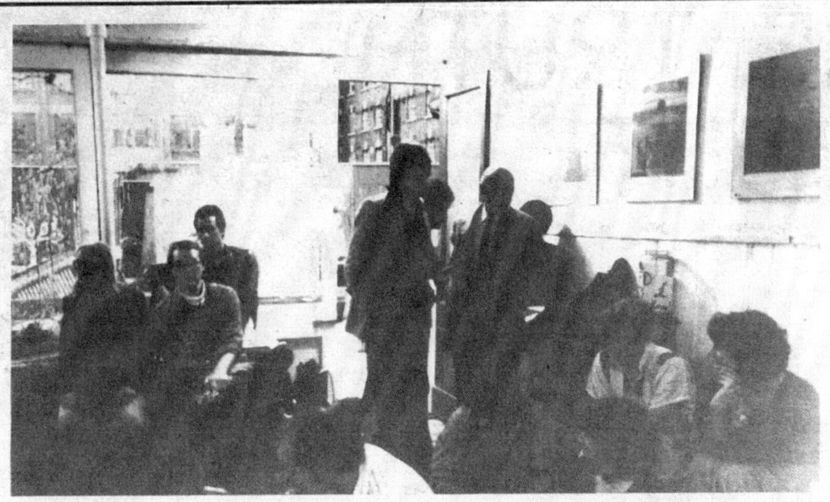

Radical, committed—and homeless

Galleries

ON THE four Sunday evenings before August 11, **Artists for Democracy** will give a farewell fling of progressive performances, music, painting and films. Then their licence to occupy 143 Whitfield Street, London W1, expires, a property company takes over and they will have to clear out of the decaying building known to some nowadays as the *Fitzrovia Cultural Centre.*

AFD have found another place but not the money to lease it. The Arts Council and Greater London Arts Association give them grants for the art they produce, but not for rent and rates, and part-time jobs don't earn them enough. They'll leave a real gap in the radical art world.

AFD are not interested in uncommitted artists or escapist art. They aim to help the liberation of the Third World. After their much-acclaimed International Festival for Chile in 1974, they came to squat at their present premises, and David Medalla, chairman, with Nick Payne, director, still live on the top floor. They are part of the group who have run many imaginatively provocative art events here — liberation of Vietnam, disintegration of Eskimo culture under commercial pressures, etc. They have also let rent-free studios and rehearsal space to some 200 artists, dancers, musicians, over the three years; a local neighbourhood association started up here; a film co-op was formed and still functions, and political discussions on Third World problems are a regular part of their programme.

Last Sunday I saw an excellent show of paintings and photographs about Sudanese culture by Ann Cloudsley (till July 31), heard inventive Asian-type percussion backed by bamboo flutes blown into water, followed by performances and a film. The atmosphere as always was friendly, informal and tight-packed. But where was "the community"? This looked an arty bunch. "True," said the director, "the art set, neighbourhood set and political set just won't mix." A pity.

The star of the evening was Tony Maples, who performed a hypnotic monologue as a disillusioned hippy passing on know-how to a greenhorn on the Singapore to Turkey trek. It was full of witty profundities: "Me 'ead's in the West, me body's in the East. There's no difference, man, between you and the meanest lousy professional beggar out there. If yer stock up nice in Malaya, yer can book 300 per cent on silks when the German tours arrive in Greece — and 'alf of it's nylon."

An exhibition in the TUC's **Congress House Foyer** till July 29 reveals "Life and Labour of the Miner" by three artists. Tom McGuinness is a 40-year-old Durham miner, a member of the re-constituted Ashington Group. He uses chalk or pen-and-paint on bright, elongated panels showing life as he knows it: long boring road passing fenced-in coal tips; slate-roofed red brick houses round a grassy space where exuberant children play on swings and climbing frames; Blackpool pier and deck-chairs under a not-too-sunny sky.

Maureen Scott's life-long involvement in the Labour movement and its history, linked to her admiration for Mexican murals, comes out in her formal symbolic figuration and in her sense of design. If her themes are sometimes too emphatic, ideologically more in tune with the days before nationalisation, there's no doubt about her decorative ability. I like her work best when its actor-like "ennobling" tendency gives way to straight portrayal, as in a bold picture of a miner with huge hands and face that reflect the man, not the artist's ideas about him.

Margaret Burlton lives in Kent, and must be one of the few women allowed to work underground. She observed and sketched in the pits, then turned drawings into tempera paintings with superb accuracy of detail. But the calm of some of her miners has a slightly holy look, as if they're testing that safety lamp in a church. Her peak is a painting with all the qualities of realism and interesting composition, "Rockfall Inspector, Betteshanger": a mining engineer in stiff yellow oilskin looks with the controlled anxiety of an expert at the tipped iron girder dripping water on to the slipped rock blocking the working space.

At the **Drian Gallery,** 7 Porchester Place, London W2, Peter Boleyn's oils are pictures to make you think. Technically he is a virtuoso; in approach, an intriguing mix. His subject-matter is near to problem picture guess-work, based on biblical texts that relate to the mental condition of the individual in today's society. His style goes back to the great mediaeval manuscript illustration, scripts and decorative borders, combined with photo-realism as intense as Alex Colville's. Like *Godspell,* he gives Christian stories up-dated truth.

Salome is a stripper, her seven veils swirling away, gradually forming words that name the seven deadly sins. "The Man Who Crossed the Bridge" — it's Hammersmith — is one who has *not* committed suicide by jumping off it. A piece of driftwood covered with graffiti forms a rough cross behind the depressed figure. So has he bridged the cross? Boleyn once worked as a sign-painter, and his craftsmanship and love of lettering may owe as much to this as to his Norwich Art School.

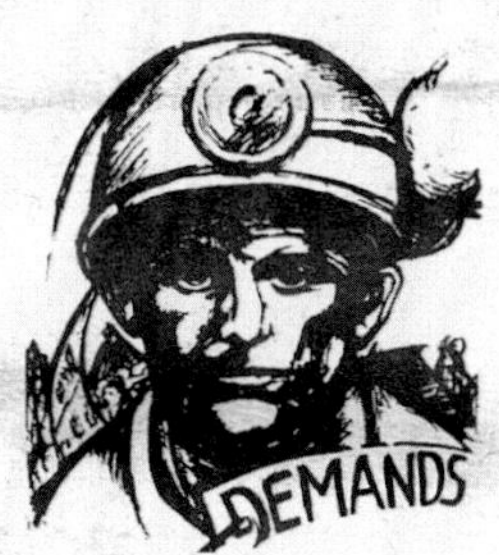

ABOVE, audience and interior of the premises soon to be vacated by Artists for Democracy (photo by Susan Adler). Right, miner's head by Maureen Scott, at Congress House.

Margaret Richards

EVENT- at A.F.D. (Artists for Democracy) Whitfield Street - August '77
on occasionof closure of A.F.D.

"WHAT I MEANT TO SAY WAS..."

Environment 22 sheets transparent polythene on which sprayed words(black)
4 sheets black plastic on which painted words (white)
Dimension of sheets 7ft. by 3ft.
Suspended in rows of 4 or 5
Distance between separate rows approx. 3ft,
Distance between hangings on separate rows approx. 1ft 6ins.

Darkness

First Section

People asked to move in amongst polythene screens to move without speaking

Person holding candle moves in amongst crowd slowly - Semi-darkness...

Glass begins to ring - (ringing obtained by running finger round brim of fine glass half filled with water)

Second Section

People still moving listening
Person with candle pronounces... Person with a torch pronounces...
"I" ...."What I meant to say was.."
"You" ...."What I meant to say was"
"He" .... etc.
"She" .... etc.
"They"............ etc.
Continuing two people to each other (Spoken repetitiously slowly flatly)

Glass begins to ring ringing increases increases
PING!
GLASS
SILENCE

Third section

Person with candle begins to read off words on screens to anyone on opposite side.
(Like throwing a 6 to begin game)
Signals person on opposite side to begin pronouncing words on polythene.
This person now has power to activate others in the same way that he/she was "freed".

Person with torch turns on tape

Begins to slowly rotate light beam

As light strongly illuminates words on transparent screens signals more people to pronounce words on polythene in passing...

Person with candle continues moving (People have already been requested to speak only through the screens)

Person with candle moves in linear fashion in and out

Person with torchlight moves in circular fashion

Glass begins to ring ringing increases increases mingling with sounds activated
PING!
GLASS

Fourth Section

Taking from initial idea....participants ad. lib.....introducing own ideas....

Now beyond control

Moving pausing naturally throughout
words through screens
Loss of coherent sentence structure indeterminate juxtapositions of word mumble gives rise to regular irregular rhythm......babel...........................

Fifth Section

Glass begins to ring over and above rhythms that may have built up
ringing increases increases

Person with torch meanwhile winds back tape to replay

Replay begins loudly audibly above all other sound drowning it

Candlelight extiguished

Torchlight goes out

Darkness

Person with torch moves amongst crowd
Dissembles screens slowly ritual
Rustle of plastic

LIGHTS GO UP

(Words on screens...abstract words with no relation to specific images...conjunctions ...certain unspecific adverbs....etc.....Limitation.......)

What I meant to say was... was my first my first ever attempted participation performance, on the closing night of the AFD space, with transparent screens, words and projected light. The audience were invited to move in and out of the space, and read out loud from the screens (conjunctions, words with no meaning). The ensuing nonsense was played back over the live sound made by the participants, with disruptive elements.

Other moments from AFD stick in my mind... In the carpark across the road, two dancers/performers [Atilio Lopez and George Isherwood] did a performance wearing nothing but a bit of cloth, like a mini skirt, and a giant python. One of them handed the python around the small gathering of onlookers, forming a circle with the snake; the other followed his co-performer and handed out precious pieces of wafer-thin scaly python skin, recently shed, to the mesmerised obeisant onlookers – aghast, or in my case, frozen in terror of such a huge snake.

There was another performance – with other scantily clad gesticulating dancer-performers – and they'd made a soft sculpture with transparent limbs with pulsating tubes as veins with blood coloured liquid and they handed bits of the soft tissue, supposed body parts, to the audience, who then passed this one lengthy piece from one to the other from the ground floor up the stairs and out onto the roof. My young daughter Ra was entranced – she wrote a story at school, describing it. This piece which was mega and perhaps the most complex use of performance art space at the time – inspired most probably by David [Medalla]'s *Stitch in Time.*

And I recall Harriet, the night club stripper and daytime go go dancer; and pyrotechnic performer Steve Cripps parachuting from the roof of AFD down onto the car park across the road; and dear Tina Keane. I also remember an erotic eastern dance by David, dressed in balletic tights and a loose gold lamé tunic with long sleeves – and someone, if it wasn't also David, was playing a flute – while he was showering the entranced onlookers with sheafs of unpaid bills and hefty demands for payment...

Anna Thew

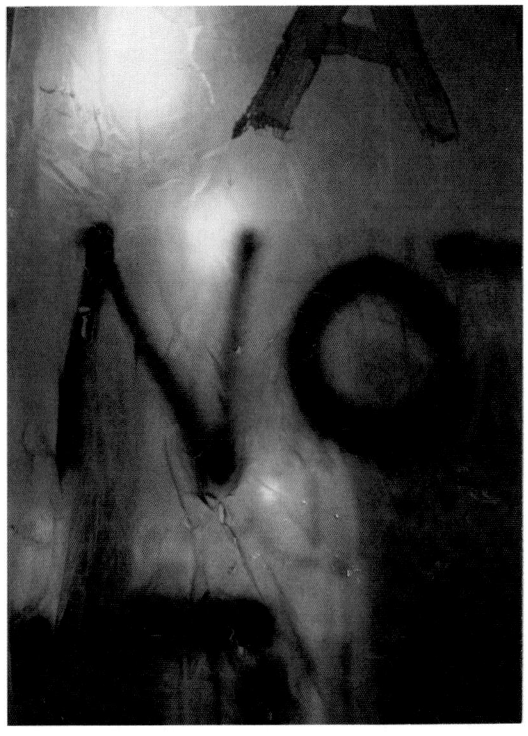

It's almost as if most of our energy had gone to trying to consolidate something here in a very short space of time, but that comes not so much from my artistic interest but a political interest and a social one. On one hand I really believe something more should be done about educating people – about situations in the Third World countries, which after all provide a great deal of the labour power, and the natural resources for developed countries – and also in those places where revolutionary situations have been occurring, consistently. New types of culture are being created, you see, and because one is away from these places doesn't mean one should be blind to what is happening there, like – you find in the Renaissance in fact that the better artists were people who were really aware of say discoveries being done in the Low Countries – which was one of the first consolidated forms of – well the early forms – not consolidated – early forms of bourgeois society – like the fact that the Florentine painters learnt a lot from a Hugo van der Goes altarpiece, the Portinari altarpiece, and the Venetian painters learnt a lot about oil painting, which was – which even Leonardo say had not – I don't think he even had the chance to experiment with, except this sort of fresco, *The Last Supper* – surely he must have found... These ideas were Transalpine ideas that were filtering into Italy. But Italy herself was in a decadent state, you know, decaying after the initial éclat, the initial brilliance of the early Renaissance. I find that is a real historical situation, that new cultures are occurring in places like Vietnam, and Guinea-Bissau, and why it is necessary to study these, and also even in say – in America, the resurgence of the American Indian Movement.

[...]

[In England] it's so difficult for artists to create models where they can be liberated from the really stultifying bureaucracy that accompanies the art world. The official art world – the kind of laissez-faire artistic production which was going on in the fifties – is not workable any more in this situation (and in the sixties) where economically, people are suffering ... and I don't have the money but I have some organisational capacity to get some space: to allow for new artists to emerge, which are not really my contemporaries, not in an artistic sense, they may be close to me in age, because I've been going on for some time, and no one is going to go out on a limb to support *some* concepts, like in AFD we've done a lot for giving an impetus to performance artists – even if several of them have started here and went elsewhere, or even if they've never been here, the fact that in our existence we were the first really to in a sense not *legitimise* it, but gave it our cachet, to the performances. It's now a known fact, it's being done now everywhere. ... [B]ecause this is a world of documentation people will believe more when we are finished, you know, there'll be a whole industry about – and more myths will come out, you know, which will have no bearing on reality. The reality is that from day to day we have to find the money just to buy milk and sugar and coffee...

David Medalla

Visual Arts

Artists for Democracy, 143 Whitfield St, W1. Warren St tube. Final Show: exhibitions by **Philippa Gray, Beryl Lerman, Jeff Rubin, Lel Green, Paul Peter Piech, David Medalla, Nick Payne, Charles Hustwick, dom Sylvester Houedard** will open on Sunday, July 3 at 8.00 + a lecture by **Paul Overy** and films by **Tina Keane** before the gallery closes on Sugust 7.

ARTISTS FOR DEMOCRACY

★ NEWSFLASH

ARTISTS FOR DEMOCRACY are closing down the Fitzrovia Cultural Centre due to lack of funds, on Sunday, August first, 1977. The Fitzrovia Cultural Centre opened in January 1975, and has been the Venue of many outstanding and memorable cultural & political events organised by Artists for Democracy.

Seeing that I was longing for it, a name
I gave it the spirit.

until further notice, David Medalla may be contacted c/o William & Glyns, Holt's Branch, Kirkland House, Whitehall, London SW1 ENGLAND! ★

STOP PRESS

Though the Fitzrovia Cultural Centre is closing down, AFD will continue elsewhere. To mark the closing of the centre, Chris Slicher has constructed a perspex, wood and plexiglas windmill on top of 143 Whitfield street. David Medalla will be performing his work, "The Pictorial Biographies of Medalla and Mozart", on the final night: August 1, 1977.

Nhân Dân 20 July 1975 HANOI

TRIỂN LÃM
NHÂN DÂN THẾ GIỚI
HỌC TẬP NHÂN DÂN
ĐÔNG DƯƠNG VÀ TỎ
LÒNG THÀNH KÍNH
ĐỐI VỚI CHỦ TỊCH
HỒ CHÍ MINH
TẠI ANH

Review of ARTISTS FOR DEMOCRACY'S VIETNAM VICTORY FESTIVAL

A million thanks to all AFD friends and supporters! As we enter the third phase of our existence, we are confident of gaining greater wisdom and strength

AFD lives on!

THE GUARDIAN

At the Fitzrovia Cultural Centre in Whitfield Street, the American Indian Movement displays the hard facts of Indian life now. This is Wounded Knee one century on, the tale of how one America suffers outrage while the other celebrates 200 years of everything that runs against what the Indian believed. Wounded Knee now means the reservation. It means 300 violent deaths, some of them at the hands of authority since 1973 in that place alone. It means anger, discrimination, alcoholism, infant mortality rates ten times the American average, suicide rates double those of white society, and a life expectancy in males of 33.3 years (34.7 for females).

Such facts are allowed to speak for themselves through photographs and printed statements. So too is the renewed pride of the Indian militants, a pride that brought half a million people on to the streets of Philadelphia on July 4 this year to support Indian claims for self-determination and an end to the trail of tears.

Sacred Circles at the Hayward Gallery until January 1977. American Indian Movement at the Fitzrovia Cultural Centre, 143 Whitfield Street, W1, until October 22.

Caroline Tisdall
Friday October 8 1976

Love from David Medalla

A.F.D. London, 7th August 1977

For David
Who with sand ways strokes the waves of the sea and kisses all the coasts around all over seas and deserts
With love.
Takis,
In Paris. 29-1-66.

Στον Δαβίδ
που με τα αφρόδη κύμματα
κι ανακατεύει τα κύμματα
της θάλασσας
και φτάνει όλες τις ακτές
γύρω σ' όλες τις θάλασσες
και ερήμους.
Χαίρε και
με αγάπη Τάκις

POETRY THE EVENING STANDARD

IF YOU feel like making knives and drums from bits and pieces collected from dustbins around Whitfield Street then head over to the Artists for Democracy Fitzrovia Cultural Centre, 143 Whitfield Street, W.1 on Sunday at 8. David Medalla has devised this curious entertainment which he describes as a "performance art work inspired initially by beautiful Eskimo poems." Admission free but it's a good idea to take food and drink. 29.IV.77

'Eskimo carver' by **DAVID MEDALLA**
opens Sunday, May First 1977 at 8 p.m., closes on June 7th, 1977.
(first floor gallery, 143 Whitfield Street. W1)

Photo by Charles Hustwick
Printed by Guy Brett

ARTISTS FOR DEMOCRACY
Fitzrovia Cultural Centre 143 Whitfield St London W1

… come to: → 'MAYFAIR Illuminations'

ARTISTS BALL

at

Hill House,

41, Berkeley Square,

London W.1.

on

Tuesday, 22nd August 1978,

starting at 11 p.m. till dawn

A night to remember

music, dancing, exhibitions, poetry, events, films, video, slides shows, performances by David Medalla & Oriol de Quadras ("Incluso Contra el Viento"), Chris Harris ("Oh Little Darling"), Miriam Bird & Charlie Pig ("Waiteress"), Gennaro Telaro ("Life is Life"), David Garcia & Annie Wright ("Eclipse"), Tina Keane, Gerry Hunt, Guy Brett, and many more .....

Featuring 'A Champagne auction' to be conducted by Oriol de Quadras & David Medalla. Note to artists: Bring a bottle of champagne to the artists Ball ("Mayfair Illuminations") with the label decorated by yourself, which we will action for your benefit. → + AFD

Donation: £1 at the door

RA: Now tell us something about Artists for Democracy (AFD). What were the motives behind AFD? And looking back do you think it was a successful venture?
DM: Well, it grew out of the Artists' Liberation Front, which was then becoming a masonic thing. A group of young artists started meeting at my place and talking about changing society, and all that idealism of youth. Then we saw the possibility of starting an organisation which, by its activities, would support liberation struggles in various parts of the world, particularly in the Third World. We actually started AFD, in 1974, with an arts festival at the Royal College of Art in support of Chilean struggle against the fascist junta there. Then in early 1975 we moved into a premises, which we squatted, at Whitfield Street. There we held many exhibitions of art as well as of documents, poetry readings, films/slide shows, discussions etc, in support of liberation struggles in Africa, in the Middle East... We organised an especial art festival in support of Vietnam, and in fact to celebrate her victory over American aggression. We also held an important exhibition in support of the American Indian Movement . . . In general we also showed the works, as individual exhibitions, of many artists. And I think as a whole it was a successful venture.
RA: As you know, I was also an active member of AFD, at least for some time. I got interested in AFD because of its orientation towards the problems of the Third World. But I think, AFD became merely a sort of support organisation and it didn't really address itself to the basic and essential ideological issues regarding the cultural relationship between the Third World and the West. Don't you think it was the failure of the AFD not to deal with this question, of cultural imperialism, particularly vis-a-vis radical artistic practice?
DM: Yes. I think it was a failure. But you see the failure had to do with the material conditions. I thought it was a failure even before the question was posed. It's like this: if people can't grasp what your question is, how can you expect an answer? We had many cultural workers, the artists, who would support all those struggles but had little knowledge of actual politics. On the other hand, there were the political radicals who came to the AFD; but they had no desire whatsoever even to look at a drawing or a painting or listen to a poem. It's the most amazing contradiction, and I saw it all the time. You see, when we had artists who did exhibitions, some only exhibited their work in the AFD because there was no other place for them to exhibit; but they were not really interested in what was happening in Brixton (London), let alone Mozambique.

AFD are evicted from 143 Whitfield Street in August 1977. A new space is found at 41 Berkeley Square, but it is not possible to maintain. 'Mayfair Illuminations', 'an artists' ball', takes place there on 22 August 1978.

AFD GRAND ARTISTS' BANQUET

A Polemic Against the Degradation of Taste in Modern Life
A Gastronomic Celebration by the Creators of Visual Art
A Joint Proposal by David Medalla and Oriol de Quadras
London, 1st September, 1978

Dear

Warm greetings!

Inspired by the success of 'Mayfair Illuminations Nos. 1&2', we have thought up the idea of a Grand Artists' Banquet, which we will organize on behalf of Artists for Democracy. We envisage the banquet to take place in London on the evening of Saturday December 16th, 1978. We will select a suitable venue for the Grand Artists' Banquet.

We are writing to you and 999 other living international artists who we feel have contributed significantly to the development of modern art. We are asking the artists, including yourself, to send us in advance their favourite recipes, preferably on sheets of paper decorated by themselves. It is our intention to publish a book of artists' recipes, once we get enough money together to publish a book; at the moment we are impecunious.

We hope the artists we have invited can come to London for the Grand Banquet. We would like the artists, if they can, to cook their favourite dishes, and to invite a maximum of three guests per artist for the banquet itself to share with them the meals they have cooked. Our friend, the English playwright Steve Thorn, has suggested that we

'Friendship dances round the world, calling to us all to awaken to the joys of a happy life'. EPICURUS.

invite the leading Chefs of the world to come to London and decorate the banqueting hall with artworks by the chefs.

We will look for suitable kitchens for the artists to cook their meals in. As for the artists who may not be able to come to London for the banquet itself, we will do our best to find members of Artists for Democracy to cook their favourite recipes.

Please send us as soon as possible your recipes for a soup, an hors d'oeuvre, an entrée, a main dish, a dessert. Please specify the drinks that you would like to accompany your meal. We also welcome any supporting documents and artworks you may care to send us that might be suitable for the banquet. Please write to us at :
David Medalla & Oriol de Quadras, BM- Quadras, British Monomark, London WCIV 6XX, England.

Our idea was inspired by the grand banquets organized by the great Italian masters (Leonardo, Titian, Giorgione, Veronese, Tintoretto) during the Renaissance, and by the famous banquet given by Apollinaire and Picasso for Douanier Rousseau at the beginning of our century. We were also inspired by the example of Ho Chi Minh, who worked as an assistant to the great chef Escoffier here in London. We look forward to the AFD Grand Artists' Banquet as a joint celebration of food and art by the 1,000 living international artists of significance.

With many thanks and best wishes,

Yours sincerely,

David Medalla & Oriol de Quadras,
Mer et Ciel, deux chefs.

P.S. Please let us know the names and addresses of other artists you feel we should invite to the banquet. Please tell your friends about the banquet itself. We welcome your ideas and suggestions.

'He brought me to the banqueting house, and his banner over me was love'. SOLOMON: 'The Song of Songs'.

CJ 30 NOV 1979

KER-u-n-n-CH!

A GAPING hole was left in a Camden street after two houses (right) suddenly crumbled and fell to the ground on Saturday.

And local MP Frank Dobson laid the blame fairly and squarely on the Tory Government which, he said, was allowing parts of London to look like something out of the blitz.

His attack came during the opening ceremony on Sunday of the Fitzrovia Play Association's new play space in Whitfield Street, which lies directly opposite the collapsed houses.

He said it was a "bloody disgrace" that the houses had collapsed but added that the Tories were cutting down the funds available for housing improvement and leaving the job to private landlords.

"They have neither the will, the skill, the commitment nor resources to do the job," he commented.

The two privately-owned houses collapsed shortly after workmen, who were renovating the buildings, pulled out the floorboards.

The empty houses next to them remained intact but are now being reinforced by workmen.

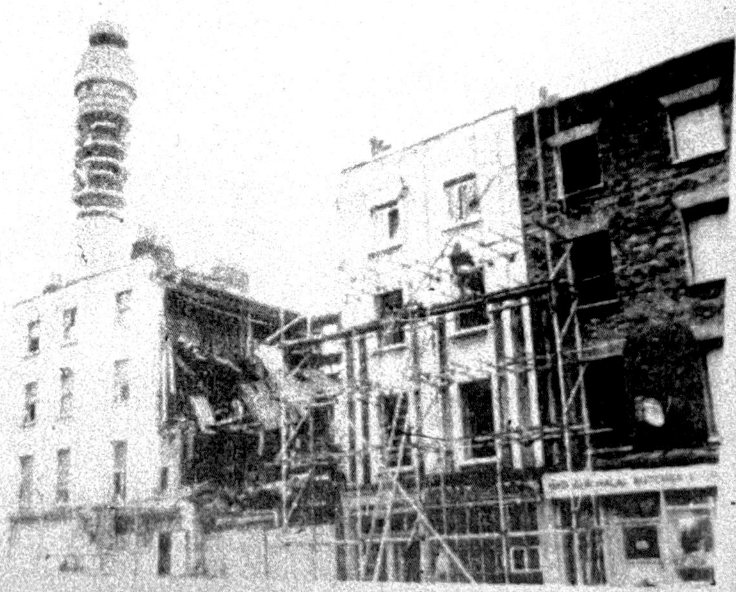

Park befor[e]

MP joins the campaign

car-pa[rk]

A FIGHT to turn a Camden car-park

On 24 November 1979, the building at 143 Whitfield Street collapses.

Acknowledgements

The editors would like to thank the authors, artists and photographers for their contributions to this book.

For support in the research process we are additionally grateful to: Katey Acquaro, Nick Aikens, Alejandra Altamirano, Maria Thereza Alves, Rasheed Araeen, Adjoa Armah, Michael Asbury, Jess Baines, Imruh Bakari, Steven Ball, John Barker, Anne Bean, John Beeson, Purissima Benitez-Johannot, Eva Bentcheva, María Berrios, Martin Berry, Steven Cairns, Virgil Calaguian, Camden Local Studies and Archives Centre, Hugh Cave, Clara Cheung, Susan Croft (Unfinished Histories: Recording the History of the Alternative Theatre Movement), CSM Collections and Archives (British Artists' Film and Video Collection), Noel Ed de Leon, Joe Desantis, Ntone Edjabe, Jane England, Rose English, Peter Fink, George Padmore Institute archive, Rose Garrard, Kylie Gilchrist, Adrian Glew, Helena Goldwater, Lewis Green, Brian Guerin (Cecilia Vicuña Studio), Hackney Archives, Christine Halsall, Ivan Hartl, Fatima Hellberg, Yaiza Hernández Velázquez, Will Holder, Charles Hustwick, May Adadol Ingawanij, Islington Borough Archives, Etienne Joseph (Hackney Archives, Libraries and Heritage Services), the family of Tina Keane, Roberta Kravitz, J.H. Kwabena Nketia Archives, Jacky Lansley, London Metropolitan Archives, LUX, Conor Macklin (Grosvenor Gallery), Lynn MacRitchie, Lani Maestro, Vali Mahlouji, Courtney J. Martin, Marx Memorial Library, MayDay Rooms, Kathleen McCreery, Arianna Mercado, Adeena Mey, Jonathan Miles, Hammad Nasar, Duong Thuy Nguyen, Kieu-Anh Nguyen, Annabel Nicolson, Ife Nii Owoo, Judith Opoku-Boateng (J.H. Kwabena Nketia Archives), Nii Kwate Owoo, Peter Oxley, Stephen Pusey, Saleem Arif Quadri, Jasia Reichardt, Adam Sach, Grace Samboh, Rosalie Schweiker, Frank Shepherd, Steve Sprung, Andrew Stahl, Stanford University Library, Lucy Steeds, Sylvia Stevens, Ingrid Swenson, Tate Library and Archive, David Teh, Verónica Tello, Jun Terra, Anna Thew, Ming Tiampo, Giles Thomas, Amy Tobin, David Toop, Eva Turner, Sarah Turner, Cecilia Vicuña, Helena Vilalta, Patricia de Villiers, Nick Wates and Mia Yu.

Research-in-progress for the present publication was shared and developed as part of a symposium of the same title, hosted online by Afterall Research Centre on 2 February 2023, supported by the Paul Mellon Centre for Studies in British Art.

RASHEED ARAEEN
was born and educated in Pakistan, and trained as an engineer before moving to London in the early 1960s, where he became one of the first artists working in minimalist sculpture in Britain. In the 1970s and 80s his work in performance, photography, painting and sculpture began to develop an overtly political content as it drew attention to the ways in which Black artists were invisible within the dominant Eurocentric culture. Through his activities as a publisher, writer and artist, Araeen has been pivotal in establishing Black voices in the British arts. He published the notable journals *Black Phoenix*, founded in 1978, which was followed by the hugely influential *Third Text*, in 1987, and *Third Text Asia*, in 2008. He also founded Kala Press in association with *Third Text* to disseminate information on the neglected contributions of African and Asian artists to post-War British art. Araeen has exhibited widely and his recent retrospective was on view at the Van Abbemuseum, Eindhoven in 2018, before internationally touring. His work is held in public collections including the Guggenheim, Abu Dhabi; Tate, London; Walker Art Gallery, Liverpool; Centre Pompidou, Paris; Fukuoka Art Museum, Japan; Kiran Nadar Museum of Art, New Delhi; MAMCO, Geneva; and Metropolitan Museum of Art, New York. Araeen lives and works in London.

GUY BRETT (1942–2021)
was a London-based art critic, curator and lecturer on art. He published widely in the international art press and authored monographic essays on Rasheed Araeen, Derek Boshier, Lygia Clark, Eugenio Dittborn, Rose Finn-Kelcey, Tina Keane, Victor Grippo, Brion Gysin, Mona Hatoum, Susan Hiller, Ghisha Koenig, David Medalla, Helio Oiticica, Lygia Pape and Aubrey Williams. From 1964 to 1975 he was an art critic at *The Times* (London) and from 1981 to 1983 arts editor of *City Limits* (London), in addition to writing extensively for the art press throughout his life. His books include *Kinetic Art: the Language of movement* (Studio Vista / Reinholdt, 1968), *Through Our Own Eyes: Popular Art and Modern History* (New Society, 1986), *Transcontinental* (Verso, 1990), *Exploding Galaxies: The Art of David Medalla* (Kala Press, 1995), *Mona Hatoum* (Phaidon, 1997), *Force Fields: An Essay on the Kinetic* (Actar in association with MACBA and Hayward Gallery, 2000), *Li Yuan-chia: tell me what is not yet said* (Iniva, 2001), *Carnival of Perception:*

Selected Writings on Art (Iniva, 2004), *Brasil Experimental: Arte/Vida Proposições e Paradoxos* (Contra Capa, 2005), *Oiticica in London* (Tate Publishing, 2007), *The Crossing of Innumerable Paths: Essays on Art* (Ridinghouse, 2019) and *Takis* (Tate Publishing, 2019).

VIRGIL CALAGUIAN
is a writer, photographer, visual and performance artist, designer, chef and gardener. Born in the Philippines, he has lived in different parts of the world and currently resides in Kamakura, Japan. In the 1970s he was active artistically between London and Manila, and lived for a while above Artists For Democracy's space at 143 Whitfield Street, London, sharing the space and collaborating artistically with David Medalla and Jun Terra. Over the years Virgil and artist Peter Oxley (formerly known as Steve) have teamed up on a wide variety of projects, ranging from performance art events, to award-winning advertising campaigns, to feature articles for international publications and art books, to Peter's acclaimed photography exhibits in such venues as the Angkor National Museum in Siem Reap, Cambodia, and Tokyo's famed Foreign Correspondents Club in Japan.

WING CHAN
is Assistant Editor at Afterall Research Centre. Her current research examines the mobility of art and language. She initiated the writing project Power Naps Post (2023), supported by Para Site, Hong Kong, and contributed to World Weather Network (2022–23), supported by m-est.org and SAHA – Supporting Contemporary Art from Turkey. She also moonlights as a translator.

GEORGE CLARK
is an artist, writer and curator focussed on moving images in the expanded field. He works across film, installation and performance with an interest in inter-local collaborative practice. Clark's projects explore non-aligned histories and geographies and seek to build new models of assembly, exhibition and moving-image production. His films have been exhibited at museums and festivals including the New York Film Festival; Hanoi Doclab; International Film Festival Rotterdam; Taiwan Biennale; Museum of Modern and Contemporary Art / MMCA, Seoul; Museo de Arte Moderno de Buenos Aires; and LA Film Forum. He is a lecturer at the University of Westminster and his work is distributed by LUX. With Cường Minh Bá Phạm he is among the members of the steering commitee of An Viet Archives, the largest known collection of documents, photographs and other objects relating to the British-Vietnamese experience.

CHARLES ESCHE
is the director of Van Abbemuseum, Eindhoven; an advisor at Jan van Eyck Academie, Maastricht; and professor of contemporary art and curating at Central Saint Martins, University of the Arts London. He received the 2012 Princess Margriet Award and the 2014 CCS Bard College Prize for Curatorial Excellence. He is a Series Editor of the *Exhibition Histories* series.

HANNAH HEALEY
is a PhD candidate and CHASE scholar at the Courtauld Institute of Art. Her research seeks to establish the full history of Artists for Democracy and the exhibitions and broader activities the group produced, with a particular focus on the ways in which AFD enacted solidarity as a creative political act. Her research interests include experimental art and politics, and the interrelation of local and international artistic political networks. She additionally works in contemporary art writing and exhibitions with institutions including Modern Art Oxford and the Royal Academy of Arts, London.

SUSAN HILLER (1940–2019)
maintained an influential art practice that extended over fifty years. Born in Tallahassee, Florida, she initially trained in anthropology but became uncomfortable with the discipline and made the decision, during a lecture on African art, to become an artist. Based mainly in London as of the late 1960s, she developed an artistic approach that used cultural artefacts to investigate overlooked, marginalised, and denigrated aspects of culture. Her work frequently explored the liminality of phenomena, from dreams and automatic writing, to near-death experiences, to collective experiences of unconscious and paranormal activity. From the 80s onwards, Hiller became known for her innovative use of multimedia technologies.

EILEEN LEGASPI-RAMIREZ
is Associate Professor at the University of the Philippines Diliman Department of Art Studies. Within UP's Doctorate in Social Development programme she pursues research into cultural work, particularly in the context of site-specific community art initiatives across the Philippines. She works across the fields of criticism and art history and presently serves as editorial collective member of the journal *Southeast of Now: Directions in Contemporary and Modern Art in Asia*.

MARÍA JOSÉ LEMAITRE MUJICA
has been Coordinator of the archive of the Museo de la Solidaridad Salvador Allende (MSSA) in Santiago since its creation in 2013. She has led international research projects related to the history and collection of MSSA and co-curated a number of its exhibitions, including 'The Resistance of a Spore: Museo de la Solidaridad returns to GAM' (2023); the MSSA chapter in the 58th Carnegie International exhibition, 'Is it morning for you yet?' (2021); and 'Debut, 43 works meet its Collection' (2018). In parallel, she has collaborated and advised the design and development of the creation of Chilean archive artists such as Lotty Rosenfeld and Carlos Ortúzar and other cultural projects in different disciplines.

DAVID MEDALLA (1938–2020)
was born in Manila and became a leading figure in kinetic and performance art, as well as a poet and an organiser. Heavily influenced by European art and literature of the nineteenth and twentieth centuries, Medalla travelled to Europe from the Philippines as a young man, arriving in Marseille in 1960, where he began to establish his peripatetic practice. In 1960s London, Medalla was instrumental in the short-lived but pioneering and influential Signals gallery (1962–64), the experimental performance collective Exploding Galaxy (1967–70) and the politically engaged Artists Liberation Front (1971–73) and Artists for Democracy (1974–77). In later years, Medalla founded the Mondrian Fan Club, in collaboration with artist Adam Nankervis (1994), and the London Biennale (1998), where processes of collaboration and exchange continued to assert their relevance to his practice. In his art, writing and activist work, Medalla maintained an ongoing dialogue with ethics of practice and questions of ecology, cultural identity and sexuality. He lived in many places, including also Paris, Venice, Berlin and New York, and the experiences of travel, place, transition and flux run throughout his work.

DAVID MORRIS
is Research Fellow and Editor at Afterall Research Centre. His work explores different approaches to artistic research, education and exhibition, with a focus on experimental and collective practice. He has organised various exhibitions, symposia and workshops, and co-edited publications including *Schizo-Culture: The Event, The Book* (with Sylvère Lotringer; Semiotext(e) / The MIT Press, 2014); *Artist-to-Artist: Independent Art Festivals in Chiang Mai 1992–98* (with David Teh; Afterall Books, 2018); and *Art and Its Worlds: Exhibitions, Institutions and Art Becoming Public* (with Bo Choy, Charles Esche and Lucy Steeds; Afterall Books, 2021). With Helena Vilalta he leads a research masters programme in Exhibition Studies at Central Saint Martins, University of the Arts London, where he is also a trade union organiser.

ANNABEL NICOLSON
creates film works and performances. She ran the gallery at the New Arts Lab, London (1969–70) and was cinema programmer at the London Film Maker's Co-op (1974, 1976–77 and 1992/93). Nicolson was a founding member of Circles–Women's Film in Distribution (1979), editorial contributor to *MUSICS* (1975–79), co-editor and publisher of *Readings* (1977). Her work is in the collection of the Belgian National Film Archive, British Film Institute, Canterbury University and Women Artists' Slide Library; her artist's book *Escaping Notice* (1977) is in the collection of the Victoria and Albert Museum, London.

NII KWATE OWOO
was born and raised in Ghana and has been producing and directing films since the early 1970s. After graduating from the London Film School, he formed Efiri Tete Films, the first Independent African film production company in the UK, under which he produced and directed his first film, the documentary *You Hide Me* (1970), about the colonisation of

African art in the British Museum. The film won the Best Short Documentary Film Prize at the Paris Short Film Festival in September 2020. From 1973 to 1975, he was Research Fellow and Co-coordinator of Film and Video at the Europe Africa Research Project in Gower Street London. In the late 70s he organised the first African Peoples Festival of Films at the Keskidee Centre in Islington. As a Research Fellow at the Institute of African Studies, University of Ghana, he founded the Media Research Unit in 1978, and collaborated on the production and direction of documentaries. He has been active in the movement for a pan-African cinema and co-produced and directed the documentary feature *OUAGA – African Cinema Now* (with Dr. Kwesi Owusu; 1988) and *AMA* (1991). In 2017 and 2019, he was Producer/Director of PANAFEST (Pan African Festival of Theatre and Arts). Since his first film, Nii Kwate has been relentlessly devoted to the research and exploration of the use of African cultural traditions and storytelling formats (orature) in film and video.

CƯỜNG MINH BÁ PHẠM

works between/in/nearby/at the intersections of sound, community and archives. He is interested in learning (and unlearning) our understandings of history, community, movement, family, sound, language and memory, and how they can inform, challenge or be influenced by power, knowledge and/or subjectivity. Sound work can encompass radio art or DJing, but also research, writing and translation. He is particularly drawn to cover songs from the pre-internet age, as he likes to speculate on how songs get translated and exchanged or how the simple act of singing can be a form of solidarity across communities and borders. He works with vulnerable communities in London, such as those who are homeless, undocumented or marginalised due to a lack of care from the state. This work ranges from translation and assisting people with accessing medical or public services to sitting on various boards. His artistic practice is heavily informed by community-based approaches that prioritise collaboration, accessibility and multivocality. Archives are the final area in which he works. He is the co-founder of the steering committee of An Viet Archives, currently held at Hackney Archives. He understands that only certain communities have had access to publishing and printing and input into how the archive is catalogued or organised. Therefore, he is a believer in community participation in the archive, which will give space to recontextualize the past, thereby allowing deeper understanding of the present and imagined futures.

VIJAY PRASHAD

is a historian and journalist working between New Delhi, Santiago and Havana. He is Chief Editor of LeftWord Books and directs Tricontinental: Institute for Social Research. Prashad is the author of *Washington Bullets: A History of the CIA, Coups, and Assassinations* (LeftWord, 2020); *Red Star Over the Third World* (Pluto Press, 2019); *The Poorer Nations: A Possible History of the Global South* (Verso, 2012); *The Darker Nations: A People's History of the Third World* (The New Press, 2008); and *The Withdrawal: Iraq, Libya, Afghanistan, and the Fragility of U.S. Power* (written with Noam Chomsky; The New Press, 2022).

BRANDON TAYLOR

is Professor Emeritus of History of Art, University of Southampton, and Senior Ruskin Tutor at the Ruskin School of Art, University of Oxford. His recent books include *The Life of Forms in Art* (Bloomsbury, 2020) and *Make It Modern: A History of Art in the 20th Century* (Yale University Press, 2022).

CECILIA VICUÑA

was born in Santiago de Chile and is a visual artist, poet, film-maker and activist. A co-founder of Artists for Democracy in 1974, she has long made poetic work in space, performance and visual arts that is considered a decolonising vision that anticipated ecofeminism. She coined the term 'arte precario' ('precarious art') in the mid-1960s in Chile, as a new, independent and non-colonised category for her structures that disappear in the landscape. These include her *quipus*, ritual acts that weave the urban landscape, rivers and oceans, as well as people, and reconstruct a sense of unity and an awareness of interconnectivity. In recent years she has exhibited at the Turbine Hall at Tate Modern, London; Solomon R. Guggenheim Museum, New York; Museum of Modern Art (MOMA), New York; Documenta 14, Athens and Kassel; Kunstinstitutt Melly, Rotterdam; MUAC, Mexico;

CA2M, Madrid; and Museo de Arte Miguel Urrutia (MAMU), Banco de la República, Bogotá, Colombia. In 2022, she received the Golden Lion Award at the 59th Venice Biennale. In 2023, her travelling retrospective 'Soñar el agua' opened at the Museo Nacional de Bellas Artes in Santiago.

CAROLL YASKY
is an art historian and, since 2013, Curator and Coordinator of the collection of the Museo de la Solidaridad Salvador Allende (MSSA) in Santiago. Her work crosses research, management and curatorial practices, and her latest co-curating projects have been the MSSA chapter in the 58th Carnegie International exhibition, 'Is it morning for you yet?' (2021); annual exhibitions of the MSSA Collection; 'Debut, 43 works meet its Collection' (2018); and 'Utopia and Crisis' (2017). She also coordinates institutional publications such as the 'catalogue raisonné' *Museo Internacional de la Resistencia Salvador Allende (1975–1990)*, about the museum and artworks donated during the exile period.

Image Credits

All artworks © the artists,
all photographs © the photographers

Courtesy An Việt Archives collection
at Hackney Archives, London
pp.116, 117, 118, 119 upper two,
120, 128 middle
Courtesy An Việt Archives collection
at Hackney Archives, London.
Photography: Hau-yu Tam
p.119 middle
Courtesy An Việt Archives collection
at Hackney Archives, London.
Photography: Hoa Lê
p.117 bottom
Courtesy Anne Bean
p.212 right
Courtesy Gui Bonsiepe
p.26
Photography: Guy Brett
p.289
Courtesy Virgil Calaguian, England & Co
pp.254, 255, 262, 266–68, 282
Courtesy Hugh Cave
pp.242, 243
Courtesy George Clark
pp.119 bottom, 128 bottom
© John Dugger Archive, England & Co
pp.101, 102, 104, 154, 155, 156, 335, 336
© John Dugger Archive, England & Co.
Design: John Dugger and David Medalla
p.28
Photography © Jane England.
Courtesy England & Co
p.244
© Jane England Archive.
Photography: England & Co
pp.230, 231, 285–86, 315
Courtesy Jane England Archive.
Photography: England & Co.
Design: Tina Keane
p.252 top
Courtesy England & Co
p.241
Photography: England & Co.
Design: Steve Thorn
p.298 top
Photography: Peter Fisher.
Courtesy England & Co
p.238
Photography: Peter Fisher,
Jane England Archive.
Courtesy England & Co
p.252 bottom left
Courtesy Bob Fitch Photography Archive,
Department of Special Collections,
Stanford University Library
p.108
Courtesy Fundación Salvador Allende,
Santiago de Chile
p.45
Courtesy Christine Halsall.
Photography: Nick Wates
pp.80, 84, 196, 203, 204, 205,
206, 207, 208
© Charles Hustwick.
Photography: England & Co
pp.276 top, 298 bottom
Photography © Charles Hustwick,
England & Co
pp.59, 287, 288
Courtesy Grosvenor Gallery
pp.57, 191, 192, 193, 218, 300–1,
303–7, 308–9
Courtesy Inti Illimani and Yanker Poster
Collection, Library of Congress Prints
and Photographs Division.
Design: Malaquias Montoya
p.109
Courtesy family of Tina Keane, LUX
pp.252 bottom right, 253
Courtesy Saleem Arif Quadri,
www.saleemquadri.co.uk
p.302

Courtesy Lynn MacRitchie
pp.66, 73, 82–83, 144–45, 150–51, 175,
177, 178, 179, 180–1, 182, 190 top, 194–95,
197, 209, 210, 214, 215, 216, 219, 220
Courtesy Lynn MacRitchie.
Design: Patricia de Villiers
p.217
Estate of David Medalla
pp.257, 283 top
© Estate of David Medalla.
Photography © England & Co
p.291 left
Courtesy Museo de la Solidaridad
Salvador Allende
pp.86, 88, 91 bottom, 92–93, 94, 97
Courtesy Cường Minh Bá Phạm
pp.121, 124, 127
Courtesy Stephen Pusey
p.31
Courtesy Frank Shepherd
pp.39, 40
Courtesy Sylvia Stevens Archive.
Photography: England & Co
pp.222–23, 281
Photography © Tate, TGA 20208
Guy Brett collection
pp.169, 170, 172, 225, 226, 228, 229,
232 top, 248, 256, 269, 271, 273, 274–75,
310, 316, 318, 319
Courtesy Tate.
Photography: Museo de la Solidaridad
Salvador Allende
p.91 top
Courtesy Jun Terra
pp.52, 71, 128 top, 149 bottom,
152, 153, 158–59, 160, 161, 168, 176,
221, 232 bottom, 233, 235, 236, 237
Courtesy Anna Thew
pp.296, 312, 313
Courtesy David Toop
pp.122, 212 left, 246–47
Photographer unknown, from Jill Drower,
*99 Balls Pond Road: The Story of the
Exploding Galaxy* (Scrudge Books, 2014)
p.35
Courtesy Unfinished Histories
p.240 top
Courtesy Cecilia Vicuña Studio
pp.37, 50 bottom, 60, 143, 146, 157, 171
Courtesy Cecilia Vicuña Studio.
Photography: James O'Hern
p.63
Courtesy Cecilia Vicuña Studio
and England & Co
p.15 and front/back cover
Courtesy the Estate of Carlos Villa
p.64

REPRINTS & EXTRACTS

p.149
'Le Chili à Londres', *Le Monde*, 28 October 1974

pp.163–67
Cecilia Vicuña, 'Organized Dreaming', trans. Christopher Winks, in *Artists for Democracy: El Archivo de Cecilia Vicuña*, Santiago de Chile: Museo de la Memoria y los Derechos Humanos / Museo Nacional de Bellas Artes, 2013, unpaginated

p.183
Margaret Richards, 'Squatter-artists with a social purpose', *Tribune*, 14 March 1975

pp.185–89
Guy Brett, 'Agriculture, Field, Decoration', in *Carnival of Perception: Selected Writings on Art*, London: Institute of International Visual Arts, 2004, pp.154–57

p.190
Caroline Tisdall, 'Artists for Democracy in London', *The Guardian*, Arts supplement, 31 March 1975

pp.198–201
Nii Kwate Owoo, 'Commentary: You Hide Me', previously unpublished, c.1970

p.205
'Film and Poster Collective: Interview', in *'Art as a Mass Political Weapon': The Poster Collective 1972–82*, London: Chimera Publications, 2020, pp.133–38

p.213
Annabel Nicolson, 'Paul Burwell and David Toop at Artists' For Democracy', *MUSICS*, no.3, August/September 1975, p.19

p.224 left
'Triển lãm: Nhân dân thế giới học tập nhân dân Đông Dương và tỏ lòng thành kính đối với Chủ tịch Hồ Chí Minh' [Exhibition: People of the World Learn from Indochina and pay homage to President Ho Chi Minh], *Nhân Dân*, 20 July 1975

p.224 right
Paul Overy, 'Aware and absent', *The Times*, 5 August 1975

p.227
Paul Overy, 'Collage: the new connexion', *The Times*, 9 December 1975

pp.234–35
David Medalla, 'Chinese Films', *Time Out*, 24–30 September 1971, pp.38–39

p.239 left
Paul Overy, 'Liverpool follows Sickert', *The Times*, 17 February 1976

p.261
Caroline Tisdall, 'Come Into the Garden', *The Guardian*, Arts supplement, 23 September 1976

pp.264–65
Marc Camille Chaimowicz, 'Performance', *Studio International*, vol.193, no.985, January/February 1977, pp.11–16

pp.266–68
Virgil Calaguian, 'Performance art – it breathes and grows', *Manila*, 1–31 May 1977, pp.22–23

p.277 left
Paul Overy, 'The indigenous Americans', *The Times*, 12 October 1976

p.277 right
Richard Cork, 'The seductive pipes of peace', *Evening Standard*, 7 October 1976

pp.278–80
Susan Hiller, 'Sacred Circles: 2,000 Years of North American Indian Art', *Studio International*, vol.193, no.985, January/February 1977, pp.56–58 [A revised version of this text was published in Alexandra M. Kokoli (ed.), *Susan Hiller: The Provisional Texture of Reality: Selected Talks and Texts, 1977–2007*, Zurich: JRP|Ringier; Dijon: Les Presses du reel, 2008, pp.93–102]

p.282
Robert Tai, in '4 for Virgil', *Readings*, no.1, February 1977, pp.7–9

pp.292–95
'David Medalla in Conversation with Brandon Taylor', *Artscribe*, no.6, 1977, pp.20–23

p.299
Suzy Adderley, '"Five Days in July" performances at Acme, and at AFD', *Artscribe*, no.8, September 1977, pp.51–52

pp.300–1
Rasheed Araeen, 'Paki Bastard', *Black Phoenix*, no.2, summer 1978, pp.12–17

pp.303–7
Rasheed Araeen, 'Preliminary Notes for a Black Manifesto', *Black Phoenix*, no.1, winter 1978, pp.3–12

p.311
Margaret Richards, 'Radical, committed – and homeless', *Tribune*, 15 July 1977

p.317
Rasheed Araeen, 'Conversation with David Medalla', *Black Phoenix*, no.3, Spring 1979, pp.10–19

p.320
'KER-u-n-n-CH!', *Camden Journal*, 30 November 1979

p.140
Guy Brett, 'Internationalism Among Artists in the 60s and 70s', in Rasheed Araeen (ed.), *The Other Story: Afro-Asian Artists in Post-War Britain* (exh. cat.), London: Hayward Gallery/South Bank Centre, 1989, p.114
Lynn MacRitchie, conversation with Adeena Mey, 2 February 2023
Jun Terra, correspondence with David Morris, 8 April 2021

p.142
Cecilia Vicuña, conversation with Courtney J. Martin, 2 February 2023
Conrad Atkinson, in *Artists for Democracy: El Archivo de Cecilia Vicuña*, Santiago de Chile: Museo de la Memoria y los Derechos Humanos/Museo Nacional de Bellas Artes, 2013, unpaginated
John Dugger, 'A Festival for Democracy/Artists for Democracy 1974', in *Artists for Democracy: El Archivo de Cecilia Vicuña*, Santiago de Chile: Museo de la Memoria y los Derechos Humanos/Museo Nacional de Bellas Artes, 2013, unpaginated

p.147
Cecilia Vicuña, 'Organized Dreaming', trans. Christopher Winks, in *Artists for Democracy: El Archivo de Cecilia Vicuña*, Santiago de Chile: Museo de la Memoria y los Derechos Humanos/Museo Nacional de Bellas Artes, 2013, unpaginated
Cecilia Vicuña, conversation with Courtney J. Martin, 2 February 2023

p.148
Stephen Pusey, correspondence with Hannah Healey, July 2023

p.153
Sylvia Stevens, in *'Art as a Mass Political Weapon': The Poster Collective 1972–82*, London: Chimera Publications, 2020, p.156
Jackie Hatfield, 'Interview with Tina Keane' for *REWIND: Artists' Video in the 70s and* 80s, 2005, available at https://sites.dundee.ac.uk/rewind/wp-content/uploads/sites/146/2021/03/TK505.pdf

p.160
Jun Terra, correspondence with Eileen Legaspi-Ramirez, 28 March 2011
Lynn MacRitchie, correspondence with David Morris, 12 May 2023

p.173
Stephen Pusey, correspondence with Hannah Healey, July 2023
Jun Terra, conversation with Arianna Mercado, 2 February 2023
Jun Terra, text shared with David Morris, 8 April 2021

p.174
Stephen Pusey, correspondence with David Morris, 20 and 27 April 2023
Jun Terra, text shared with David Morris, 8 April 2021
Jackie Hatfield, 'Interview with Tina Keane' for *REWIND: Artists' Video in the 70s and* 80s, 2005, available at https://sites.dundee.ac.uk/rewind/wp-content/uploads/sites/146/2021/03/TK505.pdf

p.179
Lynn MacRitchie, unpublished statement on 'The World in a Grain of Sand', 2020

p.192
Amra Ali, 'Ruptures of Rasheed Araeen in the Politics of Visual Art: Toward a New Art Discourse in Pakistan', in Sasanka Perera and Dev Nath Pathak (ed.), *Intersections of Contemporary Art, Anthropology and Art History in South Asia: Decoding Visual Worlds*, London: Springer Nature, 2019, p.263

p.196
Jonathan Miles, conversation with Wing Chan, David Morris, Nii Kwate Owoo and Ife Nii Owoo, 2 February 2023
Nii Kwate Owoo, conversation with Wing Chan, Jonathan Miles, David Morris and Ife Nii Owoo, 2 February 2023

p.202
James Leahy, 'You Hide Me', *Vertigo*, vol.1, issue 2, Summer-Autumn 1993, available at https://www.closeupfilmcentre.com/vertigo_magazine/volume-1-issue-2-summer-autumn-1993/you-hide-me/
Ife Nii Owoo, correspondence with Wing Chan, 4 May 2023

p.206
Steve Sprung, in *'Art as a Mass Political Weapon': The Poster Collective 1972–82*, London: Chimera Publications, 2020, p.159
Steve Sprung, conversation with David Morris, 12 June 2023

p.211
Lynn MacRitchie, correspondence with David Morris, 9 June 2023
Jonathan Miles, in *'Art as a Mass Political Weapon': The Poster Collective 1972–82*, London: Chimera Publications, 2020, p.150

p.217
Rose English, correspondence with David Morris, 17 March 2021 and 17 July 2023
Kathleen McCreery, correspondence with Wing Chan, 6 June 2023

p.218
Jun Terra, conversation with Wing Chan and David Morris, 27 April 2023

p.224
Lynn MacRitchie, conversation with Adeena Mey, 2 February 2023

p.233
Guy Brett, *Exploding Galaxies: Art of David Medalla*, London: Kala Press, 1995, pp.119–21
Jun Terra, correspondence with Wing Chan, 15 August 2023
Jun Terra, correspondence with David Morris, 10 July 2023

p.243
Hugh Cave, correspondence with David Morris, 10 June and 10 July 2023

p.244
Paul Burwell and Stephen Cripps, 'Interview on 29 March 1976', in *Stephen Cripps: Performing Machines* (exh. cat.), Vienna: VfmK Verlag für moderne Kunst, 2017, pp.159–60

p.249
Giles Thomas, correspondence with David Morris, 27 June 2022

p.254
Virgil Calaguian, correspondence with David Morris, 21 July 2023
Virgil Calaguian, 'Performance art – it breathes and grows', *Manila*, 1–31 May 1977, pp.22–23

p.257
David Medalla, interview with Purissima Benitez-Johannot, 30–31 March 1992, in P. Benitez Johannot (ed.), *The Life and Art of David Medalla*, Quezon City: Vibal Foundation, 2012, pp.234–35

p.258
Nick Payne, in 'Artists' thoughts on the seventies in words and pictures', *Studio International*, vol.195, no.991–92, 1981, p.56

p.263
Virgil Calaguian, correspondence with David Morris, 21 July 2023

p.272
Guy Brett, *Exploding Galaxies: Art of David Medalla*, London: Kala Press, 1995, pp.85–87
David Medalla, conversation with Steve Thorn, 22 May 1977. Guy Brett collection, Tate Archive TGA20208

p.284
Nick Payne, in 'Radical Attitudes to the Gallery; Artists' Contributions', *Studio International*, vol.95, no.990, 1980, p.44

p.287
Anne Bean, untitled reflection on AFD, 6 September 2022
David Medalla, conversation with Steve Thorn, 22 May 1977. Guy Brett collection, Tate Archive TGA20208

p.290
Guy Brett, 'Elasticity of Exhibition', *Tate Papers*, issue 12, Autumn 2009, available at https://www.tate.org.uk/documents/331/tate_papers_12_guy_brett_elasticity_of_exhibition.pdf
David Medalla, conversation with Steve Thorn, 22 May 1977. Guy Brett collection, Tate Archive TGA20208

p.297
Charles Hustwick, correspondence with David Morris, 29 June 2023

p.298
Roberta Kravitz, correspondence with Wing Chan, 7 July 2023
Charles Hustwick, correspondence with David Morris, 12 April 2023

p.302
Saleem Arif Quadri, correspondence with David Morris, 15 and 24 April 2023

p.313
Anna Thew, correspondence with David Morris, 14 June 2023

p.314
David Medalla, conversation with Steve Thorn, 22 May 1977. Guy Brett collection, Tate Archive TGA20208

7:84 Theatre Company 32

Acme
19, 140, *298*
African Party for the Independence of Guinea and Cape Verde (PAIGC) 24
African Students' Union (also 'The Basement')
78, 202
'After Year Zero: Geographies of Collaboration'
21
Alberti, Rafael 76
Alegría, Fernando 108
Allende, Salvador
14, 24–27, 30, 36, 43, 45, 72, 75, 87, 89, 90, 95, 99, 100, 103, 106, 108–11, 132, 133, 142, 148, 160, 164, 166, *back cover*
Altamirano, Alejandra
87, 90, *94*, *97*
Álvarez, Santiago 132
American Indian Movement (AIM)
33, 42, 47, 107, 111, 272, 314
'American Indian Movement 1976 Exhibition'
31, 38, *39*, *40*, 41, 139, 270–80
Amich, Candice 61
Amnesia International Dance Company
229, *232*
An Viet Foundation
13, 117, *120*, 122, 126, *128*
Anti-University 20
Arab Society 75
Araeen, Rasheed
12, 13, 17, 21, 22, 25, 33, 47, 48, 55–58, 62, 138, 139, 192, 193, *219*, 257, 302, 303–07
Arce, José Pérez de 164
Arguedas, José María 165
Art Against Apartheid collection
20
Art Combine 32
Art Meeting Place
19, *50*, *60*, 85
Art Workers Coalition 140
Artists Liberation Front
30, 55, 233, 243
Artists Meeting for Cultural Change
140
Artists Placement Group 20
Artists Union 142
Arts Council of Great Britain 35
'Arts Festival for Democracy in Chile'
11, *15*, 22, 25, 26, 30, 32, 36, 37, 43, 46, 55, 56, 60, *66*, 69, 70, 75, 78, 105, 107, 139, 141–71
Arts Lab
19, 249
Ashton, Dore
89, 96
Association for Radical East Asian Studies (AREAS)
71, 79
Atkinson, Conrad
138, 142

Balmes, José 89
Bandung Conference 21
Banner Arts 20
Banner Books & Crafts 76
Barber, Tamsin 117
Bean, Anne
57, 60, 138, 287
Bean, Gerlin 78
Beau Geste Press 20
Beuys, Joseph
60, 139, *285*, 287
Black Panther Party
107, 111
Black People's Free Store 107
Blackman, Peter 32
Bloomsbury Group 298
Boal, Augusto 136
Bogle-L'Ouverture Publications 32
Braden, Su 23
Brecht, Bertolt
34, 227
Brett, Guy
13, 27, 30, 35, 36, 44, 45, 58, 60, 78, 89, 90, 97, 138, 139, 140, 142, 148, 153, 165, 166, *170*, 173, 185–89, *190*, 227, *232*, 233, 272, *286*, 290
Brittain, Bernadette 153
British Society for Social Responsibility in Science *177*
Brixton Artists Collective 19
Brixton Black Women's Group 78
Broadside Mobile Theatre Group
216, 217
Bulosan, Carlos
53, 54
Bunster, Álvaro
36, 87
Burwell, Paul
57, 122, 126, 129, *212*, *213*, *246–47*
Bussi, Hortensia
103, 107, 113

Caboo, Roy
32, *132*
Cabral, Amílcar
33, 131, 196, *204*
Cafe Oto 129
Calaguian, Virgil
13, *52*, 53, 138, 139, 174, *176*, *235*, *237*, 254, *255*, *262*, 263, 266–68, 297
Campaign for Homosexual Equality (CHE) 46, 297
campamento
46, *158–59*, 160, 165
Caribbean Artists Movement (CAM)
32
Carnation Revolution
24, 131
Cave, Hugh
78, 138, 139, 148, *242*, 243
Celis, Silvia
86, 87, 90
Centre d'Etude des Musiques Orientales
125
Centro de Arte y Comunicación 17
Chaimowicz, Marc Camille
264–65
Chapman, Nicky *273*
Chapman, Veronica *271*
'Chile Britain' 89
Chile Solidarity Campaign
25, 36, 95, 99, 102, 103, 106, 107, 113, 142
Chimurenga 21
'China Show'
128, 139, 229–39
Cinema Action
32, 148, 196, *197*, 206
Clark, Harriet
230, *232*
Clark, Lygia
148, 165
Clifford, James 58
Cloudsley, Anne
139, *310*
Clough, Prunella
90, *91*
Cohen, G.A. 298
Cohen, Philip
210, 229, 257
Collets 76
Collins, Rob *284*

Columbia University 131
Committee of Concerned Asian Scholars 79
Commonwealth Immigrants Act 18
Communist Party of the Democratic Republic of Vietnam 120
Communist Party of the Philippines (CPP) 76
Communist Youth Party of Chile 125
Congress for Cultural Freedom 133
Conservative Party (UK) 106
'Conversation Future Tense' 139
Coracle Press 20
Cork, Richard 21, 42, *277*
Covent Garden Community 174
Covent Garden Independent News 85
Cripps, Stephen 138, 139, 244, *245–47*, 313
Cross, Peter 139, *191*
cultural worker 11, 14, 18, 22, 25, 26, 33, 36, 43, 68, 77, 85, 134, 135, 139

Dadzie, Stella 78
Darley, Andy 153
de Quadras, Oriol 140, *318–19*
Destruction in Art Symposium 20
Dihavina 124
Dillons 129
Disques Bam 125
Do-It-Yourself (or DIY) 23, 55, 140
documenta 30, 103
Dorfman, Ariel 75
Dugger, John 12, *15*, 27, *28*, 29, 30, 34, 36, 55, 78, 87, 90, *91*, 95, 99–115, 138, 139, 142, *143*, *148*, 165, 166, *170*, 243, *335*, *336*
Durham, Jimmie 33

El-Enany, Nadine 18
'El tren popular de la cultura' ('The Popular Culture Train') 45
'End of an Era: Hand in Life and Art' 139, *256*
England, Jane *231*
English, Rose 33, 138, 217
Escoffier, Auguste 11
'Eskimo Carver' 48, 56, 58, *59*, 60, 136, 139, 286–91, 297
Estado Novo 24
Estes, Nick 38
Equipo de Contrainformación 74
Event Structure Research Group 20
Exploding Galaxy 20, 29, 34, *35*, 46, 249, 272

Facop 19
Fedorov, Nikolai 45
FESTAC '77 17, 21
Feuchtwang, Stephan 79
'Final Show' 139, *315*
Fisher, Jean 58
Fisher, Peter 47
Fitch, Bob 108
Fleming, Alan 232, 236
Flores, Patrick 27
Folkways Records 126
Fonda, Jane 41
Fox, Dave 153
Free International University 20
Frelimo *196*, *203*, *205*, *206*
'Fruits of the Earth in Decorative Art' 44, 139, *184*, *187*, *188*, *190*
Fundación Gilberto Alzate Avendaño 37

Gallery House 140
Galván, José María Moreno 89
Gatehouse, Mike 113
Gay Liberation Front (GLF) 46, 297
General Will Theatre Company *240*
Glide Memorial Church 107–11, 114
Glynn, David *177*
Gorman, John 103, 104
Goytisolo, José Agustín 95
Gramsci, Antonio 62
Grogan, Martha *152*, *162*
Grove White, Annie 153
Grunwick strikes 56
Guanghwa Bookshop 76, 233
Guillen, Nicolas 76
Gulf Committee 75

'Haciendo barrio' 96
Hackney Black People's Association 32
Hall, Stuart 106
Halliday, Fred 75
Halliday, Jon 75
Halsall, Christine 153
Harrison, Margaret 74
Hart, Judith 107
Havana Biennale 48, 61
Hayward Gallery 38, 272, 284
Hayward, Ron 106
Heartfield, John 34, 139, *227*
Heath, Edward 106
Heath, Vic 103
Henderson, Roberta Hunter *194–95*
Heresies Collective 55
Hernandez, Amado 76
Hernandez, Miguel 76
Hikmet, Nizam 76
Hiller, Susan 13, 42, 257, 278–80
Ho Chi Minh 11, 13, 37, 76, 123, 132
Hockney, David 89, 148
Hok Thye 229
Holder, Mitch 202
'Homenaje a Vietnam' ('Homage to Vietnam') *37*
Houédard, Dom Sylvester 76, *210*
Hughes, Alice 174
Hulten, Pontus 72
Hunt, Kay 74
Huntley, Accabre 32, *152*
Huntley, Eric 32
Huntley, Jessica 32
Husband, Bertha 139, 140, *210*, 211, 257
Hustwick, Charles 46, 138, *276*, 297, 298

Ifriqiyah Films 197, 202
Immigration Act 1971 18, 240
'Inaugural Show' 139, *175*
Indo-China People's Solidarity Front *209*
Institute of Contemporary Arts (ICA) 27, *28*, *88*, 89, 142
'International Art Exhibition for Palestine' 20
International Committee for Freedom in the Philippines *225*
International Committee of Artistic Solidarity with Chile 89
International Indian Treaty Council (IITC) 41
International Marxist Group 76, 103
International Mass Media Research Center 75
International Socialists 103
Inti Illimani 107, 109–11
Isherwood, George *248*, 313
Ivens, Joris 165

Jagger, Mick 206
Japan, Asian, African and Latin American Artists' Association (JAALA) 20
Jenkins, Jane 129
'Joseph Beuys' Coyote' 139, *285*

Kabataang Makabayan 27, 71, 77, 126
Kapur, Geeta 48
Katz, Judith 217
Keane, Tina 138, 139, 140, 148, *153*, 174, *252*, *253*, 257, 313
Keeler, Paul 35
Kelly, Mary 74
Kerala Kathakali dance company 29
Khan, Naseem 47
Kim, Andrew 'Pop' 47, 148
Kim, U Cha 76, *210*
King, Martin Luther, Jr 106
Knox, Sonia 140, *194–95*, 257
Kravitz, Roberta 138, 298
Kuo Mo-Jo 76, *210*

La Peña Cultural Center 110–14
Labour Party (UK) 12, 103, 105–07, 114, 142
Lansley, Jacky 33, *216*, 217
Last Poets 57
Law Long 229
League of Socialist Artists 30
Léger, Fernand 34
Levi, Carlo 89
Lewis, Beryl *273*
Lewis, Lester 32
Lewis, Terry 41, *273*
Leymarie, Jean 89
Limited Dance Company 33, *216*
'Living Words, Living Images: Festival of Progressive Poetry and Art' 76, 139, *210*

London Biennale
55, 72
London Calling Arts Festival
139, *260–61*, 263, 264–65
London Film-makers Co-op 20
Lopez, Atilio 313
Lu Hsun (also Lu Xun)
66, 70, 76, *210*, 211, *229–32*
Lynd, Juliet 63

Machel, Josina
76, *210*
Machida, Margo 54
MacRitchie, Lynn
33, 44, 45, 54, 55, 72–75, 81, *82–83*, 138, 139, 140, 148, *158–59*, 160, 177–82, 211, *222–23*, 224
Maestro, Lani 61
Mai Thu 125
Manchanda, Abhimanyu *209*
Mangrove Nine 32
Mao Tse-Tung
30, 34, *52*, 76, 103, 263
Mapuche
37, 51, 164–65
Marinetti, F.T. 34
Martin, Courtney J. 56
Marcos, Ferdinand, Jr.
12, 51
Marcos, Ferdinand, Sr. 53
Matta, Roberto
148, *161*, 165
Mattelart, Armand
74, 75
May First Movement 32
May Fourth Movement 70
Mayakovsky, Vladimir
34, 76
Mayfair Illuminations
11, 140, *316*, 317, *318*
McCarthy, Mary 165
McCreery, Kathleen
138, 217
Medalla, David
12, 13, *15*, 18, 25–30, 32, 34, 35, 44, 48, 53–58, *59*, 60, 62, 72, 78, *128*, 136, 138, 139, 140, 142, *149*, *152*, 153, *155*, 166, *170*, 174, 192, 202, 206, 211, 217, 218, *225–26*, *228*, 229, *230*, *232*, 233, *238*, 243, *248*, 249, *256*, 257, *269*, 272, *283*, 286–95, *296*, 297, 298, 313–15
Miles, Jonathan
79, 138, 140, 148, *152*, 153, 173, *176*, 196, 206, *210*, 211
MIR (Movimiento de Izquierda Revolucionaria, also Revolutionary Left Movement)
22, 36, 166, 173
Mme Mong Trung 125
Mohaiemen, Naeem 20
Molina, Sandra 111
Monday Club 106
Monkey Theatre 20
Moore, Henry 89
Morris, Olive 78
'Murals, Images of Women'
139, *210*
Murguía, Alejandro 108
Museo de Arte Latinoamericano Contemporáneo de Managua/en Solidaridad con Nicaragua
20–21
Museo de la Solidaridad Salvador Allende (MSSA, also Museum of Solidarity)
12, 20, 72, 86–97, 166

Nazareth, H.O.
33, 76, *210*, 211
National Liberation Front (Viet Cong, South Vietnam)
76, 121, 123
National Liberation Front (the Philippines) 69
National Liberation Movement (the Philippines) 70
National Front (UK) 56
National Union of Public Employees (NUPE)
81, *82–83*
Neruda, Pablo
30, 43, 76, 107, 148, *210*
'Net'
139, *191*
New International Economic Order 24
newen
51, 65
Newham Women's Action Group
217
Nguyen Quang Than
76, *210*
nhạc đỏ (red music) 125
Nicolson, Annabel
13, 122, *213*
Nii Owoo, Ife
78, 79, 81, *84*, 138, 153, 202
Nukkad Natak (corner theatre) 134

O Productions 20
Oiticica, Hélio 165
Oldenberg, Claes 148
'On Meat & Metaphysics, of mice & men'
139, *254*
'Operación verdad' ('Operation Truth')
72, 87
Organisation of Women of Asian and African Descent (OWAAD)
78, 81
Organization of Solidarity with the People of Asia, Africa and Latin America (OSPAAAL) 132
'Other Story: Afro-Asian Artists in Post-War Britain' 58
Overy, Paul
42, *224*, *227*, *239*, *277*
Oxley, Steve (also Peter Oxley)
139, 154, *262*, 263
Owoo, Nii Kwate
13, 18, 138, 196, 198–202

Palestine Action 75
Palestine, Gulf, Yemen Solidarity Committee 75
Pan-Afrikan Connection 20
Parot, Raquel 87
Parra, Violeta
135, *152*
'Past Disquiet' 21, 45
Pavilions in the Parks 19
Payne, Nick
138, 140, *236*, *248*, *256*, 258, *259*, 283, *284*, *298*
'Peasant Painting from Huhsien County'
27
Pedrosa, Mário
87, 89, 90, 96
Penn, Mavis
103, 148
Penrose, Roland
86, 87, 89, 90, *91*, 165
'People of the World Learn from Indochina'
123, 136, 139, 214–26
'People Weave a House!'
27, *28*
Perón, Juan Domingo 74
Phạm Duy
117, 120, 121

Philippine Solidarity Campaign *225*
Phương Dung 121
Plachek, James W. 108
Plaid Cymru 41
Polish, Peter
102, 142
Polytechnic of Central London Students' Union 72
Popper, Frank 23
Poster Collective (also Poster-Film Collective)
20, 78–81, *84*, 140, 153, 196, 197, 202–08
Potter, Sally
33, *216*, 217
Pound, Ezra 34
Prashad, Vijay
10, 48, 130–36
Project Cybersyn 26
Puffin Books 71
Pulang Tala Press 77
Pusey, Stephen
30, *31*, 77, 78, 138, 139, 148, 173, 174

Quach, Georgina 117
Quadri, Saleem Arif
138, 302
Quilapayún
95, 125

Rebelo, Jorge
76, *84*, *210*
Red Ladder Theatre Company
32
Red Power movement 38
Red Star Shadow Puppet Theatre
66, 69
Reedy, Carlyle
166, 257
Renzi, Juan Pablo 74
Reyes, Cid
232, 233
Richard, Nelly 61
Richards, Margaret
73, *183*, *311*
Riley, Bridget 89
Rimbaud, Arthur
76, *210*
Roberts, Eleanor 61–62
Roja, Clarita
76, *210*
Roldan, Norberto 61

'Sacred Circles: Two Thousand Years of North American Indian Art'
38, 272, 278–80
Said, Edward 126
Saigon Radio 125
Salkey, Andrew 32
Salon de la Jeune Peinture 20
San Juan, Epifanio, Jr.
57, 62
Schiesari, Nancy 153
Scratch Orchestra 20
Seeger, Pete 95
Shepherd, Fredda 273
Shigeharu, Nakano
76, *210*
Shivtansani, Siddhartha 217
Siegelaub, Seth 75
Signals gallery
27, 35, 249
Signals Newsbulletin 27
Sining Kamalig 263
Sinn Fein 41
Sison, Jose Maria
76, 77, *220*
Socialist Republic of Vietnam 124
Society for Anglo Chinese Understanding (SACU)
27, 104, 229, *234*

Sóng Nhạc 121
Soto, Jesus-Rafael 206
'Southern Constellations: The Poetics of the Non-Aligned' 21
Southeast Asian Research Centre 117
SPACE 19
Sprung, Steve 79, 138, 140, 148, 153, 206
'State of British Art' 21
Stevens, Sylvia 79, 138, 140, 148, 153, *176*, 206, 217, *222–23*
'Strike at Brannans' 142
Sublime Frequencies 122
Synoptic Realists 249
Szeemann, Harald 89

Ta Kung Po 77
Tai, Robert *282*
Tatlin, Vladimir 34, 269
Taylor, Brandon 13, 292–95
Telero, Gennaro 140
Terra, Jun 27, *52*, 53, 55, *66*, 69–71, 77, 79, 126, 138, 140, 160, *161*, 173, 174, *210*, 211, 218, *232*, 233, *236*, 297
Thatcher, Margaret 106
Thew, Anna 138, *312*, 313
Third World Communications 107
Third World Troubadours 32
Thomas, Giles 46, 138, 139, 233, 249, 297
Thomas, Trevor 46, 297
Thorney Island Reception Centre 116
Thunder Hawk, Madonna 41
Ting Theatre of Mistakes 20
Tisdall, Caroline 139, 142, *190*, *261*, *285*
Toop, David 122, 126, 129, *213*
Tone Place Seminars 20
Townsend, Peter 102
Trà, My Hickin 117
Trail of Broken Treaties 38
Trần Quang Hải 129
Trần Văn Khê 123, 125, 129
Tribu No collective 55
Tricontinental Conference 132
Trịnh Công Sơn 125
Trinh T. Minh-ha 121–23
Trouillot, Michel-Rolph 12, 69

UHURU Arts Group 32
Unidad Popular (Popular Unity) 72, 75, 90, 99, 100, 106, 109, 111, 132, 164
United Farm Workers 107, 111
United Nations 24, 33, 38, 217
Unity Bookshop 76
Universidad Técnica del Estado 111

Vallejo, Cesar 76, *210*
Văn Cao 124
Varas, Paulina 164, 166
'Vernacular Art in Camden' 48, 139, 297, 298
'Victory to People's War' 31, 139, *197*
Vicuña, Cecilia 9, 12, 13, *15*, 18, 26, 37, 48, *50*, 51, 54–56, *60*, 61, *63*, 65, 67, 78, 87, 100, 102, 109, 112, 132, 139, 142, *146*, 147, 148, *157*, 160, 163–68, *170*
Vietnam Women's Union 76
Villa, Carlos 54, 55, 61, *64*
Vũ Khánh Thành 116, *117*, 120, *128*
Vu, Toan 117

Walker, Martin 153
Waugh, Carmen 87, 90
'We Want People to Know the Truth: Patchwork Pictures from Chile' 90, 92–94, 95
Westminster Central Hall 33, 107, 114
Wilde, Eduard de 89
Williams, Cecil 107–10
Williams, Hugo 35
Willis, Beverly 108
Wilson, Harold 106
'Women of Sudan Omdurman' 139, *310*
Women's Art History Collective 20
'Work, Wages and Prices' 142
'Works 1959–1975' 139, 191–93
World Federation of Democratic Youth 135
World Festival of Youth and Students 135
'World in a Grain of Sand' 44, 72–74, 139, 177–82
Wounded Knee 38

Y Vân 121

Zurita, Raúl 132

Precarious Solidarities:
Artists for Democracy 1974–77

Edited by Wing Chan
and David Morris

First published 2023 by Afterall in association with Asia Art Archive; Center for Curatorial Studies, Bard College; documenta Institut; and the Faculty of Fine, Applied and Performing Arts, University of Gothenburg

Exhibition Histories Series Editors
Lauren Cornell, Tom Eccles, Charles Esche, Pablo Lafuente, Sneha Ragavan, Lucy Steeds, John Tain, Felix Vogel, Mick Wilson and Mi You

Managing Editor
David Morris

Assistant Editor
Wing Chan

Copy Editor
Deirdre O'Dwyer

Design
Pedro Cid Proença

Printed and bound by
die Keure, Bruges

Distribution

Europe
Verlag der Buchhandlung Walther und Franz König (verlag@buchhandlung-walther-koenig.de)

UK & Ireland
Cornerhouse Publications Ltd. (publications@cornerhouse.org)

Outside Europe
D.A.P. / Distributed Art Publishers, Inc. (orders@dapinc.com)

Afterall
Central Saint Martins
Granary Building
1 Granary Square
London N1C 4AA
www.afterall.org

Afterall is a Research Centre of University of the Arts London and was founded in 1998 by Charles Esche and Mark Lewis.

Director
Mark Lewis

Associate Directors
Chloe Ting
Adeena Mey

Project Coordinator
Camille Crichlow

ISBN 978-3-7533-0426-7 (Koenig)
ISBN 978-1-84638-267-3 (Afterall)

Front and back covers: Artists for Democracy stickers created by artists including John Dugger, David Medalla and Cecilia Vicuña, for 'Arts Festival for Democracy in Chile', Royal College of Art, London, 1974. Courtesy Cecilia Vicuña Studio and England & Co

ASIA ART ARCHIVE

CCS BARD

DOCUMENTA INSTITUT

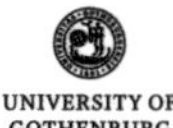
UNIVERSITY OF GOTHENBURG

ual: central saint martins

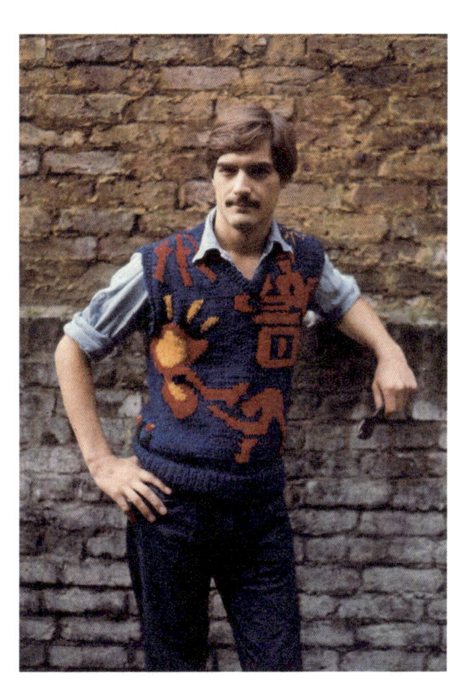

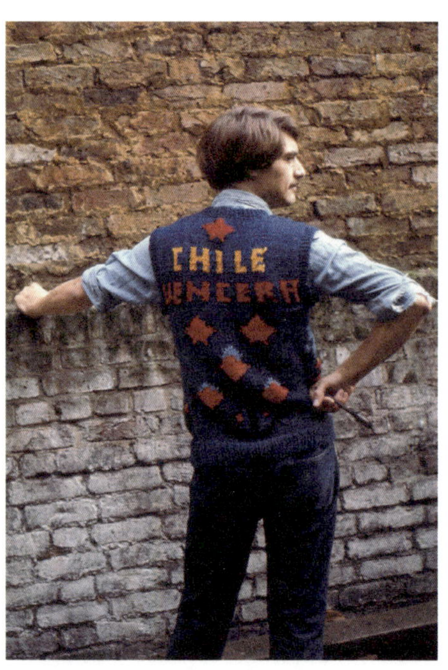
CHILE